REAL WORLD SHAREPOINT® 2010

FOREWORD xxvii

INTRODUCTION. xxix

CHAPTER 1   Building a Perfect Test Environment for SharePoint Server 2010. 1

CHAPTER 2   Upgrading to SharePoint Server 2010 — The Hybrid Approach. 35

CHAPTER 3   Monitoring SharePoint 2010. 69

CHAPTER 4   SharePoint 2010 Security Under the Hood —
Claims-Based Authentication 105

CHAPTER 5   Using PowerShell with SharePoint 2010 129

CHAPTER 6   Backing Up and Restoring SharePoint 2010. 165

CHAPTER 7   Working with SharePoint Designer 2010. .205

CHAPTER 8   Building Sandboxed Solutions 247

CHAPTER 9   SharePoint 2010 Web Parts 269

CHAPTER 10   Automating Business Processes. 335

CHAPTER 11   Building Custom Service Applications for the Right Situations. 375

CHAPTER 12   Managing the SharePoint Application Lifecycle. 407

CHAPTER 13   Using Silverlight 4 with SharePoint 2010. 441

CHAPTER 14   Business Connectivity Services 525

CHAPTER 15   Using PerformancePoint Services 2010 551

CHAPTER 16   Managing Metadata with SharePoint Server 2010 577

CHAPTER 17   Understanding SharePoint 2010 Search 605

CHAPTER 18   Understanding Branding in SharePoint 2010 637

CHAPTER 19   Planning, Designing, and Administering a
Multimedia Assets Management Solution. 671

CHAPTER 20   Accessing SharePoint Data 703

CHAPTER 21   Finding Answers to Your SharePoint 2010 Questions 745

INDEX. 763

Real World SharePoint® 2010

Real World SharePoint® 2010

INDISPENSABLE EXPERIENCES FROM 22 MVPs

Scot Hillier (Editor)

Reza Alirezaei   Darrin Bishop   Todd Bleeker

Robert Bogue   Karine Bosch   Claudio Brotto

Adam Buenz   Andrew Connell   Randy Drisgill   Todd Klindt

Gary Lapointe   Igor Macori   Jason Medero   Ágnes Molnár

Chris O'Brien   Joris Poelmans   Asif Rehmani   John Ross

Nick Swan   Mike Walsh   Randy Williams   Shane Young

WILEY

Wiley Publishing, Inc.

Real World SharePoint® 2010

Published by
Wiley Publishing, Inc.
10475 Crosspoint Boulevard
Indianapolis, IN 46256
www.wiley.com

Copyright © 2011 by Wiley Publishing, Inc., Indianapolis, Indiana

Published by Wiley Publishing, Inc., Indianapolis, Indiana

Published simultaneously in Canada

ISBN: 978-0-470-59713-2
ISBN: 978-1-118-01395-3 (ebk)
ISBN: 978-1-118-01396-0 (ebk)
ISBN: 978-1-118-01323-6 (ebk)

Manufactured in the United States of America

10 9 8 7 6 5 4 3 2 1

For general information on our other products and services please contact our Customer Care Department within the United States at (877) 762-2974, outside the United States at (317) 572-3993 or fax (317) 572-4002.

Wiley also publishes its books in a variety of electronic formats. Some content that appears in print may not be available in electronic books.

Library of Congress Control Number: 2010934748

I would like to dedicate this book to my sister and brother, Nazanin and Ali, and their wonderful families: Marjan, Jack, Kiana, Romina, and Sam. This dedication is my silent way of saying that no matter how far we get from each other, we're still together, here in my heart. I love you all.

— REZA ALIREZAEI

I've always had the privilege of being free in all my choices, with the unconditioned support of my family. It wasn't easy, I have to admit. This book is dedicated to all of them.

— CLAUDIO BROTTO

Dedicated to all the SharePoint CSS. Thank you for keeping me gainfully employed and allowing me to live the SharePoint lifestyle to which I've become accustomed.

— RANDY DRISGILL

To my ever-patient and encouraging wife, Pamela, and to Tessa, my brilliant daughter who is also an aspiring writer — I couldn't have done any of this without you!

— GARY LAPOINTE

The enthusiasm, passion, and determination that I put in my work are possible thanks to the support of Betta, my girlfriend, and Torri, my cat.

— IGOR MACORI

To my husband, son, and daughter, and all my family for their permanent support. And to all of my friends who believed in me.

— ÁGNES MOLINÁR

To my boys, Armaan and Ayaan, for always giving me a reason to smile.

— ASIF REHMANI

To Ben and Julia, thanks for making me smile even on the toughest days.

— JOHN ROSS

I would like to dedicate my chapter to Sophie, and our cats, Fluffy and Carragher.

— NICK SWAN

To Nicola and Grant: I love you both. Thank you for your support and for always being there for me.

— SHANE YOUNG

ABOUT THE TECHNICAL EDITORS

ROBERT BOGUE, MCSE (NT4/W2K), MCSA (Security, A+, Network+, Server+, I-Net+, IT Project+, E-Biz+, CDIA+), is the president of Thor Projects LLC. Thor Projects LLC provides SharePoint consulting services to clients around the world. Bogue has contributed to more than 100 book projects and numerous other publishing projects. He has been a part of the Microsoft Most Valuable Professional (MVP) program for the past seven years, and was most recently awarded for Microsoft Office SharePoint Server. Before that, Bogue was a Microsoft Commerce Server MVP, and, before that, a Microsoft Windows Servers-Networking MVP. He is also a Microsoft Patterns and Practices Champion, and a team member for the SharePoint Guidance. Bogue is the president of the SharePoint Users Group of Indiana (SPIN, www.spindiana.com). He blogs at www.thorprojects.com/blog. You can reach Bogue at Rob.Bogue@thorprojects.com.

STACY DRAPER is a founder of Wild Wires, LLC (a consulting firm based in South Florida), author, and member of PMI. He holds an MCSD certification and has been twice awarded Microsoft MVP. Being involved with Web development since 1993, Draper has led his life in a very interesting direction. He started out in UNIX and, since 1997, has had a strong concentration in Microsoft technologies. Draper enjoys public speaking and has spoken at conferences, code camps, and user groups.

JENNIFER MASON has dedicated the last seven years to working with SharePoint. She started out as an intern focused on SharePoint and eventually began working as a full-time SharePoint consultant. She is currently working as a Senior SharePoint Consultant with the team at SharePoint911. Her focus has been on strategy, project planning, project management, governance, and best practices for implementing business solutions using SharePoint Technologies. She has worked with a range of companies at different points in the lifecycles of their SharePoint implementation. She is passionate about SharePoint, and loves using the out-of-the box features to bring immediate ROI to the organization. Jennifer is involved in the SharePoint community and is one of the founding members of the Columbus Ohio SharePoint Users Group. You can learn more about Jennifer by viewing her blog at www.sharepoint911.com/blogs/jennifer/default.aspx.

CREDITS

ACQUISITIONS EDITOR
Paul Reese

PROJECT EDITOR
Kevin Shafer

TECHNICAL EDITORS
Robert Bogue
Stacy Draper
Jennifer Mason

PRODUCTION EDITOR
Daniel Scribner

COPY EDITOR
Kim Cofer

EDITORIAL DIRECTOR
Robyn B. Siesky

EDITORIAL MANAGER
Mary Beth Wakefield

FREELANCER EDITORIAL MANAGER
Rosemarie Graham

ASSOCIATE DIRECTOR OF MARKETING
David Mayhew

PRODUCTION MANAGER
Tim Tate

VICE PRESIDENT AND EXECUTIVE GROUP PUBLISHER
Richard Swadley

VICE PRESIDENT AND EXECUTIVE PUBLISHER
Barry Pruett

ASSOCIATE PUBLISHER
Jim Minatel

PROJECT COORDINATOR, COVER
Lynsey Stanford

COMPOSITOR
Craig Johnson,
Happenstance Type-O-Rama

PROOFREADER
Publication Services, Inc.

INDEXER
Ron Strauss

COVER DESIGNER
Michael E. Trent

COVER IMAGE
© Jim Schemel/istockphoto.com

ACKNOWLEDGMENTS

FIRST AND FOREMOST, I would like to thank Igor Macori, who co-authored the chapter about Digital Assets Management with me. Igor is a great friend, and this makes writing and working together much easier and enjoyable than it could ever be without him. Being part of this team was amazing. My special "thank you" goes to Scot Hillier, Paul Reese, Kevin Shafer, and all the people at Wrox who performed excellent work in coordinating and turning our drafts into a book. Finally, a huge "Grazie" to my friends and colleagues at Green Team. We find plenty of hurdles and gratifications in our everyday work, and it's great to share both with you!

— Claudio Brotto

I COULDN'T HAVE GAINED an understanding of building custom service applications without the help of quite a few people in order to author my chapter in this book. I'd like to thank the service application Senior Program Manager, Umesh Unnikrishnan, and Test Lead, Stephen Clark, on the SharePoint product team at Microsoft for answering countless questions and working through various samples. I'd also like to acknowledge Ted Pattison, my business partner and good friend, who gave me the time and asked those thought-provoking questions about service applications. No authoring experience can happen either without the full buy-in from your family, in my case specifically my wife, Meredith, son, Steven, and daughter, Kathryn. In addition, I'd like to thank Paul Oakenfold, Paul van Dyk, and DJ Bolivia for the best development music to work to (techno helps you dive into the code!).

— Andrew Connell

THANKS TO MY BEAUTIFUL WIFE, Jackie, my parents, Pat and Tom Drisgill, my in-laws, Debbie and Dave Auerbach, and all my friends for being there when I need you and for putting up with me for the past few months while I worked on this and my other book. Also, thanks to my fellow SharePoint911 coworkers, Elisabeth Olson from Microsoft, and all the other professional SharePoint branders, including Heather Solomon and Heather Waterman, for letting me bounce ideas off them and for providing different perspectives for SharePoint 2010 branding.

— Randy Drisgill

FOR AS LONG AS I CAN REMEMBER, I've wanted to be published. When I was presented with this opportunity to contribute to a book where my chapter would sit alongside those of some of the most talented individuals in the industry, I just couldn't pass it up. I want to especially thank Scot Hillier for organizing this book and for inviting me to contribute to it, and Kevin Shafer and Paul Reese for making it all happen. I try to provide a lot of my experiences and knowledge to the community through my blog as a way to give back to all those out there who have written blog posts and forum questions and answers, from which I have derived so much of my own knowledge. As such, the information provided within my chapter is, in many ways, the result of all those whom I have learned from in the community. So, to all the bloggers and forum users out there I say, "Thank you!" And finally, I am nothing without my beautiful wife and daughter, who have both been so patient and encouraging — to them I owe everything.

— GARY LAPOINTE

THANKS TO CLAUDIO BROTTO, I accomplished my second editorial experience in English, after 18 of my books have been published in Italy. I definitely hope that this can be a little contribution from Italy to the SharePoint community worldwide.

— IGOR MACORI

FIRST AND FOREMOST, I would like to thank God for giving me the strength to work on this project, even when I was not motivated to do so. Additionally, I would like to thank my working family at B&R for always challenging each other and bringing out the best of each other. These guys really have a passion for this technology, and it's nice to share the same passion with such a great group. Last, but not least, I would like to thank my loving wife for dealing with my long nights and always providing me with a smile. I would like to dedicate the work that I contributed to this book to my mother, Helene Strutton, and father, Jesus Medero, for being the best parents a son could have. I love you guys.

— JASON MEDERO

FIRST, I THANK GOD FOR the opportunity to contribute to this book and all the other opportunities that have come my way. Writing a book is never an easy feat. It requires hard work and support from friends and family. I want to thank my very awesome wife, Anisa, for supporting me throughout this process, and for letting me skip out on things as needed so I could hit my deadlines. I'm also very thankful to my boys, Armaan and Ayaan, for the comic relief they provide every time I start stressing out about little things. There is a lot of material in this book, and I'm thankful to be joined by all the wonderful co-authors to provide a thorough breakdown of all the awesome bells and whistles that ship with SharePoint 2010.

— ASIF REHMANI

I WOULD LIKE TO THANK my lovely wife, Vanessa. You are the best. I love you! And to my kids, Ben and Julia, I love you both. To my family and friends, I hope to be spending more time with you all now that this book is done. See, I wasn't just making it up when I said I couldn't do something because I had to write a book. Last, but not least, I'd like to thank the entire SharePoint911 team; I couldn't ask for a better group of people to work with. You guys are the best!

— JOHN ROSS

WRITING IS AN INVESTMENT made by the whole family. My love and appreciation goes to Gigi for her patience and understanding while I was locked up "in my cave."

— RANDY WILLIAMS

CONTENTS

FOREWORD

INTRODUCTION

xxvii

xxix

CHAPTER 1: BUILDING A PERFECT TEST ENVIRONMENT FOR SHAREPOINT SERVER 2010

1

Getting Ready

Windows

2

2

What About Windows 7 or Vista?

3

Installing Windows 2008 R2

3

Setting a Computer Name

4

Making the VM a Domain Controller

5

Configuring Windows

7

SQL Server

12

Installing SQL Server 2008 R2

12

SharePoint 2010

15

Installing SharePoint 2010

15

Setting Up Some User Data

25

SQL Server Reporting Services

29

Other Software

33

Summary

33

About the Author

34

CHAPTER 2: UPGRADING TO SHAREPOINT SERVER 2010 — THE HYBRID APPROACH

35

Understanding the New SharePoint 2010 Upgrade Process

36

System Requirements for a SharePoint 2010 Upgrade

36

SharePoint 2010 Upgrade Improvements

37

Pre-Upgrade Checker

38

Upgrade Logging

40

Visual Upgrade

41

Database Test cmdlet

44

Expected Downtime

44

Central Administration Status Page

45

Site Access During an Upgrade

46

Dealing with Large Content Databases

46

Upgrading with Custom Site Definitions   47
Choosing the Right Upgrade Approach   50
   In-Place Upgrade Approach   50
   In-Place Upgrade Under the Hood   52
   Post In-Place Upgrade   54
   Database Attach Upgrade Approach   58
   Post Database Attach Upgrade   61
SharePoint 2010 Hybrid Upgrade Approach   61
   Read-Only Databases Hybrid Approach   62
   Detach Databases Hybrid Approach   66
Summary   68
About the Author   68

CHAPTER 3: MONITORING SHAREPOINT 2010   69

ULS   69
Trace Logs   70
   Configuring Log Settings with PowerShell   74
   Using Logs to Troubleshoot   77
   Methods for Consuming the Trace Logs   80
Windows Event Logs   85
Logging Database   86
   Configuring the Logging Database   88
   Consuming the Logging Database   90
Health Analyzer   94
   Reviewing Problems   94
   Rule Definitions   97
Timer Jobs   98
   Timer Job Management   98
   Timer Job Status   100
Summary   102
About the Author   102

**CHAPTER 4: SHAREPOINT 2010 SECURITY UNDER THE HOOD —
CLAIMS-BASED AUTHENTICATION**   105

Introducing the Identity Metasystem   106
Identity in a Claims-Based World   107
The Security Token Service (STS)   108
The Problem with Multiple Identities   110
Claims Impact on Delegation   112
Mapping Technology to Components   113

Active Directory Federation Services (AD FS) 113
Windows Identity Foundation (WIF) 114
CardSpace 114
Configuration of SharePoint Claims **114**
SharePoint's Trusted STS 114
Configuring Claims-Based Authentication Using the AD FS 2.0 STS 115
Architecture of SharePoint Claims **120**
Internal Enterprise Claims (IEC) 120
Public Cloud Claims (PCC) and the LDAP Provider 122
Enterprise Identity Federation (EIF) 124
Summary **126**
About the Author **127**

CHAPTER 5: USING POWERSHELL WITH SHAREPOINT 2010 **129**

Understanding PowerShell Basics **130**
An Object-Based Scripting Language 131
The Extended Type System 133
The Object Pipeline 136
Formatting Object Data 138
Filtering and Iterating 139
Functions and Scripts 141
Using SharePoint 2010 Cmdlets **144**
Finding What You Need 144
PipeBind Objects 146
Commonly Used Cmdlets 147
Handling Disposable Objects 154
Creating Custom Cmdlets **156**
When to Create Custom Cmdlets 157
Common Base Classes 157
Custom PipeBind Objects 159
Packaging and Deploying Using Visual Studio 2010 161
Summary **164**
About the Author **164**

CHAPTER 6: BACKING UP AND RESTORING SHAREPOINT 2010 **165**

Operations Planning **166**
Importance of a Disaster Recovery Plan 166
Types of Recovery **168**
Content Recovery 168
Disaster Recovery 169

What's New in 2010   **170**

Farm Configuration Backup and Recovery   170

Changes to Central Administration   171

PowerShell   172

SQL Database Snapshots   172

Unattached Content Database Recovery   173

List Import and Export   174

Search Recovery Improvements   175

Understanding the Types of Backups   **175**

Granular Backups   176

Farm Backups   184

Recovery Scenarios   **194**

Item-Level Recovery   194

Site-Collection Recovery   197

Content Database Recovery   198

Farm Disaster Recovery   198

Recommendations   **201**

Keeping a Change Log   201

Using SharePoint Solutions for Custom Code   202

Other Items to Protect   202

Content Database Sizing   203

Performing Trial Restores   203

Third-Party Solutions   203

Summary   **204**

About the Author   **204**

CHAPTER 7: WORKING WITH SHAREPOINT DESIGNER 2010   **205**

Evolution of SharePoint Designer   **205**

Who Should Use SharePoint Designer?   **206**

Requirements for Using SharePoint Designer 2010   **207**

What's New?   **208**

Overview of the New User Experience   208

Restricting Access to SharePoint Designer   213

Branding   217

Views and Forms   224

Workflows   230

Data Sources   239

Using SharePoint Designer Effectively in Your Environment   **243**

Managing Sites   243

Workflows   243

Branding   244
Prototyping Development Tasks   245
Summary   **245**
About the Author   **246**

CHAPTER 8: BUILDING SANDBOXED SOLUTIONS   **247**

The Push to No-Code Solutions   **248**
Understanding the Concept of a Sandboxed Solution   **249**
Understanding the Execution of Declarative Code   253
Understanding What You Can and Can't Do   253
Your First Sandbox Project   **255**
Getting Out of the Sandbox   **259**
Exploring Alternatives to the Sandbox   **265**
Understanding When to Use Sandboxed Solutions   **266**
Summary   **267**
About the Author   **267**

CHAPTER 9: SHAREPOINT 2010 WEB PARTS   **269**

Web Part History   **270**
Historical Perspective   270
Web Part Goals   271
What's New   274
Web Part Development   **276**
Step 1: Prepare Environment   277
Step 2: Create Project   277
Step 3: Add Item   278
Step 4: Configure Feature   278
Step 5: Configure Solution   278
Step 6: Write Code   279
Step 7: Deploy Assets   279
Step 8: Test Solution   279
Step 9: Secure Code   280
Step 10: Deliver Solution   280
Web Part Basics   **280**
Web Parts Defined   280
Web Part Benchmarks   281
Web Part Framework   282
Web Part Ribbon   289
Web Part Properties   293
Web Part Resources   294

Creating a Simple Visual Web Part   **295**
    Prepare Environment   295
    Create Project   295
    Add Items   298
    Configure Feature   301
    Configure Solution   302
    Write Code   305
    Deploy Assets   309
    Test Solution   312
    Secure Code   316
    Deliver Solution   320
Enhancing the Visual Web Part   **320**
    Write Code   320
    Deploy Assets   322
    Test Solution   322
Adding an Editor Part   **323**
    Write Code   323
    Deploy Assets   329
    Test Solution   329
Adding Web Part Verbs   **330**
    Write Code   331
    Deploy Assets   332
    Test Solution   332
Summary   **332**
About the Author   **332**

CHAPTER 10: AUTOMATING BUSINESS PROCESSES   **335**

Using InfoPath and SharePoint Designer Individually   **336**
    Building Powerful Forms Using InfoPath   336
    Using SharePoint Designer to Build Solutions on Top of SharePoint   344
Combining InfoPath and SharePoint Designer   **349**
    Creating InfoPath Forms for the Browser   350
    Automating Processes Using SharePoint Designer Workflows   360
    The Final Product   371
Summary   **373**
About the Author   **373**

CHAPTER 11: BUILDING CUSTOM SERVICE APPLICATIONS FOR THE RIGHT SITUATIONS 375

Understanding Services in SharePoint 376
History of Services in SharePoint 376
SharePoint Portal Server 2003 376
Office SharePoint Server 2007 377
SharePoint 2010 Service Architecture Framework 377
SharePoint 2010 Service Application Extensibility 378
What the Service Application Framework Offers 379
Determining Whether or not to Build a Custom Service Application 379
Creating the Wingtip Calculator Service Application 380
Configuring the Visual Studio 2010 Project 381
Creating the Application Server Components 384
Creating the Web Front End Server Components 396
Creating the Service Consumers 401
Summary 405
About the Author 405

CHAPTER 12: MANAGING THE SHAREPOINT APPLICATION LIFECYCLE 407

Provisioning with Solution/Feature XML Versus .NET Code 408
Generating Feature XML Using Site Templates 409
Upgrading a SharePoint Application 415
Feature Upgrade in SharePoint 2010 415
An Example of Feature Upgrade 416
Upgrading Different Artifacts 428
Assembly Versioning in a SharePoint Application 431
Versioning of .NET Assemblies 431
Using the BindingRedirect Element in a WSP Manifest 432
Versioning Strategies in SharePoint Applications 435
ALM and Sandboxed Solutions 437
Solution Upgrade Model 438
Feature Upgrade 438
Assembly Versioning 438
Summary 438
About the Author 439

CHAPTER 13: USING SILVERLIGHT 4 WITH SHAREPOINT 2010 441

The Silverlight News Banner 442
Developing a SharePoint Web Part Hosting a Silverlight Application 453
Adding a Custom Ribbon to the Web Part 459
Changes Made to the Silverlight News Banner 464

Deployment Possibilities and Accessibility Scope Impact **465**
Developing a SharePoint Custom Field Type Hosting a Silverlight
Application **466**
   The Picture Service 467
   The Silverlight Picture Picker 470
   The PicturePicker Field 476
   The News List Definition 480
Developing a SharePoint Application Page That Hosts Several
Communicating Silverlight Applications **485**
   The SLNewsItemsListBox Silverlight Application 486
   The SLNewsItemDetails Silverlight Application 495
   The News Manager Application Page 502
Hosting a Silverlight Application in the Master Page **505**
   The Marquee Server Control 505
   The Custom Master Page 507
   Deploying the Custom Master Page 507
Using Business Connectivity Services **510**
   Defining the External Content Type 510
   Defining the External List 512
   Developing the WCF Service 512
   Modifying the News Banner Web Part 515
   Modifying the News Banner Silverlight Application 517
Using Silverlight from within a Sandboxed Solution **520**
Summary **524**
About the Author **524**

CHAPTER 14: BUSINESS CONNECTIVITY SERVICES **525**

A Brief Look Back **526**
Terminology Changes **526**
Welcome to SharePoint 2010 **527**
Existing BDC Applications During an Upgrade **529**
BCS Features Available in SharePoint Foundation **529**
   External Lists 529
   External Data Column 530
BCS Features Available in SharePoint Server 2010 **531**
   Business Data Web Parts 532
   Search 532
   User Profiles 534
   Office Client Integration 534
Using Tools to Create ECTs **536**
   SharePoint Designer 2010 536

Visual Studio 2010   539
BCS Meta Man   548
Developing Against the BCS Object Models   **548**
Summary   **548**
About the Author   **549**

CHAPTER 15: USING PERFORMANCEPOINT SERVICES 2010   **551**

The Case for Business Intelligence   **552**
Why Does a Company Need BI?   552
Asking the Right Questions   552
How Can PerformancePoint Services Help?   553
PerformancePoint Services 2010 Overview   **553**
PerformancePoint Services Architecture   553
Configuring and Enabling PerformancePoint Services   **555**
Configuring the Unattended Service Account   555
Configuring Trusted Locations   556
Enabling PerformancePoint Services on a Site   557
Configuring the Client   558
Creating a PPS Dashboard   **559**
Creating PPS Content   561
Creating the Workspace   561
Deploying Dashboards and Dashboard Components   573
Securing Dashboards   574
About the Author   **576**

CHAPTER 16: MANAGING METADATA WITH SHAREPOINT SERVER 2010   **577**

Information Architecture   **577**
Taxonomy and Metadata   **578**
Taxonomy Versus Folksonomy   **580**
Metadata and Taxonomy Platform Enhancements   **580**
Applying Centrally Stored Metadata   581
Working with the Term Store Management Tool   583
Using the Service Application   587
Understanding Location-Based Metadata   590
Understanding Metadata Navigation Settings   591
Document Sets and Metadata Behavior   593
Using Content Organizers   595
Understanding Content Type Syndication   596
Understanding Social Tagging and Metadata   598
Extending Social Networking   599

Programmatic Access to the EMM Service   **600**
Using the Taxonomy API   600
Remote Access to the Term Store   603
Summary   **604**
About the Author   **604**

CHAPTER 17: UNDERSTANDING SHAREPOINT 2010 SEARCH   **605**

New and Improved SharePoint 2010 Search   **606**
SharePoint 2010 Search Engines   **608**
SharePoint 2010 Search Engine   608
FAST Search Server 2010 Engine   611
Deploying SharePoint 2010 Search   **613**
Deploying a New Search Service Application   613
Crawling and Indexing   615
Queries and Results   616
Reports   617
Deploying FAST Search Server   **617**
Installing FAST Search Server 2010 for SharePoint   617
Deploying FAST Search Service Applications   619
Using PowerShell Commands   **620**
Building the Search Architecture   **621**
Defining Content Sources   621
Using Scopes   624
Scheduling Crawls   624
Using Search Federation   625
Understanding Keywords and Best Bets   627
User Context in FAST Search   628
Using People Search   628
Customizing User Interfaces   **630**
Understanding Centralized and Decentralized UIs   630
Using Search Centers   631
Using Search Web Parts   631
Customizing the Refinement Panel   632
Integrating the Client   632
Improving "Findability" and "Searchability"   **633**
Using Managed Metadata   633
Using Metadata Properties   634
Improving Keywords and Best Bets   635

Improving People Search 635
Improving the User Context in FAST Search 635
Understanding SEO and SharePoint 2010 635
Summary **636**
About the Author **636**

CHAPTER 18: UNDERSTANDING BRANDING IN SHAREPOINT 2010 **637**

Introduction to SharePoint Branding **637**
Comparing SharePoint Foundation 2010 and SharePoint Server 2010 638
Types of SharePoint Sites 638
How Branding Works in SharePoint 642
Approaches to Branding SharePoint 2010 647
Exploring New Branding Features **647**
Adhering to HTML Standards 648
Expanded Browser Support 649
Master Page Improvements 650
Wiki Pages 651
Dialog Boxes 652
Multi-Lingual User Interface (MUI) 654
Visual Upgrade 655
Creating a Branded SharePoint 2010 Site **655**
Working with SharePoint 2010 Themes and Alternate CSS 656
Creating a Custom Master Page 663
Summary **669**
About the Author **669**

CHAPTER 19: PLANNING, DESIGNING, AND ADMINISTERING A MULTIMEDIA ASSETS MANAGEMENT SOLUTION **671**

Looking at Digital Assets Management Scenarios **671**
Facing Challenges in Multimedia Solutions Design and Implementation 672
Infrastructure Deployment **674**
Remote BLOB Storage 675
Bit Rate Throttling Module 677
BLOB Cache 679
Branch Cache 680
Designing the Data Foundation **682**
Planning Asset Content Types 682
Delivering Content through Asset Libraries 683

Configuring and Developing the User Experience   **685**

Using the Out-of-the-Box Multimedia Web Part   685

Multimedia Field Type   687

Content Query Web Part   689

Designing Custom Skins for Multimedia Players   689

Media Player Advanced Configuration   691

Designing Custom Asset Library View Styles   **693**

Packaging the Solution in a Custom Site Definition   **695**

Asset Library Feature Activation   696

Definition of a Data Structure   696

Creation of Asset Library Instances   697

Definition of Custom Asset Libraries   697

Notes from the Field   **699**

Choosing a Farm Topology   699

Monitoring the Bandwidth Usage   700

Planning Content Storage   701

Facing a High Number of Concurrent Users   701

Improving the Responsiveness for Users in Branch Offices   701

Handling Large Files Stored Inside SharePoint   701

About the Authors   **702**

CHAPTER 20: ACCESSING SHAREPOINT DATA   **703**

Data Modeling   **703**

Data Access Options   **704**

Creating Sample Lists   **706**

Accessing SharePoint Data Using the Server-Side Object Model   **707**

Query Optimization   707

Working with Collections   708

LINQ to SharePoint   721

Accessing SharePoint Data Using the Client-Side Object Model   **730**

ClientContext Object: The Entry Point   731

Querying Lists Using JavaScript   731

Manipulating SharePoint Data Using JavaScript   735

JavaScript IntelliSense   737

Accessing SharePoint Data Using Web Services   **738**

WCF Data Services   738

Legacy ASP.NET Web Services   742

Accessing SharePoint Data Using No-Code Solutions   **743**

Summary   **744**

About the Author   **744**

CHAPTER 21: FINDING ANSWERS TO YOUR SHAREPOINT 2010 QUESTIONS   745

Looking for Books   **745**
Continually Expanding Your Knowledge   **747**
     Microsoft Sites   748
     MSDN Site   749
     TechNet Site   749
     Microsoft Office Site   750
     Webcasts   750
     Microsoft Knowledge Base Articles   751
     Magazines   752
     Blogs   752
     Newsgroups and Forums   753
     RSS Feeds   756
Solving Sudden Problems   **757**
     Searching   757
     Asking a Question in a Forum   758
About the Author   **762**

INDEX   *763*

FOREWORD

I HAD THE PLEASURE TO LEAD SharePoint Technical Product Management and be part of launching SharePoint 2010 to market in May 2010. SharePoint 2010 presents a tremendous amount of opportunity for customers and partners to build solutions with the rich investments we've made in features and platform capabilities. The number of man-hours across our engineering and product management teams to build this release is mind boggling to me! This wouldn't be possible without members of the SharePoint community who provided deep real-world feedback on the challenges and opportunities.

SharePoint 2010 delivers a platform that can host a number of solutions from collaboration self-service sites to business intelligence (BI) dashboards to high-end Internet sites. This allows organizations to consolidate their IT investments in a single place, and deliver a unified productivity experience to their end users. To realize this promise, it's important to carefully plan and leverage best practices to avoid common pitfalls and sub-optimal designs. With a new product in market, the challenge is always finding these real-world best practices.

This book is written by a special group of individuals, many of whom I've known and worked with over the last many years. They have been supporters of SharePoint for the last several releases, and have contributed greatly to the larger community, and provided continuous input to us. As part of the Most Valuable Professional (MVP) program, many have had access to SharePoint 2010 since July 2009. Since then, they've had the opportunity to test the software and push it to its limits, which has helped us deliver a high-quality product! Each chapter is written by an expert in the community who has spent a significant amount of hands-on time with that specific topic. So, whether you are a SharePoint developer or an IT implementer, I highly recommend this book as you look to realizing the potential of SharePoint 2010!

ARPAN SHAH
Director, Microsoft
Blog: http://blogs.msdn.com/arpans
Twitter @ arpanshah
September 2010

INTRODUCTION

SHAREPOINT 2010 IS A TRULY MASSIVE PLATFORM that can be thought of as an operating system for Information Workers. In this context, it is becoming increasingly difficult for any single individual to know everything about SharePoint. Instead, the community of SharePoint professionals is specializing. Some of us are workflow experts, others are web content management experts, still others are focused on data integration. Furthermore, it is now impossible to collect all of the end user, administration, and development knowledge for SharePoint into a single resource. Dedicated SharePoint professionals have shelves full of books, or maybe just a fully loaded Kindle, with titles covering the spectrum of subjects from installation and configuration, through customization and development. Additionally, Microsoft provides MSDN, TechNet, and several SDKs.

The size and scope of SharePoint 2010 makes the community of SharePoint technologists more important than ever before. SharePoint professionals have come to rely on blogs, forums, screencasts, and social networking as primary sources for education and problem resolution. These free resources are often at the leading edge of new thought, and routinely identify solutions to perplexing problems.

Microsoft recognizes key individuals who contribute significantly to the SharePoint community through the Microsoft Most Valuable Professional (MVP) award. These individuals are active authors, speakers, bloggers, tweeters, and innovators. They are also skilled network engineers, developers, trainers, designers, and architects. Additionally, they represent experience and perspectives from around the globe.

This book presents core areas of SharePoint 2010 from the perspective of the community leaders who work with it every day. The idea behind the book is to help administrators and developers get up to speed quickly, and avoid common missteps. The authors were selected based on their expertise in a given area.

WHO THIS BOOK IS FOR

This book is for the community of SharePoint professionals. That means architects, designers, developers, administrators, and engineers will all find something useful in its pages. It is not necessary to read the book from the beginning. Instead, you are invited to immediately turn to a chapter of interest where you will find an article written by a single SharePoint MVP.

Chapters in the book generally assume a firm technical background with SharePoint. For example, some chapters require a strong programming background, whereas others may assume knowledge of various security protocols, SharePoint permissions, or maintenance activities. The ideal reader is a technologist in the SharePoint community.

HOW THIS BOOK IS STRUCTURED

This book is an anthology, a collection of articles by MVPs in the SharePoint community. Although the articles are arranged in a logical order, each of the chapters is intended to stand alone. Following is a brief description of each chapter.

➤ *Chapter 1: "Building a Perfect Test Environment for SharePoint Server 2010"* — This chapter covers the steps necessary to create a test environment for SharePoint. Both administrators and developers will find this chapter useful for setting up an environment that can be used throughout the book.

➤ *Chapter 2: "Upgrading to SharePoint Server 2010 — The Hybrid Approach"* — This chapter covers the process for upgrading to SharePoint 2010. Readers will find this chapter useful in preparing for real-world upgrade scenarios.

➤ *Chapter 3: "Monitoring SharePoint 2010"* — This chapter covers how to monitor the health of a SharePoint 2010 farm. Administrators will find this chapter especially useful.

➤ *Chapter 4: "SharePoint 2010 Security Under the Hood — Claims-Based Authentication"* — This chapter covers the new claims-based administration model in SharePoint 2010. Readers will learn how claims authentication works, and why it is important.

➤ *Chapter 5: "Using PowerShell with SharePoint 2010"* — This chapter covers the PowerShell capabilities of SharePoint 2010. Both administrators and developers will get value from this chapter.

➤ *Chapter 6: "Backing Up and Restoring SharePoint 2010"* — This chapter covers basic maintenance activities for SharePoint. Administrators will find this chapter valuable for planning maintenance for their farms.

➤ *Chapter 7: "Working with SharePoint Designer 2010"* — This chapter covers the new capabilities of SharePoint Designer 2010. With many new features, this chapter is a great way to learn how to customize SharePoint with no code.

➤ *Chapter 8: "Building Sandboxed Solutions"* — This chapter covers the new Sandboxed Solution deployment model in SharePoint 2010. Both administrators and developers should read this chapter.

➤ *Chapter 9: "SharePoint 2010 Web Parts"* — This chapter covers development of SharePoint web parts in depth.

➤ *Chapter 10: "Automating Business Processes"* — This chapter covers workflow development techniques for automating business processes.

➤ *Chapter 11: "Building Custom Service Applications for the Right Situations"* — This chapter covers how to develop a service application. Though the chapter requires strong development knowledge, administrators can read it to gain a good understanding of the shared service infrastructure.

➤ *Chapter 12: "Managing the SharePoint Application Lifecycle"* — This is a developer-focused chapter. Development team leads will benefit from the guidance.

➤ *Chapter 13: "Using Silverlight 4 with SharePoint 2010"* — This chapter presents Silverlight 4 development techniques for SharePoint. Many samples make this a good read.

➤ *Chapter 14: "Business Connectivity Services"* — This chapter covers the fundamentals of Business Connectivity Services (BCS). Developers will learn the basics for creating solutions that integrate external data into SharePoint 2010.

➤ *Chapter 15: "Using PerformancePoint Services 2010"* — This chapter covers the setup and usage of PerformancePoint Services. This chapter is for any reader looking to create dashboards in SharePoint.

➤ *Chapter 16: "Managing Metadata with SharePoint Server 2010"* — This chapter covers the new Enterprise Managed Metadata (EMM) service. Anyone interested in organizing information in SharePoint 2010 should read this chapter.

➤ *Chapter 17: "Understanding SharePoint 2010 Search"* — This chapter covers the search capabilities of SharePoint 2010. All readers will benefit from better knowing how to retrieve information in SharePoint.

➤ *Chapter 18: "Understanding Branding in SharePoint 2010"* — This chapter covers the creation of master pages and styles for SharePoint 2010. Readers needing to customize the look and feel of SharePoint 2010 should read this chapter.

➤ *Chapter 19: "Planning, Designing, and Administering a Multimedia Assets Management Solution"* — This chapter examines a specific solution for managing multimedia assets in SharePoint.

➤ *Chapter 20: "Accessing SharePoint Data"* — This chapter covers a variety of approaches for accessing data in SharePoint lists. This chapter is a good read for SharePoint developers.

➤ *Chapter 21: "Finding Answers to Your SharePoint 2010 Questions"* — This chapter provides a listing of resources for getting answers to questions. All readers will benefit from the sources and guidance provided here.

WHAT YOU NEED TO USE THIS BOOK

To use this book successfully, readers should have a development or test SharePoint environment where they can work through chapters. Many of the chapters have step-by-step examples that can be put to work immediately. Some chapters may require only SharePoint Foundation, but many assume an environment built on SharePoint Server, Enterprise Edition.

CONVENTIONS

To help you get the most from the text and keep track of what's happening, we've used a number of conventions throughout the book.

 Boxes with a warning icon like this one hold important, not-to-be-forgotten information that is directly relevant to the surrounding text.

 The pencil icon indicates notes, tips, hints, tricks, or asides to the current discussion.

As for styles in the text:

➤ We *italicize* new terms and important words when we introduce them.

➤ We show keyboard strokes like this: Ctrl+A.

➤ We show filenames, URLs, and code within the text like so: `persistence.properties`.

➤ We present code in two different ways:

```
We use a monofont type for most code examples.
We use bold to emphasize code that is particularly important in the
    present context or to show changes from a previous code snippet.
```

SOURCE CODE

As you work through the examples in this book, you may choose either to type in all the code manually, or to use the source code files that accompany the book. All the source code used in this book is available for download at www.wrox.com. When at the site, simply locate the book's title (use the Search box or one of the title lists) and click the Download Code link on the book's detail page to obtain all the source code for the book. Code that is included on the website is highlighted by the following icon:

Available for
download on
Wrox.com

Listings include the filename in the title. If it is just a code snippet, you'll find the filename in a code note such as this:

Code snippet filename

 Because many books have similar titles, you may find it easiest to search by ISBN; this book's ISBN is 978-0-470-59713-2.

Once you download the code, just decompress it with your favorite compression tool. Alternatively, you can go to the main Wrox code download page at www.wrox.com/dynamic/books/download .aspx to see the code available for this book and all other Wrox books.

ERRATA

We make every effort to ensure that there are no errors in the text or in the code. However, no one is perfect, and mistakes do occur. If you find an error in one of our books, like a spelling mistake or faulty piece of code, we would be very grateful for your feedback. By sending in errata, you may save another reader hours of frustration, and at the same time, you will be helping us provide even higher-quality information.

To find the errata page for this book, go to www.wrox.com and locate the title using the Search box or one of the title lists. Then, on the book details page, click the Book Errata link. On this page, you can view all errata that has been submitted for this book and posted by Wrox editors. A complete book list, including links to each book's errata, is also available at www.wrox.com/misc-pages/booklist.shtml.

If you don't spot "your" error on the Book Errata page, go to www.wrox.com/contact/techsupport .shtml and complete the form there to send us the error you have found. We'll check the information and, if appropriate, post a message to the book's errata page and fix the problem in subsequent editions of the book.

P2P.WROX.COM

For author and peer discussion, join the P2P forums at p2p.wrox.com. The forums are a web-based system for you to post messages relating to Wrox books and related technologies, and interact with other readers and technology users. The forums offer a subscription feature to e-mail you topics of interest of your choosing when new posts are made to the forums. Wrox authors, editors, other industry experts, and your fellow readers are present on these forums.

At http://p2p.wrox.com, you will find a number of different forums that will help you, not only as you read this book, but also as you develop your own applications. To join the forums, just follow these steps:

1. Go to p2p.wrox.com and click the Register link.

2. Read the terms of use and click Agree.

3. Complete the required information to join, as well as any optional information you wish to provide, and click Submit.

4. You will receive an e-mail with information describing how to verify your account and complete the joining process.

 You can read messages in the forums without joining P2P, but in order to post your own messages, you must join.

Once you join, you can post new messages and respond to messages other users post. You can read messages at any time on the web. If you would like to have new messages from a particular forum e-mailed to you, click the Subscribe to this Forum icon by the forum name in the forum listing.

For more information about how to use the Wrox P2P, be sure to read the P2P FAQs for answers to questions about how the forum software works, as well as many common questions specific to P2P and Wrox books. To read the FAQs, click the FAQ link on any P2P page.

Building a Perfect Test Environment for SharePoint Server 2010

By Shane Young

Over the past few years, I have been living the glorious "rock-star" life. You know the one — sleeping in different hotels, visiting cities I have never heard of, never seeing my family, and doing gigs to pay the rent. If I just had a beater conversion van and a mullet, life would be perfect. While I have been "on tour," the one thing I have to have with me at all times is a great virtual machine (VM) to do my demos with. A big part of that VM is all of the SharePoint goodness that is configured and running, but the real secret is getting all of the other pieces installed. That is where this chapter comes in.

This chapter examines the building of my current SharePoint 2010 VM — not just the SharePoint pieces, but everything. So, in this chapter you learn a bit about installing Windows, setting up Active Directory (AD), adding SQL Server with Reporting Services in SharePoint Integration mode, deploying SharePoint, and then getting little things like Office and Visio on there. This is lots of fun, to say the least. I will also share with you things like how long the operation took for me so that you have a point of reference when you get that nagging feeling of "that didn't seem right."

This is the same VM that the SharePoint911 team uses for their book writing, demos, and consulting engagements. It has served them well, and should be a great addition to your arsenal. Now, keep in mind that this is all about building a test/demo VM, not a production server. You can take the lessons learned to build that production server, but this is a recipe for disaster if you start "dcpromoing" your production SharePoint server. You have been warned.

GETTING READY

It is only fair to tell you all of the things I had in front of me before I started so that you can get your proper ingredients ready ahead of time if you want. Or, you can acquire them as you go, because each section of this chapter includes details on why that piece was chosen.

Following are my ingredients:

➤ *My laptop* — Dell M4400, running Windows 7 Ultimate 64-bit. I have 8 GB of RAM, Intel Core 2 Extreme CPU running at 3.06 GHZ. I also have an OCZ Vertex II 120 GB SSD hard drive. The big takeaway from this is that the hard drive made a huge difference in performance. Also, the fact that I can allocate 5 GB of RAM to my VM helps. This is a great setup if you are looking for a new rig to do VMs with. Figure 1-1 shows my Windows Experience Index.

Component	What is rated	Subscore	Base score
Processor:	Calculations per second	6.6	
Memory (RAM):	Memory operations per second	6.6	
Graphics:	Desktop performance for Windows Aero	6.4	**6.4**
Gaming graphics:	3D business and gaming graphics performance	6.4	Determined by lowest subscore
Primary hard disk:	Disk data transfer rate	7.4	

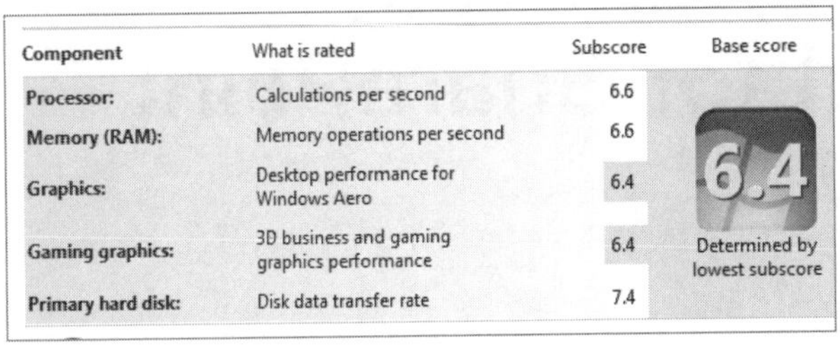

FIGURE 1-1: Author's Windows Experience Index

➤ *My software* — I am using VMWare Workstation 7.1. The key thing is that you need to be running virtualization software that supports 64-bit guest operating systems. Hyper-V is another popular choice, and is what I have running on two production servers. But it is not supported on laptops, so that makes it a no-go for me.

➤ *Software to install* — I have a TechNet Plus subscription, so all of my downloads came from there. I have downloaded Windows Server 2008 R2 Standard, SQL Server 2008 R2, SharePoint Server 2010 Enterprise, Office Web Applications, Office 2010 Professional Plus 32 bit, SharePoint Designer 32 bit, and Visio Premium 2010. I actually keep all of this in a folder on my laptop so I can build a new VM at any point in time without needing the Internet.

WINDOWS

The first step is to create a new VM guest operating system (in other words, create a new VM) so that you can install Windows 2008 R2. To avoid any holy wars, I am going to let you choose on your own which product to use. And, because the steps for creating a new blank VM are 100 percent different for each product, I will skip that, assuming you have already reached that point.

As you configure this VM, it is important to consider the hardware recommendations. As a minimum for a test VM, you should have at least 4 GB of RAM. If possible, you should have slightly more than that. On my laptop with 8 GB of RAM, I typically run the VM with 5 GB of RAM, which seems to give it that little cushion it needs. Based on my experience, if you give the VM less than 4 GB of RAM, you will get weird, inconsistent behavior, and generally wish you had read this paragraph.

SharePoint 2010 is particular about the version of Windows you install. You can use Windows 2008 64-bit SP2 or later, or Windows 2008 R2. Web, Standard, Enterprise, and Datacenter are all supported. Standard or Enterprise are the normal choices, with Enterprise being capable of a few fancy extra things that have nothing to do with SharePoint.

What About Windows 7 or Vista?

Yikes! So, you have already heard that the 64-bit versions of both Windows 7 and Vista operating systems are supported. Well, aren't you smart. If the truth be told, they are both supported for a development-only environment. So, if your developers want to install SharePoint on their local 64-bit workstation, they can.

Now, keep in mind that if you do this install, it will do a single-server install (that is, a basic install), so you cannot use real SQL Server, and everything will be automatically configured using a system account or network service. That's not really the ideal scenario for replicating production.

If you decide to go this route, ensure that anything a developer creates in this environment is put on a real test server before being deployed to production. This is because it is very possible that the developer's code will run just fine in that self-contained, not-reality-based world, but will freak out when deployed to a real SharePoint farm.

The install process is a little tricky when installing on a client operating system. You must manually install the prerequisites, and you must modify the `config.xml` file to get it to work. I recommend you follow the steps outlined at `http://msdn.microsoft.com/en-us/library/ee554869(office.14).aspx` for building on Windows 7 or Vista.

Installing Windows 2008 R2

For this example, you will use Windows 2008 R2 Standard edition. You can download a trial from `http://www.microsoft.com/windowsserver2008/en/us/trial-software.aspx`. Once on that site, click the button and enter your registration information to gain access to the download. Of course, if you already have a Windows ISO or DVD handy, you can use it.

Follow these steps:

1. Depending on your virtualization software, the first time you start the VM, a couple of different things might happen. Some of the products have a wizard that will run through the configuration of Windows for you. Others will prompt you to choose what edition of Windows you want installed before finishing things up. For this example, I have chosen Standard edition.

2. When Windows finishes installing, you will be brought to the Ctrl + Alt + Del screen. Press Ctrl+Alt+Del and then click the Administrator user to log in. When you first get to the login screen, you will get the message, "The user's password must be changed before logging on the first time." Click OK.

3. Enter a new password and click the arrow. To make my life simpler, all of my VMs use the password of `pass@word1`, but that doesn't work well for international folks, because the @ can be hard to type. So, in that case, use `Password1`.

4. You should then get the message, "Your password has been changed." Click OK.

After a minute of processing, you should get the server desktop. Just for a point of reference, it has taken my VM about 15 minutes to get to this point of Windows being installed and a password set. Also, some of the VM programs will install integration tools automatically after the first login, and will automatically reboot. This is actually a good thing, and when it finishes, you just need to log in to the VM again as Administrator to continue.

Setting a Computer Name

To set a computer name, follow these steps:

1. The Initial Configuration Tasks window will open. Although you can do lots of helpful things from this screen, it is also a pain to deal with, so select the box at the bottom left that says, "Do not show this window at logon," as shown in Figure 1-2. Then click Close.

FIGURE 1-2: Checkbox selected not to show window

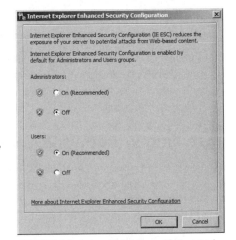

2. Server Manager will automatically open. This screen has a couple of useful nuggets. The first one is turning off the Internet Explorer (IE) Enhanced Security Configuration (ESC) feature. To do this, look down the right-hand side of the window, and click Configure IE ESC. A window will open, as shown in Figure 1-3.

3. Select the radio button for Off under Administrators, and click OK. This will reduce all of the prompts you get about whether you trust this site when opening IE.

4. From the next screen, change the server name to something a little more manageable. From the column on the right side of the window, click Change System Properties.

FIGURE 1-3: Internet Explorer Enhanced Security Configuration dialog

5. A window will open for System Properties, and you will be on the Computer Name tab. Click Change.

6. Now, set the computer name to something you would like. I am the creative type, so I usually use Server1, but on this special occasion, I will do BookServer to show you I can be cool. You, of course, can go crazy and use your favorite Star Wars character, or the name of your favorite pet. Once you set the new name, click OK.

7. Click OK at the screen, "You must restart your computer to apply these changes."

8. Click Close on System Properties, which will bring you to a screen with a Restart option.

9. Click Restart Now.

Making the VM a Domain Controller

To get the right feel in the VM, I always make it a domain controller. SharePoint 2010 doesn't like using local server accounts, so why use them in your demo world? Also, making the server a domain controller allows you to play with a domain consequence free.

If you are going to make your VM a domain controller, you should always do that step right away. The process of promoting a server to a domain controller changes a lot on the machine, and can really upset SharePoint or SQL Server if they are already installed. So, this is always the very first thing I do.

Follow these steps:

1. Once your VM finishes rebooting, log back in as Administrator.

2. After a moment, Server Manager will open again. Now, you must scroll down the page to the Roles Summary section and click Add Roles.

3. From the Before You Begin screen, click Next.

4. From the Select Server Roles screen, select Active Directory Domain Services. This will cause a window to pop up to add the .NET Framework 3.5.1 Features. Click the Add Required Features button.

5. Back at the Before You Begin window, click Next.

6. At the Active Directory Domain Services screen, click Next.

7. At the Confirm Installation Selections window, click Install.

8. At the Installation Results screen, confirm that everything was successful and click Close.

9. You may have a warning that Windows automatic updating is not enabled, as shown in Figure 1-4. You can safely ignore this. Click Close.

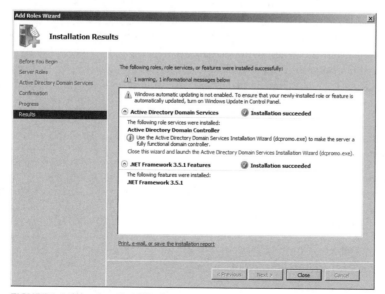

FIGURE 1-4: Warning that Windows updating is not enabled

Active Directory Domain Services are now installed, but still must be configured. You need to define your forest status and a domain name.

To do this, follow these steps:

1. Click Start ➪ Run. Type in **dcpromo** and click OK.

2. At the Welcome screen, click Next.

3. At the Operating System Compatibility screen, click Next.

4. From the Choose a Deployment Configuration screen, select "Create a new domain in a new forest" and click Next.

5. Now, you must enter the domain name you want to use. Most Microsoft VMs use `contoso` `.com`, so that is what will be used for this example. You can use anything you like, though. Once you choose a name click Next.

> *If this VM will be on the network/Internet, you should not use anything for a domain name that will cause a conflict. For example, I am tempted to use* `SharePoint911.com` *because that is my domain, and I want to build this VM to mimic my production domain. The problem is that I will get domain name and server conflicts if I put this VM on the network. So, make up something creative and avoid the pesky errors.*

6. A screen pops up that checks to ensure that you don't have any domain conflicts. If you do have a conflict, you will get a message that your domain name was set to something different. Then you will see a message like that shown in Figure 1-5. If you get this, it is recommended you go back and choose a domain name that is

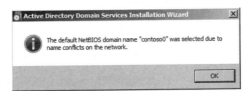

FIGURE 1-5: Active Directory Domain Services Installation error message

not in use. Remembering to type **contoso0**, for example, is going to cause you hours of grief in the future. Click Back on the Domain NetBIOS Name and try a more creative domain name.

7. From the Set Forest Functional Level screen, select Windows Server 2008 R2 and click Next.

8. From the Additional Domain Controller Options screen, confirm that DNS Server is selected and click Next.

9. A pop-up screen similar to the one shown in Figure 1-6 will appear and warn you that you don't have a static IP address assigned. In a real domain, this would be a horrible idea. But for this little VM that should be as portable as possible, a DHCP address will work fine. Click Yes to continue.

10. More than likely, another warning message appears about not being able to contact the authoritative parent zone for DNS. This is not a problem at all for the VM. Click Yes to continue.

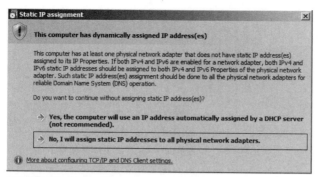

FIGURE 1-6: Static IP assignment screen

11. For the file locations, the defaults are fine, so click Next.

12. To give you a chance to restore AD later (which, for this VM, you probably will never do), you must set a password. Set it to something simple, like `pass@word1`, and click Next.

13. At the Summary screen, click Next.

14. A wizard window will pop up to let you know where it is in the process. It took my VM about 3 minutes to run this step. Once it is complete, click Finish.

15. A pop-up window will appear and ask you to restart now or later. Click Restart Now.

Configuring Windows

After a couple of minutes, your VM will finish rebooting. Log back in as Administrator. In this series of steps, you will do all the little random things people overlook that cause headaches later on.

DisableLoopbackCheck

The loopback check is a Windows security feature that, although it allows you to sleep well at night, causes SharePoint administrators countless hours of pain and suffering. For this VM, let's disable the feature altogether. If you want to read more about it and other options for disabling it in production, check out `http://support.microsoft.com/kb/896861`. The Knowledge Base makes it sound as if it is not relevant because it speaks of IIS 5.1, but I promise it is.

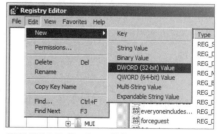

FIGURE 1-7: Registry Editor menu selection

To disable it, follow these steps:

1. Click Start ⇨ Run. Type in **regedit** and click OK.

2. Navigate to `HKEY_LOCAL_MACHINE\System\CurrentControlSet\Control\Lsa`.

3. With Lsa highlighted, click Edit ⇨ New ⇨ DWORD (32-bit) Value, as shown in Figure 1-7.

4. Type in **DisableLoopbackCheck** as shown in Figure 1-8 and press Enter.

5. Double-click DisableLoopbackCheck.

6. As shown in Figure 1-9, enter **1** for "Value data" and click OK.

7. Close the Registry Editor.

 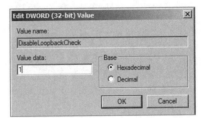

FIGURE 1-8: Entering DisableLoopbackCheck in the Registry Editor

FIGURE 1-9: Setting the value data

Adding the Desktop Experience

For things like Explorer view and other WebDav features to work inside the VM, you need to add the Desktop Experience feature in Windows. Follow these steps:

1. From Server Manager (which should still be open from when you first logged in to Windows), click Features.

2. On the right side of the window, click Add Features.

3. Select Desktop Experience.

4. Another window will pop up and tell you that you must add Ink Support. Click Add Required Features.

5. Click Next.

6. At the confirm screen, click Install.

7. At the Installation Results screen, click Close. There will be warnings about Restart Pending that you can ignore for now.

8. You will also get a pop-up dialog asking if you want to restart now. Click No.

9. Close Server Manager.

Disabling Password Expiration

Nothing annoys me more in my VMs than when I have to reset pass@word1 to pass@word2, then change it back again, and then reboot. This is the Windows operating system's way of punishing me for keeping my VM for more than a month. To disable this nuisance, follow these steps:

1. Click Start ⇨ Administrative Tools ⇨ Group Policy Management.

2. Expand your Forest and find your domain under Domains. Expand it.

3. Click Default Domain Policy.

4. At the pop-up screen, click OK.

5. Right-click Default Domain Policy and click Edit, as shown in Figure 1-10.

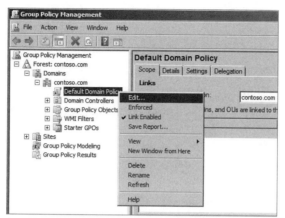

FIGURE 1-10: Menu options to edit the default domain policy

6. The Group Policy Management Editor will open. Expand Computer Configuration ➪ Policies ➪ Windows Settings ➪ Security Settings ➪ Account Policies ➪ Password Policy, as shown in Figure 1-11.

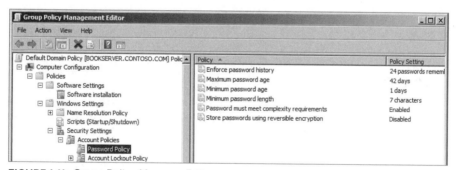

FIGURE 1-11: Group Policy Manager Editor

7. Double-click "Maximum password age."

8. Change 42 days to 0 days to keep passwords from expiring. Click OK.

9. Close the Group Policy Management Editor.

10. Close the Group Policy Management screen.

Disabling UAC

User Account Control is a great feature for production machines to keep you out of trouble by constantly asking, "Are you sure?" But for your VM, you probably don't care that much, so let's just turn it off by following these steps:

1. Click Start ⇨ Control Panel.

2. Click System and Security.

3. Click "Change User Account Control settings."

4. Move the slider to the bottom position for "Never notify."

5. Click OK. You may notice a quick pop-up dialog reminding you to reboot. Ignore it for now.

6. Close the Control Panel.

Enabling Remote Desktop

Quite often, I find the need to remote from a desktop into my VM. This is usually because I want to hide the fact I am using VMWare (smile), but whatever your motivation, you must enable it to use it:

1. Click Start. Right-click Computer and select Properties.

2. From the top-left, click "Remote settings."

3. Check the box for "Allow connections from computer running any version of Remote Desktop (less secure)."

4. You will get a pop-up screen that firewall exceptions will be enabled. Click OK.

5. Click OK.

Creating Some Users

To install and configure SQL and SharePoint, you must create some AD accounts. You will create just the ones you need here, but you may want to create some additional users for testing.

Follow these steps:

1. Click Start ⇨ Administrative Tools ⇨ Active Directory Users and Computers.

2. Double-click the `Users` folder.

3. Repeat Steps 4–11 for the following users:

   a. `sp_farm`

   b. `sp_serviceapp`

   c. `sp_apppool`

   d. `SQL_service`

4. Click Action ⇨ New ⇨ User.

5. Enter **sp_farm** in the "Full name" text box.

6. Enter **sp_farm** in the "User logon name" text box.

7. Click Next.

8. For password and confirm password, enter **pass@word1**.

9. Deselect "User must change password at next logon."

10. Click Next.

11. Click Finish.

12. Close the "Active Directory Users and Computers" screen.

Windows Updates

Windows Updates is a tough topic. I have been burned in the past by enabling them on my VM because they chose to do the install right as I was doing a demo, or they installed something that upset the delicate balance that is my primary demo VM — something broke right before going on stage at TechEd. But, on the other hand, they are nice, because they keep your VM at the same patch level as production servers, so you have more consistency.

For this VM, let's enable them, but set them to never automatically install. Follow these steps:

1. From the System Properties window, click Windows Update in the bottom-left corner.

2. Click the button for "Turn on automatic updates."

3. It will automatically start checking for updates. From the left, click "Change settings."

4. For my VM, I am choosing "Check for updates but let me choose whether to download and install them," as shown in Figure 1-12. You can choose whatever you like. Once you do, click OK.

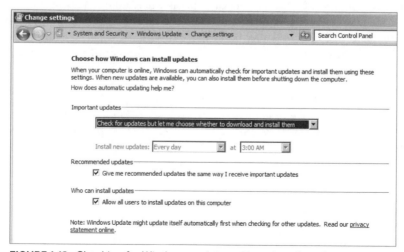

FIGURE 1-12: Checking for Windows updates without installing them

5. It will go back to checking for updates. If your VM is connected to the Internet, you should find quite a few to be installed. Click "Install updates" to install all of the important updates. You can also browse through the optional updates to see if any of them tickle your fancy.

6. If you get any pop-up windows for licensing and such while installing the updates, click through them and click Finish.

> *The amount of time this step will take to complete will depend on the number of updates and the speed of your Internet connection. In July 2010, I had 37 updates with a total size of 86.8 MB. They took about 30 minutes on my VM, but I think this was because my VM was in a bad mood, and not because that was typical.*

7. When complete, you get a big button to Restart Now. Click it.

8. Once the reboot finishes, log back into the VM as Administrator. This reboot will take longer than usual because some updates will need to finish installing, and it may even reboot multiple times.

9. After logging back in, you will also see a screen where the Desktop Experience installation continued and succeeded. Click Close.

10. Finally, Windows Update may have more things to install. If you want to install those, feel free to do so now.

SQL SERVER

SharePoint is very dependent on SQL Server, because that is where all of your content and most of your settings are stored. SharePoint supports SQL 2005, 2008, or 2008 R2. You must use a 64-bit version, and for 2005 and 2008, there is a requirement of service pack, plus cumulative updates. For more details and links to the exact versions needed, see `http://technet.microsoft.com/en-us/library/cc262485.aspx`.

> *Also, SQL Server can be running on an older version of Windows without consequence. We had a client who had SQL 2005 64-bit running on Windows 2003, and wanted to make sure that would be supported. It was.*

Installing SQL Server 2008 R2

For my VM, I used SQL Server 2008 R2 Enterprise from my TechNet Plus subscription. If you do not have a copy readily available, you can download the trial of SQL Server 2008 R2 from `http://www.microsoft.com/sqlserver/2008/en/us/trial-software.aspx`. I chose Enterprise edition because it has additional features, like snapshots, transparent database encryption, and back-up compression capabilities that I occasionally like to demo. Enterprise is not required, but it can be fun.

Also, if you want to try out the new PowerPivot stuff, it is dependent on Enterprise. I do not have PowerPivot installed on my VM. If you are planning on adding it to your VM, I recommend you read up on TechNet before continuing. It seems that in some scenarios it is better to install PowerPivot before configuring your SharePoint farm. You can find more details at `http://technet.microsoft` `.com/en-us/library/ee210682.aspx`.

The first step will be to expose the SQL software to the VM so that you can install it. This could be accomplished by mounting an ISO, copying the EXE to the VM, or running it from a network file share. Because this process is different for everyone, let's assume that you have connected the bits before continuing with the step-by-step instructions.

Now, follow these steps:

1. If the SQL splash screen isn't loaded yet, run `setup.exe` from your files.

2. From the splash screen, click Installation on the left side of the screen.

3. At the top, click "New installation or add features to an existing installation."

4. At Setup Support Rules, click OK.

5. At the Product Key screen, enter your key (if necessary) and click Next.

6. Click "I accept the license terms" and click Next.

7. At the Setup Support Files screen, click Install.

8. After the files finish installing, you will be brought to the Setup Support Rules screen. You will see a warning about Computer Domain Controller and Windows Firewall. You can ignore these warnings and click Next.

9. From Setup Role, choose SQL Server Feature Installation and click Next.

10. From Feature Selection, choose the options you would like to install. For this VM, let's go with all of the bells and whistles, as shown in Figure 1-13. Once you choose the options for your VM, click Next.

11. The Installation Rules screen will confirm that you are all set. Click Next.

12. For Instance Configuration, accept the defaults and click Next.

13. At the Disk Space Requirements screen, click Next.

14. For Server Configuration, click the button "Use the same account for all SQL Server services."

15. Enter **contoso\SQL_service** in the account name text box.

16. Enter **pass@word1** for the password.

17. Click OK.

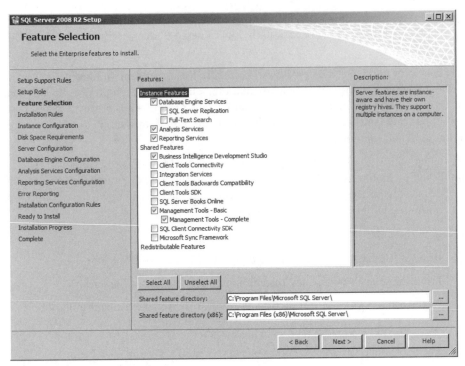

FIGURE 1-13: Feature Selection screen

18. Click Next.

19. For Database Engine Configuration on the Account Provisioning tab, click Add Current User.

20. Accept the other defaults and click Next.

21. For Analysis Services Configuration, click Add Current User.

22. Click Next.

23. For Reporting Services Configuration, select "Install, but do not configure the report server."

24. Click Next.

25. For Error Reporting, make your choice and click Next.

26. For Installation Configuration Rules, click Next.

27. For Ready to Install, click Install.

28. After a bunch of minutes (about 15 for me), you will get a Complete screen. Congratulations! SQL is ready to go. Click Close.

29. Close the SQL Server Installation Center.

At this point, rebooting might not be a bad idea just to free up as many resources as possible on your VM. If you do reboot, be sure to log back into the VM as Administrator when it completes.

SHAREPOINT 2010

Now, you have all those pesky prerequisites out of the way, and your VM is ready for you to install SharePoint. This would be a great time to take a snapshot of your VM or save off a copy. That way, you can always come back to this point.

The steps presented in this section show you how to install SharePoint Server 2010 Enterprise with the Office Web Applications, but you might want to come back later and try installing just Foundation or something like that.

Again, this is a great time for a snapshot. During the beta, I used snapshots and had multiple branches from here. One branch had just Foundation and the other Server. This way, I had one VM, but, depending on what snapshot I loaded at the time, I could play with different installs, giving me some more insight when I was comparing the two versions. That worked well, other than the fact that they both couldn't run at the same time. But, then again, my laptop didn't have the horsepower for that, so it didn't matter.

Installing SharePoint 2010

Once again, I am going to use my TechNet Plus subscription to get a copy of SharePoint 2010. As mentioned, I will be using the Enterprise edition. If you don't have access to the files, you can go to `http://sharepoint.microsoft.com/en-us/Pages/Try-It.aspx` and follow the link to register for the 180-day trial version.

As part of the install process, I am going to also show you how to install the Office Web Applications, because they are an amazing feature and are easiest to install when you are building the farm. The Office Web Applications can be difficult to evaluate because they do not have a trial edition, and they also cannot be installed on SharePoint Server 2010 Trial edition. For more information check out `http://technet.microsoft.com/en-us/office/ee815687.aspx`.

Extracting the EXE

If your download is an `.exe` file (such as `SharePointServer.exe`), the first thing to do is to extract that `.exe` file so you have access to the full files directly, instead of storing them in some temporary folder.

Follow these steps:

1. Open a command prompt by clicking Start ➪ Run. Type in **cmd** and press Enter.

2. From the command prompt, navigate to the folder where you copied the `SharePointServer.exe` file.

3. Then run the command-line `SharePointServer.exe /extract:c:\install`.

4. A pop-up dialog shows you the extraction progress. Click OK when it completes.

5. Close the command prompt.

6. To free up space on your VM, it is now also safe to delete the `.exe` you downloaded.

Installing the Prerequisites

SharePoint 2010 developed such a passion for software prerequisites that it now comes with its own tool for installing these pieces. It will also configure IIS for you so that you don't have to mess with all of that clicking as well.

The bad news is that about 70 MB of installers are needed to get SharePoint ready, and they don't come with the SharePoint download. The good news is the prerequisite installer will automatically go to the Internet and download these for you.

Follow these steps:

1. Open Windows Explorer to `c:\install`.

2. Double-click `PrerequisiteInstaller.exe`.

3. From the Welcome screen, click Next.

4. Click "I accept the terms of the License Agreement(s)" and click Next.

5. When it completes, it may prompt you to reboot. If it does, let the reboot happen, and log back into the VM when it completes. When you log back in, the prerequisite installer will continue automatically.

6. Click Finish at the Installation Complete screen. This took me about 7 minutes, including a reboot in the middle of the process.

An Extra Install for Windows 2008 R2 and 7

According to my developer friends, there is a bug where some .NET something doesn't get installed correctly by the prerequisite installer. They have explained it to me a couple of times, but I just hear the Charlie Brown teacher's voice and I get a headache. So, to make them happy, I will tell you that, if you are running SharePoint Server 2010 on Windows 2008 R2 or Windows 7, you should download and install the patch from `http://www.microsoft.com/downloads/details.aspx?FamilyID=3e102d74-37bf-4c1e-9da6-5175644fe22d&displaylang=en`.

Installing SharePoint Server 2010 Enterprise

The man, the myth, the legend — this is what you have been waiting for — actually installing SharePoint. Although there are several different versions, all of the installs (including just plain Foundation) should feel exactly the same.

Follow these steps:

1. From `c:\install`, double-click `setup.exe`.

2. Enter your product key on the first screen and click Continue. Be careful to enter the correct key. The key determines what version of SharePoint you get; there is no "select your version screen" later.

3. Click "I accept the terms of the agreement" and click Continue.

4. For the "Choose a file location" screen, accept the defaults and click Install Now.

 You may have noticed you were not prompted to choose Server Farm or Standalone. The reason for this is SharePoint 2010 is smart. Standalone installs are not supported if the SharePoint Server is a domain controller, which is the case on this example VM, so it doesn't even let you choose that silly, silly option.

5. About 4 minutes later on my VM, I am brought to the Run Configuration Wizard screen. Because you want to install the Office Web Applications, you must deselect the "Run the SharePoint Products Configuration Wizard now" checkbox. Then click Close.

Installing Office Web Applications

If you don't have access to the Office Web Applications, you can skip this section without a problem. It is also possible to install them at a later time, but that does require extra work. Because I am lazy, let's install them now. Remember, there is no trial download available for this product, so that is why there isn't a link.

Follow these steps:

1. Run `setup.exe` from your Office Web Application media. In my case, I mounted the ISO file I downloaded from TechNet.

2. On the first screen, enter your Product Key and click Continue.

3. Check the box for "I accept the terms of this agreement" and click Continue.

4. From the "Choose a file location" screen, click Install Now.

5. After less than 2 minutes, I get the Run Configuration Wizard screen. Leave the box selected and click Close.

The Configuration Wizard

The configuration wizard in SharePoint 2007 was so successful that Microsoft has chosen to provide more than one wizard in 2010. You have the same configuration wizard from last time, but Microsoft has also added another configuration wizard. Because I am not smart enough to keep the two wizards straight, I have renamed them. The wizard you are about to run I call the "gray wizard" because it comes first, and because the screen is gray in color. The other wizard is mainly a white screen, so I call it the "white wizard." I may have been watching the Lord of the Rings when I had this bright idea.

The gray wizard is in place to help you either to connect to an existing farm, or to create a new SharePoint farm. When you think of "farm," think of configuration database. Do you have one you want to connect to? If yes, then you are joining a farm. If no, then you are creating a new database. For this VM, you will be creating a new farm.

The wizard will also do things like provision Central Administration for you, and will set up all the file security and registry settings that SharePoint needs in place to run. This is really a pretty handy little tool.

If you don't have the configuration wizard open already, you can launch it manually by going to Start ⇨ All Programs ⇨ Microsoft SharePoint 2010 Products ⇨ SharePoint 2010 Products Configuration Wizard.

Follow these steps:

1. At the Welcome screen, click Next.

2. At the Warning pop-up screen, click Yes to continue.

3. From the "Connect to a server farm" screen, select "Create a new server farm."

4. Click Next.

5. Fill out the screen as shown in Figure 1-14. For "Database server," this is the name of the local VM you chose earlier. For "Database name," I always recommend the default for the sake of simplicity. "Username" is the sp_farm account created earlier. The account is just a regular domain user that SharePoint will elevate permissions for as necessary. This account will be one of the most important accounts in your farm. The Central Administration application pool and the SharePoint timer service will both use this account. Also, it will be the database owner (DBO) of all of your SharePoint databases. Click Next.

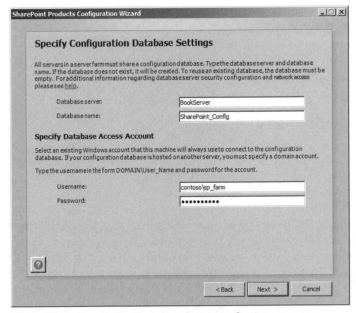

FIGURE 1-14: Specify Configuration Database Settings screen

6. Enter a farm passphrase and confirm it. The passphrase you use here must be complex, and you must remember it. Click Next.

You will need this password to add or remove servers to the farm later and, if you lose it, you are up a creek without a paddle. This is not a big deal for this VM. But if you are thinking about production, this would be critical.

7. On the Configure SharePoint Central Administration Web Application screen, check the box for "Specify port number" and enter an easy number for you to remember. I like to use 5555. That way, I always know I can go to `http://servername:5555` to access Central Administration. Click Next.

8. At the Completing screen, click Next.

9. After about 4 minutes, I get the Configuration Successful screen. Hooray! Click Finish.

The Initial Farm Configuration Wizard

New to 2010 is the Initial Farm Configuration Wizard. Because this is another configuration wizard, I prefer to call this gem the "white wizard." This wizard will set up a managed account for you, and then automatically create the service applications that you select with default settings. This may be very handy, but, at the same time, it may be kind of annoying that all of the database names it provisions will have GUIDs on the end. Let's take the good with the bad and use it to set up the example VM.

Follow these steps:

1. First, let's perform a touch of housekeeping. Because this is the first time you have opened Internet Explorer, you must deal with the Welcome screen. Click Next.

2. Click "No, don't turn on for Suggested Sites" and click Next.

3. Select "Use express settings" and click Finish.

4. A Welcome tab will open. Close the tab.

5. Now you are prompted to help make SharePoint better. Choose whether or not you will participate, and click OK.

6. You are now prompted whether you would like help with configuring your farm. Click the button for "Start the Wizard."

7. Seven steps later, you are at the Initial Farm Configuration Wizard (the "white wizard"), ready to make some configuration choices. The first choice is to determine what account you want the application pool for your service applications to run as. For the VM, you created an account called `contoso\sp_serviceapp` to use. Enter that with a password of `pass@word1`.

8. Now you can select which service applications you would like to provision for your farm. Because this is a VM that is meant to be a happy playground, I would recommend you select all of the boxes. By default, the Lotus Notes Connector is not connected. Leave that one unchecked unless you have specific plans for it. Once you have made your selections, click Next.

9. Assuming that you left the "User profile" service application selected before the wizard completes, you will get a screen prompting you to create a site collection. Enter a Title and select a template. I usually call it Team and choose the Team Site template. Click OK.

> *What is this site collection? The user profile service application automatically creates a SharePoint web application at* `http://servername` *and then creates a site collection for* `http://servername/my` *to be the My Site Host site collection.*

10. When you get the Complete screen, click Finish. Congratulations! You have a functional SharePoint 2010 farm at this point.

Manual Configuration Steps

Now that you have service applications configured, there are still a few things you must set up on your own — things like profile imports, Secure Store, search schedules, and so on. This section walks you through these tasks.

Configuring a Profile Import

The profile import architecture for SharePoint 2010 is all new and, consequently, is a little "awkward" to get running. Microsoft now uses the same .NET connectors that Search and the Business Data Catalog (BDC) are using, instead of having other types of connections for the import. For this VM, it will not be too bad, but when you go to do production, it will be a challenge. For production, I recommend you read `http://technet.microsoft.com/en-us/library/ee721049.aspx` and follow these steps to the letter.

The first series of steps is to start the User Profile Synchronization Service:

1. From Central Administration, click System Settings.

2. Under Servers, click "Manage services on server."

3. Scroll down the page and find User Profile Synchronization Service. Click Start to the right of the service.

This is your first awkward moment. See the account name listed? For me it is `contoso\sp_farm`. That account must be a local administrator on all servers this service is started on. That is this VM, but because this VM is a domain controller, it does not have a local administrators group. So, to get around this, you must make this account a domain administrator. Follow these steps:

1. Click Start ⇨ Administrative Tools ⇨ Active Directory User and Computers.

2. Find the account in the list and double-click it.

3. Click the Member Of tab.

4. Click Add.

5. For "Enter the object names to select," type in **domain admins** and click OK, as shown in Figure 1-15.

6. Click OK.

7. Close Active Directory User and Computers.

8. Now, this is another awkward moment. To get this change to take full effect and make SharePoint happy, you must reboot. Sorry.

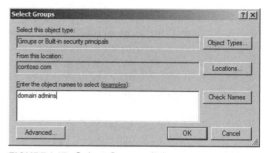

FIGURE 1-15: Select Groups dialog

9. After the reboot, log back in and go to SharePoint Central Administration.

10. Return to the start service screen, enter and confirm the password for the account, and click OK.

11. Now, show great patience. On my VM, the service took about 3 minutes to start. TechNet warns that it can take as long as 10. As long as you are hitting the screen and hitting refresh, and it says Starting, you are good. Once it changes to Started, you can continue.

12. Click Application Management.

13. Under Service Applications, click "Manage service applications."

14. Scroll down the page and click User Profile Service Application.

15. If you get the message, "An unexpected error has occurred," that is ironically expected. You need to do an iisreset. Click Start ➪ Run, type in **cmd**, and press Enter.

16. Type **iisreset** and press Enter.

17. When it completes, type **exit** and press Enter.

18. Back in Internet Explorer, hit Refresh.

19. No more error. (Did I mention this was all so very awkward?) Under Synchronization, click Configure Synchronization Connections.

20. From the menu bar, click Create New Connection.

21. For Connection Name, enter **Primary AD**.

22. For "Forest name," enter **Contoso** (or whatever name you are using).

23. For account name, enter **contoso\sp_farm** (or whatever account you used in the earlier steps).

24. Enter and confirm the password.

25. Click Populate Containers.

26. Expand the tree and check the box next to Users.

27. Click OK.

You now have the profile synchronization service running and configured. You could have selected other organizational units (OUs) in the previous step to really drill down on the profiles you wanted to import, but for your VM, you don't have a lot of complexity. You just want the basics to work.

Now, you just need to start a full import and ensure that you get accounts. Follow these steps:

1. Click Application Management.

2. Under Service Application, click "Manage service applications."

3. Scroll down the page and click User Profile Service Application.

4. Under Synchronization, click Start Profile Synchronization.

5. Select the radio button for Start Full Synchronization and click OK.

6. After a moment, refresh the "Manage Profile Service: User Profile Service Application" screen. You should see the status on the right change from Idle to Synchronizing. After a few minutes, refresh and you will see it change back to Idle, and the "Number of User Profiles" will change from 0 to a bigger number. For me, it took about 9 minutes, and I had 8 profiles. I took these few minutes to get a beverage of choice. I figured I deserved one; this is hard work. I recommend you do the same.

Now that it is complete, you will have user profiles and can start to play with the social experience in 2010.

Enabling the Activity Feed Timer Job

To get the full social experience, you must enable the activity feed timer job. This can be a simple task, but very frustrating if you don't know you need to do it.

Follow these steps:

1. Click Monitoring from the left-hand side of the page.

2. Under Timer Jobs, click "Review job definitions."

3. Scroll down the page and click "User Profile Service Application - Activity Feed Job."

4. Click the Enable button.

Running a Search Crawl

The "white wizard" automatically configured search for you, but, by default, there is no search schedule. This means your index is empty. Now, because VM performance can be so fragile, I don't recommend defining a search schedule, but instead going in from time to time and manually running a full crawl.

Follow these steps:

1. Click Application Management from the left-hand side of the page.

2. Under Service Applications, click "Manage service applications."

3. Scroll down the page and click Search Service Application.

4. On the left, under Crawling, click Content Sources.

5. Hover over the Local SharePoint sites content source and click the drop-down arrow.

6. Click Start Full Crawl, as shown in Figure 1-16.

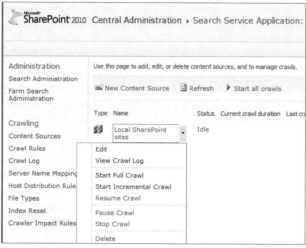

FIGURE 1-16: Starting a search crawl

7. From the left column, click under Administration and then click Search Administration.

8. Scroll to the middle of the page and look under Crawl History. You can click the refresh icon to refresh periodically to wait and see when the crawl finishes.

You will not have too many items right now, because you don't have any real SharePoint content, but you now know how to do a full crawl once you get some data to actually index. Chapter 17 is full of SharePoint 2010 search fun.

Setting Up the Secure Store

The Secure Store is the new version of the old Single Sign On (SSO) database from 2007. However, this time it is actually functional. Because some of the service applications (such as PerformancePoint) count on this service application running, I always set it up properly from the beginning so that I don't have to remember later.

Follow these steps:

1. Return to the homepage of Central Administration.

2. Click Application Management.

3. Under Service Applications, click "Manage service applications."

4. Scroll down the page and click Secure Store Service.

5. You will see a red warning. Right above that is a button for Generate New Key. Click the button.

6. Enter and confirm a passphrase. (I use `pass@word1`.) Click OK.

Now, if any of the service applications need to register themselves with the Secure Store, they can. This may seem like a trivial thing, but it is one less thing to troubleshoot and only took you 2 minutes to do. You're done, so let's move on.

Adding Some Managed Metadata

The managed metadata is probably going to be one of the most popular features for the Information Worker in SharePoint 2010, so playing with it now isn't a bad idea. Once again, because I am lazy, instead of adding a bunch of terms on my own, I take advantage of the sample data and import it. Then I can play without actually doing any real work.

Follow these steps:

1. Click Application Management from the left side of the page.

2. Under Service Applications, click "Manage service applications." (Do you have that *déjà vu* feeling yet?)

3. Scroll down the page and click Managed Metadata Service.

4. Now, you cannot do much in here until you add yourself as an administrator. To do that, in the center of the page, add your account (`contoso\administrator` for my VM) to the Term Store Administrators box, as shown in Figure 1-17. Scroll down the page and click Save.

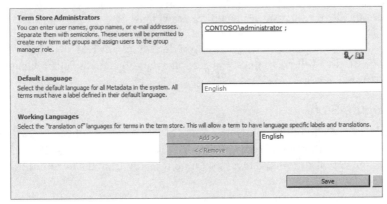

FIGURE 1-17: Adding yourself as an administrator

5. Now, from right above the administrator section, there is a blue link for "View a sample import file." Right-click the link and click "Save target as."

6. From the "Save as" box, click your desktop and click Save.

7. In the "Download complete" window, click Close.

8. Now, on the left side of the page, hover over Managed Metadata Service, click the drop-down arrow, and click New Group, as shown in Figure 1-18.

9. In the orange box, type in **Company Data**.

10. Hover over Company Data, click the drop-down arrow, and click Import Term Set.

11. Click Browse.

12. From your desktop, select `ImportTermSet.csv` and click Open.

13. Click OK.

FIGURE 1-18: Selecting New Group

Now you have the Political Geography term set with lots of terms to play with. To play with it in a SharePoint list, you would add a column of the type Managed Metadata. Check out Chapter 16 for the full scoop.

Setting Up Some User Data

You are so close. You now have a SharePoint farm configured and you are ready to rock-'n'-roll. You just need to add some simple data. In this section, I show you the basics of creating a web application and a site collection. Then, filling in your sample data is up to you.

For the SharePoint911 demo VM, I set up a few different web applications:

➤ I have a `www.contoso.com` web application for showing off publishing and branding.

➤ I have a `team.contoso.com` web application for showing off fundamental SharePoint Foundation features with ad hoc demos.

➤ I created `demo.contoso.com` and used most of the concepts from the SharePoint 2010 Walkthrough guide available at `http://www.microsoft.com/downloads/details.aspx ?displaylang=en&FamilyID=8c619bef-008b-4af2-9687-8a05848fea97`. (I helped write the guide and really like some of the functionality, so I re-created it in our VM.)

➤ And, finally, I have `portal.contoso.com`, which is a mock intranet combining a little bit from all of the other web applications from a functionality perspective.

So, have fun building out the right demo/test/play data you need to make your VM rock.

Creating a Managed Account

Did you ever try to change the password for your service accounts in SharePoint 2007? It was somewhere between calculus and rocket science in complexity.

In SharePoint 2010, Microsoft has introduced a new concept called *managed accounts* to alleviate this issue. With managed accounts, you will create the account in Active Directory like you always did, but then you will go to SharePoint and register the account as a managed account. Now, when you are specifying a service account or application pool account, you will choose one of these managed accounts.

The best feature of managed accounts is that once you register them with SharePoint 2010, you can be as hands-off with password management as you would like. Do you need to change the password every 60 days to meet domain security requirements? No problem. You can tell SharePoint to automatically do it for you. Or, if you are not comfortable with that, you can tell SharePoint just to send you an e-mail reminding you of the required change. That's pretty cool. There are a lot more features, but that is the quick run-down.

Before you can continue, you need to register one. Follow these steps:

1. From the homepage of Central Administration, click Security.

2. From the General Security section, click "Configure managed accounts."

3. Notice that your farm and service application account are already listed. SharePoint set those up for you automatically with the gray and white wizards, respectively. Click Register Managed Account.

4. For "User name," enter **contoso\sp_apppool**.

5. For Password, enter your password. For my VM, it is `pass@word1`.

6. Leave the other boxes as is and click OK.

Creating a Web Application

Web applications are the core unit that exists inside of IIS. This is the actual URL you are going to use when you connect to SharePoint. This is also the spot where you get to choose your authentication method and determine your Content Databases.

Follow these steps:

1. Return to the homepage of Central Administration.

2. Click Application Management.

3. From the ribbon, click New.

4. For Authentication, accept the default of Classic Mode Authentication. If you want an explanation of claims-based authentication, check out Chapter 4.

5. For IIS Web Site, set Port to 80 and Host Header to `team.contoso.com`, as shown in Figure 1-19.

The key here is to use something meaningful to your users. If you are the only user, it isn't a big deal, but it is good to be in the practice of not using web applications named after your crazy computer name. Remember, though, whatever name you use (for example, `team.contoso.com`), you must ensure that your users can resolve. So, create a DNS entry for them. After you finish creating this web application, you will make the necessary DNS entry.

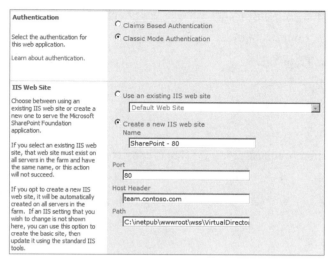

FIGURE 1-19: Configuring an IIS website

6. For Security Configuration and Public URL, accept the default settings.

7. For Application Pool, choose "Create new application pool" and accept the default application pool name.

8. For "Select a security account," choose the account previously specified as a managed account. For my VM it was `contoso\sp_apppool`.

9. For "Database name," specify `WSS_Content_Team`. I always use a database name that matches up directly to my host header. That makes life easier when the DBA asks, "What is this database for?"

10. Accept all the other defaults and click OK.

11. After about a minute, you will get an Application Created pop-up screen. Click OK.

Creating a Site Collection

This is the last thing and your SharePoint world is ready for you to come and play. You must create a root site collection in your new web application.

Follow these steps:

1. From the homepage of Central Administration, click Application Management.

2. From the Site Collections section, click "Create site collections."

 In case you were wondering, a personal pet peeve of mine is the fact it says "collections." You can only create one at a time, not multiple.

3. From the Web Application drop-down, click Change Web Application.

4. Click "SharePoint - team.contoso.com."

5. For Title, enter **Contoso Team Site**.

6. Leave Description blank.

7. Ensure that the URL drop-down has "/."

8. For Template, use Team Site.

9. For Primary Site Collection Administrator User Name, enter **contoso\administrator**.

10. Click OK.

11. After less than a minute, you will get a successful message. Click OK.

Adding a DNS Entry

So, I said your SharePoint fun was done, but because you used a custom host header of `team .contoso.com`, you must define that in DNS before you can resolve the address.

Follow these steps:

1. Click Start ➪ Administrative Tools ➪ DNS.

2. Expand the tree until you see Forward Lookup Zone.

3. Under Forward Lookup Zone, find your zone and right-click the zone. Select New Host, as shown in the Figure 1-20.

4. For Name, enter **team**.

5. For "IP address," enter **127.0.0.1**. That way, the VM can always find it, and you don't have to worry about the changing IP address.

6. Click Add Host.

7. At the successful message, click OK.

8. To save you from coming back later, add another DNS entry now. For Name, enter **rs**.

9. For "IP address," enter **127.0.0.1**.

10. At the successful message, click OK.

11. Click Done.

12. Close DNS Manager.

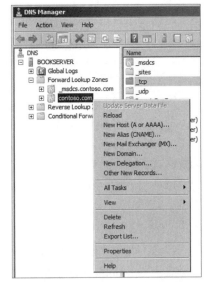

FIGURE 1-20: Selecting a new host in DNS Manager

Confirming You Are Done

Let's make sure that the site opens in Internet Explorer. Follow these steps:

1. Open a new IE window.

2. When prompted, enter **administrator** for the username and **pass@word1** for the password.

3. After a little less than a minute, you should see your SharePoint team site. Hooray!

4. To make things smoother going forward, I would add the site to your local intranet zone in IE. From the IE toolbar, click the Tools drop-down menu and select Internet Options.

5. Click the Security tab.

6. Click the "Local intranet zone" icon.

7. Click the Sites button below it.

8. Click the Advanced button.

9. Confirm http://team.contoso.com is the box, and click Add.

10. Click Close.

11. Click OK.

12. Click OK.

Now, you have no more login prompts and no worries of odd behaviors of functionality not working because IE doesn't trust your SharePoint site. And that is a wrap, folks! You now are ready to play with SharePoint 2010 and all of those fun new features.

SQL Server Reporting Services

Before you read this section, don't get too excited. This section explains how to set up SQL Server Reporting Service (SSRS) 2008 R2 for this single VM, and not for a multi-server farm. That is a topic for another day, and possibly an entire book. I know; I spend hours every week setting up those multi-server farms for clients. So, no complaints. But, once you are finished with this system, you will be able to play with SQL Server Reporting Services and see all of the fancy features.

Configuring SSRS for SharePoint Integration Mode

SSRS has two modes. *Native mode* is the traditional "build reports by hand and then look at them" model. Boring. SharePoint *Integration mode* allows you to add Reporting Services content types to SharePoint, and then build and manage your reports from SharePoint where you and your users are so very comfortable. Even better yet, teach them how to use Report Builder to build their own reports. This is too much fun.

Follow these steps:

1. Click Start ⇨ All Programs ⇨ Microsoft SQL Server 2008 R2 ⇨ Configuration Tools ⇨ Reporting Services Configuration Manager.

2. At the pop-up window, click Connect.

3. From the left-hand side of the window, click Web Service URL.

4. Click the Advanced button.

5. Click Add for the HTTP section.

6. Select Host Header Name and enter **rs.contoso.com**.

7. Click OK.

8. Highlight the "all assigned listener" item above it and click Remove.

9. Click OK.

10. Click Database on the left.

11. Click the Change Database button.

12. Select "Create a new report server database" and click Next.

13. For "Connect to Database Server," accept the defaults and click Next.

14. For Report Server Mode, select SharePoint Integrated Mode.

15. Click Next.

16. For Authentication Type, leave Service Credentials and click Next.

17. From the Summary screen, click Next.

18. After less than a minute, everything will be successful, and you can click Finish.

19. All other settings should work as is, so click Exit in the bottom right-hand corner.

Configuring Central Administration to Use SSRS

Now that SSRS is running in SharePoint Integrated mode, you must tell SharePoint how to use it. You do this from Central Administration.

Follow these steps:

1. Return to the homepage of Central Administration.

2. Click General Application Settings from the left-hand side of the page.

3. From the Reporting Services section, click Reporting Services Integration.

4. For Report Server Web Service URL, enter **http://rs.contoso.com/reportserver**.

5. For Authentication Mode, choose Windows Authentication.

6. For Credentials, enter **contoso\administrator** and the password of **pass@word1**.

7. Click OK.

8. After about a minute, you should get a screen back with three green checks. This means your configuration was successful. Click Close.

Adding the Reporting Service Content Types

Now, all that is left is to add the content types and build a quick fake report. Follow these steps:

1.   Open IE to `http://team.contoso.com`.

2.   From the left, click Shared Documents.

3.   From the ribbon, click Library.

4.   From the far right of the ribbon, click Library Settings.

5.   Under General Settings, click "Advanced settings."

6.   From Content Types, select Yes for "Allow management of content types."

7.   Scroll down the page and click OK.

8.   Scroll down the page and, from the Content Types section, click "Add from existing content types."

9.   From the "Select site content types from" drop-down, choose Report Server Content Types.

10.   Add all three content types, as shown in Figure 1-21.

11.   Click OK.

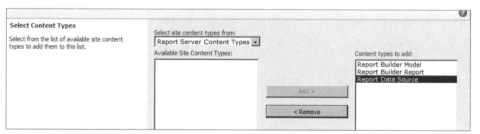

FIGURE 1-21: Adding content types

12.   From the left, click Shared Documents.

13.   From the ribbon, click Documents.

14.   Hover over New Document, click the drop-down arrow, and choose Report Builder Report.

15.   You will get an "Application Run - Security Warning." Click Run.

This will automatically download and install for you Report Builder 3.0 from your SharePoint Server. You will only have to do this once.

16.   After less than a minute, Report Builder 3.0 opens. From the New Report section, click "Table or Matrix Wizard."

17. Click Next to create a dataset.

18. For Data Source Connections, click New.

19. Next to "Connection string," click Build.

20. For Server name, enter your VM name. For my example I used `BookServer`.

21. For "Connect to a database," click the drop-down for "Select or enter a database name."

22. From the picker, choose SharePoint_Config.

 In production, this is a horrible idea. But, for this example, it is one database everyone has.

23. Click OK.

24. Click OK.

25. Back at "Choose a connection to a data source," click Next.

26. Expand Tables and select Objects.

27. Click Next.

28. Drag Properties to Values.

29. Click Next.

30. For "Choose the layout," click Next.

31. For "Choose a style," select Finish.

32. From the top-left corner, click the Save icon.

33. Select your Shared Documents library and click Save.

34. Close Report Builder.

35. In IE, refresh the Shared Documents page.

36. Click Untitled.

You now have a screen full of data. Don't be alarmed if it takes a couple of minutes to load. Hooray! You have shown you can pull data from SSRS. Now, the sky is the limit for your reporting/ business intelligence options. You may also want to take a look at the SQL Server Business Intelligence Development Studio (BIDS) that is in the SQL Server 2008 R2 `Programs` folder for more advanced report creation.

OTHER SOFTWARE

Now you have that awesome VM that I promised. To make it truly complete, you should now consider installing some additional software. I will not guide you through this part, but just provide some suggestions and a link on where to get it.

Microsoft Office 2010 Professional Plus would be the next step. You need to be able to create all of those fancy Word documents so that you can play with the different features like Office Web Applications. You can get a trial copy from `http://technet.microsoft.com/en-us/office/ee263913.aspx`.

SharePoint Designer 2010 is a must. You need to play with workflows and branding and all that fun jazz. Get the full version. It is free, after all, from `http://sharepoint.microsoft.com/en-us/product/Related-Technologies/Pages/SharePoint-Designer.aspx`.

Visio Premium 2010 is an interesting tool, and worth checking out. What's most interesting is that you can now build SharePoint workflows in Visio, and then import them to SharePoint Designer. It's worth a look. Get the trial from `http://technet.microsoft.com/en-us/evalcenter/ee390821.aspx`.

Visual Studio 2010 is all the rage with developers these days. Of course, I cannot program my way out of a paper bag, so it does me no good. Hopefully, you are smarter than I am. Download the trial at `http://msdn.microsoft.com/en-us/vstudio/default.aspx`.

`AdventureWorks` databases would be handy if you want to play more with SSRS. It is now available as a Codeplex project you can find at `http://msftdbprodsamples.codeplex.com/`. Be sure to get the correct version based on what edition of SQL Server you are using.

Other considerations before you disconnect this VM from the Internet would be Silverlight (`http://www.silverlight.net/`), Fiddler (`http://www.fiddler2.com/fiddler2/`), and Firefox (`http://www.mozilla.com/en-US/firefox/`). They are all handy things to have up and running before you hit the road.

SUMMARY

This chapter was hopefully a fun thrill ride for you building the essential tool in any IT rock star's toolbox. You now have a solid VM that has everything ready to go. So, when the client says he or she needs to see some random SharePoint feature demoed that you have never heard of, you will know your trusty VM has the power. Remember, not everything in this walkthrough is best practice for building a production farm, but hopefully working through this VM, you did get some solid ideas that will help you with that farm. You now have a safe place to try something out. Just remember to take a snapshot first.

ABOUT THE AUTHOR

Shane Young is a recovering Server Farm Administrator and active SharePoint zealot. From his home base in Cincinnati, Ohio, he travels the country, and sometimes the world, supporting, teaching, and evangelizing for all things SharePoint. He is the founder of his own SharePoint consulting company, SharePoint911.com. When he is not living the glamorous life of a Microsoft MVP, he can be found spending time with his lovely wife, Nicola, his son, Grant, and their dogs, Tyson and Pugsley.

Upgrading to SharePoint Server 2010 — The Hybrid Approach

By Jason Medero

IT professionals, developers, and even end users will eventually come across the terms "upgrade" and "migration." When these groups hear these terms, they immediately begin to shiver with fear and anxiety. Quickly following the fear and anxiety are lots of questions regarding what will change and what the overall effect will be. This chapter provides answers to questions about upgrading to SharePoint Server 2010 from Microsoft Office SharePoint Server 2007 (MOSS 2007) utilizing the hybrid approaches.

While reading this chapter, you should take notice of the planning guidelines and best practices referenced frequently. And you should always keep in mind what the requirements are for your organization. Even though I may lean toward preferring a specific approach over another, it will be up to you to choose an approach that best fits your scenario.

This chapter unveils the complexities surrounding upgrades, and provides insights from real-world experiences to better prepare you for what to expect during an upgrade and, more specifically, using the hybrid upgrade approach.

The discussion begins with some key background information and an overview of what's new with the SharePoint 2010 upgrade. Later, the discussion examines details surrounding the various upgrade options.

UNDERSTANDING THE NEW SHAREPOINT 2010 UPGRADE PROCESS

The release of SharePoint Server 2010 brings with it a couple of new database attach upgrade choices when moving from MOSS 2007 to SharePoint Server 2010. These options include two new hybrid database migration approaches that have benefits over simply using the in-place or the standard database attach approaches, which are also supported in SharePoint Server 2010.

The SharePoint Server 2010 upgrade options have changed from the options offered in previous versions. The in-place and the database attach upgrade options are still available, but the gradual upgrade option has been deprecated from the upgrade options list.

Microsoft's thinking behind deprecating the gradual upgrade option was that, if not done properly, upgrades were going terribly wrong and blowing up mid-upgrade. In my experiences, I have never had any issues with the gradual upgrade as long as I methodically followed my refined procedure for performing the gradual upgrade. On the other hand, if you didn't follow strict protocol while performing the gradual upgrade, there were plenty of things that could potentially be disastrous. It was too easy for many different avenues to destroy an upgrade, and this is why, in my opinion, Microsoft decided to not make the gradual upgrade option available in SharePoint Server 2010.

Even though Microsoft has removed the gradual upgrade capability, it has supplemented it with other capabilities that provide a somewhat similar experience. Probably the biggest addition is the Visual Upgrade Feature, which allows users to seamlessly switch the look and feel back and forth between versions. The Visual Upgrade Feature will be a commonly leveraged utility when using either of the hybrid upgrade methods that are explained thoroughly in this chapter.

Additionally, Microsoft has provided a slew of improvements to the platform as a whole when performing upgrades to SharePoint Server 2010. Utilizing these improvements and the additional new tools that have been made available will ensure a much more successful upgrade to SharePoint Server 2010.

SYSTEM REQUIREMENTS FOR A SHAREPOINT 2010 UPGRADE

The hardware and software requirements may come as a shock to those who have been living under a rock for the past few years. I say this in a joking manner, of course. But if you have been involved in the IT industry in some way or another, you must have seen this coming.

There has been a bit of lag with the widespread adoption of moving an existing MOSS 2007 environment to 64 bit. This is primarily because of the concerns regarding the expense, difficulty, and the time-consuming process that organizations presume the effort will take. Microsoft believes that these concerns are exaggerated, and the potential benefits far outweigh the investment of time and money.

Throughout the past few years especially, Microsoft has realized that many advantages exist to running an application on 64-bit hardware and software. Therefore, just as was the case with Exchange 2007 in the past, there is now a 64-bit mandatory requirement for SharePoint Server 2010.

In addition to the 64-bit hardware requirement, 64-bit edition software requirements also must be installed for use with SharePoint Server 2010. For example, SharePoint Server 2010 now requires the installation of a 64-bit edition Microsoft SQL Server. Even when using the built-in database for evaluation purposes, SharePoint will install a 64-bit version SQL Server 2008 Express Edition.

Table 2-1 shows the minimum hardware/software and client browsing requirements for SharePoint Server 2010.

TABLE 2-1: System Requirements for SharePoint Server 2010*

HARDWARE	SOFTWARE	CLIENT BROWSER
4 GB RAM for evaluation use	64-bit Windows Server 2008 Standard w/SP2	Internet Explorer 7 (32-bit), Internet Explorer 8 (32-bit), Mozilla FireFox 3.5, or Apple Safari 4.x
8 GB RAM for single server/ multi-server deployments	64-bit SQL Server 2005 Standard Edition with Service Pack 3 (SP3) and cumulative update package 3 for SP3	
64-bit, quad-core, 2.5 GHz per core minimum processor	64-bit SQL Server 2008 Standard/Express Edition with Service Pack 1 (SP1) and cumulative updated package 2 for SP1	
80 GB hard disk for installation		

*This table does not include any additional services and roles that must be implemented prior to installing SharePoint Server 2010. It includes only the minimum hardware, additional software that must be installed, and the client browsers that are supported for browsing SharePoint Server 2010.

SHAREPOINT 2010 UPGRADE IMPROVEMENTS

As mentioned, the gradual upgrade option in SharePoint Server 2010 has been removed, and is no longer a supported upgrade path. When I first received word of this, I thought for sure that there was going to be some pretty nasty backlash. I, for one, had many questions wondering how Microsoft was going to fill this gap. In the upgrade approaches to MOSS 2007, my go-to approach in most scenarios was the gradual upgrade. The biggest benefit of the gradual migration was being able to upgrade sites in real time, while not incurring any downtime for end users.

Of course, the gradual upgrade approach also had some downsides to it, and one of the biggest was the storage size and processing power of the infrastructure to run the two versions side by side. In some cases, this was a deal-breaker for the gradual upgrade approach.

So, what upgrade improvements does SharePoint Server 2010 provide to ease the pain and some of the complexities of performing an upgrade? I think it's a good idea to take a step back and work from the very beginning, even prior to selecting what upgrade method you will take. This is the very place where SharePoint Server 2010 has made the most improvements so that the upgrade team can be better prepared for what to expect during an upgrade.

Pre-Upgrade Checker

Technically speaking, the *pre-upgrade checker* tool is actually not a tool at all. Rather, it is a custom STSADM extension that Microsoft has made available to customers who have upgraded to MOSS 2007 Service Pack 2 (SP2). Simply put, you can use the pre-upgrade checker command if you have downloaded and installed MOSS 2007 SP2 in your SharePoint environment.

This is a very nifty extension that, in my opinion, is much better than its long-distant cousin, prescan.exe, of the SharePoint Portal Server 2003 days. This STSADM extension can be run on your current MOSS 2007 production farm and, unlike its cousin (prescan.exe), it will not modify any data.

The pre-upgrade checker STSADM command is a rule-based checker operation that scans the server on which it is executed. This command has two goals:

➤ The first one is to determine whether your servers in your existing SharePoint environment meet the core requirements for upgrading to SharePoint Server 2010.

➤ Secondly (and most importantly), it is to be used by the upgrade team to determine what currently exists inside of their SharePoint farm to better prepare for the upgrade to SharePoint Server 2010.

The STSADM command can be run locally from any server in your farm. The pre-upgrade command should be run locally on each server in your farm to ensure that your farm has the same components across the board. When I say "components," I am talking about Features, site definitions, list definitions, language packs, and so on. This will prevent you from scratching your head come upgrade time when, for some unexpected reason, a server from within your farm is failing to upgrade.

Following is an example of the command that does farm-level checks without any additional parameters:

```
STSADM -o preupgradecheck
```

It is possible to check the local server only by using the -localonly parameter. Once executed, the command will begin to take an extensive inventory of your SharePoint environment and document such things as the following:

➤ Servers in the farm

➤ Web applications

➤ Office Server Search topology information

➤ Information about supported upgrade types to SharePoint Server 2010

➤ Site/list definitions

➤ Missing or invalid farm configuration settings

➤ Database upgrade eligibility (set to read/write)

➤ Installed features/language packs

➤ Custom workflow actions

➤ Alternate access mapping information

➤ Customized list/field types that will not be upgraded

After the pre-upgrade checker command has finished scanning the SharePoint environment and taking inventory, it creates a report. Now, the report it creates is not perfect, and could be organized a bit better, but this is light-years ahead of past versions. My guess is that Microsoft provided literally everything at once, instead of just the customizations to the SharePoint environment.

I am certainly not complaining, but it would have been nice for Microsoft to provide a parameter to weed out all of the out-of-the-box items, and just show the customizations. On the other hand, I can see how this could become fairly subjective as to what exactly is considered a customization and what is not.

Figure 2-1 provides a glimpse into some of the more important information included in this report. Pay special attention to the section labeled "Supported upgrade types," because this will provide you with what methods you should initially consider.

The preupgrade checker needs to be run on each of these servers in order to get a complete list of issues that might affect upgrade. For more information about this rule, see KB article 954758 in the rule article list at http://go.microsoft.com/fwlink/?LinkID=120257.

Information Only : The components from this farm
This sharepoint software currently running on this farm is 12.0.0.6421. The farm contains the following components:

- 3 servers
- 10 web applications
- 10 content databases, approximately total size = 18244960256 bytes
- 40 Site collections

For more information about this rule, see KB article 954759 in the rule article list at http://go.microsoft.com/fwlink/?LinkID=120257.

Information Only : Supported upgrade types
The current farm supports the following upgrade types:

- Inplace Upgrade
- Content Database Attach

FIGURE 2-1: Report generated by the pre-upgrade checker

 The only time you will not see the "in-place upgrade" option is if your current SharePoint environment is running on 32-bit hardware. This chapter does not focus on the process of moving your SharePoint environment to 64-bit hardware. However, to perform either of the hybrid methods described in this chapter, you must be currently running on 64-bit hardware.

I find myself running the pre-upgrade checker command multiple times against my environment throughout the upgrade process. The first time is to get a preliminary picture of the current environment, and each time thereafter is to see if the environment has changed any since the last time the tool was run. Think of it as uncovering any new potential issues that you will have to face during the upgrade. Running this tool (whether your MOSS 2007 environment is large or small) should certainly be included in your overall upgrade strategy. Not running it would be simply asking for trouble.

Upgrade Logging

Each time that you instantiate an upgrade (whether it is an in-place or database attach upgrade), SharePoint will create two logs for you:

➤ One will be the actual upgrade procedure log with a naming convention like "Upgrade-TimeOfUpgrade."

➤ The other will be an associated error log to that of the instantiated upgrade in the form of "Upgrade-TimeOfUpgrade-Error."

Figure 2-2 shows what the actual logs will look like. These logs will be located in the default LOGS folder within the directory C:/ProgramFiles/CommonFiles/MicrosoftShared/ WebServerExtensions/14/LOGS.

Upgrade-20100202-171518-90	2/2/2010 5:16 PM	Text Document	1,036 KB
Upgrade-20100202-171518-90-error	2/2/2010 5:15 PM	Text Document	3 KB
Upgrade-20100202-171121-396	2/2/2010 5:12 PM	Text Document	1,038 KB
Upgrade-20100202-171121-396-error	2/2/2010 5:11 PM	Text Document	3 KB
Upgrade-20100202-165551-569	2/2/2010 4:56 PM	Text Document	13 KB
Upgrade-20100202-165551-569-error	2/2/2010 4:56 PM	Text Document	5 KB
Upgrade-20100202-142717-396	2/2/2010 2:29 PM	Text Document	1,388 KB
Upgrade-20100202-142717-396-error	2/2/2010 2:27 PM	Text Document	2 KB

FIGURE 2-2: Sample log listing

Those who can remember as far back as 2007 will recall that you had to deal with one long upgrade log. If you wanted a new log each time you started an upgrade, you had to actually delete the old one.

This time around, things have changed for the better, and you now have an upgrade log each time you kick off an upgrade, as well as an associated upgrade error log. The error log is the log that you should be going to first if your upgrade is failing for any reason. This log will report all errors and additionally state any warnings that may be logged along the upgrade process.

For example, a common warning in larger MOSS 2007 environments might be something like, "The orphaned sites could cause upgrade failures. Try to detach and reattach the database that contains the orphaned sites." This error means that you have some orphaned sites that were probably found by the pre-upgrade checker, but were overlooked. For those who are not familiar with what *orphans* are, simply put, they are the name for objects in a SharePoint schema that live without a parent or child relationship in the database. The main source of orphans comes from the create and delete transactions within your SharePoint farm.

There is an STSADM command that can be run to repair your Content Databases and remove these orphaned sites or other objects. In the case when your upgrade fails, these logs will be invaluable for finding the root cause of the failure.

When performing an upgrade (whether it's an in-place, a database attach, or a hybrid of the two approaches), the upgrade log, along with the upgrade error log, will be created each time an upgrade is instantiated. These logs (especially the error log) contain key information in the event that your upgrades were to fail. Even when upgrades I have done succeeded, I have made it a habit to check the upgrade error log for any warnings that might have come up during the upgrade that I should be aware of. This is good practice. Just because your upgrade succeeded does not mean that there are not some minor things still missing in the background that you will only know about when you review the logs.

Visual Upgrade

In my mind, Microsoft had to provide the *Visual Upgrade Feature* because of the deprecation of the gradual upgrade approach. Whether you choose to upgrade using the in-place, database attach, or hybrid approach, you are bound to run into the Visual Upgrade Feature.

This feature allows site collection administrators (and, if allowed, site owners) to preview sites with the new SharePoint 2010 look and feel. SharePoint 2010 ships with the SharePoint 2007 default master pages and style sheets. Because of this, administrators have the capability to switch back and forth between the SharePoint 2007 and SharePoint 2010 look and feel to take advantage of the Visual Upgrade Feature.

During the actual upgrade, administrators have the capability to select whether or not they want the sites to use the SharePoint 2007 or the SharePoint 2010 look and feel when the sites are upgraded. It is important that you understand what a customized page is prior to going through the two options.

A *customized page* in SharePoint 2007 is a page that is referenced in the database instead of the filesystem. A customized page is created when a user opens up a page in SharePoint Designer 2007, makes a direct change to the settings or interface of a page, and then saves the change. Once this occurs, that instance of the page is now being referenced in the Content Database instead of the filesystem.

With that understanding of what a customized page is, the two Visual Upgrade options that administrators have during the upgrade are as follows:

➤ *Preserve the user interface* — This option allows site collection owners and site owners to have control over whether their site collection and sites use the SharePoint 2007 or SharePoint 2010 look and feel.

➤ *Upgrade to new user interface* — A couple of options actually exist within this option. When upgrading to SharePoint 2010, administrators can either choose to preserve customized pages, or force all sites (customized and un-customized, including all admin pages) to use the SharePoint 2010 look and feel.

You should select the "preserve the user interface" option when upgrading, or you should select "upgrade to the new user interface," but preserve customized pages. This will minimize the amount of possible broken sites when the initial upgrade completes.

This is especially important for customized sites, because forcing the sites to use the new user interface will reset the site back to its site definition. Simply put, all customizations that users have made to the look and feel of the site through SharePoint Designer 2007 will be lost. In some cases, this could cause the sites to not be functional.

If you are performing a trial upgrade, and are looking to see what breaks so that you can document the issues and resolutions, then that's one thing. But, during a production upgrade, it is best to select the option to keep the SharePoint 2007 look and feel, unless, of course, you are looking for a ton of support calls and a big headache. Regardless of the Visual Upgrade option that you select, the upgraded farm will be able to receive all of the SharePoint 2010 infrastructure benefits.

Once the sites have been upgraded, administrators will notice a new option under the Site Actions menu. This new option is called Visual Upgrade. By selecting this option administrators will be taken to what looks like the title and description page for that specific site. Looking a bit further down the page, site owners will notice the new Visual Upgrade option, as shown in Figure 2-3.

FIGURE 2-3: Visual Upgrade option on Site Settings page

This section of the page allows administrators to select whether they would like to keep the SharePoint 2007 look and feel, preview the site with the SharePoint 2010 look and feel (preview mode), or finalize the site with the SharePoint 2010 look and feel. These options provide the administrator with some flexibility during an upgrade to preview the site and identify potential issues before finalizing the look and feel of the site.

When a site is in preview mode, some features are not available. These include such things as navigational options, inheritance of page layouts, master pages, cascading style sheets (CSS), and subsite templates. This is especially prevalent if the root site collection is in Visual Upgrade preview mode.

Inheriting options will be grayed out and unavailable until you finalize the Visual Upgrade settings with the SharePoint 2010 look and feel. These types of restrictions should be communicated to the site owners and users who have more than contributor access to the site. This measure should be taken into consideration, or else you will have a sudden influx of help desk support calls.

At the site-collection level, site-collection administrators have the capability to force all subsites underneath that site collection to use any of the three options previously mentioned. Once the upgrade completes, the Visual Upgrade options can be controlled only through the user interface (site settings) on a site-collection basis. For example, there is not an option in the user interface to force all site collections in the farm to be put in preview mode.

However, just because it's not in the user interface does not mean that it cannot be done. Thanks to the use of PowerShell, this kind of job can easily be performed. Following is an example of how you can use PowerShell to loop through all of the sites and get the information that you need to change the user interface by calling Get-SPSite:

```
$gc = Start-SPAssignment
$sites = $gc | Get-SPSite -Limit All -Url http://*
$ver = 3
$sites | % {Set-UIVersion $_ $ver $true}
$gc | Stop-SPAssignment
```

Once a site-collection administrator or site owner has finalized the Visual Upgrade settings through the user interface, the Visual Upgrade option will not be configurable again through the user interface. If, for some reason, the look and feel needs to be reversed back to the old look and feel, PowerShell or the object model will have to be used.

When configuring your sites to be in preview mode, there are some features that are not available to configure within the site itself — such things as navigational options, inheritance of page layouts, master pages, CSS, and selection subsite templates. This is especially prevalent if the root site collection site is in Visual Upgrade Preview mode. Options that involve inheriting from the top-level site collection will be grayed out and unavailable until you finalize the Visual Upgrade settings for the top-level site collection with the version 4 (V4) look and feel.

As you can tell, the Visual Upgrade Feature will be an integral part of the upgrade planning and strategy. This feature should be used temporarily while site owners work through each of their sites to determine and identify issues with the look and feel of the site. Organizations should provide some timelines around how long sites will be allowed to be in SharePoint 2007 mode or preview mode. This will enforce consistency across your newly upgraded SharePoint 2010 farm.

The Visual Upgrade Feature will be especially valuable for organizations that have allowed site owners to customize the look and feel of their sites with SharePoint Designer. In my experience, these sites have a much higher rate of running into complications during an upgrade, particularly with the user interface components. The reason for this is that because of the WYSIWYG nature of SharePoint Designer, users who are not trained and not provided guidelines about what they can and cannot do unfortunately can very quickly do damage to the site. The site may look and work as normal, but behind the scenes, components that are needed for the upgrade may have been deleted and, thus, the upgrade may not be successful.

Database Test cmdlet

A very useful PowerShell cmdlet called `Test-SPContentDatabase` is now included. This cmdlet can be used to test a Content Database against a web application to verify that all customizations (that is, Features that contain a wide variety of customizations) currently being stored in that Content Database are also installed within the web application you are testing against. This cmdlet will also identify potential issues with data orphans, missing assemblies, missing site definitions, and missing Features.

In the context of an upgrade, you can use this cmdlet in conjunction with the pre-upgrade checker described earlier to ensure that your new SharePoint 2010 environment has all the necessary installed components. This takes a lot of the guesswork out of the equation, because if you are missing anything in regard to what lives inside of the sites within the Content Database, this cmdlet will throw up a red flag. This makes the database attach upgrade portion of the hybrid approach a smoother procedure.

This cmdlet can be run against Content Databases only. The Content Database can be of the 2007 or 2010 version, and this includes Microsoft Windows SharePoint Services (WSS) and SharePoint Foundation (SPF). The Content Database can either be attached or unattached to the SharePoint 2010 farm.

One thing to keep in mind if the Content Database is large and is under heavy load is the overhead that running this command can cause while the scan is in progress. This cmdlet should not be used against a Content Database that is currently attached to the farm and is under heavy load.

This cmdlet is something that should be utilized prior to upgrading and post-upgrade. It can be used as a troubleshooting and validation tool throughout your SharePoint deployment, and not simply for upgrades. This is certainly not a tool that you throw away after your upgrade is successfully completed. You will find yourself using this command in the following scenarios:

➤   Upgrading from SharePoint 2007 to SharePoint 2010

➤   Moving Content Databases from one environment to another (development, staging, production)

➤   Moving Content Databases from one web application to another

Expected Downtime

Microsoft has also addressed the amount of downtime caused by performing an upgrade, especially with large upgrades (think 15 or more Content Databases, each at more than 250 GB). Upgrading to SharePoint 2010 using either of the hybrid approaches explained in this chapter allows you to upgrade multiple Content Databases in parallel. In the case that you have a large farm with many large Content Databases, an administrator can manually initiate the upgrade for more than one Content Database at a time.

This is the biggest advantage of using the database detach upgrade approach instead of the in-place upgrade approach. The in-place upgrade will automatically initiate the upgrade of one Content Database at a time. So, in large farms, this can cause a ton of downtime, because the farm is not available during an in-place upgrade.

As you can imagine, the caveat to initiating the upgrade of multiple Content Databases at once is the performance impact that this can cause. It is important when performing a trial upgrade that you test the number of upgrade threads that the hardware on which you are running can handle at one time. This number really depends on how much horsepower the hardware on which you are running your upgrade has.

Now, that doesn't mean that you should try to attach all of your Content Databases at once if you are lucky enough to be running your upgrade on a server with 64 GB of RAM and 32 processors. There is some dependency on the structure of your databases, so you should first try two or three at once, and then move on from there. It may be quicker to do them in batches of three than, say, batches of five, because the time it takes for the batch of three to complete might not be as long as it takes for the batch of five. Your miles will vary, and the only real way to approach this is to perform a trial upgrade and document your findings. This is by far one of the best improvements when it comes to upgrading a large SharePoint 2007 farm to SharePoint 2010.

Central Administration Status Page

Another awesome improvement that is worth mentioning is the upgrade status page that is provided through Central Administration in SharePoint 2010. This provides some great insight into the upgrades that are running (and have run) by furnishing a history with some information on each initiated upgrade.

This upgrade status page can be used with the in-place upgrade or the database attach approach. It is especially useful when using the database attach upgrade because you can see the status of each Content Database as it's being upgraded. This is night and day compared to the little blinking cursor inside of the command prompt that appeared when upgrading to MOSS 2007 using the database attach method.

Figure 2-4 shows the new upgrade status page within Central Administration.

FIGURE 2-4: SharePoint 2010 upgrade status page

Site Access During an Upgrade

You can now use read-only databases to provide users with continuous access to their sites throughout an upgrade. With the release of MOSS 2007 SP2, setting your MOSS 2007 farm to read-only is now supported.

This plays into the hybrid upgrade scenario quite well, because now you can have a farm still serving read-only requests throughout the upgrade, instead of the entire farm being unavailable throughout the entire upgrade procedure. This all occurs while the new farm upgrades a restored copy of all of the Content Databases. Once the new farm is upgraded, an administrator simply must redirect traffic from the old farm to the new farm. Although users cannot contribute to the read-only farm, they can at least access content without interruption of the upgrade.

DEALING WITH LARGE CONTENT DATABASES

While performing discovery on your environment prior to the actual upgrade, it is imperative to look for large site collections. *Large site collections* are defined as any site collections that have more than 100 GB of content. If your environment has large Content Databases (150 GB or more) that contain multiple large site collections, it is a best practice to separate these large site collections into their own Content Databases prior to performing the upgrade.

The reason behind scaling out your site collections has to do with the way the content is stored inside of the Content Databases in SharePoint 2007. In SharePoint 2007, all content is stored in large tables. In large collaborative environments, there were potential performance implications that were affected by SQL Server locks. In some cases, with very large Content Databases during a large update, SQL would execute row- and table-level read locks, therefore preventing updates, inserts, and deletes. For example, if many people were trying to access the same content all at once, SQL Server locked the large table, thus causing performance issues until the lock was released.

With that said, architecturally speaking, you are much better off if your organization has one large site collection in one Content Database than having multiple large site collections living in one Content Database. These site collections should be scaled out to their own database if they are getting large. When I say "large," I mean site collections that are growing quickly (gigabytes per month) that potentially could reach 100 GB.

My past experience has shown that it is much easier to upgrade multiple smaller Content Databases than one large beast of a Content Database. You are less likely to run into timeout issues during the upgrade. Additionally, the recommended Content Database size limit in SharePoint Server 2010 is 200 GB. This limit is not a hard limit, but rather a guide to follow based upon Microsoft's internal testing.

One other thing to note is that, in SharePoint Server 2010, Content Database sizes up to 1 TB are supported, but only for large, single-site collection repositories with non-collaborative I/O usage patterns. A great example of this type of repository is a Records Center. These larger database sizes are supported for this type of scenario because they have been designed for such, and have been tested at these scales.

The main point to understand here is that splitting up these large site collections in multiple Content Databases is a best practice. This process will ease the upgrade process, and will allow for additional growth following sizing best practices in the future.

SharePoint 2007 SP1 included a new STSADM command, Mergecontentdbs, which was the command to easily move site collections into new Content Databases. Unfortunately, in some very rare cases, this command can fail and cause data corruption. This has not changed, and I do not recommend using this command to move site collections. Instead, you should use the Batch Site Manager included in the SharePoint Administration Toolkit, which you can download from Microsoft TechNet at http://technet.microsoft.com/en-us/library/cc508851%28office.12%29.aspx.

Once you have installed the toolkit, you will be able to use and access the Batch Site Manager tool through Central Administration to move one or more site collections between existing Content Databases. If all of your Content Databases are large, you may have to create the Content Databases through Central Administration first, because the tool will not create these for you.

An alternative to the Batch Site Manager tool is to simply use the STSADM backup and restore commands, which would look something like this:

```
stsadm -o backup -url http://YourSiteCollection -filename e:\test1.bak
stsadm -o restore -url http://YourSiteCollection -filename e:\test1.bak
```

You will first need to create the Content Database for the web application you will be using. If you have more than one Content Database, you will need to turn all of the databases to offline through the UI to make sure that your site collection gets restored in the newly created Content Database. If you do not turn all of the existing content databases offline (by clicking on each of them and selecting offline in the status drop-down box), you run the risk of restoring your site collection into the wrong database. Once you are finished restoring your site collection, you can proceed to turn each of the Content Databases back on.

If you are trying to move more than one site collection at a time, then the Batch Site Manager tool is worth using, because it allows you to move multiple site collections at once.

In short, keeping your Content Databases at a size that is manageable and meets your organization's Service Level Agreement (SLA) policies is something that is commonly overlooked. If not administered properly, issues can arise, not only related to an upgrade, but also to your backup/ restore policies and acceptable user performance.

UPGRADING WITH CUSTOM SITE DEFINITIONS

Creating a custom site definition was a commonly supported practice in SharePoint 2007. Custom site definitions are commonly created when you need a unique identifier for a collection of sites so that they can be targeted. You can then use that unique identifier to staple your Features to them, therefore deploying modular components that can affect a collection of sites at once.

In SharePoint 2007, site definitions were very lightweight and composed of scoped Features that were stapled to the site definition and activated when a new site was created from that specific site definition. So, what is the story like when moving your custom site definitions from SharePoint 2007 to SharePoint 2010? I guess that might be a loaded question, and the answer depends on how you architected your custom site definition.

Let's be sure you understand what a site definition is. A *site definition* is the blueprint for newly created sites. Each out-of-the-box site that you create in SharePoint 2007 and SharePoint 2010 will have an associated site definition. It defines what is to be added to the site when the site is created. Such things as what lists, document libraries, files, content types, and web parts are defined by what is in the ONET.xml file. A site uses the ONET.xml file only once upon site creation.

Now, the out-of-the-box site definitions have an ONET.xml file, and the way that Microsoft created content and capabilities in its site definitions is by using the Feature framework. The Feature is declared inside of the ONET.xml file, and can be activated during the site provisioning process. If you open up an ONET.xml file, you will see Feature IDs scoped at different levels. If you have followed the way that Microsoft created the out-of-the-box site definitions, then come upgrade time, you are in good shape.

In fact, if you have not heavily customized the ONET.xml file that you copied from the original out-of-the box ONET.xml file, you will be in much better shape when it comes to upgrade time. Such things as simply adding your own custom Features and essentially following what Microsoft did to create new functionality will be the key to an easier upgrade when it comes to upgrading an environment with custom site definitions. Your site should render in both version 3 (V3) and V4 user interfaces, as long as you have a V4 master page associated with it.

When upgrading your sites to SharePoint 2010, SharePoint uses *upgrade definition files* (UDFs) to map and transform sites from MOSS 2007 to SharePoint 2010. The site UDF maps and upgrades all of the sites and all content (including all of the list data) within these sites to a subsequent version — in this case, SharePoint 2010. SharePoint 2010 includes UDF files that it uses to map all of the out-of-the-box site definitions during upgrade time. A site UDF contains all the site mapping information, along with list upgrade templates that describe how particular columns of a list map to content types in SharePoint 2010.

You can create and register your own UDF for a site definition by giving it a unique filename per custom site definition that you have in your environment. Once you have created your custom UDF, if you place it in the `%ProgramFiles%\Common Files\Microsoft Shared\web server extensions\ 14\Config\Upgrade` folder of the setup directory, your UDF will then be processed during the upgrade. If you have created custom site definitions in your MOSS 2007 environment, then most likely you will need to create your own UDF files for mapping to SharePoint 2010.

With all that being said, if you have minimally used and customized your custom site definitions, you may not need to create a custom UDF. During the trial upgrade, if you notice sites that are completely being skipped and still have the old look and feel, that is a clear indication that you will need to create your own site UDFs. Unfortunately, without testing, there really isn't an indicator that provides this information.

When upgrading with custom site definitions, SharePoint has a process that it goes through to decide between what upgrade definition it will use if one is not specified. SharePoint upgrades websites based on the previous product version, prioritizing (as much as possible) migration of data. I am not going to describe the entire process that it goes through, but keep in mind that you should document how your environment reacts during a trial upgrade, and whether or not you need to create a UDF or start from scratch and create new Features. This will dictate the changes that will need to be made to upgrade your custom site definition.

The best option for upgrading site definitions with minimal customizations is to use a current SharePoint 2010 equivalent site definition, and then use the SharePoint 2010 Feature upgrade feature for upgrading Feature elements used in MOSS 2007.

In SharePoint 2010, every Feature has a corresponding version number that is specified in the `feature.xml` file. The feature versioning in SharePoint 2010 allows Features once activated to have an associated version number and, therefore, these Feature instances can be more easily tracked. This new functionality provides developers with a way to upgrade their custom MOSS 2007 Features that they may have been using to add functionality to their sites. This is a best-case upgrade scenario, because, in this case, you will not have to worry about site UDFs as mentioned previously. You must simply create upgrade actions in the new `feature.xml` file for SharePoint 2010.

The `feature.xml` file in SharePoint 2010 has a specific section that can be used to declare the upgrade actions that are required to upgrade a particular Feature instance from an earlier version to the most current version. The new Feature upgrade infrastructure queries the `feature.xml` file for Feature instances that need upgrading, and then proceeds to upgrade. The scope order in which the Features are upgraded is as follows:

1. The server farm
2. The web application level
3. The site collection level
4. The specific web level

At the web level, the Features at the root web are upgraded first, and then all sub-webs. During the upgrade process, if an error occurs, it will be logged in both the ULS and upgrade logs. The upgrade process will continue to upgrade the remaining Feature instances, whether it fails on a specific Feature instance or not.

Upgrading Features in SharePoint 2010 is not handled through Central Administration, PowerShell, or STSADM out of the box. It requires writing custom code, but there is a tool on Codeplex built by fellow MVP Chris O'Brien that you might want to check out at `http://spfeatureupgrade.codeplex.com/`. This tool will help you facilitate upgrading your MOSS 2007 Features after the upgrade has been completed.

 For more information on Feature upgrading, see the MSDN library at `http://msdn.microsoft.com/en-us/library/ee535723.aspx`.

Because there have been some fundamental changes in the ONET.xml file from SharePoint 2007, it may be easier to just start from scratch — especially in the case where your environment is using many different language packs. SharePoint relies heavily on resource expressions and resource files to work with different languages. A lot of changes will need to be made to the XML files of the previous versions.

Additionally, if your organization has directly edited the ONET.xml file to create custom capabilities for newly created sites based on a custom site definition in V3, it is best to create this functionality and wrap it up into Features. If not, your other option is to edit the ONET.xml file to make it more consistent with a V4 site definition.

As you can imagine, this can be very problematic, and it may be a lot easier to create a new site definition for new sites to use during site creation. Old sites can still take advantage of the new capabilities because, during the upgrade, all site objects and Features will be upgraded to the current version using the UDF that you have the option to create. But, for new sites, my experience has shown that it's usually easier to create a new custom site definition to use if you have to, or use an out-of-the-box one and staple your Features to it. It really all depends on the level of customization that has been done to the ONET.xml file, and the practices that were used to edit that file.

The takeaway from this section should be that prior to creating a UDF and re-working your custom site definition, you should first perform a trial upgrade to see how your custom site definition(s) work. In some cases (especially if you used the Feature framework to add capabilities), everything may come across unscathed and work normally.

 For more information on site UDFs and how they are processed, check out the MSDN article found at http://msdn.microsoft.com/en-us/library/ms439232.aspx.

CHOOSING THE RIGHT UPGRADE APPROACH

So, what approach should your organization select when pursuing an upgrade from SharePoint 2007 to SharePoint 2010? Because the hybrid approach is actually a combination of the two approaches (in-place and database attach), it is pivotal to understand what occurs underneath the hood of each. This section briefly describes each of the different supported approaches, and provides clear direction with the advantages and disadvantages of each.

Once you have an understanding of both approaches, you will then be prepared for the discussion later in this chapter about combining both of these approaches into their own upgrade approach.

In-Place Upgrade Approach

The first approach to examine is the in-place upgrade. The in-place upgrade is definitely simpler with regard to the number of steps you must follow to upgrade. But, there is a lot going on in the background when you kick off an in-place upgrade — some of which you can and can't control. When using the in-place upgrade approach, you will roughly follow these steps:

1. Install SharePoint 2010 on all of your SharePoint 2007 servers.

2. Run the SharePoint Products Configuration Wizard (SPCW) on the server running Central Administration website first. Then pause when prompted and run it on the other servers.

3. Select the desired Visual Upgrade options for your newly upgraded sites.

4. Complete the running of the SPCW on the server running Central Administration, and then complete it on the rest of your SharePoint servers.

5. Check the upgrade status for sites within Central Administration, or use the `localupgradestatus` operation within `STSADM.exe`.

6. Verify for upgrade failure or success, including the following:

> ➤ Review upgrade log files.

> ➤ Validate new configurations for the environment and sites (service applications, My Sites, search components, profiles, and so on).

> ➤ Review application logs and server diagnostic logs.

These steps are by no means a complete and exhaustive list that you will need to work through when using an in-place upgrade. But it should provide you with an idea of the amount of effort that it actually takes to start the upgrade procedure.

Table 2-2 lists the pros and cons of the in-place upgrade.

TABLE 2-2: In-Place Upgrade Advantages and Disadvantages

ADVANTAGES	DISADVANTAGES
Capability to upgrade entire farm at once.	Can only upgrade to the same type of installation.
Capability to upgrade while conserving farm-wide configuration settings.	No capability to pause or roll back the upgrade once it has started.
Easiest direct upgrade path.	The server farm is unavailable for user requests during the actual upgrade process.
Can upgrade multi-server farms.	The length of time for the upgrade could be significant, and depends on the number of Content Databases, as well as the size of each.
If SharePoint 2007 is running on 64-bit hardware, there is no need to rebuild server(s) or deal with moving customizations, which, in most cases, can upgrade directly.	The upgrade will process only one Content Database at a time. There are no parallel Content Database upgrades.
Can be combined with the database attach approach to provide hybrid advantages to a hybrid approach.	This upgrade approach cannot be used if the current environment is running on 32-bit hardware.

The biggest advantage of the in-place upgrade approach is that it has the capability to migrate all your farm configuration settings. However, the number one barrier to entry with using this approach is that the hardware on which SharePoint 2007 is running must be 64-bit. This is not just for the web tier. This requirement applies to the application and the database server tiers as well.

This is an issue that will need to be overcome with organizations that have failed to update their hardware.

To overcome this issue, the process of moving to 64-bit is not very complex, but will require some planning to avoid downtime. The biggest thing to keep in mind if this is something that your organization is considering is that it is unsupported (not that it won't necessarily work) to mix and match 32-bit and 64-bit architectures at the tier level. For example, having one Web Front-End (WFE) that is 32-bit and one WFE that is 64-bit is unsupported.

As everyone knows, the easiest approach is most likely never the best, and usually is the most risky. This holds true for the in-place upgrade, because once the upgrade starts, there is no going back, and the procedure requires downtime. The amount of downtime is dependent upon how much content is being stored in the Content Databases that belong to the farm being upgraded.

As reflected in Table 2-2, another disadvantage of the in-place upgrade is that using the in-place upgrade only allows the server farm to be upgraded to the same type of installation. For example, if you are currently running a standalone server environment, you cannot scale out during the upgrade to a medium server farm, and vice versa. So, organizations looking to scale out at the same time as the upgrade will have to wait until after the upgrade has completed on the current server farm configuration.

Those who can remember back to the upgrading to SharePoint 2007 days will remember the in-place upgrade and the recommendations that Microsoft made available on deciding whether to choose this approach. The guidelines were that the in-place upgrade approach was to be used only on very small server farms (15 GB of data or less).

Furthermore, many in-place upgrades that were performed on server farms with large Content Databases experienced timeout issues within the upgrade process. The timeout issue was especially prevalent in virtualized environments that ran on (for lack of a better word) "underpowered" hardware. Microsoft has promised that the timeout issue has been rectified, but only time will tell.

If there is a failure with the in-place upgrade approach, Microsoft has provided administrators with a "resume" feature for the upgrade. This enables the in-place upgrade procedure to continue upgrading sites where it left off prior to the failure. The in-place upgrade approach today has improved considerably, and even though Microsoft has not released any guidance as of this writing, more organizations will consider using the in-place upgrade approach in comparison to its counterpart when upgrading to 2007.

In-Place Upgrade Under the Hood

The in-place approach takes very little time to get going. But in the background, a few things are happening that are important to understand.

During an in-place upgrade, all services infrastructure and configuration settings are upgraded to the SharePoint 2010 equivalent. In MOSS 2007, the Shared Service Provider (SSP) hosted one or more reusable services. During an in-place upgrade to SharePoint 2010, SSPs are converted to service applications and service application groups (also known as *proxies*). One service application is created per service.

For example, for each SSP that existed in the farm prior to the upgrade, the upgrade process automatically creates a *Search service application*. All settings from the OSearch service in the MOSS 2007 SSP are copied to the corresponding search service application. The settings that are copied include the search scopes, crawl rules, content sources, and managed properties.

In SharePoint 2010, two services are used for user profiles and the new taxonomy metadata store. These services are called the *User Profile Service* and the *Managed Metadata Service*. During an in-place upgrade, these two services are automatically enabled and configured.

The user profile data from MOSS 2007 is upgraded from the SSP database into a new user profile database. Properties that are related to the profiles such as the My Site host URL (which are stored in the configuration database) are preserved during the in-place upgrade. The SSP database is not kept or upgraded; rather, it is broken out into different service applications that have their very own databases. After an in-place upgrade has completed successfully, and all configurations have been verified, the old SSP admin site can be safely deleted.

All scheduled timer jobs will need to be reconfigured after an in-place upgrade. This is because all timer jobs are set back to their default times, so be sure to document these prior to kicking off an upgrade.

The in-place upgrade will handle the export and import of all administrator-deployed form templates (.XSN files) and data connection files (.UDCX files). If the URL is going to change after the upgrade, the farm administrator can run the Update-SPInfoPathAdminFileUrl Windows PowerShell cmdlet to update links that are used in the .XSN files.

With regard to Excel Services, the in-place upgrade handles all of the configuration information stored in the SSP database. The configuration information is upgraded and moved into the configuration database. After the upgrade is completed, the farm administrator must provision a new unattended service account by using the Secure Store Service to use with Excel Services.

The in-place upgrade also does a pretty good job with the Business Data Catalog (BDC) data. All of the BDC data that was stored in the SSP database is moved and upgraded to a separate database. For each BDC service that was running in SharePoint 2007, two new services are created for use with the new SharePoint 2010 Business Data Connectivity Services (BCS).

One service, the Business Data Connectivity Service, is used to store BDC models, which are compatible with the new SharePoint 2010 BCS object model.

The second service is called Application Registry Service, which is used to store application definitions that are compatible with the SharePoint 2007 BDC object model. Essentially, this is a backward-compatible service that is used to manage old BDC connections that use the older SharePoint 2007 BDC object model. During the in-place upgrade, a copy of each application definition that was being stored in the BDC is moved to the Application Registry Service, and an upgraded version that is based on the new object model is placed in the BCS.

Using the in-place upgrade approach is supported for upgrading custom solutions that are based on the BDC. This is not something that will always work automatically, but the majority of the grunt work is done for you. If you are using the BDC or Excel Services in conjunction with Single Sign-On (SSO), you must perform some work to migrate SSO data to the Secure Store Service, which is explained in detail later in this chapter.

It is recommended to slowly begin updating your BDC models to be compatible with the new BCS object model to take advantage of all of the new features that come with the new BCS for SharePoint 2010.

SSO has been replaced with the Secure Store Service in SharePoint 2010. Neither of the upgrade approaches available provides a direct upgrade path for the data and settings from SSO to the Secure Store Service. As mentioned previously, this will require some manual re-working, which will involve migrating data from the SSO database that your organization was using to a new Secure Store database.

The story is the same if you were using SSO for Excel Services, because it requires the use of the Secure Store Service to also function correctly. Application definitions that were using the Microsoft SSO service provider will be updated to refer to the Secure Store Service.

 For more information on moving SSO data from Microsoft SSO to the Secure Store service, see `http://technet.microsoft.com/en-us/library/cc262889.aspx#SecureStore`.

Post In-Place Upgrade

During the in-place upgrade, SharePoint will handle upgrading all of the existing MOSS 2007 services and SSPs. If your organization wants to leverage any of the new services that come with SP 2010, these services will need to be enabled. You can enable these new services by creating service applications to host these new services. Service applications have replaced SSPs in SP 2010. Service applications in SP 2010 enable the platform to become even more scalable and modular with respect to service consumption and the publishing of services.

A new option in SP 2010 to configure several services and create service applications very quickly is to use the farm configuration wizard. The farm configuration wizard is recommended to be used in development environments only. You should certainly not be using the farm configuration wizard to enable and create services post upgrade in a production environment.

The configuration wizard provides very little control over the naming of services and service applications, as well as segmenting what accounts are used to run these services. It is highly recommended that you manually create and configure only the services that you foresee using in your environment currently. It is not good practice to turn every service on just because you can, and this will only add unneeded load on the servers in your environment.

In addition to enabling your new SP 2010 services, you can also add proxies for your service applications. Service application proxies enable administrators to connect web applications to only the services that they will be using. In comparison to SP 2007 (where you only could associate a web application to an SSP that included all of the services), this model is much more versatile.

Profile properties data in SharePoint 2007 was stored in the SSP database, which was a part of the profile services data. Profile data in SharePoint 2010 is stored in the User Profile Services profile database. The new SharePoint 2010 service application that handles all of the taxonomy data is called the *Managed Metadata Service (MMS)*. These service applications must be enabled after you have completed the in-place upgrade. From there, you can use Windows PowerShell cmdlets to upgrade the profile and taxonomy data, and migrate everything to the taxonomy and user profile databases.

The cmdlet to upgrade the taxonomy data is `Move-SPProfileManagedMetadataProperty`. You must first get the ID of the newly created User Profile Service application by using the cmdlet `Get-SPServiceApplicationProxy`. Next, you need the name to use as the identity for the managed metadata property when you upgrade the taxonomy data (that is, user profile properties) when using the `Move-SPProfileManagedMetadataProperty` cmdlet.

You must run the `Move-SPProfileManagedMetadataProperty` cmdlet for each user profile property that you would like to move, because there is not currently an option to specify all properties. It is important to note that, if you are upgrading taxonomy data, the User Profile Service application proxy and the MMS application proxy must be in the same proxy group.

After an in-place upgrade, the profile picture store must be updated. To update the photo store you can use the cmdlet `Update-SPProfilePhotoStore`. This cmdlet will copy the user photos from where they were stored in SharePoint 2007, and will move them to the user photos library on the My Site host. Prior to migrating the user profiles, ensure that the quota set for My Site sites has enough space to store the photo. This cmdlet must be run only once for each My Site host URL.

If your SharePoint 2007 web applications were configured to use forms-based authentication (FBA), the web applications must be converted to claims authentication before FBA will work correctly in SharePoint 2010. Additionally, you must take some steps prior to getting FBA to work within SharePoint 2010.

 TechNet has a decent article that goes through the different tasks that will need to be completed to get FBA working with claims authentication. You can find the article at `http://technet.microsoft.com/en-us/library/ee806890.aspx#section5`.

Now that you understand the major components that need to be configured/enabled post-upgrade, let's cover the verification steps that you should be going through:

1. Check the upgrade status page to ensure that the upgrade has finished successfully.

2. Configure/enable services appropriately for your environment, as described previously in this section.

3. Check the upgrade logs and work through any outstanding issues.

4. Check the application log (event viewer) for potential issues.

5. Run a full crawl and go through the crawl log looking for potential issues.

6. Review the health analyzer reports from SharePoint 2010 monitoring in Central Administration.

7. Review upgraded sites to identify issues that must be corrected when the upgrade is run in the production environment .

Once you have gone through these steps, and the upgrade status page says 100 percent successful, the first thing you should review is the upgrade log. As mentioned earlier, the upgrade log will provide valuable insight into your newly upgraded servers.

The application log (event viewer) on each of the servers in the farm should also be reviewed to see if anything is wrong. If the issue is coming up in the application log, it is more than likely also being reported in the SharePoint 2010 diagnostic logs as well. Most of the time, what is reported in the application log is identical to what you will find in the diagnostic log. That is not to say that I don't always check the diagnostic log anyway, because sometimes you can get a bit more information about the events occurring that led up to the issue. That's right, those context clues that you were taught in elementary school come in handy even today!

Even though the SharePoint 2010 health analyzer reports may seem pretty rudimentary, they can still be useful. For example, in the configuration category, you may see an error with the title of "Missing server side dependencies." This is helpful when determining if you are missing Features or solutions that you have overlooked and not installed on the farm. Additionally, this error message can also identify potential data orphans. Figure 2-5 shows an example of this error and should demonstrate the value of these reports.

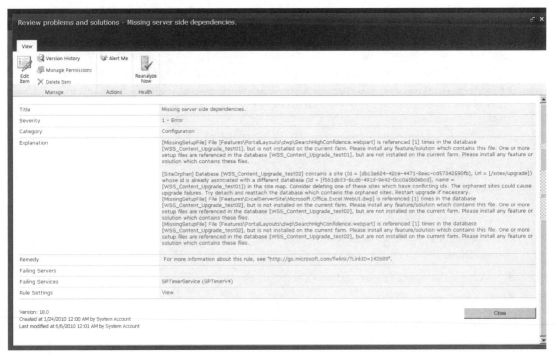

FIGURE 2-5: Health analyzer report

TRIAL UPGRADES

When performing an upgrade using any of the approaches mentioned, prior to performing an upgrade in a production environment, the best practice is to perform a trial upgrade first. The trial upgrade setup should mimic production as closely as possible from hardware all the way to the actual data. The trial upgrade will give your team a good glimpse into what they will be facing when it comes time to perform the actual production upgrade.

When performing a trial upgrade, I make sure to document all issues and resolutions from the backup and restore of the content all the way down to the .dlls that are included in the solution packages that have been deployed. This is critical in the preparation of the production upgrade, because it will allow your team to be more confident to quickly resolve issues that they have already seen. Because upgrades have a lot of moving parts, you may not catch everything with the trial upgrade, but I can guarantee that you will see the bigger show-stopping issues.

The trial upgrade also provides a good opportunity for the site owners to go through their sites and ensure that nothing has gone horribly wrong. This gives the upgrade team time to work through the issues that come up, and also gives the site owners a sense of confidence, because they know what to expect when their sites get upgraded in production.

It is very common (and a recommendation of mine) to spin up virtual machines for your trial upgrade. Everything but SQL Server should be virtualized. The reason behind not virtualizing SQL Server is because I have seen timeout issues when performing an upgrade with a virtualized SQL Server. At the end of the day, it all depends on the amount of resources you can devote to the SQL Server virtual machine. The best part about using virtualization technology is that you can leverage the "snapshotting," and if something gets really messed up, you can very easily revert back to the last stable snapshot. If virtualization technology is available, I think this a total no-brainer.

To me, there are so many advantages to a trial upgrade that not going through with one is just insane. Even if budget and time are an issue, I always go back to my SharePoint mantra, which is, "Short-term gains equal long-term pains." This means that it is better to invest the time and money now into doing a trial upgrade than it is to potentially ruin your production environment with a botched upgrade. Upgrading from SharePoint 2007 to SharePoint 2010 is not a simple task, and planning should be involved. A trial upgrade is a major key to the success of the production upgrade.

Database Attach Upgrade Approach

The database attach upgrade approach involves upgrading the content in your environment only. The configurations that come along with SharePoint 2007 will not come across when using this approach. Keep in mind that, to use this approach, you will need an available SharePoint 2010 environment that you can use to attach the SharePoint 2007 databases to in order to initiate the upgrade.

This approach has some advantages along with some disadvantages. This approach is useful in the scenario where you are changing existing hardware. The common example is if your SharePoint 2007 environment is currently running on 32-bit hardware. You cannot use the in-place approach because it requires 64-bit hardware. So, you are stuck with either using the database attach approach, or using one of the hybrid approaches described later in this chapter.

Table 2-3 describes the pros and cons of the database attach upgrade approach.

TABLE 2-3: Database Attach Upgrade Advantages and Disadvantages

ADVANTAGES	DISADVANTAGES
Capability to upgrade multiple Content Databases simultaneously. This translates into quicker upgrades in environments with large Content Databases.	SharePoint 2007 configuration settings are not upgraded to the new SharePoint 2010 environment, and must be configured manually.
If you have multiple farms that you would like to combine, you can attach the Content Databases to the new SharePoint 2010 environment and initiate an upgrade.	All customizations must be moved to the new SharePoint 2010 environment.
	Need to be versed in using SQL Server tools to back up and restore Content Databases if moving to a new SQL Server.
The cleanest upgrade path with the most control over newly configured services and naming conventions.	Will incur downtime if new hardware to build SharePoint 2010 is not available.
Can be combined with in-place upgrade approach to provide a hybrid upgrade approach.	SharePoint 2010 environment must be built and configured prior to attaching Content Databases and initiating the upgrade.
	Once a database upgrade is initiated, this process cannot be rolled back.

The biggest downside of the database attach is that this approach does not migrate all of your SharePoint 2007 configuration settings to your new SharePoint 2010 environment. This is a big issue for environments with many customizations and custom configurations. This is not that painful if you have used the SharePoint 2007 solutions (WSP) framework. You must copy over all of your solution packages and deploy them to your SharePoint 2010 environment.

If, for some reason, you missed the boat on using SharePoint 2007 solution packages to deploy your customizations, you are in for a bit more work. You must hunt down each customization and manually move it over to the new SharePoint 2010 environment, and then deploy accordingly. These customizations include (but are not limited to) the following:

➤ Custom site definitions

➤ web.config changes

➤ Assemblies/dlls

➤ Features that were installed and deployed outside of solution packages

➤ Custom master pages and CSS that were deployed to the filesystem

All of these custom elements must be installed in the newly installed SharePoint 2010 environment. These elements should be installed on all of the WFE servers in your farm. As mentioned earlier in this chapter, the pre-upgrade checker STSADM command and the test-spcontentdatabase cmdlet will provide you with the information you will need to determine whether you are missing customizations.

When performing the database attach upgrade, you will want to document all customizations throughout a trial upgrade. This will be critical when it comes time to perform the database attach in production.

Another item worth mentioning is that it is important to not introduce any new custom components into the production environment from the time a trial upgrade is performed until production has been upgraded. This is so you don't end up with unexpected surprises come production upgrade time. In larger environments, this may be difficult to accomplish, so instead, some restrictions on what is introduced into the existing environment prior to production upgrade should be defined.

If your organization is heavily using InfoPath forms (in particular, administrator-approved form templates and data connection files in Central Administration libraries), you must perform some additional steps when upgrading the following types of files:

➤ Form templates (.XSN) that were uploaded to the Manage Form Templates library through the Central Administration site

➤ Data connection files (.UDCX) that were uploaded to the Manage Data Connection Files library through the Central Administration site

These libraries in MOSS 2007 were stored in the configuration database, which does not get upgraded when using the database attach upgrade method. Therefore, the administrator-approved form templates and data connection files will need to be exported from your MOSS 2007 environment, and imported into the newly configured SharePoint 2010 environment prior to upgrading your Content Databases.

It is important to note that, if you have deployed your form templates and data connection files via Features, you can simply deploy your Features containing these files into your SharePoint 2010 environment. To export these files from your MOSS 2007, use the following command:

```
STSADM -o exportipfsadminobjects -filename <output path where the CAB file
    will be created>
```

The export will create a CAB file containing all of your deployed objects. You will need the path to run the import using the following PowerShell cmdlet:

```
Import-SPInfoPathAdministrationFiles -path "Path to exported CAB in previous step"
```

Once the objects are imported, the InfoPath Forms service will need to be configured. The import strictly imports templates and data connection files, and does not migrate over any of the settings from your MOSS 2007 environment. Additionally, if your URL is going to change after the upgrade, the links that the forms and the form templates use may have to be updated to use the new URL. These links include (but are not limited to) form data to the form template file location or links in the form template to data connection files.

To update links that are being used in the user data connection files or user form templates, you can use the PowerShell Update-SPInfoPathUserFileUrl cmdlet. For the administrator-approved form templates and data connection files, you can use the cmdlet Update-SPInfoPathAdminFileUrl. These cmdlets will essentially perform a find-and-replace of the old URL with the new URL.

Outside of preparing the new SharePoint 2010 environment and moving over elements and customizations, the database attach upgrade approach involves the following steps:

1. Use SQL Server tools to back up all Content Databases and SSP database(s) (if you have more than one SSP in your SharePoint 2007 farm).

2. For your SharePoint service account that you will be using on SQL Server, verify that permissions have been granted for a member of the db_owner database role for the Content Databases and SSP databases.

3. Run the pre-upgrade checker (not mandatory, but a good thing to run) to identify any potential issues that must be addressed prior to the upgrade.

4. Restore a copy of the backed-up SSP databases and Content Databases to SQL Server using SQL Server tools.

5. Attach your Content Databases (preferably the Content Database with the root site collection first) to a previously created web application in your SharePoint 2010 environment using the Mount-SPContentDatabase cmdlet or AddContentDb STSADM operation.

6. Once that succeeds, you can then upgrade the rest of the Content Databases and then all of the SSP databases using either of the commands mentioned previously.

It is important to note, that, as mentioned previously, if you are upgrading My Sites, you must have configured the User Profile Service application and the MMS in your SharePoint 2010 environment prior to upgrading My Sites Content Databases. Additionally, you must upgrade the SSP database(s) prior to upgrading My Site websites.

Upgrading the SSP database consists of attaching your SSP database as the new profile database that your new User Profile Service application will use. By attaching your old SSP database to the new User Profile Service application, you are essentially migrating all of the profile information for the User Profile Service application to use. You can do this through the SharePoint 2010 management shell command prompt by entering the following command:

```
New-SPProfileServiceApplication -applicationpool <ApplicationPoolName>
    -Name <ServiceApplicationName> -Profiledbname <DatabaseName>
    [-Profiledbserver <ServerName>]
```

The *Profiledbname* will be the name of your SSP database. If you have multiple SSP databases, you will create a User Profile Service application for each SSP and run the command shown here.

Once all of your SSP databases have been upgraded and attached to your new User Profile Service application, you can then attach the remaining Content Databases to your new SharePoint 2010 environment.

Using the database attach upgrade method from MOSS 2007 to SharePoint 2010, administrators have the option of upgrading multiple databases at once. During your trial upgrade, you should test the number of databases that can be attached simultaneously before performance degradation occurs. Because the number of databases that can be upgraded simultaneously is highly dependent on the horsepower of hardware, it is important to use hardware similar to what is used in production during your trial upgrade.

To initiate an upgrade on multiple databases at once, you must simply open up another instance of Windows PowerShell or STSADM and run the commands mentioned in the steps outlined earlier.

Post Database Attach Upgrade

The post-upgrade steps for the database attach are fairly similar to the in-place upgrade post-upgrade steps. A couple of differences should be noted:

> ➤ When performing a database attach, farm administrators, by default, will have permissions to all services and service applications in your farm. Permissions must be delegated accordingly after the upgrade has completed.

> ➤ The database attach does not automatically upgrade the form templates or data connection files. These must be exported and imported accordingly, as described earlier.

I find that there are fewer things to worry about configuring post database attach. This is primarily because prior to attaching the databases for upgrade, you are configuring a new environment from scratch. You also have more control in the configuration of your environment, and setting up things the proper way.

In my opinion, this is a much cleaner approach than what the in-place upgrade gives you, with many of the defaults that the approach uses through the upgrade without giving the administrator a choice. At the end of the day, the in-place upgrade is for the "set it and forget it" types, whereas the database upgrade is more hands-on and requires more upfront work, which is a good thing when it comes to upgrades.

SHAREPOINT 2010 HYBRID UPGRADE APPROACH

The hybrid upgrade approach is a combination of the two approaches described previously, with some special sauce mixed in.

The first hybrid upgrade approach to be examined here is the database attach read-only flavor. With the read-only farm capabilities introduced with MOSS 2007 SP2, you can use this feature to minimize the amount of downtime during the actual upgrade. Essentially, you can run your MOSS 2007 farm Content Databases in a read-only state. It is important to note that, in a SharePoint 2007 read-only farm, only the Content Databases can be put into read-only. All other databases (including the Central Administration Content Database, configuration database, search database, and SSP databases) are read-write.

So, the read-only flavor of the hybrid approach consists of setting your current SharePoint 2007 production environment to a read-only state. Once you have done this, you can then back up all of your SSP databases and Content Databases, and then copy them from SQL Server to your newly configured SharePoint 2010 farm.

The second hybrid approach examined here is a combination of the in-place upgrade and database attach. In performing this hybrid method, your team will perform an in-place upgrade, but first detach all of the Content Databases. Then, once the in-place upgrade is complete, you can begin to attach Content Databases to the newly in-place upgraded SharePoint 2010 farm. This approach allows you to take advantage of the good features of both the in-place and database attach approaches.

The next couple sections delve into detail about each one of these hybrid approaches, and also describe how you can put your SharePoint 2007 farm in read-only mode.

Read-Only Databases Hybrid Approach

The major benefit to using the read-only approach is that it limits downtime to a minimum. Users can still access their data as needed, instead of not being able to access their data at all. Not only that, but, in my opinion, the database attach method is a much cleaner approach. More work may have to go into the planning, but your SharePoint 2010 environment will have been configured from the ground up with no worries about legacy items being left behind.

SharePoint has become a critical application at many organizations, and downtime of any kind just may not be acceptable. If downtime is a concern, this hybrid approach should be the preferred approach.

To begin upgrading using this approach, you must first put your current SharePoint 2007 farm in read-only mode. To run a farm that uses read-only databases, you must first ensure that all of your Content Databases are in a read-only state. Once that is confirmed, you must then disable the timer jobs that write to these Content Databases, which are now in read-only mode.

To set your SharePoint 2007 farm to a read-only state, follow these steps:

 This procedure should not be performed on mirrored or log-shipped Content Databases. Additionally, you must have sufficient privileges in SQL Server to perform these steps on the databases.

1. Open SQL Server Management Studio.

2. Right-click the Content Database that you want to change to read-only, and then click Properties.

3. Select the Options page, and, in the "Other options" list, scroll to the State section.

4. On the Database Read-Only entry, click the arrow next to False, select True, and then click OK.

When a farm is in read-only mode, some timer jobs will fail and must be disabled. To satisfy this requirement, follow these steps:

1. Open up SharePoint 2007 Central Administration.

2. Click the Operations tab.

3. Find the Global Configuration section on the right-hand side of the screen. Click Time Job Definitions.

4. Click the following timer jobs and click the Disable button:

- ➤ Bulk workflow task processing
- ➤ Change Log
- ➤ Database Statistics
- ➤ Dead Site Delete
- ➤ Disk Quota Warning
- ➤ Expiration policy
- ➤ Hold Processing and Reporting
- ➤ Immediate Alerts
- ➤ Information management policy
- ➤ Profile Synchronization
- ➤ Quick Profile Synchronization
- ➤ Records Center Processing
- ➤ Recycle Bin
- ➤ Scheduled Approval
- ➤ Scheduled Page Review
- ➤ Scheduled Unpublish
- ➤ Search and Process
- ➤ Shared Services Provider Synchronizing Job
- ➤ Site Collection: Delete
- ➤ Usage Analysis
- ➤ Variations Propagate Page Job Definition
- ➤ Variations Propagate Site Job Definition

➤ Windows SharePoint Services Watson Policy Update

➤ Workflow

➤ Workflow Auto Cleanup

➤ Workflow Failover

5. Click OK.

When you have finished performing these steps for each of the Content Databases in your environment, SharePoint 2007 will officially be in a read-only state. If you now go through the environment that you just put in read-only mode, you will notice that some UI elements have been modified so that users cannot perform tasks that require writing to the database. With the exception of creating subsites (webs) and some other little nuisances here and there, the Content Databases for MOSS 2007 with SP2 are in read-only mode.

Now that your original farm is in read-only mode, you can start making copies of all of your SSP databases and Content Databases. Then you can move the databases to your newly configured SharePoint 2010 farm for the upgrade of data.

Prior to kicking off the upgrade of your copied SSP databases and Content Databases, you will first want to check and double-check that you have transferred all customizations from your SharePoint 2007 environment to the new SharePoint 2010 farm. It is a good idea to run the `Test-SpContentDatabase` cmdlet mentioned earlier in this chapter on each of the Content Databases prior to initiating the upgrade. This is your last chance to ensure that you have deployed all customizations before you have to begin searching through the upgrade logs if your upgrade begins to fail because of a missing customization.

Once you have set your current production farm to read-only, you can essentially follow the database attach method steps when working through the rest of the upgrade. The only difference between the two approaches is that, with the hybrid read-only approach, you have a SharePoint 2007 read-only farm running in parallel with a newly configured SharePoint 2010 farm. You are initially using the new SharePoint 2010 farm to upgrade your SSP databases and Content Databases. This means that you can take advantage of all the nice features of the database attach upgrade method, particularly the use of parallel Content Database upgrades.

When all of your databases have been upgraded successfully and you have performed all of the post-configuration steps mentioned earlier in this chapter, you can then redirect traffic to your new SharePoint 2010 farm. This will usually involve a DNS change if you have a single WFE server or standalone environment to point to the new SharePoint 2010 WFE. If you have multiple WFEs in your environment and are using a hardware or software network load balancer (NLB), a change will be required to point to the new SharePoint 2010 WFEs.

Figure 2-6 illustrates what the read-only hybrid approach looks like from the architecture standpoint.

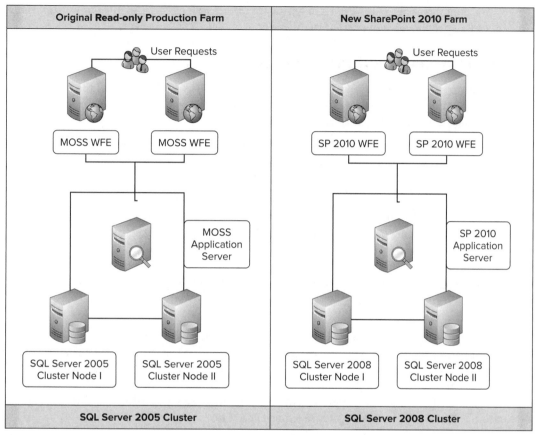

FIGURE 2-6: Architectural view of read-only hybrid approach

A unique strategy for this hybrid approach in environments that have multiple WFEs and that are running on compatible hardware is to try to reuse/rebuild on current hardware where possible. It is possible to rotate servers out of the current SharePoint 2007 farm, and then rebuild and join them as members to your new SharePoint 2010 farm. Following are some items to think about before attempting this:

➤ If you pull a WFE out of your SharePoint 2007 environment, will the performance of the other WFEs be substantial enough to serve web requests for current users?

➤ Does the hardware that you intend to reuse meet the minimum hardware requirements for SharePoint 2010?

If you are thinking about reusing current hardware for your SharePoint 2010 environment, these two questions are the most important to think about.

Detach Databases Hybrid Approach

This hybrid approach is fundamentally a combination of the in-place upgrade and the database attach approaches. This hybrid approach allows you to take advantage of all of the good things in each of the out-of-the-box upgrade approaches.

The greatest thing about this approach is the fact that the in-place upgrade takes care of migrating all of your configuration settings, which were mentioned earlier in this chapter. Minimal post-upgrade configurations will be needed after using this approach because the in-place part of the upgrade will handle them.

Unless you use a separate farm from your original production farm, the farm will be unavailable for the in-place upgrade part of the upgrade. You could potentially follow the steps described earlier for the read-only databases hybrid approach to put your original SharePoint 2007 farm in read-only mode. Then, restore your SharePoint 2007 production farm onto new hardware and perform the hybrid approach described in this section. This will allow for minimal downtime, and also allow you to take advantage of the automatic configurations that take place with the in-place upgrade method.

The detach databases hybrid approach encompasses two different phases of the actual upgrade. The important part of the process is to first detach all of the Content Databases in the current SharePoint 2007. The reason behind this is that, during a normal in-place upgrade, the process will first upgrade the farm, all of the settings, and the configurations, and then move your SSP to services and service applications. Lastly, the in-place upgrade will normally then begin upgrading the Content Databases that are attached to the farm being upgraded one at a time.

Therefore, if you leave your Content Databases attached during the in-place phase of the upgrade, SharePoint will attempt to upgrade them one by one. Furthermore, you will not be able to reap the performance benefits of upgrading multiple Content Databases in parallel. This is the primary advantage of this hybrid method. All of your configurations and settings will be upgraded. Once that has finished, you can re-attach your Content Databases (multiple at once, if desired) and begin the upgrade of your content. This is especially beneficial for organizations that have many large Content Databases and need to minimize the amount of time it takes to complete the upgrade.

An organization that has terabytes of data stored in SharePoint 2007 and only has one weekend to complete an upgrade will most likely not be able to complete the upgrade in that time frame by using the in-place method. To cut down on the time it takes to upgrade the Content Databases, multiple databases will have to be upgraded simultaneously.

Following are the necessary steps to perform this two-part hybrid upgrade on the same farm.

First, you must detach the Content Databases. This is so that the in-place upgrade does not attempt to upgrade one Content Database at a time. To detach each of the Content Databases, run the following STSADM command for each Content Database attached to your farm's web application(s):

```
Stsadm.exe -o deletecontentdb -url http://URL_OF_Web_Application
    -databasename NameOfContentDatabase
```

Next, you must perform in-place upgrade of the current farm by following these steps:

 This procedure will upgrade farm settings, configurations, and convert SSP(s) to services and service applications. For more detailed step-by-step instructions, see the TechNet article at `http://technet.microsoft.com/en-us/library/cc263212.aspx.`

1. Install all prerequisites using the prerequisites installer on all servers in the farm.

2. Install SharePoint 2010 on all servers in the farm by running `setup.exe`.

3. Install all language packs for SharePoint 2010 that you are currently using in SharePoint 2007.

4. Run the SharePoint Configuration Wizard (SPCW) on the server that is running Central Administration first (that is, the server that is running Central Administration services).

5. Run the SPCW on the rest of the member servers in your farm.

Now you must attach the SharePoint 2007 databases and upgrade content. The Content Databases that you detached previously should be attached to your newly upgraded SharePoint 2010 farm. Attaching them will automatically initiate the upgrade sequence for that Content Database. If used, the `UpdateUserExperience` parameter will upgrade all sites within that specific Content Database to be set to preview the new SharePoint 2010 user experience. If the parameter is not used, the old user experience will be set after upgrade.

Follow these steps:

1. Add a Content Database to web application using the following Windows PowerShell cmdlet:

```
Mount-SPContentDatabase -Name <ContentDatabaseName> -DatabaseServer
-<DbServerName>
        -WebApplication <URL_Of_Web_Application> [-UpdateUserExperience]
```

2. Verify a successful upgrade of the first database. If possible, you should upgrade the Content Database that contains the root site collection first, with the other Content Databases to follow.

3. Repeat Step 1 for the rest of the Content Databases that need upgrading. Databases can be upgraded simultaneously, but caution should be taken to not consume too many server resources by upgrading too many databases at once.

Optionally, you can also use a temporary SharePoint 2010 farm to upgrade your Content Databases if you are under time constraints and have many large Content Databases. This will require you to back up the Content Databases from the original farm, and restore the backup copy, unless you are using the same SQL Server for both farms.

During this upgrade process, it is a good idea to temporarily make your farm unavailable by either changing DNS/NLB to point to a custom maintenance site, or just completely making the sites inaccessible. By default, your farm will not be accessible while the in-place part of the upgrade is running. However, once your Content Databases are successfully upgraded, if you have not redirected user request traffic, users will be able to hit these sites if you are using the same URL.

Once each of your Content Databases has been successfully attached and upgraded, you should sweep through the farm a couple times before releasing it back to users. Some things to look over are the event logs, SharePoint 2010 diagnostic logs, upgrade logs, and the health analyzer page. These tools will provide a good indication of the stability of your farm post-upgrade. You should follow each of the post-upgrade steps mentioned earlier in the chapter for both the in-place upgrade and the database attach upgrade.

SUMMARY

SharePoint 2010 has experienced many improvements from the previous version when it comes to upgrading. You now have many tools to assist you throughout the upgrade process, no matter what approach is chosen.

This chapter has made you aware of the improvements and provided guidance for the new upgrade approaches that are available when upgrading from SharePoint 2007 to SharePoint 2010. You have seen that SharePoint 2010 inherently is a bit more complex with regard to the moving pieces, architecturally and functionally speaking. It is important to understand the architectural changes in SharePoint 2010, and plan for them prior to beginning the upgrade process.

I would say that about 50–60 percent of my effort during an upgrade project goes into planning all aspects of the upgrade. I cannot reinforce enough how important it is to run through a trial upgrade and put all of that planning into action. This includes running multiple tests with real production data on similar (if not identical) hardware configurations. It also makes sense in large environments to perform a successful trial upgrade and have users preview their own sites. There is no way in large environments your team will be able to check each and every site, so this will help weed out issues early that can be documented as known issues. Documenting any known issues and resolutions during the trial upgrade will make the production upgrade that much easier.

No matter what approach you select, performing an upgrade is an undertaking in its own right, and requires a knowledgeable team to complete successfully. At least now you have some good options to choose from, which allows you to select an upgrade approach that best meets your business requirements.

ABOUT THE AUTHOR

Jason Medero (MCP, MCT, MCTS, and MVP for WSS) is a systems architect with a concentration in Microsoft Office SharePoint Server (MOSS) and its related Microsoft technologies. He is a managing partner of B&R Business Solutions, a central New Jersey-based firm specializing in SharePoint and surrounding technologies, infrastructure, real-time communications (OCS), and application development. He is an active member of the SharePoint User Group in the New Jersey/New York City area, where he sits on the speaker selection committee. He speaks frequently at SharePoint events across the country. He also contributes his SharePoint knowledge as a mentor for some of the popular forums (for example, TechNet and Yahoo groups). You can visit his blog at www.sharepointblogs.com/JasonMedero, or visit his company's page at www.bandrsolutions.com. Finally, he would like to dedicate his contribution to this book to his mother Helene and father Jesus for being the best parents that a son could ever ask for.

3

Monitoring SharePoint 2010

By Todd Klindt

Getting SharePoint up and running is only half the battle. Keeping it up and running is another thing entirely. Once you have SharePoint installed and configured, and you have end users telling you how great it is (and you are), it's easy to get comfortable and just admire your handiwork. Don't be lulled into a false sense of security. Forces are working against you and your poor, innocent SharePoint farm.

It's your job to keep these problems at bay and keep SharePoint spinning like a top. Using the tools you read about in this chapter, you will be able to see what SharePoint is doing behind the scenes, as well as see ways to predict trouble before it happens. After you're finished with this chapter, you'll almost look forward to experiencing problems with SharePoint so that you can put these tools to good use and get to the bottom of the issues.

ULS

The Unified Logging Service (ULS) is the service responsible for keeping an eye on SharePoint and reporting what it finds. It can report events to three different locations:

- ➤ SharePoint trace logs
- ➤ Windows Event Log
- ➤ SharePoint logging database

Where the event is logged (and if it's logged at all) depends on the type of event, as well as how SharePoint is configured. The ULS is a passive service, which means that it only watches SharePoint and reports on it; it never acts on what it sees.

Let's take a look at each of the three locations and see how they differ.

TRACE LOGS

The trace logs are the logs you think of first when discussing SharePoint logs. They are plain old text files that are tab delimited and can be opened with any tool that can open text files. You learn about methods for consuming them later in this chapter.

By default, trace logs are located in the LOGS directory of the SharePoint root (also called the *14 Hive*) at C:\Program Files\Common Files\Microsoft Shared\Web Server Extensions\14. Figure 3-1 shows how the directory looks. Later in this chapter you learn how to move these files to a better location.

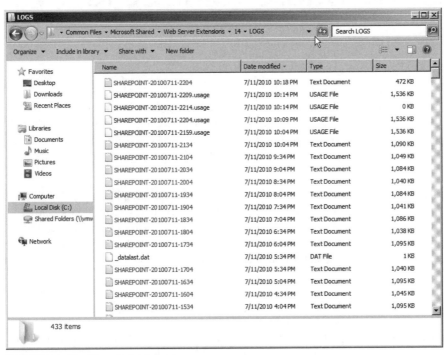

FIGURE 3-1: The SharePoint trace logs

The naming format for the trace log files is *machinename*-YYYYMMDD-HHMM.log, in 24-hour time. By default, a new log file is created every 30 minutes. This can be changed using Windows PowerShell with the Set-SPDiagnosticConfig command. The following code snippet configures SharePoint to create a new trace log every 60 minutes:

```
Set-SPDiagnosticConfig Set-SPDiagnosticConfig -LogCutInterval 60
```

For more information about using PowerShell with SharePoint 2010, check out Chapter 5.

Trace logs existed in previous versions of SharePoint, but they have undergone some improvements in SharePoint 2010. For starters, they take up less space, but still provide better information. It's a classic "eat all you want and still lose weight" situation.

The trace logs are smaller than their SharePoint 2007 counterparts for a couple of reasons. First, a lot of thought has gone into what gets written to the trace logs by default. Anyone who has perused through a SharePoint 2007 ULS log or two has seen a lot of repetitive and mostly unhelpful messages. These messages add to the bloat of the file, but do not provide much in return. In SharePoint 2010, many of these messages have been removed from the default settings, which makes the log files smaller.

Also, SharePoint now leverages Windows NT File System (NTFS) file compression for the LOGS folder, which also decreases the amount of space the logs occupy on disk. Figure 3-2 shows the compression on a trace log file.

The log file shown in Figure 3-2 is 9.62 MB, but it is only taking 3.30 MB on disk, thanks to NTFS compression. This allows you to keep more logs, or logs with more information, without as much impact on the drive space of your SharePoint servers.

Finally, in SharePoint 2010 you have much better control over which events are written to the trace logs, and better control over getting things put back after you have customized them. In SharePoint 2007, you had some control over which events were written to the trace logs, but there were two significant drawbacks:

> You didn't know which events in the interface to more heavily monitor.

> Once you cranked up one area, there was no way to set it back to its original setting after you had successfully solved a problem.

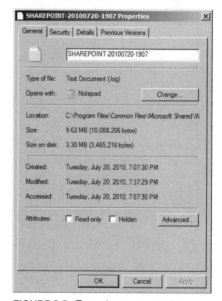

FIGURE 3-2: Trace log compression

With SharePoint 2010, there's now good news, because both of those issues have been addressed. You have a very robust event throttling section in Central Administration that enables you to customize your logs to whatever area your issue is in, and then dial it back easily once the problem is solved.

In Central Administration, click Monitoring on the left, and then select Configure Diagnostic Logging under the Reporting section. You will see a screen similar to Figure 3-3.

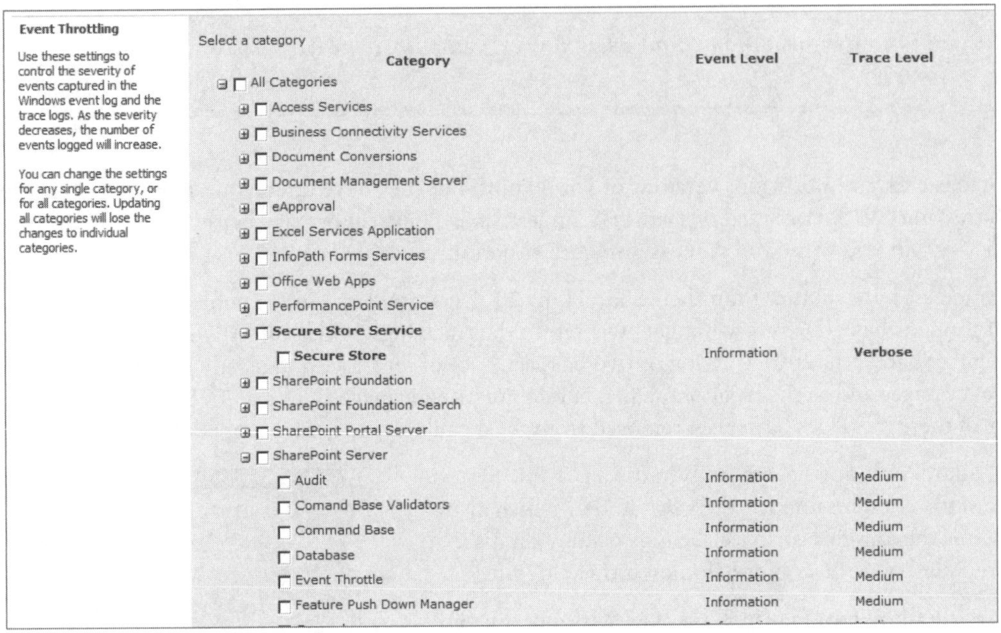

FIGURE 3-3: Event Throttling

Two things should jump out at you. The first is the sheer number of options you have to choose from. The Enterprise SKU of SharePoint Server has 20 different categories, each with subcategories. This means that if you are troubleshooting an error that only has to do with accessing External Data with Excel Services, you can crank up the reporting only on that without adding a lot of other unhelpful events to the logs. The checkbox interface also means that you can change the settings of multiple categories or subcategories at one time. So, the interface makes it easy to change a single area, or a large area.

The second thing that should jump out at you in Figure 3-3 is that one of those options, Secure Store Service, is bolded. In SharePoint 2007, after you had customized an event's logging level, there was no way to go back to see which levels you had changed. And, if, by some strange twist of fate, you were able to remember which events you had changed, there was no way to know what level to change them back to.

In most cases, one of two things happened. You either left the events alone (in their chatty state), or you found another SharePoint 2007 installation and went through the settings, one by one, to compare them. Neither solution was great.

Fortunately, SharePoint 2010 addresses both of those issues swimmingly. As you can see in Figure 3-3, the Secure Store Service is bolded in the list of categories. That's SharePoint 2010's way of saying, "Hey! Look over here!" Any category that is not at its default logging level will appear in bold, making it very easy to discover which ones you need to change back. That's only half the battle though.

How do you know what to set it back to? SharePoint 2010 covers that, too. As shown in Figure 3-4, in the list of "Least critical events to report to the trace log" drop-down, there is a shining star at the top, "Reset to default." This little number will set whichever categories are selected back to their default logging settings. This means that you can crank up the logging as much as you want, knowing that you can easily put it back once you are finished. Microsoft has even provided an "All Categories" checkbox at the top of the category list (see Figure 3-3) to make it even easier to fix in one fell swoop.

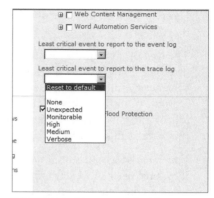

FIGURE 3-4: "Reset to default" setting

Setting the event levels that are logged to the trace logs is just one of the settings you can customize. Probably the most important change you can make to your trace logs is their location. As mentioned, the default location for these files is `C:\Program Files\Common Files\Microsoft Shared\Web Server Extensions\14\LOGS`. That location is fine, because the logs get to hang out with the rest of their SharePoint 2010 friends. But space on the `C:\` drive is sacred, and if something can be safely moved to another drive, it should be.

Fortunately, it is very easy to move these files to a new location, where they can't do any harm to your `C:\` drive. To do this, go into Central Administration ➪ Monitoring ➪ Configure Diagnostic Logging. Figure 3-5 shows the bottom of this page, where you can enter a new location to store your trace logs.

FIGURE 3-5: Moving trace logs

Change the default location to a location on another drive. An excellent choice is something like `D:\Logs\SharePoint` or `E:\Logs\SharePoint`, depending on where your server's hard drives are located.

 Keep in mind that this is a farm-level setting, not server level, so every server in your farm must have that location available. If you try to set a location that is not available on all of the servers in the farm, you'll get an error message. You'll also need to keep this in mind when adding new servers to your farm. Your new server must have this location as well.

Figure 3-5 shows a couple of other settings you can use to control the footprint your trace logs have on your drives.

The first option allows you to configure the maximum number of days the trace logs are kept. The default is 14 days. This is a good middle-of-the road setting. Resist any temptation to shorten this time period unless your servers are really starving for drive space. If you ever need to troubleshoot a problem, the more historical data you have, the better off you are. The only downside to keeping lots of information is the amount of time and effort it takes to go through it. You learn more about this later in this chapter.

You can also assign a finite size to the amount of drive space your trace logs can consume, whether they have reached 14-day expiration or not. The default value is 1 TB, so be sure to change that value if you want to restrict the size in a more meaningful way.

Configuring Log Settings with PowerShell

Every SharePoint 2010 administrator should get cozy with Windows PowerShell. It is the best way to do repetitive tasks, and manipulating the trace logs is no exception. So far in this chapter, you have learned about using Central Administration to interact with trace logs. In this section, you learn how to use PowerShell to make those same configuration changes.

SPDiagnosticConfig

The first tool in the PowerShell arsenal is the `Get-SPDiagnosticConfig` cmdlet and its twin brother, `Set-SPDiagnosticConfig`. The former is used to retrieve the diagnostic settings in your farm; the latter is used to change them. Figure 3-6 shows the output of `Get-SPDiagnosticConfig`, and it reflects changing the log cut interval to 60 minutes, as you did previously.

FIGURE 3-6: Get-SPDiagnosticConfig output

Seeing the settings that `Get-SPDiagnosticConfig` displays gives an idea of what values its brother `Set-SPDiagnosticConfig` can set. Using PowerShell's built-in `Get-Help` cmdlet is also a good way to get ideas on how best to leverage it, especially with the `-Examples` switch, like this:

```
Get-Help set-SPDiagnosticConfig -Examples
```

This shows a couple of different methods of using `Set-SPDiagnosticConfig` to change the diagnostic values of your farm. The first method uses the command directly to alter values. The second method assigns a variable to an object that contains each property and its value. You can alter the value of one or more properties, then write the variable back with `Set-SPDiagnosticConfig`. Either way works fine; it's a matter of personal opinion as to which way you go.

Earlier, you learned that it's a good idea to move the location of the ULS trace logs. By default, they are located in the `Logs` directory of the SharePoint root. While they are fine there, space on the `C:\` drive is almost holy ground. If the `C:\` drive gets full, then Windows gets unhappy, and everyone (including IIS and SharePoin)t are unhappy. To help prevent that, you can move your trace logs to another location, freeing up that precious space. The following PowerShell command will move the log location to `E:\logs`:

```
Set-SPDiagnosticConfig -LogLocation e:\Logs
```

It is important to note that this only changes the location that new log files are written to. It will not move existing log files. You will have to move them yourself.

SPLogLevel

You learned previously that you have some flexibility in configuring how different aspects of SharePoint log events. You saw how to look at these settings and change them in Central Administration. You can also use PowerShell to get and set that same information with the `SPLogLevel` cmdlets.

You can get a list of the cmdlets that deal with the log levels by running the command `Get-Command -Noun SPLogLevel` in a SharePoint Management Shell. The results should look like Figure 3-7.

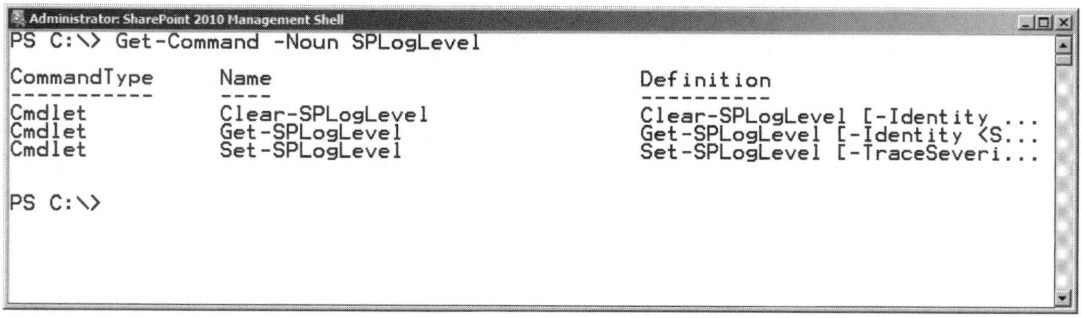

```
Administrator: SharePoint 2010 Management Shell
PS C:\> Get-Command -Noun SPLogLevel

CommandType     Name                Definition
-----------     ----                ----------
Cmdlet          Clear-SPLogLevel    Clear-SPLogLevel [-Identity ...
Cmdlet          Get-SPLogLevel      Get-SPLogLevel [-Identity <S...
Cmdlet          Set-SPLogLevel      Set-SPLogLevel [-TraceSeveri...

PS C:\>
```

FIGURE 3-7: SPLogLevel cmdlets

Let's start an examination of the available options by taking a look at `Get-SPLogLevel`, which reports the current logging level in the farm. With no parameters, it will list through every category and subcategory, and report their trace log and event log levels. Using `Get-Member`, you can see that

`Get-SPLogLevel` will report information that is not available in Central Administration, like what the default trace and event log logging levels are.

The `SPLogLevel` objects have a property named `Area` that corresponds to the top-level categories in Central Administration. Running the PowerShell command `Get-SPLogLevel | select -Unique area` displays those categories. To get all of the settings from a particular area takes a little work.

The `-Identity` parameter of `Get-SPLogLevel` corresponds to the second column (or `Name` column) of the log levels, which maps to the subcategories in Central Administration. This means you cannot use `"Access Services"` for the `Identity` parameter, but you could use `"Administration"`, which is the first subcategory under `"Access Services"`. To get all of the logging levels for `"Access Services"`, use a command like this:

```
Get-SPLogLevel | Where-Object {$_.area.tostring() -eq "Access Services"}
```

This uses the `Area` property of the log level, converts it to a string, and then displays the log level objects that match `"Access Services"`, as shown in Figure 3-8.

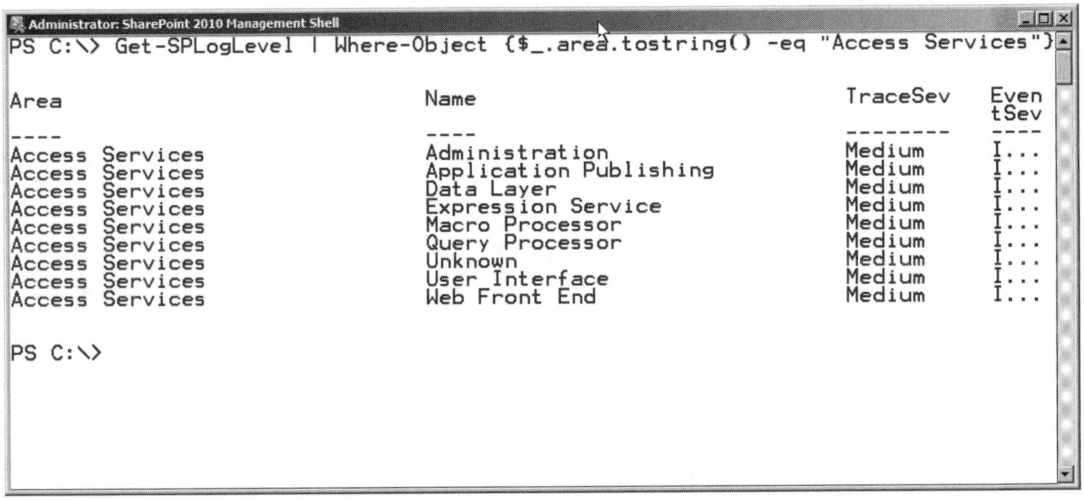

FIGURE 3-8: Access Services event categories

Now that you've mastered `Get-SPLogLevel`, let's look at `Set-SPLogLevel`, its complementary cmdlet. You can use this one to set a specific log level to the trace or event logs for a category or group of categories.

Suppose you are having trouble with the Office Web Applications and you want as much debugging information as you can get. Of course, you could go into Central Administration and check the box next to "Office Web Apps," but that's no fun. Let's use PowerShell instead.

The following command uses PowerShell to get all of the `SPLogLevel` objects that are in the Office Web Applications category, then pipes them through `Set-SPLogLevel` to set their trace logging level to `verbose`:

```
Get-SPLogLevel | Where-Object {$_.area.tostring() -eq "Office Web Apps"} |
    Set-SPLogLevel -TraceSeverity verbose
```

In one fell swoop, you have set all of the logging levels you need. Now you can reproduce the error, then go through your trace logs, and discover what the problem is. Once you have conquered that Office Web Applications problem, you must return the logging levels back to normal. That's where the third SPLogLevel cmdlet, Clear-SPLogLevel, comes into play.

Much like in Central Administration, there is an easy way to reset all of your logging levels back to the default. The Clear-SPLogLevel cmdlet clears out any changes you have made, and sets the logging levels to their default values for both trace and event logging. If you run it with no parameters, it resets all of the logging levels to their defaults. Like Get-SPLogLevel and Set-SPLogLevel, you can also pass it optional parameters to reset specific categories or areas.

Using Logs to Troubleshoot

Having lots and lots of beautiful logs files does you no good unless you can crack them open and use them to hunt down problems. In this section, you learn about some things to look for in the trace logs, and a variety of ways to look at them.

Introducing the Correlation ID

The first time anyone opens up a SharePoint trace log, he or she feels the same sense of helplessness and being overwhelmed. It's like being dropped into an unfamiliar city, in the middle of rush hour. So many things are going on at once all around you, and none of it looks familiar.

Fortunately, SharePoint has provided a bit of a road map for you, the correlation ID. The *correlation ID* is a globally unique identifier GUID that is assigned to each conversation a user or process has with SharePoint. When an error occurs, an administrator can use the correlation ID to track down all of the events in the trace logs that pertain to the conversation where the problem occurred.

This is very helpful in those very, very rare occasions when end users contact the help desk because something is broken and, when asked what they were doing, they reply, "Nothing." Now, with correlation IDs, those conversations with SharePoint can be tracked and you can see exactly what was happening when the error occurred. Figure 3-9 shows a screen an end user might get with the correlation ID in it.

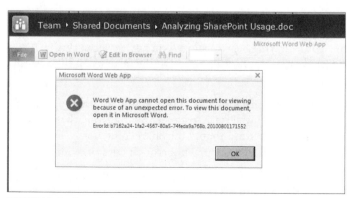

FIGURE 3-9: Correlation ID in action

In this example, you know that the user was trying to view a Word document with the Office Web Applications and it failed. Once you get the correlation ID, `b7162a24-1fa2-4567-80a5-74feda9a768b`, `20100801171552`, you can figure out why the document wouldn't open.

Because each entry in the trace logs has a correlation ID, you can just open up the trace log in Notepad and look for the lines that reference this conversation. Figure 3-10 shows what you would find in this example.

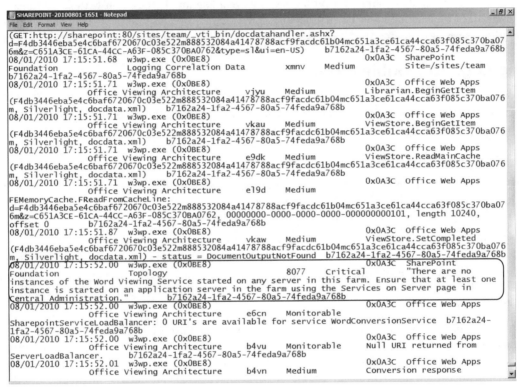

FIGURE 3-10: Hunting down the problem with the correlation ID

By following the correlation ID through the trace log, you might stumble across a pretty telling error: "There are no instances of the Word Viewing Service started on any server in this farm. Ensure that at least one instance is started on an application server in the farm using the Services on Server page in Central Administration."

That does sound like a problem. Sure enough, by checking in Central Administration, you see that no servers in the farm are running the Word Viewing service instance. By following that correlation ID through the logs, you can learn all kinds of fun stuff about how SharePoint works. For example, SharePoint looks to see if there is a cached copy of that document before it tries to render it.

As you have seen, the correlation ID is exposed when an error page is displayed, and throughout the trace logs. It is also referenced in events in the Windows Event Log, when it is appropriate. You can also use a correlation ID when doing a SQL trace on SharePoint's SQL traffic. The correlation ID is considered by many administrators to be one of the best new features in SharePoint 2010.

The Developer Dashboard

You aren't always handed the correlation ID all tied up with a bow like you were in Figure 3-9. Sometimes the page will render, but there are problems with individual web parts. In those cases, you can use the Developer Dashboard to get the correlation ID and hunt down the problem.

Despite what the name may suggest, this dashboard is not just for developers. The Developer Dashboard is a dashboard that shows how long it took for a page to load, and which components loaded with it, as shown in Figure 3-11.

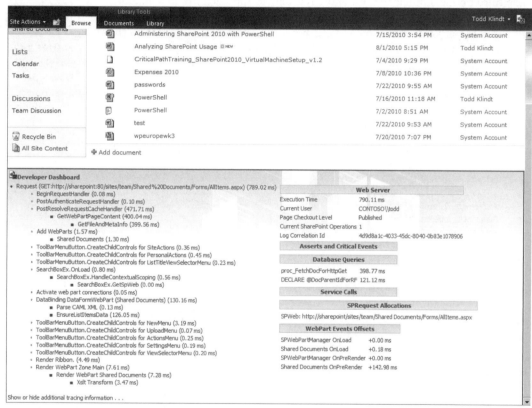

FIGURE 3-11: The Developer Dashboard

This dashboard is loaded at the bottom of your requested web page. As you can see, the dashboard is chock full of information about the page load. You can see how long the page took to load (790.11 ms), as well as who requested it, its correlation ID, and so on. This can be used when the help desk gets those ever popular "SharePoint's slow" calls from users. Now you can quantify exactly what "slow" means, as well as see what led up to the page load being slow.

If web parts were poorly designed and did a lot of database queries, you'd see it here. If they fetched large amounts of SharePoint content, you'd see it here. If you're really curious, you can click the link on the bottom left, "Show or hide additional tracing information," to get several pages worth of information about every step that was taken to render that page.

Now that you're sold on the Developer Dashboard, how do you actually use it? As previously mentioned, it is exposed as a dashboard at the bottom of the page when it renders. The user browsing the page must have the `AddAndCustomizePages` permission (site collection admins and users in the Owner group, by default) to see the Developer Dashboard, and it must be enabled in your farm.

By default, it is shut off, which is one of the three possible states. It can also be on, which means the dashboard is displayed on every page load. Not only is that tedious when you're using SharePoint, but it also has a performance penalty.

The third option, on demand, is a more reasonable approach. In on demand mode, the Developer Dashboard is not on, but it's warming up in the on-deck circle, waiting for you to put it into action. When the need arises, a user with the correct permission can turn it on by clicking the icon shown in Figure 3-12. When you are finished with it, you can put it back on the bench by clicking the same icon.

FIGURE 3-12: Enabling the Developer Dashboard when it's on demand

How do you go about enabling the Developer Dashboard to make this possible?

You can use Windows PowerShell, as shown here:

```
$dash = [Microsoft.SharePoint.Administration.SPWebService]
    ::ContentService.DeveloperDashboardSettings;
$dash.DisplayLevel = 'OnDemand';
# $dash.DisplayLevel = 'Off';
# $dash.DisplayLevel = 'On';
$dash.TraceEnabled = $true;
$dash.Update()
```

The `DisplayLevel` can be one of three values: `Off`, `On`, or `OnDemand`. The default value is `Off`.

Notice that at no point do you specify a URL when you're setting this. It is a farm-wide setting. Never fear, though, users with `AddAndCustomizePages` permission will see it, so hopefully it won't scare too many users if you must enable it for troubleshooting. If you have enabled MySites, each user is the site collection owner of their site collection, so they will see it.

Methods for Consuming the Trace Logs

So far, you've learned what the trace logs are, and a little bit about how to configure them and their contents. In this section, you learn about some ways to mine them and get out the information that you need.

The Basics

These wonderful trace files, which will help you do all this troubleshooting, are just text files. This may be very confusing — information-packed text files, but text files nonetheless. The trace logs have the following columns:

➤   *Timestamp* — The date and time of the event in local time

➤   *Process* — The name of the process that generated the log entry

➤ *TID* — The thread ID

➤ *Area* — The area the event is from

➤ *Category* — The category of the area that the event is from

➤ *EventID Level* — An undocumented ID

➤ *Message* — The text of the message

➤ *Correlation* — The correlation ID

As you saw in Figure 3-10, these trace logs can be opened with any program that can open text files, including humble old Notepad.exe. Although Notepad is good (because it exists on every SharePoint server), it can be very unwieldy to work with. If you have a correlation ID, you can just do a find with Ctrl+F and jump right to its location in the log. You will have better luck if you only search on the first group of characters in the GUID (b7162a24 in the previous example), instead of the whole GUID. Not only is it easier to manage, but some screens that display the correlation ID place a space at the end, or do not have hyphens in them — both of which can prevent you from finding the correlation ID in your log files.

Although you can load the logs into Notepad, there are better ways to handle them. Let's look at a couple.

Using Excel

Not only are those beloved trace logs text files, they are tab-delimited text files. This means that Excel can import them easily and put each column of information into its own column. Once trace logs are in an Excel spreadsheet, you can use Excel's sort and filtering to locate the events of interest. You can also resize the columns or hide them completely for readability. You can even paste several log files into one spreadsheet to look for trends of errors.

Whereas Notepad gets sluggish with large files, Excel handles them with ease.

Using MSDN ULS Viewer

Though it's frustrating that SharePoint does not come with a log viewer, Microsoft has redeemed itself a bit. It released a free, dedicated (though unsupported) ULS Viewer. You can download it at http://code.msdn.microsoft.com/ULSViewer. Because this utility was built from the ground up to read SharePoint's ULS, it does it quite well.

It allows real-time monitoring of the ULS logs, and will do smart highlighting (where it highlights all events that have the same value of the field you are hovering over). For example, if you hover over the category "Taxonomy," it will automatically highlight all categories that match.

It also offers extensive filtering that includes filtering out event levels like Verbose or Medium. You can also filter by any value in any column. Right-clicking any correlation ID allows you to set a highlight for any matching row, or simply only show the rows that match. Figure 3-13 shows how to filter the logs based on a single correlation ID.

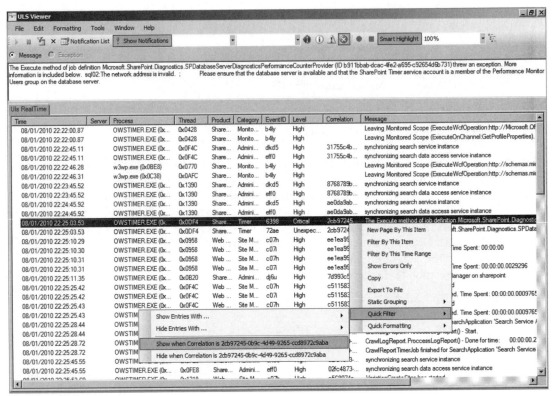

FIGURE 3-13: The MSDN ULS Viewer

The interface has a lot of options, and is laid out very well. Because it's a free tool, it's worth every penny. If you're not comfortable installing it on your production servers, you can install it on your workstation and copy the ULS files over when trouble occurs.

Using SPLogEvent and SPLogFile

The last method to discuss is using the PowerShell cmdlets that deal with consuming the trace logs. The first, `Get-SPLogEvent`, retrieves log events from the trace logs. As with the other cmdlets you have learned about, using `Get-Help` with the `-Examples` parameter provides a good foundation to learn the different ways you can use this cmdlet. Let's take a look at a few examples.

If you just run `Get-SPLogEvent` with no parameters, it will spit back every record from every trace log it can find on your local machine. Hopefully, you are sitting in a comfortable chair if you do that, because it's going to take a while. Fortunately, you have many ways to limit the number of results you get, making it easier for you to separate the wheat from the chaff.

First, you can use the PowerShell cmdlet `Select` to pare down the results. The following examples demonstrate getting the first and last events in the logs:

```
Get-SPLogEvent | Select -First 5
Get-SPLogEvent | Select -Last 5
Get-SPLogEvent | Select -First 20 -Last 10
```

Depending on how many trace logs you have, it could take a while for the last results to show up. It's still walking through the whole list of events; it's just not displaying them all.

A better way is to use `Get-SPLogEvent`'s `-StartTime` parameter to limit the events it reads. The following command returns the last ten events in the last five minutes:

```
Get-SPLogEvent -StartTime (get-date).addminutes(-5) | Select -Last 10
```

This will return results much more quickly, and likely will give you better results. You can also specify an end time, if you want to more tightly narrow down your window. You can also specify which levels you would like to see returned. The following line returns all of the `"high"` level events in the last minute:

```
Get-SPLogEvent -MinimumLevel "high" -StartTime (get-date).addminutes(-1)
```

In most cases, when you use `Get-SPLogEvent`, it will be to get all of the events for a particular correlation ID. This is as easy as piping `Get-SPLogEvent` through a `Where-Object` clause and filtering for a specific correlation ID. The following command will return all of the events in the last ten minutes with a blank correlation ID:

```
Get-SPLogEvent -StartTime (Get-Date).addminutes(-10) |
    Where-Object {$_.correlation
    -eq "00000000-0000-0000-0000-000000000000"}
```

If you want a real correlation ID to work with, you can get one quickly with this command:

```
Get-SPLogEvent -StartTime (Get-Date).addminutes(-1) | select correlation  -First 1
```

You might have to run it a couple times to get a correlation ID that's not all zeros.

Figure 3-14 shows how this looks with its output. Once you have it, you can paste it into the previous statement to get all of the events that pertain to that correlation ID.

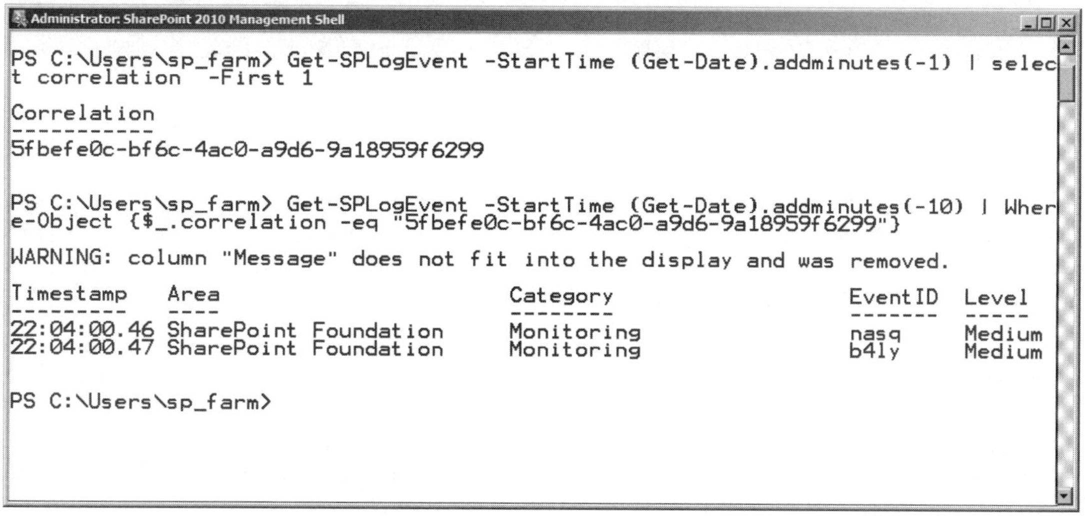

FIGURE 3-14: Getting a random correlation ID

You have some other cmdlets at your disposal for pruning through those trace logs. A good one to use when troubleshooting is New-SPLogFile.

This tells SharePoint to close out the current log file and create a new one. You saw earlier that, by default, SharePoint rolls its logs over every 30 minutes. If you've ever loaded up those logs and tried to look for a specific event, you know it can be quite daunting.

With New-SPLogFile, you can run it before and after an event you are troubleshooting. For example, if the User Profile service instance won't start on a particular server, you could use New-SPLogFile to create a new log file right before reproducing the problem. Then, after you've tried to start the service, you can create another new log file. This will isolate into one file all the events created during your attempt, making it easier to follow.

If you have multiple servers in your farm, browsing through trace logs can be daunting, because you must constantly collect them from all of your servers. If only there were a way to merge the logs from all of your servers into one file.

Stop the presses! There is! SharePoint 2010 comes with a cmdlet, Merge-SPLogFile, that does exactly that. Merge-SPLogFile will merge the trace logs from all of the SharePoint servers in your farm into one, easy-to-consume (or, at least, easier-to-consume) log file. All the tools that you used previously to work with trace files work with the merged log file as well.

By default, Merge-SPLogFile only merges events from the last hour from each machine. Using the same -StartTime and -EndTime parameters that you can use with Get-SPLogEvent, you can customize that window. If the error you are chasing happened in the last ten minutes, you can make it shorter. If you want to archive all of the events from your servers from the last three hours, you can make it longer. Figure 3-15 shows Merge-SPLogFile in action.

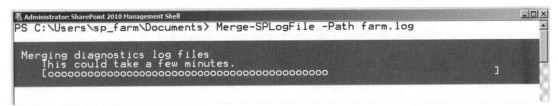

FIGURE 3-15: Merging log files

You can see from Figure 3-15 that all Merge-SPLogFile needs to run is a path to write the newly created log file to. When you run it, it creates a timer job on all of the machines in the farm. This timer job collects the logs requested, and then copies them over to the server where Merge-SPLogFile is running. That's why you are warned that it may take a long time.

Although Merge-SPLogFile is happy to run with no parameters, you do have the option of trimming down the results, should you choose to. Get-Help Merge-SPLogFiles provides a list of parameters you can use, including (but not limited to) Area, EventID, Level, Message, and Correlation ID. Figure 3-16 shows how you can use the last one, the correlation ID, to get a single log file that tracks one correlation ID from across your farm. This can be very handy when chasing down a problem.

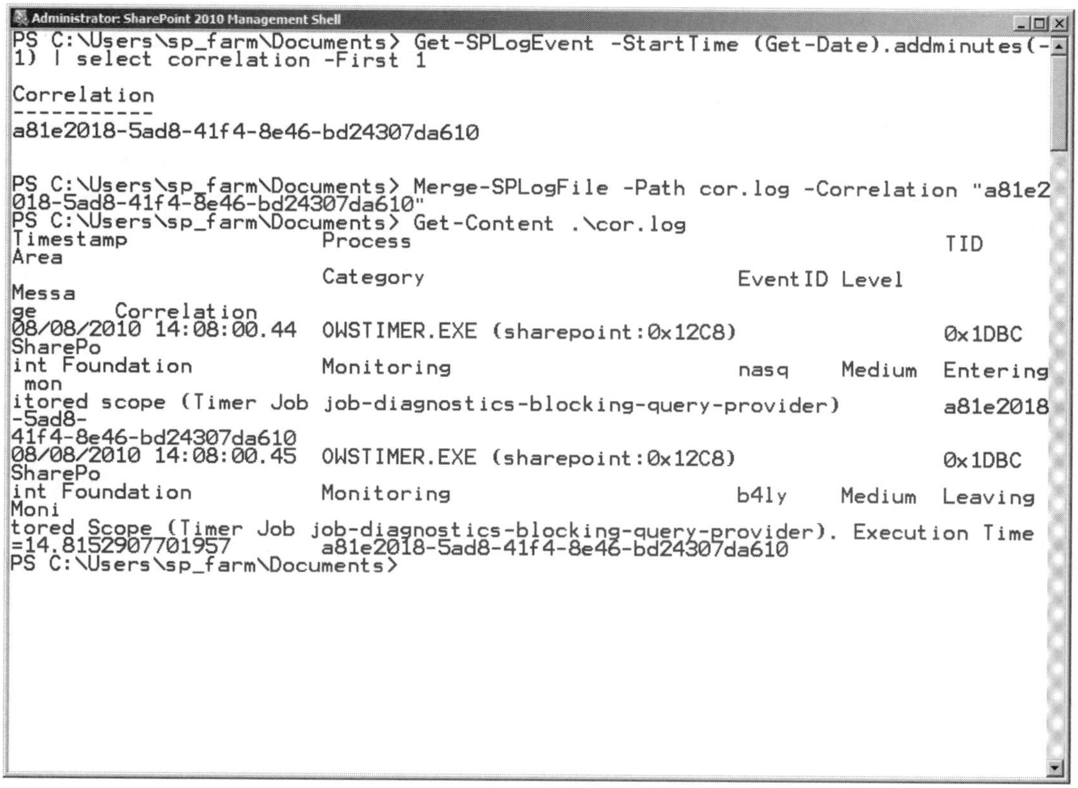

FIGURE 3-16: Merging events with a common correlation ID

Because Get-SPLogEvent supports a -directory switch, you can point it at a location other than your standard LOGS directory when searching for events. This can be used to speed up your searches if you copy the applicable logs to a different directory and point Get-SPLogEvent there. You can also point it to the directory where you save a merged log file created by Merge-SPLogFile and use it to filter those results as well.

As previously mentioned, Merge-SPLogFile is good for troubleshooting, but it is also very handy for archiving log events.

WINDOWS EVENT LOGS

In addition to the trace logs, another part of the ULS is Windows Events. These are the events that you are used to viewing in the Windows Event Viewer. While SharePoint 2010 will write to its own trace logs, it also writes events here as well.

You can configure how much information SharePoint writes to the Windows Event Logs in the same way you can control how much it writes to the trace logs. In Central Administration, under

Monitoring ⇨ "Configure diagnostic logging," you can set the threshold of events that are written to the Windows Event Logs, just like you can with the trace log.

You have several levels of events to choose from, including "Reset to default," which resets the logging level back to its default. For Windows Events, you have an additional setting, event log throttling. If you enable event log throttling, SharePoint will not repeatedly write the same event to the Windows logs if there is a problem. Instead, it will only write events periodically, telling you the event is still being throttled. This keeps your Windows Event Logs from being overrun by the same message.

In Central Administration, you can only enable or disable this feature. In Windows PowerShell, using `Set-SPDiagnosticConfig`, you can enable or disable throttling, as well as change some of the settings. Table 3-1 shows a list of these settings, a description of what they do, and their default values.

TABLE 3-1: Settings for Set-DiagnosticConfig

SETTING	DESCRIPTION	UNITS	DEFAULT VALUE
Threshold	Number of events allowed in a given time period (`TriggerPeriod`) before flood protection is enabled for this event	Integer — value must be between 0 (disabled) and 100 (maximum)	5
TriggerPeriod	The timeframe in which the threshold must be exceeded in order to trigger flood protection	Minutes	2
QuietPeriod	The amount of time that must pass without an event before flood protection is disabled for an event	Minutes	2
NotifyPeriod	The interval in which SharePoint will write an event notifying you that flood protection is still enabled for a particular event	Minutes	5

Earlier in this chapter, Figure 3-6 showed the Event Log Flood Protection settings as they are displayed with `Get-SPDiagnosticConfig`. These settings can be changed with the complementary cmdlet, `Set-SPDiagnosticConfig`.

LOGGING DATABASE

Microsoft has always made it pretty clear how it feels about anyone touching the SharePoint databases. The answer is always a very clear and concise, "Stop it!" Microsoft didn't support reading from, writing to, or even looking crossly at SharePoint databases — period. End of story. That became a problem, however, because not all of the information administrators wanted about their farm or servers was discoverable in the interface, or with the SharePoint object model. This resulted in rogue administrators, with the curtains pulled, quietly querying their databases, hoping to never get caught.

SharePoint 2010 addresses this by introducing a logging database. This database is a farm-wide repository of SharePoint events from every machine in your farm. It aggregates information from many different locations, and writes them all to a single database. This database contains just about everything you could ever want to know about your farm, and that's not even the best part. The best part is that it is completely supported for you to read from and write to this database, if you would like, because the schema is public.

Following are some of the types of information that is logged by default:

- Feature Usage
- Search Queries
- Timer Jobs
- Content Import Usage
- Server Farm Health Data
- SQL blocked queries
- Site Inventory
- Search Query statistics
- Page Requests
- Site Inventory Usage
- Rating Usage
- Content Export Usage
- NT Events
- SQL high CPU/IO queries
- Search Crawl
- Query click-through

Microsoft had well-intentioned reasons for forbidding access to databases before. Obviously, writing to a SharePoint database potentially puts it in a state where SharePoint can no longer read it and render the content in it. Everyone agrees that this is bad.

What is less obvious, though, is that reading from a database can have the same impact. A seemingly innocent, but poorly written SQL query that only reads values could put a lock on a table — or the whole database. This lock would also mean that SharePoint could not render out the content of that database for the duration of the lock. That's also a bad thing.

However, because this logging database is simply just a copy of information gathered from other places, and it is not used to satisfy end-user requests, it's safe for you to read from it or write to it. If you destroy the database completely, you can just delete it and let SharePoint re-create it. The freedom is invigorating.

Let's take a look at some details behind this change of heart.

Configuring the Logging Database

How do you use this magical database and leverage all this information? By default, health data collection is enabled. This builds the logging database. To view the settings, open SharePoint Central Administration and go into the now-familiar Monitoring section. Under the Reporting heading, click "Configure usage and health data collection." This brings up the page shown in Figure 3-17.

Let's start by looking at the settings at the top. The first checkbox on the page determines whether the usage data is collected and stored in the logging database. This is turned on by default, and here is where you would disable it, should you choose to.

The next section enables you to determine which events you want reported in the log. By default, all eight events are logged. If you want to reduce the impact that logging has on your servers, you can disable events for which you don't think you'll want reports. You always have the option to enable events later. You may want to do this if you find yourself wanting to investigate a specific issue. You can turn the logging on during your investigation, and then shut it off after the investigation is finished.

The next section determines where the usage logs will be stored. By default, they are stored in the LOGS directory of the SharePoint root, along with the trace logs. The usage logs follow the same naming convention as the trace logs, but have the suffix .usage. As with the trace logs, it's a good idea to move these logs off of the C:\ drive if possible. You also have the capability to limit the amount of space occupied by the usage logs, with 5 GB being the default.

The next section, Health Data Collection, seems simple enough — just a checkbox and a link. The checkbox determines whether SharePoint will periodically collect health information about the members of the farm. The link takes you to a list of timer jobs that collect that information. When you click the Health Logging Schedule link, you're taken to a page that lists all of the timer jobs that collect this information. You can use this page to disable the timer jobs for any information you don't want to collect. Again, the more logging you do, the greater the impact on performance.

The amount of information SharePoint collects about itself is quite vast. Not only does it monitor SharePoint-related performance (such as the User Profile Service Application Synchronization Job), it also keeps track of the health of non-SharePoint processes (such as SQL Server). It reports SQL blocking queries and Dynamic Management Views (DMV) data. Not only can you disable the timer jobs for information you don't want to collect, but you can also decrease how frequently they run, to reduce the impact on your servers.

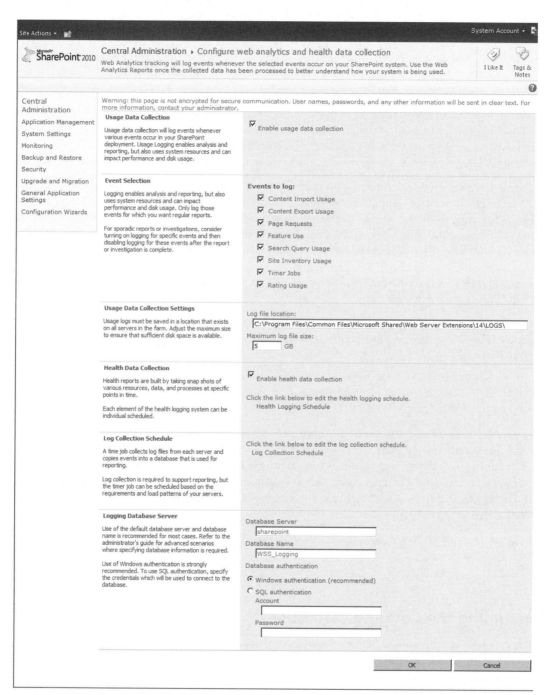

FIGURE 3-17: Configuring the logging database

The next section of the "Configure web analytics and health data collection" page is the Log Collection Schedule. Here you can configure how frequently the logs are collected from the servers in the farm, and how frequently they are processed and written to the logging database. This lets you control the impact the log collection has on your servers. The default setting collects the logs every 30 minutes, but you can increase that to reduce the load placed on the servers.

The final section of the page displays the SQL instance and database name of the reporting database itself. The default settings use the same SQL instance as the default Content Database SQL instance, and use the database name WSS_Logging. The page says that it is recommended that you use the default settings. However, there are some pretty good reasons to change its location and settings.

Considering the amount of information that can be written to this database, and how frequently that data can be written, it might make sense to move this database to its own SQL Server instance. Though reading from and writing to the database won't directly impact end-user performance, the amount of usage this database could see might overwhelm SQL Server, or fill up the drives that also contain your other SharePoint databases. If your organization chooses to use the logging database, keep an eye on the disk space that it uses, and the amount of I/O activity it generates. On a test environment with about one month's worth of use by one user, the logging database grew to more than 1 GB. This database can get huge.

If you must alter those settings, you can do so in Windows PowerShell with the Set-SPUsageApplication cmdlet. The following PowerShell code demonstrates how to change the location of the logging database:

```
Set-SPUsageApplication -DatabaseServer <Database server name>
    -DatabaseName <Database name> [-DatabaseUsername <User name>]
    [-DatabasePassword <Password>] [-Verbose]
```

Specify the name of the SQL Server instance where you would like to host the logging database. You must also specify the database name, even if you want to use the default name, WSS_Logging. If the user running the Set-SPUsageApplication cmdlet is not the owner of the database, provide the username and password of an account that has sufficient permissions. Because this database consists of data aggregated from other locations, you can move it without losing any data. It will simply be repopulated as the collection jobs run.

To get the full list of PowerShell cmdlets that deal with the Usage service, use Get-Command as follows:

```
get-command -noun spusage*
```

Consuming the Logging Database

Thus far, you've read a lot about this logging database, what's in it, and how to configure it. But you haven't learned how you can enjoy its handiwork. There are many places to consume the information in the logging database.

The first place to look is Central Administration. Under Monitoring ➪ Reporting, there are three reports that use information in the logging database. The first is a link that says "View administrative reports." Clicking that link takes you to a document library in Central Administration that contains a few canned administrative reports. Out-of-the-box, there are only search reports, but any type of reports could be put here. Microsoft could provide these reports, or they can be created by SharePoint administrators.

The documents in this library are simply web pages, so you can click any of them to see the information reported in them. These particular reports are very handy for determining the source of search bottlenecks. This enables you to be proactive in scaling out your search infrastructure. You are able to see how long discrete parts of the search take, and then scale out your infrastructure before end users are affected.

The next reports in Central Administration are the health reports. These reports enable you to isolate the slowest pages in your web application, and the most active users per web application. Like the search reports, these reports enable you to be proactive and diagnose issues in your farm. Running these reports will allow you to see details about the slowest pages being rendered, so you can take steps to improve their performance. Figure 3-18 shows part of the report. To view a report, click the "Go" button on the top of the page.

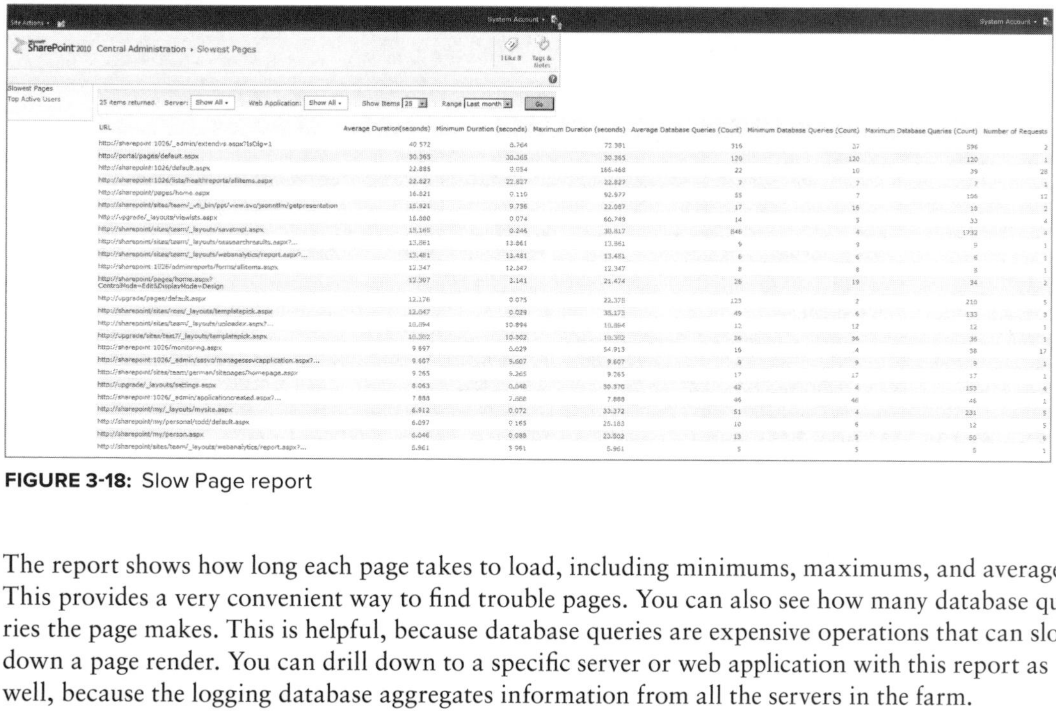

FIGURE 3-18: Slow Page report

The report shows how long each page takes to load, including minimums, maximums, and averages. This provides a very convenient way to find trouble pages. You can also see how many database queries the page makes. This is helpful, because database queries are expensive operations that can slow down a page render. You can drill down to a specific server or web application with this report as well, because the logging database aggregates information from all the servers in the farm.

You can also pick the scope of the report you want, and click the "Go" button. The reports are generated at run-time, so it might take a few seconds for them to appear. After the results appear, you can click a column heading to sort by those values.

Web Analytics reports in Central Administration are also fed from the logging database. These reports provide usage information about each of the farm's web applications, excluding Central Administration. Clicking the "View Web Analytics reports" link takes you to a summary page listing the web applications in the farm, along with some high-level metrics like total number of page views and total number of daily unique visitors.

When you click a web application on the Summary page, you are taken to a Summary page for that web application that provides more detailed usage information. This includes additional metrics for the web application, such as referrers, total number of page views, and the trends for each, as shown in Figure 3-19.

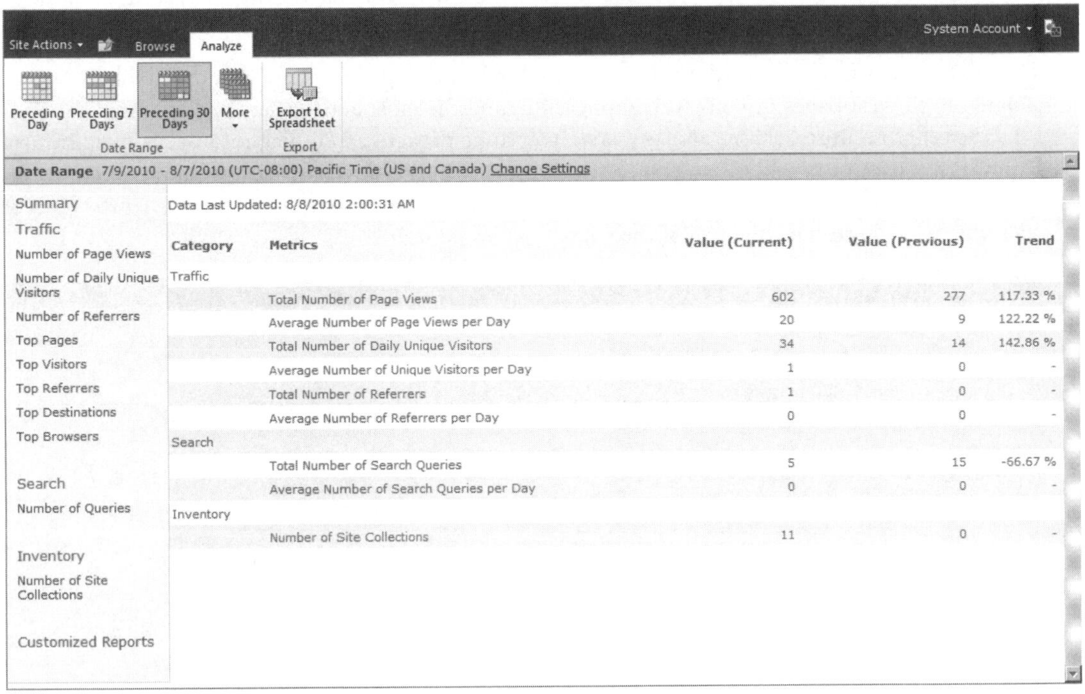

FIGURE 3-19: Web Analytics report

The web application Summary report also adds new links on the left. These links enable you to drill further down into each category. Each new report has a graph at the top, with more detailed information at the bottom of the screen.

If you want to change the scope of a report, you can click Analyze in the ribbon. This then shows the options you have for the report, including the date ranges included. You can choose one of the date ranges provided, or choose custom dates. This provides the flexibility to drill down to the exact date you want. You can also export the report out to a comma-separated value (CSV) file by clicking the "Export to Spreadsheet" button. Because this is a CSV file, the graph is not included — only the dates and their values. These options are available for any of the reports after you choose a web application.

As previously mentioned, the Web Analytics reports do not include Central Administration. Although it's unlikely that you'll need such a report, it is available to you. The Central Administration site is simply a highly specialized site collection in its own web application. Because it is a site collection, usage reports are also available for it. To view them, click Site Actions ⇨ Site Settings. Under Site Actions, click "Site Web Analytics reports." This brings up the same usage reports you just saw at the web application level. You also have the same options from the ribbon, with the exception of being able to export to a CSV file.

Because these reports are site-collection Web Analytics reports, they are available in all site collections, and not in Central Administration. This is another way to consume the information in the logging database. To view the usage information for any site collection or web application, open Site Actions ⇨ Site Settings to get the Web Analytics links. You have two similar links: Site Web Analytics reports and Site Collection Web Analytics reports. These are the same sets of reports, but at different scopes. The site-collection level reports are for the entire site collection. The site-level reports provide the same information, but at the site (also called *web*) level. You have a further option of scoping the reports at that particular site, or that site and its subsites.

Another option that was not available in the Central Administration Web Analytics reports is the capability to use workflows to schedule alerts or reports. You can use this functionality to have specific reports sent to people at specific intervals, or when specific values are met. This is another way that you can use the logging database and the information it collects to be proactive with a SharePoint farm.

There is one final way to consume the information stored in the logging database: directly from SQL. Although it might feel like you're doing something wrong, you're not. Microsoft said it's okay. You have several ways to access data in SQL Server databases, but let's take a look at how to do it in SQL Server Management Studio with regular SQL queries.

SQL Server Management Studio allows you to run queries against databases. Normally, it is a very bad thing to touch any of the SharePoint databases, but the logging database is the only exception to that rule. To run queries against the logging database, you open up Management Studio and find the WSS_Logging database.

The database has a large number of tables. Each category of information has 32 tables to partition the data. It is obvious this database was designed to accommodate a lot of growth. Because of the database partitions, it is tough to do SELECT statements against them. Fortunately, the database also includes views that you can use to view the data.

Expand the Views node of the database to see which views are defined for you. In Figure 3-20, you can see how to get the information from the Usage tables. Right-click the view and click "Select Top 1000 Rows."

This figure shows both the query that is used, and the results of that query. You can use this view and the resulting query as a template for any queries you want to design. If you do happen to do any damage to the logging database, you can simply delete it, and SharePoint will re-create it.

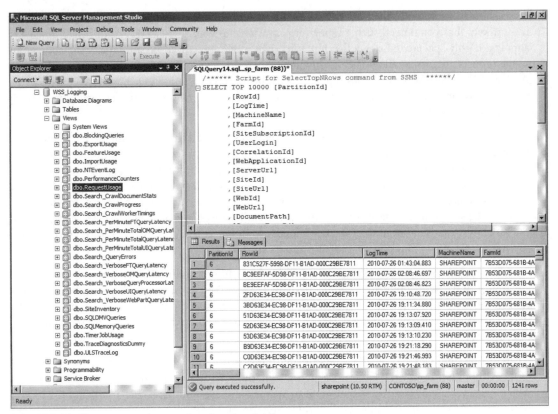

FIGURE 3-20: Usage request query from logging database

HEALTH ANALYZER

By now, you've seen that you have a lot of ways to keep an eye on SharePoint. What if there were some magical way for SharePoint to watch over itself? What if it could use all that fancy monitoring to see when something bad was going to happen to it, and just fix it itself?

Welcome to the future. SharePoint 2010 introduces a feature called the Health Analyzer that does just that. The Health Analyzer utilizes timer jobs to run rules periodically, and to check on system metrics that are based on SharePoint best practices. When a rule fails, SharePoint can alert an administrator in Central Administration, or, in some cases, just fix the problem itself. To access all this magic in Central Administration, you just select Monitoring ➪ Health Analyzer.

Reviewing Problems

How do you know when the Health Analyzer has detected a problem? When you open up Central Administration and there's a red or yellow bar running across the top, as shown in Figure 3-21, that's the Health Analyzer alerting you that there's a problem in the farm. To review the problem, click the "View these issues" link on the right of the notification bar.

Site Actions
Browse
Page
SharePoint 2010 Central Administration
The SharePoint Health Analyzer has detected some critical issues that require your attention. View these issues.

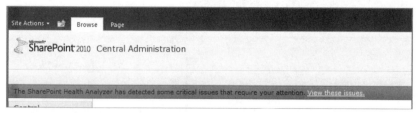

FIGURE 3-21: The Health Analyzer warning

When you click the link, you are taken to the "Review problems and solutions" page. (If there are no problems, you can also get there by clicking Monitoring ⇨ "Review problems and solutions" in Central Administration.) This page shows you all the problems that the Health Analyzer found in the farm. Figure 3-22 shows some problems common with a single-server farm after installation.

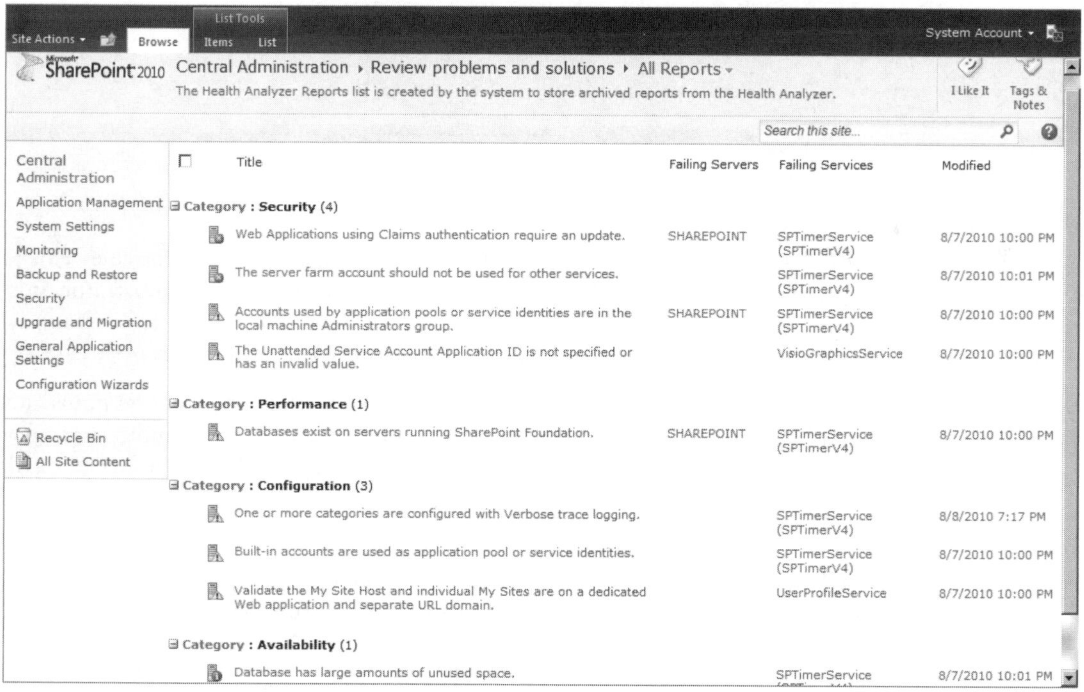

List Tools
Site Actions
Browse
Items
List
System Account
SharePoint 2010 Central Administration ▸ Review problems and solutions ▸ All Reports
The Health Analyzer Reports list is created by the system to store archived reports from the Health Analyzer.
I Like It
Tags & Notes
Search this site...
Central Administration
Application Management
System Settings
Monitoring
Backup and Restore
Security
Upgrade and Migration
General Application Settings
Configuration Wizards
Recycle Bin
All Site Content
Title
Failing Servers
Failing Services
Modified
Category : Security (4)
Web Applications using Claims authentication require an update. SHAREPOINT SPTimerService (SPTimerV4) 8/7/2010 10:00 PM
The server farm account should not be used for other services. SPTimerService (SPTimerV4) 8/7/2010 10:01 PM
Accounts used by application pools or service identities are in the local machine Administrators group. SHAREPOINT SPTimerService (SPTimerV4) 8/7/2010 10:00 PM
The Unattended Service Account Application ID is not specified or has an invalid value. VisioGraphicsService 8/7/2010 10:00 PM
Category : Performance (1)
Databases exist on servers running SharePoint Foundation. SHAREPOINT SPTimerService (SPTimerV4) 8/7/2010 10:00 PM
Category : Configuration (3)
One or more categories are configured with Verbose trace logging. SPTimerService (SPTimerV4) 8/8/2010 7:17 PM
Built-in accounts are used as application pool or service identities. SPTimerService (SPTimerV4) 8/7/2010 10:00 PM
Validate the My Site Host and individual My Sites are on a dedicated Web application and separate URL domain. UserProfileService 8/7/2010 10:00 PM
Category : Availability (1)
Database has large amounts of unused space. SPTimerService 8/7/2010 10:01 PM

FIGURE 3-22: Problems with a SharePoint farm

Clicking any of the issues will bring up the definition of the rule, and offer remedies for it. Figure 3-23 shows details about one of the problems.

FIGURE 3-23: Problem details

As you can see toward the top of Figure 3-23, SharePoint provides a summary of the rule. This particular error indicates that one of the application pool accounts is also a local administrator. In most situations, this is a security issue, so SharePoint discourages it. SharePoint categorizes this as having a severity level of 2, being a Warning. It also tells you that this problem is in the Security category.

The next section, Explanation, describes what the problem is and to which application pools and services it pertains. The following section, Remedy, points you to the Central Administration page where you can fix the problem, and provides an external link to a page with more information about this rule. This is a great addition, and gives SharePoint the capability to update the information dynamically.

The next two sections indicate which server is affected by the issue, and which service logged the failure. The final section provides a link to view the settings for this rule. You learn more about the rule definitions later in this chapter.

That's a rather in-depth property page, and it's packed with even more features. Across the top is a small ribbon that gives you some management options.

Starting on the left, the first button is Edit Item. This lets you alter the values shown on the property page. You could use this to change the error level or category of the rule. It isn't recommended that you alter these values, but if you do, you can keep track of the versions with the next button to the right, Version History. The next button, Alert Me, enables you to set an alert if the item changes. You have these options because these rules are simply items in a list, so you have many of the same options you have with regular list items.

There is another button that deserves mention. For each rule, you have the option to Reanalyze Now. This lets you fire off any rule without waiting for its scheduled appearance, which is great for ensuring that a problem is fixed once you have addressed it. You won't have to wait for the next time the rule runs to verify that it has been taken care of.

Some problems are not only reported, but can be fixed in the property page as well. Figure 3-22 shows another problem that appears under the Configuration category. It notes that one or more of the trace log categories were configured with Verbose trace logging. This configuration issue can contribute to unnecessary disk I/O and drive space usage. The Health Analyzer alerts you when this value is set. This problem is fairly easy to fix. Simply set the trace logging level back to its default. For problems like this, SharePoint offers another option, Repair Automatically, shown at the top of Figure 3-24.

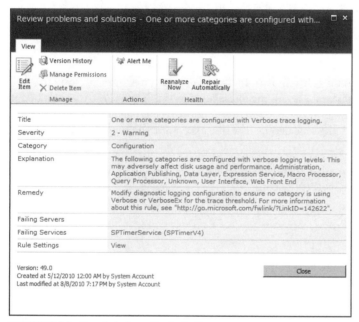

FIGURE 3-24: Repair Automatically button

Clicking the Repair Automatically button allows SharePoint to fix the problem. Then, click the Reanalyze Now button, click Close on the property page, and reload the problem report page. The trace logging problem should no longer be listed. This is almost bliss for the lazy SharePoint administrator.

Rule Definitions

The real power of the Health Analyzer lies in its impressive set of rules. Out-of-the-box, SharePoint 2010 comes with 60 rules. You can see the entire list and details about each rule by clicking Monitoring ⇨ Health Analyzer ⇨ "Review rule definitions" under Health Analyzer.

The rules are broken down by category: Security, Performance, Configuration, and Availability. The default view shows several pieces of information about each rule, including the Title, the Schedule of how often it runs, whether it's Enabled to run, and whether it will Repair Automatically. Wait, did you just read "Repair Automatically"? You read that right. Some rules can be configured to automatically repair problems when they find them.

One example of a rule that automatically fixes itself is "Databases used by SharePoint have fragmented indices." Once a day, SharePoint checks the indices of its databases, and if their fragmentation exceeds a hard-coded threshold, SharePoint will automatically defrag the indices. If the indices are not heavily fragmented, it does nothing. This is a great use of Repair Automatically. It's an easy task to automate, and there's no reason it should need to be done manually by an administrator.

Some rules, like "Drives are running out of free space," don't seem like quite as good a candidate for SharePoint to fix by itself. You don't want it deleting all those copies of your resume, or your Grandma's secret chocolate-chip cookie recipe.

If you want to change the settings of any of the rules (including whether or not it Repairs Automatically), you simply click the rule title, or click the rule's line and select "Edit Item" in the ribbon. Here, you can enable or disable whether or not a rule will run. In a single-server environment, it might make sense to disable the rule that reports databases on the SharePoint server. It's nothing that can be fixed, so getting alerts about it does you no good. You could also choose to change how often the rule is run, but it is not a best practice to change the details of a rule except for enabling the rule and Repair Automatically.

Finally, the rules are simply items in a list. This illustrates how the rules list is extensible. More rules can be added later by Microsoft, or by third parties.

TIMER JOBS

Timer jobs are one of the great unsung heroes of SharePoint. They have been around for several versions of SharePoint, and they get better with age.

Timer jobs are the workhorses of SharePoint. At the most basic level, timer jobs are tasks defined in XML files in the configuration database. Those XML files are pushed out to the members of the farm, and are executed by the Windows service, "SharePoint 2010 Timer." Most configuration changes are pushed out to the farm members with timer jobs. Recurring tasks like Incoming E-Mail also leverage timer jobs.

In SharePoint 2010, timer jobs get another round of improvements. A lot of the functionality covered in this chapter relies on timer jobs, so you have seen some of those improvements already. This section drills down a little deeper into how timer jobs have improved.

Timer Job Management

When you enter Central Administration, it is not immediately obvious that timer jobs have received such a shiny new coat of paint. They have links to essentially the same two items in SharePoint 2010 that they do in SharePoint 2007 — job status and job definition. In SharePoint 2010, the timer job links are under the Monitoring section, because there no longer is an Operations tab. Figure 3-25 shows their new home.

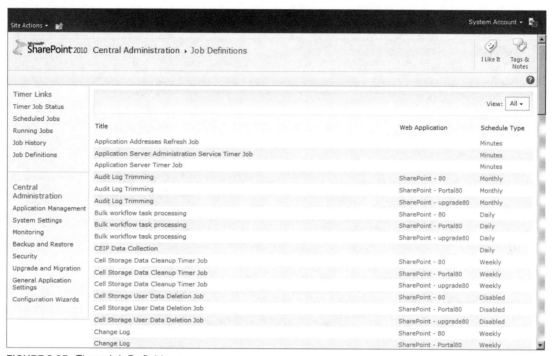

FIGURE 3-25: Timer Job Definitions

The timer job definition page is largely unchanged from its SharePoint 2007 counterpart. You get a list of the timer jobs, the web application they will run on, and their schedule. You can also change the jobs that are shown by filtering the list with the View drop-down in the upper right-hand corner.

To really see what's new, click one of the timer job definitions. Hopefully you're sitting down, because otherwise the new timer definition page shown in Figure 3-26 might knock you over. It includes all of the same information provided in SharePoint 2007, including the general information on the job definitions screen, and the buttons to disable the timer job. However, there are two new, very exciting features.

First, you can change the timer job schedule in this screen. In SharePoint 2007, you needed to use code to do this. This provides a lot of flexibility to move timer jobs around if your farm load requires it. That's a great feature, but it's not the best addition.

The best addition to this page (and arguably to timer jobs in SharePoint 2010) is the button on the bottom of the page, Run Now. You now have the capability to run almost any timer job at will. This means no more waiting for the timer job's scheduled interval to elapse before knowing if something you fixed is working. It is also how Health Monitoring (discussed earlier in this chapter) can fix issues and re-analyze problems. You are no longer bound by the chains of timer job schedules. You are free to run timer jobs whenever you want. That alone is worth the cost of admission.

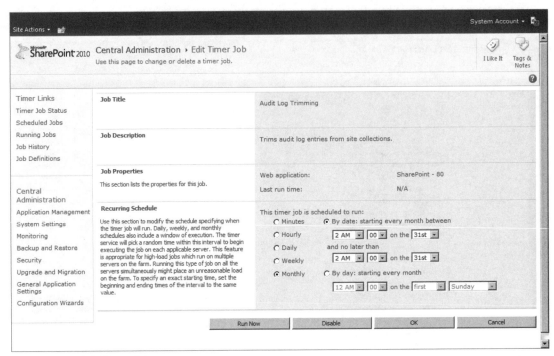

FIGURE 3-26: Edit Timer Job page

Timer Job Status

The other link related to timer jobs you have in Central Administration is "Check job status." This serves the same purpose as its SharePoint 2007 counterpart. However, like the timer job definitions, it has received a new coat of paint. Figure 3-27 shows the new Timer Job Status page. Like the SharePoint 2007 version, it shows you the timer jobs that have completed, when they ran, and whether they were successful.

SharePoint 2010 takes it a step further. The "Succeeded" status is now a hyperlink. If a timer job fails or succeeds, you can click this link to the status and get more information. You also have the capability to filter and view only the failed jobs. That helps with troubleshooting, because you can see all the failures on one page, without all those pesky successes getting in the way. To take it a step further, you can click on a failure and get information about why that particular timer job failed.

The Timer Job Status page serves as a dashboard. You've already seen how it shows the timer job history, but it also shows the timer jobs that are scheduled to run, as well as the timer jobs that are currently running. If you want more complete information on any of these sections, you can click the appropriate link on the left under Timer Links. This provides a page dedicated to each section.

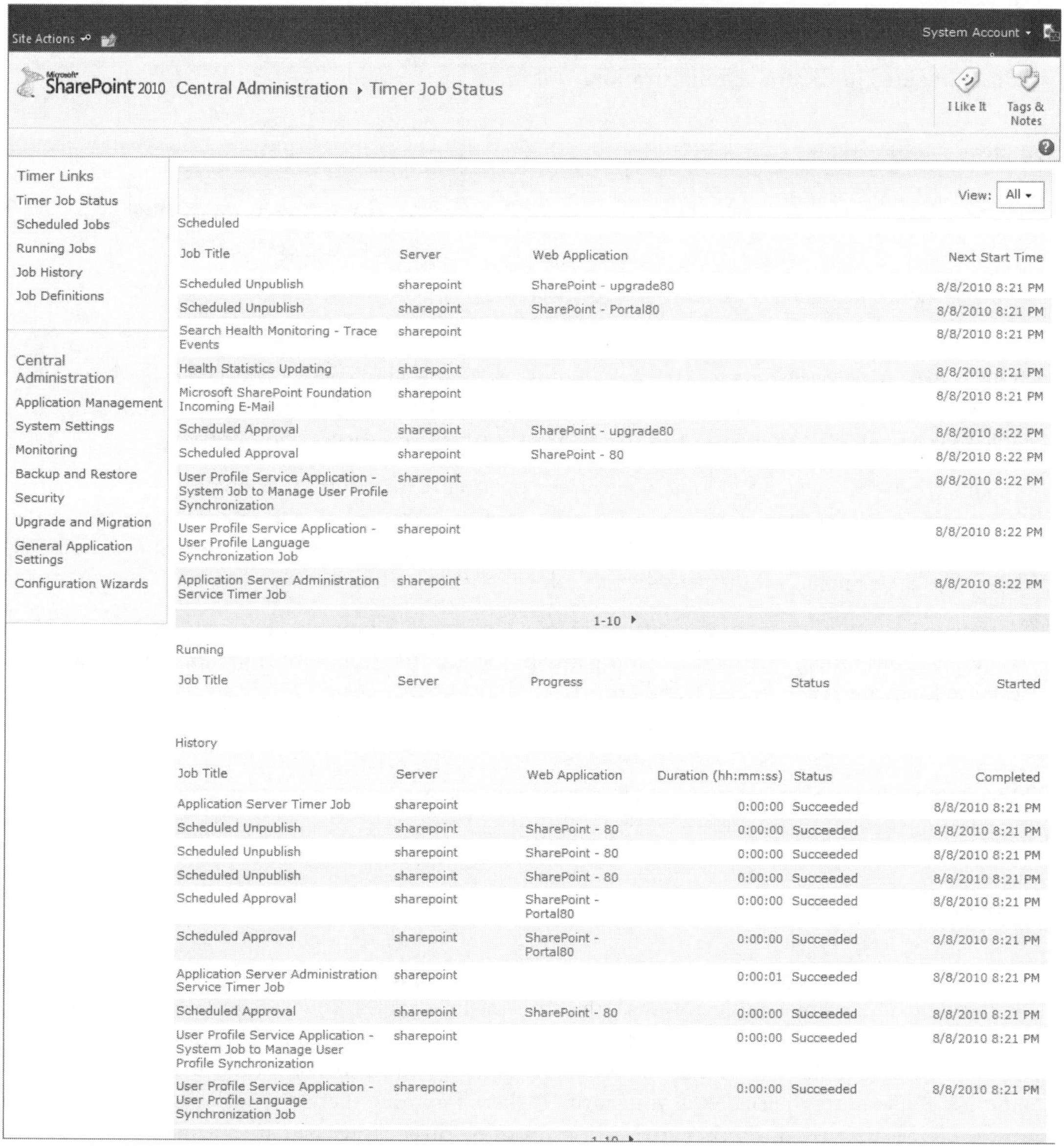

FIGURE 3-27: Timer Job Status page

Along with showing the timer jobs that are running, you can also see the progress of how far along each job is, complete with a progress bar. If you have many jobs running at once, you can click "Running Jobs" in the left Navigation pane to access a page dedicated to reporting the timer jobs that are currently running.

Here's one final timer job improvement: SharePoint 2010 introduces the capability to assign a pre-ferred server for the timer jobs running against a specific Content Database. Figure 3-28 shows how it is configured in Central Administration.

FIGURE 3-28: Configuring Preferred Timer Job Server

This setting is set per Content Database, so it is set on the Manage Content Database Settings page (that is, Central Administration ➪ Application Management ➪ Manage Content Databases). Being able to set a particular server to run the database's timer jobs serves two purposes.

From a troubleshooting standpoint, you can use this to isolate failures to a single box, if you're hav-ing trouble with a specific timer job or Content Database. You can also use this to move the burden of timer jobs to a specific server. This server could be one that is not used to service end-user requests, so having it be responsible for timer jobs will allow another scaling option.

Although you can do a lot to manage timer jobs in Central Administration, you can't forget about Windows PowerShell. Five cmdlets ship with SharePoint that deal with timer jobs. To discover them, use the following `Get-Command` cmdlet:

```
PS C:\> Get-Command -noun SPTimerJob
```

You can use PowerShell to list all of your timer jobs using `Get-SPTimerJob`, and then choose to run one with `Start-SPTimerJob`.

SUMMARY

This chapter picked up where your installation experience left off. You have a SharePoint farm that is installed and running perfectly. With the tools in this chapter, you have learned how to keep an eye on that farm to ensure that it continues to run well. If there is trouble in your farm, you are now armed with the tools to hunt it down and fix it. You will know to check the Health Analyzer and see if it has found any problems with your farm. If there's nothing there, you will also know how to use the ULS logs to track down that error. After finishing this chapter you are a lean, mean, SharePoint monitoring machine.

ABOUT THE AUTHOR

Todd Klindt has been a professional computer nerd for 15 years, and an amateur computer nerd before that. After finding out in college that his desires for food and shelter and his abilities at pro-gramming were not compatible, he decided to try being an administrator instead. He got his MCSE in 1997 and spent a lot of time taming Windows Server, Exchange Server, and the unlucky SQL Server here and there. In 2002, he was tasked with setting up a web page for his IT department. He couldn't program, and he couldn't design HTML to save his life. He found SharePoint Team Services on an Office XP CD and decided to give it a shot. It turned out that SharePoint was just what the doctor ordered. As each version of SharePoint was released, Klindt became more and more enamored with it. In 2005, Klindt was awarded Microsoft's MVP award for Windows SharePoint Services. Since then, he has contributed to a couple of SharePoint books, written a couple of magazine articles, and had the pleasure of speaking in more places than he can believe. To pay the bills, he's a SharePoint consultant and trainer with SharePoint911. He can be found on Twitter dispensing invaluable SharePoint and relationship advice as @ToddKlindt. He lives in Ames, Iowa, with his lovely wife, Jill, their two daughters, Lily and Penny, and their two feline masters, Louise and Spike.

SharePoint 2010 Security Under the Hood — Claims-Based Authentication

By Adam Buenz

For organizations that require more complex SharePoint security architectures, working with multiple identities from various sources can be an extremely difficult task. While determining where assorted identity information exists may be a one-dimensional assessment, deciding which identity technology to use to traverse technology and organizational boundaries can be a challenging decision. However, before assessing and implementing an identity technology, you must understand specifically what an identity is.

An *identity* can be an arduous concept to define. In the context of the physical world, it can take on many forms, and attempts to define it can quickly transform into a metaphysical discussion. In the digital world, an identity is more easily defined, but can also take on multiple structures.

Because of its indistinctness, an identity can be any number of things, including persons, computers, applications, or other various assets. As such, a *digital identity* can simply be described as an object that has distinguishable properties differentiating it from other objects. However, it is more common that an identity is associated directly with a specific user, and differentiated by common characteristics such as username, job role, and age.

For enterprise applications such as SharePoint 2010 that can commonly be accessed and authenticated through several diverse means, numerous diverse identity sources and courses of access may have to be explored. Inherently, such strategies imply that SharePoint integration may be complex because appropriate federation with identity sources (be it a directory service, database, or other storage medium) can be particularly intricate.

For SharePoint environments that necessitate participation from multiple identity sources, such problems in the past have been historically resolved with overly complex solutions. Examples of such solutions are custom Internet Server Application Programming Interface (ISAPI) filters used to intercept the request before the loading of relevant SharePoint filters (`STSFLTR.DLL`) in Windows SharePoint Services 2.0, or the use of Active Directory Federation Services (ADFS) in Windows SharePoint Services 3.0. Though some level of interoperability exists under these constrained circumstances, a single interoperable identity approach is notably more advantageous. Not only does this improve the lives of everyone leveraging the particular technology, but it also implies a large paradigm shift in how identity works.

Consider one of the most common types of authorization in SharePoint, NT LAN Manager (NTLM). NTLM is commonly used in situations where authorization is bound to the orchestrating control of Windows Access Control Lists (ACLs) over what resources are accessed. As such, NTLM is known as a *resource-based identity*. However, NTLM is limited because it is dependent on one Source of Record (SoR), remote sources may require delegation, and the security context of the caller must flow between the application and back end.

On the other hand, Kerberos uses secret key cryptography to provide strong authentication and cryptography over a network. As opposed to directly leveraging Windows assets such as ACLs, Kerberos uses a key distribution center (KDC) to safeguard information and broker ticket issuance. As such, Kerberos is commonly known as *network-based identity*, because the Kerberos protocol provides third-party authentication where a user proves his or her identity by the use of a centralized server.

Resource-based and network-based identities are both constrained because they don't support both omni-directional (responsive in all directions equally) public identities and unidirectional (responsive in a single direction) enterprise entities. True universal identity, however, must both equally embrace the differences between identity sources, while allowing the recognition of various identity data concurrently. This type of thinking is the precursor to the identity metasystem and claims-based authentication.

INTRODUCING THE IDENTITY METASYSTEM

This type of technology fragmentation is certainly not limited to identity scenarios. For example, consider the evolution of network-aware software. In the past, applications had to be written to target a specific network type, such as Token Ring or X.25. Writing a new application or retrofitting a preexisting application for different network types was notoriously difficult.

This restricting problem was solved by the establishment of Internet Protocol (IP). IP provided a baseline that leveraged preexisting underlying technologies, even when from multiple vendors. Most importantly, IP did not replace these technologies, but employed them, providing the means for new technologies to be rapidly adopted with less integration friction as they were invented.

In this sense, the advent of IP provided a needed metasystem, or system of systems, tying individual systems into a larger interoperable system. By permitting diverse network systems to work jointly following a unified programming paradigm, the metasystem abstracts the concern regarding the progression and adoption of explicit underlying technologies, reducing risk and increasing the speed with which individual technology can evolve.

This equivalent metasystem paradigm within the context of identity forms the fundamental constitution for claims-based identity in SharePoint 2010, as well as for claims authentication as a whole. Providing a single, interoperable approach tailored to traverse the various identity barriers that an organization might encounter, a claims-based identity allows standardized mechanisms to harness identity information, regardless of whether it exists within an organization, at a separate organization, or on the cloud.

Some SharePoint environments don't require such complicated security architectures, but can still take advantage of claims architectures. Consider an internal-facing, straightforward small farm environment utilizing NTLM/Kerberos and Active Directory Domain Services (AD DS). A large amount of the mandatory application-level security configuration for this type of environment is automatically handled on the SharePoint back end (not including the other configuration steps required to appropriately organize Kerberos authentication) during provisioning.

In this simplistic design, SharePoint doesn't require that you know much regarding users. Because all the users subsist within the organization context, a majority of the traditional identity barriers are not applicable. There are two principal situations where the use of classic authentication (as opposed to claims authentication) begins to break down:

➤ NTLM and Kerberos are not accommodating when providing extended information concerning a user — frequently requiring tapping into separate (and even orphaned) sources to gather the required data. This can be challenging, or, in some cases, entirely not practicable.

➤ When extending the environment to share identity across security domains, broad-spectrum identity barriers (either organizational or technological) will begin to crop up.

Although viable solutions to these identity problems have certainly existed in the past, the majority are a medley of configurations and compromises to ensure proper functioning. The most suitable solution is that which claims-based authentication promotes — providing a solitary interoperable approach to leverage widely recognized industry standards, and abstracting underlying technology, provider, and vendor considerations. As part of the solution, organizational and technology boundaries can be more effortlessly hurdled, because the uniform approach provides the required ambiguity to traverse such barriers.

This unified, broadly supported approach is exactly what claims-based identity is meant to provide.

IDENTITY IN A CLAIMS-BASED WORLD

Regardless of what the identity is representing, bundled identity information in the digital context is often referred to as a *token*, or *security token*. These semantics are present in a claims-based environment, with a security token containing any number of arbitrary claims. Each individual claim represents a piece of information regarding the specific user, as shown in Figure 4-1.

As demonstrated in Figure 4-1, a claim can represent any information regarding an identity. In the context of a user, this can be more ordinary information (such as name or position title) to more idiosyncratic attributes (such as user interests or projects they are working on). These pieces of information or attributes are referred to as *assertions*, whose moniker is discussed shortly.

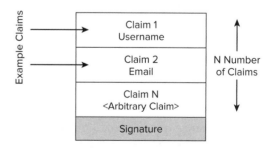

FIGURE 4-1: Token structure and example claims contents

Each of the tokens is digitally signed to ensure the validity of its content, to support non-repudiation, to protect against unauthorized changes, and to provide overall token security. Thus, from a high-level perspective, a token can be broken up into two main segments — the serialized set of claims it contains, and the appended signature verification from the issuing authority to provide cryptographic assurance.

An essential feature of claims structure is the comprehensive identity information that it can provide, which can naturally couple with built-in user intelligence capabilities such as SharePoint User Profiles. The source for the extended attributes can contrast, from orphaned directory services to a generic data store existing on some other medium. Though a token can be unwrapped and the claim information used as a key to harvest further data from detached sources, this situation should be considered atypical, and multiple data source queries kept very lean as a best practice.

In this process, claims are extracted from security tokens for each respective run-time (all within the same security realm) to interact with, one of the claims being a unique identifier. Under the hood, this process is interesting to disseminate at a programmatic level to understand the object interaction, and how the actual identity is built.

First, the required context information about the user is harvested to build an `IClaimsPrincipal` object. The `IClaimsPrincipal` interface defines the data and behavior of the identities associated with an execution context — in this case, the SharePoint context. Once the `IClaimsPrincipal` is built, the `Identities` property can be used to get an `IClaimsIdentity` object, which, in turn, has a `Claims` property containing a queryable `ClaimsCollection`. The key, as described in the aforementioned uncharacteristic claims situation, can be extracted at this point, and leveraged as desired.

Some of this queryable claims information can even be relayed as parameters for other decisions within SharePoint, a situation in some custom environments when role attributes are transported (which is explored shortly) within the claim and security access decisions occurring in SharePoint. From both an architectural and development perspective, this situation simplifies SharePoint security integration, because the platform can simply expect that the required identity information is present within the token.

THE SECURITY TOKEN SERVICE (STS)

Each of the created tokens in a claims-based environment is generated by a *security token service* (*STS*). STSs are specified in the WS-Trust standard that targets mutual use by web service clients and providers. The WS-Trust specification describes how to request and accept security tokens, as well as brokering trust relationships, and, thus, is a vital part of the STS architecture. Consider Figure 4-2, which illustrates the condensed STS processing actions when integrated in a SharePoint environment.

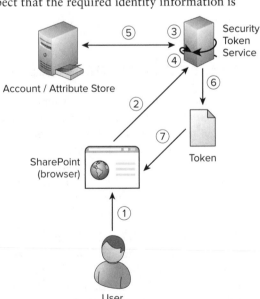

FIGURE 4-2: Abridged STS processing diagram

First, a client issues a request to the enterprise SharePoint instance using a passive client. Once the request is received, SharePoint will query the STS leveraging WS-Trust in order to issue a request for a token with the suitable claims for the specific user. The STS processes the authentication for the request, acting as the issuing authority and, thus, including cryptographic endorsements. Once authentication occurs, the STS examines the request, which contains the SharePoint URI and the required user information to indicate for whom the token should be constructed. Once the information is retrieved, it is used to generate the appropriate token. Once generated, the token is returned to the requester.

The STS in the described process is possessed by an *identity provider* (*IdP*), which is also known as the *issuer*. An IdP can be largely defined as hosted service responsible for publishing identity information based on relationships, thus responsible for implementing the STS. The IdP is accountable for issuing (hence, the "issuer" title) digital identities and acting as the producer of assertions, and the service consumer (SharePoint) employs the fashioned assertions.

The consumer (SharePoint) acting on behalf of the user is known as the *Relying Party* (*RP*). In fact, any application that makes use of claims is given this designation. In the previously described process, the IdP is being hosted by SharePoint, a situation known as a *Identity Provider Security Token Service* (*IdP-STS*). This is extraordinarily common, because SharePoint comes baked within its own STS, already configured for AD DS. Later in this chapter, you learn about the architecture of this STS, along with how to exploit it.

If the STS exists in a location outside of the SharePoint farm, it is known as a *Relying Party Security Token Service* (*RP-STS*), where the partner STS has a trust relationship with an IdP-STS.

When considering some types of issuing authority authentication (as well as most RP-STS SharePoint scenarios with portability across otherwise autonomous security domains), it is easiest to think of the SharePoint STS acting as a *claims transformer*. When the token is initially requested from the STS, there is some level of authentication that occurs using the issuing authority, such as the presentation of a Kerberos TGT (Ticket-Granting Ticket). In a sense, this ticket is a series of claims, albeit limited in scope.

The STS will leverage the TGT to authenticate the request, producing a separate serialized token. This token is represented in a different format, being a Security Assertion Markup Language (SAML) token, as opposed to a Kerberos TGT. Thus, it is viable to extrapolate the major functions of an STS into web service client actions and web service provider actions.

On the client end, the STS converts a security token (that is used locally) into a standard SAML security token containing the user's identity that is shared with the web services provider. On the web service provider side, the STS corroborates incoming security tokens, and can produce a new local token for consumption by other applications. These various situations are discussed in more detail later in this chapter.

When architecting STSs, it is considered a best practice to define a *Token Policy* (*TP*) providing a description of an STS implementation and also defining a *Token Practice Statement* (*TPS*) describing the TP enforcement rules for an STS. The purpose of these is to identify policies and levels of assurance an STS can provide through a commonly used and widely adopted security policy.

While developing and implementing such security policies, it is important to remember that true organizations do not have static policies, particularly when it comes to the mutable identity and security space. Policies (while providing the definition for such matters as enterprise token encryption standards) are dynamic, subject to transition, and not autonomously enforced. Policies must be consistently imposed and adapted to the fluctuating business landscape in accordance with the standards, guidelines, and even other policies within the organization. Implementation of the policies is generally particular to each organization. However, this is commonly tackled through security awareness and training within areas of responsibility.

THE PROBLEM WITH MULTIPLE IDENTITIES

When users have multiple identities (an ordinary situation within organizational environments), this becomes a cause of concern, because it is characteristic that a user will use various identities as opposed to just one. For example, consider Figure 4-3 and Table 4-1, where the user is afforded only one identity to select. (The numbers in the figure correspond to entries in the table.)

The user described in this process must authenticate depending on the issuing authority configuration against the STS to produce the necessary token. Thus, once it consumes the token, SharePoint will not need to re-authenticate again during this session.

However, there is the implied assumption that the user will be leveraging one identity, and this identity will be used against any number of applications. In the real world, this is not practical, because a user will want to send varying sets of identity information based on application requirements, even though there might be some shared level of consistency present among claims.

For example, two general forms of identification are a driver's license and a birth certificate. Though these documents may share some identical information, they cannot be used in the same situation. This is similar to identities in a claims environment — different identities are used for specific applications based on the application requirements, each issued for an unambiguous purpose with the focus on providing the right user information to SharePoint. A distinctive STS will issue tokens with certain claims tailored to provide the appropriate information to the right application. Thus, the tokens, while sharing some attributes, are not the same.

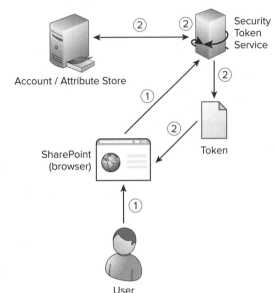

FIGURE 4-3: Abridged claims processing

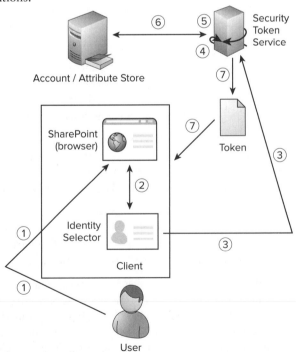

FIGURE 4-4: Identity selector integration

To provide a way around this issue, a component called an *identity selector* is introduced. Using the previous scenario, an identity selector acts as a type of wallet and distribution source for a mixture of user identities. As shown in Figure 4-4 and Table 4-2, when an identity selector is introduced in the claims process, the flow becomes more complete. (The numbers in the figure correspond to entries in the table.)

TABLE 4-1: Abridged Claims Processing

FIGURE	INTERACTION	EXPLANATION
1	Client SharePoint STS	A client issues a request to the SharePoint instance, who, acting on the behalf of the user, queries the STS.
2	SharePoint STS	The STS processes the request and authenticates the user, resolves the user information to generate a token, and returns it to SharePoint, which processes it for authentication.

TABLE 4-2: Identity Selector Integration

FIGURE	INTERACTION	EXPLANATION
1	Client SharePoint	A client issues a request to the SharePoint instance.
2	SharePoint CardSpace	Gathering the claims requirements, the identity selector presents a visual identity selection interface.
3	STS CardSpace	A query is issued to the STS based on the selected identities, requesting a token with the appropriate claims for the user.
4	STS	The STS processes the authentication for the request.
5	STS	Once authenticated, the STS will examine the request, which should contain the SharePoint URI and the user to build the token for.
6	STS	After the STS determines the specific user, the required information is queried out of the local STS database.
7	STS SharePoint	Once the information is queried, it is used to generate a token. Following token generation, it is returned to the requester.

The expanded process still begins with the SharePoint RP, configured to know the claims required in the token, as well as the trusted IdPs. These requirements are relayed to the client, which will trigger the identity selector, providing a visual selection interface of the accessible identities that meet the requirements that SharePoint has sent back. The user will select the identity he or she wants SharePoint to use, and the selector will query the trusted IdP STS to generate a token. The token is presented to SharePoint for processing, verifying the token and exposing the claims content.

When considering this more expanded demonstration of the claims process components, it is important to note the built-in vendor neutrality powered by the use of the numerous WS* specifications. Consider three overarching examples:

➤ SharePoint relays the claims requirements through WS-SecurityPolicy (for requests made via SOAP) or HTML (for requests made via HTTP). There is no compulsory token format, as long as an application and the STS agree. WS-SecurityPolicy is the WS* specification that extends other WS* specifications by providing policy assertions that can characterize distinctive security requirements and restrictions.

➤ Policy use comes into play when an STS is encapsulating the assertions. Retrieved policies are facilitated through an HTTP GET, and the policy is prepared according to the WS-Policy specification. WS-Policy provides a means of policy information exchange, allowing brokering of policy requirements between a provider and consumer.

➤ The exposed STS endpoints implement the WS-Trust specification, describing how to request and accept security tokens. Beyond this, WS-Trust also provides a means to institute and manage trust exchanges.

Most STSs today issue SAML tokens, which, as discussed previously, is an industry-recognized XML vernacular for interoperable claims.

CLAIMS IMPACT ON DELEGATION

In the context of security information being propagated from a caller to a called object, *delegation* is a principal concept in claims-aware SharePoint environments that use the platform for both the built-in features and an "application launching pad." Another way to think of delegation is impersonating the current user as a different identity that has rights to execute certain tasks — in essence, a casting of identity with potentially dissimilar privileges to provide to the access control mechanism. For example, for orphaned application launching, assume that there must be some level of impersonation required, whereby an identity is delegated for discrete application invocation. Furthermore, assume that there are service-dependent components being used, where one service may depend on another. In these situations delegation is a critical concept to consider.

As a condensed example, let's say that a user invokes a claims-aware SharePoint application, following the orthodox steps to retrieve a token for SharePoint to consume. Part of this user request may also invoke a separately hosted claims-aware Service A through a web service leveraging WCF. Both of the applications leverage a shared AD FS 2.0 STS.

To authenticate against Service A, a token must be relayed to Service A with the appropriate claims. Acting on behalf of the user, SharePoint can access Service A, learning its token requirements and trusted IdPs. SharePoint can issue a token request for Service A through the shared STS, signifying it will act as the original user.

Under the pretenses of an AD FS 2.0 STS, it may control policies regarding what applications are allowed to access which other applications using delegation. The STS will confirm this with the policy, and, in this particular example, allow SharePoint to invoke Service A on behalf of this user. The AD FS 2.0 STS will then issue the requested token, allowing SharePoint to call Service A on this user's behalf. Service A will verify the token using Windows Identity Foundation (WIF), making use of the claims.

Another way to control delegation is to make SharePoint a trusted subsystem. In this case, it gathers complete access to other services. Though this can work, this grants SharePoint questionably large security latitude. This becomes increasingly important when considering an organization that might be subject to auditing requirements. Because of such an expansively open security configuration, this will make it impossible for other services to know what SharePoint is delegating access to.

MAPPING TECHNOLOGY TO COMPONENTS

Several components are required to build a claims-aware SharePoint environment, many of which have already been discussed. However, the discussion thus far has assumed that the different features simply exist, without mentioning the particular platform that's responsible for each.

To help provide a robust claims environment, technologies exist that help when designing a claims-based security strategy, and knowing each will aid in gauging whether each is wise from an infrastructure investment standpoint. Some are baked into the SharePoint platform, and, therefore, are not elective.

 Although the focus of this particular section is centered on Microsoft technologies, it should be noted that many other products also exist that can be considered outside of the Microsoft stack, depending on requirements and infrastructure investments.

Active Directory Federation Services (AD FS)

The central component in a claims-based environment is the STS, and the Microsoft platform for a more robust STS is Microsoft Active Directory Federation Services (AD FS) Version 2.0 (which, while in development, was known as the "Geneva" server). This platform should not be confused with the limitations of its previous version based on its name. Though the title does include the same federation semantics, the capabilities of the platform far outreach simple federation scenarios.

AD FS 2.0 has broad support for claims-based identity, providing a ready-to-use STS, issuing SAML tokens in response to WS-Trust requests. Furthermore, eliminating the limitation of its predecessor (which was restricted to use strictly within browsers), AD FS 2.0 supports both active and passive clients. Thus, it can be used from a web and client environment. While being more commonly deployed as a cross-federation source within an organization, the AD FS 2.0 STS can leverage any identity provider. None of this is to imply that Geneva server is required for SharePoint claims-based authentication. SharePoint can leverage any STS, from any vendor, even if the STS is built in-house.

Windows Identity Foundation (WIF)

Known during its development as the "Geneva Framework," WIF is leveraged by the SharePoint platform, allowing externalization of user access through claims. It is distributed as a shared library inclusive of the necessary classes to handle claims authentication. This library contains the essential functions for things such as token reception handling and signature verification. The library is mutually present in the AD FS 2.0 STS and SharePoint STS. The implications of this are beneficial, because a custom STS with tailored features can be more easily implemented using the two existing examples.

CardSpace

CardSpace is the Microsoft identity selector. Built off the preexisting CardSpace platform, the identity selector interface can be used under both active and passive clients. CardSpace is truly the most voluntary component in a claims environment, whereas pieces such as the STS are requisite. This certainly doesn't imply that it should not be considered in a claims design, because without an identity selector (be it CardSpace or another), users will have no consistent, instinctive interface to get a practical representation of their available identities.

The CardSpace interface is rationally laid out, with each identity being represented by an information card. Each card is a simple XML file, specifying the IdP relationship. The card metadata defines how the communication is brokered between the trusted IdP servicing the STS, and how the token return should be structured. It is important to note that the information card contains no claims data. When the card is selected by a user, CardSpace will issue a request for a token from the associated identity provider, generally prompting the user for authentication, depending on the issuing authority. While all this is taking place behind the scenes, the user is simply shown a hold screen representing card exchange.

Considering all of these features, it is important to keep in mind that each is mutually exclusive. Each is implemented with standardization in mind, and, thus, can operate independently. For example, CardSpace isn't limited in use to the AD FS 2.0 STS. It's assumed to be like any other STS, because token requests are sent using the standard WS-Trust protocol.

CONFIGURATION OF SHAREPOINT CLAIMS

Before discussing claims design, it is helpful to get under the hood of SharePoint claims and to see how it fits within an organizational security strategy.

SharePoint's Trusted STS

By default, SharePoint 2010 includes a trusted STS, more commonly referred to as the *Security Token Service* web application because of its interface title. You'll find the web services associated with the STS in the `SecurityTokenService` application under SharePoint Web Services in Internet Information Server (IIS).

To support this type of functionality, there are several moving parts. However, the most visibly evident is the introduction of numerous new `HTTPModules` from the `Microsoft.SharePoint.IdentityModel` namespace — namely, `FederatedAuthentication`, `SessionAuthentication`, and `SPWindowsClaimsAuthentication`. These features are also backed by two important web service protocols:

➤ *SharePoint Claim Provider Service Web Service Protocol Specification (MS-CPSWS)* — MS-CPSWS is the protocol responsible for providing access to returned claims and their relevant metadata to execute queries against. It is important to note that the protocol does not define how claim providers interface with identity providers, or how identity providers store data.

➤ *SharePoint Security Token Service Web Service Protocol Specification (MS-SPSTWS)* — MS-SPSTWS builds on the WS-Trust model, allowing control over other protocols for interoperability between the protocol server, and allowing authentication to be properly implemented.

The restrictions propped by MS-SPSTWS take on two forms: those dealing with `RequestSecurityToken` (RST) messages and `RequestSecurityTokenResponse` (RSTR) messages. An RST message offers facilities for issuing a request for a token from an STS, and an RSTR message (as the name implies) responds to the token request by returning a token.

Configuring Claims-Based Authentication Using the AD FS 2.0 STS

Although SharePoint ships with its own STS, even in this most basic claims design some preparation is required. Such obligatory preparation is evident when, as you are creating a new web application, you attempt to configure claims-based authentication, and the Federated Identity Provider option is grayed out with a message, "There are no Trusted Providers defined."

You can structure the default SharePoint trusted identity provider by using all PowerShell scripting. All the useful claims commands are also done with PowerShell. For example, if you receive the trusted provider error and believe that you have already set up a trusted provider, SharePoint might not have been set up with the appropriate identity claim mapping when the trusted provider was built.

In this case, you can use the `Get-SPTrustedIdentityTokenIssuer` PowerShell command. By examining the `IdentityClaimTypeInformation` value, it is possible to find out exactly what claims SharePoint is expecting — so that you can avoid the STS issuing a token without this claim, or an empty claim of that type.

Before getting started with any configuration for claims authentication, it is necessary to define what you will use as the STS. Though it may be practical, using the SharePoint IdP-STS scenario is a limited example. Therefore, for this demonstration, the environment will make use of the AD FS 2.0 STS.

The AD FS 2.0 instance will be hosted on a separate server, because, by default, AD FS 2.0 makes use of the Default Web Site, and also implements a self-signed certificate. If it is desirable to leverage a preexisting SQL database for storage, you cannot use `FsConfigWizard.exe` (the AD FS 2.0 configuration wizard), but instead must use a command line. Otherwise, configuration information is stored in a SQL 2008 Express Edition instance locally by default.

After AD FS 2.0 has been installed and the default configuration is in place, it is best to verify that the communications setup is indeed well formed before proceeding. To do so, follow these steps:

1. On the Start menu, select All Programs.

2. Select the "ADFS 2.0 Management console."

3. Expand the `Services` folder.

4. Select Certificates.

5. Double-click the Service Communications certificate and ensure that the properties are correct.

6. Ensure that you can navigate to the Federation Metadata by browsing to `https://<ADFS Server>/FederationMetadata/2007-06/federationmetadata.xml`.

As is discussed shortly, an X.509 certificate is required to be passed as a parameter to the `SPTrustedIdentityTokenIssuer` you will be creating. You can retrieve the certificate from AD FS 2.0 through the Management console. Follow these steps to do so:

1. On the Start menu, select All Programs.

2. Select "ADFS 2.0 Management console."

3. Expand the `Services` folder.

4. Select Certificates.

5. Right-click the certificate under the Token-Signing Certificate header and select View Certificate.

6. Select the Details tab, and then select "Copy to File." Save to a familiar location.

Now that a certificate is in place and accessible, you must use a SharePoint-specific configuration to bring the certificate over to the SharePoint server. Keeping in mind previously discussed problems regarding claim mapping (that is, adding the mapping on token issuer creation), it is possible to sort out the appropriate PowerShell commands to build a proper `SPTrustedIdentityTokenIssuer`.

In this example, you will also build out an identity claim mapping something unique — an e-mail address. You will also build out a role claim to nicely match up with the built-in role security features that SharePoint presents.

Follow these steps:

1. On the Start menu, select All Programs.

2. Select Microsoft SharePoint 2010 Products.

3. Select SharePoint 2010 Management Shell.

In the PowerShell command, you must first define a certificate by creating a new x509Certificate2 object that specifies a path to a unique X.509 certificate. The certificate used to hydrate the object is the one previously exported from the STS. When creating the new SPTrustedIdentityTokenIssuer, it expects this certificate for the ImportTrustCertificate parameter, but it is important to note that you can use the certificate only once to create an SPTrustedIdentityTokenIssuer. Thus, if you wanted to associate it with a different SPTrustedIdentityTokenIssuer, you must disassociate it from its web applications and delete the certificate.

It is important to note that if you receive an error that reads, "The root of the certificate chain is not a trusted root authority," you must export the root CA for the certificate that is used for token signing in your STS.

Next, you create the two mapped claims. Initially the e-mail (identity) claim is mapped using the New-SPClaimTypeMapping command, as shown here:

```
$mapX = New-SPClaimTypeMapping -IncomingClaimType
    "http://schemas.xmlsoap.org/ws/2005/05/identity/claims/emailaddress" -
    IncomingClaimTypeDisplayName "EmailAddress" -SameAsIncoming
```

Then, the role claim is created. The role claim is one of the nicest claim types, because it can increase or decrease, depending on group memberships.

```
$mapY = New-SPClaimTypeMapping -IncomingClaimType
    "http://schemas.microsoft.com/ws/2008/06/identity/claims/role" -
    IncomingClaimTypeDisplayName "Role" -SameAsIncoming
```

When creating the SPTrustedIdentityTokenIssuer, both of these claims will be included as parameters. In the New-SPTrustedIdentityTokenIssuer command, you can see that, instead of pointing to the default SharePoint STS, you are pointing to the ADFS STS. If the default SharePoint STS were being used, the URL to that would be used instead. In the following code, the realm can be set by specifying a string value, or you can automate it through the use of environmental variables:

```
$ap = New-SPTrustedIdentityTokenIssuer -Name "ADFS v2" -Description "ADFS v2" -
    Realm "yourRealmName" -ImportTrustCertificate $yourCert -ClaimsMappings
    $mapX,$mapY -SignInUrl "https://urlToYourAdfsServer/adfs/ls" -
    IdentifierClaim http://schemas.xmlsoap.org/ws/2005/05/identity/
    claims/emailaddress
```

Several things must be taken into account with this process. First, when creating the SPTrustedIdentityTokenIssuer, you are explicitly setting the claims. If you include other unnecessary claims, they will not be leveraged by SPClaim when SharePoint receives them. Claims are immutable once the SPTrustedIdentityTokenIssuer is created in the current version of SharePoint.

Now, a new identity provider under the name specified in the Name switch of the New-SPTrustedIdentityTokenIssuer command will be available.

Follow these steps:

1. Open SharePoint Central Administration.

2. Select Web Application Management.

3. Highlight a web application.

4. Select Authentication Providers in the ribbon.

5. Look in the Federated Identity Provider section.

By default, generally, Windows authentication and Claims authentication (dual authentication on a single zone, an improvement from SharePoint 2007) are left on, because there has been no RP configuration done, and the environment is still not fully built. The next hurdle is that AD FS 2.0 federation requires Secure Socket Layers (SSL).

The easiest way to accomplish this is to simply add the Active Directory Certificate Services (AD CS) roles to the SharePoint WFE, and request a new certificate in IIS. Once the certificate is in place, you can set up the RP trust relationship with SharePoint from AD FS 2.0.

Follow these steps:

1. On the Start menu, select All Programs.

2. Click "ADFS 2.0 Management console."

3. In the `Relying Party Trusts` folder, right-click and select Add Replying Party Trust. This will start the Add Relying Party Trust Wizard.

4. On the Select Data Source screen, select "Enter data about the relying party manually."

5. Click Next.

6. On the Specify Display Name screen, enter the display name and any helpful notes.

7. Click Next.

8. On the Choose Profile screen, select "AD FS 2.0 profile."

9. On the Configure Certificate screen, you can specify whether SAML tokens should be encrypted. This isn't required.

10. Click Next.

11. On the Configure URL screen, select "Enable support for the WS-Federation Passive Protocol" and specify the site collection URL with the `/_trust/` suffix. Because the federation requirements specify the need for SSL as previously discussed, this requirement will bubble up an error if not met.

12. On the Configure Identifiers screen, clear the default value. The value for this should be the realm specified when executing the `New-SPTrustedIdentityTokenIssuer` command. As detailed in previous sections, if this value is not available, simply use `Get-SPTrustedIdentityTokenIssuer`, and examine the `ProviderRealm` attribute.

13. On the Choose Issuance Authorization Rules screen, select "Permit all users to access this relying party."

14. Click Next.

15. On the "Ready to Add Trust" screen, review your settings and click Complete.

16. In the "ADFS 2.0 Management console" screen, right-click the Relying Party Trust (the one just created) and select Edit Claim Rules.

17. At Choose Rule Type, select "Send LDAP Attributes as Claims."

18. Click Next.

19. On the Edit Rule Screen, keep the "Claim rule name" as "Pass through LDAP claims" and ensure that the Attribute store is using Active Directory.

20. In the "Mapping of LDAP attributes to outgoing claims types" section, ensure that the E-mail Addresses address attribute is mapped to the E-mail Address outgoing claim type. Also ensure that the SAM-Account-Name is matched to the Name outgoing claim type.

After you have followed these steps, you can access the SharePoint instance, but you will receive an "access denied" message. This is because you have not configured an account for any roles in SharePoint. Before the user is added as a site collection administrator, ensure that a valid e-mail is provided in AD DS, because this is mapped in the claims.

Follow these steps:

1. Open SharePoint Central Administration.

2. Select Site Collection Administrators.

3. At the top of the Site Collection dialog, ensure that you are working with the right site collection.

4. In the Primary Site Collection Administrator box, use the people picker to search using the e-mail specified in AD DS for the required account.

5. Click OK.

Now, the specified site collection should be accessible through this account. However, other users will still not be able to access the site because you have only added the site collection administrator. Thus, it is beneficial to add all the ADFS authenticated users to the instance.

Follow these steps:

1. Navigate to the site collection that users should be added into.

2. Select Site Actions.

3. Select Site Permissions.

4. Select the group to add the users into, and select New ➪ Add Users.

5. Select the All Users security group and add them.

ARCHITECTURE OF SHAREPOINT CLAIMS

SharePoint claims authentication is utilized in a variety of different designs. However, there are three logical boilerplate designs whose canned architecture can demonstrate extending a claims application.

To exhibit these environments, AD FS 2.0 and CardSpace claims components will be integrated. However, it should be noted that SharePoint ships with an operational STS that is preconfigured to use the local AD DS instance for authentication. Interestingly, this is, in fact, the default setting, and represents a push by Microsoft to move SharePoint 2010 toward a claims-based, rather than classic, authentication.

For this discussion, let's focus on using a separate IdP-STS with the SharePoint STS acting as the RP-STS.

Internal Enterprise Claims (IEC)

The most frequently used claims architecture is claims usage within the enterprise, also known as *Internal Enterprise Claims (IEC)*. Logically, this architecture is the easiest to understand, because an organization owns the identity provider. Using the previously described pieces of technology in this design, building a claims-based environment is a fairly simple task, as shown in Figure 4-5 and Table 4-3. (The numbers in the figure correspond to entries in the table.)

The benefit of using a claims-based environment should be apparent in this process. Besides the initial hydration of user information to populate the claims with the required user information, there is no other lookup for user data that's required. Everything can be handled within the initial token hydration, thereby reducing possible complex security integration.

TABLE 4-3: IEC Architecture

FIGURE	INTERACTION	EXPLANATION
1	AD DS SharePoint	A user logs in receiving a Kerberos TGT that was issued by the Kerberos KDC.
2	SharePoint	A user issues a request to the SharePoint environment, learning what kinds of tokens it accepts, and what claims those tokens must contain.
3	CardSpace	If CardSpace is being used, the user will be shown the card-selection interface.
4	CardSpace STS	CardSpace will issue a token request for this identity, using the Kerberos TGT to authenticate the user.
5	STS AD DS	The ADFS 2.0 server STS will verify the TGT, and subsequently query AD DS for the required information needed to construct the requested token.

FIGURE	INTERACTION	EXPLANATION
6	SharePoint STS	Once the token has been created, the AD FS 2.0 STS will send it back to the user, which will be relayed to SharePoint. If transformation of the claim is required, it can be relayed to the SharePoint STS.
7	SharePoint	SharePoint will use WIF to verify the token's signature and expose the claims for use.

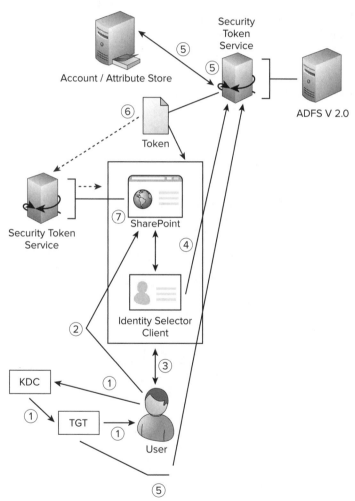

FIGURE 4-5: IEC Architecture

Public Cloud Claims (PCC) and the LDAP Provider

It is not unusual for SharePoint implementations to be used both internally and externally, some-times with a more limited internal STS for remote employee access, or a fully cloud-facing deploy-ment with a public STS. When using claims, even when the SharePoint deployment is externally facing, the security approach can remain unchanged. As such, an architecture that should be explored is configuring the LDAP provider for forms authentication.

You must first use SharePoint's Central Administration to configure a claims web application to use an LDAP provider. Then, you must adjust the LDAP `web.config` files for the claims web applica-tion, Central Administration, and security token service. In the `web.config` file for each, ensure that the following grouping is included in the `<system.web>` group:

```
<membership defaultProvider="AspNetSqlMembershipProvider">
    <providers>
      <add name="membership"
       type="Microsoft.Office.Server.Security.LdapMembershipProvider,
            Microsoft.Office.Server, Version=14.0.0.0, Culture=neutral,
            PublicKeyToken=71e9bce111e9429c"
          server="server.com"
          port="389"
          useSSL="false"
          userDNAttribute="distinguishedName"
          userNameAttribute="sAMAccountName"
    userContainer="OU=UserAccounts,DC=company,DC=corp,DC=organization,DC=
       distinguishedName"
          userObjectClass="person"
          userFilter="(ObjectClass=person)"
          scope="Subtree"
          otherRequiredUserAttributes="sn,givenname,cn" />
    </providers>
  </membership>
  <roleManager enabled="true" defaultProvider="AspNetWindowsTokenRoleProvider" >
    <providers>
      <add name="roleManager"
          type="Microsoft.Office.Server.Security.LdapRoleProvider,
              Microsoft.Office.Server, Version=14.0.0.0,
              Culture=neutral, PublicKeyToken=71e9bce111e9429c"
          server="yourserver.com"
          port="389"
          useSSL="false"
          groupContainer="DC=location,DC=corp,DC=organization,DC=
             distinguishedName"
          groupNameAttribute="cn"
          groupNameAlternateSearchAttribute="samAccountName"
          groupMemberAttribute="member"
          userNameAttribute="sAMAccountName"
          dnAttribute="distinguishedName"
          groupFilter= ***SEE LEGEND***
          userFilter=*** SEE LEGEND***
          scope="Subtree" />
    </providers>
  </roleManager>
```

Use the filters shown in Table 4-4 for the role manager decoration.

Additionally, it is considered a best practice to set up some optional configuration, because it supports single-server deployments. In the STS `web.config` file, decorate the `connectionUserName` and `connectionPassword` as follows:

```
connectionUsername="domain\administrator"
connectionPassword="password"
```

An external identity provider existing on the cloud can also be used internally with an organization, as opposed to providing a separate identity provider. This is known as a *Public Cloud Claims* (PCC), and is shown in Figure 4-6 and Table 4-5. (The numbers in the figure correspond to entries in the table.)

TABLE 4-4: Filter Values for the Role Manager

WEB.CONFIG	FILTER
Central Administration	`groupFilter="((ObjectClass=group)"`
	`userFilter="((ObjectClass=person)"`
Security token service	`groupFilter="(&amp;(ObjectClass=group))"`
	`userFilter="(&amp;(ObjectClass=person))"`
Web application	`groupFilter="(&amp;(ObjectClass=group))"`
	`userFilter="(&amp;(ObjectClass=person))"`

TABLE 4-5: PCC Architecture

FIGURE	INTERACTION	EXPLANATION
1	SharePoint	The external user accesses SharePoint and learns what kinds of tokens it will accept.
2	CardSpace	If CardSpace is being used, the user will be shown the card selection interface with the identities that match requirements.
3	CardSpace STS	CardSpace queries the external identity provider and requests the token.
4	STS SharePoint	The token is returned to the user or to the SharePoint STS for transformation, and then is submitted to SharePoint.
5	SharePoint	SharePoint uses the token and the claims it contains.

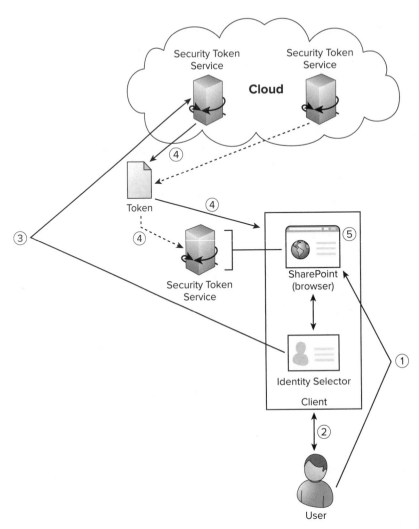

FIGURE 4-6: PCC Architecture

 In this example, although the external identity provider being used is owned by Microsoft, no propriety links exist. Any STS can be leveraged in this situation, assuming that SharePoint trusts the claims generated by the identity provider.

Enterprise Identity Federation (EIF)

Federating identities between organizations is one of the most common security problems that a SharePoint architect will encounter. For example, consider a scenario in which partner firms want to make data available within the internal SharePoint deployment exposed to external organizations without an overcomplicated security strategy. The least-complicated way to enable these users to have access to the SharePoint instance is to allow them to use their own identities through a direct federation. This is known as *Enterprise Identity Federation (EIF)*.

Though this will naturally bring about concerns regarding legal agreements between the two organizations, several technological considerations must also be taken into account. The approach required to allow the users to surpass this identity barrier can be overcome by implementing AD FS 2.0.

In the example shown in Figure 4-7 and Table 4-6, two organizations are used, Organization A and Organization B. (The numbers in the figure correspond to entries in the table.) With the prescribed solution, you will avoid two problems:

➤ First, you assume that the STSs are not already configured to trust each other.

➤ Second, because you don't know the number of STSs that must be configured, you implement a certain configuration.

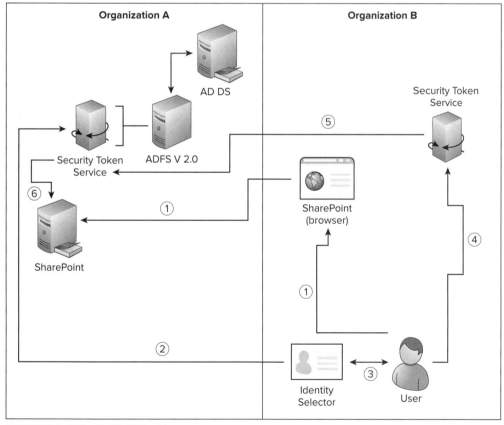

FIGURE 4-7: EIF with ADFS Architecture

TABLE 4-6: EIF with ADFS Architecture

FIGURE	INTERACTION	EXPLANATION
1	SharePoint	A user in Organization B accesses Organization A's SharePoint instance. SharePoint is configured to trust only the Organization A SharePoint instance.
2	CardSpace	CardSpace will issue a request to the STS in Organization A to determine the token requirements. CardSpace has built-in intelligence to traverse this type of relationship.
3	CardSpace	The user will be prompted to select an identity that matches these requirements.
4	STS	A request is issued to build a token from the Organization B STS. However, SharePoint will not accept this token because of a lack of trust.
5	STS	This token is sent to the Organization A STS, which acts as a federation partner, transforming the incoming token to one the SharePoint instance will accept. The federation partner will also verify the signature on the token.
6	SharePoint	The token is sent to SharePoint.
	STS	

SUMMARY

Claims-based authentication is an exciting new security feature of SharePoint 2010 that allows deployment in much more extended designs. Taking advantage of claims environments provides the capability to both consume and provide identity information in modern, refined ways based on widely accepted industry standards.

Several components build up the claims-based identity context, and a strong foundation is available with AD FS 2.0, CardSpace, and WIF. Using claims enables the capabilities of a SharePoint implementation to be easily employed by users outside of an organization, allowing a larger return on the infrastructure investment to be realized, as well as increasing adoption.

Configuring claims-based authentication is a combination of administrative operation in Central Administration and using PowerShell commands. There are important considerations to take into account when creating the claim mapping, and it is always important to double-check your commands before executing them, because this adjusts security context. Several types of claims environments exist, including Internal Enterprise Claims (IEC), Cloud Enterprise Claims (CEC), and Enterprise Identity Federation (EIF).

ABOUT THE AUTHOR

Adam Buenz is a SharePoint architect and developer for ARB Security Solutions, LLC (sharepointsecurity.com). He focuses on security-centric collaboration environments that build off the SharePoint and .NET Framework. Focusing heavily on the security of SharePoint, along with integration of sister Microsoft platforms into SharePoint (such as ForeFront, ISA, MIIS, and DPM), he has developed against several of the largest health care, financial, and federal implementations of SharePoint within the United States. He is co-author of *Professional SharePoint 2007 Development* (Indianapolis: Wiley, 2007) and co-author of *7 Microsoft Office Business Applications for Office SharePoint Server 2007* (Redmond, WA: Microsoft Press, 2007). He lives wherever he is contracted, and can be contacted at adam@sharepointsecurity.com.

5

Using PowerShell with SharePoint 2010

By Gary Lapointe

SharePoint is an incredibly powerful and complex application that takes considerable time and effort to master. I started working with the enterprise version of SharePoint 2007 (MOSS) shortly after it released, and I became quickly overwhelmed by the amount of configuration settings it took to get the product up and running properly. I was creating what turned out to be a rather massive document detailing every configuration and taxonomy change that was needed for an upgrade from my company's SharePoint 2003 environment to SharePoint 2007. It quickly became apparent that tracking all the necessary changes using a document was a pointless and tedious exercise. That's when I discovered the true power of STSADM, the command-line tool used to automate SharePoint 2007.

It turned out that STSADM was easily extendable, allowing developers to supplement the existing 184 out-of-the-box commands with additional commands as necessary. Using this information, I began developing a series of batch files that not only used the out-of-the-box commands, but also used numerous custom command extensions that I built. The end result was that I was easily able to script an entire farm configuration, everything from creating and provisioning farm components, to adding items to lists and migrating site collections.

However, with all the power that STSADM exposed, it was, in many ways, extremely limited. Conditional logic was very difficult to achieve using batch files. If no command was available to manipulate a setting, a custom command would have to be created. And performance was poor because of the inability to re-use objects across command calls. Enter *PowerShell*.

PowerShell is Microsoft's next-generation scripting language offering direct access to .NET objects, complex flow and structure capabilities, and an object pipeline that makes passing objects from one command to another extremely easy. Administrators and developers slowly began to use PowerShell with SharePoint 2007, but there was no direct support from the product itself, thus forcing users to be intimately familiar with the SharePoint API. Adoption has been extremely slow as a result of this.

With the latest release of the SharePoint platform, SharePoint 2010, administrators and developers now have full support for PowerShell at their disposal. Almost every aspect of the platform can be manipulated using any of the more than 500 out-of-the-box *cmdlets* (pronounced "command-lets") or by creating custom cmdlets that can be developed and deployed just like any other core SharePoint artifact. STSADM is still present in SharePoint 2010, but its prominence has been greatly reduced.

This chapter examines the basic PowerShell concepts that every SharePoint administrator and developer should know. I share with you the tips, tricks, and techniques that have helped me understand the technology, and how best to use it. I then show how, why, and when to create custom cmdlets using Visual Studio 2010. The intent of this chapter is not to provide a comprehensive understanding of PowerShell, but rather to provide you with the core skills you need to get started with the technology, as it relates to SharePoint 2010.

UNDERSTANDING POWERSHELL BASICS

To use PowerShell with SharePoint, you must first make the PowerShell environment aware of the SharePoint cmdlets and assemblies. The easiest way to do this is to open PowerShell using the SharePoint 2010 Management Shell, which you can find under the Microsoft SharePoint 2010 Products folder in the Start menu. But what is the "Management Shell"?

> A cmdlet *(pronounced "command-let") is the term used to describe commands within the PowerShell language. Cmdlets are always named using a verb-noun pattern, but it is possible to create an alias for easier access. For example, the* Get-Help *cmdlet has an alias of* help. *Thus, typing* help Add-PsSnapin *or* Get-Help Add-PsSnapin *both output the same results.*

If you right-click the shortcut and select Properties, you'll see the following for the Target field:

```
C:\...\PowerShell.exe -NoExit
    " & ' C:\...\14\CONFIG\POWERSHELL\Registration\sharepoint.ps1 ' "
```

From this, you can see that the SharePoint 2010 Management Shell is just a PowerShell instance that loads the sharepoint.ps1 script file, which is as follows:

```
$ver = $host | select version
if ($ver.Version.Major -gt 1) {$Host.Runspace.ThreadOptions = "ReuseThread"}
Add-PsSnapin Microsoft.SharePoint.PowerShell
Set-location $home

# SIG # Begin signature block
# MIIXUAYJKoZIhvcNAQcCoIIXQTCCFz0CAQExCzAJBgUrDgMCGgUAMGkGCisGAQQB
```

```
# gjcCAQSgWzBZMDQGCisGAQQBgjcCAR4wJgIDAQAABBAfzDtgWUsITrck0sYpfvNR
...
# NwyRMmAJgiCXGmPkQYEPjWHFS7Xtxfb09AYHswf+66VAYvDSJ0xf8qdaRSwRsknW
# 7bKQc8uuhw=
# SIG # End signature block
```

The third line of this script file is the most critical, and the only one that matters right now. (The implications of the second line are addressed later in this chapter.) `Add-PsSnapin` is a PowerShell cmdlet that is used to register new cmdlets that are packaged up in what is called a *snap-in*. When the SharePoint 2010 binaries are installed on a server (or Windows 7 workstation), the assemblies that contain the SharePoint PowerShell cmdlets are also installed and registered with the system. However, those assemblies will not be available to PowerShell until they are added using the `Add-PsSnapin` cmdlet.

The significance of this is that you can easily work with the SharePoint PowerShell cmdlets in editors other than the SharePoint Management Shell (or, specifically, the PowerShell console window). In fact, my general recommendation is to not use the SharePoint Management Shell and instead use a script editor such as the *Windows PowerShell Integrated Scripting Environment (ISE)*, or a third-party scripting editor. The Windows PowerShell ISE is available only with PowerShell V2 and can be loaded by going to Start ⇨ All Programs ⇨ Accessories ⇨ Windows PowerShell.

If you choose to use the PowerShell ISE, you must manually execute the `Add-PsSnapin Microsoft .SharePoint.PowerShell` command. But you will now have the benefit of integrated debugging capabilities, syntax highlighting, and, of course, a simple editor in which you can construct your routines without having to execute them line by line.

An Object-Based Scripting Language

Once you have started PowerShell, the SharePoint assemblies and cmdlets are registered. So, now what? Start by looking at a simple example that demonstrates using the new `Get-SPFarm` cmdlet:

```
PS C:\> $farm = Get-SPFarm
PS C:\> $farm.GetType().FullName
Microsoft.SharePoint.Administration.SPFarm
PS C:\>
```

If you've worked with the SharePoint object model before, you should immediately recognize the type name `Microsoft.SharePoint.Administration.SPFarm`. The `Get-SPFarm` cmdlet returns back a first-class .NET object that can be used and manipulated just like any other .NET object.

To prove this, pass the `$farm` variable you just created into a standard PowerShell cmdlet called `Get-Member`. (In the following code snippet, I've omitted some of the output details for the sake of brevity.)

```
PS C:\> Get-Member -InputObject $farm

    TypeName: Microsoft.SharePoint.Administration.SPFarm

Name                             MemberType Definition
----                             ---------- ----------
AddBackupObjects                 Method     System.Void AddBackupObje...
Clone                            Method     System.Object Clone()
```

```
CurrentUserIsAdministrator                    Method       System.Boolean CurrentUse...
Delete                                        Method       System.Void Delete()
...
AllowAggregationCalendar                      Property     System.Boolean AllowAggre...
AlternateUrlCollections                       Property     Microsoft.SharePoint.Admi...
BuildVersion                                  Property     System.Version BuildVersi...
CanBackupRestoreAsConfiguration               Property     System.Boolean CanBackupR...
CanMigrate                                    Property     System.Boolean CanMigrate...
...
```

The `Get-Member` cmdlet takes in any object and outputs information about the object's public methods and properties. Take a minute to think about what this means. This means that you have a fully featured, real-time compiler that allows you to manipulate virtually any object in a SharePoint farm, and you have convenient, easy-to-use cmdlets that provide quick access to those objects!

But what if there's no cmdlet that provides access to what you need? No problem, you can still get to any .NET object either indirectly by accessing the object via a container (for example, retrieve an `SPList` object using the `SPWeb` object, which can be retrieved using the `Get-SPWeb` cmdlet), or directly by loading the object's assembly and creating a new instance of the object, or by using a static method or property. The following example demonstrates this by retrieving the `SPFarm` object directly, rather than via the `Get-SPFarm` cmdlet:

```
PS C:\> [System.Reflection.Assembly]::LoadWithPartialName("Microsoft.SharePoint")

GAC     Version         Location
---     -------         --------
True    v2.0.50727      C:\Windows\assembly\GAC_MSIL\Microsoft.SharePoint\14.0...


PS C:\> $farm = [Microsoft.SharePoint.Administration.SPFarm]::Local
```

This code performs a one-time, in-memory load of the `Microsoft.SharePoint` assembly using the static `LoadWithPartialName` method of the `System.Reflection.Assembly` class. It then calls the `SPFarm`'s static `Local` property to retrieve an instance of the `SPFarm` object. The SharePoint assembly is automatically loaded when the snap-in is registered, but you load just this one assembly individually rather than the snap-in, if desired. Typically, you won't do this with SharePoint 2010, but, if you're still working against SharePoint 2007, this approach is your only option.

In PowerShell, an object's type is represented by wrapping the object in brackets (for example, [*type name*]). This is most commonly seen when accessing a static method or property of a type, such as the `LoadWithPartialName` method or the `Local` property. However, rather than using a period to access the object member, you use a double colon (::).

To instantiate new objects, you use the `New-Object` cmdlet, as shown in the following example that demonstrates creating new quota templates:

```
$webService = [Microsoft.SharePoint.Administration.SPWebService]::ContentService
$quota = New-Object Microsoft.SharePoint.Administration.SPQuotaTemplate
$quota.Name = "Team Site"
$quota.StorageMaximumLevel = 2GB
$quota.StorageWarningLevel = 1.5GB
$webService.QuotaTemplates.Add($quota)
```

This example loads an SPWebService object via the static SPWebService.ContentService property, which is used to save the quota template that is instantiated on the next line via the New-Object cmdlet. If you type **Get-Help New-Object** in your PowerShell console, you'll be presented with a detailed explanation of how the cmdlet works, including how to pass arguments into the object's constructor.

> *Notice in the example that the property values are set using the standard* GB *and* MB *units. PowerShell recognizes these as standard types, and automatically converts them to the number of bytes specified. Try it for yourself. Simply enter* 1GB *in your PowerShell console window. You should see an output of* 1073741824.

Tons of great books on the market focus on teaching you how to use PowerShell. What you will soon discover, however, is that the trick to being successful with PowerShell is to learn the object model of the application you want to manipulate; the rest is just syntax.

The Extended Type System

When I first started working with PowerShell, the first thing I did was declare a variable. As a C# programmer, the first thing I noticed was that I didn't have to declare the type of that variable. Look at an example from earlier:

```
PS C:\> $farm = Get-SPFarm
```

Variables in PowerShell are defined by prefixing a name with a dollar sign. The variable $farm stores an instance of the Microsoft.SharePoint.Administration.SPFarm class. This is great, because you don't have to think about what type a cmdlet returns.

However, sometimes you'll want to be more explicit with your variable declarations, especially when creating script files that will need to be managed for months or years to come. To declare the same variable, but explicitly set the type, simply prefix the variable with the type name surrounded by brackets, as shown here:

```
PS C:\> [Microsoft.SharePoint.Administration.SPFarm]$farm = Get-SPFarm
```

Try another example that demonstrates what is called the *adaptive type system* in PowerShell. In Listing 5-1, you use the Get-Content cmdlet to load data from an XML file and output the type returned.

LISTING 5-1: FarmConfigurations.xml

```
<Farm FarmAccount="wrox\spfarm"
      ConfigDB="SharePoint_ConfigDB"
      AdminContentDB="SharePoint_Content_Admin"
      DatabaseServer="spsql1"
      Passphrase="Pa$$w0rd">
  <CentralAdmin Port="1234" AuthProvider="NTLM">
    <Servers>
```

continues

LISTING 5-1 *(continued)*

```
            <Server Name="spsvr1" />
        </Servers>
    </CentralAdmin>
</Farm>
```

Code file [FarmConfigurations.xml] available for download at Wrox.com

For the first example, load the `FarmConfigurations.xml` file without specifying the type:

```
PS C:\> $settings = Get-Content .\FarmConfigurations.xml
PS C:\> $settings.GetType().FullName
System.Object[]
PS C:\> $settings[0].GetType().FullName
System.String
```

Notice that the `$settings` variable is a `System.Object[]` type, or an object array, where each element is of type `System.String`.

So, what happens if you prefix the variable with a specific type such as the `System.Xml.XmlDocument` type (which has been conveniently aliased as `xml`)? If you're a C# programmer you'd expect a cast exception to occur. But, fortunately, PowerShell has an adaptive type system that allows objects to be seamlessly converted from one type to another, as shown here:

```
PS C:\> [xml]$settings = Get-Content .\FarmConfigurations.xml
PS C:\> $settings.GetType().FullName
System.Xml.XmlDocument
```

But wait, there's more! The PowerShell designers were nice enough to provide a specific type adapter just for working with XML files. What this means is that you can access the `Farm` node of the XML file by simply accessing the nodes as though they were properties, as shown here:

```
PS C:\> [xml]$settings = Get-Content .\FarmConfigurations.xml
PS C:\> $settings.Farm

FarmAccount     : wrox\spfarm
ConfigDB        : SharePoint_ConfigDB
AdminContentDB  : SharePoint_Content_Admin
DatabaseServer  : spsql1
Passphrase      : Pa$$w0rd
CentralAdmin    : CentralAdmin
```

Look at this a little closer and use the `Get-Member` cmdlet to see the details of the `Farm` property. (In the following code snippet, some details have been removed for brevity.)

```
PS C:\> Get-Member -InputObject $settings.Farm


   TypeName: System.Xml.XmlElement

Name        MemberType      Definition
----        ----------      ----------
ToString    CodeMethod      static System.String XmlNode(PSOb...
```

```
AppendChild          Method                    System.Xml.XmlNode AppendChild(Xm...
Clone                Method                    System.Xml.XmlNode Clone()
...
WriteContentTo       Method                    System.Void WriteContentTo(XmlWri...
WriteTo              Method                    System.Void WriteTo(XmlWriter w)
Item                 ParameterizedProperty     System.Xml.XmlElement Item(String...
AdminContentDB       Property                  System.String AdminContentDB {get...
CentralAdmin         Property                  System.Xml.XmlElement CentralAdmi...
ConfigDB             Property                  System.String ConfigDB {get;set;}
DatabaseServer       Property                  System.String DatabaseServer {get...
FarmAccount          Property                  System.String FarmAccount {get;set;}
Passphrase           Property                  System.String Passphrase {get;set;}
```

Notice how the attributes that are defined within the Farm XML element show as properties of the object, and that the TypeName is System.Xml.Element. Do you notice anything missing? How about the OuterXml property or the Name or OwnerDocument properties, all of which are public members of the System.Xml.XmlElement class?

What's happened is that PowerShell has created a "special" object, of type PSObject, which wraps the System.Xml.XmlElement object, dynamically adds all of the child attributes and elements of the XML document as properties, and hides the built-in properties. To be clear, the built-in properties are still there; they're just not showing up when you query for them using the Get-Member cmdlet.

Fortunately, PowerShell provides a way for you to see them using a property called PSBase, as shown here:

```
PS C:\> Get-Member -InputObject $settings.Farm.PSBase


   TypeName: System.Management.Automation.PSMemberSet

Name                 MemberType                Definition
----                 ----------                ----------
AppendChild          Method                    System.Xml.XmlNode AppendChild(Xm...
Clone                Method                    System.Xml.XmlNode Clone()
...
WriteContentTo       Method                    System.Void WriteContentTo(XmlWri...
WriteTo              Method                    System.Void WriteTo(XmlWriter w)
Item                 ParameterizedProperty     System.Xml.XmlElement Item(String...
Attributes           Property                  System.Xml.XmlAttributeCollection...
BaseURI              Property                  System.String BaseURI {get;}
...
Prefix               Property                  System.String Prefix {get;set;}
PreviousSibling      Property                  System.Xml.XmlNode PreviousSiblin...
SchemaInfo           Property                  System.Xml.Schema.IXmlSchemaInfo ...
Value                Property                  System.String Value {get;set;}
```

Typically, you won't need to use the PSBase property, because you can still access the core properties directly, as in the following example:

```
PS C:\> $settings.Farm.OuterXml
```

The only time you're likely to need the `PSBase` property is when an XML element or attribute conflicts with a core property name. (For example, if you had an attribute in your XML called `Prefix`, you would need to use `$settings.Farm.PSBase.Prefix` to access the `XmlElement`'s implementation of the property.)

PowerShell's adaptive type system allows you to do all sorts of really cool things with very little coding effort. Consider the following example:

```
PS C:\> $user = @{}
PS C:\> $user.Name = "Tessa"
PS C:\> Write-Host "User name = $($user.Name)"
User name = Tessa
```

This example creates a hash table object and stores it in the `$user` variable. It then sets the `Name` property and outputs the value, which you can see matches the value set. What's happening here is similar to what is happening with the `XmlElement` object in the previous examples. PowerShell is creating a dynamic property that maps to the key of the hash table.

> *One additional point of interest in the previous example is the fact that* `$user.` `Name` *is wrapped in parentheses with a leading dollar sign —* `$($user.Name)`. *Wrapping variables in* `$()` *allows PowerShell to evaluate the contents of the parentheses, and then return the results of that evaluation as a new variable.*

Another common thing you'll run into when working with PowerShell is the need to create arrays of objects. Again, PowerShell makes this easy. Simply separate your values with a comma, as shown here:

```
PS C:\> $users = "Tessa", "Pamela"
PS C:\> $users[0]
Tessa
PS C:\> $users[1]
Pamela
```

The values can be any type, and you can mix and match types. SharePoint 2010's PowerShell cmdlets make significant use of arrays of objects, which play a huge role when working with the *object pipeline.*

The Object Pipeline

In the simplest sense, PowerShell's object pipeline provides the means to pass an object from one command to another. Think of the pipeline as an assembly line where each stage in the assembly line performs some sort of operation, and then passes the results of that operation to the next stage of the assembly line. If you've worked with the console before, then "piping" information from one command to another is not new. You simply use the "pipe" operator (|) to separate the commands. The difference with PowerShell is that you are passing fully qualified objects, which gives you much more flexibility and power.

Consider the following example that uses the Get-SPWeb cmdlet and then "pipes" the resultant SPWeb objects to the Where-Object cmdlet to filter the results to just those that use the new v4.master master page:

```
PS C:\> Get-SPWeb http://portal/* | where {$_.MasterUrl -like "*/v4.master"}

Url
---
http://portal
http://portal/SiteDirectory
http://portal/SearchCenter
http://portal/News
http://portal/Docs
```

This code passes in a wildcard-based URL to the Get-SPWeb cmdlet to return back all SPWeb objects under the http://portal/ web application, and then passes those objects to the Where-Object cmdlet. (Notice how this example uses the where alias, rather than the full name of the cmdlet.) The variable $_ represents the current object within the script block. (This is discussed in more detail later.)

The next question you should be asking is how do you know what parameters can be piped into a cmdlet? The easiest way is to get the help for the cmdlet and look at the description for the various parameters. If you execute help Get-SPWeb -full, you see the following parameter descriptions (among others):

```
PARAMETERS
    -Identity <SPWebPipeBind>
        The name or full or partial URL of the sub-site. If you use a relative
        path, you must specify the Site parameter.
        A valid URL in the form of "http://server_name" or a relative path in t
        he form of "/SubSites/MySubSite".

        Required?                 false
        Position?                 1
        Default value
        Accept pipeline input?    False
        Accept wildcard characters? false

    -AssignmentCollection <SPAssignmentCollection>
        PShell_param_AssignmentCollection
        PShell_param_AssignmentCollection_Note

        Required?                 false
        Position?                 Named
        Default value
        Accept pipeline input?    True
        Accept wildcard characters? false
```

From this snippet, you can see that the Get-SPWeb cmdlet can take an SPAssignmentCollection object (which is discussed later) via the pipeline, but you cannot pass the Identity parameter via the pipeline. (You can also pass in an SPSitePipeBind object via the pipeline. PipeBind objects are discussed shortly.)

An important thing to keep in mind when working with PowerShell is that, by default, every time a new "pipe" is executed, that command is executed in a new thread. So, essentially, every time you press the Enter key, PowerShell is executing the entered line in the context of a single thread. (Note that the SharePoint 2010 Management Shell alters this default behavior.) This introduces some problems when working with certain SharePoint objects, which are examined in detail later in this chapter.

Formatting Object Data

Four cmdlets are available to help you format data in the PowerShell console window:

```
PS C:\> Get-Command -verb format

CommandType     Name                       Definition
-----------     ----                       ----------
Cmdlet          Format-Custom              Format-Custom [[-Property] <...
Cmdlet          Format-List                Format-List [[-Property] <Ob...
Cmdlet          Format-Table               Format-Table [[-Property] <O...
Cmdlet          Format-Wide                Format-Wide [[-Property] <Ob...
```

The cool things about these cmdlets are that you can specify which properties of the object you'd like to have displayed, and you can use wildcards, regular expressions, and script blocks:

```
PS C:\> $site = Get-SPSite http://portal
PS C:\> $site | Format-List Url, Allow*, {[int]($_.Usage.Storage/1MB)}


Url                        : http://portal
AllowUnsafeUpdates         : True
AllowRssFeeds              : True
AllowDesigner              : True
AllowRevertFromTemplate    : False
AllowMasterPageEditing     : False
[int]($_.Usage.Storage/1MB) : 5
```

This simple example gets an SPSite object and uses the Format-List cmdlet (which can also be abbreviated using the fl alias) to return back the Url property using the exact name of the property, all the properties that start with Allow using the wildcard character *, and, finally, a script block to return the amount of space consumed by the site collection in megabytes. You can add a label to the column by changing the script block to the following:

```
@{Expression={ [int]($_.Usage.Storage/1MB) }; Label="Size"}).
```

If you just want to see all the properties, just pipe the object to the desired formatter without specifying any properties (with the exception of Format-Wide, which is meant to show a single property). Now run the same command, but use the Format-Table cmdlet, and then the Format-Custom cmdlet:

```
PS C:\> $site | Format-Table Url, Allow*, {[int]($_.Usage.Storage/1MB)}

Url          AllowUnsafe AllowRssFee AllowDesig AllowRever AllowMaste [int]($_.U
             Updates             ds        ner tFromTempl rPageEditi sage.Stora
                                              ate         ng    ge/1MB)

---          ----------- ----------- ---------- ---------- ---------- ----------
http://p...        True        True       True      False      False          5
```

```
PS C:\> $site | Format-Custom Url, Allow*, {[int]($_.Usage.Storage/1MB)}

class SPSite
{
  Url = http://portal
  AllowUnsafeUpdates = True
  AllowRssFeeds = True
  AllowDesigner = True
  AllowRevertFromTemplate = False
  AllowMasterPageEditing = False
  [int]($_.Usage.Storage/1MB) = 5
}
```

If you try the same command using `Format-Wide`, you'll receive an exception, because the `Format-Wide` cmdlet can take only one property at a time.

Filtering and Iterating

With all of these objects, eventually you'll need to filter the set of objects down to a subset, and/or iterate over those objects and perform some additional operation. The most common way to filter down the results that come back is by using the `Where-Object` cmdlet. This cmdlet (which is aliased as `where` and `?`) operates on the client side, which means that all the results will be passed into the cmdlet and filtered based on the expression specified in the provided script block.

```
PS C:\> Get-SPSite -Limit All | where {$_.Owner -like "wrox\spadmin"}

Url
---
http://mysites
http://portal/sites/Test1
```

This example gets all the site collections within the farm where the `Owner` of the site collection is equal to the `wrox\spadmin` account. The `where` command is just an alias for the `Where-Object` cmdlet, and you're passing to that cmdlet what is known as a *script block* — anything wrapped in curly braces (`{` and `}`). The `Where-Object` cmdlet iterates over the collection of objects passed to it, and executes the code within the script block for each object. You can get access to the current object by using the `$_` variable.

As mentioned earlier, the `Where-Object` cmdlet does its filtering after all the objects have been returned. This can result in really slow performance if, for example, you must process a subset of site collections within a large farm (especially if you are using PowerShell's remoting capabilities). To address this issue, several SharePoint cmdlets provide `-Filter` parameters to facilitate filtering of the results before passing to the pipeline. The same query shown earlier can be rewritten using the `-Filter` parameter, as shown here:

```
PS C:\> Get-SPSite -Limit All -Filter {$_.Owner -eq "wrox\spadmin"}

Url
---
http://mysites
http://portal/sites/Test1
```

The -Filter parameters are much more limiting in their capabilities, but if your requirements fit within those limits, you should use this parameter instead of doing pipeline filtering.

 The -Filter *parameter for the* Get-SPSite *cmdlet can only accept script blocks that use* -eq, -ne, -like, *or* -notlike *operators, and you can only filter on* Owner, SecondaryOwner, *or* LockState.

The Where-Object cmdlet is doing some iterating internally, but, as you can imagine, you can construct your own script blocks that iterate over objects using constructs that are very similar to those available in C#. Specifically, you can create foreach, do, while, and for loops. In addition to these constructs, there is also a ForEach-Object cmdlet. The foreach and ForEach-Object cmdlets require some special attention to clarify how the two work, so the remainder of this section focuses on those differences, and leaves you to research the other constructs.

The ForEach-Object cmdlet takes pipeline data in and iterates through each object executing the code in the provided script block — similar to the way the Where-Object cmdlet works. One point of confusion stems from the fact that the ForEach-Object cmdlet is aliased as foreach. It is critical to note that this is not the same as the foreach loop construct. The key difference is that the ForEach-Object cmdlet does not support the use of the continue and break statements.

To illustrate the point, consider the following examples:

```
PS C:\> 1..10 | ForEach-Object {
>>      if ($_ -eq 5) {continue}
>>      Write-Host $_
>> }
>>
1
2
3
4
PS C:\> foreach ($i in 1..10) {
>>      if ($i -eq 5) {continue}
>>      Write-Host $i
>> }
>>
1
2
3
4
6
7
8
9
10
PS C:\>
```

Notice how the `continue` statement, when used within the `ForEach-Object` cmdlet, appears to break out of the loop, rather than continue to the next iteration. In fact, what is happening is that it is attempting to locate an outer loop, which causes any code following the `continue` (including code outside of the script block) to not execute. If an outer loop were found (that is, if the call to the `ForEach-Object` cmdlet were running within a loop), that loop would skip to the next iteration. Where this all gets confusing is when you use the `foreach` alias for the `ForEach-Object` cmdlet, as shown here:

```
PS C:\> 1..10 | foreach {
>>      if ($_ -eq 5) {continue}
>>      Write-Host $_
>> }
>>
1
2
3
4
PS C:\>
```

The key thing to remember is that if you are passing the objects to be iterated upon via the pipeline, you should not use the `continue` or `break` statements.

Functions and Scripts

Up until now, the examples you've seen have been one or two simple lines of code that you could easily enter directly into the PowerShell console. Reusability hasn't been a factor with these simple examples, but, in the real world, you'll most likely be creating more complex logic that you'll want to reuse, and possibly make that logic vary based on simple or complex parameters.

To accomplish this, PowerShell has the capability to create functions that operate very much like cmdlets. Though they can be created directly in the console window, these functions are typically stored in a script file for either direct execution or inclusion in other script files.

Functions can be created with or without parameters. To demonstrate this, create a simple function that prompts the user for credentials, which are then used to create a SharePoint managed account:

```
function New-ManagedAccount {
    $cred = Get-Credential "wrox\spfarm"
    return New-SPManagedAccount -Credential $cred
}
```

This function can be typed directly into the PowerShell console, which will then make it available to be called directly, or you can save it in a script file with an extension of `.ps1`. The script file can then be loaded into memory by using what is known as "dot source notation":

```
PS C:\> . .\Functions.ps1
```

Using this syntax, you tell PowerShell to load the script into memory for later use. If any code exists outside of functions, that code will be executed. Now that the function exists in memory, you can call it as though it were a cmdlet:

```
PS C:\> New-ManagedAccount

UserName            PasswordExpiration    Automatic ChangeSchedule
                                          Change

--------            ------------------    --------- --------------
WROX\spfarm         3/30/1975 1:02:38 AM  False
```

Now, tweak the function so that it takes the account name to create as a parameter:

```
function New-ManagedAccount([string]$accountName) {
    $cred = Get-Credential $accountName
    return New-SPManagedAccount -Credential $cred
}
```

It will be necessary to reload the script into memory after you've modified it. To call this new version, you simply add the parameter value as an argument:

```
PS C:\> New-ManagedAccount "wrox\spfarm"
New-SPManagedAccount : Account WROX\spfarm has already been registered.
At line:3 char:32
+     return New-SPManagedAccount <<<<  -Credential $cred
    + CategoryInfo          : InvalidData: (Microsoft.Share...wManagedAccount:
    SPCmdletNewManagedAccount) [New-SPManagedAccount], InvalidOperationExcepti
   on
    + FullyQualifiedErrorId : Microsoft.SharePoint.PowerShell.SPCmdletNewManag
   edAccount
```

In this case, you get an error if you try to create a managed account for a credential that already exists. So, this function should probably be improved to add some logic to check whether the account exists before attempting to create it:

```
function New-ManagedAccount([string]$accountName) {
    $account = Get-SPManagedAccount $accountName -ErrorAction SilentlyContinue
    if ($account -eq $null) {
        $cred = Get-Credential $accountName
        $account = New-SPManagedAccount -Credential $cred
    }
    return $account
}
```

You can now use this simple function to retrieve an SPManagedAccount object, and, if one does not exist, create the managed account before returning it. A function like this can be very useful when doing a scripted deployment of SharePoint, particularly when setting up the various application pools that may be necessary for the various services available within SharePoint 2010.

Notice that it is incorrect to wrap function (or script) parameters in parentheses, or to use a comma to separate parameter values when calling functions. Assuming the function has been modified to take two parameters (account name and password), the following syntax is incorrect, and will not produce the expected results:

```
PS C:\> New-ManagedAccount("wrox\spfarm", "password")
```

Instead, you would call the function using the following syntax:

```
PS C:\> New-ManagedAccount "wrox\spfarm" "password"
```

However, this is not true when calling functions on .NET objects that require parentheses to wrap parameters, which must be separated by a comma.

Functions, however, are not the only things that can take parameters. Script files themselves can also take in parameters, as shown in the following example, which takes the path to an XML file as a parameter:

```
param(
   [string]$settingsFile = "Configurations.xml"
)
[xml]$settings = Get-Content $settingsFile
$settings.Farm.Accounts.Account | ForEach-Object {
    New-ManagedAccount $_.Name
}
```

Save this code in a file named CreateManagedAccounts.ps1. The script has a single parameter named settingsFile. If the parameter is not provided, the value is defaulted to Configurations.xml. The script then loads the settings into an XmlDocument object using the Get-Content cmdlet. The <Account /> nodes are then passed to the ForEach-Object cmdlet, which iterates through each item and calls the previously created New-ManagedAccount function to create the specified managed accounts. The XML structure that is passed in looks like this:

```
<Farm>
    <Accounts>
        <Account Name="wrox\spfarm" />
        <Account Name="wrox\spportalapppool" />
    </Accounts>
</Farm>
```

With all of the elements in place, you can now load the script and pass in the path to the XML settings file:

```
PS C:\> ..\CreateManagedAccounts.ps1 "Configurations.xml"

UserName            PasswordExpiration   Automatic ChangeSchedule
                                         Change
--------            ------------------   --------- --------------
WROX\spfarm         5/4/1975 12:30:02 PM False
WROX\SpPortalApp... 3/30/1975 1:20:23 AM False
```

For both functions and scripts, you can also specify the parameter values using a name/value syntax, as shown here:

```
PS C:\> . .\CreateManagedAccounts.ps1 -settingsFile "Configurations.xml"
```

It is considered a best practice to create your functions and scripts in a test environment using a tool such as the PowerShell ISE or similar tools such as PowerGUI. These tools allow debugging, syntax highlighting, and, in some cases, IntelliSense — all of which make creating and debugging functions and scripts considerably easier.

A final critical point about functions and scripts is that the execution of functions and scripts takes place within a single thread. The importance of this will become clear in the following discussion.

USING SHAREPOINT 2010 CMDLETS

The most difficult part of working with PowerShell is learning the semantics and structure of the language. Once you have that down, the next challenge is finding the cmdlets and object model properties and methods that are required to complete a task. SharePoint 2010 then adds some additional complexities because of the way in which various objects within the object model are implemented.

This section demonstrates how to use some PowerShell cmdlets to help find what you need to complete a task. You learn about some common cmdlets that everyone should be familiar with, and, finally, you learn about disposable objects and how to deal with them.

Finding What You Need

When you first start working with SharePoint, one of the first challenges that you will face is finding the cmdlets that are needed to accomplish a particular task. This can be especially difficult when that task requires the use of several cmdlets that must be executed in a specific order, or when a specific cmdlet for the task doesn't exist, thus requiring the use of the SharePoint object model.

In most cases, the best way to locate the cmdlets or .NET objects, methods, or properties that you'll need is to use the SharePoint SDK or your favorite search engine, because you'll be able to search by common terms related to the task that you need to perform. However, you can also do some basic searching within the PowerShell console. Two cmdlets facilitate this:

➤   `Get-Command` — This is aliased as gcm.

➤   `Get-Member` — This is aliased as gm.

You can use the `Get-Command` cmdlet to return back any and all cmdlets registered with the PowerShell console. Look at a few examples that demonstrate the various ways in which you locate cmdlets.

In this first example, you return back all the SharePoint 2010 cmdlets:

```
PS C:\> Get-Command -pssnapin Microsoft.SharePoint.PowerShell
```

Running this example isn't extremely helpful because it returns way too much information. Assume that you want to create service applications using PowerShell, so you must see all the cmdlets that are related to services. The easiest way to do this is to filter by SPService, as shown here:

```
PS C:\> Get-Command -noun SPService* | Sort Noun | ft Name

Name
----
Install-SPService
Set-SPServiceApplication
Unpublish-SPServiceApplication
Remove-SPServiceApplication
Publish-SPServiceApplication
Get-SPServiceApplication
Get-SPServiceApplicationProxy
Remove-SPServiceApplicationProxy
Remove-SPServiceApplicationProxyGroup
New-SPServiceApplicationProxyGroup
Get-SPServiceApplicationProxyGroup
Remove-SPServiceApplicationProxyGroupMember
Add-SPServiceApplicationProxyGroupMember
Get-SPServiceApplicationSecurity
Set-SPServiceApplicationSecurity
Get-SPServiceContext
Set-SPServiceEndpoint
Get-SPServiceEndpoint
Get-SPServiceInstance
Stop-SPServiceInstance
Start-SPServiceInstance
```

This list is much more manageable because you can see all cmdlets that apply to service applications. Of course, there may be additional cmdlets needed for specific services such as the Metadata Service Application. Try another search for anything with the term metadataservice in it:

```
PS C:\> Get-Command -noun *metadataservice* | Sort Noun | ft Name

Name
----
New-SPMetadataServiceApplication
Set-SPMetadataServiceApplication
Get-SPMetadataServiceApplication
Set-SPMetadataServiceApplicationProxy
Get-SPMetadataServiceApplicationProxy
New-SPMetadataServiceApplicationProxy
```

Once you have identified the cmdlets you need, you can then use the Get-Help cmdlet to learn more about how to use the cmdlets.

Eventually, you'll get to the point where the available cmdlets fail you, and you must resort to working with the object model. Again, the SDK is a great resource for you, but oftentimes just seeing a list of available methods and properties is enough to get you started.

To accomplish this, you can use the `Get-Member` cmdlet, which returns a listing of all the properties and methods that you can work with. To use this cmdlet, you must pass an instance of the target object into it:

```
PS C:\> Get-SPSite http://portal | Get-Member
```

You can pass in additional parameters to the `Get-Member` cmdlet to either filter the results down to just properties, for example, or to see the original members of the .NET object without any extension or adaptation. So, previously where you looked at the properties and members of the `System.Xml.XmlElement` object and could not see items such as `OuterXml` or `OwnerDocument`, you could have simply added a `View` attribute and specified a value of `All` or `Base` to see those core properties:

```
PS C:\> $settings.Farm | Get-Member -View Base
```

PipeBind Objects

As you look through the various SharePoint cmdlets you will notice that most cmdlets have one or more parameters that take a special object type called a `PipeBind` object. In an earlier example, you saw a snippet of the help text for the `Get-SPWeb` cmdlet. Following is the relevant piece:

```
-Identity <SPWebPipeBind>
    The name or full or partial URL of the sub-site. If you use a relative
    path, you must specify the Site parameter.
    A valid URL in the form of "http://server_name" or a relative path in t
        he form of "/SubSites/MySubSite".
```

Within SharePoint, many objects (such as the `SPWeb` and `SPSite` objects) can be represented differently. An `SPSite` object, for example, can be represented using either a URL, a GUID (unique identifier), or an actual `SPSite` object. `PipeBind` objects allow you to use either of these representations for the parameter value.

 One thing to watch out for is that the name is a bit misleading. Not all `PipeBind` parameters can accept input from the pipeline.

The following example demonstrates how to use the `SPSitePipeBind` object with the `Get-SPWeb` cmdlet to return all the `SPWeb` objects within the specified site collection:

```
$site = Get-SPSite http://portal
$webs = $site | Get-SPWeb
$webs = $site.ID | Get-SPWeb
$webs = "http://portal" | Get-SPWeb
```

As you can see, you first get an `SPSite` object and then use that to pipe into the `Get-SPWeb` cmdlet using the three possible representations. Each approach returns the same information.

Commonly Used Cmdlets

If you have ever created a scripted install of SharePoint 2007, you'll be familiar with `psconfig.exe` and how to use it to create or connect to a farm. With SharePoint 2010, `psconfig.exe` still exists, but its use has been made obsolete by some new PowerShell cmdlets.

Table 5-1 details the cmdlets that are necessary to create or connect to a farm. (These are listed in the order in which they would be utilized.)

TABLE 5-1: Farm Creation Cmdlets

CMDLET NAME	DESCRIPTION
New-SPConfigurationDatabase	Creates a new configuration database, and, therefore, a new SharePoint farm. This cmdlet is run only once per farm.
Connect-SPConfigurationDatabase	Connects a server to an existing configuration database, thus adding the server to the farm. This cmdlet is run once per server in the farm after the first server is provisioned using New-SPConfigurationDatabase.
Initialize-SPResourceSecurity	Sets required file, folder, and registry access control lists (ACLs) for the local server. This cmdlet must be run for each server in the farm.
Install-SPService	Installs the services in the farm. This cmdlet is run once per farm. In a standalone configuration, it is possible to automatically provision the services by running the cmdlet again, providing the -Provision parameter, as shown here: `PS C:\> Install-SPService`

Install-SPFeature	Installs all the features available to the farm. This cmdlet is run once per farm using the -AllExistingFeatures parameter, as shown here:
	
	`PS C:\> Install-SPFeature`
	`-AllExistingFeatures`

New-SPCentralAdministration	Provisions a Central Administration site on the local server. This cmdlet is typically run only once per farm, but can be run on additional servers as needed.
Install-SPHelpCollection	This optional cmdlet installs the help files that are used throughout the farm. This cmdlet is run only once per farm on the same server as the first Central Administration site, unless installing new help collections (custom or third party). Provide the -All switch when calling this cmdlet for farm setup, as shown here: `PS C:\> Install-SPHelpCollection -All`

continues

TABLE 5-1 *(continued)*

CMDLET NAME	DESCRIPTION
Install-SPApplicationContent	This optional cmdlet installs any application content for the Central Administration site. This cmdlet is run only once per farm on the same server as the first Central Administration site.

Using these cmdlets, you can easily construct a simple, reusable, script that will create a new farm or connect a server to an existing farm. To make the script more manageable, you use an XML file (Listing 5-2) that can be passed to the script (Listing 5-3).

Available for
download on
Wrox.com

LISTING 5-2: FarmConfigurations.xml

```xml
<Farm FarmAccount="wrox\spfarm"
      ConfigDB="SharePoint_ConfigDB"
      AdminContentDB="SharePoint_Content_Admin"
      DatabaseServer="spsql1"
      Passphrase="Pa$$w0rd">
    <CentralAdmin Port="1234" AuthProvider="NTLM">
        <Servers>
            <Server Name="spsvr1" />
        </Servers>
    </CentralAdmin>
</Farm>
```

Code file [FarmConfigurations.xml] available for download at Wrox.com

Available for
download on
Wrox.com

LISTING 5-3: Sample Farm Creation Script — BuildFarm.ps1

```powershell
function Install-SharePointFarm([bool]$connectToExisting,
    [string]$settingsFile = "Configurations.xml") {

    [xml]$config = Get-Content $settingsFile

    $farmAcct = Get-Credential $config.Farm.FarmAccount

    $configDb = $config.Farm.ConfigDB
    $adminContentDb = $config.Farm.adminContentDb
    $server = $config.Farm.DatabaseServer
    if ($config.Farm.Passphrase.Length -gt 0) {
        $passphrase = (ConvertTo-SecureString $config.Farm.Passphrase `
            -AsPlainText -force)
    } else {
        Write-Warning "Using the Farm Admin's password for a passphrase"
        $passphrase = $farmAcct.Password
```

```
    }

    #Only build the farm if we don't currently have a farm created
    if (([Microsoft.SharePoint.Administration.SPFarm]::Local) -eq $null) {
        if ($connectToExisting) {
            #Connecting to farm
            Connect-SPConfigurationDatabase -DatabaseName $configDb `
                -DatabaseServer $server -Passphrase $passphrase
        } else {
            #Creating new farm
            New-SPConfigurationDatabase -DatabaseName $configDb `
                -DatabaseServer $server `
                -AdministrationContentDatabaseName $adminContentDb `
                -Passphrase $passphrase -FarmCredentials $farmAcct
        }
        #Verifying farm creation
        $spfarm = Get-SPFarm -ErrorAction SilentlyContinue -ErrorVariable err
        if ($spfarm -eq $null -or $err) {
            throw "Unable to verify farm creation."
        }

        #ACLing SharePoint Resources
        Initialize-SPResourceSecurity

        #Installing Services
        Install-SPService

        #Installing Features
        Install-SPFeature -AllExistingFeatures
    } else {
        Write-Warning "Farm already exists. Skipping creation."
    }

    $installSCA = (($config.Farm.CentralAdmin.Servers.Server | `
        where {$_.Name -eq $env:computername}) -ne $null)
    $url = "http://$($env:computername):$($config.Farm.CentralAdmin.Port)"
    $sca=[Microsoft.SharePoint.Administration.SPWebApplication]::Lookup($url)
    if ($installSCA -and $sca -eq $null) {
        #Provisioning Central Administration
        New-SPCentralAdministration -Port $config.Farm.CentralAdmin.Port `
            -WindowsAuthProvider $config.Farm.CentralAdmin.AuthProvider

        #Installing Help
        Install-SPHelpCollection -All

        #Installing Application Content
        Install-SPApplicationContent
    }
}
```

Code file [BuildFarm.ps1] available for download at Wrox.com

You can then call the script using the following syntax:

```
PS C:\> . .\buildfarm.ps1
PS C:\> Install-SharePointFarm $false "FarmConfigurations.xml"
```

Once you have a farm created, the next thing you are likely to do is to create web applications and associated site collections. To accomplish this, you can use the core set of cmdlets shown in Table 5-2.

TABLE 5-2: Site Structure Creation Cmdlets

CMDLET NAME	DESCRIPTION
New-SPManagedAccount	Creates a new managed account that can be used when creating application pools.
New-SPServiceApplicationPool	This cmdlet is specific to creating application pools for use with service applications and should not be used when creating application pools for web applications. To create an application pool for a web application, use the appropriate parameters of the New-SPWebApplication cmdlet.
New-SPWebApplication	Creates a new web application.
New-SPContentDatabase	Creates a new content database for a specific web application.
New-SPManagedPath	Creates a managed path under the specified web application.
New-SPSite	Creates a new site collection (watch for disposal issues!).
New-SPWeb	Creates a new site within a site collection (watch for disposal issues!).
Set-SPDesignerSettings	Sets the actions that users can perform using SharePoint Designer (SPD).

Just like you did for the farm creation, you can do the same for creating your site structure. Listing 5-4 shows an XML file that defines the web application, application pool, content databases, and site collections that you then create by using the buildwebapps.ps1 script file shown in Listing 5-5. The XML can be modified to include multiple web applications, content databases, or site collections, making it extremely useful for building out your site structure.

LISTING 5-4: WebAppConfigurations.xml

```
<WebApplications>
    <WebApplication Name="SharePoint Portal (80)"
                DefaultTimeZone="12"
```

```
                          DefaultQuotaTemplate="Portal"
                          AllowAnonymous="false"
                          AuthenticationMethod="Kerberos"
                          HostHeader="portal"
                          Path="c:\sharepoint\webs\portal"
                          Port="80"
                          LoadBalancedUrl="http://portal"
                          Ssl="false">
          <ApplicationPool Name="SharePoint Portal App Pool"
                          Account="wrox\spportalapppool" />
          <SPDesigner AllowDesigner="true" AllowRevertFromTemplate="true"
                          AllowMasterPageEditing="true" ShowURLStructure="true" />
          <ContentDatabases>
              <ContentDatabase Server="spsql1"
                              Name="SharePoint_Content_Portal1"
                              MaxSiteCount="100" WarningSiteCount="80"
                              Default="true">
                  <SiteCollections>
                      <SiteCollection Name="Portal"
                                      Description=""
                                      Url="http://portal"
                                      LCID="1033"
                                      Template="SPSPORTAL#0"
                                      OwnerLogin="wrox\siteowner1"
                                      OwnerEmail="siteowner1@wrox.com"
                                      SecondaryLogin="wrox\spadmin"
                                      SecondaryEmail="spadmin@wrox.com">
                      </SiteCollection>
                  </SiteCollections>
              </ContentDatabase>
          </ContentDatabases>
      </WebApplication>
  </WebApplications>
```

Code file [WebAppConfigurations.xml] available for download at Wrox.com

LISTING 5-5: Site Structure Creation Script — BuildWebApps.ps1

```
function Start-WebApplicationsBuild(
    [string]$settingsFile = "Configurations.xml") {
    [xml]$config = Get-Content $settingsFile

    #Creating individual web applications
    $config.WebApplications.WebApplication | ForEach-Object {
        $webAppConfig = $_
        $webApp = New-WebApplication $webAppConfig

        #Configuring SharePoint Designer Settings
        $spd = $webAppConfig.SPDesigner
        $allowRevert = ([bool]::Parse($spd.AllowRevertFromTemplate))
```

continues

LISTING 5-5 *(continued)*

```
        $allowMasterEdit = ([bool]::Parse($spd.AllowMasterPageEditing))
        $webApp | Set-SPDesignerSettings `
            -AllowDesigner:([bool]::Parse($spd.AllowDesigner)) `
            -AllowRevertFromTemplate:$allowRevert `
            -AllowMasterPageEditing:$allowMasterEdit `
            -ShowURLStructure:([bool]::Parse($spd.ShowURLStructure))

        $webAppConfig.ContentDatabases.ContentDatabase | ForEach-Object {
            #Creating content database
            $db = New-SPContentDatabase -Name $_.Name `
                -WebApplication $webApp `
                -DatabaseServer $_.Server `
                -MaxSiteCount $_.MaxSiteCount `
                -WarningSiteCount $_.WarningSiteCount

            $_.SiteCollections.SiteCollection | ForEach-Object {
                #Creating site collection
                $gc = Start-SPAssignment
                $site = $gc | New-SPSite `
                    -Url $_.Url `
                    -ContentDatabase $db `
                    -Description $_.Description `
                    -Language $_.LCID `
                    -Name $_.Name `
                    -Template $_.Template `
                    -OwnerAlias $_.OwnerLogin `
                    -OwnerEmail $_.OwnerEmail `
                    -SecondaryOwnerAlias $_.SecondaryLogin `
                    -SecondaryEmail $_.SecondaryEmail `
                Stop-SPAssignment -SemiGlobal $gc
            }
        }
    }
}

function New-WebApplication([System.Xml.XmlElement]$webAppConfig) {
    $poolAccount = $null
    $tempAppPool = $null
    $poolName = $webAppConfig.ApplicationPool.Name
    if ([Microsoft.SharePoint.Administration.SPWebService]::ContentService
        .ApplicationPools.Count -gt 0) {
        $tempAppPool = [Microsoft.SharePoint.Administration
            .SPWebService]::ContentService.ApplicationPools | ? {$_.Name -eq $poolName}
    }
    if ($tempAppPool -eq $null) {
        $accountNode = $webAppConfig.ApplicationPool.Account
        Write-Host "Getting $($accountNode) account for application pool..."
        $accountCred = Get-Credential $accountNode
        $poolAccount = (Get-SPManagedAccount -Identity $accountCred.Username `
            -ErrorVariable err -ErrorAction SilentlyContinue)
```

```
        if ($err) {
            $poolAccount = New-SPManagedAccount -Credential $accountCred
            }
        }

    $allowAnon = [bool]::Parse($webAppConfig.AllowAnonymous.ToString())
    $ssl = [bool]::Parse($webAppConfig.Ssl.ToString())

    $db = $null
    if ($webAppConfig.ContentDatabases.ChildNodes.Count -gt 1) {
        $db = $webAppConfig.ContentDatabases.ContentDatabase | `
            where {$_.Default -eq "true"}
        if ($db -is [array]) {
            $db = $db[0]
        }
    } else {
        $db = $webAppConfig.ContentDatabases.ContentDatabase
    }

    #Create the web application
    $webApp = New-SPWebApplication -SecureSocketsLayer:$ssl `
        -AllowAnonymousAccess:$allowAnon `
        -ApplicationPool $poolName `
        -ApplicationPoolAccount $poolAccount `
        -Name $webAppConfig.Name `
        -AuthenticationMethod $webAppConfig.AuthenticationMethod `
        -DatabaseServer $db.DatabaseServer `
        -DatabaseName $db.DatabaseName `
        -HostHeader $webAppConfig.HostHeader `
        -Path $webAppConfig.Path `
        -Port $webAppConfig.Port `
        -Url $webAppConfig.LoadBalancedUrl `
        -ErrorVariable err

    return $webApp
}
```

Code file [BuildWebApps.ps1] available for download at Wrox.com

To help keep the script a bit easier to read, I broke out the code that creates the application pool and the web application from the rest of the code. You can then call the script, as shown here:

```
PS C:\> . .\buildwebapps.ps1
PS C:\> Start-WebApplicationsBuild "WebAppConfigurations.xml"
```

With more than 500 cmdlets available to you, the few that have been highlighted here are just the tip of the iceberg. As you get deeper into a deployment, you'll find a variety of cmdlets that you must understand very well, many that you use only use once, and others that you may use almost daily. Hopefully, this brief illustration of some of the more prevalent cmdlets will aid you in your investigations of the other cmdlets available to you.

Handling Disposable Objects

As you have been reading through this chapter and studying the various cmdlets that come with SharePoint 2010, you will hopefully have noticed one particular parameter that is available to every single cmdlet:

```
[-AssignmentCollection <SPAssignmentCollection>]
```

The purpose of the SPAssignmentCollection is to store objects that implement the IDisposable interface — specifically, objects such as SPSite, SPWeb, and SPSiteAdministration.

When working with objects of these types, it is necessary to "dispose" of the objects when you are done working with them to free up the unmanaged resources that they consume. (Internally, these objects use an unmanaged Component Object Model, or COM, object that must be properly released when no longer needed.) If these objects are not disposed of properly, you run the risk of memory leaks, which could potentially make a server temporarily unusable. The issue is compounded because of the way in which PowerShell handles threads.

As mentioned previously in this chapter, the default behavior of PowerShell is that each line of code entered at the console is executed in its own thread. So, even if you call the Dispose() method, that call is happening on a new thread, which means that, though the managed heap is freed, the unmanaged heap is not. To help work around this, PowerShell V2 introduces a new host model that allows you to run each line in the same thread.

Let's revisit the sharepoint.ps1 script that is loaded when the SharePoint Management Shell is loaded:

```
$ver = $host | select version
if ($ver.Version.Major -gt 1) {$Host.Runspace.ThreadOptions = "ReuseThread"}
```

This code is changing the way in which PowerShell does threading by telling it to use the same thread for each line of code. (Note that functions and scripts will always execute in the same thread, as will multiple commands separated by a semicolon.) This is important if you are manually loading the cmdlets in your own PowerShell window or editor (such as the PowerShell ISE), instead of using the SharePoint Management Shell, which sets this thread option for you.

However, the SharePoint team decided to provide another mechanism to help avoid these disposal issues, and to eliminate the need to explicitly call Dispose() on the objects. That's where the SPAssignmentCollection object and the -AssignmentCollection parameters come in. Two cmdlets allow objects to be stored in the SPAssignmentCollection and subsequently disposed from it: Start-SPAssignment and Stop-SPAssignment.

You create a new assignment collection by calling the Start-SPAssignment cmdlet. You can then optionally pass the created assignment collection object into your subsequent calls either by using the pipeline, or by directly setting the parameter.

Take a look at the "help" text for this cmdlet to understand this better:

"The Start-SPAssignment cmdlet properly disposes of objects used with variable assignments.

Large amounts of memory are often required when SPWeb, SPSite, or SPSiteAdminisitration objects are used. So the use of these objects, or lists of these objects, in Windows PowerShell scripts requires proper memory management. By default, all Get commands dispose of these objects immediately after the pipeline finishes, but by using SPAssignment, you can assign the list of objects to a variable and dispose of the objects after they are no longer needed. You can also ensure that the objects remain as long as you need them, even throughout multiple iterations of commands.

There are three levels of assignment:

➤ No assignment — The object is not assigned to a variable and is disposed of after each iteration of the command.

➤ Simple assignment — All objects are assigned to the global assignment store. This is done by using the Global parameter. When using this level, all objects are assigned to a global store and are disposed of when the Stop-SPAssignment command is called.

➤ Advanced assignment — Objects are assigned to named stores for disposal. You can dispose of objects by using the -Identity parameter with the Stop-SPAssignment command. Regardless of the level used, all objects are disposed of when the PowerShell runspace is closed."

As you can see from the "help" text, there are three levels of assignment:

➤ No assignment (dispose immediately)

➤ Simple assignment (use a global store)

➤ Advanced assignment (use a named store)

The syntax for the cmdlet is as follows:

```
Start-SPAssignment [-Global] [-AssignmentCollection <SPAssignmentCollection>] [
-Verbose] [-Debug] [-ErrorAction <ActionPreference>] [-WarningAction <ActionPre
ference>] [-ErrorVariable <String>] [-WarningVariable <String>] [-OutVariable <
String>] [-OutBuffer <Int32>]
```

If you specify the -Global switch, you do not need to store the returned object, or pass it into your cmdlets. Internally, this cmdlet stores the object in a static variable that is used by all subsequent calls. This is the "simple assignment" method mentioned in the "help" text.

If you do not specify the -Global switch, you must do the following (referred to as the "advanced assignment" in the "help" text):

➤ Store the returned object in a variable

➤ Pass that variable into all subsequent cmdlet calls that return disposable objects

➤ Provide the variable to the Stop-SPAssignment cmdlet via the -SemiGlobal parameter

What about the "no assignment" option? The "no assignment" option is basically when you do not create an SPAssignmentCollection using the Start-SPAssignment cmdlet, which causes cmdlets that return disposable objects to dispose of the object immediately after the call to WriteObject (an internal method that all cmdlets call to write out results). So, as long as the pipeline is active, the object remains undisposed. But, at the end of the pipeline, the object is disposed.

Now take a look at the syntax for the Stop-SPAssignment cmdlet:

```
Stop-SPAssignment [[-SemiGlobal] <SPAssignmentCollection>] [-Global] [-Assignme
ntCollection <SPAssignmentCollection>] [-Verbose] [-Debug] [-ErrorAction <Actio
nPreference>] [-WarningAction <ActionPreference>] [-ErrorVariable <String>] [-W
arningVariable <String>] [-OutVariable <String>] [-OutBuffer <Int32>]
```

If you used the -Global switch for the Start-SPAssignment cmdlet, you'll use it here. Otherwise, you would use the -SemiGlobal parameter and pass the variable you created earlier.

Here's a complete example demonstrating both approaches:

```
#Use of the Global assignment variable
Start-SPAssignment -Global
$site = Get-SPSite "http://portal"
$site | fl
Stop-SPAssignment -Global

#Use of a semi-global, or named variable
$gc = Start-SPAssignment
$site = $gc | Get-SPSite "http://mysites"
$site | fl
$gc | Stop-SPAssignment
```

The second example passes in the variable using the pipeline, rather than setting the parameter directly (for both the Get-SPSite cmdlet and the Stop-SPAssignment cmdlet). I could have easily set the parameter names directly, but this just results in less code (only the -SemiGlobal parameter of the Stop-SPAssignment cmdlet accepts input from the pipeline).

 Keep in mind that, if you have not set the thread options to "ReuseThread," this mechanism will not work as expected because the objects will live in the wrong thread, and will not be disposed when Stop-SPAssignment is called.

If you are unsure when you should be doing this, the easiest solution is to always use the global assignment collection. This ensures that any cmdlets that participate in this disposable mechanism will be properly disposed. It's important to note, however, that though every cmdlet accepts an SPAssignmentCollection, only Get-SPSite, New-SPSite, Get-SPWeb, and New-SPWeb actually participate by adding the returned objects to the collection.

CREATING CUSTOM CMDLETS

SharePoint 2010 provides so many cmdlets and exposes so much via the object model that you're probably thinking there isn't anything you can't do with what is provided. In a way, you'd be correct. However, certain core, repeatable tasks would require constantly loading up script files, which could be extremely complex and prone to error because of the lack of good compile-time checking and debugger support. If you are doing a lot with PowerShell and SharePoint, inevitably, you will start wondering whether it makes sense to create your own cmdlets to achieve a particular task.

Fortunately, creating and deploying custom cmdlets with SharePoint 2010 is extremely easy. The process now follows the same pattern as any other SharePoint development effort (unlike with SharePoint 2007, where you had to create custom setup packages and your own snap-in installer). With SharePoint 2010, you can now use Visual Studio 2010 to create a *SharePoint Solution Package* (*WSP*) and deploy that package to the farm, like any other WSP package.

When to Create Custom Cmdlets

So, when is it appropriate to create a custom cmdlet?

Generally speaking, you'll want to create a cmdlet when you are performing building block tasks that are not specific to a particular business, and are used frequently. For example, SharePoint 2010 does not provide any cmdlets for working directly with SPList objects (corresponding to SharePoint Lists and Libraries). If you do a lot of list manipulations using PowerShell, you may want to create a custom cmdlet to speed up the process of retrieving those lists, and setting common properties in a consistent manner, rather than relying on scripts to achieve the same tasks.

Creating cmdlets also allows administrators to access the functionality from any server in the farm, or even from a remote PowerShell session, without the need to copy scripts around, or set security on shared drives to allow script execution.

Another good example of when you'll need to create custom cmdlets is when you create custom service applications. Service applications require several custom cmdlets to handle the creation of the application and proxy, as well as setting various configuration options.

Also, if you are an independent software vendor (ISV), it is generally considered a best practice to provide PowerShell cmdlets with your shipping application to allow users to script the management of that application.

Common Base Classes

When creating custom cmdlets, the first decision you must make is from what base class to inherit. For SharePoint cmdlets, you should choose one of five available classes, each found in the Microsoft.SharePoint.PowerShell namespace:

- ➤ SPCmdlet
- ➤ SPRemoveCmdletBase<TCmdletObject>
- ➤ SPSetCmdletBase<TCmdletObject>
- ➤ SPGetCmdletBase<TCmdletObject>
- ➤ SPNewCmdletBase<TCmdletObject>

Note that SPCmdlet derives from PSCmdlet (which is found in the System.Management.Automation namespace), and the four variable operator base classes all derive from SPCmdlet. When deciding which base class to use, consider whether the cmdlet you are creating is meant to deal with persistent data, non-persistent data, or perform an action.

Persistent data cmdlets would be ones that work with objects that could be set to a variable and used in a later call. For cmdlets that work with persistent data, use the following:

➤ Get *cmdlets* — SPGetCmdletBase<TCmdletObject>

➤ Set *cmdlets* — SPSetCmdletBase<TCmdletObject>

➤ New *cmdlets* — SPNewCmdletBase<TCmdletObject>

➤ Remove *cmdlets* — SPRemoveCmdletBase<TCmdletObject>

An example of a non-persistent cmdlet would be one that created a text-based report or some other unstructured data, or one that set properties on a variety of different objects without returning anything specific. For cmdlets that work with non-persistent data, use the following:

➤ Get *cmdlets* — SPCmdlet

➤ Set *cmdlets* — SPCmdlet

For action cmdlets, use SPCmdlet.

By having all your cmdlets inherit from one of these five base classes, you ensure that users have a consistent experience when using common parameters such as the AssignmentCollection parameter, which is defined in SPCmdlet.

Listing 5-6 shows an example of a simple Get cmdlet that returns an SPList object.

LISTING 5-6: SPCmdletGetSPList.cs

```csharp
using System.Collections.Generic;
using Microsoft.SharePoint;
using Microsoft.SharePoint.PowerShell;
using System.Management.Automation;

namespace Wrox.SharePoint.PowerShell
{
    [Cmdlet(VerbsCommon.Get, "SPList", SupportsShouldProcess = false),
    SPCmdlet(RequireLocalFarmExist = true)]
    internal sealed class SPCmdletGetSPList : SPGetCmdletBase<SPList>
    {
        [Parameter(Mandatory = true,
        ValueFromPipeline = true, Position = 0)]
        public SPListPipeBind Identity { get; set; }

        protected override IEnumerable<SPList> RetrieveDataObjects()
        {
            List<SPList> lists = new List<SPList>();

            SPList list = Identity.Read();
            if (list != null)
            {
                AssignmentCollection.Add(list.ParentWeb);
                AssignmentCollection.Add(list.ParentWeb.Site);
```

```
                    lists.Add(list);
                }

            return lists;
        }
    }
}
```

Code file [SPCmdletGetSPList.cs] available for download at Wrox.com

This class has a single SPListPipeBind property named Identity, and implements the required RetrieveDataObjects() method. The SPListPipeBind object is detailed in the following discussion. Within the RetrieveDataObjects() method, I call the SPListPipeBind object's Read() method, and add the resultant SPList object to a generic List<SPList> collection, which is then returned.

One additional thing to point out is the call to the SPAssignmentCollection's Add() method. Because SPList objects depend on a valid SPWeb and SPSite object, you must add those objects to the assignment collection so that they can be properly disposed when Stop-SPAssignment is called.

Custom PipeBind Objects

If you have any custom objects that can be represented using more than one mechanism (a URL and a GUID, for example), you should consider creating a custom PipeBind object so that either representation of the object can be passed to your cmdlet. A common example of a PipeBind object is the SPSitePipeBind object that is used whenever an SPSite object is needed. The SPSitePipeBind type allows a URL, a GUID, or an actual SPSite object to be passed into any SPSitePipeBind parameter.

To create a custom PipeBind object, you inherit from SPCmdletPipeBind<TCmdletObject>. You must then have at least one public constructor that can be used by the PowerShell run time to load the parameter specified. When the run time parses the parameter, it attempts to bind it to a constructor that matches the parameter type. If no constructor can be found, an error is thrown.

You must also override the Read() and Discover(TCmdletObject) methods. The Read() method inspects the values stored by the constructors, and returns an object of the specified type. The Discover(TCmdletObject) method takes in an object and should store the object, or an alternate representation of the object, which can then be used when the Read() method is called.

Listing 5-7 demonstrates a simplified implementation of an SPListPipeBind class that allows either an actual SPList object or a URL pointing to an SPList object to be accepted as a valid parameter. Note that, for production-ready code, proper error handling should be added.

LISTING 5-7: SPListPipeBind.cs

Available for
download on
Wrox.com

```
using System;
using Microsoft.SharePoint;
```

continues

LISTING 5-7 *(continued)*

```csharp
using Microsoft.SharePoint.PowerShell;

namespace Wrox.SharePoint.PowerShell
{
    public sealed class SPListPipeBind : SPCmdletPipeBind<SPList>
    {
        private string m_ListUrl;

        public SPListPipeBind(SPList instance) : base(instance)
        { }

        public SPListPipeBind(string inputString)
        {
            this.m_ListUrl = inputString.Trim();
        }

        public SPListPipeBind(Uri listUri)
        {
            this.m_ListUrl = listUri.ToString();
        }

        protected override void Discover(SPList instance)
        {
            this.m_ListUrl = instance.ParentWeb.Site.MakeFullUrl(
                instance.RootFolder.ServerRelativeUrl);
        }

        public override SPList Read()
        {
            // We don't dispose here as we'll add these objects
            // to the SPAssignmentCollection
            SPSite site = new SPSite(ListUrl);
            SPWeb web = site.OpenWeb();
            SPList list = web.GetList(ListUrl);

            if (list == null)
                throw new SPCmdletPipeBindException(
                    string.Format("SPList PipeBind object not found ({0})",
                        ListUrl));
            return list;
        }

        public string ListUrl
        {
            get { return this.m_ListUrl; }
        }
    }
}
```

Code file [SPListPipeBind.cs] available for download at Wrox.com

The Read() *method of your custom* PipeBind *object must always return back a new instance of the base object type, and never the actual instance that was passed in. This allows any custom cmdlet code to freely dispose of the object without impacting the original caller of the cmdlet.*

Packaging and Deploying Using Visual Studio 2010

With previous versions of SharePoint and Visual Studio, you had to undergo a difficult and tedious process to create, package, and deploy custom cmdlets. The process involved creating a custom snap-in and installer, along with several hacks if you needed to deploy to a 64-bit environment. Thanks to the new SharePoint capabilities within Visual Studio 2010, creating and deploying custom cmdlets is simple and straightforward, and follows the same pattern as all other SharePoint artifact deployments.

To see how simple this process can be, take the two classes shown earlier and put them into a Visual Studio 2010 project, which can create a SharePoint Solution Package that you can deploy to any SharePoint 2010 farm.

1. Open Visual Studio 2010 and choose File ➪ New ➪ Project. In the New Project dialog, select Installed Templates ➪ Visual C# ➪ SharePoint ➪ 2010.

    a. Select Empty SharePoint Project.

    b. Name the project `Wrox.SharePoint.PowerShell`.

    c. Click OK to close the window and proceed to the SharePoint Customization Wizard.

    d. Provide a valid URL to an existing SharePoint site, and select Deploy as a Farm Solution.

    e. Click Finish to create the project.

2. SharePoint PowerShell cmdlets require a project reference to the `Microsoft.SharePoint.PowerShell.dll` and the `System.Management.Automation.dll` assemblies. When adding references, these two assemblies do not show in the .NET references tab, so it is necessary to browse to their location in the global assembly cache (GAC).

    a. Right-click the `References` folder and select Add Reference.

    b. Browse to `%SYSTEMROOT%\assembly\GAC_MSIL\Microsoft.SharePoint.PowerShell\{version}` and select `Microsoft.SharePoint.Powershell.dll`.

    c. Click OK to add the assembly reference.

    d. Repeat for `%SYSTEMROOT%\assembly\GAC_MSIL\System.Management.Automation\1.0.0.0__31bf3856ad364e35\System.Management.Automation.dll`.

3. When the SharePoint PowerShell snap-in is loaded, it looks at all the XML files in the `CONFIG\ PowerShell\Registration` folder found in the SharePoint root folder on the `C:/` drive. The solution package will deploy a custom XML file defining custom cmdlets to this folder.

a. Right-click the project file in the Solution Explorer and select Add ⇨ SharePoint Mapped Folder.

b. Select `{SharePointRoot}\CONFIG\PowerShell\Registration`.

c. Click OK to add the mapped folder.

d. Delete the `Wrox.SharePoint.PowerShell` folder created under the `Registration` folder. (The registration XML file must be in the root of the `Registration` folder.)

e. Right-click the `Registration` folder and select Add ⇨ New Item.

f. In the Add New Item dialog, select Installed Templates ⇨ Visual C# ⇨ Data ⇨ XML File.

g. Name the file `Wrox.SharePoint.PowerShell.xml` and click Add to add the file.

h. Open the new XML file and add the following XML to the file:

```xml
<?xml version="1.0" encoding="utf-8" ?>
<ps:Config xmlns:ps="urn:Microsoft.SharePoint.PowerShell"
  xmlns:xsi="http://www.w3.org/2001/XMLSchema-instance"
  xsi:schemaLocation="urn:Microsoft.SharePoint.PowerShell SPCmdletSchema.xsd">

  <ps:Assembly Name="$SharePoint.Project.AssemblyFullName$">
    <ps:Cmdlet>
      <ps:VerbName>Get-SPList</ps:VerbName>
      <ps:ClassName>Wrox.SharePoint.PowerShell.SPCmdletGetSPList</
ps:ClassName>
      <ps:HelpFile>Wrox.SharePoint.PowerShell.dll-help.xml</ps:HelpFile>
    </ps:Cmdlet>
  </ps:Assembly>
</ps:Config>
```

The registration XML file defines the cmdlet by specifying the cmdlet name and corresponding class name, along with the assembly within which the class is defined. Note that the value for the `<ps:HelpFile />` element is required, but the help file itself is not. This allows you to create and test your cmdlet without going through the effort of creating a help file, but does add some confusion because it implies that the file does, in fact, exist.

4. Now that you have the registration XML file in place, you can add the code from the `SPListPipeBind.cs` and `SPCmdletGetSPList.cs` classes that you defined earlier.

a. Right-click the project name and select Add ⇨ Class.

b. Name the class file `SPListPipeBind.cs` and click Add to add the new class.

c. Open the new class file and add the `SPListPipeBind` class defined earlier.

d. Repeat for the `SPCmdletGetSPList.cs` class file.

5. Once you've added the registration XML file and required class files, you can then deploy and test the project.

    a. Right-click the project name and select Deploy.

    b. Open the SharePoint 2010 Management Shell. (If you have an instance open already, you will need to close and re-open it.)

    c. Enter **Get-Command Get-SPList | fl** and verify that the cmdlet details are returned, as shown here:

```
PS C:\> Get-Command Get-SPList | fl

Name             : Get-SPList
CommandType      : Cmdlet
Definition       : Get-SPList [-Identity] <SPListPipeBind> [-AssignmentCollecti
                   on <SPAssignmentCollection>] [-Verbose] [-Debug] [-ErrorActi
                   on <ActionPreference>] [-WarningAction <ActionPreference>] [
                   -ErrorVariable <String>] [-WarningVariable <String>] [-OutVa
                   riable <String>] [-OutBuffer <Int32>]

Path             :
AssemblyInfo     :
DLL              : C:\Windows\assembly\GAC_MSIL\Wrox.SharePoint.PowerShell\1.0.
                   0.0__d8914da6275b7d87\Wrox.SharePoint.PowerShell.dll
HelpFile         : C:\Program Files\Common Files\Microsoft Shared\Web Server Ex
                   tensions\14\CONFIG\PowerShell\Help\Wrox.SharePoint.PowerShel
                   l.dll-help.xml
ParameterSets    : {[-Identity] <SPListPipeBind> [-AssignmentCollection <SPAssi
                   gnmentCollection>] [-Verbose] [-Debug] [-ErrorAction <Action
                   Preference>] [-WarningAction <ActionPreference>] [-ErrorVari
                   able <String>] [-WarningVariable <String>] [-OutVariable <St
                   ring>] [-OutBuffer <Int32>]}
ImplementingType : Wrox.SharePoint.PowerShell.SPCmdletGetSPList
Verb             : Get
Noun             : SPList
```

    d. Enter **Get-SPList** *http://portal/pages* and verify that list details are returned. (Be sure to provide a URL to a valid list.)

If you've completed all the steps correctly you should have a project structure that looks like Figure 5-1.

As you can see, the only complex part of creating custom cmdlets is creating the business logic that defines the actual cmdlet. Packaging and deployment has been reduced to a rather trivial task, thanks to Visual Studio 2010's excellent solution packaging capabilities.

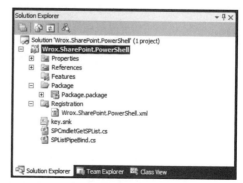

FIGURE 5-1: Solution Explorer

SUMMARY

This chapter provided an overview of the core PowerShell features and SharePoint-specific implementation details that every administrator and developer should know when working with SharePoint 2010.

You should now have the foundational knowledge necessary to accomplish basic tasks using PowerShell and SharePoint 2010. With this knowledge, you can more confidently do further research into more complex PowerShell capabilities (such as error handling, script-based cmdlets, modules, dynamic script execution, and remoting, to name but a few).

PowerShell is an amazingly powerful tool, and can be rather confusing to even the most seasoned developers and administrators. Stick with it, don't get frustrated, and always test your scripts in a test or development environment before attempting anything on production equipment, and you're sure to be successful.

ABOUT THE AUTHOR

Gary Lapointe is an independent consultant and SharePoint MVP who has been planning and implementing SharePoint solutions since early 2007. A developer by trade, Lapointe spends most of his time developing tools that enable IT professionals to be more productive so that they can focus on solving business problems and satisfying their customers' needs. Lapointe's blog at `http://stsadm.blogspot .com` has become the definitive source for all things related to the automated deployment and management of SharePoint 2007 and SharePoint 2010. He lives in Colorado Springs, Colorado, with his wife and daughter. When he's not architecting SharePoint solutions or writing code, he's usually playing ice hockey, snow skiing, or off on a hike in the mountains.

Backing Up and Restoring SharePoint 2010

By Randy Williams

Welcome to backup and restore! For system deployments, and certainly not just SharePoint, this is the part of a project or operations task where most recognize its importance, but few do what is really necessary to protect the system. For SharePoint, this can be particularly dangerous, because it has quickly progressed into a mission-critical application for many organizations.

The good news is that Microsoft has made a number of backup-and-restore investments in SharePoint 2010. These investments cover nearly every aspect of those operations, including enhanced UI options, PowerShell scripting, complete backup of a farm's configuration, and, most importantly, numerous restore improvements. These investments are part of SharePoint Foundation 2010. So, whether you are running SharePoint Foundation 2010 or SharePoint Server 2010, they apply to you.

In this chapter, you learn about the following:

- ➤ Operation planning concepts
- ➤ What's new with backup and restore in SharePoint 2010
- ➤ Content recovery and disaster recovery
- ➤ Concepts and steps to perform each type of backup and restore
- ➤ How to apply concepts by studying different recovery scenarios
- ➤ Recommendations to further protect your SharePoint investment

OPERATIONS PLANNING

Many IT administrators do their jobs from the seat of their pants. Of course, don't interpret that statement literally — I mean quite the opposite, because they are usually busy reacting to the next emergency, never finding time to effectively plan. This is especially true for SharePoint deployments, because many of these deployments begin as grass-root efforts, maybe even pilot projects that just somehow become entrenched in the organization.

Here's a common problem:

> *Chief Executive Officer*: I can't find my budget presentation in SharePoint. I think someone deleted my department site.
>
> *IT Admin*: I didn't know you had a site. This is supposed to be a proof of concept just for the Acme project team.
>
> *Chief Executive Officer*: I did, and I need it back in time for my afternoon meeting.
>
> *IT Admin*: I'll try, but we're not doing regular backups yet.

This is a scary problem — and not just from a recovery standpoint. It speaks to a larger problem of governance needed in this organization. Governance is a very big topic, so this section just briefly examines one aspect that relates to the discussion in this chapter — the importance of a disaster recovery plan.

Importance of a Disaster Recovery Plan

Unfortunately, the *disaster recovery* (*DR*) plan is perceived as either a minor nuisance or the out-right bane of many IT administrators. In contrast, it should be the administrator's ally. One of the primary goals of the plan is to publish clearly defined management expectations and operational service levels. In this way, it's like a contract. You might be wondering how this is a good thing. Let me explain.

As an IT administrator, it gives you protection. It delineates where and when the service begins and ends. It requires the organization to be clear with its needs and expectations, and allows you to publish costs for that service. In other words, it allows you to justify your labor and materials budget.

The plan also provides instructional guidance to the team on how to execute. In a real disaster, you really don't want to be trying to figure out how to perform what should be a simple task.

Because this chapter focuses mostly on the technical aspects of backing up and restoring SharePoint 2010, how to create a DR plan is well outside of this scope. However, take a look at a little guidance just to get you thinking about it. This will also help explain concepts that I refer back to later in the chapter.

Alignment with Business Continuity Plan

Many organizations (especially larger ones) have some form of a *business continuity plan (BCP)*. You can think of the BCP as a larger, more holistic recovery plan for the organization at large. It encompasses not just systems, but personnel to ensure that essential services and functions can continue in the event of a crisis.

If you have (or will be creating) a DR plan, make sure you inquire whether or not you have a BCP as well, and do your best to ensure that they are in alignment with each other. In many cases, the DR plan is a part of the BCP.

To learn more about what should be included in a BCP, or how to implement one, see http://www.businesscontinuityplan.org.

Defining Recovery Objectives

When constructing a DR plan, or when you are just clarifying recovery expectations, three key targets should be defined:

➤ *Recovery time objective (RTO)* — An RTO defines the maximum amount of time a recovery process should take in the event of failure. In other words, how much downtime can the organization afford? If a SharePoint website must be recovered from backup, how long should it take? The RTO is usually expressed in a time span such as minutes, hours, or days. Of course, what you are restoring may dictate how long it will take, so multiple RTOs may be defined. How much data must be restored and how fast the recovery is must be considered when meeting an RTO.

➤ *Recovery point objective (RPO)* — An RPO defines the maximum amount of data that can be lost in the event of failure. In transaction processing systems, it's fairly easy to define. For example, a company that takes orders over the Internet cannot afford to lose any orders that have already been accepted. For SharePoint, it's a bit more difficult, because transaction units are not as obvious. Instead, you might express the RPO with a time span as well. For example, when restoring a site collection, at most only two hours of loss is acceptable. How frequently you back up must be considered when meeting an RPO.

➤ *Recovery level objective (RLO)* — An RLO defines the level of granularity needed when you restore. This is very pertinent to SharePoint, and it could refer to very granular levels such as a single document, or a wider level such as a Content Database. Critical service applications such as Search or Managed Metadata Service should also be considered when defining an RLO.

Together, these three objectives tell you what your recovery goals are. Of course, getting the organization to help define and agree on these is a separate challenge, but somehow, you should try to define them. If you're not even sure where to start, go with a 24-hour RTO and an 8-hour RPO, and adjust from there.

When setting the objectives, keep in mind that there may be significant costs associated with achieving them. This is related to the exorbitant cost for delivering "5 nines" of uptime (that is, 99.999 percent). Figure 6-1 shows a graph that explains this.

The reasoning here is that the more you lower the RTO, the more the costs exponentially increase. Where the sweet spot is on the curve will depend on the organization — in particular, the importance of the systems and the budget used to invest in the DR infrastructure.

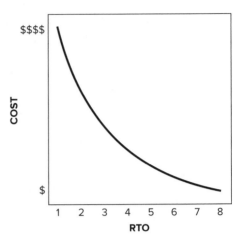

FIGURE 6-1: Recovery time objective cost curve

TYPES OF RECOVERY

Before getting into the specific backup-and-recovery features in SharePoint 2010, this section defines the two primary types of recovery — *content recovery* and *disaster recovery*. This will allow you to better recognize which option works best in a given situation.

Content Recovery

Content recovery is used in cases where information has been incorrectly modified or deleted. This typically refers to a small amount of information such as a single document or a library within a website. In many cases, the end user or a site collection administrator can perform this type of recovery without IT involvement. This is solved by restoring from one of the recycle bins, or restoring a previous version.

When possible, it's always best to restore using one of these methods, because it's easy to do, and, in general, less intrusive. For example, if a folder is accidentally deleted in a library, it is better to restore this from a recycle bin than restoring the whole website from last night's backup.

Some consider website recovery as a form of content recovery. The distinction made here is that, if a farm administrator must perform the operation, it's considered disaster recovery.

A FEW POINTS ABOUT THE RECYCLE BIN

Though this chapter won't go into detail on basic recycle bin use or version recovery, here are some important, not-so-well-known details about the recycle bins that farm administrators should be aware of. Knowing these will help ensure that you recognize how best to use the two recycle bins.

➤ Files that are aged from the first-stage recycle bin do not go into the second. For example, say you are using the default of 30 days for your recycle bin setting. If you delete a document on March 1, it will go into the first-stage recycle bin for the website. If no one touches it, it will be automatically deleted on March 31.

➤ This age countdown starts when the file is originally deleted. Continuing with the previous example, say that the website recycle bin is emptied on March 30. The document goes into the second-stage recycle bin for the site collection, and will stay for just one day before being deleted.

➤ If you turn off your recycle bins for the web application, it will immediately empty all recycle bins for all site collections in that web application.

➤ Space used by all first-stage recycle bins is part of your site collection quota. Space used by the second-stage recycle bin goes against a specified percentage of this quota (by default 50 percent).

➤ A website that is deleted is not stored in any recycle bin. This must be restored using other means.

➤ Developers can write code to delete items that bypass both recycle bins and are permanently deleted.

Disaster Recovery

This section takes a look at disaster recovery, the other type of recovery that will be the primary focus for most of this chapter. The use of the word "disaster" is not meant to be melodramatic. Whether these are truly a disaster depends on your recovery objectives within your DR plan. If you have a solid plan in place that is well understood, even these types of restores can be easily performed.

Nonetheless, for definition purposes, these are recovery efforts that are more significant, and tend to be done by farm administrators, not content managers or site collection administrators.

In general, these types of recoveries include website, site collection, Content Database, and farm. As you learn more about the recovery options, you will see that other types do exist.

WHAT'S NEW IN 2010

SharePoint 2010 has added a number of improvements to the backup-and-restore story. For those who already have a good understanding of backup and restore in SharePoint 2007, this section highlights many of the key changes found in this new release.

 Throughout this chapter, references are occasionally made to SharePoint 2007. To be clear, this is a reference to both Windows SharePoint Services (WSS) 3.0 and Microsoft Office SharePoint Server (MOSS) 2007.

Farm Configuration Backup and Recovery

For the past several releases, SharePoint has centralized much of the farm's configuration in a single database. This is great, because it provides a single repository for important farm settings (such as web applications, servers in the farm, timer jobs, and services that are running). Unfortunately, though you could back up this farm configuration database, it could never be restored through SharePoint. This means that if you ever had to do a farm recovery or wanted to duplicate a farm (for example, when creating a test environment), you would need to create a brand new farm, rebuild the web applications, and manually apply many of the farm's settings.

In SharePoint 2010, you have true farm configuration backup and recovery. Many of the farm settings found in the configuration database are now serialized into backup files. These settings are not tied to the actual servers, allowing you to much more easily recover or duplicate a farm to different machines.

Following are a few of the configuration details that are part of the backup:

- ➤ Web application settings, including alternate access mappings (AAM), managed paths, and Content Databases
- ➤ Farm Solutions (WSP packages)
- ➤ Incoming/outgoing e-mail settings
- ➤ Timer jobs
- ➤ Diagnostic logging settings

Yes, this is great, but before you get too excited, you should know that it still does not back up everything. For example, manual changes to the SharePoint root (now the 14 folder), manual changes to `web.config` files, as well as most configuration settings specific to IIS (such as SSL certificates and NLB settings) are still not included. So, some manual steps still need to be both documented and manually backed up. You learn more about the details in the farm recovery scenario later in this chapter.

In addition to having this farm configuration backup, there is a configuration-only backup-and-restore option as well. This allows you to quickly back up or restore just the configuration settings, including the Central Administration web application, but excluding all other web applications, Content Databases, and service applications.

Changes to Central Administration

As you already know, the SharePoint 2010 user interface (UI) has undergone major cosmetic surgery, including Central Administration. As part of this redesign, the "Backup and Restore" section has some different options. Figure 6-2 shows how the category now appears on the Central Administration home page.

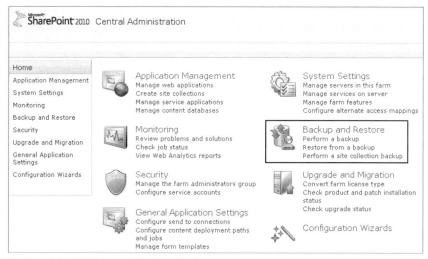

FIGURE 6-2: "Backup and Restore" category

When you click the category title, a new page displays a summary of the major improvements, as shown in Figure 6-3. These are covered in detail later in this chapter.

FIGURE 6-3: Backup and restore commands

As you can see, you can now issue many different types of backups, such as farm backup, configuration-only backup, and site collection. You can even export a website or list.

Granularity options are much improved when choosing items to back up within a farm. You can individually select farm solutions, service applications, and InfoPath Forms Services settings, among others. The same granularity applies to items when you want to restore.

In case you're wondering, there is still no way to schedule backups directly through Central Administration. The recommended approach is to still write a script and schedule it through the Windows Task Scheduler. And, with PowerShell scripting, as you'll see next, you have enormous scripting power.

PowerShell

In this new version of SharePoint, PowerShell becomes the de-facto command-line management console. Yes, STSADM operations are still in the product, and they undergo some small changes to support some of the new backup-and-restore features. But, by far, the power and flexibility comes with PowerShell. Officially, Microsoft now considers STSADM deprecated, and it recommends porting these scripts over to PowerShell.

Though PowerShell does have a steeper learning curve — it can be pretty imposing the first few times you use it — trust me, you will get better at it, and the time is well spent. SharePoint 2010 has more than 500 PowerShell commands with about 10 of these specific to backup and restore. Many of these commands have options that are not available when using Central Administration or STSADM. Aside from the plethora of commands and scripting, the PowerShell engine is also so much more performant compared to traditional STSADM operations.

Following are the six most commonly used PowerShell commands when it comes to backup and restore:

➤ Backup-SPFarm

➤ Restore-SPFarm

➤ Backup-SPSite

➤ Restore-SPSite

➤ Export-SPWeb

➤ Import-SPWeb

The details and syntax for these are covered later in this chapter.

 For all PowerShell commands covered in this chapter, I assume you will be using the SharePoint 2010 Management Shell, which preloads all of the SharePoint cmdlets.

SQL Database Snapshots

SQL Server 2005 first introduced support for SQL database snapshots, but SharePoint 2007 did not support them. The idea behind them is very simple. A database snapshot functions like a separate, read-only copy of a regular database that is made at a specific point in time. One of the big advantages is that it is not a byte-for-byte duplicate of a database, meaning that the actual space used by the snapshot is quite small, at least initially.

When you create a database snapshot, SQL Server tells Windows to create a special type of file called a *sparse file* that is not allocated any actual space. This sparse file grows only when modifications to the source database are made. Before a change to the original database is applied, the *data pages* (the allocation units SQL Server uses) that will be changed are first copied into the snapshot database. When reading from the snapshot database, SQL effectively merges the source and snapshot databases together to get a complete, point-in-time view of data at the time the snapshot was created.

You might be curious as to how this benefits SharePoint. The primary benefit is when you perform a site collection backup. Since the Service Pack 2 build in SharePoint 2007 and continuing in 2010, SharePoint marks a site collection as read-only during a site collection backup. This is done to prevent changes to the data that could cause corruption, such as orphaned sites.

The problem is that no user can make changes while a site collection backup is running. Site collection backup commands in SharePoint 2010 now have an option (UseSqlSnapshot) to create SQL database snapshots as an alternative to marking it as read-only. When employed, SharePoint creates a database snapshot and runs the site collection backup from it instead. When the backup finishes, the snapshot is deleted. This option is also available when you export a website or list.

It's a bit early to share the best practices on when to use this feature, but here's some common sense advice. Because Content Databases can contain multiple site collections, you would be ill-advised to use this option when backing up small site collections within large Content Databases.

 To learn more about database snapshots, see an article in SQL Server Books Online at http://msdn.microsoft.com/en-us/library/ms175158.aspx.

 SQL Database snapshots are supported only in the Enterprise and Developer editions of SQL Server 2005 and 2008.

Unattached Content Database Recovery

In SharePoint 2007, you need a recovery farm for many restore operations. For example, say that you needed to recover a single website from a farm backup. Here are the usual steps:

1. Restore the Content Database from a backup.

2. Attach it to your recovery farm.

3. Perform an export operation on the recovery farm (STSADM -o export).

4. Import to the production farm (STSADM -o import).

In SharePoint 2010, you have a new feature that allows you to recover data from a Content Database, even though it's not attached to a farm. Here's a new way to recover the single website:

1. Restore the Content Database from a backup.

2. Use Central Administration to connect to the database, browse, and then export the website.

3. Import to the production farm (use the `Import-SPWeb` PowerShell cmdlet).

You can restore your database to any network-accessible SQL Server. You can use one of your production SQL servers used by SharePoint, but if you do, be very careful that you restore it to a different database name. It won't save you a lot of time since the steps are similar, but you will not need a recovery farm. In the "Recovery Scenarios" section later in this chapter, you see more details on how to perform recovery using unattached Content Databases.

List Import and Export

Those who know their stuff on SharePoint 2007 probably noticed a new command in the earlier description of unattached Content Database recovery. In SharePoint 2010, you can now back up a single list or library, giving you another level of restore granularity. You can perform the export operation from Central Administration, STSADM, or PowerShell. Importing is done from STSADM or PowerShell, as you see later in this chapter.

When using Central Administration, the GUI is very similar to what you just saw in the previous section. You first select the site collection, then the website, then the list, and, lastly, some export options. Figure 6-4 shows you how it looks when exporting the Shared Documents library from a team site.

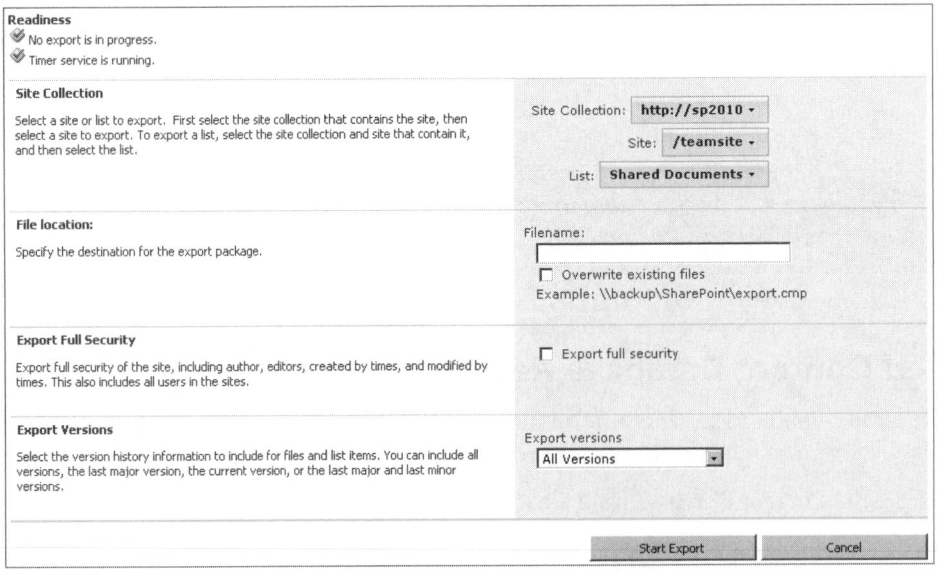

FIGURE 6-4: Site or list export

Search Recovery Improvements

Architectural improvements with the SharePoint Server 2010 Search enable you to perform either a farm restore or a restore of the Search application, without having to run a full crawl of all the content sources. SharePoint now uses a point-and-time approach, so that when the restore finishes, you only need to run an incremental crawl, saving hours or days to rebuild all of your indexes.

UNDERSTANDING THE TYPES OF BACKUPS

SharePoint supports a number of different backup types, each with distinct advantages and disadvantages. This section examines each type of backup that is supported out-of-the-box. In some cases, this will slightly overlap what was discussed in the previous section, "What's New in 2010," but this section covers the specific syntax, important caveats, and other details.

The backup engine in SharePoint is only capable of making disk-based backups, either to a local or Universal Naming Convention (UNC) path. Direct backup to tape is not an option.

To classify all the types of backups, you can group them into two primary backup categories: *granular* and *farm*. Granular backups have two main types: *site collection* and *website/list*. As you can see, this focuses on content within a single Content Database. Farm backups, on the other hand, are more comprehensive, and consist of settings such as farm configuration, solution packages, web applications, whole Content Databases, service applications, and some others.

As this discussion progresses through each type of backup, you will see how to use Central Administration to perform the operation. Because Central Administration has no scheduling engine, it is suitable only for ad-hoc backup-and-restore operations. Therefore, the syntax and examples are examined using STSADM and PowerShell, which you can automate using Task Scheduler. Because PowerShell is now the preferred management console for SharePoint 2010, more emphasis will be placed on it.

Even though this discussion does not explain how, all backup and restore operations that are covered in this chapter can also be run using the SharePoint Object Model. This allows .NET developers to perform these same operations within custom applications that are developed.

To learn more about the SharePoint Object Model, check out the SharePoint 2010 Software Development Kit (SDK) located at `http://msdn.microsoft.com/en-us/library/ee557253.aspx`.

Granular Backups

Granular backups are content backups that work on the site collection, website, or list level. Granular backups can be made against the regular Content Databases that are attached to a farm, or against unattached Content Databases. These backups can be performed using Central Administration, STSADM, or PowerShell commands.

Site Collection Backups

Site collections are the largest backup unit within granular backups. One big advantage of site collection backups is that they are full-fidelity backups. This means that not only are all websites and list items fully preserved, but the plethora of site collection details (such as users, groups, permissions, galleries, alerts, workflow status, feature activation, navigation, and everything else) are also preserved. Another advantage is that they are the fastest of all granular backup types.

Despite these advantages, you should be aware of some disadvantages as well. Though faster than other granular types, they are much slower than Content Database backups. Site collection backups also put a sizeable performance load on your farm. For these reasons, it is not recommended to run site collection backups if your site collection is larger than around 15 GB.

Another disadvantage is that, by default, a site collection backup will place a read-only lock on site collection, preventing any write access during the backup. However, this can be solved by using database snapshots that were introduced earlier in this chapter. A final disadvantage is that a site collection backup can only be restored in its entirety. That is, you are not able to restore just a portion (such as a single website) from a site collection backup.

Performing a Site Collection Backup

Let's take a closer look at how you run site collection backups. You can issue a site collection backup directly from Central Administration, STSADM, or PowerShell. Keep in mind that whichever way you run it, the format of the backup file is the same.

Figure 6-3 shows you where to start a site collection backup in Central Administration. After you click the link, you are presented with the screen shown in Figure 6-5, where you select the site collection and specify the filename.

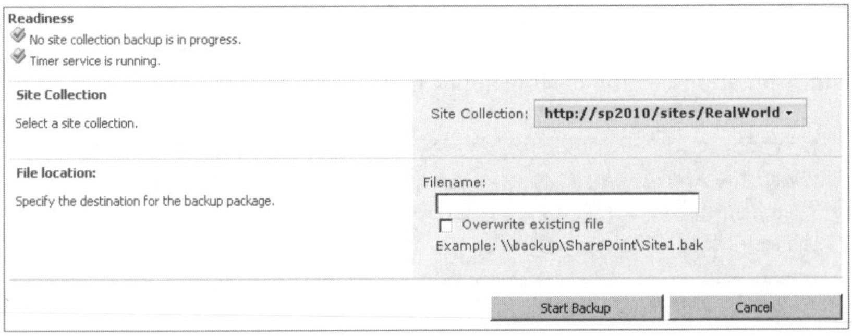

FIGURE 6-5: Site collection backup

As you can see, a site collection backup is stored in a single file. The path to the file can either be a local path (for example, e:\backup) or a UNC path (for example, \\backupserver\SharePoint). For any remote UNC paths, you must ensure that the farm administrator account has read/write permissions to both the share and the NTFS folder. After you click Start Backup, a timer job will be created and the backup will start.

All backup and restore commands issued from Central Administration create jobs that are executed by the timer service. Thus, you must ensure that the timer service (SPTimerV4) is running for the job to run.

Site collection backups can also be easily issued with STSADM. Because these commands are becoming deprecated in favor of PowerShell, the following shows you just the basic syntax:

```
STSADM -o backup -url <url> -filename <filename>
```

Here is a sample:

```
STSADM -o backup -url http://sp2010/sites/realworld -filename
    e:\backup\realworld.bak
```

The most flexibility in running site collection backups comes with the Backup-SPSite PowerShell cmdlet. Here is the complete syntax:

```
Backup-SPSite [-Identity] <SPSitePipeBind> -Path <String>
    [-AssignmentCollection <SPAssignmentCollection>]
    [-Confirm [<SwitchParameter>]] [-Force <SwitchParameter>]
    [-NoSiteLock <SwitchParameter>] [-UseSqlSnapshot <SwitchParameter>]
    [-WhatIf [<SwitchParameter>]] [<CommonParameters>]
```

The syntax can be imposing if you're not used to PowerShell, so this section looks at just a few examples that better explain how easily it can be used. To back up a single site collection just like the STSADM example shown previously, you can use the following form:

```
Backup-SPSite http://sp2010/sites/realworld -path e:\backup\realworld.bak
```

To back up a site collection and use a SQL Database Snapshot (requires SQL Enterprise), you can use the following form:

```
Backup-SPSite http://sp2010/sites/realworld -path
    e:\backup\realworld.bak -UseSqlSnapshot
```

To prevent a read-only site collection lock from being issued, you can use the following form:

```
Backup-SPSite http://sp2010/sites/realworld -path
    e:\backup\realworld.bak -NoSiteLock
```

If the backup file already exists, and you want to overwrite it, use the -force switch, as shown here:

```
Backup-SPSite http://sp2010/sites/realworld -path e:\backup\realworld.bak -force
```

One of the strengths of PowerShell is the capability to chain several commands together, which not only gives you much more flexible commands, but also precludes your writing lines of script. Here is a command that backs up all the site collections individually within a given web application:

```
Get-SPWebApplication "SharePoint - 80" | Get-SPSite -limit all |
    ForEach-Object { $filename = "e:\backup\" +
    $_.Url.replace("http://","").replace("_","__").replace("/","_") +
    ".bak" ; backup-spsite $_.Url -path $filename -force}
```

Or, you can just back up the site collections within a single Content Database, as shown here:

```
Get-SPContentDatabase "SP_Portal_Content" | Get-SPSite -limit all |
    ForEach-Object { $filename = "e:\backup\" +
    $_.Url.replace("http://","").replace("_","__").replace("/","_") +
    ".bak" ; backup-spsite $_.Url -path $filename -force}
```

Performing a Site Collection Restore

Restoring a site collection is also a simple operation, but it cannot be done using Central Administration. This means that you will probably be using STSADM or PowerShell commands.

When restoring a site collection, you should be aware of a few important details. First, you can restore a site collection backup into a different managed path. So, if you have a site collection backed up from http://sp2010/sites/hr, you can restore it to http://sp2010/hr. This is handy if you need to either move or duplicate a site collection.

However, there is a caveat to this that you should know. A site collection backup preserves all the internal details, including the internal Globally Unique IDs (GUIDs), and you cannot have duplicate site collection GUIDs in the same Content Database. This means that if you backup and restore the HR site collection as shown previously, you must drop the original site collection before the restore, or ensure that the destination Content Database is different from the source.

Restoring a Content Database will not automatically create a managed path for the web application. Continuing the previous example, if you want to move the HR site collection from http://sp2010/sites/hr to http://sp2010/hr, you must create the HR managed path first.

With some of those details out of the way, take a look at the basic restore syntax using STSADM, as shown here:

```
STSADM -o restore -url <url> -filename <filename> [-overwrite]
```

The syntax is quite straightforward using STSADM. You have a few optional features such as overwrite, which will automatically delete the site collection if one exists at the URL specified.

Using PowerShell to restore is equally easy using the Restore-SPSite cmdlet, but it gives you many more options. Here is the complete syntax for one of the ways to run it:

```
Restore-SPSite [-Identity] <String> -Path <String> [-AssignmentCollection
    <SPAssignmentCollection>] [-Confirm [<SwitchParameter>]]
    [-ContentDatabase <SPContentDatabasePipeBind>] [-Force <SwitchParameter>]
    [-GradualDelete <SwitchParameter>] [-HostHeaderWebApplication <String>]
    [-WhatIf [<SwitchParameter>]] [<CommonParameters>]
```

Look at some examples to better understand how to run restore commands. Here is the simplest form:

```
Restore-SPSite http://sp2010/hr -Path e:\backup\hr.bak
```

If you want to overwrite the existing site collection located at the managed path, use the `-force` optional parameter, as shown here:

```
Restore-SPSite http://sp2010/hr -Path e:\backup\hr.bak -force
```

Of particular interest is the fact that you can specify a specific Content Database when you restore your site collections. This allows you to easily work around the problem where you are unable to have a duplicate site collection in a Content Database. It's also helpful if you just want better control over where your site collections are located.

This next example assumes that another Content Database named `SP_HR_Content` has already been created and attached to the `http://sp2010` web application:

```
Restore-SPSite http://sp2010/hr -Path
    e:\backup\hr.bak -ContentDatabase SP_HR_Content
```

If you do not specify a Content Database as shown here, SharePoint 2010 selects what is sometimes called the "most available" Content Database. This is the same as it was in SharePoint 2007.

 For details on how this is done, see the article at `http://www.synergyonline` `.com/blog/blog-moss/Lists/Posts/Post.aspx?ID=65.`

When running site collection backup or restore commands, log entries are created in the SharePoint ULS logs (by default `14\LOGS`). The correlation token GUID can be used to link the related log activities together into a single story.

 If you will be restoring a site collection backup to a different farm, it is best to match the build numbers (that is, patch level) of the farms to help ensure a clean restore. At a minimum, the destination farm must be at the same or newer build for the restore command to attempt the restore. Also, you cannot restore SharePoint 2007 site collection backups on a SharePoint 2010 farm.

Web and List Exports

In a number of cases a full site collection backup is more than you need, such as when you have a large site collection storing all of the projects in your organization. Most of these project websites are closed, and you only want to back up the active ones. Or, say, you will be performing some customizations using SharePoint Designer 2010, and you want to back up the one website in the event that something is damaged. You can also just export a single list or library to narrow in on the important area of content.

For these situations, SharePoint 2010 allows you to export websites and lists. Because of the unique way in which this type of backup is run, this operation is called an "export." When you issue an export for a website, it will export not just that website, but the whole website hierarchy from that level on down.

Figure 6-6 shows a very simple project hierarchy of websites. For this example, if you issue an export command and specify the project root site, you'll get all five websites in your backup. If you specify just Project B, you'll only get two websites. If the project is the top-level, root Web for the site collection, it will export the whole site collection. But, be careful, because this is not the same as with the site collection backup.

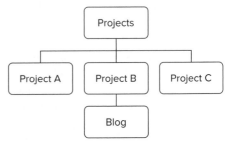

FIGURE 6-6: Simple website hierarchy

If you are exporting just a list, as you would expect, you just get that one list, and only that list.

Export and import operations are also commonly used to copy or move content such as website hierarchies around within your environment. In this way, you can think of them like a prune-and-graft operation. You can copy websites within site collections or between them. You can also copy to other farms. To be clear, the export and import will only copy the websites. To make it a real move operation, you will want to delete the source website after the import is complete, and certainly after you've verified that all is correct!

Unlike a site collection backup, exports are not full-fidelity. This means that some characteristics of the websites and lists are not included in the backup. Settings not preserved are workflow associations and instances, file check-out status, alert subscriptions, tags and notes, and personal Web part settings.

Another caveat for exports is that it will take a long time and place a large burden on your farm. For this reason, it is not recommended to use this for anything other than small website hierarchies or lists. As a general rule, you should try to keep the size of the export under 1 GB.

Performing an Export

Like site collection backups, you can run export commands from Central Administration, STSADM, or PowerShell. The output format of the export is the same when using any of these programs. When running an export, SharePoint serializes the website or list content and other details into various XML and binary files. At the end, these files can be combined together and compressed into a cabinet (CAB) file format. Depending on the size, you may get multiple cabinet files that are treated as one logical set for the export operation.

To run an export using Central Administration, simply click the Export a Site or List link from the Granular Backup menu shown in Figure 6-3. From here, specify the site collection, the website, the list (which is optional), the filename, and whether you want to export security details and item version history. If you do not select a list, you get a website export. Figure 6-7 shows a sample backup of a team site.

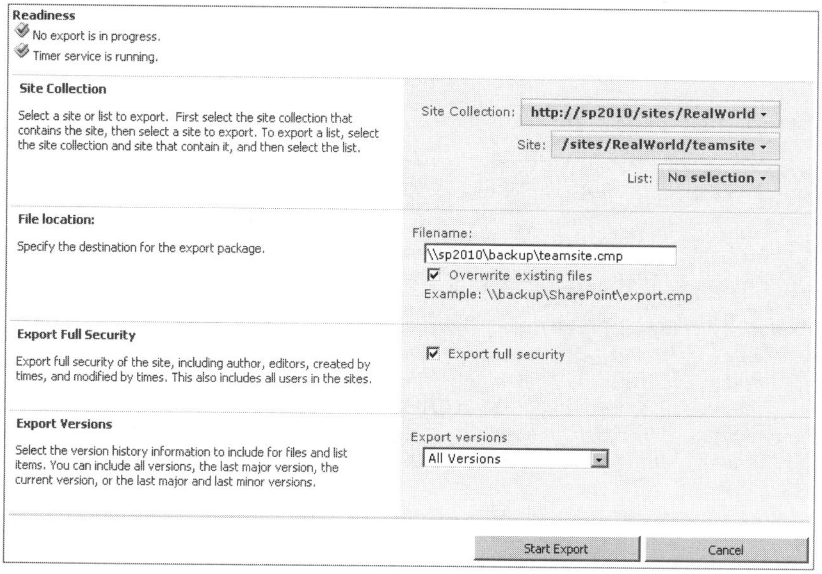

Readiness
- No export is in progress.
- Timer service is running.

Site Collection

Select a site or list to export. First select the site collection that contains the site, then select a site to export. To export a list, select the site collection and site that contain it, and then select the list.

Site Collection: `http://sp2010/sites/RealWorld ▾`

Site: `/sites/RealWorld/teamsite ▾`

List: `No selection ▾`

File location:

Specify the destination for the export package.

Filename:
`\\sp2010\backup\teamsite.cmp`
☑ Overwrite existing files
Example: \\backup\SharePoint\export.cmp

Export Full Security

Export full security of the site, including author, editors, created by times, and modified by times. This also includes all users in the sites.

☑ Export full security

Export Versions

Select the version history information to include for files and list items. You can include all versions, the last major version, the current version, or the last major and last minor versions.

Export versions
`All Versions ▾`

[Start Export]   [Cancel]

FIGURE 6-7: Exporting a website using Central Administration

Clicking Start Export creates a timer job and redirects you to the granular backup job status screen. Here you can see the status of the current backup jobs, and this page will automatically refresh every 30 seconds. The export will be shown in the lower half of the screen where it says Content Export, as shown in Figure 6-8.

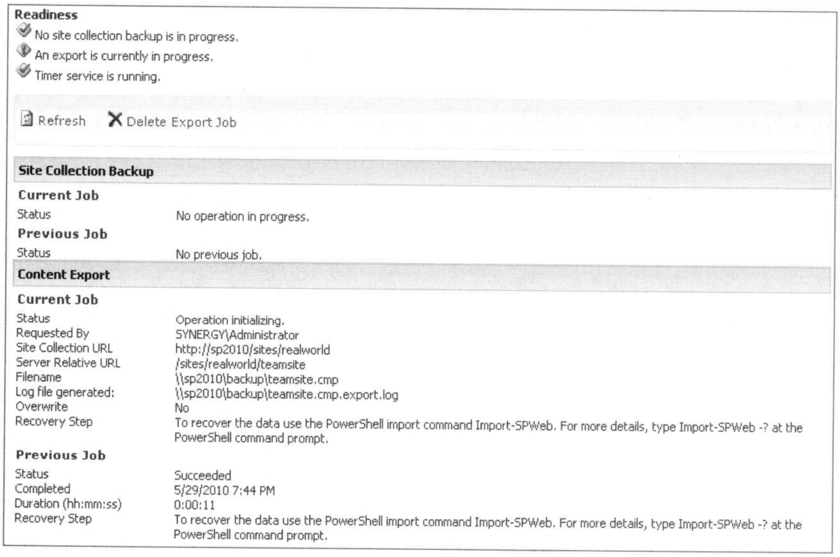

Readiness
- No site collection backup is in progress.
- An export is currently in progress.
- Timer service is running.

🔃 Refresh   ✖ Delete Export Job

Site Collection Backup

Current Job
Status   No operation in progress.
Previous Job
Status   No previous job.

Content Export

Current Job
Status   Operation initializing.
Requested By   SYNERGY\Administrator
Site Collection URL   http://sp2010/sites/realworld
Server Relative URL   /sites/realworld/teamsite
Filename   \\sp2010\backup\teamsite.cmp
Log file generated: \\sp2010\backup\teamsite.cmp.export.log
Overwrite   No
Recovery Step   To recover the data use the PowerShell import command Import-SPWeb. For more details, type Import-SPWeb -? at the PowerShell command prompt.

Previous Job
Status   Succeeded
Completed   5/29/2010 7:44 PM
Duration (hh:mm:ss)   0:00:11
Recovery Step   To recover the data use the PowerShell import command Import-SPWeb. For more details, type Import-SPWeb -? at the PowerShell command prompt.

FIGURE 6-8: Granular backup job status

To run an `export` command from `STSADM`, use the `-o export` operation. Here is the basic syntax:

```
STSADM -o export -url <url> -filename <filename>
```

Here is a more complete form that matches the same export run from Central Administration:

```
STSADM -o export -url http://sp2010/sites/RealWorld/teamsite -filename
    \\sp2010\backup\teamsite.cmp -includeusersecurity -versions 4
```

To run an `export` command from PowerShell, use the `Export-SPWeb` cmdlet. As you would expect, it provides the most flexibility. Here is the complete syntax:

```
Export-SPWeb [-Identity] <SPWebPipeBind> -Path <String> [-AssignmentCollection
    <SPAssignmentCollection>] [-CompressionSize <Int32>]
    [-Confirm [<SwitchParameter>]] [-Force <SwitchParameter>]
    [-HaltOnError <SwitchParameter>] [-HaltOnWarning <SwitchParameter>]
    [-IncludeUserSecurity <SwitchParameter>]
    [-IncludeVersions <LastMajor | CurrentVersion | LastMajorAndMinor | All>]
    [-ItemUrl <String>] [-NoFileCompression <SwitchParameter>]
    [-NoLogFile <SwitchParameter>] [-UseSqlSnapshot <SwitchParameter>]
    [-WhatIf [<SwitchParameter>]] [<CommonParameters>]
```

Take a look at many of the important switches through a few examples. Start with the simplest form that just exports a website hierarchy with no options specified:

```
Export-SPWeb http://sp2010/sites/RealWorld/teamsite -path
    \\sp2010\backup\teamsite.cmp
```

If you want to just export the Shared Documents document library, use the `-ItemUrl` option, as shown here:

```
Export-SPWeb http://sp2010/sites/RealWorld/teamsite -path \\sp2010\backup\
    teamsite.cmp -ItemUrl "Shared Documents"
```

If you want to include user security (which includes users, groups, and the item created and last modified timestamps), use the `-IncludeUserSecurity` switch, as shown here:

```
Export-SPWeb http://sp2010/sites/RealWorld/teamsite -path \\sp2010\backup\
    teamsite.cmp -IncludeUserSecurity
```

When it comes to preserving item versions, you have four different choices for the `-IncludeVersions` option. In following example, all major and minor versions for all list items are being preserved. This also overwrites the previous backup file, if one exists.

```
Export-SPWeb http://sp2010/sites/RealWorld/teamsite -path \\sp2010\backup\
    teamsite.cmp -IncludeVersions All -force
```

If the backup size exceeds 25 MB, you might want to adjust `CompressionSize` to prevent the backup from spanning across multiple files. If you do get multiple files in your export, you must ensure that all files are present in order to do an import. The following example adjusts the maximum size of a single file to 100 MB:

```
Export-SPWeb http://sp2010/sites/RealWorld/teamsite -path \\sp2010\backup\
    teamsite.cmp -CompressionSize 100000000
```

Performing an Import

To import websites and lists that have been exported, you can use STSADM or PowerShell. The import process is very different from the site collection restore, so this section examines these important distinctions first before looking at the syntax.

When you import a website, the top-level website with a matching site definition must already exist at the destination URL. For example, suppose you exported the five project websites shown in Figure 6-6. When you import these to a new location, you must ensure that a website for Projects already exists, and it must be based on the same site definition (for example, team site, blank site, meeting workspace, and so on). There doesn't need to be any content in it, so you can literally just create a new website prior to the import.

SharePoint can automatically create the descendant websites (Project A, Project B, Blog, and so on), but you must create the top-level one. If descendant websites do already exist, they must also match the site definition of the corresponding website. In this way, you can think of the import as being more like a merge operation than a pure restore.

When importing from a list, if the list does not exist, it will be created using the same list template as the source. If the list does exist, it must be the same template.

This merge concept has some great benefits. Say that you export only a single website, such as Project A. Then, say that several files in a document library are deleted. You can run an import operation from the original export, and SharePoint restores the files that were deleted. New files that were added after the export are not disturbed, so you have effectively just restored the missing files.

STSADM provides a number of options when importing, but here is the basic syntax:

```
STSADM -o import -url <url> -filename <filename>
```

To use PowerShell to import, the cmdlet is Import-SPWeb. Like STSADM, it also has many options. Here is the full syntax:

```
Import-SPWeb [-Identity] <SPWebPipeBind> -Path <String>
    [-ActivateSolutions <SwitchParameter>]
    [-AssignmentCollection <SPAssignmentCollection>]
    [-Confirm [<SwitchParameter>]]
    [-Force <SwitchParameter>] [-HaltOnError <SwitchParameter>]
    [-HaltOnWarning <SwitchParameter>] [-IncludeUserCustomAction <None | All>]
    [-IncludeUserSecurity <SwitchParameter>]
    [-NoFileCompression <SwitchParameter>]
    [-NoLogFile <SwitchParameter>] [-UpdateVersions
    <Append | Overwrite | Ignore>]
    [-WhatIf [<SwitchParameter>]] [<CommonParameters>]
```

Using the UpdateVersions switch allows you to define how version updates are applied. If you want to only restore files that were deleted, you can use the following form to ignore files that already exist:

```
Import-SPWeb http://sp2010/sites/RealWorld/teamsite -Path \\sp2010\backup\
    teamsite.cmp -UpdateVersions Ignore
```

To preserve the security information (including item created and last modified timestamps), use the `IncludeUserSecurity`, just like with the `Export-SPWeb` cmdlet.

```
Import-SPWeb http://sp2010/sites/RealWorld/teamsite -Path \\sp2010\backup\
        teamsite.cmp -IncludeUserSecurity
```

Unlike a site collection backup, log files for the import and export operations are stored in the same folder as the backup file(s). These text files are quite verbose and, hence, may be large. The most important area to notice are the last two lines where warning and error totals are displayed.

> *In SharePoint Designer 2007, commands existed that you could use to back up and restore websites using this same export/import design. There were numerous problems with this. In particular, a 25 MB size limit was a real pain. In SharePoint Designer 2010, this feature is no longer present.*

Farm Backups

Now that you understand granular backups, it's time to focus on farm backups. *Farm backups* come in many forms, such as complete farm, configuration-only, individual web applications, individual Content Databases, individual service applications, and others. This variety of farm backups makes them fairly granular as well. It's just that the unit of backup isn't at a low level such as a site collection or website, but at a higher, more encompassing one.

For a number of important reasons, farm backups must be a part of your backup strategy. If you back up nothing else, just make farm backups and you'll be fairly well-protected. With improvements in SharePoint 2010, you can use farm backups to recover from virtually any recovery scenario. Whether your recovery needs span from a single list to the whole farm, and anywhere in between, you'll see that farm backups have you covered.

> *Farm backups also ensure that the transaction log files for your SQL Server databases are regularly truncated. This will prevent runaway log files from eating up all the space on your SQL Server!*

Performing a Farm Backup

The easiest type of backup to run is the complete farm. As the term implies, it is the most complete backup form, and it gives you the most restore choices. A complete farm backup can be issued from Central Administration, `STSADM`, or PowerShell.

First take a look at how it works from Central Administration. You perform the backup by first clicking Perform a Backup from the top-level Central Administration screen, or from the Backup and Restore screen shown in Figure 6-3. You are then presented with a tree view that gives you all the options for your farm backup. In Figure 6-9, some of the categories have been collapsed and then the Farm component has been checked, which automatically selects all sub-components, yielding a complete farm backup.

Readiness

- No backup or restore in progress. Backup and Restore Job Status
- Timer service is running.
- Administration service is running.

Select component to back up

Select the top-level component to back up. You can also click the name of a Web application to browse its contents.

Select	Component	Type	Description
☑	⊟ Farm	Farm	Content and configuration data for the entire server farm.
	SP_Farm_Config	Configuration Database	Configuration data for the entire server farm.
☑	⊞ Solutions	Solutions	Collection custom solutions.
☑	⊞ InfoPath Forms Services	Server Settings and Content	Administrator-approved content and settings for the server farm.
☑	⊞ SharePoint Server State Service	State Service	Service for storage of temporary state information used by various SharePoint Server features.
☑	⊞ Microsoft SharePoint Foundation Web Application	Microsoft SharePoint Foundation Web Application	Collection of Web Applications
	⊞ WSS_Administration	Central Administration	Collection of Web Applications
☑	⊞ SharePoint Server State Service Proxy	State Service Proxy	
☑	⊞ SPUserCodeV4	Microsoft SharePoint Foundation Sandboxed Code Service	Settings for the Sandboxed Code Service.
	Microsoft SharePoint Server Diagnostics Service	Microsoft SharePoint Server Diagnostics Service	Settings for the diagnostics service.
☑	Global Search Settings	Search object in configuration database	Crawler impact rules for the farm
☑	Application Registry Service	Application Registry Service	Backwards compatible Business Data Connectivity API.
	Microsoft Office Web Apps Diagnostics Service	Microsoft Office Web Apps Diagnostics Service	Settings for the diagnostics service.
	Microsoft SQL Server Reporting Services Diagnostics Service	Microsoft SQL Server Reporting Services Diagnostics Service	Settings for the diagnostics service.
	Microsoft SharePoint Foundation Diagnostics Service	Microsoft SharePoint Foundation Diagnostics Service	Settings for the diagnostics service.
☑	⊞ Shared Services	Shared Services	Shared Services of the server farm.

[Next]   [Cancel]

FIGURE 6-9: Specifying a complete farm backup

After you click Next, you have a few other choices. One is that you can specify whether this is a full or differential backup. To choose differential, you should have already have run a full backup. Like typical differential backups, it captures the only changes that were made since the last full backup. Not every component supports differential backups, but all database backups do. If a component doesn't support a differential backup, you'll just get a full backup for that component instead.

You can also specify whether to back up all content and configuration settings, or just configuration settings. The configuration-only backup was discussed earlier in the section, "What's New in 2010."

Lastly, specify a folder location where the backup will be stored. For a farm backup, it is imperative to use a UNC path (for example, \\backupserver\sharepoint), rather than a local one (for example, e:\backup). This is because your SQL Servers will be issuing backups of their content and service application databases, and they will all be writing directly to this network share. To ensure that the backup succeeds, make sure that the service accounts that are running the SQL Server engine services have read/write permissions to both the share and NTFS folders.

> *If your SQL Server engine service (*MSSQLSERVER *or* MSSQL$InstanceName*) is running under a local system account, you should grant permissions to the machine account instead. This machine account is* domain\servername$*, where servername is the NetBIOS computer name of the SQL Server (for example,* domain\sqlprod01$*).*

Figure 6-10 shows the configuration options chosen for this example of a complete farm backup.

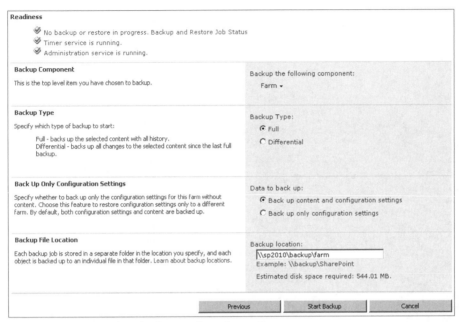

FIGURE 6-10: Setting farm backup configuration options

After you click Start Backup, as you have now seen, a timer job is created and you are taken to the job status screen. How long the backup takes depends on several factors, including the size of your Content Databases, the speed of your farm servers (in particular, the SQL Servers), and the speed of the network in between the farm servers and the UNC share. Despite possibly taking several hours to run, it is, by far, faster in megabytes per second than a site collection backup, making this the recommended backup type to run in terms of performance.

Now that you have seen the complete farm backup, take a look at some other granular options that Central Administration provides for farm backups. Going back to the farm backup options in Figure 6-9, instead of selecting the whole farm, you can instead select any other component that is shown. For example, you can choose to just back up all solution packages, or all web applications, or just a single service application like the User Profile Service application. Figure 6-11 shows the selection of a single web application named "SharePoint - 80."

It is important to note that you can select only one component per backup job. If it is a parent node (such as a web application), all nodes within this hierarchy are also automatically selected. In other words, you are unable to back up, for example, just two of the four Content Databases in a web application. Similarly, you are unable to only back up just the solutions and service applications. To do this, you would need to run two backup jobs. This limitation also extends to STSADM and PowerShell farm backups, so it's not just Central Administration.

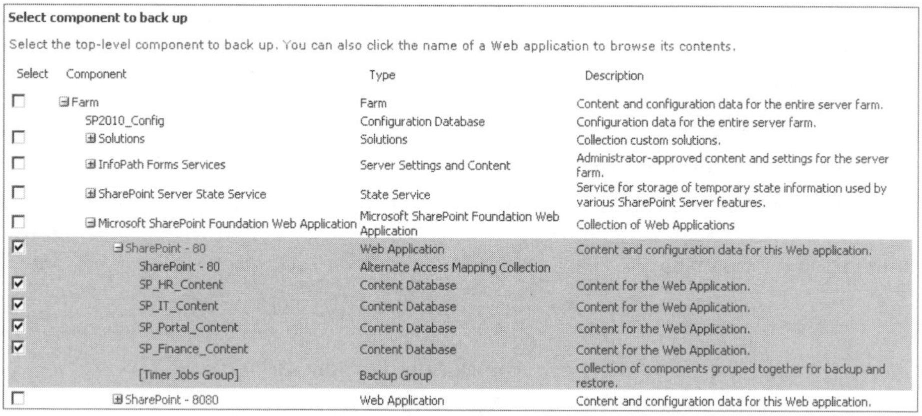

FIGURE 6-11: Backing up a single web application

Now that you have a basic understanding of farm backups, you can see how they work with the command-line tools STSADM and PowerShell. Knowing how to perform backups this way is essential, because there is no scheduling engine for Central Administration backups.

Using STSADM, you can perform a complete farm backup by using a different form of the backup operation you learned about in the discussion of site collection backups earlier in this chapter. Here is the basic syntax for a farm backup:

```
STSADM -o backup -directory <UNC path> -backupmethod <full | differential>
```

Thus, to run a complete farm backup equivalent to the one shown in Figure 6-10, here is the proper syntax:

```
STSADM -o backup -directory \\sp2010\backup\farm -backupmethod full
```

You can also specify individual component items to back up. The following code snippet backs up just a single Content Database:

```
STSADM -o backup -directory \\sp2010\backup\farm -backupmethod full
    -item SP_Portal_Content
```

PowerShell is equally easy to use when running farm backups. The cmdlet that you use is Backup-SPFarm. It can be run two different ways. First look at the complete syntax for both:

```
Backup-SPFarm -BackupMethod <String> -Directory <String> [-AssignmentCollection
    <SPAssignmentCollection>] [-BackupThreads <Int32>]
    [-ConfigurationOnly <SwitchParameter>] [-Confirm [<SwitchParameter>]]
    [-Force <SwitchParameter>] [-Item <String>]
    [-Percentage <Int32>] [-WhatIf [<SwitchParameter>]] [<CommonParameters>]

Backup-SPFarm -ShowTree <SwitchParameter> [-AssignmentCollection <
    SPAssignmentCollection>] [-ConfigurationOnly <SwitchParameter>]
    [-Confirm [<SwitchParameter>]] [-Item <String>]
    [-WhatIf [<SwitchParameter>]] [<CommonParameters>]
```

The purpose of the first `Backup-SPFarm` form is to actually perform a complete farm or single component backup. The second one (with the `-ShowTree` option) is used to enumerate all of the components that can be individually backed up. This list matches what Central Administration displays in the tree view shown in Figure 6-9.

Here is the syntax for a basic, but complete, farm backup:

```
Backup-SPFarm -BackupMethod full -Directory \\sp2010\backup\farm
```

Here is a configuration-only backup:

```
Backup-SPFarm -BackupMethod full -Directory \\sp2010\backup\farm -ConfigurationOnly
```

Here is a backup of just the User Profile Service Application component:

```
Backup-SPFarm -BackupMethod full -Directory \\sp2010\backup\farm
      -item "User Profile Service Application"
```

The following will show the tree of all components that can be individually backed up:

```
Backup-SPFarm -ShowTree
```

To define the number of threads used for the backup, use the `BackupThreads` option. This will cause multiple backup tasks to be done in parallel, possibly increasing the overall backup speed. The downside is that the more threads that you use, the more difficult it is to interpret the log file, because many operations are all writing concurrently to the file, affecting the normal sequence you'd expect to see. The default number of threads is 3.

```
Backup-SPFarm -BackupMethod full -Directory \\sp2010\backup\farm -BackupThreads 5
```

Understanding Farm Backup Sets

Before examining how to restore from a farm backup, spend some time understanding how these backup sets are organized and stored. This becomes very helpful when you want to do an unattached Content Database restore.

As you have seen, when you run a farm backup from Central Administration, STSADM, or PowerShell, you specify a UNC folder for the backup location. In this folder, SharePoint creates and maintains an XML file named SPBRTOC.XML that stores the history for each backup set. It contains useful details such as the start and finish time, the backup type (full or differential), the folder where the backup is stored, and other information. Here is how one entry looks for a complete farm backup:

```
<SPHistoryObject>
  <SPId>9ce00db8-3862-49e1-a25a-caf18d92b875</SPId>
  <SPParentID>7b556ff7-0b5f-429e-baaf-01ed67c49fd8</SPParentID>
  <SPRequestedBy>SAP\administrator</SPRequestedBy>
  <SPBackupMethod>Full</SPBackupMethod>
  <SPRestoreMethod>None</SPRestoreMethod>
  <SPStartTime>04/28/2010 14:28:57</SPStartTime>
  <SPFinishTime>04/28/2010 15:03:05</SPFinishTime>
  <SPIsBackup>True</SPIsBackup>
  <SPConfigurationOnly>False</SPConfigurationOnly>
```

```
    <SPBackupDirectory>\\sp2010\backup\farm\spbr0002\</SPBackupDirectory>
    <SPDirectoryName>spbr0002</SPDirectoryName>
    <SPDirectoryNumber>2</SPDirectoryNumber>
    <SPTopComponent>Farm</SPTopComponent>
    <SPTopComponentId>0d9c1711-68be-4372-83d2-442145a5af24</SPTopComponentId>
    <SPWarningCount>0</SPWarningCount>
    <SPErrorCount>0</SPErrorCount>
  </SPHistoryObject>
```

As shown here, the SPBackupDirectory node points to the folder where this backup set is stored. In this case, the folder is spbr0002. Incidentally, the naming convention is elementary — it starts at spbr0000, then increments to spbr0001, and continues on. Take a look into one of these folders to get a closer look at how each backup is stored.

In here you'll find a bunch of .bak files. Some of these are XML-based, some of these are database backups, and some are just unreadable binary files. In addition, you'll find two important text files, spbackup.log and spbackup.xml. The .log file is simply the detailed log file for that backup set. It can be a bit difficult to read, especially if you are using a lot of backup threads. However, the last part is easy to read and contains a summary, along with every component item (for example, a Content Database) in the tree, and whether or not it was backed up. To know if a component item is part of the backup set, look for an asterisk next to it. If you see an asterisk, it tells you that this item is not included in the backup, and cannot be restored.

The spbackup.xml file is also very useful and provides great detail about each and every object in the backup. The Content Database backups are likely to be the most practical. In Figure 6-12, you can see the Content Database SP_Portal_Content, which corresponds to the file 000000E0.bak.

```
- <SPBackupObject Name="SP_Portal_Content">
    <SPBackupRestoreClass>Microsoft.SharePoint.Administration.SPContentDatab
    PublicKeyToken=71e9bce111e9429c</SPBackupRestoreClass>
    <SPBackupSelectable>True</SPBackupSelectable>
    <SPRestoreSelectable>True</SPRestoreSelectable>
    <SPName>SP_Portal_Content</SPName>
    <SPId>187f3de5-a955-4bbb-8749-1150e3206b14</SPId>
    <SPCanBackup>True</SPCanBackup>
    <SPCanRestore>True</SPCanRestore>
    <SPCurrentProgress>100</SPCurrentProgress>
    <SPLastUpdate>04/28/2010 14:50:24</SPLastUpdate>
    <SPCurrentPhase>Done</SPCurrentPhase>
  - <SPParameters>
    - <SPParameter Key="187f3de5-a955-4bbb-8749-1150e3206b14STATE.xml">
        <![CDATA[ 00000023.bak ]]>
      </SPParameter>
    - <SPParameter Key="dcsql:SP_Portal_Content.dat">
        <![CDATA[ 000000E0.bak ]]>
      </SPParameter>
    - <SPParameter Key="InstanceId">
        <![CDATA[ 36e5fd47-005f-4a06-a1de-077194f940af ]]>
      </SPParameter>
    - <SPParameter Key="ServerId">
        <![CDATA[ a0d33f19-ac0d-41d2-820a-4a4cd8647c46 ]]>
      </SPParameter>
    - <SPParameter Key="SPDescription">
        <![CDATA[ Content for the Web Application. ]]>
      </SPParameter>
```

FIGURE 6-12: Examining the backup for a Content Database

This is useful because, with this knowledge, you can easily restore just a single database from a complete farm backup. By restoring the database, you can then use SharePoint's unattended Content Database recovery to extract any bit of content you want — from a site collection, to websites, even a list. This provides a great deal of flexibility, provided you have made a complete farm backup. You see how to do this later in this chapter during the examination of various recovery scenarios.

Scripting Your Backups

As mentioned previously, Central Administration is not capable of scheduling backups. You also know how important farm backups are for recovery, so you really need to have some automated backup system in place. Some organizations choose to use good-old Windows Task Scheduler for their scheduling needs. If you have another scheduling engine that works, feel free to use that instead.

The following PowerShell script will not only run the farm backup, it will also delete old backup sets for you. This is useful so that you can better manage the amount of space used. There are two initial parameters ($days and $backupFolder) that you'll want to adjust. Here is the full script:

```
#FarmBackupScript.ps1

Add-PsSnapin Microsoft.SharePoint.PowerShell

# Parameter: Days of backup that should be retained
$days = 7

# Parameter: Backup Folder
$backupFolder = "\\sp2010\backup"

# Run complete backup.
#Backup-SPFarm -BackupMethod full -Directory $backupFolder

# Archive older backup sets

# Location of TOC
$spbrtoc = $backupFolder + "\spbrtoc.xml"

# Import the Sharepoint backup report xml file
[xml]$sp = gc $spbrtoc

# Find backup sets in TOC
$archive = $sp.SPBackupRestoreHistory.SPHistoryObject | ? { $_.SPStartTime -lt
    ((get-date).adddays(-$days)) }
if ($archive -eq $Null) { write-host "No backups older than
    $days days found" ; break}

# Delete the old backups from the Sharepoint backup report xml file
$archive | % { $sp.SPBackupRestoreHistory.RemoveChild($_) }

# Delete the physical folders in which the old backups were located
$archive | % { Remove-Item $_.SPBackupDirectory -recurse }

# Save the revised backup TOC
$sp.Save($spbrtoc)
```

```
Write-host "Backup(s) entries older than $days days have been removed
        from spbrtoc.xml and $backupFolder"
```

Code file [FarmBackupScript.ps1] available for download at Wrox.com

To automate it, first save the script into a file named `FarmBackupScript.ps1`. A common practice is to typically put scripts like this into a scripts folder such as `d:\scripts`. Then, just create a new scheduled task using Task Scheduler, as shown in Figure 6-13.

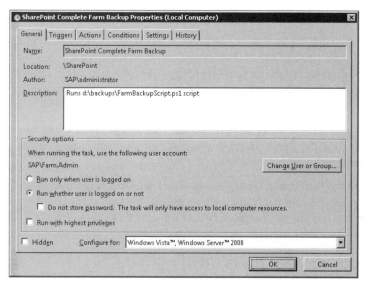

FIGURE 6-13: Farm backup scheduled task

Following are the important settings for the task:

➤ Use your farm admin account to run the task. If you're not sure which account this is, it is the identity of your SharePoint 2010 Timer service.

➤ Run the task whether or not the user is logged in.

➤ Under the Triggers tab, choose the schedule that best fits your recovery objectives. If possible, try to run a complete farm backup at least weekly. You might consider running multiple jobs, one for a weekly farm, and one for a daily differential. Running a farm backup will introduce a load on your servers, so schedule this during off-peak hours.

➤ Under the Actions tab, start a program. The program is `PowerShell.exe`. For arguments, provide the path to the previous script (for example, `d:\backups\FarmBackupScript.ps1`).

➤ Adjust the settings under the Conditions and Settings tabs as appropriate for your environment. I usually leave these unchanged.

If you are using a combination of full and differential backups, ensure that the $days parameter in the script goes back far enough to include your last full backup. For example, if you're scheduling weekly backups, do not set your $days variable to anything less than 7. A differential backup is useless without the full backup.

Performing a Farm Restore

Though we all hope we never have to do a farm restore, we must be prepared in the event that a farm disaster occurs. Additionally, performing a farm restore is a common way to duplicate your farm into a separate environment, such as for test or development purposes. Fortunately, with the farm's configuration preserved in the backup, the effort in recovering your farm with SharePoint 2010 is much easier than with prior versions of SharePoint.

This section walks you through the steps using Central Administration, and introduces the basic syntax using STSADM and PowerShell. Later in this chapter, you learn about other recovery issues you must consider within the context of different recovery scenarios.

In most cases, you should do farm restores using Central Administration. This is because these are usually one-time operations, and, depending on the type of restore, it is very difficult to accurately key in all the settings from the command prompt. After walking through the steps for a farm restore, you'll see what I mean.

In Central Administration, you perform a farm restore by using the Restore from a Backup link from the Farm Backup and Restore category shown in Figure 6-3. This starts a three-step wizard.

The first step is to select the backup set you want to restore. If you don't see the backup you want, ensure that the backup directory location is set correctly. Incidentally, all this screen is doing is reading from the spbrtoc.xml file found in the backup location.

In the second step, it reads the details for that backup and displays a tree view of what can be recovered. Just like a backup, when restoring, you can select only a single component per restore job. When you restore, however, you can restore just a subset of what you backed up. For example, if you did a complete farm backup, you could restore any individual component (or component hierarchy), such as a single web application and all of its Content Databases.

In the third step, you must provide SharePoint with a number of details as to how the farm restore should be done. Depending on how complex your environment is, this may be a very large screen. Figure 6-14 shows the top portion of what is asked.

As you can see, the whole farm including content, or just the farm configuration, can be restored. You also must specify whether you will be restoring to the same environment or a new one. If you are performing an actual recovery and will be using the same SQL Server and application server names, you can choose Same Configuration. You would choose New Configuration if anything has changed, or you are restoring into a different environment.

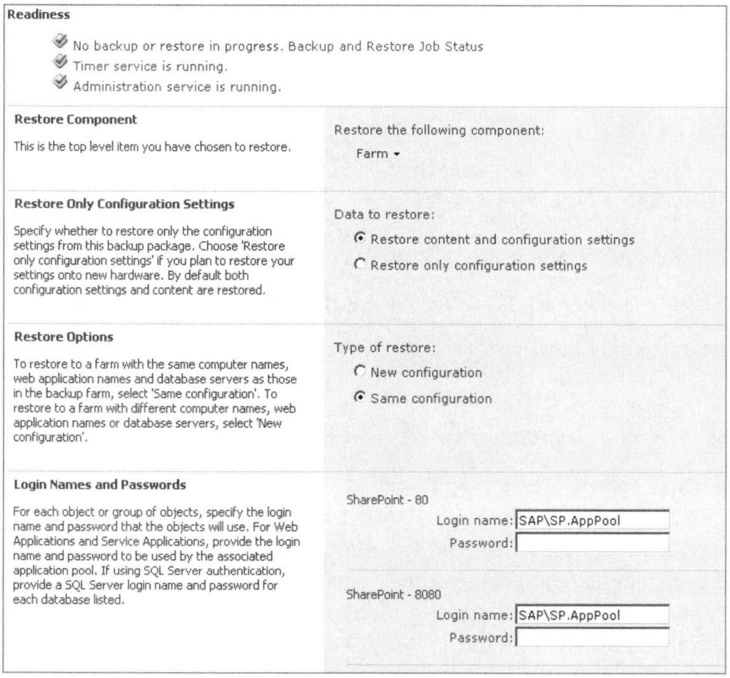

Readiness

- No backup or restore in progress. Backup and Restore Job Status
- Timer service is running.
- Administration service is running.

Restore Component

This is the top level item you have chosen to restore.

Restore the following component:

Farm ▾

Restore Only Configuration Settings

Specify whether to restore only the configuration settings from this backup package. Choose 'Restore only configuration settings' if you plan to restore your settings onto new hardware. By default both configuration settings and content are restored.

Data to restore:

- ⦿ Restore content and configuration settings
- ○ Restore only configuration settings

Restore Options

To restore to a farm with the same computer names, web application names and database servers as those in the backup farm, select 'Same configuration'. To restore to a farm with different computer names, web application names or database servers, select 'New configuration'.

Type of restore:

- ○ New configuration
- ⦿ Same configuration

Login Names and Passwords

For each object or group of objects, specify the login name and password that the objects will use. For Web Applications and Service Applications, provide the login name and password to be used by the associated application pool. If using SQL Server authentication, provide a SQL Server login name and password for each database listed.

SharePoint - 80

Login name: SAP\SP.AppPool

Password:

SharePoint - 8080

Login name: SAP\SP.AppPool

Password:

FIGURE 6-14: Selecting farm restore options

Next, you will need to supply the current passwords for the application pool accounts that were in use. For security reasons, the passwords for these managed accounts are not included in the backup. If you don't know the password, or if it was automatically changed, just reset it within Active Directory and enter it here.

If you chose New Configuration for the restore, you then need to adjust all of the database directory names, database names, and SQL Server names for your web and service applications. Initially, these are filled out with what was in use on the farm at the time of backup. If you are restoring a Search application, you will also need to specify local paths and server names for query partitions. This data-entry part becomes very tedious if you are using STSADM or PowerShell to restore the farm, so having a graphical interface is much easier to work with, and less error-prone.

 Before you start the restore, double- and triple-check your settings. The restore may take hours, or even longer, and you don't want to find out after the fact that a small setting was wrong.

As you have seen before, a restore job is created, and you are taken to the job status screen, which auto-refreshes. If this is a complete farm restore, do not be alarmed if you receive an IIS error somewhere during the restore during a screen refresh. This is normal, because, during the farm recovery,

IIS application pools are being created. Wait a minute or two and refresh the screen to get it to redisplay.

Now look how command-line tools can also be used to restore the farm. To restore a farm using STSADM, here is the basic syntax you use:

```
STSADM -o restore -directory <UNC> -restoremethod <overwrite | new>
    [-backupid <GUID>] [-item <from showtree>]
```

You have a number of other options as well. See STSADM -help restore to see all of them.

To restore a farm using PowerShell, use the Restore-SPFarm cmdlet. Here is the basic syntax:

```
Restore-SPFarm -Directory <UNC> -RestoreMethod <overwrite | new>
    [-BackupId <GUID>] [-Item <from showtree>]
```

To see all the other options, use get-help Restore-SPFarm.

When using STSADM or PowerShell to restore a farm, the BackupId value is the backup GUID found in the <SPId> element in the spbrtoc.xml file. overwrite means you want to restore to the same configuration, and new means you want to restore to a new configuration. The Item parameter tells SharePoint what component of the farm backup gets restored. This can be determined by looking at the spbackup.xml file (see the Name attribute of the SPBackupObject element), or just by using the -showtree option when running the restore command.

During the restore process, you will be prompted for various input that is needed. This is the same as when you used Central Administration. If you are using the new restoremethod type, expect to be prompted repeatedly for database names, server names, and so on.

RECOVERY SCENARIOS

Now that you have learned about each type of backup and how to restore, in this section you see how to practically apply this to a number of common recovery scenarios. This section looks at item-level recovery, site collection recovery, Content Database recovery, and, the big one, farm disaster recovery. As you will see, having a complete farm backup is your best protection to recover from each of these situations.

Item-Level Recovery

If your RLO requires you to provide item-level recovery, unfortunately, SharePoint 2010 does not have a built-in way to do this. However, a number of ways exist to address the problem.

One way is to use the unattached Content Database restore, which is what is examined here. Following are the three steps you go through to recover a single document:

1. Restore the Content Database from your complete farm backup.

2. Point SharePoint to this database and perform a list export.

3. Import this list into a temporary website to extract the file.

For Step 1, first identify the specific Content Database in which this file is stored. If you're not sure which one, you can look at the URL to identify the managed path. From here, go into View All Site Collections from the Application Management menu.

Once you know the Content Database, review the backup set you want (`spbrtoc.xml` file). Then, go into the backup folder and look at the `spbackup.xml` file. This will tell you which `.bak` file in the backup folder needs to be restored. Details on this were discussed earlier in the section, "Understanding Farm Backup Sets."

When restoring, you can restore to any SQL Server, provided that SharePoint can connect to it on the network. If you are going to restore to the same SQL Server that is hosting the live Content Database, be very careful to ensure that you restore under a different database name.

 For specific steps on how to restore a database using SQL Server Management Studio, see `http://msdn.microsoft.com/en-us/library/ms177429.aspx`.

For Step 2, use Central Administration. From the Backup and Restore menu shown in Figure 6-3, select Recover Data from an Unattached Content Database in the Granular Backup section. Figure 6-15 shows the screen you then see.

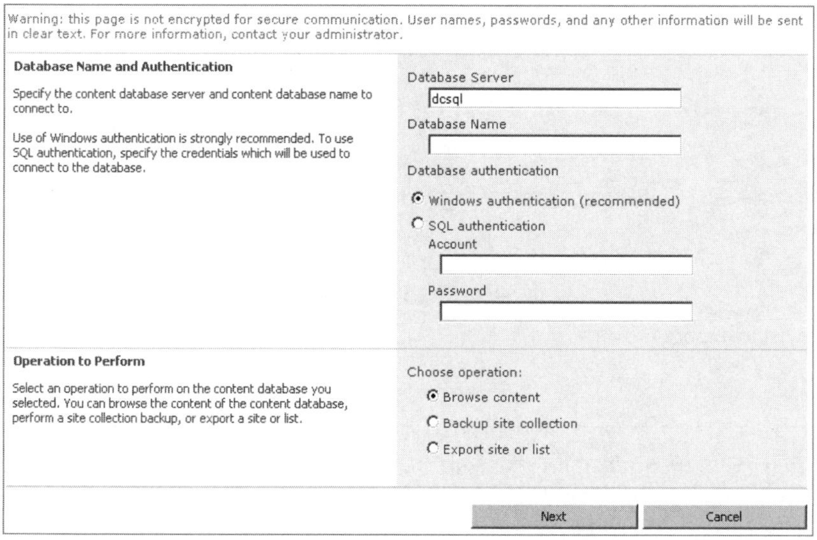

Warning: this page is not encrypted for secure communication. User names, passwords, and any other information will be sent in clear text. For more information, contact your administrator.

Database Name and Authentication

Specify the content database server and content database name to connect to.

Use of Windows authentication is strongly recommended. To use SQL authentication, specify the credentials which will be used to connect to the database.

Database Server
`dcsql`

Database Name

Database authentication

⦿ Windows authentication (recommended)
○ SQL authentication
Account

Password

Operation to Perform

Select an operation to perform on the content database you selected. You can browse the content of the content database, perform a site collection backup, or export a site or list.

Choose operation:

⦿ Browse content
○ Backup site collection
○ Export site or list

[Next]   [Cancel]

FIGURE 6-15: Unattached Content Database recovery

From here, just enter in the SQL Server and database name, and choose Export Site or List, shown toward the bottom of Figure 6-15. This might seem odd, because you are trying to restore a file, yet SharePoint is asking you to export. This is necessary, because SharePoint is not capable of directly importing (or restoring) from this unattached Content Database. So, you must first export the list from the unattached database, and you can then import into an attached one. Click Next to continue.

 If you use Windows authentication, the farm administrator account will be used to connect, so ensure that this account has a SQL Server login on the server. This login must also have a user account in the newly restored database with db_owner *role membership.*

In the next screen, browse to the site collection, website, and list where the document is located. Then, specify the path to where the export should be stored. Figure 6-16 shows you how this looks.

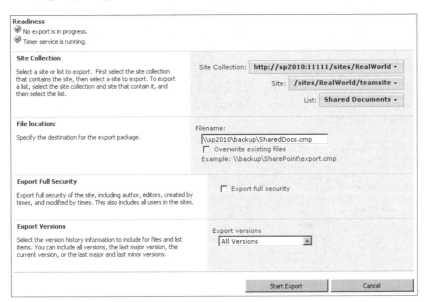

FIGURE 6-16: Selecting a list to export

 Another oddity is the web application that is displayed on the screen. If you look at Figure 6-16 again, you'll see that the web application displayed is http://sp2010:11111. *This is not the web application where this Content Database was located; it's the Central Administration web application. SharePoint does this because it doesn't know which web application this Content Database was attached to. Don't let this confuse you. Just focus on the managed path portion only (*/sites/RealWorld *in this example).*

When you click the Start Export button, a timer job will be created, and the export operation will start. You must wait for the job to finish before you proceed to Step 3.

For Step 3, just run an `Import-SPWeb` PowerShell command. In this example, you first create a website named `tempsite` to temporarily hold the document library you'll be importing. The following shows how you would restore the library:

```
Import-SPWeb http://sp2010/sites/RealWorld/tempsite -Path \\sp2010\backup\
    SharedDocs.cmp -UpdateVersions Overwrite
```

After this is done, just move or copy this file back into the original document library. After you have confirmed the recovery is successful, you can remove the restored SQL database and temporary website because they are no longer needed.

The process to recover a website is very similar to these steps. The only difference is that you are selecting the website instead of a list. Remember, however, that it will export and import this website and all descendant websites (that is, the whole hierarchy).

 For more seamless item-level recovery, you might want to consider using AvePoint's DocAve Recovery Manager. It is free, and makes this type of recovery much easier. See http://www.avepoint.com/docave-recovery-manager -for-sharepoint.

Site-Collection Recovery

You can also use unattached Content Database recovery for site collection recovery, and the steps are very similar to item-level recovery. In this scenario, follow these three steps:

1. Restore the Content Database from your complete farm backup.

2. Point SharePoint to this database and perform a site collection backup.

3. Restore the site collection back into the original web application.

I won't spend time walking you through these, because you have already learned how to do each of them. Instead, the following PowerShell script will help automate the second step and third step:

```
# Backup the site collection from the Unattached content database
Get-SPContentDatabase -ConnectAsUnattachedDatabase
    -DatabaseName SP_Portal_Content_Temp -DatabaseServer dcsql |
    Get-SPSite -limit all | where {$_.Url -like "*/sites/RealWorld"} |
    Backup-SPSite -Path \\sp2010\backup\realworld.bak

# Restore the site collection and overwrite the current one
Restore-SPSite http://sp2010/sites/RealWorld -Path
    \\sp2010\backup\realworld.bak -force
```

For this script, following are the values that you'll need to replace with your own settings.

➤ `SP_Portal_Content_Temp` refers to the unattached content database that you have restored from Step 1.

➤ `dcsql` is the name of your SQL Server.

➤ `*/sites/RealWorld` is the name of the site collection found in the unattached content database. (Note that this must be preceded with an asterisk.)

➤ `\\sp2010\backup\realworld.bak` is the filename of the site collection backup.

➤ `http://sp2010/sites/RealWorld` is the full URL of the site collection where the site collection will be restored.

Content Database Recovery

A Content Database recovery is a snap, assuming you have a complete farm backup. The easiest way to do this is to use Central Administration and go through a farm restore, but select only the single Content Database that you want to restore. This will automatically restore it on top of the current one in use. Of course, you should be careful that you choose the correct Content Database.

You can also restore the database directory using SQL Server. This would be similar to Step 1 as described for item-level recovery.

Farm Disaster Recovery

You have already learned how to do a farm backup and restore. This is critical knowledge, and a major part of a farm disaster recovery, but not the only part. This section provides some additional real-world guidance to help you perform all the necessary steps to ensure that a full farm recovery in a disaster can be a success.

The scenario used here is a fairly typical farm for smaller organizations. It consists of one physical server that is running Hyper-V with two virtual machines. The first virtual machine is a dedicated Web Front End and Application Server. The second is a dedicated SQL Server.

The physical server has suffered a hard disk failure that is unrecoverable. Both servers are dead — the farm is down, and it's your job to fix it! Fortunately, you have a full backup from last night stored on a network attached storage (NAS) appliance. The plan is to recover the farm shown in Figure 6-17 using this backup.

SPS_WFE
Windows Server 2008 R2
SharePoint Server 2010
Web Front End
All Service Apps

SPS_SQL
Windows Server 2008 R2
SQL Server 2008 R2

NAS01
Network Applicance
Backups are stored on
\\NAS01\SharePoint

FIGURE 6-17: Server farm to recover

You start by building the new host environment with Windows Server 2008 R2. You then install Hyper-V and create two new virtual machines. On both of these, you install 64-bit versions of Windows Server 2008 R2. These two servers are named SPS_WFE and SPS_SQL just like before, and joined to the AD domain.

On SPS_SQL, you install SQL Server 2008 R2. On SPS_WFE, you install SharePoint Server 2010 along with any language packs that were used. You then create a complete farm, specifying SPS_SQL as the database server. When entering the database access account, you use the farm administrator account that you had in the original farm.

At this point, you have a brand new farm. The next step is to follow the steps described earlier in this chapter to do a complete farm recovery. The summary is to use Central Administration to point to the backup location, \\NAS01\SharePoint, select last night's full backup, and restore this to the Same Configuration (instead of New Configuration), as shown in Figure 6-14. The recovery may take several hours or longer to complete.

After the restore, you think you're done, but start to notice a number of problems while doing initial testing. For example, certain websites do not work, some pages with custom Web parts show errors, and Search is broken. What happened?

The first thing to point out is that, though SharePoint does a great job of restoring SharePoint's configuration and data, this is not quite everything that makes up your farm. There are still operating system, filesystem, and IIS details that should be included in an end-to-end backup strategy. Here is a list of the most important items that are not covered by SharePoint's complete farm backup:

➤ Manual changes made to IIS, such as using dedicated IP addresses, and loading and binding of SSL certificates

➤ Manual changes made to web.config files

➤ Manual changes made to SharePoint root

➤ Files manually deployed into the global assembly cache (GAC)

➤ Installation of any third-party applications, including Office Web Apps

 For more details on what is not included in the SharePoint farm backup, see http://technet.microsoft.com/en-us/library/ee663490.aspx.

Back to the recovery scenario, after doing some investigation, you learn that you were using a custom site definition, and before, it was manually deployed into the SharePoint root on SPS_WFE. Also, there is a third-party application that provides Web parts that need to be reinstalled. After some scrambling, you get these working again, and the only remaining problem seems to be Search.

After testing a bit more, you also notice that user profiles are not displayed properly. After more testing, you find that Excel Services is also not functioning. It seems there is a problem with most service applications. You go into Central Administration and decide to click the Manage Services on Server link. Figure 6-18 shows you some of the services for SPS_WFE.

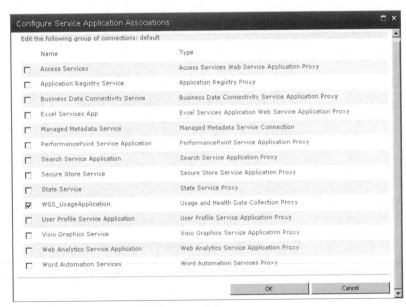

Server:	SPS_WFE ▾	View:	Configurable ▾

Service	Status	Action
Access Database Service	Stopped	Start
Application Registry Service	Stopped	Start
Business Data Connectivity Service	Stopped	Start
Central Administration	Started	Stop
Claims to Windows Token Service	Stopped	Start
Document Conversions Launcher Service	Stopped	Start
Document Conversions Load Balancer Service	Stopped	Start
Excel Calculation Services	Stopped	Start
Lotus Notes Connector	Stopped	Start
Managed Metadata Web Service	Stopped	Start
Microsoft SharePoint Foundation Incoming E-Mail	Started	Stop
Microsoft SharePoint Foundation Sandboxed Code Service	Stopped	Start
Microsoft SharePoint Foundation Subscription Settings Service	Stopped	Start
Microsoft SharePoint Foundation Web Application	Started	Stop
Microsoft SharePoint Foundation Workflow Timer Service	Started	Stop
PerformancePoint Service	Stopped	Start
Search Query and Site Settings Service	Stopped	Start
Secure Store Service	Stopped	Start
SharePoint Foundation Search	Stopped	Start
SharePoint Server Search	Stopped	Start

FIGURE 6-18: Services running on SPS_WFE

As you can see, the farm restore does not automatically start the services that were running on this server, so you manually start these. However, that doesn't seem to fix the problem, because Search and Excel Services still do not work. You then decide to check out your service application associations. You click this link from the Application Management menu. You can see that your web application is properly associated with the default application proxy group, but none of the service applications are. Figure 6-19 shows what you see.

Configure Service Application Associations   ⬜ ✕

Edit the following group of connections: default

	Name	Type
☐	Access Services	Access Services Web Service Application Proxy
☐	Application Registry Service	Application Registry Proxy
☐	Business Data Connectivity Service	Business Data Connectivity Service Application Proxy
☐	Excel Services App	Excel Services Application Web Service Application Proxy
☐	Managed Metadata Service	Managed Metadata Service Connection
☐	PerformancePoint Service Application	PerformancePoint Service Application Proxy
☐	Search Service Application	Search Service Application Proxy
☐	Secure Store Service	Secure Store Service Application Proxy
☐	State Service	State Service Proxy
☑	WSS_UsageApplication	Usage and Health Data Collection Proxy
☐	User Profile Service Application	User Profile Service Application Proxy
☐	Visio Graphics Service	Visio Graphics Service Application Proxy
☐	Web Analytics Service Application	Web Analytics Service Application Proxy
☐	Word Automation Services	Word Automation Services Proxy

OK   Cancel

FIGURE 6-19: Service application associations

The associations are not restored properly, so you manually check these as needed. Finally, Search, Excel Services, and other service applications are working, and your recovery is complete!

 A great improvement in SharePoint Server 2010 is that you will not need to do a full crawl of your content sources after a farm restore. You will need to restart crawls, because these become paused after you perform a restore. After you restart, it will only need to do an incremental crawl.

RECOMMENDATIONS

Before closing out this chapter, I would like to leave you with a number of additional recommendations that should help prepare and protect you during your backup and recovery operations.

Keeping a Change Log

As discussed in the farm disaster recovery scenario section, you must know a number of details about your farm to help ensure that a complete recovery succeeds. This is also important to better communicate the farm's history to consultants, co-workers, and others who may also be supporting the environment. It doesn't need to be fancy or formal. You just need to add an entry for each activity that changes your farm. Table 6-1 shows an example.

TABLE 6-1: SPS_WFE Change Log

DATE	NAME	ACTIVITY
May 5, 201x	Wen	Built farm. Added servers. More details about the installation.
June 11, 201x	Steve	Installed and deployed `custom.wsp` to all web applications.
July 22, 201x	Chris	Installed Adobe PDF IFilter. Edited `DocIcon.xml` to add PDF icon.
Nov 1, 201x	Todd	Applied SP1. Farm build is now 14.x.y.z.

No firm rules exist about what should go into a change log, so use your best judgment. At a minimum, you should log any manual changes made to `web.config` files, manual changes to IIS, files added to the SharePoint root, installation of software, patches applied to the operating system or SharePoint, and any servers added or removed from the farm. You should also document what service application proxy groups you have, what services they contain, and how they are associated to web applications.

Regarding where to store this change log, the first thought would be to keep this in SharePoint — maybe stored in a custom SharePoint list. This is not a bad idea, but keep in mind that this log is essential for SharePoint recovery, and if your farm is down, you can't get access to it. Therefore, make sure you have another copy that you keep in a separate environment. Or, keep an updated hard copy on hand. You might even consider keeping this in a physically separate location.

Using SharePoint Solutions for Custom Code

I insist on only a few things for a SharePoint environment. One of them is to use SharePoint solution packages for any custom code you will deploy into your SharePoint environments. Solution packages typically have a `.WSP` extension, but are just cabinet files that can contain code, data files, configuration files — essentially any file that gets deployed to your farm servers.

These are not only critical to drastically simplify the effort involved in deploying custom code into your environments, but they also ensure the changes are consistently and correctly applied. If you ever need to recover your farm (such as the disaster farm recovery scenario), SharePoint will restore and redeploy custom solutions automatically. This could shorten your recovery time by days, not to mention avoiding the frustration of having to manually re-apply the changes. If you expect to be deploying custom code in your SharePoint environments, insist that the development team build solution packages for all deployed artifacts.

> *To learn more about solutions, see* `http://msdn.microsoft.com/en-us/library/aa543214.aspx.`

> *SharePoint 2010 offers support for a new type of solution package, called a sandbox or user solution. These are different in that they are deployed directly into site collections, and not into the filesystem of your farm servers. You can read more about these in Chapter 8.*

Other Items to Protect

During the farm disaster recovery scenario, you learned that a complete farm backup does not offer full protection. As part of your end-to-end backup strategy, ensure that you are also including these other SharePoint-related items in your DR strategy:

➤ *SSL certificates* — If you don't already have a protected backup, export these and store them in a secure location. You should include the private key in the export, and secure it with a strong password.

➤ *IIS* — Though IIS has a built-in backup mechanism using `appcmd.exe`, it is not recommended to use this for SharePoint recovery. Instead, document manual changes made to IIS in your change log.

➤ `Inetpub\wwwroot\wss\VirtualDirectories` *and SharePoint root* — Just create a `.zip` file for these folders, or include them as part of a filesystem backup.

Content Database Sizing

Most forms of recovery in SharePoint are done at the Content Database level, and this is definitely the case if you expect to do any unattached Content Database restores. Because of this, the size of your Content Database has a major impact on how long a recovery process will take. For example, if many of your Content Databases are 500 GB in size, your recoveries will probably take several hours, depending on the hardware and network speeds. Most SharePoint experts agree that you should target your Content Databases to grow no larger than 100 GB. Because site collections cannot span Content Databases, this means that you should also keep your site collections under this size as well.

 When I suggest a 100 GB limit, I am referring to the amount of actual data space in use. The easiest way to measure this is to look at the size of the database backup. When you look at the size of the database in SQL Server Management Studio, you will see data and log space, plus empty space, which is not a true reflection of actual data space.

Performing Trial Restores

I can't tell you how many customers I have worked with who are convinced that their backups are fine. When I ask how often they verify them by doing a trial restore, most say "never." The purpose of doing a trial restore is not only to validate that the backup works, but it also ensures that you actually know how to do a restore. To me, these are equally important.

The best way to safely do this with SharePoint is to have a staging or recovery environment. All you need to do is periodically apply your production farm backup to another environment. If it's a staging environment, it's also a great way to ensure they are consistent.

Performing a farm recovery is stressful enough. You don't want to have to figure out how to do it during an actual disaster. Also, keep in mind that many live recoveries are done during off hours, which could mean that you would otherwise be sleeping. Because you might not be at your best, if you're well-prepared, you're much less likely to make a careless mistake.

Third-Party Solutions

During this entire chapter, I have been covering out-of-the-box recovery strategies. You should also know that a number of third-party solutions exist that augment what SharePoint can do. Many are quite powerful. I won't offer any opinions on any of them, but here is a list of products you might consider for your environment:

➤ Data Protection Manager 2010 by Microsoft (www.microsoft.com/dpm)

➤ DocAve by AvePoint (www.avepoint.com)

➤ NetVault: Backup by BakBone (www.bakbone.com)

➤ Recovery Manager for SharePoint by Quest (www.quest.com)

➤ Simpana by CommVault (www.commvault.com)

➤ NetWorker Module for Microsoft Applications by EMC (www.emc.com/products)

SUMMARY

In this chapter, you have learned how to plan, implement, and perform backup and restore procedures for SharePoint 2010.

This chapter covered a bit of the operations planning guidance you'll need to set recovery expectations. You learned the differences between content recovery and disaster recovery. You should also be comfortable with each of the backup types, including farm level, site collection level, website, and list level. You even learned how to practically apply these backup types to a number of farm recovery scenarios.

➤ Finally, you have been provided with a number of recommendations to ensure a complete recovery strategy. With this, you should have all the knowledge you need to preserve your SharePoint investment, whether it's mission-critical or just a proof of concept.

ABOUT THE AUTHOR

Randy Williams is a Senior Solution Architect and Trainer for Synergy Corporate Technologies. He has 20 years of eclectic IT experience, and his focus for the last 13 years has been architecting and developing Microsoft-based Web and database solutions. Williams writes for *Windows IT Pro* magazine and contributes to books. He has a master's degree in Information Systems, along with a number of Microsoft certifications. For 2009 and 2010, he was awarded the Microsoft Most Valuable Professional (MVP) in SharePoint Server. Williams is currently based in Singapore, and runs Synergy's operations there. When not working, he enjoys hiking and spending time with his wife and best friend, Gigi.

7

Working with SharePoint Designer 2010

By John Ross

SharePoint Designer (SPD) is a powerful tool for editing sites in SharePoint. It is a product with a long list of capabilities that entire books have been dedicated to. This chapter takes you on a tour of the most notable changes to SharePoint Designer 2010, with a special focus on the SharePoint capabilities that are unique to SPD. It's time to put on some of your favorite music, turn up the volume, and get psyched up to experience the awesomeness of SPD 2010.

EVOLUTION OF SHAREPOINT DESIGNER

SPD began life several years ago as a product called FrontPage. For users who are new to the product, this may sound like just an interesting bit of trivia. However, most likely many of you have strong feelings about FrontPage that may have evolved when SharePoint Designer 2007 was released. Before getting too far into this overview of SPD, let's clear the air on the controversy surrounding FrontPage.

When Microsoft FrontPage was released, it was designed to be a tool that made creating websites easy — too easy in many cases. Bad websites created with FrontPage began to pop up with more frequency. To many web designers, the mention of FrontPage would normally make them shudder. In fact, there have been stories of web designers not being hired because they listed FrontPage on their resumes.

The toxic reputation of FrontPage didn't stop with just web designers. It was also the tool of choice for customizing sites in SharePoint 2003. For users, it had many of the same quirks with SharePoint as it had with editing traditional HTML (such as frequently rewriting HTML for no good reason). However, it wasn't until organizations started trying to upgrade to SharePoint 2007 that the full extent of the problems caused by FrontPage were realized. Entire migration efforts were made significantly more difficult because of how FrontPage customized sites.

For more information on customization check out Andrew Connell's MSDN article, "Understanding and Creating Customized and Uncustomized Files in Windows SharePoint Services 3.0," at `http://msdn.microsoft.com/en-us/library/cc406685.aspx`*. Although the article was written for the previous version of SharePoint, the concepts are still applicable to SharePoint 2010.*

Around the same time that SharePoint 2007 was released, FrontPage was eventually split into two products. These two products were called Microsoft Office SharePoint Designer 2007 and Expression Web Designer. You might notice that the name FrontPage is absent from both product names, and this was intentional to try to diffuse some of the bad feelings about the previous product. SharePoint Designer 2007 was designed to be the primary way for users not only to customize the user interface of SharePoint, but also build applications to improve business processes that did not require any code. With SharePoint Designer 2007, business users had the capability to create functionality (such as a custom workflow) that previously required a developer.

Despite a name change and new functionality, SharePoint Designer 2007 was unable to shake many of the negative perceptions. Though many users described SharePoint Designer 2007 as being a very powerful product, they'd also typically describe it as being very quirky. Common complaints about SharePoint Designer 2007 included instances where HTML was rewritten, or functionality in the product seemed unreliable. For example, SharePoint Designer 2007 allowed users to back up sites as long as they were not larger than 24 MB. Anything larger would cause an error.

Another big issue was related to governance. One of the biggest problems cited with SharePoint Designer 2007 was that there wasn't an easy way for farm administrators to prevent users from using the product. It wasn't uncommon for a user without proper training to open a site with SPD and unknowingly cause issues. Multiply this type of situation across a large organization and there's the potential for a big mess.

There is a happy ending to this story. Although FrontPage and SharePoint Designer 2007 both had issues, all of these things are now in the past. SharePoint Designer 2010 was redesigned with many of these frustrations and complaints in mind.

This chapter covers these areas that may have caused your blood pressure to rise and explains how SharePoint Designer 2010 has improved and evolved. As you'll see, there have been a number of changes that are far more than just cosmetic. SharePoint Designer 2010 is an evolution of the product that brings about some welcome fundamental changes.

WHO SHOULD USE SHAREPOINT DESIGNER?

SPD has always been designed to be a tool for Information Workers (IW). These are the business users who might be referred to as "power users" in most organizations. They are subject matter experts (SMEs) for their particular areas, and they use SharePoint to organize, collaborate, and improve business processes. Because many of these users aren't developers, SPD enables them to create custom, no-code solutions to business problems without the aid of a developer.

It should be noted, though, that SPD is a powerful tool, and it is important for any user of the product to have a basic level of training to ensure that he or she is using the product in accordance with the internal governance policies of the user's organization. I'll assume for the remainder of this discussion that all users who will be using SPD have been trained on how to use it properly.

SPD is ideal for the following users:

➤ *Information Workers* — This represents the primary audience for the tool. SPD enables users to manage and customize their sites without having to rely on the IT department to make the changes for them.

➤ *Developers* — SPD is an important tool for developers to learn for a number of reasons. Specifically, often when requirements are provided to developers and they are asked to estimate something, they must know the various approaches that can be used to solve a problem. It is often quicker and easier to build a solution in SharePoint Designer than to develop a custom application. It is also a useful tool for developers to quickly prototype functionality before developing it.

➤ *Administrators* — Administrators are ultimately the ones who are responsible for the servers. With SharePoint Designer 2010, they are also the ones who have the capability to control who can use SPD. If a user requests the capability to use SPD 2010, it is important that administrators understand what they are agreeing to. What do you want to allow? What do you want to restrict? To make the best decision, it is important that administrators have an understanding of SPD's capabilities.

As you can see, SPD can be useful for many groups of users, but it should be noted that plenty of users shouldn't be using SPD. This whole section shouldn't be interpreted as a message that says everyone in your organization should be using SPD, because that is definitely not the case. Users must have a good business reason to use SPD, such as process improvement, or some other requirement that could help to streamline activities, as well as a basic understanding of the implications of developing small-scale solutions. Basically, if you aren't someone on your organization's SharePoint team or a site owner, you're probably not someone who should be using SPD unless you have a good business reason.

REQUIREMENTS FOR USING SHAREPOINT DESIGNER 2010

On April 2, 2009, Microsoft announced that SharePoint Designer 2007 would be available as a free download. The reasoning behind the decision concerned Microsoft's view on the original cost of SharePoint Designer 2007. It was a line item that many companies just decided to cross off their purchase orders.

When SharePoint Designer 2010 was announced, many wondered if the tool would still be offered as a free product. The good news is that SharePoint Designer 2010 is indeed available as a free download at www.microsoft.com/spd.

> *SharePoint Designer 2010 works only with SharePoint 2010. (This includes both SharePoint Foundation and SharePoint Server.) If you were to try to open your SharePoint 2007 sites with SharePoint Designer 2010, it wouldn't work. Although this might be frustrating for some users, it was a necessary decision made by the SPD product team in order to implement all of the changes for the product.*

In environments where SharePoint 2007 and SharePoint 2010 are both installed, it might be necessary to have SharePoint Designer 2007 and SharePoint Designer 2010 installed side by side on the same machine. If this applies to you, ensure that you install the same version of SharePoint Designer 2010 that you did with SharePoint Designer 2007. Because SharePoint Designer 2007 only came in 32-bit, if you wanted to install SharePoint Designer 2010 on the same machine, it would be necessary to install SharePoint Designer 2010 32-bit.

WHAT'S NEW?

The changes to SharePoint Designer 2010 can be summed up by saying that the product is now much more focused on SharePoint. It sounds pretty strange to say that something with "SharePoint" in the name at one point wasn't SharePoint-focused. But the fact is that SharePoint Designer 2007 was essentially a web editor with SharePoint extensions. SharePoint Designer 2010 is a SharePoint editor that also does web editing.

SharePoint Designer 2010 allows users to manage almost all aspects of their sites quickly and easily from the user interface. Things like creating sites, managing users, lists, and libraries, and even content types and site columns can all be done without ever leaving SharePoint Designer 2010. However, it is still a powerful tool for branding, creating workflows, and connecting to external data sources. In fact, almost across the board, all of the capabilities have been enhanced to allow the user to do even more than ever without having to write a single line of code. Last, but certainly not least, there have been significant changes to how access to SPD can be controlled to make it easier for organizations to govern the product.

The changes to SharePoint Designer 2010 have made it a must-have tool for all SharePoint power users to have in their bags of tricks.

Overview of the New User Experience

As soon as you open SharePoint Designer 2010, it should be obvious that there have been substantial changes to the user interface. Of course, SharePoint Designer 2010 now includes the ribbon, but the entire user interface has been updated to reflect the stronger focus on SharePoint itself. The new interface makes it easier to see all of the components of a site, and how they relate to each other.

Changes can be made to these components directly from SPD without needing to go to a settings page in the browser. For example, with SharePoint Designer 2007, if you wanted to make a change to the settings of a list, you needed to open up a web browser, go to the list, open its settings page, and then make the corresponding change. With SharePoint Designer 2010, most settings that can be adjusted through the web browser for a site can now be centrally accessed from SharePoint Designer 2010. This includes site permissions and settings, list and library settings, and creation of site columns and content types, just to name a few.

To open SPD, click Start ⇨ All Programs ⇨ SharePoint, and then click Microsoft SharePoint Designer 2010.

The first screen that appears is the Sites page of the Microsoft Office Backstage Feature. As shown in Figure 7-1, the screen is divided into four self-explanatory areas: Open SharePoint Site, New SharePoint Site, Recent Sites, and Site Templates.

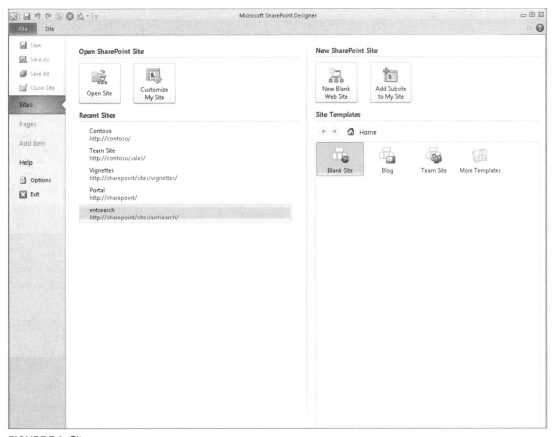

FIGURE 7-1: Sites page

By default, you'll only see three options in the Site Templates section: Blank Site, Blog, and Team Site. Clicking one of these templates opens a dialog that enables you to create a new site once a URL is specified. To create a site using a different template, you can click the More Templates button, and enter the URL of a site with more options for templates. For example, if you entered the URL for a site that was created using the Enterprise Wiki template, you'd be able to choose from the Enterprise Wiki as well as other templates (such as a Publishing Site, and so on).

With SharePoint Designer 2010, you must be connected to a site to use the tool. Although it was possible to edit local copies of master pages or page layouts with SharePoint Designer 2007, this is no longer possible. For example, you wouldn't be able to email yourself a copy of a master page and expect to be able to edit it if you didn't have access to a SharePoint server at home. If you did try to edit the file without first opening a site, you'd get the error shown in Figure 7-2.

If you've never opened SPD, the Recent Sites area will be blank, and you'll need to click the Open Site button. Once the dialog opens, you can type in the URL of your site and then click Open.

The first page you'll see when your site opens is referred to as the *settings page*. From this screen you'll see information about your site, such subsites, and so on. The settings page is used as the central hub for making all of the changes to your site.

FIGURE 7-2: Error received when attempting to edit a file without opening a site

Once you've opened up a site, the new user interface shown in Figure 7-3 is divided into the following three main sections. (Note that the numbers in parentheses refer to the boxed numbers shown in Figure 7-3.)

➤ *Navigation (1)* — This pane at the left shows the various components that make up a site, including lists, libraries, master pages, page layouts, workflows, content types, and so on. Clicking one of the links takes you to a gallery page.

➤ *Ribbon (2)* — As with the rest of SharePoint, selecting an object causes the ribbon to display menus and options for customizing that object.

➤ *Gallery and Summary (3)* — This main area in the center of the screen displays the lists of each component type or summary information about the component.

Most users will find that the Navigation pane is the most convenient way to navigate through the different components in their sites. The Navigation panel is always visible, no matter which gallery has been selected. This allows users to quickly jump between galleries, or click the Site link (listed first in the Navigation area) to return to the settings page for the site.

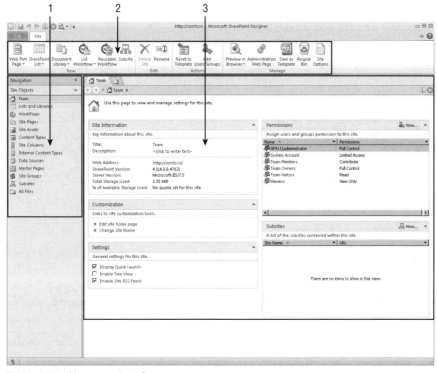

FIGURE 7-3: New user interface

The gallery pages show a high-level view of each component of the site. Click a gallery and you will see a list of all of the components of a certain type — for example, you'll see all of the lists for the site, or all of the workflows. Once the gallery is selected, the ribbon will change context to show buttons related to the components in the gallery. This means that if you click the "Lists and Libraries" gallery, you'll see options in the ribbon specifically related to lists and libraries. Clicking the Workflow gallery changes the context of the ribbon to show items specifically related to workflows, and so forth.

It is also possible to pin a gallery to open a "mini-gallery" below the Navigation pane. To do this, hover your mouse over the link for a gallery and you'll see a pin icon, as shown in Figure 7-4. Clicking the pin icon opens the mini-gallery, which continues to show even if another gallery is selected. This makes it easy to reference the items in a gallery at any time. However, it should be noted that it is only possible to pin one gallery at a time.

When looking at the items in a gallery, clicking the name of an item once opens its settings page. Double-clicking the name of the item opens its editor. So, if you were to open the "Lists and Libraries" gallery, and click the Shared Documents library, the settings page would open, which would let you change general settings, such as versioning, create and modify views, or update permissions for the library. However, double-

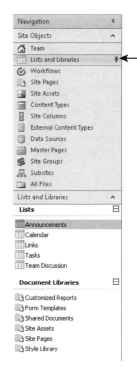

FIGURE 7-4: Pin icon used to open a mini-gallery

clicking Shared Documents would take you to the editor for the library, which would allow you to create and modify the columns.

 Opening the editor for an object can be deceptively tricky, because the name of the object is actually a link. If you double-click the name itself, the settings page will normally open because of the link. To open the editor directly, be sure to double-click away from the name of the object, but still on the same row. For example, it might be easier to double-click the row near the Type column, rather than the Name column.

Breadcrumbs, Tabs, and Navigation

The way you get around in SharePoint Designer 2010 has also changed. It's already been mentioned that if you click the Navigation panel, you can easily hop to different elements of your site. Although the Navigation panel is likely to be the most common way people use to get around, it isn't the only way. Users who are familiar with Windows 7 especially should feel right at home with the new navigation aspects of SharePoint Designer 2010.

The first thing to note is that, as users navigate through their sites with SharePoint Designer 2010, the interface functions very similarly to how a web browser does. As you click around to different elements of the site, new tabs will open so that you can quickly hop between different open areas or specific files, as shown in Figure 7-5. Additionally, each tab maintains its own history, and just like a web browser, back and forward buttons can be used to easily move between recent pages. If you have a mouse that has back and forward buttons, these can also be used to move between page history.

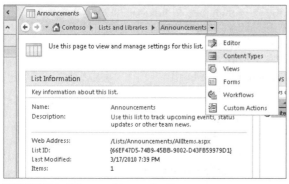

FIGURE 7-5: Tabs used for navigation

To the right of the back and forward buttons, there's also a breadcrumb navigation that shows where you are within the site. If you happened to be in the Shared Documents library, the breadcrumb would have a link for each level in the hierarchy. This would enable you to quickly jump from editing a site column back to any level above.

Additionally, the breadcrumbs themselves can be expanded, which provides even more navigation flexibility. Using the example just mentioned, you could go from editing a column in the Shared Documents library, click the drop-down for "List and Libraries" in the breadcrumb, and go directly to the Announcements list, as shown in Figure 7-6.

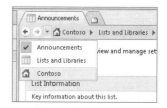

FIGURE 7-6: Navigation using breadcrumbs

The File Tab

You may have noticed a big orange button in the upper-left corner that says "File." For more than the last decade, most of us have become familiar with the idea of an application's File menu that enables functionality such as opening a new file, saving, saving as, or even exiting the program. The File tab for SharePoint Designer 2010 is very similar in concept to the traditional idea of a File menu on the toolbar. In fact, many of the options that you'd expect to exist in a File menu are here.

This menu is the place for changing the options for SPD, opening new sites, or closing the program. Another thing to remember is that the Help menus are located here, along with the version number for SharePoint Designer 2010. Most users typically look for the Help menu along the top toolbar, so it might take a little time to get used to the idea that the Help and version information actually are found under the File tab. Finally, if you've clicked the File tab and want to return to your site, you can click the tab immediately to the right of the File tab and you should be returned to the exact place you were previously viewing.

Checking and Changing the Current User

Let's pretend for a second that you've logged in to a machine — maybe it is a virtual machine that's used for development. When you open SPD, it automatically logs you in with the same credentials you used to log in to the machine. In this scenario, you might be logged in with an administrator account. If you wanted to test something as a different user, how would you do that?

There's a very easy way to check the current user's account and switch to a different user, but it certainly isn't very obvious. With SPD open, if you look in the bottom-left corner, you'll see a tiny little person icon, as shown in Figure 7-7. Hovering over the icon with your mouse shows the name of the user currently logged in. Clicking the icon allows you to log in with a different account.

FIGURE 7-7: Icon for checking user account

Restricting Access to SharePoint Designer

Earlier in this chapter, you learned that one of the biggest issues with SharePoint Designer 2007 was the governance challenge it presented. This was one of the primary sources for many of the negative feelings among IT professionals concerning SharePoint Designer 2007. When the product was made free, it only served to fuel the fire.

Many companies tried to address the problem by writing lengthy governance documents that outlined how SPD should be used in the environment. There were methods for restricting the capability to use SPD, but they required changes typically made by developers, and were often beyond the capabilities of the administrators responsible for the servers. Obviously, a certain level of access is required to use SPD, but the biggest challenge was how you gave users full control to a site, but still prevented them from using SPD. The bottom line is that it certainly was possible, but required a lot more effort than it probably should have.

For many SharePoint administrators, the biggest change for SharePoint Designer 2010 is that it is now possible through the web user interface to control how SPD can be used in your organization. This is an important and necessary change, which provides companies who use SPD with the peace of mind that it can be safely deployed to users and easily controlled. This means that not only can administrators control the capability for whether SPD can be used at all, but additional options have been added. These new options would, for example, allow SPD to be used, but prevent the files from being customized by detaching them from the site definition. Essentially, the same potential issues from customization with SharePoint Designer still exist in SharePoint 2010, but there are now easier ways to control it.

Some of you might be familiar with the concept of Contributor Settings in SharePoint Designer 2007. They weren't heavily used because they were complex, and users were able to bypass the settings and still make changes. This was because Contributor Settings did not fully integrate with the SharePoint permission model. The new functionality for SharePoint 2010 to control SPD does integrate directly with the permission model to effectively prevent unwanted changes to sites.

SharePoint 2010 has the following settings in both Central Administration and at the Site Collection level to control how SPD can be used:

➤ *Enable SharePoint Designer* — Determines whether SPD can be used at all.

➤ *Enable Detaching Pages from the Site Definition* — Allows edited pages to be customized, which detaches them from the site definition.

➤ *Enable Customizing Master Pages and Layout Pages* — Enables the Master Page link from the Navigation pane. When disabled, it prevents users from updating master pages and layout pages.

➤ *Enable Managing of the Web Site URL Structure* — Enables the All Files link on the Navigation pane, which allows users to manage all of the folders and files for a given site. This is useful for advanced configuration and modification for a site, and should be reserved for experienced users, to prevent accidentally modifying or deleting system files.

These new options enable organizations to control SPD 2010 at the level appropriate to their requirements. SharePoint 2010 allows access to SPD to be controlled at two different levels:

➤ *Central Administration* — Accessed from the General Application Settings menu, this enables farm administrators to control SPD at the web application level. Disabling the options here prevents site collection administrators from enabling the functionality from within a site collection. Site collection administrators are also not able to make edits with SPD.

➤ *Site Collection* — Accessed from the Site Collection Administration section in Site Settings, this enables site collection administrators to control SPD access for designers and site owners. When disabled, only site collection administrators will be able to make customizations.

The following example walks you through the process of updating the SPD settings from Central Administration:

1. Open Central Administration from your SharePoint server by clicking Start ⇨ All Programs ⇨ Microsoft SharePoint 2010 Products ⇨ Microsoft SharePoint 2010 Central Administration.

2. Click General Application Settings in the left Navigation pane.

3. From the SharePoint Designer section, click Configure SharePoint Designer Settings, as shown in Figure 7-8.

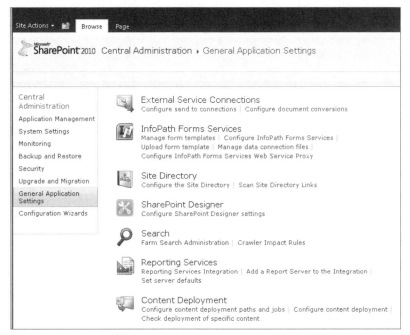

FIGURE 7-8: SharePoint Designer section

4. From the Settings page, select the appropriate web application from the drop-down at the top right. By default, all the options should be selected. Leave the first box checked, which enables the use of SPD, but remove the checks from the other boxes, as shown in Figure 7-9. Click OK.

5. To test the changes, navigate to the URL of the site collection in your web browser to be used for testing, and log in as a site collection administrator. For this example, let's use http:// contoso. For this example to work, the ID that is used must be a site collection administrator. If you were to test with an account that has more permissions (such as a farm administrator account), you might not notice any changes. Because administrator accounts have more rights to the site collection, these changes won't impact the capability of those administrators to use SPD.

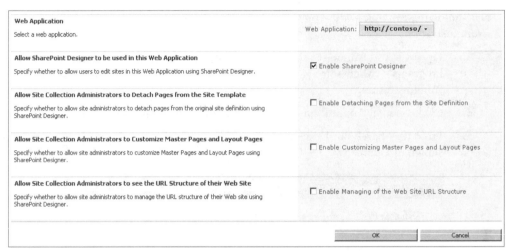

FIGURE 7-9: Options to select in the Settings page

6. From the Site Actions button, choose "Edit in SharePoint Designer," as shown in Figure 7-10.

7. SPD should open. Note that the Master Page, Page Layouts (only shows in sites with Publishing enabled), and All Sites links should be missing from the left-hand Navigation pane, as shown in Figure 7-11. If the links are still there, verify that you are logged in as a site collection administrator, not a farm administrator. You can check by clicking the icon in the bottom-left corner of the SPD window, which displays the name of the logged-in user (as explained in the earlier section, "Checking and Changing the Current User").

FIGURE 7-10: "Edit in SharePoint Designer" option

FIGURE 7-11: Navigation pane without links

Also, if you were to click Site Pages and try to edit the `home.aspx` page, you would notice that Advanced mode is grayed out, as shown in Figure 7-12. The page can only be edited in Normal mode, which means that only content in Web part zones can be edited. Conversely, Advanced mode allows users to edit the files themselves (such as the page itself or the master page), which would cause the files to become detached from the site definition. This is also referred to as *customizing the page*. If this setting is enabled, it is important that all SharePoint Designer users are sufficiently trained on using the tool responsibly in accordance with your organization governance policies.

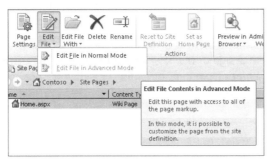

FIGURE 7-12: Advanced mode grayed out

8. For the next step, let's test what happens when you completely disable SPD access. Close the instance of SPD that you were using for the previous example. It's OK to leave your web browser open.

9. Repeat Steps 1–3 and remove the check from the Enable SharePoint Designer box. Click OK.

10. Repeat Step 5. Now, when you try to open SPD, you should see the prompt shown in Figure 7-13.

FIGURE 7-13: Prompt informing user editing is not allowed

Branding

When users see the name "SharePoint Designer," the first thing that usually comes to mind is that it is primarily a tool for designing websites. That's a fair assumption, considering that the product evolved from FrontPage, which was itself a tool for designing websites. Even SharePoint Designer 2007 had a primary focus on the page editing experience. When you opened SharePoint Designer 2007, you were presented with a blank HTML page. Although SharePoint Designer 2010 has put less of a focus on the page-editing experience, it is still the primary tool for customizing the SharePoint user interface. The common term for this task is *branding*.

Branding is discussed in more detail in Chapter 18, but simply put, it refers to the objects that work together to create the visual aspects of the site. This includes the master pages, page layouts, cascading style sheets (CSS), HTML, fonts, and so on. Specifically, for SharePoint branding, let's focus on the following elements:

➤ *Cascading style sheets (CSS)* — These are used heavily throughout SharePoint to specify the overall look and feel. Branding a SharePoint site usually requires creating custom CSS.

➤ *Master page* — Registers many of the SharePoint controls on the page, and then arranges them via HTML, CSS, and content placeholders. This is a primary factor that influences the look and feel of a site or page. Every page that is rendered in SharePoint requires a master page.

➤ *Page Layout* — A template for content. Using field controls, users enter content that is then rendered as a web page based on the design of the page layout itself. This can be thought of as a more heavily styled version of entering content into a list. Page layouts are available only with sites where Publishing has been enabled.

The experience for creating a master page or page layout hasn't changed noticeably in this version — aside from the fact that many of the options for creating, editing, and deleting are now controlled by buttons in the ribbon. The process for creating page layouts is made easier because site columns and content types can now be created directly from SPD, which prevents a user from having to jump between the browser and SPD.

Modifying CSS

If you've ever tried to do any amount of branding in SharePoint, you've likely seen how much of an impact CSS has on the user interface. Making changes to the look and feel of a site usually requires modifying CSS. Essentially, almost everything you see on the page has CSS applied to it. For example, if you wanted to hide something like the All Site Content link in the left Navigation pane, you'd need to make a change to the CSS. You have two basic ways to do this — either edit the out of the box CSS, or create your own custom CSS that overrides the system CSS. Which option do you think is preferred? If you said create your own CSS that overrides the system CSS, you made the right choice!

For this example, consider that the All Site Content link might have five styles that apply to it. Because of the cascading nature of CSS, whichever style is applied last to the object is the one that counts. There are some exceptions to this, but the goal here isn't to get into the mechanics of CSS. All you must do is ensure that your custom CSS is applied after the system CSS, which can safely be done in a couple different ways:

➤ *Apply the styles inline* — This just means that CSS is referenced directly from the master page inline with the other code. This is a more simplistic approach, but also means that to change the CSS in the future, you'll have to modify the master page so it is generally not recommended.

➤ *Create a custom CSS file* — Styles can be placed in a separate CSS file and referenced in the master page. As long as the custom CSS file is referenced after the out of the box CSS, the custom styles will safely be applied. This method allows the CSS to be modified separately from the master page.

New features have been added to SharePoint Designer 2010 that enable you to more easily work with CSS. A new feature called *Skewer Click* makes it easier for you to find which style is being applied to a given element. By clicking the Skewer Click button on the ribbon, you can select an element on the page and see what CSS is being used. Then, new styles can safely be applied either inline or by creating a custom CSS file.

The process of creating the new CSS is now automated by SharePoint Designer 2010. All you must do is right-click the style and select whether to apply the style inline or in a separate file, and SharePoint Designer 2010 does the rest.

Perhaps the biggest change when it comes to branding isn't what has been added, but rather what's been removed. Throughout SharePoint Designer 2007, there was functionality geared toward modifying non-SharePoint sites, which only served to confuse users. For example, if you were editing a file and wanted to publish it, you would often right-click the file and select "Publish." It certainly makes sense, but, unfortunately, this functionality didn't do what you would have expected. What you really should have done was right-click and select "Check in the file," which would then prompt you to publish a major version.

Removing these non-SharePoint related features from the product has made SPD more intuitive and easier to use.

Working with Master Pages and CSS

Editing master pages is covered in more detail in Chapter 18, but SPD offers some new functionality that makes the branding process even easier. The following example walks you through the process of creating a custom master page to add a footer, as well as hiding the All Site Content and Recycle Bin links from the left Navigation pane. Both of these tasks are fairly common requests in many organizations, and this example shows off some of the new capabilities of SharePoint Designer 2010.

For this example, be sure you are logged in as a user who has permission to edit master pages. Also, in this example, you'll be making changes to a Team Site, so, if your site uses a different template, the steps might be slightly different.

1. Open your site in SPD and click the Master Pages link in the Navigation pane.

2. Right-click v4.master and select Copy. Then right-click and paste another copy of the file into the Master Pages gallery.

 It is always recommended that you make copies of any of the out of the box files before making changes.

3. From the Master Pages gallery, click next to the filename for the master page that was just created. From the ribbon, click the Rename button. Rename the file CustomFooter.master.

4. Select the file CustomFooter.master and then, from the ribbon, click the Edit File button.

5. Ensure that either the Split or Code view is showing. Near line 624, after
`<SharePoint:DeveloperDashboard runat="server"/>`, add the following code snippet,
as shown in Figure 7-14:

```
<div class="s4-notdlg" style="clear: both; background-color:
        #FEAD30; padding: 10px;">
    &copy; Copyright 2010 Contoso Manufacturing
</div>
```

 For demonstration purposes, this example applies the CSS inline. It is generally preferred to add custom CSS by referencing a specific CSS class that can be used in throughout the page or from other pages.

FIGURE 7-14: Adding code to CustomFooter.master

6. After you've made the change, save the file by clicking the Save icon in the upper left-hand corner of the screen. You will get a dialog that warns you that you are about to customize the file from the site definition. Click Yes to continue.

7. Click the Master Page link again from the Navigation pane on the left to return to the Master Pages gallery.

8. To apply the changes to the site, select `CustomFooter.master` and then, from the ribbon, click the "Set as Default" button.

If you open your site in the web browser, you'll see that a footer has been applied to your site, as shown in Figure 7-15. If your browser is already open to the site, you might need to refresh.

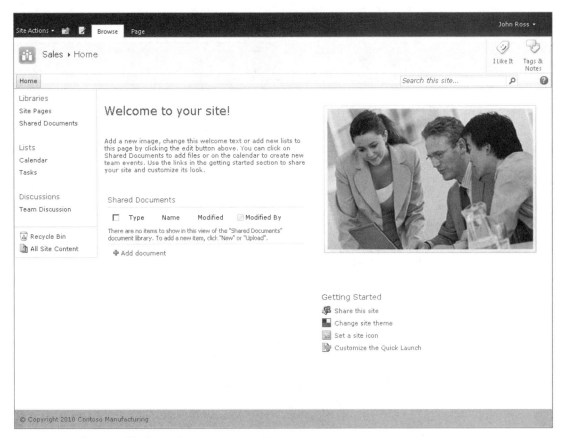

FIGURE 7-15: Footer added to a site

Now that the footer has been added, let's hide the Recycle Bin and All Site Content links from the Navigation pane. This is a common request that many organizations make because they feel the links in the Navigation pane are confusing or add too much clutter.

The following steps walk you through the process of making this common SharePoint customization:

1. Edit the `CustomFooter.master` file again from SPD.

2. From the ribbon, click the Skewer Click button, as shown in Figure 7-16. This enables you to see the CSS that is being applied to a specific object.

3. With Skewer Click selected, hover over the area near where the Recycle Bin and All Site Content links are located. Move your mouse around the area and you should see the name `PlaceHolderQuickLaunchBottom` appear faintly. Select it and another window will open displaying a list of styles. Click the style called `ul.s4-specialNav...`, as shown in Figure 7-17.

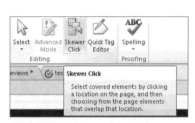

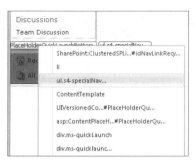

FIGURE 7-16: Skewer Click button

FIGURE 7-17: Selecting a style

4. Before you can edit the CSS, you must first add a new panel to SPD. From the ribbon, click the Style tab and select the CSS Properties button, as shown in Figure 7-18.

5. When the new panel opens, you'll see the top section is called Applied Rules, as shown in Figure 7-19. The style you want to modify (.s4-specialNavLinkList) should already be selected. It may be tough to read the entire name of the style, so it might be easier to make the right panel a little wider. Right-click the style and select New Style Copy.

FIGURE 7-18: CSS Properties button

FIGURE 7-19: Applied Rules section

6. At the top of the New Style dialog shown in Figure 7-20, set the new style to be defined in the "Current page." Be sure to check the box "Apply new style to document selection." Then select the Layout category and set the "visibility" to "hidden." Click OK.

7. Save the changes made to the master page.

When you view the site now, the links for All Site Content and the Recycle Bin will be hidden. You might get a warning after you save the file that says, "Saving your changes will customize this page so that it is no longer based on the site definition." Click Yes to continue. When you browse back to your site, the All Site Content and Recycle Bin links are now hidden, as shown in Figure 7-21.

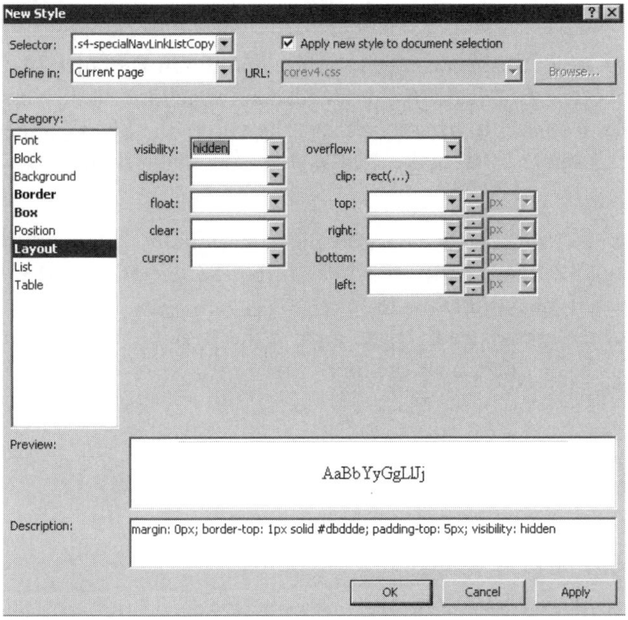

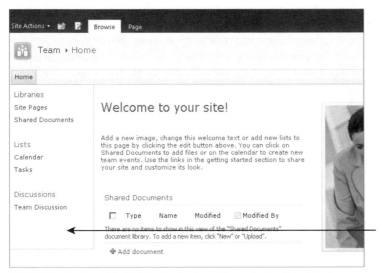

FIGURE 7-20: New Style dialog

FIGURE 7-21: Site with All Site Content and Recycle Bin links hidden

Learning from the Example

In this example, you used the New Style Copy Feature, which is new to SharePoint Designer 2010. This approach of overriding the out-of-the-box CSS is the recommended approach for modifying styles in your site. It is a common mistake for users to directly change the out-of-the-box CSS files, but these new capabilities of SharePoint Designer 2010 make it easier to safely make changes to the CSS in your site.

By following the steps in this example, when using the New Style Copy functionality, you made a copy of the style you wanted to edit. Then, SPD automatically updated the CSS reference on the object you were modifying. In this case, that meant SPD made a copy of `.s4-specialNavLinkList` and made the changes inline at the top of the master page. If you look at the Design view of the master page, you'll see the following code has been added near the top:

```
        <style type="text/css">
.s4-specialNavLinkListCopy
{
        margin: 0px;
/* [ReplaceColor(themeColor:"Light2-Lightest")] */    border-top: 1px solid #dbddde;
        padding-top: 5px;
        visibility: hidden;
}
</style>
```

Notice that the style was copied and appended with "Copy." Simply selecting New Style Copy creates this reference, but it is necessary to check the "Apply new style to document selection" option, which changes the reference of the style you want to change to the copied style. Without checking the box, you'd need to make manual changes to get the style to apply your changes properly. In this example, this would have meant that the previous code would be added to the top of the master page, but the links for the Recycle Bin and All Site Content wouldn't be hidden until the new style was applied by referencing the new copied style.

Instead of applying the styles inline, you can also choose to apply the changes to a separate CSS file. The result is the same, but instead of the code being inline, the custom CSS file would be automatically referenced. If you are making several changes to CSS, it is recommended that you use the option to reference a separate CSS file to keep the master page code cleaner.

Views and Forms

Most companies spend a considerable amount of time planning for how they are going to store content in SharePoint. This is definitely an important consideration, but it is really only part of the equation. Once you have a place for all of that content, how will you capture and display that content in a highly usable way? In SharePoint 2010, forms are used to capture the information. Views and the XSLT Web part are the most common ways to display list and library information.

Forms

In an electronic form, you have a list of fields that you enter data into and submit it. Often, when the term "forms" was used when talking about SharePoint 2007, the first thing that came to mind was InfoPath. One of the most common questions related to InfoPath was when you should use an InfoPath form, or, in other words, when would a SharePoint list do just as well? The answer ultimately was that it depended on what you were trying to do.

Out of the box, most list forms in SharePoint 2010 are ASP.NET forms. However, with SharePoint Server 2010 Enterprise, it is possible to edit these forms, or even create new ones, using InfoPath 2010. If you don't have enterprise licensing, it is still possible to create new ASP.NET list forms without code using SharePoint Designer 2010.

If you do have SharePoint Server 2010 Enterprise, you can edit a list for from SPD by going to the "Lists and Libraries" link in the Navigation pane and open up one of the settings pages, you'll notice that there's a link on the ribbon called "Design Forms in InfoPath." Clicking this allows you to customize the list form. You could do something as simple as just putting a custom header on the form, or maybe add some additional instructions to the form.

InfoPath forms are also automatically created for workflows when using SharePoint Server 2010 Standard or Enterprise. For example, if you have a workflow that assigns a task meant to be an approval, you could edit the task form and change it to provide more clarification for what is expected during the step. Perhaps you could change the labels on the button, or explain what it means for a user to approve the task.

Views and the XSLT List View Web Part

Views are the primary way that content from lists and libraries is displayed to the user. Conceptually, very little has changed since SharePoint 2007. Views are still used to filter and sort data to display a set of data in a unique way. However, there have been some significant changes to how views work, and how they are created, especially as it relates to SharePoint Designer 2010.

For starters, views can still be created in the web browser just as they always could be, but they can now also be created directly from SPD. By clicking the settings page for any list or library, you should see a list of views. Creating a new view is as simple as clicking the New button and entering a name for the view. Once the new view has been created, it will be added to the list of views — nothing too earth shattering there. But if you click the name of the view in SPD, this is where things start to get interesting.

With SharePoint 2007, all views were based on Collaborative Application Markup Language (CAML). If you aren't familiar with the term, that's okay. The important thing to know is that, aside from picking some options on what columns to show, filter criteria, sorting, and grouping (all of which was possible through the SharePoint user interface), it was very difficult to customize.

That's all been changed with SharePoint 2010. All views are now based on Extensible Stylesheet Language Translation (XSLT), and can be easily customized from SharePoint Designer 2010. When you click the view name from the list or library settings page, a new page will open showing the XSLT List View Web part.

Users familiar with the Data View Web part (DVWP) in SharePoint 2007 will find the functionality to be very similar. You can customize the columns to be displayed, create filters, customize sorting and grouping, apply conditional formatting, and even apply various out-of-the-box layouts to quickly change the look and feel of the Web part. Additionally, if you happened to be an XSLT guru, or had access to someone who was, you could further customize the look and feel.

If you counted yourself among the group who had used the DVWP, you might be asking the question, "Although the DVWP was powerful and could do a lot of useful things, once it was deployed, it wasn't easy to update without going back to SPD, so has that been fixed?" That's a great question! The XSLT List View Web part provides the power and flexibility of the DVWP, but doesn't take away the capability to edit and modify the Web part through the SharePoint user interface. You can actually create a custom XSLT List View Web part with custom columns and conditional formatting that would be treated just like any old view in SharePoint.

Editing Views and Forms with SharePoint Designer

This example walks you through the various options available in SharePoint Designer 2010 for creating and editing views and forms. You create a list with a few fields, customize the list form in InfoPath, edit the view to add conditional filtering, and then create a custom view. Although views can still be created through the user interface as they were in SharePoint 2007, SharePoint Designer 2010 provides for much greater power and flexibility through the use of the new XSLT List View Web part.

This example shows off these new capabilities and demonstrates some concepts that can be reused and expanded on in your organization. Let's get started by following these steps:

1. Open SPD and connect to a site.

2. From the Navigation pane on the left, click "Lists and Libraries" to open the gallery.

3. To create a new list, click the Custom List button on the ribbon.

4. Name the list `Employee Review` and click OK.

5. The new list should be added to the gallery. Click the name of the list to open its summary page.

6. From the summary page, in the Customization section located in the middle of the center panel, click the "Edit list columns" link. This opens the editor for this list.

7. There should already be a column on the list called `Title`. Single-click the name of column and change the name to `Employee Name`.

8. For the next column, click the Add New Column button on the ribbon once again and select to add a Choice column. The Column Editor dialog window opens and allows you to customize the choices for the drop-down. For the choices, enter the following values on separate lines, as shown in Figure 7-22:

   ➤ Exceeds Expectations

   ➤ Meets Expectations

   ➤ Does Not Meet Expectations

FIGURE 7-22: Entries for Choice column

9. While still in the Column Editor, delete the value from the "Default value" field, leaving the field empty, and click OK. You'll be returned to the screen showing the columns on the list. Be sure to name the new column `Rating`.

10. Add one more column. For this column, choose the type "Multi lines of text." Call it `Comments`.

11. The list is created and the fields are updated, but you'll need to save the list for the changes to be applied. Click the Save icon in the upper-left corner of the browser.

Now that the list has been created, you can view it from the web browser by going to the site. If the site is a Team Site, the link for the list should show in the left Navigation pane. Clicking the list name should display the list with all of the custom fields. There's nothing too fancy here. If you click to add a new item to the list, you'll see the standard form with the various fields displayed. Because this is a special list, you can customize this form using SPD and InfoPath.

Let's do that now by following these steps:

1. From SPD, navigate to the new `Employee Review` list summary page by clicking the "Lists and Libraries" link in the Navigation pane on the left, if it isn't already open.

2. On the ribbon, click the button called "Design Forms in InfoPath." As shown in Figure 7-23, another small window will open below the button. Click Item and the form will open in InfoPath.

FIGURE 7-23: "Design Forms in InfoPath" button

3. After the form opens in InfoPath, give the form a title and remove the `Attachments` row, because you won't be using that. You can do this by clicking your mouse somewhere in the `Attachments` row, right-clicking, and selecting Delete ⇨ Rows. When you've completed your changes, click the Quick Publish button in the upper-left corner, as shown in Figure 7-24. You should get a message that says your form was published successfully.

4. Now, if you open your browser and try to create a new item on the list, you'll see the customized form. Try entering a few items into the list. As you enter items, choose different values for the `Ratings` field. With the items entered into the list, you can now create a custom view to help visualize and filter the data.

FIGURE 7-24: Quick Publish button

5. Click "Lists and Libraries." Then click the `Employee Reviews` list to get to the list settings page. Click the All Items view to edit it, as shown in Figure 7-25. For this example, you'll be editing the All Items view. In a production environment, however, the best practice would be to create a new view, rather than modify this one.

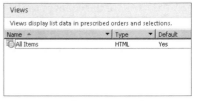

FIGURE 7-25: Selecting the All Items view

6. The XSLT List View Web part will open. The first thing you do is remove the Attachments icon from the left column because you already removed the `Attachments` field from the entry form. Click the icon in the header of the table and press the Delete key.

7. After you delete the paper clip icon for the heading, the left column should still be there. Select the left cell on the first row with data below the headings. It is important that the whole cell be selected. (Note that if the whole cell is selected, it will be gray. If it isn't selected, it will only show the border, but the center will be white.) If the cell isn't selected, click the small "td" tab above the cell, as shown in Figure 7-26. To add conditional formatting to this cell, click the Conditional Formatting button in the ribbon and choose Format Column.

8. In the Condition Criteria window shown in Figure 7-27, use the following criteria for the condition:

➤ Field Name — Rating

➤ Condition — Equals

➤ Value — "Does Not Meet Expectations"

When you have finished, click the Set Style button.

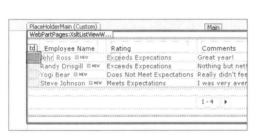

FIGURE 7-26: Cell selected for conditional formatting

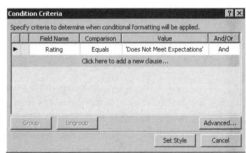

FIGURE 7-27: Condition Criteria window

9. In the Modify Style window shown in Figure 7-28, choose the Background category. Change the background color to #FF0000 (red) and click OK.

10. Save the changes to the view by clicking the Save button in the upper-left corner.

11. You'll notice now that any `Employee Reviews` that were entered with the Rating of "Does Not Meet Expectations" will have the highlighted (red) cell, as shown in Figure 7-29. (This would be similar to how you could create a simple KPI for any list or library, no matter which version of SharePoint you had.)

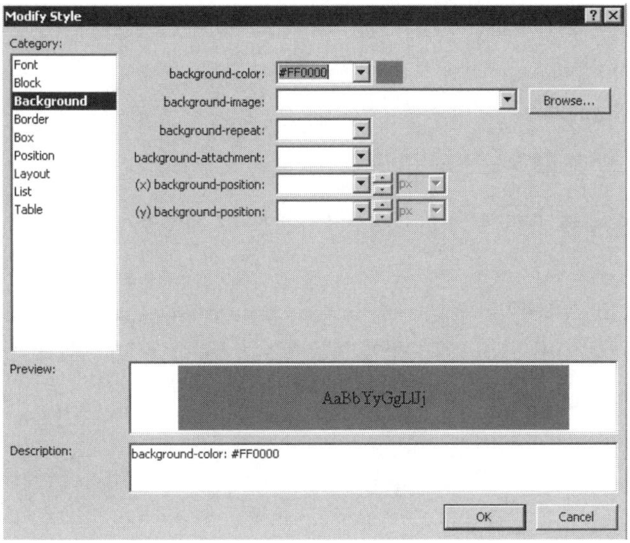

Modify Style

Category:
Font
Block
Background
Border
Box
Position
Layout
List
Table

background-color: #FF0000
background-image: Browse...
background-repeat:
background-attachment:
(x) background-position: px
(y) background-position: px

Preview:

AaBbYyGgLlJj

Description:
background-color: #FF0000

OK   Cancel

FIGURE 7-28: Modify Style window

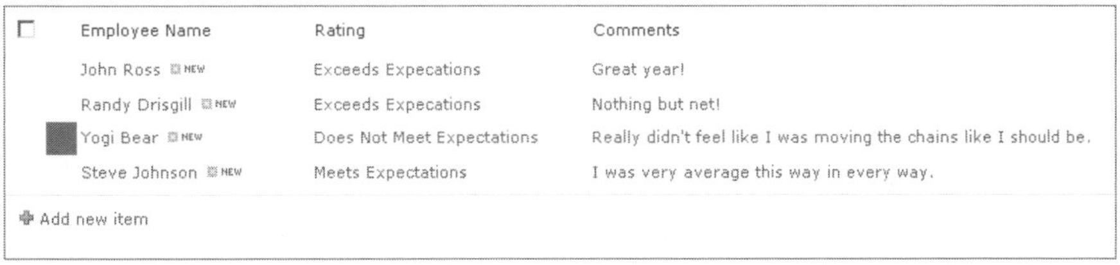

☐	Employee Name	Rating	Comments
	John Ross ☑ NEW	Exceeds Expectations	Great year!
	Randy Drisgill ☑ NEW	Exceeds Expectations	Nothing but net!
	Yogi Bear ☑ NEW	Does Not Meet Expectations	Really didn't feel like I was moving the chains like I should be.
	Steve Johnson ☑ NEW	Meets Expectations	I was very average this way in every way.

⊕ Add new item

FIGURE 7-29: Highlighted cell

The final step is to create a custom view that shows only the values of the employees who have given themselves a low rating. To do this, follow these steps:

1. Click "Lists and Libraries" and once again open the settings page for the `Employee Review` list. In the Views section, click the New button to create a new view. The Create New List View dialog will open up. Call the view `Low Ratings` and click OK.

2. The new view will be created and appear in the list of views. Click the new name of the new view to edit it.

3. Click the Filter button on the ribbon, as shown in Figure 7-30. If you don't immediately see it, select the Options tab under List View Tools.

FIGURE 7-30: Filter button on ribbon

4.   For the Filter Criteria, set the values to the following criteria:

   ➤   Field Name — Rating

   ➤   Comparison — Equals

   ➤   Value — "Does Not Meet Expectations"

5.   Click OK. Before viewing the changes, you'll need to click the Save button in the upper left-hand corner.

The new view has been created. To test it, open the site in the web browser again and navigate to the list. When the list opens, it will show the All Items view by default. To switch to the new view, hover your mouse over the All Items link in the breadcrumb. You'll be able to switch to the Low Ratings view, which will now display only the employees who have given themselves low scores, as shown in Figure 7-31.

FIGURE 7-31: Low Ratings view

This example walked you through many of the common tasks related to views and forms in an organization. SharePoint Designer 2010 makes it easy to customize the display of information with the XSLT List Web part and integration with InfoPath forms.

Workflows

You'll normally find workflows among the list of top reasons why most companies purchase SharePoint. Just about every organization has business processes that can be streamlined through the use of a workflow. Although SharePoint has several workflows available out-of-the-box through the web UI, their flexibility is limited, and many processes require more customization than these allow. This is where SPD comes in handy. It is the preferred tool for creating custom, no-code workflows.

The topic of workflows in SharePoint 2010 is covered in much more detail in Chapter 10, but this section focuses specifically on the options available in SharePoint Designer 2010.

New Types of Workflows

One of the common complaints about workflows in SharePoint Designer 2007 was that they were directly tied to a list or library and couldn't be reused. What often happened was that someone would make a request for a custom workflow to be created with SPD and it would be created in a test location. Once the workflow was approved, the only way to move the workflow was to re-create the workflow again on the production library. Additionally, once you created a workflow, there simply wasn't a way to use it anywhere else. It simply wasn't possible to create a standard workflow that could be used on different sites across the organization without re-creating it over and over again.

SharePoint Designer 2010 has added new types of workflows that not only address this issue, but also expand the capabilities that are possible with the product. SharePoint Designer 2010 supports the following types of workflows:

- ➤ *List workflow* — These are workflows that are directly associated with a list. This was the only type of workflow supported by SharePoint Designer 2007.

- ➤ *Reusable workflow* — These are workflows that can be associated with many lists, or libraries. Reusable workflows are based on a specific content type and can be reused throughout your SharePoint sites as needed.

- ➤ *Site workflow* — These workflows are not associated with a specific list or content type.

- ➤ *Globally Reusable Workflow* — When you look in the workflow gallery in SPD, you'll notice that the out-of-the-box workflows (Approval, Collect Feedback, and Collect Signatures) are listed as Globally Reusable Workflows. The workflows can be edited with SPD, or used as the basis to create new workflows. Keep in mind that, when working with these workflows, it is best to make copies of the workflows and make any modifications to the new copy.

With workflows in SharePoint Designer 2010, it is still possible to create workflows associated directly with a list or library, but you now have the additional flexibility to create workflows that are associated with a content type, create a reusable workflow, or even create a site workflow that doesn't really have to be associated with anything specific.

This new flexibility isn't going to eliminate the need for custom developed workflows. But it does mean that you have more options for creating workflows to automate a business process that don't require development.

Workflow Designer

Another major complaint about SharePoint Designer 2007 had to do with the Workflow Designer itself, which was more of a wizard-type interface. Although it was still possible to create effective workflows, the interface made it challenging for users to create workflows unless they were fairly familiar with the process.

The Workflow Designer in SharePoint Designer 2010 has been substantially changed to allow you to see the entire workflow on a single screen. The new interface makes it easier for you to visualize workflows to ensure that all of the conditions and actions needed for the workflow are accounted for.

SPD uses declarative rule-based workflows. These workflows use conditions and actions to define the process. This simply means that when a workflow runs on an item, it evaluates each condition, starting with the first one, until a condition is found that applies.

To open the Workflow Designer, click the Workflows link from the Navigation pane, and then click one of the workflow buttons in the New section on the ribbon. Any of the options will open the

Workflow Designer. Once the Workflow Designer is open, you can add conditions and actions to your workflow steps:

➤ *Conditions* — These are the rules or criteria that are applied to the workflow. When the workflow is started, the conditions are compared against the item being processed by the workflow. If the condition is found to be true, whatever is contained within the condition will be processed. Conditions are compared, starting with the first condition, then the second, and so forth, in order. Clicking the Condition button on the ribbon displays the complete list of conditions.

➤ *Actions* — These determine what activities are performed by the workflow. Some common examples would be to send an e-mail or set a value in a field. Actions can be applied without the use of conditions. Clicking the Actions button on the ribbon shows the complete list of actions available for workflows.

As conditions and actions are added to the workflow, you'll see that they have links that are used to more specifically define the criteria. Anyone who's ever created a rule in Microsoft Outlook should find this behavior very familiar. For example, if you were to add an action to send an e-mail, you'd need to click the link, which would open up a dialog to define the e-mail recipient, subject, and body text of the e-mail.

New Workflow Functionality

A number of other new capabilities have also been added to workflows in SharePoint Designer 2010. The following is a summary of some of the most notable changes.

Parallel Blocks

Traditionally, events in an SPD workflow are processed in a *serial* fashion — in other words, Step 1 is processed, and then, once completed, Step 2 is processed, and so on. However, many times workflows require that steps happen in *parallel* — in other words, both Steps 1 and 2 could be executed simultaneously. Workflows in SharePoint Designer 2010 now support parallel blocks within steps, which allows for more flexibility when you are creating workflows.

Impersonation Step

By default, when an SPD workflow runs, it does so under the identity of the user who is logged in to the machine. This means that if you have a workflow that writes to a list, the user initiating the request must have access to the list.

For example, maybe you have an expense report workflow and want to ensure that, when users fill out the form, an item is created in a list that the user doesn't have access to. Previously, this wasn't possible without custom code. However, SharePoint Designer 2010 adds the capability to create an *impersonation step* to address this scenario. An impersonation step can be created by clicking the button on the ribbon, and any actions within the step will be run as the user that associated the workflow to the list or library. In the case of the example expense report workflow, a user could submit his or her expense report, and then it could be written to a secure list.

Using an impersonation step also enables you to use a series of new actions that can manipulate the permissions of an item:

➤ Replace List Item Permissions

➤ Remove List Item Permissions

➤ Inherit List Item Permissions

The names of the actions are self-explanatory as to what they do. However, they open the door to numerous capabilities that previously required custom coding. For example, it is now possible to create a workflow that writes an item to a list, and set permissions so that all users wouldn't have permission to see the list until a certain criterion was met. Also, you could conditionally set permissions based on the values set in the workflow.

 It should be noted that, although this capability can come in handy, creating item-level permissions on a list or library with a large number of items can cause problems if proper planning isn't done before implementing.

Lookup from Profile

Many business processes involve submitting some type of information and having it automatically sent to the user's manager, or possibly looking up other information from the user's profile. SharePoint Designer 2010 now has the capability to pull information from a user's profile and use it in a workflow. This allows for much more dynamic workflows that can be routed differently based on the submitting user.

 For this functionality to work, it is important that the values that are to be looked up are defined and populated in the user profile.

Modify the Out-of-the-Box Workflows

The out-of-the-box SharePoint 2010 workflow templates can be copied from SharePoint Designer 2010 and modified as needed. This is useful if the out-of-the-box workflows are close, but not exactly what you are looking for, and prevents the need to rebuild a workflow entirely from scratch.

 You should avoid modifying the workflow templates in the top-level site in your site collection. These templates are used as the basis for workflows across the entire site collection. If you modify one of the out-of-the-box workflow templates, it is best to make a copy and modify the copy.

Import and Export Workflows to and from Visio 2010

Most workflows are created to complement an existing business process and, in most organizations, those workflows are created by business analysts. SharePoint Designer 2010 workflows can now be modeled in Visio 2010 by a business analyst. Once the workflow is complete, it can be saved and then imported to SharePoint Designer 2010, where the steps can be refined. In other words, Visio 2010 can be used to create all of the conditions and actions. Once imported into SharePoint Designer 2010, the specific details must be defined. For example, if an e-mail is to be sent, the action would be listed in the Workflow Designer, but who it gets sent to and what it says would still need to be defined.

Additionally, it is also possible to export workflows from SharePoint Designer 2010 back to Visio 2010 to be further modified if necessary. Not all of the details will be visible in Visio but they will be preserved for re-import into SharePoint Designer.

Creating a Site Workflow that Writes to a Custom List

Creating standardized forms that have basic workflows is a common scenario in many companies. The following example uses a site workflow to capture employee reviews submitted by employees, which their managers will then need to review and approve.

To do this, you'll create a custom list, customize the fields on the form that are used to start the workflow, look up the manager of the person submitting the workflow, write it all to a list, and then assign a task to the manager. Follow these steps:

1. Open your site in SPD and click "Lists and Libraries" in the Navigation pane on the left.

2. Click the Workflows link in the Navigation pane on the left.

3. From the ribbon, click the Site Workflow button shown in Figure 7-32 to create a new workflow.

FIGURE 7-32: Site Workflow button

4. Name the workflow `Employee Reviews` and click OK. The Workflow Designer for the new workflow will automatically open.

5. With the Workflow Designer open, you should see a blinking horizontal orange line, which is used to indicate where the next action or condition will be inserted. But, before you add any steps to this workflow, from the ribbon, click the Initiation Form Parameters button shown in Figure 7-33. This allows you to define parameters that are used to collect data when the workflow is started. In this case, you want the user to fill out the form and then use the information that was entered throughout the workflow.

FIGURE 7-33: Initiation Form Parameters button

6. From the "Association and Initiation Form Parameters" dialog, click the Add button.

7. Name the field `Employee Name`, choose "Single Line of Text" as the Information type, and click Next. Leave the default value blank and click Finish.

8. Once you've completed adding the first parameter you should be returned to the "Association and Initiation Form Parameters" dialog. You need to create another parameter, so click the Add button and name the field `Rating`. Choose Choice as the Information type (that is, a menu to choose from), and click Next. On the Column Settings screen, enter the values shown in Figure 7-34 and click Finish.

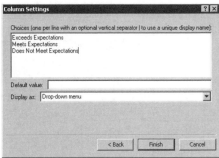

9. Click the Add button to add another field. Name this field `Comments`, set it as "Multiple lines of text," and click Next. Then click Finish. Click the OK button from the "Association and Initiation Form Parameters" screen.

FIGURE 7-34: Column Settings values

 Workflows make use of two concepts that are sometimes confused: variables and parameters. Variables are defined during the workflow process and can be referenced throughout the workflow. In this example, the name of the initiator's manager is a variable that is later written to a field in a list. Parameters are user-entered information that's captured during the workflow. In Steps 9 and 10, parameters are defined that will be filled out by the user before the workflow process begins.

10. The Workflow Designer should open and there should be a horizontal, orange blinking cursor in a box titled Step 1. From the ribbon, click the Action button and then click "Send an Email" from under the Core Actions section, as shown in Figure 7-35. Optionally, instead of clicking the Actions button, you can start typing and SPD will try to figure out what you want it to do.

11. The new action will be added to the workflow, but it still must be configured. To do that, click the "these users" link in the action, which will open the Define E-mail Message dialog.

12. Click the phone book icon at the right of the "To:" field to open the Select Users dialog. Select "Workflow Lookup for a user", then click the Add button. Choose the following values from the "Lookup for Person or Group" dialog shown in Figure 7-36:

➤ Data Source — Workflow Context

➤ Field from source — Initiator

➤ Return field as — Email

Once complete, click OK and you'll be taken back to the Select Users dialog. Click OK again on this screen to define the rest of the fields in the e-mail.

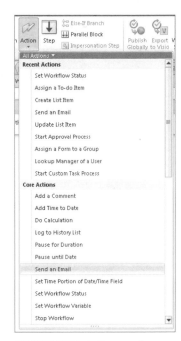

FIGURE 7-35: Actions options

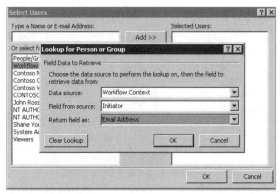

FIGURE 7-36: "Lookup for Person or Group" dialog

13. For the "Subject" field, enter the text **Employee Review Received**. Optionally, here you could also click the ellipsis (…) button to open the string builder to create a dynamic subject that could pull values from the user, or from the workflow itself.

14. In the body field of the e-mail, enter the text **Your review has been sent to your manager who will schedule a meeting within the next week,** as shown in Figure 7-37. Again, you can optionally click the "Add or Change Lookup" button in the bottom-left corner of the dialog to add dynamic text from the workflow itself. When you are finished, click the OK button to return to the Workflow Designer.

15. From the ribbon, click the Action button and select Create List Item. This adds the action to the workflow. To configure it, click the "this list" link in the action, which opens the Create New List Item dialog.

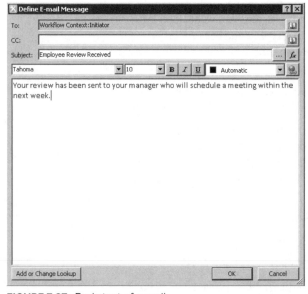

FIGURE 7-37: Body text of e-mail

16. Click the Add button to open the Value Assignment dialog. Select the field to set as `Employee Name`. Then, to assign the value, click the function button. Choose the following values:

➤ Data Source — Workflow Variables and Parameters

➤ Field from source — Parameter: Employee Name

➤ Return field as — As String

When you have finished, click OK, and then click OK again to return to the Create New List Item dialog.

17. Repeat Step 16 to add the `Rating` and `Comments` fields from the parameters captured in the form, as shown in Figure 7-38. Once you have added all of the fields, click OK.

18. Back in the Workflow Designer, click the Action button again and choose "Assign a To-do Item."

19. Click the link for "a to-do item" and the Custom Task Wizard will open. Click Next. On the second page of the wizard, enter **Employee Review** in the Name field and click Finish.

20. Next, from the Workflow Designer, click the "these users" link in the "create to-do item" action that you've been editing. From the Select Users dialog, click "Workflow Lookup for a User," and then click Add. The "Lookup for Person or Group" dialog window will open.

21. Set the following values for the lookup in the top section of the window:

➤ Data source — User Profiles

➤ Field from source — Manager

➤ Return field as — Login Name

22. For the fields at the bottom of the "Lookup for Person or Group" dialog shown in Figure 7-39, choose Account Name from the drop-down menu for the Field value. Next, click the function button to the right of the Value field. In the dialog that opens, set the fields as follows:

➤ Data source — Workflow Context

➤ Field from source — Initiator

➤ Return field as — Login Name

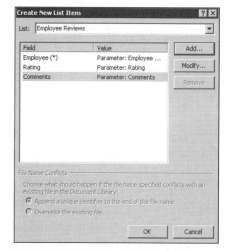

FIGURE 7-38: Adding the Rating and Comments fields

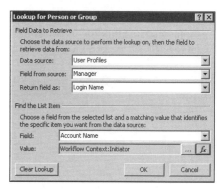

FIGURE 7-39: Selecting Account Name

The name of the manager is being returned for the purpose of assigning a task to the manager, which is why the Login Name is used as the return field.

Step 22 requires that you have user profile imports configured and a value in the Manager field in the profile. If you don't have that configured, choose another value for that such as yourself. It won't be as elaborate, but it will still demonstrate the concept of assigning a task to a user.

23. Click OK on all the dialogs to accept the changes.

24. The workflow is now complete and should look similar to Figure 7-40. From the ribbon, click the Save button. Before the workflow can be used, it must first be published. To do so, click the Publish button on the ribbon, as shown in Figure 7-41.

FIGURE 7-40: Result of completed workflow

FIGURE 7-41: Publish button

To try the site workflow, go back to your site and click Site Actions ➪ View All Site Content. At the top of the page, click the Site Workflows link.

Click the Employee Reviews link, as shown in Figure 7-42, which opens the page where you can fill out the form to start the workflow. Fill out the form and click Start. To make this form easier to access, you can copy the form's URL and create a link directly to the form.

You can see the workflow has kicked off by clicking Site Actions ➪ View All Site Content, and then clicking the Site Workflows link. The workflow task will be listed under the My Running Workflows section. Click the link for the workflow to go to the Task Item that's been created. You should see that the task has been assigned to the manager of the user who started the workflow, as shown in Figure 7-43.

FIGURE 7-42: Employee Reviews link

FIGURE 7-43: Task being assigned to a manager

Hover your mouse over the Title of the workflow task item and select it to edit the task item. If you log in as a user who can edit the task, you can click the "Complete task" button. When you view the status of the workflow, the outcome should show as Completed.

If you go back to the Employee Review list, you'll see that a new item has been created and the information entered into the form has been added, as shown in Figure 7-44.

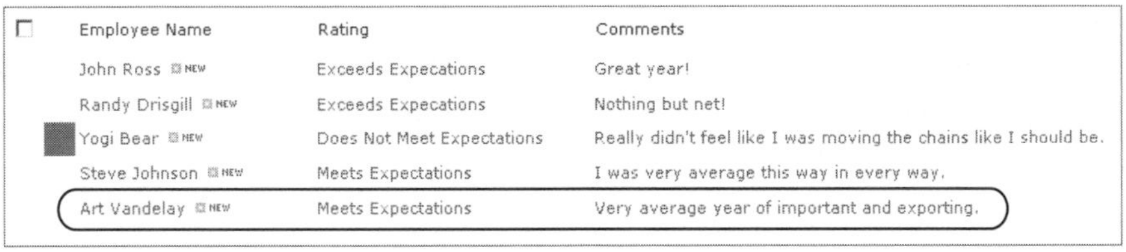

	Employee Name	Rating	Comments
	John Ross ⊠ NEW	Exceeds Expectations	Great year!
	Randy Drisgill ⊠ NEW	Exceeds Expectations	Nothing but net!
	Yogi Bear ⊠ NEW	Does Not Meet Expectations	Really didn't feel like I was moving the chains like I should be.
	Steve Johnson ⊠ NEW	Meets Expectations	I was very average this way in every way.
	Art Vandelay ⊠ NEW	Meets Expectations	Very average year of important and exporting.

FIGURE 7-44: New item added with information

This example showed how you can create a workflow that captures information into a form, sends an e-mail, writes information to a list, and then assigns a task to the user's manager. Although this was a very basic workflow example, these concepts can be expanded and repeated to create much more robust and complex workflows that don't require any custom code.

Data Sources

The generic term used by SharePoint Designer 2010 to refer to all sources of SharePoint content is *data sources*. This could be data coming from SharePoint, or the data could be coming from external sources such as a SQL Server database or web service. You can see the data sources link in the Navigation pane. From the gallery page for the data sources, you'll see all of the different types listed in your site. By default, you might only see lists and libraries, but if you look at the options on the ribbon, you'll see that several other data sources are supported.

Lists and Libraries

Lists and libraries are the most basic types of data in SharePoint. Not much has changed, other than lists and libraries can be created and managed directly from SharePoint Designer 2010. Clicking the "Lists and Libraries" link in the Navigation pane opens up the gallery, which shows all of the lists and libraries associated with the site. The ribbon will change context, which will make it easier to create and update your lists and libraries.

Data Source Connections

Clicking the Data Sources link in the Navigation pane opens the gallery and displays all data sources related to the site. At first glance, it looks very similar to the "Lists and Libraries" gallery simply because that's probably the majority of what you'll see listed. But if you look at the ribbon, you'll notice several new options that reflect the various data source connections that are supported:

- ➤ External Database
- ➤ SOAP Web Service

➤ REST Web Service or RSS Feed

➤ XML File Connection

Clicking one of the buttons on the ribbon opens a wizard that walks you through the process of connecting to the respective data source. Once the connection has been made to the data source, SharePoint Designer 2010 can be used to combine the data from multiple sources into a single view. This is commonly referred to as a *mashup*, but, in SharePoint terminology, this is referred to as a *composite application*. An example of this would be if you combined customer address information from a SQL Server table with Bing maps to show a visual representation of where your clients were located.

External Data Integration

The Business Connectivity Service (BCS) is a new feature in SharePoint 2010 that enables SharePoint to connect with line of business (LOB) systems such as SQL Server, Oracle, PeopleSoft, and others. It is the evolution of the Business Data Catalog (BDC) functionality that existed in SharePoint 2007. Although the BDC was able to integrate critical business data with SharePoint, there were a few obstacles that often made it challenging for organizations to implement.

Connecting to a LOB system with SharePoint 2007 required an XML file called an *application definition*, which essentially helped to define the connection between SharePoint and the LOB system. The application definition was extremely complex and too difficult to create by hand in most cases. Most companies preferred to use a third-party tool to create the file, which was an additional expense. Once companies were able to connect to the LOB systems by default, data was only pushed in one direction to SharePoint. This meant that it wasn't possible to edit the data from SharePoint and have it write back to the LOB system without custom development.

Through the use of the BCS and SharePoint Designer 2010, the entire process of connecting to LOB systems has been greatly simplified. It is now possible for SharePoint Designer 2010 to create the connection to the LOB systems quickly and easily. Once the connection is made, the information can be surfaced as an external content type (ECT) in an external list. This allows users to interact with the external data just as if they were editing any other SharePoint list. Although the data is coming from an LOB system, users can make changes directly from SharePoint, and changes will be written back to into the LOB system.

 The BCS is covered in more detail in Chapter 14.

Connecting to a SharePoint Web Service with a Data View Web Part

Did you know that the site directory is gone from SharePoint 2010? Well, if you didn't, sorry to be the bearer of bad news. If you weren't familiar with the site directory, it listed all of the sites in your site collection grouped by categories that you specified. Many organizations used it as a way to quickly show all of their sites in one place.

This example walks through how you can connect to one of the out-of-the-box SharePoint web services to get a list of all of the sites in a site collection. This isn't a complete replacement for the site directory, but it will enable you to show a dynamic display of sites in a site collection.

Follow these steps:

1. Click the Data Sources link in the Navigation panel.

2. The Data Sources gallery will open and the ribbon will change context to reflect the options available for connecting to different data sources. Click SOAP Service Connection on the ribbon, as shown in Figure 7-45.

FIGURE 7-45: SOAP Service Connection button

3. The Data Source Properties dialog will open with the Source tab selected. In the "Service description location" field, enter the URL `http://contoso/_vti_bin/webs.asmx?WSDL`, which should point to the top-level site in your site collection. Then, click the Connect button.

4. On the Data Source Properties page, leave all of the options set to the default except for the Operation drop-down, which should be set to `GetAllSubWebCollection`, as shown in Figure 7-46. When you have finished, click OK. You'll be returned to the Data Sources gallery and notice that the new SOAP Services connection has been added.

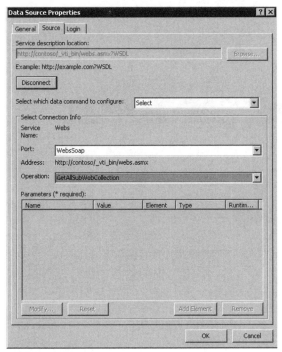

FIGURE 7-46: Operation drop-down in Data Source Properties window

5. Click the Site Pages link in the Navigation panel. Then, from the ribbon, click the Web Part Page button. Choose the first option, which is called "Full Page, Vertical." Change the name of the file to AllSites.aspx.

6. Select the new page and the click the Edit File button from the ribbon.

7. The page will open in edit mode. Be sure to first click inside PlaceHolderMain in the body of the page to select it. Next, to add the new data source to the page, click the Insert tab from the top of the ribbon. Then, click the Data View button and select the data source, which will be listed under the SOAP Services section, as shown in Figure 7-47.

FIGURE 7-47: Selecting the data source

8. You'll see that the Data View immediately starts showing a list of all of the sites in your site collection. However, the URL isn't clickable. To change that, click the URL listed for the first item, and then click the arrow to the right of the field to edit the formatting. Select to format the field as a Hyperlink, as shown in Figure 7-48. You'll get a warning, but click Yes. A new window will open that enables you to further customize the link. It is safe to ignore the warning and click OK.

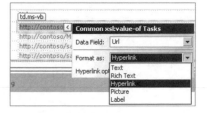

FIGURE 7-48: Formatting as a hyperlink

9. Click Save on the form from the upper left-hand corner. If you go back out to your site, you can see your new page by going to the Site Pages library and clicking the link. You could further customize the DVWP by adding filtering, changing the grouping or sorting, or even adding conditional formatting to display the list of sites however you wanted.

This was a very basic example of connecting to a web service using SPD and the DVWP. Whether you are using one of the out-of-the-box SharePoint web services, or connecting to an external source, SPD makes it quick and easy to make the connection and display the information to users without custom development.

USING SHAREPOINT DESIGNER EFFECTIVELY IN YOUR ENVIRONMENT

Thus far in this chapter, you have learned about the new capabilities of SharePoint Designer 2010 and what it can do. However, just because the tool can do something doesn't necessarily mean you should use for it a task. So, the question is ultimately, "When is SPD the best tool for the job?"

This section examines many of the typical scenarios that SPD is used for, and briefly discusses considerations for determining whether SPD is the best option. At a high level, the best approach for any custom requirement for SharePoint is to consider your options out-of-the-box, with SPD, and with custom development. There's no "one size fits all" answer, and there are definitely pros and cons to the various approaches. So, it is important to understand all of your options and weigh them fairly.

Managing Sites

SharePoint Designer 2010 is an ideal tool for site owners to use to manage all aspects of their sites quickly and efficiently. The new UI for SPD makes it easy to make changes from a central location without having to click through countless menus like you'd have to do from the web interface.

Why wouldn't you want to give SPD to your site owners? For starters, it is still a very powerful tool that requires control from the administrative side. Additionally, those who are identified as being potential SPD users should be given an appropriate amount of training to ensure that they understand how to properly use the tool. Handing SPD out to your users without proper training and controls is a big risk. It doesn't guarantee that something bad will happen, but why leave anything to chance? Properly controlling your environment will make it more reliable, and well-trained users will have a better experience with SharePoint, so everyone wins.

Workflows

Workflows are the classic example that's typically used to determine the best tool for the job. Often, organizations will be faced with a business requirement to add workflows and are convinced that the internal group of ace .NET developers can knock out a custom SharePoint workflow in no time. However, even relatively simplistic SharePoint workflows have been known to bring many .NET developers to tears. Workflow development in SharePoint is an advanced task that requires not only a deep understanding of .NET, but also a deep understanding of SharePoint development, which simply takes time to acquire.

Following are the typical options for creating custom workflows in an organization:

➤ *Out-of-the-box* — This provides limited options for workflows and limited customization capabilities through the web UI. These are easy to create and use. They are good for very simplistic workflows, such as approval and feedback workflows.

➤ *SharePoint Designer* — This provides declarative, rule-based workflows that are capable of medium complexity. These are ideal for the majority of workflows that require more complexity than the out-of-the-box options. They are quick to create, and easy to change and support. The out-of-the-box workflows can also be imported and modified by SPD to further extend their capabilities.

➤ *Custom Development* — This provides nearly unlimited options, and are very flexible, which provides the capability to support the most complex scenarios. These require a highly skilled developer and a significant amount of time to create.

How do you know which one to pick? The answer is that you should pick the easiest method that will meet your requirements. In most environments, most workflow requests can be addressed either through the use of the out-of-the-box or SPD workflows. Custom developed workflows definitely have a place, but they should be reserved for the most complex workflows. There's no need to go through the effort of writing something custom that could easily be created with another method. This is just another reason why it is important for developers to learn SPD.

Branding

SPD is an ideal tool for branding SharePoint for both big and small projects. For small projects, it is the obvious choice because of the simple page editing capabilities. But SPD is also an integral part for complex SharePoint branding projects. Professional SharePoint branders start with SPD to create their master pages and page layouts. The typical process normally is something like this:

1. A SharePoint brander creates the mockup of the design to implement.

2. The master pages and page layouts are created and styled using SPD in a development environment. SharePoint Designer 2010 makes this process of creating page layouts even easier because site columns and content types can be created directly from SPD.

3. Custom branding assets (master pages, page layouts, CSS, images, and so on) are exported from SPD and given to a developer, who packages the assets up as a WSP with one or more features.

These are high-level steps, and might vary depending on the people doing the work and the specific project. Many might be surprised to learn that SPD is used even in complex projects, but the reason why it is an effective tool is because it allows SharePoint branders to make changes and see them reflected immediately in the site. Often, a custom SharePoint design requires lots of small adjustments to CSS to get the pixels exactly where they need to go. SPD is the ideal tool for these types of changes. Once all of the changes have been made to the assets, they can be exported to Visual Studio 2010 for packaging and deploying as a feature and WSP.

Prototyping Development Tasks

One of the most overlooked scenarios for SPD is to use it to quickly prototype development tasks in your environment. Most of you can relate to the idea that your users or clients make requests for custom functionality all the time. They are coming to you because you are the SME for SharePoint in your environment, and they think you have the answer to every possible request they could dream up. The fact is that many users don't understand that they might be the only person on the face of the earth to make the request they are making. But before you can estimate or agree to do the project, sometimes it is best to prototype the idea to prove if it's even possible. SPD is the ideal tool for rapidly prototyping many development tasks.

Let's be clear about what is meant by "prototyping." This is the idea of proving a concept. That doesn't mean that you are trying to get it working on the first shot. It simply means that you are determining whether it is possible to do what's being asked.

An example of this could be a manager from a department requesting a custom workflow. You use SPD to create a prototype that provides a good idea about how the workflow works and demonstrates concepts, but it is far less refined than the actual production workflow will be. In this example, it would even be possible to mock up the workflow in SPD, and then export to Visual Studio 2010 where it could be further customized and refined.

SPD is also a good way to prototype development tasks involving connection to external data sources, such as web services or LOB systems. The information from these sources can be returned, and SPD can display the data using the DVWP. Once the concepts are proven by connecting to the external systems, developers can use this information to help them formulate more accurate estimates about how to create a custom solution to address the business requirement in a more formal way.

SUMMARY

This chapter discussed the many capabilities of SharePoint Designer 2010. Users who are familiar with SharePoint Designer 2007 should appreciate the improvements made to this latest version, which include the following highlights:

➤ The user interface for SharePoint Designer 2010 has been redesigned to put more focus on the various SharePoint objects, and less focus on being a page editor.

➤ SharePoint Designer 2010 has been divided into three areas: Navigation pane, ribbon, and Gallery and Summary.

➤ Access to SPD can be controlled by farm administrators from Central Administration, or by site collection administrators from the site settings page.

➤ To prevent users from getting into trouble, you can restrict SPD by customizing specific pages, or more broadly, by removing the permission to use SPD altogether.

➤ SPD is the primary tool for customizing the look and feel of your SharePoint site.

➤ SPD 2010 enables users to quickly customize views using the XSLT List View Web part.

➤ List forms can be customized in InfoPath directly from SPD.

➤ Declarative workflows can be created with SPD, which enables you to create no-code solutions to streamline business processes.

➤ The three types of SPD workflows are List, Reusable, and Site.

➤ Connections to data sources can be made right from SPD, including LOB systems such as external databases, REST web services, SOAP web services, and XML files.

➤ SPD is an invaluable tool for many different tasks across the organization for all users, including information workers, administrators, and developers.

ABOUT THE AUTHOR

John Ross is a Senior Consultant for SharePoint911from Orlando, Florida, with more than seven years of experience implementing solutions for clients ranging from small businesses to Fortune 500 companies, as well as government organizations. He has been involved with a wide range of SharePoint solutions that include public-facing Internet sites, corporate intranets, and extranets. Additionally, Ross is co-founder of the Orlando SharePoint User Group (`http://www.orlandosharepoint.com`). His blog can be found at http://www.sharepoint911.com/blogs/john.

8

Building Sandboxed Solutions

By Robert Bogue

Since SharePoint Portal Server 2001, end users have been finding ways to get things done. Getting things done didn't always mean writing code and deploying it to the server. Little "hacks" started to show up around the time of SharePoint Portal Server 2003, and particularly with SharePoint 2007. These little "hacks" may have been a little bit of JavaScript, a cute bit of CSS, an InfoPath form, or even a special Word or Excel template file. The fact that these little "hacks" existed has flown mostly below the radar of the IT professional trying to manage the system. Generally, they didn't cause much harm (if any) and, in the end, the IT professionals had bigger issues to worry about.

In 2007, SharePoint began to emerge as a valid development platform. As of this writing in 2010, many people have caught on to the fact that SharePoint is a valid development platform — even if it's not without its difficulties and limitations. That has created more and more solutions that IT professionals were asked to deliver to their SharePoint 2007 farms.

It is, of course, predictable that when the IT professionals were trying to deliver numerous solutions quickly, some of those solutions had performance and stability problems. The end result was that the entire SharePoint 2007 farm's stability and performance were threatened or impacted by as little as one quickly written solution. This has been a problem that IT professionals have been trying to solve.

This situation (where one poorly written solution could bring down the whole farm) exposed a conflict — a conflict between an individual business unit just trying to get work done, and the IT Pro who just didn't want to have to be awakened at 3 a.m. to deal with a server farm that has crashed for no apparent reason. This conflict — between getting things done quickly and ensuring that systems are maintainable — is one of the areas of focus for improvement in SharePoint 2010.

This chapter focuses on all of the options that SharePoint 2010 brings to bear for the developer and quasi-developer to create business solutions, while respecting the need for the IT professional to keep the platform performing and available — no matter what the business throws at it.

THE PUSH TO NO-CODE SOLUTIONS

SharePoint 2007 offered two different ways to deploy code to the server. Both of those methods leveraged the SharePoint Solution (.WSP) infrastructure. (I've gone quite public on the fact that if you're not using WSPs to deploy your code, you are doing something wrong. You can see one of my blog posts about this topic at http://www.thorprojects.com/blog/archive/2009/05/30/why-we -build-wsps-and-option-explicit.aspx.) Following are the two options:

➤   Deploy in the BIN folder of the web application and apply code access security (CAS) policies.

➤   Deploy to the global assembly cache (GAC).

The .NET CAS policies are not well understood by most folks — even those with experience in SharePoint. Typical security is managed through the authorization of the user. Whatever the user can do, the code can do as well. When .NET was created, it was already understood that there are some times when it may not be appropriate to allow a program to do anything the user can do.

As a result, CAS was added to .NET. It's a set of policies that control which functions can be performed by code based on a set of identification criteria. For example, execution of code that is hosted on a network share is disabled by default.

SharePoint is by far the most popular application built on top of ASP.NET that leverages this technology to allow a subset of activities to be performed based on CAS. Policies are written in XML, so they can be visually inspected by administrators and security personnel before a DLL is installed. This provides the capability to ensure that code written by a third party doesn't perform operations that it shouldn't — such as write to the local filesystem, access a database directly, and so on.

One of the key things to understand about CAS policies is that they do not apply to any assembly that's located in the GAC. All assemblies in the GAC are automatically granted a full CAS policy, and can do anything, and are, therefore, more difficult to perform a security review on.

One of the key problems with the CAS approach is that it wasn't well understood, and writing the CAS policies was a bit of trial and error. The net effect was that it was more likely for an organization to perform a security code review on its code instead of implementing CAS policies. Most of the BIN/CAS deployments were from third-party vendors who were looking for their solutions to be as widely accepted as possible.

The BIN/CAS approach had the benefit of being able to restrict the code from performing some operations. However, the BIN/CAS option wasn't available for timer jobs, feature receivers, event receivers, and workflows. And, using the BIN/CAS approach did nothing to prevent the code from entering an endless loop, doing very expensive operations on the system, or generally consuming resources — in other words, generally creating a performance problem. Worse yet, there's no protection against consuming too much memory. Code that consumes (and doesn't release) too much memory will force the application pool serving SharePoint's web application to recycle — and, therefore, cause an outage, even if it's brief.

In short, the protection offered by the 2007 models just wasn't sufficient to protect the SharePoint farm from the evils that could be done by some bad code. To work around this, various techniques were attempted.

IT professionals could call upon developers they trusted to perform automated analysis of the solutions that were being proposed for the farm. Tools like SPDisposeCheck and FXCop (or Visual Studio Code Analysis) could provide some level of automated checking for obvious issues.

Both SPDisposeCheck and FXCop perform what is known as *static analysis* — that is, they look at the code and identify potentially bad patterns. They do not monitor the application at run-time to determine for certain whether there is a problem or not. SPDisposeCheck looks at the output DLL that was created from the code and identifies patterns specific to SharePoint that may indicate that memory was leaked. FXCop does an analysis of the source code and looks for numerous issues. The most relevant is the failure to dispose of an object that implements IDisposable.

However, neither of the tools was foolproof — they both provided false positives, and failed to identify all of the potential issues in code. Furthermore, they did nothing to identify heavy-duty processing, the potential for endless loops, or other potentially bad behaviors.

In some organizations, an actual code-review process was instituted. This process involved a more detailed review by a set of trusted developers, where the developers would try to understand the entire solution, and identify those situations that might negatively impact the farm. However, because this process relied on humans, it was not only expensive, it was not always reliable. Its effectiveness was very dependent upon the person (or persons) doing the review.

As a result, some organizations resorted to putting high prices via internal charge backs for custom code to deter the business from writing(or having written) code that had to be deployed on the shared farm. Others just prohibited it outright. The end result was an even greater push toward the no-code solutions.

UNDERSTANDING THE CONCEPT OF A SANDBOXED SOLUTION

SharePoint 2010 offers a whole new set of tools to work around the problems caused by bad code in the execution models of SharePoint 2007. Sandboxed solutions provide developers with a flexible development environment, while providing site administrators the capability to manage applications in their site collection, and providing farm administrators with peace of mind that this development is not endangering the farm.

In addition to code deployed in the sandbox, many new client opportunities exist with better support for JavaScript, REST, Ajax, and Silverlight. This all adds up to a variety of techniques that can get the code that users need, as you will see later in this chapter. Because of these options, it's easier to restrict what the code can do on the server — or remove the code from the server altogether.

As mentioned previously, code for SharePoint 2007 was written by the developers and the infrastructure team deployed it all in the same process. In SharePoint 2010, the process is still the same for what are called *farm solutions* that are deployed by the administrator. One of the key decisions to be made by developers as they begin their projects is whether to develop a new sandboxed solution or a more traditional farm solution. The sandbox versus farm solution question is one of the two things that are asked during the first step in the new project wizard.

From a developer perspective, it is important to understand the limitations to developing code for the sandbox (which will be examined shortly). It does also represent a change in where the developers' solutions are deployed. With a sandboxed solution, the individual site collection administrators can deploy the solution into a special solutions gallery of each site collection. This means that site administrators have the power to control which solutions are deployed to their sites — but it also means that they'll have to take responsibility for installing their own solutions. If the developer chooses the farm solution, only the farm administrator will have the capability to add the new solution to the farm.

Who can deploy the solution — and where it goes — may be important, but that's only half of the story. Why should the IT professionals want to allow users to upload code to their environments?

Figure 8-1 shows conceptually how farm solutions are executed. Notice that all of the code is in the same box. Everything runs together with few barriers to prevent one piece of code from overrunning the space of another.

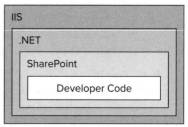

FIGURE 8-1: Full-trust execution

However, an entire class of solutions called *sandboxed solutions* can be installed by SharePoint 2010 site collection administrators. These solutions are processed differently.

Sandboxed solutions are different because SharePoint spins up a separate application domain and runs the sandbox code inside this application domain, as shown in Figure 8-2. The application domain that SharePoint creates is inside an entirely different process than the IIS process that hosts ASP.NET and the SharePoint code for web pages — SPUCHostService.exe. This application domain has a tiny set of things that it can do. Essentially, in the sandbox, code can access anything inside the same SharePoint site collection — but nothing else. (You learn more about what the code can or cannot do later in this chapter.) You'll notice that there's a complete gap between where the code is running and the IIS host process that SharePoint is running in. This gap is what prevents sandboxed applications from impacting SharePoint.

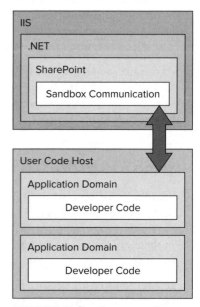

FIGURE 8-2: Sandbox execution

In addition to imposing limits on what sandboxed code can do, SharePoint does two other critical things to items in the sandbox:

➤   Because, at any given time, there's only one thing in this unique application domain that will be running, SharePoint will terminate the sandboxed code if it executes for too long. The default is 60 seconds. This means that no sandboxed solution can bring the server to its knees — at least not for very long.

➤ All of the resources used by the solution are tracked. These resources are assigned points, and ultimately the system administrator allocates a maximum set of points to a site collection. The system administrator can change how individual actions and granular resource usages are converted into the points that they allocate. However, this isn't generally done, because the defaults are reasonable. Table 8-1 shows the resources that are tracked, and how they are converted into resource points.

TABLE 8-1: Sandbox Counters and Default Values

COUNTER NAME	RESOURCE POINTS
AbnormalProcessTerminationCount	1
CPUExecutionTime	200
CriticalExceptionCount	10
IdlePercentProcessorTime	100
InvocationCount	100
PercentProcessorTime	85
ProcessCPUCycles	1E+11
ProcessHandleCount	10000
ProcessIOBytes	10000000
ProcessThreadCount	10000
ProcessVirtualBytes	1000000000
SharePointDatabaseQueryCount	400
SharePointDatabaseQueryTime	20
UnhandledExceptionCount	50
UnresponsiveprocessCount	2

The site collection's resource quota is set at a site-collection level, and it doesn't specify specific things that can be executed, or events that can happen — just like a storage quota doesn't control how much storage can be consumed by a document library or a sub-site. The goal is to allocate points in a way that they represent a relatively accurate load on the system.

The product team has said that an abnormal process termination (first entry in the table) is twice as bad as an unresponsive process (the last entry in the table). They've said that the sandbox terminating an unresponsive process is roughly 25 times more impactful than an unhandled exception. All of these counters are added up for each solution in the site collection (slightly behind when they are used), and the individual solution usages are aggregated and compared against the site's quota. As long as, in aggregate, the total is lower than the quota, everything runs fine.

Once the site collection reaches its quota of resource points, the solutions in the site collection are shut down for the remainder of the day. Of course, the farm administrator can always grant more points. However, reaching this quota provides a way to identify that a solution is either becoming popular, or some sort of coding issues may be leading to performance problems.

The implementation of the sandbox is flexible in that you can have the host supporting the user code on the Web Front End (WFE) servers or on another set of servers. For larger farm environments, you can completely isolate the performance of all sandboxed code onto other servers so that the core SharePoint operations are unaffected. All communication in and out of the sandbox is done via serialization, so it's possible to transport the communication across the network to another server.

You have a choice of whether to do local sandbox execution or remote sandbox execution. It may be easier to do local execution, particularly if you don't have an abundance of servers in your farm. However, you should keep in mind that sandboxed solutions will have an impact on your WFEs — even if that impact is mitigated.

The idea of protection afforded by the sandbox relies upon the concept of a .NET *application domain*, or the execution environment in which code runs. Each application domain is separate and distinct from all of the other application domains in the process. This allows the SPUCHostService.Exe process to kill application domains when they've run for too long — without impacting other solutions. It also allows you to define CAS policies for the entire application domain. This means that you can (and, in the case of the sandbox, Microsoft did) severely restrict what you can do from a CAS policy perspective.

 The Microsoft Patterns and Practices SharePoint Guidance for SharePoint 2010 has extensive coverage of execution models, including sandbox execution details. If you're interested in the technical details of the architecture, including detailed diagrams, you can go to http://msdn.microsoft.com/en-us/ library/ff798382.aspx. *If you want to look through all of the guidance, you can go to* http://www.microsoft.com/spg.

Another SharePoint 2010 technology that helps to protect the platform is *query throttling*. Set at a web application level, query throttling prevents queries from running if they will return more than 5,000 rows. This protects the system from having large queries eat up performance across the system. The default of 5,000 rows isn't an accident. It's the default value where SQL server will promote row-level locks to a table-level lock. When SQL has converted a query to a table-level lock, no write operations (including adding new rows and updating existing rows) can take place until the query has been completed. This can have substantial impacts on performance.

Despite very good reasons to prevent large queries from running most of the day, certain things generally require large queries. Things like timer jobs and reporting often require more than 5,000 records at a time. There are three solutions to this:

➤ Administrators have a different row quota that applies to them. You can override the query limit by changing settings and by using an override setting on the query.

➤ Administrators can switch off query throttling for certain lists via a property on the list.

➤ "Happy hour" is a time of day where the query throttling is turned off for the whole application. This exclusion allows you to schedule all of your reports and administrative jobs for an hour (or a few hours) during the evening when the queries won't have as big of an impact on end user performance. This setting is available from Central administration web application resource throttling.

Understanding the Execution of Declarative Code

One difficulty when learning about the sandbox is the fact that the sandbox actually refers to two distinct things:

➤ The first is the Solution Gallery in a site collection, as well as the SharePoint Solutions (WSPs) that are in it. This is *sandboxed deployment*.

➤ The second is the SPUserHostService.exe process. This is where code deployed to the sandbox is executed.

What's the difference?

Well, consider for a moment Collaborative Application Markup Language (CAML), Extensible Object Markup Language (XOML), and declarative elements that have no code. These non-code items aren't executed inside of the sandbox. Instead, they're considered to be inherently safe, and are, therefore, run directly inside of the IIS worker process.

This distinction is often confusing, because, once CAML runs to create a list instance, the list instance itself isn't considered to be a part of the sandbox. Similarly, if you have a declarative workflow that consists of XOML and XML, it's not executed inside of the SPUCHostService.exe process — it cannot because, in fact, workflow requires full trust.

Don't get tangled up by the fact that declarative items are handled differently. Just know that only code gets special treatment in the sandbox.

Understanding What You Can and Can't Do

Two primary restrictions are applied to the sandbox. As mentioned previously, one restriction is CAS policies. The second restriction is related to a process token. Let's first zero in on CAS.

Three basic permissions are granted to sandbox application domains:

➤ SecurityPermission.Execution

➤ AspNetHostingPermission.Level = Minimal

➤ SharePointPermission.ObjectModel

Together, these permissions allow the code to run, inspect its basic operating environment, and access SharePoint objects. However, the SharePoint objects are further restricted. It's not possible to access anything in the Microsoft.SharePoint.Administration namespace. This includes enumerations — which should inherently be safe.

Numerous other limitations exist, as shown in Table 8-2.

TABLE 8-2: Sandbox Restrictions on SharePoint Objects

ALLOWED NAMESPACE	OBJECTS NOT ALLOWED
`Microsoft.SharePoint` except	`SPSite` constructor
	`SPSecurity` object
	`SPWorkItem` and `SPWorkItemCollection` objects
	`SPAlertCollection.Add` method
	`SPAlertTemplateCollection.Add` method
	`SPUserSolution` and `SPUserSolutionCollection` objects
	`SPTransformUtilities`
	`Microsoft.SharePoint.Navigation`
`Microsoft.SharePoint.Utilities` except	`SPUtility.SendEmail` method
	`SPUtility.GetNTFullNameandEmailFromLogin` method
`Microsoft.SharePoint.Workflow`	All objects in this namespace
`Microsoft.SharePoint.WebPartPages` except	`SPWebPartManager` object
	`SPWebPartConnection` object
	`WebPartZone` object
	`WebPartPage` object
	`ToolPane` object
	`ToolPart` object

Other objects, such as `SPGridView`, should be allowed, but are not. It may seem obvious that things like logging to the Unified Logging Service (ULS) is not allowed — but it's certainly frustrating if you want to do the right thing and log from your code.

The other type of limitations in the sandbox relate to the processes. These limitations are designed to prevent the code from accessing anything outside of the site collection to which the sandboxed solution is deployed. Earlier, you learned that the `SPSite` constructor was blocked (actually only the URL one — if you use the GUID constructor with the current site GUID, it works). However, what's not clear in the object restrictions is that the process has had all of its permissions stripped as well.

There's no way to create a TCP connection to another server from inside of the sandbox. This rules out doing anything with web services, calls to web pages, or reading RSS feeds, as well as connecting to a database or any kind of back-end system. It also means that some operations from the sandbox won't work as intended. You won't be able to do operations on an external list that uses the user's identity because the user's identity is destroyed in the sandbox — that is, except for the

`SPUser` object. The result is that if you're going to access an external list from the sandbox, the external list must be set up through the Secure Store Service to use an alternate set of credentials.

Of course, there's still a lot that can be done inside the sandbox. You can create web parts and use them to operate on data inside the site collection. For many solutions, this is all that is needed.

YOUR FIRST SANDBOX PROJECT

The sandbox doesn't have to be scary. Let's walk through the process of creating your first sandbox project step-by-step. As is customary, let's start with "Hello World."

To begin, create a new Empty SharePoint Project. To do this, follow these steps:

1. Open Visual Studio 2010.
2. Choose File ➪ New Project.
3. In the left-hand pane of the New Project dialog shown in Figure 8-3, select SharePoint.
4. In the center pane, select Empty SharePoint Project.
5. In the Name textbox, enter **HelloWorld**.
6. Click the OK button.

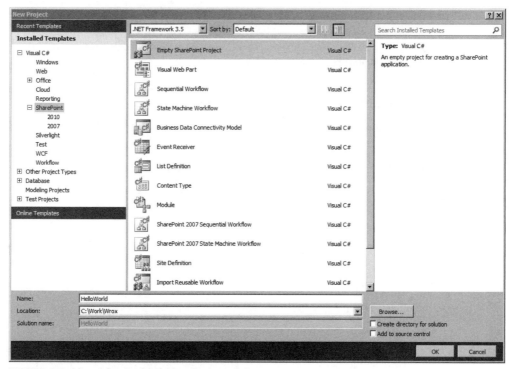

FIGURE 8-3: Visual Studio 2010 New Project dialog

Next, follow these steps to use the SharePoint Customization Wizard shown in Figure 8-4:

1. Enter a valid site (such as `http://localhost`) in the textbox that says, "What local site do you want to use for debugging?"

2. Verify that the "Deploy as a sandboxed solution" option is selected.

3. Click the Finish button.

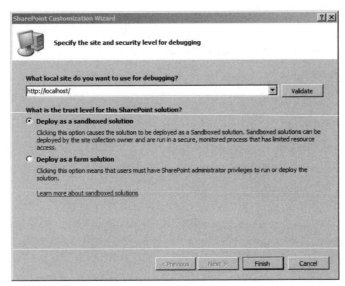

FIGURE 8-4: SharePoint Customization Wizard

Add a Hello World web part by following these steps:

1. In the Solution Explorer window right-click the `HelloWorld` project and select Add ➪ New Item.

2. In the center pane of the Add New Item dialog shown in Figure 8-5, select Web Part.

3. In the Name textbox on the bottom, enter **HelloWorldWebPart.**

4. Click the Add button.

Add the following line to the `CreateChildControls()` method to cause the web part to display "Hello World."

```
Controls.Add(new LiteralControl("Hello World"));
```

Press F5 to run the application.

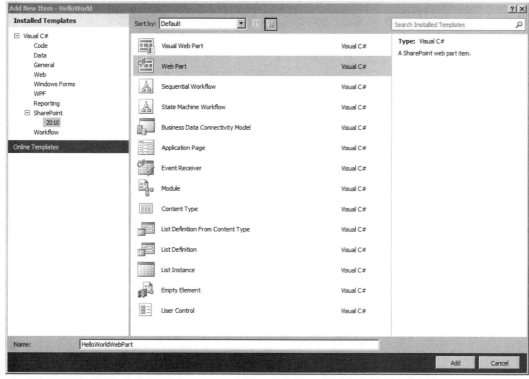

FIGURE 8-5: Add New Item dialog

Add the web part to the default page by following these steps:

1. In Internet Explorer, on the ribbon, click Page ➪ Edit Page.

2. In the left web part zone, click "Add a Web Part."

3. In the Categories pane on the left, click Custom.

4. Verify that HelloWorldWebPart is selected, as shown in Figure 8-6.

5. Click the Add button.

6. In the Page ribbon, click Stop Editing.

Verify sandbox deployment by following these steps:

1. Click Site Actions ➪ Site Settings.

2. In the Galleries group, click Solutions, as shown in Figure 8-7.

3. Verify that the HelloWorld solution appears.

Close Internet Explorer to end the debugging session.

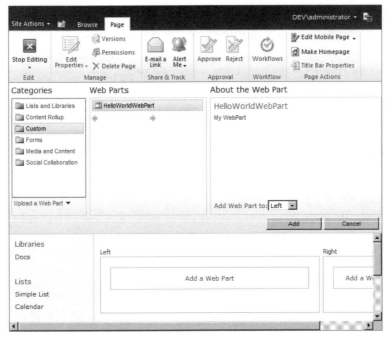

FIGURE 8-6: Adding HelloWorld

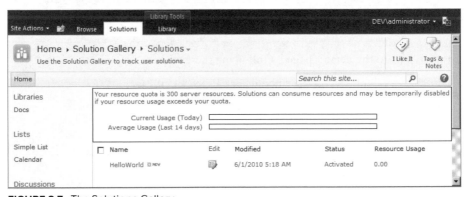

FIGURE 8-7: The Solutions Gallery

When you create a sandbox solution project, Visual Studio 2010 does much of the "heavy lifting" to get the project going. When you add the new web part, Visual Studio automatically creates a Feature in your project to deploy the .webpart file to the Web Part Gallery, so you could add the web part from the web user interface. Visual Studio 2010 also creates the WSP package behind the scenes with the information stored in the packaging designer. When Visual Studio creates the Feature for the project, it adds it automatically to the package.

With the package created, Visual Studio 2010 deploys the SharePoint Solution file (WSP) to the site collection's Solution Gallery, where all sandboxed solutions go. Visual Studio then activates the solution in the gallery.

You can also create your own Features, rename the default Feature, and change the way the package is created, all from within the Visual Studio environment.

It should be noted that sandboxed WSPs refer to the included assemblies as being deployed to the GAC. Despite this, they are not. This is, however, the only supported value for assemblies deployed as a part of sandboxed solutions. You cannot change this setting even if you want your solution package to deploy.

 Shortly after the release of Visual Studio 2010, the Visual Studio 2010 SharePoint Power Tools were released. With the Power Tools, you get two things. First, you get a visual web part that works in the sandbox. Second, you gain the capability to receive an error at compile time when something won't work in the sandbox. Both of these are indispensible additions to Visual Studio that every SharePoint developer should have. You can find more at `http://msdn.microsoft.com/en-us/vstudio/bb980963.aspx`.

GETTING OUT OF THE SANDBOX

With all of the restrictions on the sandbox, it's fairly easy to get stuck wanting to create a solution that just won't fit inside the sandbox. Whether it's a need to call a web service or connect to a required database, that one need might force you out of the sandbox completely. However, there is a solution that allows you to keep your solution mostly in the sandbox and call out to more trusted code that can do things that can't be done directly from the sandbox.

Implementing a proxy is a matter of overriding (or creating) two classes — an arguments class and an operations class — and registering your proxy to SharePoint. To call a proxy, you create the arguments class and pass this to SharePoint, along with the fully qualified object that you want to execute.

The arguments class must derive from `SPProxyOperationArgs` and must be serializable. This object must be executable from both inside the sandbox and outside. The other class must be derived from `SPProxyOperation`, and must be executable from outside the sandbox. This means that it should be installed to the GAC and should allow partially trusted callers, so that it can be called from items with more restrictive CAS policies.

The biggest limitation to a sandbox proxy is that it requires full trust to deploy it. That means that you can't just create one and use it; you must get it deployed to the farm. Depending on the complexity of the solution and the corporate policy, this may be easy, or it may be impossible. There's no free pass when it comes to the proxy. You must have someone drill that hole out of the sandbox for you.

The following example creates a proxy assembly and a simple sandbox proxy consumer web part. The consumer web part will use the proxy to make an `HttpWebRequest` to get data from a file that resides in another site collection. This operation is not otherwise supported in a sandbox web part.

To begin, create the Full Trust Proxy Project by following these steps:

1. Open Visual Studio and select File ⇨ New Project.

2. In the left pane of the New Project dialog, select SharePoint.

3. In the center pane, select Empty SharePoint Project, as shown in Figure 8-8.

4. In the Name textbox, enter **WebProxy**.

5. Check the box for "Create directory for solution."

6. Click the Finish button.

FIGURE 8-8: Selecting Empty SharePoint Project in the New Project dialog

Follow these steps to use the SharePoint Customization Wizard:

1. Enter a valid site (such as `http://localhost`) in the textbox that says, "What local site do you want to use for debugging?"

2. Select the "Deploy as a farm solution" option.

3. Click the Finish button.

Next, create the proxy arguments class by following these steps:

1. In the Solution Explorer window, right-click the WebProxy project and click Add ⇨ Class.

2. Enter **WebProxyArgs.cs** in the Name textbox.

Code file [WebProxyArgs.cs] available for download at Wrox.com

---

3. Click the Add button.

4. Change the class declaration to the following:

```
public class WebProxyArgs : SPProxyOperationArgs
```

5. On the class declaration, right-click SPProxyOperationArgs and then click "Resolve — using Microsoft.SharePoint.UserCode."

6. Declare the Url, Response, ExceptionText, and ExceptionOccurred properties that will be used for the request and the response by adding the following lines to the class:

```
public string Url { get; set; }
public string Response { get; set; }
public string ExceptionText { get; set; }
public bool ExceptionOccurred { get; set; }
```

7. Add ProxyAssemblyName and ProxyTypeName static properties to the class (ignoring the fact that WebProxyOps doesn't resolve yet) so that it is possible from the arguments class to determine the operation it's mated to:

```
public static string ProxyAssemblyName { get { return
    (typeof(WebProxyOps).Assembly.FullName); } }
public static string ProxyTypeName { get { return
    (typeof(WebProxyOps).FullName); } }
```

Now, create the proxy operations class by following these steps:

1. In the Solution Explorer window, right-click the WebProxy project and click Add ⇨ Class.

2. Enter **WebProxyOps.cs** in the Name textbox.

Code file [WebProxyOps.cs] available for download at Wrox.com

---

3. Click the Add button.

4. Change the class declaration to the following:

```
public class WebProxyOps : SPProxyOperation
```

5. On the class declaration, right-click SPProxyOperationArgs then click "Resolve — using Microsoft.SharePoint.UserCode."

6. Add an override for the `Execute` method to actually perform the request, as shown in the following code:

```
public override object Execute(SPProxyOperationArgs args)
{
  WebProxyArgs webProxyArgs = args as WebProxyArgs;
  try
  {
    WebRequest req = HttpWebRequest.Create(webProxyArgs.Url);
    req.Credentials = CredentialCache.DefaultCredentials;
    using (WebResponse resp = req.GetResponse())
    {
      using (Stream respStrm = resp.GetResponseStream())
      {
        using (StreamReader rdr = new StreamReader(respStrm))
        {
          webProxyArgs.Response = rdr.ReadToEnd();
        }
      }
    }
  }
  catch (Exception excpt)
  {
    webProxyArgs.ExceptionOccurred = true;
    webProxyArgs.ExceptionText = excpt.ToString();
  }
  return webProxyArgs;
}
```

Add a static method that can be called from inside the sandbox to perform the request by adding the following code:

```
public static WebProxyArgs ProxyWebRequest(string url)
{
  WebProxyArgs args = new WebProxyArgs();
  args.Url = url;
  args = SPUtility.ExecuteRegisteredProxyOperation(WebProxyArgs.ProxyAssemblyName,
    WebProxyArgs.ProxyTypeName, args) as WebProxyArgs;
  return args;
}
```

Add a Feature to register the proxy class by following these steps:

1. In the Features node of Solution Explorer, right-click and select Add Feature.

2. In the Title field enter **Web Proxy Activation Feature**.

3. In the Scope drop-down list, select Farm.

4. Click the Manifest tab at the bottom.

5. Click the plus sign to the left of Edit Options.

6. Add `Hidden="TRUE"` to the `<Feature>` node.

7. Right-click the `Feature 1` node in Solution Explorer and click Add Event Receiver.

8. In the `Feature1.EventReceiver.cs` file, add the following code to register and unregister the proxy:

```
public override void FeatureInstalled(SPFeatureReceiverProperties properties)
{
   SPUserCodeService ucService = SPUserCodeService.Local;
   SPProxyOperationType proxyOp = new
      SPProxyOperationType(WebProxyArgs.ProxyAssemblyName,
      WebProxyArgs.ProxyTypeName);
   if (!ucService.ProxyOperationTypes.Contains(proxyOp))
   {
      ucService.ProxyOperationTypes.Add(proxyOp);
      ucService.Update();
   }
}
public override void FeatureUninstalling(SPFeatureReceiverProperties
properties)
{
   SPUserCodeService ucService = SPUserCodeService.Local;
   SPProxyOperationType proxyOp = new
      SPProxyOperationType(WebProxyArgs.ProxyAssemblyName,
      WebProxyArgs.ProxyTypeName);
   if (ucService.ProxyOperationTypes.Contains(proxyOp))
   {
      ucService.ProxyOperationTypes.Remove(proxyOp);
      ucService.Update();
   }
}
```

Code file [Feature1.EventReceiver.cs] available for download at Wrox.com

Now, set the `AllowPartiallyTrustedCallers` property so that the proxy can be called from the sandbox. To do this, follow these steps:

1. In the Solution Explorer, expand the Properties folder and double-click the `AssemblyInfo.cs` file.

2. Add the following line to the end of the file:

```
[assembly: AllowPartiallyTrustedCallers]
```

Turn off auto retract so the project isn't accidentally retracted while you're debugging the client application. Follow these steps:

1. In the Solution Explorer, right-click the `WebProxy` project and select Properties.

2. In the tabs on the left, select SharePoint.

3. Uncheck the "Auto-retract after debugging" option.

Now, create the `ProxyCaller` project by following these steps:

1. In the Solution Explorer, right-click the `WebProxy` solution and select Add ⇨ New Project.

2. In the center pane, confirm that Empty SharePoint Project is selected.

3. Enter a name of **ProxyCaller**.

4. In the SharePoint Customization Wizard, click Finish.

Add a reference to the WebProxy class so that the ProxyCaller can use the classes. Follow these steps:

1. Right-click the WebProxy\References node and select Add Reference.

2. Verify WebProxy is selected and click OK.

Create the WebProxyCaller web part with calls to SharePoint by following these steps:

1. Right-click the ProxyCaller project and click Add ⇨ New Item.

2. In the center pane, click Web Part.

3. In the Name textbox, enter **WebProxyCaller**.

> *Code file [WebProxyCaller.cs] available for download at Wrox.com*

4. Click the Add button.

5. Replace the contents of the WebProxyCaller class with the following property and CreateChildControls override:

```
private string url = "http://localhost/_layouts/viewlsts.aspx";
[WebBrowsable(true), WebDisplayName("Url"),
    WebDescription("The url to retrieve"), Category("Proxy")]
public string Url { get { return (url); } set { url = value; } }

protected override void CreateChildControls()
{
  WebProxyArgs args = WebProxyOps.ProxyWebRequest(url);
  if (args.ExceptionOccurred == false)
  {
    Controls.Add(new LiteralControl("Received : "));
    Controls.Add(new LiteralControl(HttpUtility.HtmlEncode(args.Response)));
  }
  else
  {
    Controls.Add(new LiteralControl("Exception : "));
    Controls.Add(new LiteralControl(HttpUtility.HtmlEncode(args.
ExceptionText)));
  }
}
```

Now you need to invoke Set Startup Projects so that both of the projects will start when you start debugging. Follow these steps:

1. Right-click the WebProxy solution and select Set StartUp Projects.

2. Click the "Multiple startup projects" radio button.

3. Click the WebProxy row and the up arrow.

4. In the `WebProxy` row, select Start.

5. In the `ProxyCaller` row, select Start.

6. Click OK.

Run the project and add the web part to the page by following these steps:

1. Press F5 to deploy and run both projects.

2. In either of the Internet Explorer windows, on the ribbon, click Page ⇨ Edit Page.

3. In the left web part zone, click "Add a Web Part."

4. In the Categories pane on the left, click Custom.

5. Ensure that `WebProxyCaller` is selected.

6. Click the Add button.

7. In the Page ribbon, click Stop Editing.

The project will show the HTML-encoded output from the All Site Content page. Although this isn't that useful, it demonstrates that you can read a web request in the sandbox through the proxy that was created.

EXPLORING ALTERNATIVES TO THE SANDBOX

The primary focus of this chapter has been the new sandbox technology of SharePoint. However, in the spirit of being complete in terms of how to create solutions for SharePoint when you don't have administrative access to the server, there are a few other technologies and approaches that you might want to consider.

Perhaps the most dramatic improvement to SharePoint 2010 is support for client programming. When SharePoint 2007 came out, it didn't even support Ajax. SharePoint 2010 offers Ajax support, Silverlight support, .NET client support, as well as a richer set of APIs that can allow users of non-Microsoft technology to create and consume content in SharePoint.

A key thing to note about the Microsoft-supported technologies is that Microsoft has provided a client object model (`ClientOM`) that roughly resembles the server object model (`ServerOM`) in the names of the classes, methods, and functions. The key difference between the `ServerOM` and the `ClientOM` is the fact that the `ClientOM` uses a data context that requires batching of operations. This is designed to be more efficient, because making hundreds (or thousands) of small requests from the client would amplify the impact of lag between the client and the server.

For non-Microsoft clients, technologies like Windows Communication Foundation (WCF) allow access via a traditional SOAP/web service interface. Thanks to ADO.NET Data Services, SharePoint lists are also exposed as REST (REpresentational State Transfer). REST services are much simpler to consume and, therefore, are usable from applications that can't call a traditional web service. The ADO.NET Data Services support return types of both ATOM XML and JavaScript Object Notation (JSON), so most clients will be able to natively read from and write to SharePoint lists from the REST interface. It should be noted that the REST interface isn't supported for external lists, so you can't use SharePoint to directly connect a front-end client web application to back-end server data.

In addition to these changes, a complete new set of WCF-based web services can be called by clients that know how to use the full SOAP Web Service syntax. This is necessary for working with non-list data and the services that SharePoint exposes.

All of these options turn the idea of working with SharePoint data on its head. In other words, none of these options have code running on the server, so, other than the impact of their data operations (including queries), there's no impact. This means that anyone can write any kind of client-side code and have that work on data on the server — whether or not they can deploy SharePoint sandboxed solutions. It also means that it is possible to write code that doesn't have the same restrictions as the sandbox — if the code is run on the client side. If you can't deploy code to the server, then deploying code that will run on the client may be the right answer.

UNDERSTANDING WHEN TO USE SANDBOXED SOLUTIONS

With all of these choices, how do you know which one to pick? Well, fortunately, there are some relatively easy answers.

If you need to do a workflow, you're building a full-trust solution. In most cases, if you're wanting to do an event receiver, you need to do this in a full-trust solution as well — so that it doesn't get shut down with the rest of the solutions if the site collection goes over its processing quota.

There's overhead to running in the sandbox, so it's not appropriate for high-volume or public-facing sites. So, if you must develop for high volume, you shouldn't do it in the sandbox.

If you need to do a web service, database call, or anything outside of the current site collection, you can't do it inside the sandbox. Though you can create proxies for this, you're creating a full-trust solution in the proxy, so it won't be completely inside of the sandbox.

If you don't have access to deploy code to the farm — or it's prohibitively expensive — you're going to need to do either sandboxed or client-based solutions.

How do you make the final decision between sandboxed code or client code? This generally breaks down to being able to ensure that the client can run. This includes problems with JavaScript breaking, an inability to ensure that the Silverlight client is deployed, and the capability to deploy other solutions to the client workstations. It is also complicated by the cost of developing for the client versus developing for the server. Generally speaking, it's quicker and easier to code for the server, because you don't have to worry about asynchronous callbacks, which can lead you to sandboxed solutions.

Ultimately, if the operations you want to perform can be done in the sandbox, and you're not doing high-volume or public sites, then the sandbox is your answer. If you can't deploy a farm solution, but need to do more than the sandbox will allow, you'll be developing a client solution.

SUMMARY

This chapter took you on a tour of the new SharePoint sandbox technology and the other technologies that allow you to deploy code to your site without administrative privileges. You learned that there are several new features in SharePoint to allow site collection administrators to deploy code to the farm. You also learned what the features are in SharePoint designed to protect the farm when the site collection administrator and their developer friends are putting code on the farm.

ABOUT THE AUTHOR

Robert Bogue, MCSE (NT4/W2K), MCSA (Security, A+, Network+, Server+, I-Net+, IT Project+, E-Biz+, CDIA+), is the president of Thor Projects LLC. Thor Projects LLC provides SharePoint consulting services to clients around the world. Bogue has contributed to more than 100 book projects and numerous other publishing projects. He has been a part of the Microsoft Most Valuable Professional (MVP) program for the past seven years, and was most recently awarded for Microsoft Office SharePoint Server. Before that, Bogue was a Microsoft Commerce Server MVP, and, before that, a Microsoft Windows Servers-Networking MVP. He is also a Microsoft Patterns and Practices Champion, and a team member for the SharePoint Guidance. Bogue is the president of the SharePoint Users Group of Indiana (SPIN, www.spindiana.com). He blogs at http://www.thorprojects.com/blog. You can reach Bogue at Rob.Bogue@thorprojects.com.

SharePoint 2010 Web Parts

By Todd Bleeker

Web parts are essential to fulfilling the fundamental objective of SharePoint — to empower the end user to self-sufficiency and self-reliance. Using web parts, end users can construct their own software solutions from personalizable chunks of pre-built functionality. Though this idea may evoke a visceral wave of panic in some, this core capability is one of the primary reasons for the unbridled success of SharePoint as a platform.

Because of web parts, end users can often be creating and populating sites, pages, lists, and libraries within just a short time after being granted access to SharePoint. Of course, education can go a long way in helping end users avoid common pitfalls or painting themselves into a corner. SharePoint can often be leveraged to replace the vast majority of end-user spreadsheet and desktop database applications with securable, web-based, scalable solutions that the end users themselves can manage, and even alter, over time. Eliminating the IT bottleneck in application provisioning and maintenance can yield an exponential return on investment (ROI).

Web parts are essential to making that reality possible. When out-of-the-box web parts become inadequate, ASP.NET provides an extensible Web Part Framework that allows developers to build their own custom web parts that can be coded to do practically anything that you can imagine. Certainly, web parts can achieve anything that can be done on a traditional website, and with some effort, they can eventually become sophisticated enough to replace entire commercial applications.

This chapter begins with the basic steps required to create custom web parts, and then ventures into several of the more advanced web part topics as well.

The technical approach to extending SharePoint with custom web parts as described in this chapter is equally applicable to both SharePoint Foundation 2010 (SPF 2010) and SharePoint Server 2010 (SPS 2010), collectively known as SharePoint 2010, or just SharePoint. Distinctions between SFP 2010, the platform (free with purchase of a Microsoft Server operating system and a SQL Server database), and SPS 2010, the product, are highlighted in this chapter only when necessary — which is rare.

This chapter does not cover the XSL List View (XLV) Web Part, the Data View Web Part (DVWP), or the Data Form Web Part (DFWP). However, these out-of-the-box web parts should be thoroughly explored before deciding to create a custom web part.

WEB PART HISTORY

Good web parts encapsulate functionality that the end user will find useful in a large variety of contexts by providing public properties the end user can set. This personalization can extend the web part's usefulness to solve the widest variety of possible use cases. What follows are some historical initiatives that led to the characteristics that web parts embody.

Historical Perspective

In 2000, the Dashboard Web Part (`*.dwp`) was available only in SharePoint Portal Server, and it came in four flavors: JScript, VBScript, XML, and HTML. These web parts were created using the Microsoft Visual Interdev (VID) plug-in for the Digital Dashboard Resource Kit (DDRK). These were very complicated to create, and required lots of client-side code, but the core concept of a web part was born.

In 2003, Windows SharePoint Services replaced Dashboard Web Parts with SharePoint web parts. These new controls derived from `System.Web.UI.WebControls.WebControl` and were much more aligned with the type of controls that developers created for themselves. Unfortunately, adding a user control as the design surface for the web part was possible, but not common. When a user control was used, it was typically deployed as a web part resource, and accessed using the physical `wpresources` folder in the home directory of the Internet Information Server (IIS) website by `BIN`-based assemblies, and using the `_wpresources` virtual directory for Global Assembly Cache (GAC) based assemblies.

In 2007, Microsoft mainstreamed web parts by adding web part capabilities directly into the .NET Framework 3.0. For backward compatibility, the SharePoint web part was recoded to inherit from the new ASP.NET web part. SharePoint 2007 supported both, but Microsoft recommended that all new custom web parts derive from ASP.NET rather than SharePoint. Again, adding a user control as the design surface for the web part was possible, but not common. When a user control was used, it was typically deployed to a subfolder in the `.\12\TEMPLATE\CONTROLTEMPLATES\` folder, and accessed using the `_controltemplates` virtual directory.

SharePoint 2010 continues in the same direction as SharePoint 2007. ASP.NET web part support remains strong. The biggest thing introduced in this release is the tooling to create web parts in Visual Studio 2010. As part of that tooling, Microsoft has embraced the idea that a user control is the ideal design surface for the web part.

So, a Visual web part template has been included in Visual Studio 2010. It deploys the user control to a subfolder in the `{SharePointRoot}\TEMPLATE\CONTROLTEMPLATES\ProjectName\` folder (see the "{SharePointRoot}" sidebar) and accesses it using the `_controltemplates` virtual directory. `Page.LoadControl` is used to dynamically load the ASCX control at run-time. Both of these characteristics require that Visual web parts must be deployed using a farm solution rather than a sandboxed solution.

{SHAREPOINTROOT}

In 2003, the primary location for infrastructure files on the filesystem of every Web Front End (WFE) server in SharePoint was `C:\Program Files\Common Files\Microsoft Shared\Web Server Extensions\60`. This was a residual of the sixth version of Front Page Server Extensions. This notorious location was commonly referred to as the 60 ("six oh") Hive.

In 2007, the primary location for infrastructure files on the filesystem was `C:\Program Files\Common Files\Microsoft Shared\Web Server Extensions\12`. This was a reflection of the platform being tied to the twelfth release of Microsoft Office. This equally notorious location was affectionately referred to as the 12 Hive.

However, with Visual Studio finally entering the picture in 2010, a more official name with a longer-term view than just this release was needed for the filesystem location that housed all SharePoint infrastructure files. With Office skipping version 13 (bad luck), the infrastructure files would be housed in `C:\Program Files\Common Files\Microsoft Shared\Web Server Extensions\14`. Visual Studio got the go-ahead from Microsoft's Legal department to call this location the `{SharePointRoot}` (including the braces).

So, the `{SharePointRoot}` will always refer to the location on the filesystem where the SharePoint infrastructure files can be found for whatever version of SharePoint is running.

Web Part Goals

In addition to end user empowerment, web parts helped achieve the following technical goals over the years:

➤ Reusability

➤ Componentization

➤ Interoperability

➤ Portability

➤ Configurability

Reusability

Web parts, by their very definition, should be reusable.

Of course, the idea of reusable widgets isn't new. For literally decades, the promise of reuse has been difficult and rarely attained. The Common Object Request Broker Architecture (CORBA) standard defined by the Object Management Group (OMG) was one of the first frameworks that claimed to enable software components written in divergent computer languages on non-homogenous platforms to seamlessly communicate to solve common business problems leading to reuse. Historically, there were various mainframe component initiatives, too.

However, the big difference in SharePoint is who is reusing the widget. The audience for web parts is the end user, not other developers or applications. End users reuse web parts, not developers.

Componentization

Web parts should encapsulate common business functionality.

Historically, on the WinTel platform (Windows running on the Intel chipset) alone there were several different C and C++ libraries, such as the set of template-based C++ classes called the Active Template Library (ATL) that facilitated the creation of small, fast Component Object Model (COM) objects. For a long period of time, COM was loved. Most developers had MTS and later COM+ to host these middle-tier widgets.

There were also widgets designed for application construction by less technical resources under the era of event-based Visual Basic development. Initially, composite controls called Visual Basic Extensions (VBX) encapsulated common user interface elements, which were followed by the Object, Linking, and Embedding Control Extentions (OCX) controls (later renamed to simply ActiveX controls). The n-tier development approach comprised of widgets in each tier was all part of the Microsoft DNA approach to software development.

But, again, web parts are widgets designed to empower the end user. Will end users lack the technical proficiency to create the same level of data integrity that can be achieved with a traditional software application? Probably. Will they repeatedly create weak solutions, only to abandon them after a period of non-productive use during which the self-assembled application will spew misleading information? Probably. Will they create dozens of similar, but disparate, data islands only to come back to IT in a crisis when they can't figure out how to consolidate and report on that data? Probably.

So, you should create web part components that help end users avoid those likely issues.

Interoperability

Web parts should facilitate a synergy using cross-part and even cross-page communication with other web parts.

In the past, competing encoding protocols such as the following provided for complicated communication scenarios:

➤ Extended Binary Coded Decimal Interchange Code (EBCDIC), which is a character-encoding protocol commonly used on IBM mainframe operating systems

➤ American Standard Code for Information Interchange (ASCII), which is a character-encoding protocol commonly used on most modern computer systems

➤ Base64

➤ Uuencoding (pronounced "you-you-n-code-ing")

➤ Unicode Transformation Format (UTF)

Electronic Data Interchange (EDI) and, later, the Simple Object Access Protocol (SOAP) moved the communication channels to a more standardized way for loosely coupled systems to interact, but they lacked compression, authentication, and versioning.

Web parts use the object-oriented concept of a class interface to ensure web parts are communicating at least on par with the level of certainty the developer coded into the web part. If all that is required is a string to satisfy a connection, that can be accommodated. However, if a validated invoice number must be used for connecting web parts, that can be accommodated as well.

Portability

Web parts should work on SharePoint websites and non-SharePoint ASP.NET websites alike.

The Web was initially constructed using HTML, DHTML, and later ASP pages, which were spaghetti-code-riddled stop gaps that proved to be a difficult-to-support approach to development on this new platform. Widgets like the *webbots* provided by FrontPage, as well as plug-in widgets like Adobe's Flash, Microsoft's ActiveX, and others, left a lot to be desired.

Real progress was made around the turn of the century when Microsoft released the .NET Framework to compete with the Java Virtual Machine (JVM) software development approach. This put the focus for future Microsoft-centric development squarely on the shoulders of the Web. In fact, constructing web pages from web controls (also known as server controls) and user controls has been a best practice of ASP.NET development since it was first released. However, allowing the non-technical masses to assemble these widgets onto a web page canvas of their own making only became a reality as a result of the introduction of SharePoint.

Configurability

The shift from a page-orientation to a part-orientation is not trivial. Developers must think differently. It's not a matter of sitting down with the end users to discuss what they'd like to see on the home page, and then what they would like to see on each child page.

Instead, the developer must help the end users understand how to create their own data repository using lists for structured data or libraries for unstructured (but decorated) data. The developer must show them how to create a site page canvas upon which to display the data collected, and to use the galleries of assets available to them for application construction. Although this primarily consists of web parts, it also includes things like site columns and content types, master pages, style libraries, image libraries, workflow, and SharePoint groups. The end users then construct their own applications and only ask the developer to fill the gaps identified.

When developers are creating a web part to fill an identified gap, they must think about all the potential ways that an end user may use it. Anything that could typically be hard-coded should usually be made available as a configurable property for personalization (see the "Tools to Effect Change in SharePoint" sidebar) by the end user.

TOOLS TO EFFECT CHANGE IN SHAREPOINT

The following tools are typically used to effect various levels of change in SharePoint:

➤ *The browser is used for personalization* — This includes choosing web parts, setting web part properties, and customizing site navigation stored as metadata within the Content Database.

➤ *SharePoint Designer (SPD) is used for customization* — This includes creating a physical copy (*unghosting*) of an altered Instance Page into the Content Database, as well as managing most of the asset galleries, including declarative workflow.

➤ *Visual Studio is used for centralization* — This includes deploying assets to the Web Front End (WFE) filesystem in a SharePoint Solution Package (WSP).

When directing corporate consistency (that is, content placement, or a look-and-feel commonly referred to as a brand) becomes more important than empowering individualistic flexibility, a Web Content Management (WCM) solution is probably in order. This is when Publishing Pages get involved.

What's New

Web parts continue to derive from `System.Web.UI.WebControls.WebParts.WebPart`, which derive from the standard `System.Web.UI.WebControls.WebControl` (also known as server control). So, anything that can be done in the context of an ASP.NET web page can be done using a web part. As previously stated, the biggest difference is who uses the final solution to assemble the application. Yet, several things that used to be difficult have been simplified or improved in this release.

For example, there are now two kinds of web parts:

➤ The imperative-only standard web part that ASP.NET introduced in ASP.NET 2.0

➤ The new Visual web part that includes both a declarative user control `.ascx` file and an imperative class

The Visual web part includes all the typical capabilities of a standard user control. The default `CreateChildControls` method uses `Page.LoadControl` to load the declarative user control from the `_controltemplates` virtual directory into the Controls collection of the web part. That requires that the `.ascx` file be deployed to the `{SharePointRoot}\TEMPLATE\CONTROLTEMPLATES\ProjectName\` mapped folder.

When an imperative solution is in order for a web part, the structure of the user interface should be constructed within the `CreateChildControls` method using the abstract web controls (also known as server controls) to generate the HTML not using strings in any of the `Render` methods. There are four things that should be done within `CreateChildControls` and no more: instantiate user interface objects, initialize non-data object properties, wire-up events, and insert (add) objects to the Controls collection.

DECLARATIVE VERSUS IMPERATIVE

In ASP.NET, there are two models for creating applications: declarative and imperative. The declarative model consists entirely of a finite set of XML elements and attributes, whereas the imperative model relies on inheritance, the creation of predefined objects, the overriding of predefined base class methods, and extensibility.

The following markup creates an ASP.NET textbox declaratively:

```
<asp:TextBox Text="Default Text" runat="server" />
```

Whereas this code creates that same textbox imperatively:

```
TextBox t = new TextBox();
t.Text = "Default Text";
Controls.Add(t);
```

Typically, the declarative approach is easier to understand, create, and support. But when its finite set of markup is inadequate, the imperative model is infinite and extensible. Of course, the two models can be intermixed, so it is typically best to attempt a solution using declarative only, and move to include imperative code when that simpler model proves inadequate.

SharePoint Designer and Visual Studio designers for `.ascx` and `.aspx` files auto-generate declarative markup as the developer adds components to the design surface. Behind the scenes, elements are generated into a companion file. It is often possible for the developer to select multiple components and set common properties simultaneously. Most developers find working with components on a design surface and a property pane to be easier than maintaining imperative-only solutions.

SharePoint's Collaborative Application Markup Language (CAML) is made up entirely of declarative elements, each with a finite set of attributes. The following files are made up entirely of declarative CAML:

➤ Site definition's `ONET.XML` file

➤ Site template's `WEBTEMP*.XML` file

➤ List definition's `SCHEMA.XML` file

➤ Feature template's `Feature.XML` file

➤ Feature definition's `Elements.XML` file

➤ Solution definition's `Manifest.XML` file

➤ Web Part template's `*.webpart` file

Workflow's Extensible Object Markup Language (XOML) is also a set of finite declarative elements.

Packaging Web Parts

Web part packaging hasn't actually changed in this release. However, several things have changed around web part packaging. There are now two kinds of SharePoint solutions (WSP): sandboxed solutions and farm solutions.

In addition to the traditional SharePoint Solution Package (WSP — previously called Windows SharePoint Services Solution Package) that continues to be deployed to the Solution Store in the farm, SharePoint Foundation 2010 (SPF) introduces a new scope for deploying limited WSPs to a Solution Gallery in each site collection.

XSL List View (XLV) Web Part

The XSL List View (XLV) Web Part replaces the List View Web Part (LVWP) for displaying most SharePoint lists. Based upon the DVWP, XSL replaces Display CAML Markup (sometimes called "CAML Spit") for most List Views. This is browser-editable.

Out-of-the-Box Web Parts

Following are new out-of-the-box web parts:

- ➤ Slideshow web part
- ➤ Silverlight web part
- ➤ What's New web part
- ➤ Virtual Earth Map web part (MWP)
- ➤ Ajax grid control

WEB PART DEVELOPMENT

As shown in Figure 9-1, web part development can be summed up in three simple 10,000-foot tasks:

1. Make a DLL

2. Write some XML

3. Deploy

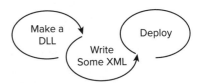

FIGURE 9-1: Three web part development tasks

There are declarative-only SharePoint solutions that don't require a DLL (an assembly), but web part development always includes at least some imperative logic. There may also be assets like images, cascading style sheets (CSS), and JavaScript to supplement the web part, but at a high level, these three steps sum up web part development quite well.

When web parts were first released, lots of trial and error was required to ferret out the best practices for creating them. When responsibility for the Web Part Framework shifted from the SharePoint product team to the .NET Framework team, there were a few more tweaks to the approach used for web part development.

Eventually, I documented and espoused a set of tried-and-true steps for speedy, iterative web part development. I called them the "ten easy steps" for web part development, and eventually generalized them for the development of any SharePoint platform extension. For nearly a decade, I refined those "ten easy steps" into a model of development best practices. You can view a picture and description of that old model on my blog at http://SharePoint.MindsharpBlogs.com/Todd/ SharePoint2007DevelopmentModel/.

However, a complete revision of that trustworthy development model was required for SharePoint 2010. The new SharePoint 2010 tools in Visual Studio 2010 required rethinking every aspect of SharePoint platform extension development. So, I spent a full year refining a new model that facilitates speedy, iterative SharePoint 2010 development right from the start. You can view a picture and description of this new model on my blog at http://SharePoint.MindsharpBlogs.com/Todd/ SharePoint2010DevelopmentModel/. The "ten easy steps" that make up the new model are briefly described here.

Step 1: Prepare Environment

Before starting a new SharePoint project, be sure that the development environment includes the necessary site, lists, and libraries (as needed) that will be used to test the SharePoint solution. These will be prompted for during the project creation, so they must exist prior to creating the SharePoint project.

Step 2: Create Project

Visual Studio will only create a SharePoint Solution Package (WSP) in the SharePoint project template. The WSP is not intended to be added to any other type of Visual Studio project. Though it doesn't have to be used, it is not intended to be removed from a SharePoint project. So, most SharePoint solutions require the creation of a SharePoint project.

A SharePoint Feature (or just Feature) is a bundle of functionality that can be activated in numerous ways at one of four scopes: Web, Site Collection, Web Application, or Farm. Web and Site Collection Features can usually be activated by the end user. Web Application Features can be activated by a farm administrator, whereas Farm Features are auto-activated when they are installed. Features can also be activated at the command line, declaratively by a Site Definition or Feature dependency, and imperatively from nearly any running code. This ubiquitous capability for activation makes Features invaluable for extending the SharePoint platform.

A SharePoint Solution Package (WSP) is a collection of assets (including Features) packaged for deployment. If the WSP is uploaded to the SharePoint 2010 Central Administration (SCA) Solution Store, its deployment can impact virtually any aspect of the SharePoint farm, including the filesystem on every server in the farm. A subset of functionality can be uploaded into a Site Collection Solution Gallery. Its deployment is sandboxed to impact aspects of the containing site collection only.

Everything deployed to a SharePoint farm should be delivered using a WSP. This includes all SharePoint Features, all files destined for `C:\Program Files\Common Files\Microsoft Shared\Web Server Extensions\14\` (also known as the `{SharePointRoot}`), all content destined for the configuration or Content Databases, all `web.config` modifications, and so on. Literally, everything deployed, altered, or configured on a SharePoint farm by non-end-users should be packaged into a WSP.

Step 3: Add Item

Typically, the first task a developer will undertake after creating a new project is to add one or more items into that project. In addition to the plethora of .NET project items that can be added, Visual Studio now includes dozens of SharePoint Project Items (SPIs). As SPIs and other items are added into a SharePoint project, Visual Studio attempts to update the Feature and solution in that project. So, whenever an item is added to the project, the following two steps should also be done.

WHAT ARE SPIs?

SharePoint Project Items (SPIs) are new to Visual Studio 2010. Historically, organizing projects into folders containing files with a type affinity for one another was common. For example, developers often organize disparate CSS files into a `styles` folder; GIFs, JPGs, and PNGs into an `images` folder; and disparate JavaScript files into a `scripts` folder. The benefit was that, if another developer had to support someone else's work, he or she would be able to anticipate where assets of a common type would be found.

SPIs are effectively folders that hold a motley collection of files with a common purpose, rather than a common type. Each file may have a unique deployment location and a unique purpose, but they are organized into the SPI folder because they work together for a common purpose — typically to create some type of SharePoint platform extension. This would be akin to keeping the CSS, images, and JavaScript in a folder along with the `.aspx` page that consumes them. The SPI model definitely takes some getting used to, but it isn't going to change any time soon — if ever. "Embrace and extend" is my motto.

Step 4: Configure Feature

Whenever a new item is added into a SharePoint project, Visual Studio attempts to auto-update the Feature and solution with its best guess as to where that item should be included. For the most part, it does a good job. But as a project's complexity increases, those guesses lack precision. So, whenever an item is added (Step 3), the Feature(s) in the project should be evaluated to determine whether Visual Studio took the correct course of action.

Step 5: Configure Solution

Similar to the need to validate Visual Studio's auto-handling of the Feature, the SharePoint solution package alterations that occur when a new item is added must also be evaluated to determine whether Visual Studio makes the correct changes.

There are some items that a developer can add to a project that do not affect the Feature or the solution. For example, adding a class only further defines the assembly, or adding another file to an existing Module Feature supplements the Module, but doesn't affect the configuration of either the Feature or the solution. Also, some items (such as mapped folders) only affect the solution. But it never hurts to check both the Feature and the solution whenever any item is added to the Visual Studio project.

Step 6: Write Code

After items have been added to the project and configured, the developer will typically begin implementing the business logic. Code-deploy-test is an iterative process, so development often returns to this step when the testing in Step 8 identifies deficiencies.

Code comes in two forms: declarative (also known as *markup* and *script*) and imperative (*compiled code*). It is best to first plumb a simple working solution and then sharpen the business logic and the rendering of the user interface. The plumbing must be in place to debug the SharePoint solution using Visual Studio.

Step 7: Deploy Assets

This is an area where Visual Studio 2010 really shines. Choosing Build ➪ Debug from the menu (or using the Alt+B+D keyboard shortcut) will save changes to any project files, compile the imperative logic (if any) into an assembly, validate the declarative logic and the solution composition, generate a WSP, upload it to SharePoint (either the farm's Solution Store or the site collection's Solution Gallery), and by default, activate the Features contained in the SharePoint solution. If the debug URL in the properties has been configured, pressing F5 will do all of those tasks, and then automatically attach to the W3WP process. If the goal is to test the upgrade of an existing SharePoint Solution, only create a WSP and manually deploy it using PowerShell.

Step 8: Test Solution

You must determine if the deployed solution's business logic meets the business need. This requires running code, often in the browser, but sometimes in other contexts such as PowerShell or a Timer Job. It can also be helpful to debug imperative code during this step.

Use the following Visual Studio keyboard shortcuts to manually attach to the process likeliest to be running the current code:

➤ W3WP — Ctrl+Alt+P, W, Enter, Enter

➤ PowerShell.exe — Ctrl+Alt+P, P, Enter, Enter

➤ SPUCWorkerProcess — Ctrl+Alt+P, S, S, Enter, Enter

 For these three examples, pressing Enter the second time is only necessary when prompted by Visual Studio for confirmation.

Step 9: Secure Code

After the functionality of the SharePoint Solution has tested complete, there may still be a need to create a Code Access Security (CAS) `IPermission`. This is only potentially necessary in farm solutions that are deployed to the `BIN` rather than the GAC. Whereas deploying assemblies to the `BIN` using a custom CAS policy was the preferred approach in SharePoint 2007, sandboxed solutions make that far less likely in SharePoint 2010.

Step 10: Deliver Solution

Finally, you must deploy the resulting SharePoint Solution (WSP) to a test environment for validation outside of the development environment. This is a great time to conduct code reviews, test the performance of the solution, and validate that the solution works in an environment that more closely resembles production (like multiple WFEs).

The WSP generated during the previous deployment can be found in the `bin\debug` folder of the current project. This can certainly be used in a shared test environment. However, an automated build or a gatekeeper in the Operations department should recompile the project in Release mode before deploying to any integration testing environments and eventually to production.

WEB PART BASICS

In the beginning, website pages were created and maintained by developers using Hyper Text Markup Language (HTML). Over the years, as websites became more dynamic, developers added script and eventually components (user controls and web controls or server controls) onto the page. But the end user was still dependent on the developer to create new pages and organize content on to the page.

Even after Content Management Systems (CMS) became commonplace, end users were expected to create pages that conformed to the corporate standard. Presentation and content placement was mostly prescribed by the enterprise. Empowering end users who can create pages that reflect their individual needs is where SharePoint really shines. Web parts are the primary vehicle for enabling that empowerment.

Web Parts Defined

Canned, parameterized (*personalizable*) functionality must be flexible on whatever page canvas the end user places it. Often, people's perception of web parts is based upon the web parts that are included in SharePoint Foundation. However, web parts can be much more diverse. Similar to the VBX, OCX, and ActiveX controls of the past, web parts can be created that alter the entire environment, not just to show content.

Web parts can influence the ABCs of a page:

- ➤ *Appearance* — Because web parts can include CSS and JavaScript, they can literally alter any aspect about the presentation or position of elements on the page.

- ➤ *Behavior* — Most SharePoint actions begin with a call to a JavaScript function. Because the last version of a JavaScript function defined on a page is the function that will be executed, and web parts can include JavaScript, web parts can most definitely influence the behavior of a SharePoint page.

➤ *Content* — Many out-of-the-box web parts demonstrate that content can readily be presented from the context of a web part. Custom web parts are no different.

Web Part Benchmarks

A custom web part must be well defined, reusable, and context-agnostic, or it will become a one-off solution. Web parts typically involve running server-side code, often for the specialized display or manipulation of data. The custom web part is a powerful, yet easy-to-use component that, when placed on a web page, results in decentralized, self-service, data-driven websites that can do the following:

➤ Be maintained, customized, updated, altered, and shared by end users via a browser

➤ Offer shared and personalized views to others

➤ Enable powerful collaboration and connection scenarios

➤ Leverage extensibility and code reuse

➤ Accommodate Internet scalability requirements

Five benchmarks must be met for a web part to run within the Web Part Framework. Each web part must meet the following benchmarks:

➤ *Compiled* — Obviously, an assembly must be assembled or it won't execute. All web parts are encapsulated in a compiled DLL.

➤ *Signed* — Although signing is not actually required in all cases, any web part created may be deployed into the GAC, which only accepts signed (that is, strongly named) assemblies. It is good practice to separate the duties of the development personnel responsible for the creation of a web part from the operational personnel (Ops) responsible for deploying it. An unsigned web part assembly robs Ops of the option of deploying the assembly wherever they see fit (potentially the GAC). Therefore, it is good practice to always sign web part assemblies. There are other benefits and arguably little downside to signing an assembly, so it is listed here as required.

➤ *Marked as safe* — A SharePoint web application will run a web part only if it is explicitly identified as `SafeControl` in the `web.config`.

➤ *Trusted* — All assemblies that execute within a web context must be trusted to do the kind of activity that they are trying to do. WSS v2 was one of the first applications to really leverage CAS, and SharePoint continues that excellent practice. Just like people are prevented from doing certain things on the corporate network, code can be prevented (no matter who is executing it) from doing things it wasn't designed to do. For example, CAS can allow/prevent an assembly access to various resources such as SharePoint object model access, the filesystem, databases, network resources, Active Directory, and the registry. It is possible to identify which assemblies have access to which resources using things such as namespace, strong name public key blob, and zone of operation.

➤ *Deployed* — If the assembly meets all of the preceding benchmarks, but isn't in the right place on every web server in the SharePoint farm, it obviously won't work.

Web Part Framework

Web parts are organized and managed within a SharePoint-enhanced version of the ASP.NET Web Part Framework. However, most of the SharePoint-specific code is included for the support of legacy SharePoint web parts that can still run in the SharePoint 2010 environment.

Web Part Makeup

As previously mentioned, a minimum of two files make up a web part:

➤ The web part definition

➤ The web part template

The web part definition always comes in the form of an assembly. That assembly can derive from either the recommended ASP.NET `System.Web.UI.WebControls.WebParts.WebPart` or from the legacy `Microsoft.SharePoint.WebPartPages.WebPart`. A web part assembly can contain any number of web parts.

Each ASP.NET web part is surfaced to the user interface using a web part template with a `.WEBPART` extension. It uses an XML format similar to the following:

```xml
<?xml version="1.0" encoding="utf-8"?>
<webParts>
  <webPart xmlns="http://schemas.microsoft.com/WebPart/v3">
    <metaData>
      <type name="Namespace.Classname, $SharePoint.Project.AssemblyFullName$" />
      <importErrorMessage>$Resources:core,ImportErrorMessage;</importErrorMessage>
    </metaData>
    <data>
      <properties>
        <property name="Title" type="string">Web Part Title</property>
      </properties>
    </data>
  </webPart>
</webParts>
```

The legacy SharePoint web part is always surfaced to the user interface using a web part template with a `.DWP` extension. `DWP` stands for Dashboard Web Part, and is a throwback to the original SharePoint Web Part Framework. It uses an XML format similar to the following:

```xml
<?xml version="1.0" encoding="utf-8"?>
<WebPart xmlns="http://schemas.microsoft.com/WebPart/v2" >
  <Assembly>$SharePoint.Project.AssemblyFullName$</Assembly>
  <TypeName>Namespace.Classname</TypeName>
  <Title> Web Part Title </Title>
</WebPart>
```

However, the web part definition and the web part template cannot be used unless there is a `SafeControl` entry in the `web.config` for the web application.

SafeControl Entry

To provide the SharePoint administrators with some level of control over which web parts they want to allow the end user to use in a given web application, SharePoint requires a `SafeControl` element to be included in the `web.config` file for each web part assembly class. It looks similar to the following:

```
<SafeControl Assembly="AssemblyName, Version=1.0.0.0, Culture=neutral,
    PublicKeyToken=xxxxxxxxxxxxxxxx" Namespace="NamespaceName"
    TypeName="ClassName" Safe="True" AllowRemoteDesigner="True"
    SafeAgainstScript="True" />
```

Table 9-1 shows the definitions of the various attributes of the `SafeControl` element.

TABLE 9-1: SafeControl Attributes

ATTRIBUTE	DESCRIPTION
Assembly	This is a full four-part, fully qualified assembly name including `Assembly`, `Version`, `Culture`, and `PublicKeyToken`. If the assembly is unsigned, the `PublicKeyToken=null`.
Namespace	The namespace in C# is found at the top of the web part class, and is prefixed with the word `namespace`. Visual Basic.NET uses a slightly different approach. Though it does support the namespace in the same location as C#, the default location for this value can be found on the Application tab of the project's properties. It is called `Root Namespace`. If both the `Root Namespace` and the namespace at the top of the class are used, they are concatenated together, separated by a period, as in `RootNamespace.ClassNamespace`.
TypeName	This is the name of the web part class, or an asterisk (wildcard indicating that all web part classes are in the assembly).
Safe	This attribute is optional and defaults to `True`, but it is usually included even if it is set to `True` (which it usually is). However, if the `Safe` attribute is set to `False`, the web part class or classes (if the value is an asterisk) are explicitly not allowed to be used by the end user in that web application.
AllowRemoteDesigner	This attribute indicates whether SharePoint Designer can use the control as a web part. It is optional, and defaults to `True`. However, this attribute cannot be set by the `SafeControl` entry in the SharePoint Solution Manifest.
SafeAgainstScript	This attribute indicates who can view/change web part properties. Just like the previous two, this attribute is optional. However, it defaults to `False`. So, the default behavior prohibits people with less than Designer permissions from viewing/editing properties. Only when set to `True` can people with Contributor permissions view/change web part properties.

The `SafeControl` element should always be added to the `web.config` file using a SharePoint solution, and never by hand. If the web part has custom dependent assemblies (such as a third-party treeview), they, too, will need `SafeControl` entries. These can be added to the web part's SharePoint Project Item `SafeControls` property.

SharePoint uses Web Part Galleries to house the collections of web part templates.

Page Terms

Pages are the canvas that the end user uses to host the web parts that developers create. As shown in Figure 9-2, several different terms are used for the various kinds of pages found in SharePoint.

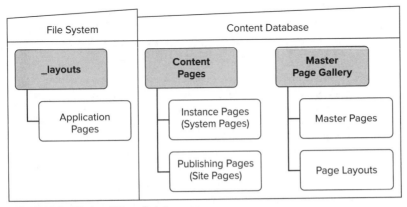

FIGURE 9-2: Kinds of SharePoint pages

Application Pages

Application Pages are always found in the `_layouts` virtual directory (`{SharePointRoot}\TEMPLATE\ LAYOUTS`) automatically added to the IIS website for every SharePoint web application. They are available to all sites on the entire SharePoint farm. They cannot be created, edited, or secured by the end user. Layout Pages are typically deployed using a SharePoint farm solution and are most frequently used for administration.

> *Publishing consists of two SharePoint Server Features (one Site Collection-scoped and one Site-scoped) that manipulate the SharePoint platform to facilitate the creation of pages within a Pages Library based upon a set of Content Type-based Page Layouts found in the Master Page Gallery. The approval of these pages is managed by a Publishing workflow. Publishing Pages are discussed later in this chapter.*

Content Pages

Always found in the SharePoint Content Database, Content Pages come in two flavors: Instance Pages and Publishing Pages.

Instance Pages

Instance Pages (also known as *System Pages* in a Publishing context) are Content Pages not based on a Page Layout. These pages use the `MasterUrl` property of the `SPWeb` object to determine which Master Page will be used.

Instance Pages are primarily used by the end user as a canvas to show whatever they need to show. There are a few other reasons to create an Instance Page rather than creating an Application Page:

- ➤ The page need not be available on all sites
- ➤ Content should be editable by the end user
- ➤ Content may include web parts
- ➤ The page must be a securable object
- ➤ The page must override a content placeholder in the underlying master page
- ➤ The page must use a unique master page

Instance Pages are virtually copied into the Content Database via a Module Feature as one of two types:

- ➤ *Ghostable (also known as Uncustomized)* — Pages are copied to a folder defined by metadata. Ghostable pages cannot be secured, and they reference an underlying filesystem page physically located in the Feature or site definition in the `{SharePointRoot}`. If the end user customizes the content for that Instance Page, then a physical copy is saved directly in the Content Database.

- ➤ *GhostableInLibrary* — Pages are configured in an `SPDocumentLibrary` as `SPFile` objects that can be secured. These pages are visible to the end user and look like they are just another document that was uploaded to the Document Library.

The following are the types of Instance Pages that can be created from the browser interface and from within SharePoint Designer:

- ➤ *Web Part Page* — This kind of Instance Page includes web part zones. By default, you can choose from eight possible web part zone configurations (eight is the maximum number of configurations because of the legacy API used to create these kinds of pages), as shown in Figure 9-3.

- ➤ *Wiki Page (also known as a Page in the Silverlight Create XAP)* — This kind of Instance Page usually only has one Rich Content area that takes up the entire main body of the page. Not only can you add static text and static images, but you can also now add web parts to this Rich Content area.

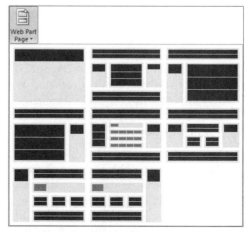

FIGURE 9-3: Web Part Page

➤ *Meeting Workspace Tab Page* — This kind of Instance Page can only be created from the context of a Meeting Workspace. Choosing Add Pages from the Site Actions menu results in a tool pane on the right edge of the existing page where a new Page Name can be provided. Choosing Manage Pages from the Site Actions menu allows the end user to specify the order of the pages on the left Navigation pane, where the Quick Launch bar is typically located. Otherwise, these pages behave much like Web Part Pages.

➤ *ASPX/HTML Page* — This kind of empty Instance Page can only be created from within SharePoint Designer. End users can add whatever web parts, static text, static images, and any other control supported by SharePoint Designer. These pages are stored entirely within the Content Database (that is, they have no reference to an underlying page on the filesystem).

The following are some examples of Instance Pages:

➤ `/default.aspx`

➤ `/Lists/Tasks/AllItems.aspx`

➤ `/Lists/Tasks/MyItems.aspx`

➤ `/SitesPages/Home.aspx`

➤ `/reports/default.aspx`

➤ `/RunOnce.aspx`

Publishing Pages

Publishing Pages (also known as *Site Pages* in a Publishing context) are always based upon a Page Layout and stored in a Pages Library. These pages use the `CustomMasterUrl` property of the `SPWeb` object to determine which Master Page will be used.

The following are some examples of Instance Pages:

➤ `/Pages/default.aspx`

➤ `/Pages/Todd.aspx`

➤ `/Pages/Bill.aspx`

End users only create Publishing Pages in a platform-generated Pages Library. There is only one Pages Library per site, and folders are discouraged in a Pages Library. In fact, a new site is typically created to create a new collection of Publishing Pages. These pages are used to collect, approve, display, and protect the actual content in every WCM implementation.

Master Pages

The master page provides the technical plumbing and custom chrome for all the content pages that reference it. This includes elements like Register tags, Import tags, Meta tags, CSS and JS includes, as well as the standard navigation and all the named rectangular placeholder controls that are meticulously juxtaposed to each other and that unify to create a consist look and feel. *Master pages* in the Master Page Gallery are used for Content Pages, whereas master pages in `_layouts` are typically used for Application Pages.

Page Layouts

Page Layouts in the Master Page Gallery are used to define what Content Type (and, therefore, what Site Columns) will be positioned where within the master page. All Publishing Pages must identify which Page Layout they are using.

Web Part Galleries

Given the web part assembly has been deployed to the server and a `SafeControl` entry has been made in the web application's `web.config` for the site collection where the web part is to be used, the web part template is hosted in what SharePoint calls *Web Part Galleries*. SharePoint uses Web Part Galleries to house collections of web part templates.

Web part templates surface web parts from several default Web Part Galleries, each with a different scope and purpose. It is possible to add other Web Part Gallery Sources using the WebPartAdderExtension Feature.

Site Collection Web Part Gallery

Web part templates uploaded to the site collection's Web Part Gallery are available anywhere within the site collection. These web part templates typically get into the site collection Web Part Gallery using a Module Feature. The bad news is that most Module Features orphan the web part template file on deactivation, which subsequently causes an error when the end user attempts to use the orphaned web part template to add the web part to the page.

Because web part templates are literally XML documents in this special Document Library, they are standard securable objects just like any other document. Each web part template can also be configured to show in a specific category on the Add Web Part dialog, including a custom category. It's possible to "new up" a web part template — that is, auto-generate its web part template into the Site Collection Gallery. You do this by following these steps:

1. Navigate to the Web Part Gallery (`_catalogs/wp/`) using Site Actions ⇨ Site Settings ⇨ Web Parts.
2. Click the New Document button.
3. Select the checkbox to the left of the desired web part.
4. Click the Populate Gallery button.

Web Application Web Part Gallery

Web part templates placed in the physical `wpcatalog` folder just off the root of the web application's IIS website root directory will show in all pages of all site collections within the web application. These web part templates typically get into the Web Application Web Part Gallery using the `DwpFiles` element of the SharePoint solution manifest. Because these files are placed directly on the filesystem, they are not securable objects, so they cannot be secured, and they can only be displayed under the Custom category.

Closed Web Part Gallery

Web parts that have been placed onto a specific page and then closed are placed into the Closed Web Part Gallery. Unfortunately, closing a web part is easier than deleting it, so often there are many web parts in the Closed Web Part Gallery that do not need to be there. The valid reason for closing a web part rather than deleting it is to retain its personalization. This makes it possible for people to add an already configured web part to the Personal view of their page. Web part templates in the Closed Web Part Gallery for a specific page are much easier to find than they have been in the past. If any exist, they show up as the last category in the Add Web Part dialog.

Imported Web Part Gallery

Web part templates can be exported to the filesystem and then uploaded into the site collection's Web Part Gallery, or directly onto a page. Web parts that have been uploaded for use on a page are temporarily added to the Imported Web Parts Gallery, so they can be subsequently added to the page.

Web Part Manager

The web part infrastructure relies on the `WebPartManager`, a control typically placed on the master page to manage all the moving parts of a web part zone, as well as the web parts in each web part zone. SharePoint Foundation 2010 does not use the standard `WebPartManager` control. Rather, it uses a SharePoint-specific `SPWebPartManager` control that is derived from the .NET `WebPartManager` class.

The primary purpose of `SPWebPartManager` is to act as the hub for all web parts on a given page. It works in conjunction with web parts that reside within the `WebPartZone`(s) to handle the following tasks:

➤ Maintain an inventory of all the controls on a specific page that supports web parts

➤ Provide a vehicle to add and remove, as well as import and export, web parts

➤ Raise web part life cycle events

➤ Change between the different web page views (such as design, page layout, and editing views)

➤ Create, delete, and manage connections between web parts

➤ Manage page and web part personalization

For developers, the `SPWebPartManager` and, when there is no `HttpContext` or page object instantiated, the `SPLimitedWebPartManager` (which provides a limited set of web part operations that can be performed in object model scenarios), serve as the gateway to all web part–related objects on a web page. Included in its long list of available members are `Connections`, `DynamicConnections`, `Controls`, `WebParts`, `Zones`, and `Personalization`. It also exposes a long list of synchronous and asynchronous events that enable granular programmatic control over the behavior and state of a web page (such as `WebPartAdded`, `WebPartAdding`, `SelectedWebPartChanged`, and `SelectedWebPartChanging`). All events are inherited from either the .NET `WebPartManager` or `Control` objects.

Web Part Zone

Similar to the SPWebPartManager class, SharePoint Foundation 2010 has a WebPartZone class that derives from the .NET WebPartZone class. Notice the SharePoint WebPartZone class does not contain an "SP" prefix like the SPWebPartManager class, even though both are derived from similar ASP.NET 2.0 classes. This is because the WebPartZone control was carried over from the Windows SharePoint Services version 2 (WSS v2) object model to support backward compatibility for SharePoint web parts. The SharePoint product team went to great lengths to ensure that code written against the WSS v2 object model would work in later versions of SharePoint.

The WebPartZone's primary role in a web page is to provide a common user interface and to control the appearance of web part controls. Each zone can contain zero or more web part controls. Along with the SPWebPartManager, WebPartZones handle all serialization of data related to web parts into SharePoint Content Databases. This is the reason a web part cannot reside on a web page without these two controls and retain all the capabilities of a web part (such as personalization). Without the WebPartZone, the web part just becomes a web control (also known as a server control).

There are two types of WebPartZones:

➤ WebPartZoneBase — Contains all the web parts on a web page

➤ ToolZone — A specialized zone that enables users to change the appearance, behavior, layout, and properties of the web parts within the selected zone

There are four different types of ToolZones, each of which is used for a very different purpose. Each of these different types is designed to contain a similar component that derives from the Part class. Table 9-2 shows the four zones, as well as the corresponding types of Part control that each contains.

The ToolZone is responsible for the common user interface of all Part controls that have been added to the specific ToolZone.

TABLE 9-2: ToolZones and Part Controls

TOOLZONE TYPE	PART CONTROL TYPE
WebPartZone	WebPart
EditorZone	EditorPart
CatalogZone	CatalogPart
ConnectionsZone	WebPartConnection

Web Part Ribbon

Like everything else in SharePoint 2010, web parts are now managed using a ribbon.

Edit Mode

There are several ways to put a page into Edit mode. The first is the tried-and-true Site Actions ⇨ Edit Page. This option seems to be ubiquitous, but doesn't involve the ribbon at all. Because this section is about the ribbon, let's consider the alternatives.

Wiki Pages (but not Web Part Pages) have an icon just to the right of the global breadcrumb that will put the page into Edit mode, as shown in Figure 9-4.

FIGURE 9-4: Edit mode icon

Choosing Page ➪ Edit (or Edit Page) will also put the page into Edit mode. Many web part options are available only when the page is in Edit mode.

The Page ➪ Stop Editing option in a Web Part Page works differently than the Page ➪ Save & Close ➪ Stop Editing option in a Wiki Page. Web Part Pages automatically save almost every change directly to the database as the end user interacts with the page. So, Stop Editing in a Web Part Page context simply takes the page out of Edit mode. On the other hand, a Wiki Page does not save any changes to the database until the end user indicates to save the changes. So, Stop Editing in a Wiki Page would abandon the changes unless the end users indicate that they want to save them; thus the prompt.

Add Web Part Dialog

Follow these steps to view the Add Web Part ribbon:

1. Use a browser to navigate to a SharePoint page.

2. Choose Page ➪ Edit (or Edit Page).

3. Position the cursor within a Rich Context area, or click on the edge of the web part zone.

4. Choose Insert ➪ Web Part.

Figure 9-5 shows the Add Web Part ribbon from the context of a Wiki Page. Similarly, Figure 9-6 shows the Add Web Part ribbon from the context of a Web Part Page. Note that there are fewer options on the ribbon.

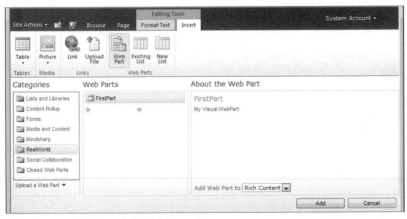

FIGURE 9-5: Wiki Page Add Web Part ribbon

FIGURE 9-6: Web Part Page Add Web Part ribbon

Upload Web Part

Follow these steps to upload a web part template directly to a page, bypassing the galleries entirely:

1. Use a browser to navigate to a SharePoint page.

2. Choose Page ➪ Edit (or Edit Page).

3. Position the cursor within a Rich Context area, or click on the edge of the web part zone.

4. Choose Insert ➪ Web Part.

5. Click the down arrow to the right of "Upload a Web Part."

6. Click the Browse button.

7. Locate the DWP or WEBPART file.

8. Click the Open button.

9. Click the Upload button.

Imported web parts are then listed in an Imported Web Parts category at the top of the Categories list in the Add Web Part dialog.

Web Part Tab Controls

Whenever a web part is selected, a Web Part Tools contextual tab set is presented in the ribbon. As shown in Figure 9-7, clicking the Options contextual tab exposes controls that reflect options that used to be available only on the web part's context menu.

FIGURE 9-7: Options contextual tab

As shown in Figure 9-8, the Web Part Properties control on the ribbon is the same as the Edit Web Part option on the context menu.

FIGURE 9-8: Web Part context menu (also known as web part verbs)

The Insert Related List control is used when in the context of an XSL List View Web Part for a List that has lookup columns to other lists. This option allows the end user to insert the related list(s) auto-connected to this web part.

Delete and Connections are still found exclusively on the web part context menu, and are available only when the page is in Edit mode.

List the Web Page Contents

Sometimes a web part will be added to a page that breaks the entire page. To see an example of a broken page, add a Content Editor web part by following these steps:

1. Use a browser to navigate to a SharePoint page.
2. Choose Page ⇨ Edit (or Edit Page).
3. Position the cursor within a Rich Context area, or click on the edge of the web part zone.
4. Choose Insert ⇨ Web Part.
5. From Categories, choose Media and Content.
6. From Web Parts, choose Content Editor.
7. Click the Add button.
8. Choose Edit Web Part from the web part's context menu.
9. Click the "Click here to add new content" link.
10. Choose Editing Tools ⇨ Format Text ⇨ HTML ⇨ Edit HTML Source.
11. Type in the code shown in Listing 9-1.
12. Click the OK button.
13. Choose Editing Tools ⇨ Page ⇨ Stop Editing.
14. If prompted to save changes, click the Yes button.

LISTING 9-1: Broken CSS

```
<style>
<!--
</style>
```

Code file [01.Broken.css.txt] available for download at Wrox.com

Notice that the comment tag in Listing 9-1 was not properly closed. This situation causes the entire page to malfunction. The ribbon tabs do not work. Clicking the Web Part menu results in a browser error. Any web parts or other content that came after the web part have stopped showing.

To recover from this problem, simply append `contents=1` to the `QueryString`. Precede it with a question mark if the URL has no other `QueryString` parameters like this:

```
http://Intranet/default.aspx?contents=1.
```

Precede it with an ampersand if there are already `QueryString` parameters like this:

```
http://Intranet/default.aspx?PageView=Personal&contents=1.
```

This will present the Web Part Page Maintenance screen shown in Figure 9-9.

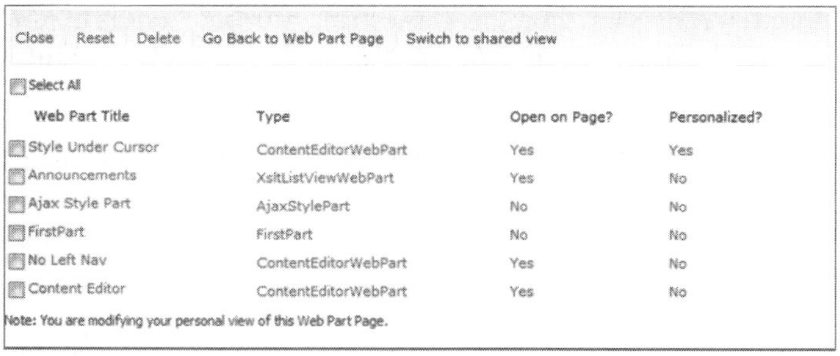

Close	Reset	Delete	Go Back to Web Part Page	Switch to shared view		

Select All				
Web Part Title	**Type**		**Open on Page?**	**Personalized?**
Style Under Cursor	ContentEditorWebPart		Yes	Yes
Announcements	XsltListViewWebPart		Yes	No
Ajax Style Part	AjaxStylePart		No	No
FirstPart	FirstPart		No	No
No Left Nav	ContentEditorWebPart		Yes	No
Content Editor	ContentEditorWebPart		Yes	No

Note: You are modifying your personal view of this Web Part Page.

FIGURE 9-9: Web Part Page Maintenance screen

This list of web parts shows the title and type of each web part on the page for either the Shared view of the page, or the Personal view of the page (shown in Figure 9-9). This is a great place to eliminate unnecessary closed web parts. Use the following steps to fix the page:

1. Select the checkbox to the left of the Content Editor web part.

2. Click the Delete option in the toolbar at the top.

 Web parts can be closed but not deleted from the Personal view.

Click the "Go Back to Web Part Page" link to see the page working again.

Web Part Properties

State management is an important part of most applications that run in a stateless environment like SharePoint. Fortunately, SharePoint provides some terrific, yet easy-to-use, built-in state management. All that is necessary is to decorate the public properties of the web part class with a few attributes, and SharePoint does the rest.

Following are the four attributes that are unique to SharePoint:

➤ `WebBrowsable` — When this Boolean is set to `true`, the end user will be able to see the property in the Editor pane. Set it to `false` to imperatively set the property's value on behalf of the end user.

➤ `WebDescription` — This string shows as a tooltip over the display name.

➤ `WebDisplayName` — This string shows as the label for the control in the Editor pane.

➤ `Personalizable` — This enum has two settings. `PersonalizationScope.Shared` indicates that SharePoint should only store one value for everyone. `PersonalizationScope.User` indicates that SharePoint should still store one common value for everyone, but allow anyone who has permission to personalize to change that value to whatever he or she would like it to be.

Literally dozens of other `System.ComponentModel` attributes can be included. They all are used the same in SharePoint as they are used in ASP.NET. `Category` is a string attribute that is used to indicate in which group the property will be displayed in the Add Web Parts dialog. The default `Category` is `Custom`.

Each public property can have a unique set of attributes. SharePoint supports several different types:

➤ `bool` — Rendered as a checkbox

➤ `DateTime` — Rendered as a textbox

➤ `enum` — Rendered as a drop-down list

➤ `int` — Rendered as a numeric-only textbox

➤ `Float` — Rendered as a numeric-only textbox

➤ `KnownColor` — Rendered as a drop-down list

➤ `string` — Rendered as a textbox

It is also possible to have a custom data-entry experience by creating an `EditorPart` that saves the value that it collects into a hidden (`WebBrowsable` is `false`) property for SharePoint to manage.

Web Part Resources

Sometimes it is necessary to include resources that will always be deployed with the web part — for example, files such as images, CSS, HTML, JavaScript, CSV, XML, and `.ascx`. These resource files are deployed based on the assembly destination:

➤ *Assemblies deployed to the* `BIN` — Resources will be copied to an assembly subdirectory of the `wpresources` directory of each IIS web application for each web part that has resources. This location is identified in the URL using the physical `wpresources` directory.

➤ *Assemblies deployed to the* `GAC` — Resources will be copied to an assembly subdirectory of the `wpresources` directory that is a sibling to the {`SharePointRoot`} for each web part that has resources. This location is identified in the URL using the virtual _wpresources directory.

➤ *Assemblies deployed to the Content Database* — In sandboxed solutions, the assembly isn't physically deployed to the file system until run-time, so the resources must be virtually copied to the Content Database using a Module Feature. This location is identified in the URL using the relative location of the document library to which the resources were copied. You cannot use the Client Script Manager from within a sandboxed solution.

CREATING A SIMPLE VISUAL WEB PART

The Visual web part demonstrated in this exercise simply outputs the date and time. It covers all the steps that a developer would go through using the new Visual Studio 2010 Tools for SharePoint. It also covers the housekeeping steps necessary whenever a Module Feature is employed.

 The steps described here correspond to the "ten easy steps" described previously in the section, "Web Part Development."

Prepare Environment

A SharePoint team site must exist to complete this exercise. This exercise uses a team site called `http://Intranet`, but the URL to any team site will do.

Create Project

I recommend that you create an empty SharePoint project and subsequently add a web part or Visual web part. Unless importing a WSP, importing a workflow, or creating a Site Definition, you should always start with an Empty SharePoint Project template and then add a SPI, rather than choosing a specific template right from the start. In this way, the approach is always consistent, and no refactoring is required (Visual Studio SharePoint Project Item refactoring was not mature as of this writing).

In Visual Studio 2010 or later, follow these steps:

1.   Choose File ➪ New ➪ Project (or use the Crtl+Shift+N key sequence), as shown in Figure 9-10.

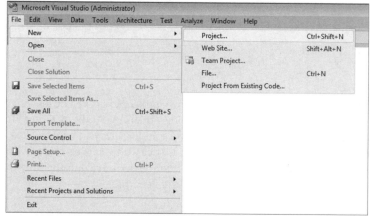

FIGURE 9-10: New Project menu option

2. Alternatively, choose New Project from the content area of the Start Page, as shown in Figure 9-11.

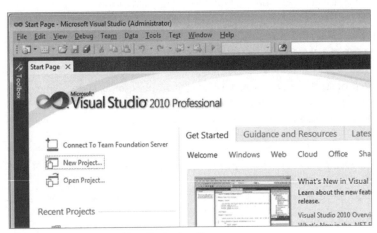

FIGURE 9-11: Alternate New Project option

The Framework Version option and the Sort By option are sticky until they are changed to another value. As of Release to Manufacturing (RTM), SharePoint 2010 could only target the .NET Framework 3.5.

In the New Project screen shown in Figure 9-12, follow these steps:

1. Select Visual C# ⇨ SharePoint ⇨ 2010.

2. From the Framework Version drop-down list near the top center, select .NET Framework 3.5.

3. Optionally, from the "Sort by" drop-down list also near the top center, select Name Ascending.

4. From the SharePoint Project Templates list, select Empty SharePoint Project.

5. In the Name textbox, replace `SharePointProjectN` with `Mindsharp.WebParts.RealWorld`. Be careful to type this in the correct case, because this field is case-sensitive.

6. Optionally, clear the "Create directory for solution" checkbox in the bottom-right corner.

7. Accept all the other defaults.

8. Click OK.

Clearing the "Create directory for solution" checkbox allows project folders to be located immediately inside the `Documents/Visual Studio 2010/Projects` folder. If Visual Studio `SLN` files are also stored in the `Projects` folder, all Visual Studio project folders and solution files can be viewed at once. This can be handy, but is not the default. The choice made here is sticky until it is reversed. Also, when the "Create directory for solution" checkbox is checked, a solution folder is used in the fully qualified file-name, which can substantially limit an already limited name length.

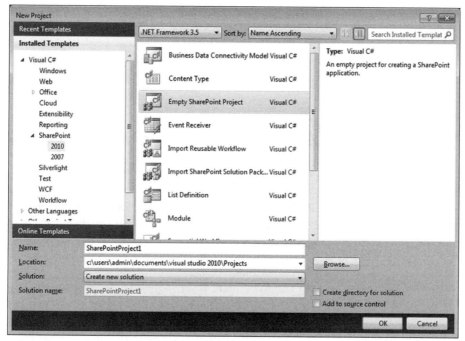

FIGURE 9-12: New Project screen

If prompted as shown in Figure 9-13, click Yes to save changes to all previously altered (but unsaved) project items.

If the dialog shown in Figure 9-14 appears and indicates that the directory already exists, either delete the old project from the filesystem, or change the name of the new project being created and try again from Step 1.

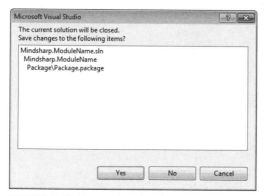

FIGURE 9-13: Unsaved project items prompt

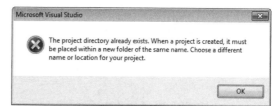

FIGURE 9-14: Dialog indicating that the directory already exists

In the SharePoint Customization Wizard dialog, follow these steps:

1. In the "What local site do you want to use for debugging" textbox, enter **http://Intranet**.

2. Click the (default) "Deploy as a sandboxed solution" radio button.

3. Click Finish.

In the Solution Explorer follow these steps:

1. Optionally, if a strong name key file (`key.snk`) is created in the project root, move the `key.snk` file into the `Properties` folder.

2. Collapse the `Properties` folder.

As projects become more complex, a lack of vertical space in the Solution Explorer makes projects more difficult to work with. Moving the `.snk` file into the `Properties` folder simply hides it in an appropriate location, freeing up that line of vertical scroll. As indicated here, this is totally optional. Often, moving the `key.snk` file will fail. Waiting five to ten seconds overcomes this issue. Keep trying until the file can be moved to the `Properties` folder.

Add Items

The following instructions can be used to add a Visual web part. Minor alterations in the code are necessary to create a standard web part instead of a Visual web part.

In the Solution Explorer, follow these steps:

1. Right-click `{ProjectRoot}`.

2. Choose Add ➪ New Item (or use the key sequence Ctrl+Shift+A), as shown in Figure 9-15.

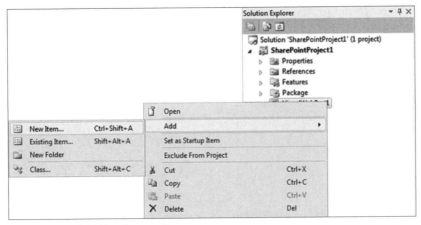

FIGURE 9-15: Add New Item option

3. Alternatively, select Project ⇨ Add New Item (or press Ctrl+Shift+A), as shown in Figure 9-16.

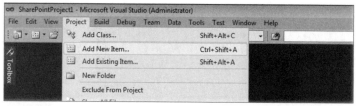

FIGURE 9-16: Alternate Add New Item option

In the Add New Item screen shown in Figure 9-17, follow these steps:

1. Select Visual C# ⇨ SharePoint ⇨ 2010.

2. Optionally, from the "Sort by" drop-down menu also near the top center, select Name Ascending..

The default sort order is non-deterministic — that is, the most commonly used templates are listed first. Initially, this sounds great. But the reality for most people is the capability to anticipate where a template will be displayed outweighs having the most common templates listed at the top. "Sort by" is a sticky setting in this dialog. Whatever value is chosen will remain the initially selected value each time this dialog is used until it is changed to something else.

3. From the SharePoint Project Item Templates list, select Visual Web Part.

4. In the Name textbox, replace the default name with **FirstPart**.

5. Click Add.

6. Wait for the connection to complete while viewing "Connecting to SharePoint" progress dialog shown in Figure 9-18.

In the FirstPart folder, double-click the Elements.xml file. In the Elements.xml editor, replace the child element of the File element with the code shown in Listing 9-2.

Available for
download on
Wrox.com

LISTING 9-2: Group Property

```
<Property Name="Group" Value="RealWorld" />
```

Code file [02.GroupProperty.xml.txt] available for download at Wrox.com

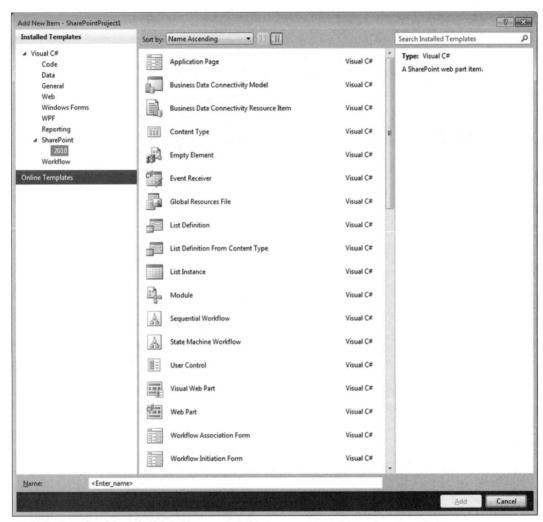

FIGURE 9-17: Add New Item screen

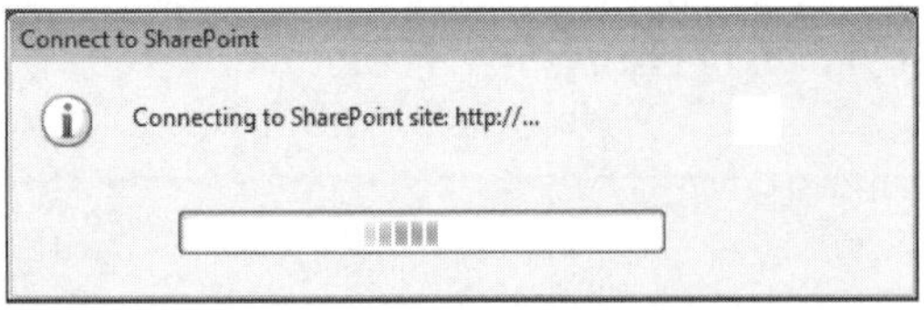

FIGURE 9-18: "Connecting to SharePoint" progress dialog

Configure Feature

The deployment destination for the `Features` folder is automatically set to `$SharePoint.Project.FileNameWithoutExtension$_$SharePoint.Feature.FileNameWithoutExtension$`. These two replaceable parameters are replaced with the actual Visual Studio project name suffixed with an underscore and the name of the Feature folder every time the project is compiled. A folder using that entire string will be deployed to `{SharePointRoot}\TEMPLATE\FEATURES\` by a farm solution, along with the contents as presented in the Feature Designer. Of course, a sandboxed solution will retain all the files for the Feature within the WSP.

In the Solution Explorer, follow these steps:

1. Expand the (default) `Features` folder.

2. Right-click the `Feature1` folder, as shown in Figure 9-19.

3. Choose the Rename option (see Figure 9-19).

4. In the textbox showing the FeatureN text, type **SiteFeature** to replace that text.

5. Press the Enter key to commit the change.

6. Double-click the `SiteFeature` folder.

FIGURE 9-19: Right-clicking the Feature1 folder

In the `SiteFeature.feature` designer, follow these steps:

1. At a minimum, delete Feature1 from the Title textbox, as shown in Figure 9-20.

2. Optionally, add some descriptive text to the Description textbox.

> *This Title and Description will be presented to the end user on the Feature Activation screen in the browser. The Visual Studio project name followed by the SharePoint Feature folder name may not be what the end user will expect. So, bearing that context in mind, the actual text used should be entered.*

3. Select (default) Site from the Scope drop-down list.

4. Verify that the `FirstPart VisualWebPart` (default) is listed in the "Items in the Feature" section.

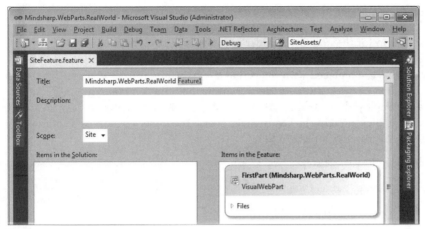

FIGURE 9-20: Alter the Feature Title

Configure Solution

Next, validate that the SharePoint Solution Package (WSP) can be deployed with the items that have been added to it. If a Visual web part was chosen in an earlier step, the validation will fail while Sandboxed Solution is set to `True`. This is because the Visual web part uses two things that can only be used in a farm solution: a mapped folder, and a `Page.LoadControl` statement (which require a GAC'd assembly to obtain Full trust).

Unless circumstances demand rare deployment options as subsequently described, the defaults will be sufficient.

In the Solution Explorer, follow these steps:

1. Right-click the `{ProjectRoot}`.

2. Choose the "Set as StartUp Project" option, as shown in Figure 9-21.

> *Choosing the StartUp Project ensures that this Visual Studio project's package will be deployed when the developer either chooses Debug ⇨ Start Debugging in the Visual Studio menu, presses the Start Debugging icon in the toolbar, or presses F5 to start debugging.*

3. Double-click the `Package` folder, as shown in Figure 9-22.

FIGURE 9-21: "Set as StartUp Project" option

FIGURE 9-22: SharePoint Solution Package in Solution Explorer

In the `Package.package` designer shown in Figure 9-23, follow these steps:

1. In rare cases, change the Name textbox. For this example, the default project name text (`Mindsharp.WebParts.RealWorld`) will be sufficient.

2. In rare cases, change the Deployment Server Type drop-down. The default is to deploy to the Web Front End (WFE) server, and it is rare that you would change the drop-down selection to deploy to the Application Server.

3. In rare cases, select the Reset Web Server checkbox to cause the Timer Job on each server where the SharePoint Solution is deployed to run an Application Pool reset.

4. Choose View ➪ Other Windows ➪ Packaging Explorer View from the Visual Studio menu.

5. Verify that the Feature is listed (default) in the "Items in the Package" section.

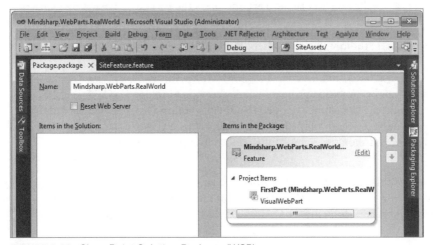

FIGURE 9-23: SharePoint Solution Package (WSP)

In the Packaging Explorer, follow these steps:

1. Right-click the top-level node.

2. Choose the Validate option, as shown in Figure 9-24.

3. Optionally, click the push pin to auto-hide the Packaging Explorer.

4. Verify that the validation succeeded by pressing Ctrl+Alt+O.

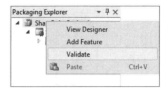

FIGURE 9-24: SharePoint Solution Package Validate option

 Validate will generate notes in the Visual Studio Output Window shown in Figure 9-25 that describe potential issues with the package. Before the SharePoint Solution package will deploy, issues must be corrected until the "Package validation completed successfully" message is seen in the Visual Studio Output Window.

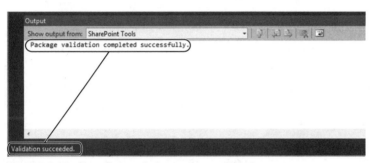

FIGURE 9-25: SharePoint solution package validation output

If the Properties window shown in Figure 9-26 does not display below the Solution Explorer, select the project and press the F4 key.

In the Properties window, if the Sandboxed Solution property is set to `True`, Visual Studio will only present the subset of IntelliSense that is valid within a sandboxed solution, and will warn the developer if assets are used that will not work within a sandboxed solution. Because this project includes a mapped folder and uses `LoadControl`, it must be changed to a farm solution, so change the Sandboxed Solution property to `False`. Once you make this change, you should see the confirmation prompt shown in Figure 9-27.

Click Yes. Ensure that the Visual Studio project's Site URL property is set to `http://Intranet` so that deployment and debugging will work in the expected context.

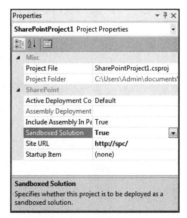

FIGURE 9-26: Project Properties window

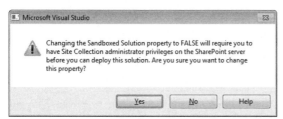

FIGURE 9-27: Changing to a Farm Solution confirmation prompt

Write Code

In the Visual Studio 2010 Release to Manufacturing (RTM), the Visual web part requires a SharePoint farm solution because the `LoadControl` statement in the `CreateChildControls` method requires Full Trust CAS (which requires the GAC), whereas the standard web part can be deployed within a SharePoint sandboxed solution. Also, the `ascx` control is always deployed to the `ControlTemplates` mapped folder. This may change in a future release.

In the Solution Explorer, follow these steps:

1. Expand the `FirstPart` folder.

2. Double-click the `FirstPartUserControl.ascx` user control to open the editor.

In the `FirstPartUserControl.ascx` editor, follow these steps:

1. Click the Design tab.

2. Drag a `Label` control from the Toolbox onto the design surface.

3. Right-click the design surface.

4. Choose View Code.

5. Inside the `Page_Load` method, enter the code shown in Listing 9-3.

LISTING 9-3: Page Load

Available for
download on
Wrox.com

```
Label1.Text = DateTime.Now.ToString();
```

Code file [03.PageLoad.cs.txt] available for download at Wrox.com

A Module Feature is used to copy the web part template (`*.webpart`) file into the Web Part Gallery. However, when a Module Feature is deactivated, it orphans that file in the Content Database. To end users, it will still look like they could add the web part, but an error occurs when they try. So, whenever a Module Feature is used, housekeeping code is required in the imperative `FeatureDeactivating` method of the Feature Receiver.

To make the housekeeping code common to all web parts, replaceable parameters can be used in the SPI properties passed into the Feature Event Receiver. .

In the `FirstPart.cs` editor, enter the code shown in Listing 9-4 above the `FirstPart` class definition.

LISTING 9-4: Class Attribute

```
[System.Runtime.InteropServices.Guid("[guid]")]
```

Code file [04.Class Attribute.cs.txt] available for download at Wrox.com

SharePoint uses GUIDs to identify most major entities. The Field (Site Column) and any reference to it must include braces, but almost everything else uses brace-less, lowercase, Registry Format GUIDs. Content Type IDs may also use a brace-less, Registry Format GUID, but they also strip out the dashes.

Create a brace-less, lowercase, Registry Format GUID as an ID for the class in the decorative attribute. You can do this by using the Tools ⇨ Create Guid option in the Visual Studio menu.

The Tools ⇨ Create Guid option is added to the Visual Studio menu if the Web Designer option is included during installation. If the menu option isn't there, use the following steps to add it to the Visual Studio menu. If no external tools are defined at all, Visual Studio will automatically present the Add options without your having to first click the Add button.

1. In Visual Studio, choose Tools ⇨ External Tools, as shown in Figure 9-28, and click Add.

2. In the Title textbox, enter **Create Guid**.

3. Type the following in the Command textbox:

    ```
    %ProgramFiles(x86)%\Microsoft SDKs\Windows\v7.0A\Bin\guidgen.exe
    ```

4. Click OK.

Now that the option has been added to the Visual Studio menu, in the Solution Explorer, choose Tools ⇨ Create Guid.

In the Create GUID dialog, follow these steps, as shown in Figure 9-29:

1. Click the "4. Registry Format" radio button.

2. Optionally, click the New GUID button repeatedly until a GUID with memorable characteristics is presented in the Result pane.

3. Click the Copy button.

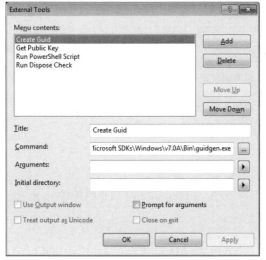

FIGURE 9-28: External Tools dialog

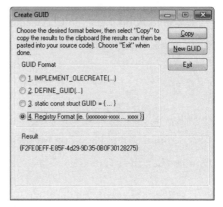

FIGURE 9-29: Create GUID dialog

 Though it's true that any GUID will do, burning a number guaranteed to be unique forever just to find one with memorable characteristics may impart a unique feeling of power over the world. To burn a GUID or not to burn a GUID — that is the question. An even bigger question is whether a GUID should ever be tweaked. What risk of unexpected GUID duplication does GUID tweaking present?

In the `FirstPart.cs` editor, follow these steps:

1. Replace the `[guid]` placeholder in the class attribute with the Registry Format GUID from the clipboard.

2. Remove the braces from the beginning and the end of the Registry Format GUID.

3. Highlight the Registry Format GUID.

4. Press the Ctrl+U keyboard shortcut to ensure that any letters in the Registry Format GUID are lowercase.

This GUID will be used in the next code block to reference this class type.

Select the `FirstPart` folder. Choose View ⇨ Properties Window (or press Ctrl+W, P, or press F4).

In the FirstPart Properties window, follow these steps:

1. Click the Feature Properties property.

2. Click the ellipsis to open the Feature Properties property editor dialog.

In the Safe Control Entries dialog, follow these steps:

1. Click Add.

2. Replace `FeatureProperty1` in the Key property with `myAssemblyQualifiedName`.

3. Type **\$SharePoint.Type.[guid].AssemblyQualifiedName\$** in the Value property.

4. Replace the `[guid]` placeholder with the brace-less Registry Format GUID decorating the `FirstPart` class.

5. Click OK.

In the Solution Explorer, follow these steps:

1. Choose Build ⇨ Build Solution (or press Ctrl+Shift+B, or press F6 to add the GUID to the class).

2. Double-click the `SiteFeature.feature` folder.

When the `SiteFeature.feature` designer appears, choose the Manifest tab at the bottom of the designer to see the token as it will be resolved.

In the Solution Explorer, follow these steps:

1. Right-click the `SiteFeature` folder.

2. Choose the Add Event Receiver option.

3. Add the code shown in Listing 9-5 to overwrite the commented `FeatureDeactivating` method.

LISTING 9-5: FeatureDeactivating

```
public override void FeatureDeactivating(
  SPFeatureReceiverProperties properties)
{
  SPSite siteCollection = properties.Feature.Parent as SPSite;

  SPWeb web = siteCollection.RootWeb;

  // Reflect Type from AssemblyQualifiedName property
  Type asmType = Type.GetType(
    properties.Feature.Properties["myAssemblyQualifiedName"].Value);

  // Cleanup the Web Part that was copied to the
  // Web Part Gallery by the Module in the Feature Elements file
  // asmType.Name contains the Class Name of the Web Part
  // which is also the name of the deployed .webpart file
  SPFile webpartFile = web.GetFile(
    string.Format("/_catalogs/wp/{0}.webpart", asmType.Name));
  webpartFile.Delete();
}
```

Code file [05.FeatureDeactivating.cs.txt] available for download at Wrox.com

While in a code context, from the Visual Studio menu, you can optionally choose Edit ⇨ Advanced ⇨ Format Document (or press Crtl+E+D, or press Ctrl+K+D) to ensure that the code is aligned according to the style rules. Some Visual Studio profiles do not show the Format Document option. However, often one of the keyboard shortcuts will work anyway.

Deploy Assets

The next phase is to deploy the project's assets to the SharePoint test site.

The Visual Studio solution is a container for Visual Studio projects and code. It should not be confused with the SharePoint solution, which is a `CAB-format` file that contains assets to be deployed to a SharePoint farm or a SharePoint site collection Solution Gallery.

In Visual Studio, follow these steps:

➤ Choose Build ⇨ Build Solution (or press Ctrl+Shift+B).

➤ If the Error List tab is displayed, fix the errors reported.

➤ If the Output Window is not showing, choose View ⇨ Output (or press Ctrl+W+O).

➤ Verify that the Build succeeded. (You can use the Ctrl+Alt+O keyboard shortcut.)

The Deploy option described at the end of this exercise will automatically build (compile) the projects from which it gets its assets. So, this build step is not technically required. Though redundant, it is a swift way to identify issues before attempting to deploy any SharePoint Solution. Build Solution only recompiles code if Visual Studio detects that the code is not up to date. If code changes are not detected by Visual Studio, choosing Build ⇨ Rebuild Solution instead will always recompile the code and run the Post Build Events. Using Rebuild Solution is highly advisable during debugging. There is also an alternative to build just one of the projects in the Visual Studio solution.

In the Solution Explorer, double-click the `Properties` folder. In the Project Properties dialog, follow these steps:

1. Select the SharePoint node, as shown in Figure 9-30.

2. Optionally, type the following into the "Post-deployment Command Line" textbox:

```
del C:\inetpub\wwwroot\wss\VirtualDirectories\
    [WebApplicationHomeDirectory]\*.bak
```

Replace [WebApplicationHomeDirectory] with the actual filesystem directory that IIS refers to as the web application's home directory.

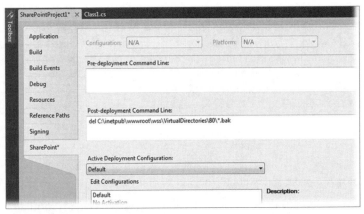

FIGURE 9-30: Project Properties SharePoint node

 Whenever SharePoint modifies the web.config *file, it creates a backup copy with a* BAK *extension. These backup files can be helpful on the occasion a previous version of the* web.config *is needed. However, for iterative development, they can accumulate a ton of unwanted files. Though certainly not required, running this DOS command after each successful deployment will keep the web application IIS home directory much tidier.*

3. Just below the Post-deployment Command Line, verify that the Default option is selected in the Active Deployment Configuration drop-down box.

4. Alternatively, you can also find the Active Deployment Configuration drop-down in the Properties window of the SharePoint Project, as shown in Figure 9-31.

Deployment conflicts can occur when an artifact with the same name and location has previously been deployed. Every SPI includes a Deployment Conflict Resolution property (shown in Figure 9-32) that instructs Visual Studio to handle these conflicts in one of the following ways:

➤ *None* — When a conflict occurs, an error is thrown.

➤ *Prompt* — A prompt allows the developer to decide what to do when a conflict occurs.

➤ *Automatic* — Visual Studio automatically tries to resolve conflicts when they occur. This is the default.

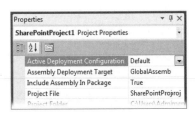

FIGURE 9-31: Active Deployment Configuration project property

FIGURE 9-32: SPI Deployment Conflict Resolution property

For example, if a Visual web part does not include `FeatureDeactivated` code that deletes the `webpart` file from the Web Part Gallery, the message shown in Figure 9-33 will be displayed in the Output Window when the Deployment Conflict Resolution is set to Automatic.

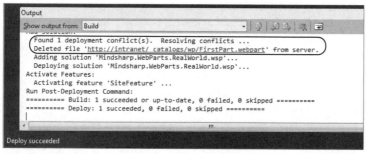

FIGURE 9-33: Resolved conflicts in Output Window

It is possible that the current package being deployed was somehow previously deployed. This most commonly happens when the developer creates a new project that happens to match a project previously created and deployed, perhaps by another developer, or from another development environment. The prompt shown in Figure 9-34 is displayed when this occurs.

FIGURE 9-34: Duplicate SharePoint Solution package prompt

This message will be presented on each deployment. Presuming the existing solution should be replaced, the easiest way to stop receiving this message is to Retract the solution once so that the conflict is eliminated, and then repeatedly use the Deploy option.

In the Solution Explorer:

1. Right-click {ProjectRoot}.

2. Choose the Deploy option (or press Alt+B, D).

3. Press Ctrl+Shift+O to verify that the Deploy succeeded, as shown in Figure 9-35.

FIGURE 9-35: Output Window showing that the deployment succeeded

USING KEYBOARD SHORTCUTS TO DEPLOY

The keyboard shortcut for *building* Visual Studio solutions is F6, or Ctrl+Shift+B (where the B stands for "Build"). The Alt+B, D key sequence works for *deploying* SharePoint solution packages, and that isn't a bad keyboard shortcut, but you may want to map a more memorable keyboard shortcut for deploying that is similar to the build keyboard shortcut.

The Ctrl+Shift+D key sequence (where the D stands for "Deploy") would be nice for deploying SharePoint solutions. Use the following steps to set up that mapping in Visual Studio. (It's a convoluted process.)

1. Choose Tools ➪ Options.

2. Expand Environment ➪ Keyboard.

3. Place the cursor in the "Press shortcut keys" textbox.

4. Press Ctrl+Shift+D. This keyboard shortcut is mapped by default to Debug .ParallelStacks.

5. In the "Show commands containing" textbox, type **deploy**. Select Build .DeploySolution.

6. Click Assign.

7. Click OK.

Then, to deploy a SharePoint Solution Package, just press Ctrl+Shift+D in any SharePoint project. Deploying a SharePoint Solution Package will also save all files and build the Visual Studio projects involved.

Test Solution

Now you must validate that the web part is operational by adding it to a SharePoint Page.

In Internet Explorer, follow these steps:

1. Browse to `http://Intranet`.

2. If a `TestPage` does not exist, choose Site Actions ➪ New Page.

 The options on the Site Actions menu vary based upon whether the Wiki Page Home Page Site Feature is activated. If the New Page option is not visible, a page can still be created by choosing the Site Actions ➪ More Options option instead.

If a New Page option is visible, the New Page dialog shown in Figure 9-36 will appear. In the "New page name" textbox, enter **TestPage**. The `.aspx` extension will be added automatically.

If a New Page option is not visible, use the Create dialog shown in Figure 9-37 and follow these steps:

1. Choose Filter By ⇨ Page.

2. Alternatively, you can further filter the list of items by choosing one of the Blank & Custom, Collaboration, Content, or Meetings categories. Or, you can type at least some of the Site Template name into the Search textbox in the top-right corner, and press Enter or click the search icon.

FIGURE 9-36: New Page dialog

3. In the Name textbox, enter **TestPage**. The `.aspx` extension is automatically added when the page is created.

4. Optionally, you can click the More Options button to set metadata. Clicking the Cancel button returns you to the original Create dialog shown in Figure 9-38.

5. If prompted to create a Wiki Page Library as shown in Figure 9-39, click the Create button.

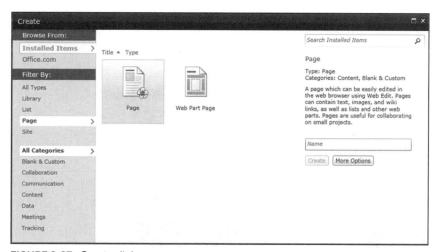

FIGURE 9-37: Create dialog

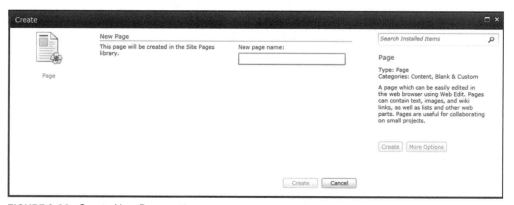

FIGURE 9-38: Create New Page options

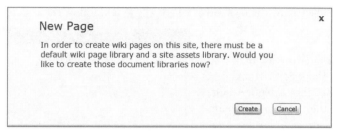

FIGURE 9-39: Create Wiki Page Library confirmation prompt

In the New Page dialog or the Create dialog, click the Create button.

The Long Running Process dialog will appear. When the Long Running Process dialog screen shown in Figure 9-40 stops processing, the new Page will be displayed.

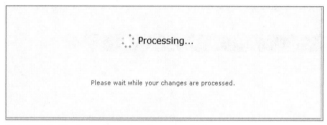

FIGURE 9-40: Long Running Process dialog

In Internet Explorer, follow these steps:

1. Click in the empty Rich Content textbox, as shown in Figure 9-41.

2. From the ribbon, choose Editing Tools ⇨ Insert ⇨ Web Part.

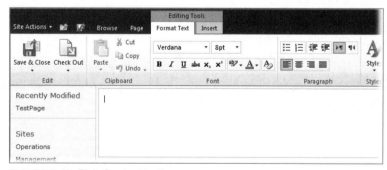

FIGURE 9-41: Rich Content textbox

In the Add Web Part panel shown in Figure 9-42, follow these steps:

1. Select RealWorld from the Categories list.

2. Select FirstPart from the Web Parts list.

3. From the "Add Web Part to" drop-down list, select Rich Content.

4. Click Add.

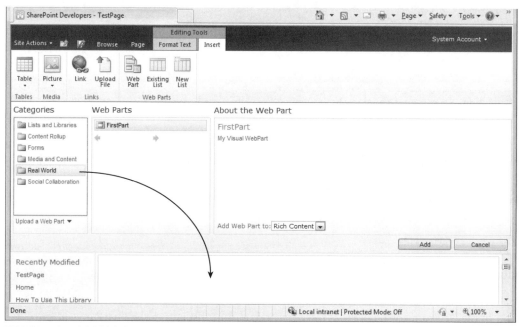

FIGURE 9-42: Add Web Part panel

On the SharePoint page, wait for the Loading dialog to complete. From the ribbon, in the Edit group, choose Page ⇨ Save & Close, as shown in Figure 9-43.

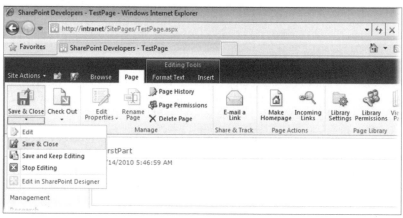

FIGURE 9-43: Save & Close option

If the content of the page is altered, and you attempt to navigate away from the page, a prompt to either save the changes or continue without saving is displayed, as shown in Figure 9-44.

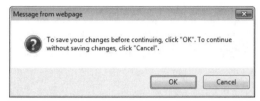

FIGURE 9-44: Save changes confirmation prompt

If you select Page ⇨ Stop Editing after altering the page content, a prompt to save the changes is presented in a different dialog box, as shown in Figure 9-45, but this accomplishes the same thing.

FIGURE 9-45: Another save changes confirmation prompt

Now, in the web part zone, note that the current date/time displays in the FirstPart web part, as shown in Figure 9-46.

FIGURE 9-46: FirstPart web part

Secure Code

Because the Feature Receiver assembly in this exercise is deployed to the GAC, which always has Full trust, the assembly will automatically have the necessary CAS permissions. Had this been a sandboxed solution, the assembly would be deployed inside of the WSP file and extracted at run-time by the User Code Service, so the CAS policy of the User Code Service would apply.

So, in SharePoint 2010, the only time that a custom CAS policy is needed is when the developer sets the Assembly Deployment Target property of a Visual Studio SharePoint Project to WebApplication, which deploys the assembly to the BIN of the web application and all of its extensions. This can only be done in a farm solution, and will typically only be done when the security of the assembly is absolutely essential.

Any of the 19 .NET Framework CAS permissions shown in Figure 9-47 can be granted to a custom assembly deployed to the BIN. (Figure 9-47 shows the .NET Framework 2.0 Configuration Wizard.)

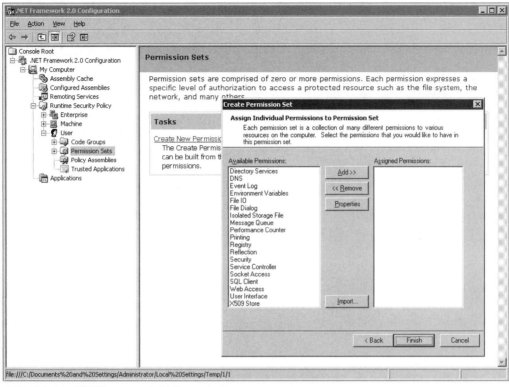

FIGURE 9-47: .NET Framework CAS permissions

There are two CAS permissions in the `Microsoft.SharePoint.Security` namespace. Figure 9-48 shows these in Redgate's .NET Reflector.

The SharePoint permissions are not given an alias in all contexts, so they should be fully qualified whenever referenced to be sure that they will be found:

FIGURE 9-48: SharePoint custom CAS permissions

➤ `WebPartPermission` (`Microsoft.SharePoint.Security .WebPartPermission, Microsoft.SharePoint.Security, Version=14.0.0.0, Culture=neutral, PublicKeyToken= 71e9bce111e9429c`) — As the name implies, this permission grants the assembly the permission to be a web part. It has a Boolean attribute called `Connections`.

➤ `SharePointPermission` (`Microsoft.SharePoint .Security.SharePointPermission, Microsoft.SharePoint .Security, Version=14.0.0.0, Culture=neutral, PublicKeyToken=71e9bce111e9429c`) — This has three Boolean attributes: `Impersonate`, `ObjectModel`, and `UnsafeSaveOnGet`.

Of course, like a CAS permission, both SharePoint permissions support the Boolean `Unrestricted` attribute.

By default, all assemblies deployed to the BIN are granted three permissions, as shown in Listing 9-6.

LISTING 9-6: Default PermissionSet for BIN-Based Assemblies

```xml
<PermissionSet
        class="NamedPermissionSet"
        version="1"
        Name="SPRestricted">
    <IPermission
            class="AspNetHostingPermission"
            version="1"
            Level="Minimal"
    />
    <IPermission
            class="SecurityPermission"
            version="1"
            Flags="Execution"
    />
    <IPermission class="WebPartPermission"
            version="1"
            Connections="True"
    />
</PermissionSet>
```

Code file [06.Default PermissionSet for BIN-based assemblies.xml.txt] available for download at Wrox.com

Assemblies deployed to the BIN can interact with the .NET Framework, participate in security, and be a web part. Note that SharePoint's custom CAS permission, `WebPartPermission`, does not need to be fully qualified because it is given an alias in every `web.config` that SharePoint deploys.

To use a custom CAS policy for a web part assembly, a `PolicyItem` must be added to the farm solution manifest. At present, Visual Studio doesn't have any tools to aid with the creation or placement of this `PolicyItem`. As an example, to allow a BIN-based web part assembly to interact with the SharePoint Object Model and query a SQL database, the `PolicyItem` shown in Listing 9-7 would be added into the `Package.Template.xml` file.

LISTING 9-7: CodeAccessSecurity PolicyItem

```xml
<CodeAccessSecurity>
  <PolicyItem>
    <Assemblies>
      <Assembly PublicKeyBlob="[blob]" />
    </Assemblies>
    <PermissionSet
            class="NamedPermissionSet"
            version="1"
```

```
            Name="SPRestricted">
        <IPermission
            class="AspNetHostingPermission"
            version="1"
            Level="Minimal"
        />
        <IPermission
            class="SecurityPermission"
            version="1"
            Flags="Execution"
        />
        <IPermission class="WebPartPermission"
            version="1"
            Connections="True"
        />
        <IPermission class="SharePointPermission"
            version="1"
            ObjectModel="True"
        />
        <IPermission
            class="SqlClientPermission"
            version="1"
            Unrestricted="true"
        />
    </PermissionSet>
  </PolicyItem>
</CodeAccessSecurity>
```

Code file [07.CodeAccessSecurity PolicyItem.xml.txt] available for download at Wrox.com

Note the two IPermission sections bolded near the bottom of Listing 9-7. Compile the project to generate the signed assembly. Then, run the strong name (sn.exe) command with the –Tp switches (to get the Token and Public Key Blob) from a Visual Studio command prompt, as shown in Figure 9-49.

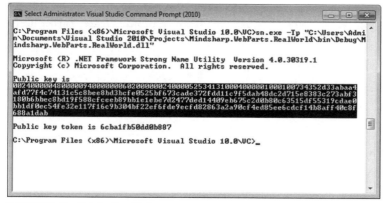

FIGURE 9-49: Public Key Blob

> *Be sure to use the proper case for the switches. Also, the entire command must be on one line.*

Copy the Public Key Blob (highlighted in Figure 9-49) and remove all line breaks. Replace the `[blob]` placeholder in Listing 9-7 with this hexadecimal value. When the farm solution is deployed, SharePoint will automatically update the CAS policy `config` files and modify the `web.config` of every web application that will be running the web part.

Deliver Solution

As previously mentioned, the WSP generated during the deployment step can be found in the `bin\debug` folder of the current project. This can certainly be used in a shared test environment. However, an automated build or a gatekeeper in Operations should recompile the project in Release mode before deploying to any testing environments, and eventually to production.

ENHANCING THE VISUAL WEB PART

Unfortunately, the default code generated by Visual Studio 2010 when a Visual web part is added to a SharePoint project does not include the capability for the web part to manipulate the user control, nor does it include the capability of the user control to access the properties exposed to the end user by the web part. This is easy to remedy.

Write Code

The following steps make changes to the FirstPart Web Part created earlier in this chapter to demonstrate how to loosely couple the web part with its design surface, the user control, using strongly typed variables and public properties. The public property on the web part provides a nice example of state management.

1. In Visual Studio, open the `Mindsharp.WebParts.RealWorld` project created earlier in this chapter.

2. In the Solution Explorer, expand the `FirstPart` folder.

3. Double-click the `FirstPart.cs` web part class.

4. In the `FirstPart.cs` editor, insert the code shown in Listing 9-8 at the top of the class.

LISTING 9-8: Web Part Property

```
// Public property, set by the end user
[WebBrowsable(true)]
[Personalizable(PersonalizationScope.Shared)]
[WebDisplayName("First Part Text")]
```

```
[WebDescription("Enter the text to display")]
[System.ComponentModel.Category("Real World")]
public string WpProperty { get; set; }
```

Code file [08.WebPartProperty.cs.txt] available for download at Wrox.com

Several of the most common attributes decorate the `WpProperty` public property.

Follow these steps:

1. In the `FirstPart` folder, double-click the `FirstPartUserControl.ascx` user control.

2. In the `FirstPartUserControl.ascx` editor, click the Design tab.

3. Expand the Toolbox.

4. Drag a `Button` control from the Toolbox onto the design surface just before the `Label`.

5. Double-click the new `Button` to wire up the `Button1_Click` event.

6. In the `FirstPartUserControl.ascx.cs` editor, replace the existing `Page_Load` and `Button1_Click` methods with the code shown in Listing 9-9.

LISTING 9-9: UcClass

```
// Public property, set by the Web Part
public string UcProperty { get; set; }

// Strongly typed pointer to parent Web Part
FirstPart thisPart = default(FirstPart);

protected override void OnInit(EventArgs e)
{
  // Establish parent Web Part
  thisPart = this.Parent as FirstPart;
}

protected void Page_Load(object sender, EventArgs e)
{
  // Display the User Control property
  Label1.Text = UcProperty;
}

protected void Button1_Click(object sender, EventArgs e)
{
  // Display the Web Part property
  Label1.Text = thisPart.WpProperty;
}
```

Code file [09.UserControlClass.cs.txt] available for download at Wrox.com

7. In the `FirstPart` folder, double-click the `FirstPart.cs` web part class again.

8. In the `FirstPart.cs` editor, replace the existing `CreateChildControls` method with the code shown in Listing 9-10.

LISTING 9-10: Web Part CreateChildControls

```
protected override void CreateChildControls()
{
  // Strongly typed design surface (User Control)
  FirstPartUserControl control =
    Page.LoadControl(_ascxPath)
      as FirstPartUserControl;

  control.UcProperty = "Set By Web Part";

  Controls.Add(control);
}
```

Code file [10.WebPartCreateChildControls.cs.txt] available for download at Wrox.com

Deploy Assets

Now you must deploy the project's assets to the SharePoint test site.

In the Solution Explorer, follow these steps:

1. Right-click `{ProjectRoot}`.

2. Choose the Deploy option (or press Alt+B, D).

3. Verify that the Deploy succeeded by pressing Ctrl+Shift+O.

Test Solution

Now validate the web part changes.

In Internet Explorer, follow these steps:

1. Browse to `http://Intranet/SitePages/TestPage.aspx`.

2. As shown in Figure 9-50, note that the text "Set By Web Part" established by setting the user control's property from the web part's `CreateChildControls` is initially displayed.

3. Choose the Edit Web Part option from the web part's context menu.

4. Collapse the Appearance Category.

5. Expand the Real World Category.

6. In the First Part Text textbox shown in Figure 9-51, enter **Set By End User**.

7. Click OK.

8. After the page refreshes, click the Button on the web part.

9. Note that the "Set By End User" text established by setting the web part's property from the Task Pane is displayed, as shown in Figure 9-52.

FIGURE 9-50: Initial text displayed

FIGURE 9-51: Custom First Part Text web part property

FIGURE 9-52: Value entered into First Part Text web part property

ADDING AN EDITOR PART

As mentioned earlier in this chapter in the "Web Part Properties" section, sometimes the default data entry options of a property is insufficient. When that happens, the property can be hidden, and its value can be collected by an editor part. These are just web controls (also known as server controls), which are just like web parts, but they are specifically designed to run in the context of the Editor pane.

Let's take a look at how to add an editor part. Again, this example follows the "ten easy steps" methodology discussed earlier in this chapter.

Write Code

The following steps make changes to the FirstPart Web Part created earlier in this chapter to demonstrate how to add a simple editor part to hide the value collected (password mode).

Follow these steps:

1. In Visual Studio, open the `Mindsharp.WebParts.RealWorld` project created earlier in this chapter.

2. In the Solution Explorer, expand the `FirstPart` folder.

3. Double-click the `FirstPart.cs` web part class.

4. In the `FirstPart.cs` editor, insert the code shown in Listing 9-11 at the top of the class.

LISTING 9-11: Web Part Property

```
// Hidden public property, set by the Editor Part
[WebBrowsable(false)]
[Personalizable(PersonalizationScope.User)]
public string Pwd { get; set; }
```

Code file [11.WebPartProperty.cs.txt] available for download at Wrox.com

The hidden public property has been decorated with attributes to prevent it from showing in the Tool Pane. If the web part is on a page in Personal view, each user can specify his or her own value for this property.

Follow these steps:

1. In the Solution Explorer, right-click the `FirstPart` folder.

2. Choose Add ⇨ Class (or press Shift+Alt+C).

3. In the Add New Item dialog, replace default name in the Name textbox with `PasswordEditorPart`.

4. Click Add.

5. In the `PasswordEditorPart.cs` editor, enter the code shown in Listing 9-12 at the top of the `PasswordEditorPart` class.

LISTING 9-12: Editor Part Import Directives

```
using System.Web.UI;
using System.Web.UI.WebControls;
using Microsoft.SharePoint.WebPartPages;
```

Code file [12.EditorPartImportDirectives.cs.txt] available for download at Wrox.com

6. Replace the generated `PasswordEditorPart` class with the code shown in Listing 9-13.

LISTING 9-13: PasswordEditorPart Class

```csharp
public class PasswordEditorPart :
  System.Web.UI.WebControls.WebParts.EditorPart
{
  TextBox txt = default(TextBox);
  CheckBox chk = default(CheckBox);

  protected override void OnInit(EventArgs e)
  {
    // Label at the top of the Editor Part
    Title = "Password Editor";
  }

}
```

Code file [13.EditorPartClass.cs.txt] available for download at Wrox.com

7.   Inside the class just above the last two end braces, insert the code shown in Listing 9-14.

LISTING 9-14: Editor Part User Interface

```csharp
// Create the structure for the User Interface
protected override void CreateChildControls()
{
  Panel div = default(Panel);

  // Label just above Textbox
  Label lbl = new Label();
  lbl.Text = "Password";

  div = new Panel();
  div.CssClass = "UserSectionHead";
  div.Controls.Add(lbl);
  Controls.Add(div);

  // Password protected Textbox
  // 176 is the default width for an Editor Pane TextBox
  txt = new TextBox();
  txt.CssClass = "UserInput";
  txt.TextMode = TextBoxMode.Password;
  txt.Width = Unit.Pixel(176);

  div = new Panel();
  div.CssClass = "UserControlGroup";
  div.Controls.Add(txt);
  Controls.Add(div);
```

```
    // Password protected Textbox
    chk = new CheckBox();
    chk.CssClass = "UserInput";
    chk.Text = "Set a blank password";

    div = new Panel();
    div.CssClass = "UserSectionHead";
    div.Controls.Add(chk);
    Controls.Add(div);
}
```

Code file [14.EditorPartCreateChildControls.cs.txt] available for download at Wrox.com

8. Inside the edit part class just above the last two end braces, insert the code shown in Listing 9-15.

LISTING 9-15: Editor Part Implementation

```
// Applies changes made in the Editor Part back to a
// hidden Web Part public property
// to maintain the specified value across sessions
public override bool ApplyChanges()
{
  // Obtain a pointer to the Web Part that
  // launched the Editor Pane
  using (FirstPart thisPart = this.WebPartToEdit as FirstPart)
  {
    // If the user has entered a value into the TextBox
    // save it to the Web Part's Pwd property
    string newPassword = txt.Text;
    if (newPassword.Length > 0)
    {
      thisPart.Pwd = newPassword;
    }

    // Set the Web Part's Pwd property to empty string
    // Reset the CheckBox
    if (chk.Checked)
    {
      thisPart.Pwd = string.Empty;
      chk.Checked = false;
    }
  }

  return true;
}
```

```csharp
// Synchronize the Web Part property values with
// the control values in the Editor Part
public override void SyncChanges()
{
  // Nothing to sync
}

protected override void OnPreRender(EventArgs e)
{

  /// This Editor Parts Controls collection contains
  /// all the Editor Parts for this Web Part
  /// including the classic SharePoint WebPartToolPart
  /// from SharePoint 2003 that shows the standard
  /// Appearance, Layout, and Advanced panels
  /// plus the Custom Property Tool Part that shows
  /// all the public properties that are WebBrowsable
  /// and the collection of buttons: OK, Cancel, and Apply
  /// To work with these panels,
  /// iterate thru the siblings of this Editor Part
  /// and when the Panel to change is found,
  /// cast it to a specific type and manipulate
  foreach (Control part in base.Parent.Controls)
  {
    // Get the classic Web Part Tool Part
    if (part.GetType().Equals(typeof(WebPartToolPart)))
    {
      WebPartToolPart wptp = part as WebPartToolPart;

      // Hide the Layouts Category
      wptp.Hide(WebPartToolPart.Properties.ZoneID);
      wptp.Hide(WebPartToolPart.Properties.IsVisible);
      wptp.Hide(WebPartToolPart.Properties.Direction);
      wptp.Hide(WebPartToolPart.Properties.PartOrder);

      // Expand the Advanced category and
      // Hide the AllowClose option
      wptp.Expand(WebPartToolPart.Categories.Advanced);
      wptp.Hide(WebPartToolPart.Properties.AllowClose);
    }

    if (part.GetType().Equals(typeof(CustomPropertyToolPart)))
    {
      CustomPropertyToolPart cptp = part as CustomPropertyToolPart;

      cptp.Expand("Real World");
    }
  }
}
```

Code file [15.EditorPartImplementation.cs.txt] available for download at Wrox.com

9. In the `FirstPart` folder, double-click the `FirstPart.cs` class.

10. In the `FirstPart.cs` editor, overwrite the existing `WebPart` class definition by using the code shown in Listing 9-16.

LISTING 9-16: IWebEditable Interface

```
public class FirstPart :
   System.Web.UI.WebControls.WebParts.WebPart
   System.Web.UI.WebControls.WebParts.IWebEditable
```

Code file [16.IWebEditable.cs.txt] available for download at Wrox.com

11. Use the code in Listing 9-17 to implement the `IWebEditable` Interface inside the web part class just above the last two end braces.

LISTING 9-17: Web Part CreateEditorParts

```
EditorPartCollection IWebEditable.CreateEditorParts()
{
   // Create a generic collection of Editor Parts
   System.Collections.Generic.List<PasswordEditorPart> editorParts =
     new System.Collections.Generic.List<PasswordEditorPart>(1);

   // Add the custom Editor Part
   PasswordEditorPart part = new PasswordEditorPart();
   part.ID = this.ID + "_PasswordEditorPart";
   editorParts.Add(part);

   // Return the Editor Part
   return new EditorPartCollection(editorParts);
}

object IWebEditable.WebBrowsableObject
{
   get { return this; }
}
```

Code file [17.EditorPartImplentation.cs.txt] available for download at Wrox.com

12. Use the code shown in Listing 9-18 to replace the existing `CreateChildControls` method.

LISTING 9-18: Display Password Text

```
Label secret = default(Label);
protected override void CreateChildControls()
{
   // Strongly typed design surface (User Control)
   FirstPartUserControl control =
```

```
        Page.LoadControl(_ascxPath)
          as FirstPartUserControl;

    control.UcProperty = "Set By Web Part";

    Controls.Add(control);

    // Add label for Pwd text, if any
    Panel div = new Panel();
    secret = new Label();
    div.Controls.Add(secret);
    Controls.Add(div);
}

protected override void OnPreRender(EventArgs e)
{
  if (!string.IsNullOrEmpty(Pwd))
  {
    secret.Text = "Your password is: " + Pwd;
  }
  else
  {
    secret.Text = "Your password is blank";
  }
}
```

Code file [18.CreateChildControls.cs.txt] available for download at Wrox.com

Deploy Assets

Now you must deploy the project's assets to the SharePoint test site.

In the Solution Explorer, follow these steps:

1. Right-click {ProjectRoot}.

2. Choose the Deploy option (or press Alt+B, D).

3. Verify that the Deploy succeeded by pressing Ctrl+Shift+O.

Test Solution

And, finally, you must validate the web part changes.

In Internet Explorer, follow these steps:

1. Browse to http://Intranet/SitePages/TestPage.aspx.

2. Choose the Edit Web Part option from the web part's context menu.

3. Type **asdf** in the Password textbox shown in Figure 9-53.

FIGURE 9-53: Populate the Password Editor Part

4. Click Apply.

5. Note that the password text typed is displayed below the button, as shown in Figure 9-54.

6. Click the "Set a blank password" checkbox.

7. Click OK.

8. Note that "Your password is blank" is subsequently displayed below the button, as shown in Figure 9-55.

FIGURE 9-54: Password display

FIGURE 9-55: Blank password display

ADDING WEB PART VERBS

Web parts have a menu that is accessible by clicking the small downward facing arrow in the upper-right corner of the rendered web part. Clicking this arrow displays a menu such as the one shown for the Announcements Web Part in Figure 9-56.

FIGURE 9-56: Web part menu

By default, the menu includes options for minimizing, closing, deleting, and editing the web part (which opens the tool pane), and connecting to other web parts.

The ASP.NET web part calls these menu items *verbs*, which are the UI elements that enable users to perform actions on the associated web part.

Developers can modify the Verbs menu by overriding the Verbs property within the .NET WebPart class. Any kind of server-side (generates postback) or client-side (JavaScript) behavior can be accommodated using a web part verb.

The Verb property returns a WebPartVerbCollection object, which contains all verbs within the Verbs menu for the web part. To add a new verb to the Verbs menu, create a new object of type WebPartVerb, set its public properties, and add it to the WebPartVerbCollection. Custom verbs can either be added to the existing collection of verbs, or replace the existing verbs altogether.

Write Code

To write the code, follow these steps:

1. In Visual Studio, open the `Mindsharp.WebParts.RealWorld` project created earlier in this chapter.

2. In the Solution Explorer, expand the `FirstPart` folder.

3. Double-click the `FirstPart.cs` web part class.

4. In the `FirstPart.cs` editor, enter the code shown in Listing 9-19 inside the web part class just above the last two end braces.

LISTING 9-19: Verbs Property Override

```
public override WebPartVerbCollection Verbs
{
  get
  {
    // Client-side Verb Part that outputs the DateTime
    WebPartVerb clientSideVerb =
      new WebPartVerb("VerbsPart_ClientSideVerb",
        "javascript:alert(new Date());"
      );
    clientSideVerb.Text = "Client-side Item";
    clientSideVerb.Description = "Calls client-side script when clicked.";
    clientSideVerb.ImageUrl = "/_layouts/images/DAY.GIF";

    // Server-side Verb Part that changes the Web Part Title
    // to include the DateTime
    WebPartVerb serverSideVerb =
      new WebPartVerb("VerbsPart_ServerSideVerb",
        new WebPartEventHandler(ServerSideVerbHandler)
      );
    serverSideVerb.Text = "Server-side Item";
    serverSideVerb.ImageUrl = "/_layouts/images/DETAIL.GIF";

    // Create an array of the two new Web Part Verbs
    WebPartVerb[] newVerbs =
      new WebPartVerb[] { clientSideVerb, serverSideVerb };

    // Return a verb collection comprising of the existing Verbs
    // along with the two new Web Part Verbs
    return new WebPartVerbCollection(base.Verbs, newVerbs);
  }
}

// Function called from server-side Verb
protected void ServerSideVerbHandler(object sender, WebPartEventArgs args)
{
  this.Title = "FirstPart Server Time: " + DateTime.Now.ToString();
}
```

Code file [19.Verbs.cs.txt] available for download at Wrox.com

Deploy Assets

To deploy the project's assets to the SharePoint test site, follow these steps:

1. In the Solution Explorer, right-click {ProjectRoot}.

2. Choose the Deploy option (or press Alt+B, D).

3. Verify that the Deploy succeeded by pressing Ctrl+Shift+O.

Test Solution

To validate the web part verbs, follow these steps:

1. In Internet Explorer, browse to http://Intranet/SitePages/TestPage.aspx.

2. Click the web part context menu.

3. Choose the Edit Web Part option from the web part's context menu, as shown in Figure 9-57.

FIGURE 9-57: Edit Web Part option in context menu

SUMMARY

This chapter provided an introduction to web parts, starting with a retrospective recap of web part history. After exploring the goals of web parts and the new capabilities added in this release, a web part development approach was defined with "ten easy steps." Several basics about web parts have been covered, including a brief definition, the web part benchmarks, the Web Part Framework, ribbon, state management, and use of resources.

This chapter included a few simple coding exercises that provided step-by-step instructions for creating a Visual web part, enhancing the coordination of the Visual web part and its user control design surface, and adding a custom Editor Part and custom verbs.

ABOUT THE AUTHOR

Todd Bleeker, Ph.D. and SharePoint MVP, is an industry leader in Microsoft-centric software development, specializing in SharePoint Products and Technologies. Bleeker is an innovative, resourceful, and competitive technologist with an intense desire to excel. He joined Mindsharp in 2004 as co-owner and Chief Software Architect (CSA) to help establish the strategic technical plan for Mindsharp's educational and consulting assets. In addition to writing and teaching cutting-edge SharePoint training courses for Mindsharp, Bleeker also architects innovative applications that help Mindsharp's clients improve their content management capabilities. He has been recognized by Microsoft for his contributions to the SharePoint Platform and the SharePoint community. As such, he is a frequent speaker at key conferences such as Microsoft TechEd and the Microsoft SharePoint Conference. Bleeker also holds a BS degree in Management Information Systems, as well as an MBA and Ph.D. in Business. In his spare time, he loves to soak up whatever technology Microsoft is churning out. He also enjoys spending countless hours in Minnesota with his wife, Kathryn, and his six "high energy" children (Landis, Lake, Lissa, Logan, Lawson, and Lexa).

10

Automating Business Processes

By Asif Rehmani

When the word "automation" comes to mind in terms of software, the first thing many people think of is the need to know coding or programming. Although writing structured code is probably the best way to achieve automation for large systems with complex requirements, that's not always the only need for automation of processes in the marketplace. More often than not, it's usually a knowledge worker sitting in an office somewhere just trying to automate a process that's currently manual in nature. That person might first try to get the folks in the IT department to tackle this project for him or her.

However, in today's world, the IT departments of most companies are already pretty busy with the projects that relate to the core business of the company, or projects that have high visibility with the executive team. The knowledge worker's projects usually get pushed down as the eleventh project on the list of top ten projects.

SharePoint to the rescue! The SharePoint platform is the perfect fit for those "eleventh projects," because it enables knowledge workers to create powerful solutions with the use of out-of-the-box technologies without the need to write any code! Because SharePoint already contains the building blocks capable of building solutions on top of this platform, the knowledge worker just needs the proper tools to help create those solutions.

This chapter examines these tools, and discusses who should use them, as well as the proper way to utilize them to their fullest potential.

This chapter focuses on the following concepts:

- ➤ Understanding the benefits of using InfoPath and SharePoint Designer
- ➤ Using InfoPath to create powerful electronic forms
- ➤ Utilizing Visio to model workflows
- ➤ Creating solutions using Visio, SharePoint Designer, and InfoPath

USING INFOPATH AND SHAREPOINT DESIGNER INDIVIDUALLY

InfoPath and SharePoint Designer both work great individually to enable power users to build powerful solutions. In the following sections, each of these products is analyzed first in its own right. Later in this chapter, the discussion continues by providing a complete picture of how they can both be used together to provide an end-to-end solution.

Building Powerful Forms Using InfoPath

Microsoft Office InfoPath first became part of the Office suite of products back in 2003. It was ahead of its time then, because this was the only product within the Office suite that utilized the inherent power of XML in its inner workings. An InfoPath form is based completely on an XML schema, and offers structural editing of the XML data. It is the most appropriate platform for gathering data in the Microsoft Office suite of applications, and the user interface provided is very much like Microsoft Word, so the ramp-up time for a new form designer is minimized. You can build dynamic data-driven forms without having a programming background.

Microsoft InfoPath 2010 is the latest revision of the product. The Fluent interface (ribbon) has been introduced in the product, which now provides it a consistent look and feel with the other Office products. There are two InfoPath programs:

➤ *Microsoft InfoPath Designer 2010* — Designer is used by the form designers to design the form.

➤ *Microsoft InfoPath Filler 2010* — The Filler is used by end users to fill out a form and save it.

Both of these products come bundled together when an InfoPath 2010 license is bought by a company. In addition to filling out the form in the Filler, you can also allow end users to fill out forms using the browser, provided that you have the enterprise license of SharePoint Server that comes along with the needed component, Forms Server, to serve up the forms. InfoPath 2010 web browser forms are compliant with Web Content Accessibility Guidelines 2.0 (WCAG 2.0) and are fully XHTML 1.0 compliant.

 You can find more information on the enterprise licensing of SharePoint Server at http://sharepoint2010.microsoft.com.

A form designer uses InfoPath to create form templates for end users to fill out. After opening the InfoPath Designer application, the first decision that a form designer must make is to choose the type of form template. The Backstage screen of Designer helps with this process. As shown in Figure 10-1, Designer has lots of form template choices.

InfoPath Designer can be utilized to edit SharePoint List or Library forms. An example of this functionality is demonstrated later in this chapter. InfoPath can be utilized completely independent of SharePoint by creating template forms that can be used on their own. Form templates can be placed on a network share or on an intranet, from where users can obtain and fill out the forms. In addition, forms can be sent directly to people's inboxes, where they can fill out the form within the Microsoft Outlook 2010 environment and submit it back to the person who sent them the form.

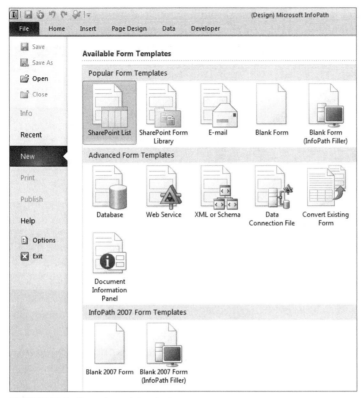

FIGURE 10-1: Form template choices

The Designer environment provides a quick-and-easy interface to get started building your forms. Assuming you begin with the Blank Form template that starts you out by providing just an empty table, you can quickly decide on a page layout for your form by selecting the Page Design tab, and picking a Page Layout template. Then pick a *theme* for your form by selecting from the provided theme choices. Figure 10-2 shows the Page Layout templates and a brief view of the available themes.

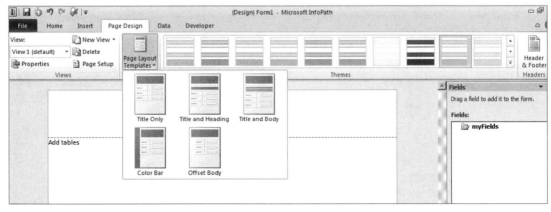

FIGURE 10-2: Page Layout templates

Form templates generally consist of labels and controls through which you want to accept user input. These elements are best arranged in a table. By clicking the Insert tab, you see a number of choices for table styles, as shown in Figure 10-3. Pick the style(s) that best suit your need.

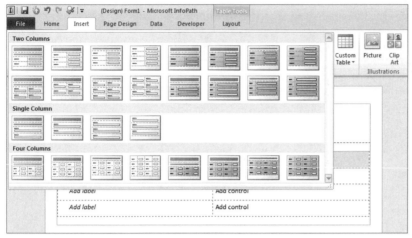

FIGURE 10-3: Table style choices

The next step in creating the form is to populate it with descriptive text and controls needed for the form. You insert the text/label simply by typing it directly onto the appropriate place in the form. The controls for the form are available through the Home tab.

This is where the true design power of InfoPath forms is realized, because you, as the designer, can use a variety of controls. As shown in Figure 10-4, controls such as TextBox, Drop-Down List, Date Picker, Button, Repeating Table, and more are all available here, ready to be placed on the form. Just place your cursor at the place you want the control to appear and click the control to insert it in the form template.

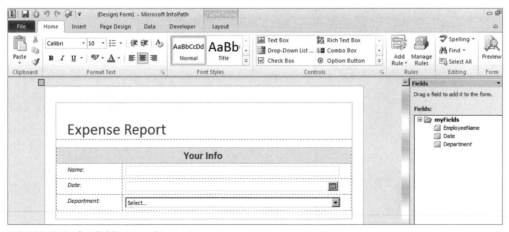

FIGURE 10-4: Available controls

The form template is aware of the controls placed on it, as well as their associated properties. Controls can be accessed by their names and used as needed by the form designer. So, a best practice to follow is to immediately name all of the controls on the form. You can access the control's name and other properties by first clicking the control, and then using the Control Tools tab that appears on the ribbon. The Fields task pane on the right side of the screen reflects that change.

Once a form template design meets your required specifications for what the form is intended to accomplish, the next step is to manage the dynamic aspects of the form by using proper validation and formatting rules. This aspect of the form is discussed next.

Enhancing Forms with Validation and Conditional Formatting

The InfoPath Designer environment allows you to use a rules engine with which you can decide how your form and the controls on the form should behave in response to the data that the end user provides. Following are the three types of rules that can be created using the rules management interface:

➤ *Validation* — Validating the entered data in controls

➤ *Formatting* — Changing the formatting of a control based on defined condition criteria

➤ *Action* — Performing an action (such as setting a field's value, submitting data, and so on) based on defined condition criteria

You can quickly get started incorporating rules in your form by using Quick Rules. A set of pre-built rules can help validate your data and make forms more dynamic. Simply click the control upon which you want to set a rule, click the Add Rule button on the ribbon, and then select the condition and subsequent action from the list of options that appear. Figure 10-5 shows how these rules are displayed.

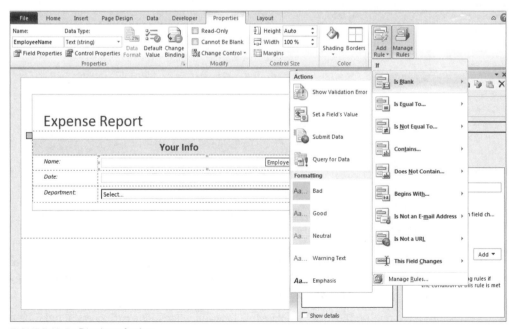

FIGURE 10-5: Display of rules

Think of Quick Rules as a wizard to get you started. Or, you can start from scratch by clicking the Manage Rules button on the ribbon, which displays the Rules task pane (on the right) to manage rules. The same task pane also appears after you have picked a Quick Rule, and lets you manage the properties of that rule further (such as changing its name). You can configure as many rules as needed for the control. The control's rules are displayed on this task pane when the control is placed in context by clicking it.

You create a new rule by clicking the New button in the Rules task pane and selecting the appropriate type of rule. A rule is set up much like a mini-workflow in which you define a condition and then a subsequent action for when the condition becomes true.

For example, you might designate a field as required to contain content so that, if the field is blank and the user tries to submit the form, a validation error is shown. An example of a formatting rule would be checking a field's value with the value of another field and, if they are not the same, changing the background color of one or both fields to red to signify the problem. Figure 10-6 shows a couple of configured rules for a control.

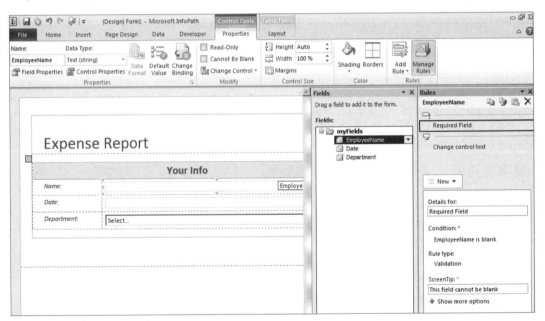

FIGURE 10-6: Configured rules

In a typical form created for business use, numerous rules might need to be created for the controls. A very useful functionality is the capability to copy and paste rules from one control to another. To copy single or multiple rules, simply select them and click the copy icon that appears within the Rules task pane. Then, select the control to which you want to paste the rule(s) and click the paste icon in the Rules task pane. All of your rules, along with their defined logic, are copied to the new control, which saves you tons of time and effort.

The end goal is for you to publish the form template to a location where users can access it and fill it out with their data. The topic of publishing is examined in more detail shortly. However, before publishing your form, it is always a good idea to use the Preview button on the Home tab of the ribbon to preview your form and run through its logic. Figure 10-7 shows how the preview screen looks.

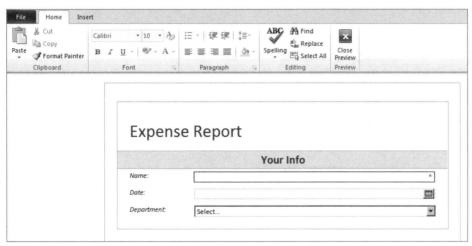

FIGURE 10-7: Preview screen

Publishing Forms to a Variety of Locations

An InfoPath form template is saved as an `.xsn` file. When the form is published, this file becomes accessible to the end users, and works very much like a Microsoft Word document template (`.dotx` file). The user opens the file and fills out the required information on the form. When the user decides to save or submit the form, it gets saved as an `.xml` file containing all of the user-provided data, and a pointer to the original `.xsn` file used to create this instance.

Publishing and sharing the form through SharePoint is the recommended option, because the SharePoint framework provides a multitude of built-in options to support the form processes. If your SharePoint instance is running with enterprise client access licenses, the only thing that the users need is the browser to fill out the forms. If SharePoint Server standard licensing or just SharePoint Foundation is deployed, the end user would need the InfoPath Filler application to fill out the forms.

When the form is published to the form library in SharePoint, it can utilize all of the base features available within every library, such as versioning, check in/check out, the capability to attach workflows to the library, and more. The form library provides a superset of features available in a document library.

In addition to all of the base features of a typical library, a form library is recognized inherently by InfoPath, which can publish forms directly to it. This process is demonstrated with an example later in this chapter. An added benefit of hosting the forms in a form library is that it contains a special built-in view called Merge View that lets you merge the information of multiple instances of the filled-out forms hosted in the library.

Figure 10-8 shows the publishing options that are available through the Publish option on the File tab in the ribbon.

FIGURE 10-8: Publishing options

In addition to the SharePoint Server, the InfoPath form template can also be published directly via e-mail to users' inboxes, or placed on a network location that's accessible to the intended audience. Both of these options require that users filling out the forms have the InfoPath Filler application available to them on their computers.

The process to publish the form to a network share is the simplest one available within the Designer environment. It entails just pointing to the location where the .xsn file needs to be saved. After the file is published to that location, you can notify your users (via e-mail or otherwise) to fill out the forms using this template. Figure 10-9 shows the wizard screen that is used to define the location and name of the form.

In a scenario where, for example, you want to quickly collect some information from your users, you can send them an e-mail with the form prominently displayed in the body of the e-mail. As long as the users have InfoPath on their computers, they will see the form ready to be filled out. The Email button in the Publish screen starts up the e-mail client and guides the form designer through the process of sending the form. When the end users receive the e-mail, all they will need to do is to fill out the form directly in the e-mail client application and submit it.

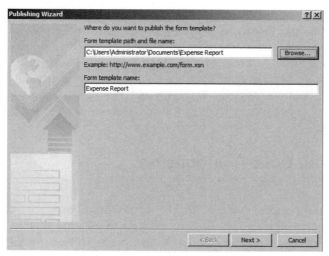

FIGURE 10-9: Publishing Wizard

The submission process of InfoPath must be configured beforehand by the form designer for this process to work. It can be configured to automatically submit the form to a variety of places, including sending the form back through e-mail, sending it to a library, or sending it to a predefined connection in SharePoint, and submitting it to a web service. The submission options are available through the Info selection under the File tab, as shown in Figure 10-10.

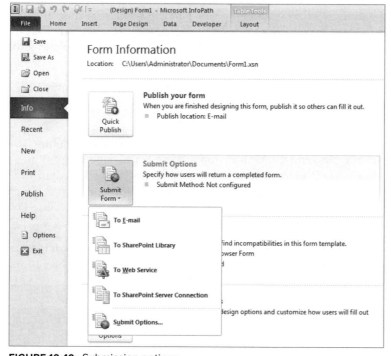

FIGURE 10-10: Submission options

The information provided thus far should give you enough guidance to get started with Microsoft InfoPath 2010. However, by no means has this discussion presented an exhaustive list of features available within InfoPath 2010. It is definitely advisable to learn more about this product by picking up a good book that's dedicated to this subject. Look for a good InfoPath 2007 book such as *Designing Forms for Microsoft Office InfoPath and Forms Services 2007* by Scott Roberts and Hagen Green (Upper Saddle River, N.J.: Addison-Wesley, 2007). This will provide you with a good basis for the internals of this product, and open your mind to the possibilities of what is achievable with this platform.

Using SharePoint Designer to Build Solutions on Top of SharePoint

SharePoint 2010 is an extremely powerful platform that contains the components to build robust solutions on top of it. If you are a programmer, there is no limit to the types of solutions you can create with the available objects in SharePoint using a tool such as Visual Studio. However, what if you are not a code jockey? What are your options then?

Well, you can always use the browser to build your solutions. It is fairly easy for a site administrator of a SharePoint site to organize information in lists and libraries, and then present that information on SharePoint pages in a variety of ways using just the browser. This option works fine until you realize that inherent limitations exist to using the browser.

First of all, because the browser is a thin client, it is always a bit slower than using a fat client application. To go from one administration screen to the next, your web page requests require a request to the server, which might take a few seconds, depending on your web server. Another thing is the inability to really take charge of creating the layout of the Web parts and Web part zones on your page. The only thing you can do there is to choose from the provided Web part page templates to build your page. Furthermore, you can use limited numbers of pre-built workflow templates through the browser.

The list of limitations goes on and on. These limitations can really keep your investment in SharePoint from truly realizing its full potential. That's where Microsoft SharePoint Designer 2010 comes into the picture.

Microsoft SharePoint Designer 2010 (SPD) is a product for knowledge workers, site administrators, and power users who want to build powerful solutions on top of SharePoint, but don't want to use code to make it happen. Until early 2009, there used to be a price tag associated with acquiring this product. However, on April 2, 2009, Microsoft decided to make this a free product so that the price point for it does not limit organizations from realizing the return on their investment in SharePoint. It can be downloaded directly from Microsoft's website (`www.microsoft.com/spd`).

SPD's charter is to let you take advantage of SharePoint's already available underlying components, and put them together to create real business solutions. It makes it easier and more efficient to work with them using this environment. One thing to keep in mind, however, is that this product is not backward-compatible, and can only be used to work on SharePoint 2010 sites.

The next couple of sections show you the potential for this product.

Manipulating SharePoint Sites and Its Components

SharePoint 2010 sites are primarily a collection of pages, lists, and libraries. All of these components (and more) are easily and efficiently provisioned and customized using SharePoint Designer 2010. SPD's work begins under a site collection. A site collection itself cannot be created through SPD. When you open up SPD, the first thing you do is to point it to a SharePoint site that it can open. Once the site is opened up in SPD, the interface is displayed in three distinct areas, as shown in Figure 10-11:

➤ *Navigation pane* — You can use the Navigation pane to explore the various components of the site.

➤ *Ribbon* — The ribbon provides the Fluent interface that is now present in all Microsoft Office applications, as well as SharePoint itself. It is context-sensitive, which means that it displays the actions you can take, depending on which component of the site is in context.

➤ *Summary page* — The main body of the screen shows the properties of the object that is currently in context. For example, in Figure 10-11, you can see the summary page of the SharePoint eLearning site, which shows information about the site, in addition to the site's permission, any subsites underneath it, and more.

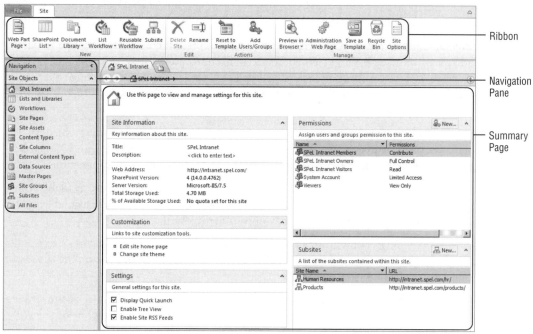

FIGURE 10-11: SPD interface

To really understand what SPD has to offer, you should explore the components on the Navigation pane. Following is a list of all of the items you see on the Navigation pane and a brief explanation for each:

➤ *<Site Name> (SharePoint eLearning in Figure 10-11)* — The summary page of the site has the information about the site at a high level. Site permissions, site navigation settings, and any subsites underneath this site are all displayed here.

➤ *Lists and Libraries* — This section shows all of the lists and libraries that currently exist on the site. This is a security-trimmed view and will not show items for which the user does not have permissions.

➤ *Workflows* — Three types of workflows can be created in SPD using this area: List, Reusable, and Site. In addition, the built-in workflows (Approval, Collect Feedback, and Collect Signatures) can be copied and modified. All of the workflows that currently exist on the site are listed in this view.

➤ *Site Pages* — This shows the wiki page library called Site Pages that gets created automatically for every new site. The home page of the site is stored here. All pages contained in this library are *wiki pages*. Each wiki page can be organically linked to other pages within the same library.

➤ *Content Types* — The content types for this site and from the parent site are all visible here.

➤ *Site Columns* — All site-based columns for this site and the parent site are visible in this view.

➤ *External Content Types* — External content types represent connections to data in back-end Line of Business (LOB) systems. These connections are created using the Business Connectivity Services (BCS), which is installed as a service application among other services in the web farm. This view shows all of the connections, not just on this site, but for the whole site collection.

➤ *Data Sources* — SharePoint sites can create connections directly to a variety of external data sources, such as databases, web services (both SOAP and REST services), and XML files. The Data Sources section in the Navigation pane shows all of the existing connections.

➤ *Master Pages* — The Master Pages section shows the master pages that are available to be used for the site. `Default.master`, `minimal.master`, and `v4.master` are available by default in a team site. If others are created, they appear here as well.

➤ *Site Groups* — SharePoint groups are used as a container for Active Directory users and groups. All the SharePoint groups, whether or not they have permissions on the site, available in the entire site collection appear here.

➤ *Subsites* — This section shows the subsites directly below this site. This list of sites is security-trimmed. If the logged-in user does not have access to a particular subsite, he or she will not see that subsite in this list.

➤ *All Files* — This view shows the URL structure of the website. The subsites, lists, libraries, hidden folders, and more all appear within this folder tree view.

Each of these Navigation areas serves the purpose of letting SPD users create new components, manipulate existing ones, and create their solutions as needed. The detailed explanation of all of these areas is not the topic of this chapter. However, you should explore them further to understand how best to take advantage of each of the areas.

In the next section, one of these areas, Data Sources, is discussed further to explain how you can surface data from external systems within a SharePoint site.

Connecting to External Data Sources

One of the most powerful aspects of SPD is the capability to reach out and fetch data from a variety of data repositories. As you have just learned, the Data Sources component on the Navigation pane helps you accomplish this. Figure 10-12 shows all of the available data connection options. Let's take a look at each connection option.

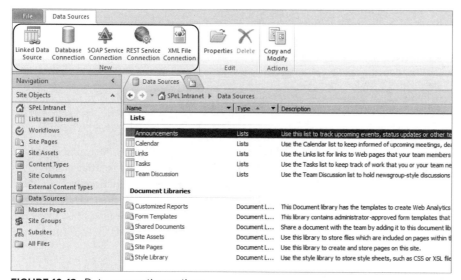

FIGURE 10-12: Data connection options

The XML file connection allows you to use an XML file as the data repository. This file could have any type of structured information. For example, as shown in Figure 10-13, you could have a file that contains the products your company carries, and various attributes of each product, such as the supplier, unit price, units in stock, and more.

When you click the XML File Connection button, you are asked about the location of the XML file that contains your data. The XML file should be hosted within the SharePoint site — preferably the Site Assets library. If it is not already within SharePoint, you can easily drag and drop the file from your computer to within the Site Assets library, and then point to it. The benefits of using an XML file as a data repository are that the data is easy to manage, and it provides a structured way to describe your data.

```
<?xml version="1.0" encoding="utf-8"?>
<ProductsRoot>
    <Products>
        <ProductID>1</ProductID>
        <ProductName>Chai</ProductName>
        <SupplierID>1</SupplierID>
        <CategoryID>1</CategoryID>
        <QuantityPerUnit>10 boxes x 20 bags</Quantit
        <UnitPrice>18</UnitPrice>
        <UnitsInStock>39</UnitsInStock>
        <UnitsOnOrder>0</UnitsOnOrder>
        <ReorderLevel>10</ReorderLevel>
        <Discontinued>0</Discontinued>
    </Products>
    <Products>
        <ProductID>2</ProductID>
        <ProductName>Chang</ProductName>
        <SupplierID>1</SupplierID>
        <CategoryID>1</CategoryID>
        <QuantityPerUnit>24 - 12 oz bottles</Quantit
        <UnitPrice>19</UnitPrice>
        <UnitsInStock>17</UnitsInStock>
        <UnitsOnOrder>40</UnitsOnOrder>
        <ReorderLevel>25</ReorderLevel>
        <Discontinued>0</Discontinued>
    </Products>
```

FIGURE 10-13: Example of information in XML file

Another option on the ribbon is to connect to a database directly by clicking the Database Connection button. This is a very powerful option, because you are provided the capability to point to any database server directly to get to its data. Within the configuration screen of this functionality, the .NET framework data providers for SQL Server and OLE DB are readily available in the Provider Name drop-down list. If that's not enough, you can check the checkbox for "Use custom connection string" and provide your own connection string to use additional data providers such as ODBC and Oracle, as shown in Figure 10-14.

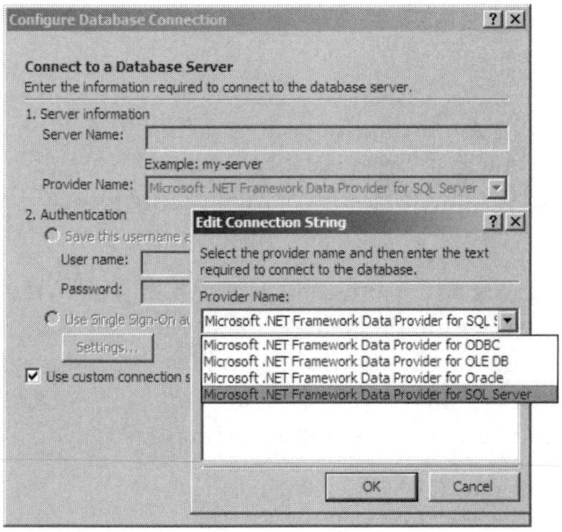

FIGURE 10-14: Configure Database Connections dialog

Also provided in this interface is a way to connect to services available on the Web. The two types of web services often used on the Web, SOAP and REST, are both supported with this platform.

SOAP is the older one of the two protocols, and is utilized by many websites such as Google and Amazon. In fact, SharePoint itself also provides 42 SOAP web services right out of the box that can be utilized by the SOAP service connection. REST web services are available on the Web through sites such as Yahoo, Flickr, eBay, and more. So, using these two web service connection options, you can get to data from any of these services, and display it directly on your SharePoint pages.

The information provided here about SPD is just the tip of the iceberg. A thorough discussion of this immense product is not the focus of this chapter. However, it is definitely recommended that you pick up a book such as *Beginning SharePoint Designer 2010* by Woodrow Windischman, Bryan Phillips, Asif Rehmani, and Marcy Kellar (Indianapolis: Wrox, 2010) to get a good understanding of how to take full advantage of this product.

COMBINING INFOPATH AND SHAREPOINT DESIGNER

Individually, both SPD and InfoPath are great products — think of them like peanut butter and chocolate. They are great flavors by themselves. However, when you put them both together, you get an even better combination.

The common denominator between InfoPath and SPD is their interaction with the SharePoint platform. InfoPath is great for creating forms that can be hosted in a form library in SharePoint. SPD, on the other hand, can be used to create workflows (among other things), and attach them to libraries — including form libraries. The rest of this chapter presents a sample solution that demonstrates this great combination.

The scenario that is used to present this solution consists of creating a form that employees fill out to request training. If the employee has already taken 100 credit hours of training or more, that employee is not eligible for attending any more training. If the current credit hour count is less than 100, the employee is eligible, and an approval from his or her manager is needed.

The scenario itself is fairly simplistic, because anything more complex would make this a far longer chapter than it already is. However, the design of the solution itself presents many learning opportunities. The scenario consists of the following steps:

1. A training request form is designed and published to a new forms library called Training Requests.

2. Visio is used to model a workflow for routing the training request form, and the workflow is exported.

3. The exported workflow file is imported into SPD and attached to the Training Requests library.

4. Workflow rules are configured within SPD and published.

Creating InfoPath Forms for the Browser

The InfoPath concepts discussed at the beginning of this chapter (in addition to a few other features) are utilized to create a brand new form for accepting training requests. To start, the SharePoint Form Library template is selected to create the skeleton of the form. This template comes with a built-in page layout with some tables in which to place your heading, labels, and controls. First, the picture of the company logo is inserted at the top and the form is given a heading, "Training Request Form." Then the labels and controls are placed on the form. The following list details which controls are being used.

➤ *Name (Textbox)* — Phone (textbox)

➤ *Date and Time (Date and Time Picker)* — Email (textbox)

➤ *Department (Drop-down List)* — Training Requested (combo box)

Once the proper layout is created, each control is given an appropriate name through the Control Tools tab. One main thing to keep in mind while naming the control is that no spaces are allowed in the name. When naming a control with two words, always use Pascal notation. Pascal notation dictates that all words are joined together without spaces, and the first letter of each word is capitalized. For example, the combo box for Training Requested is named TrainingRequested. The benefit of using this notation is that SharePoint recognizes it, and it separates the two words automatically with a space in between when you later publish this form to the form library in SharePoint.

Next, the table column widths are adjusted and the extra rows are deleted. Figure 10-15 shows the completed layout of the form.

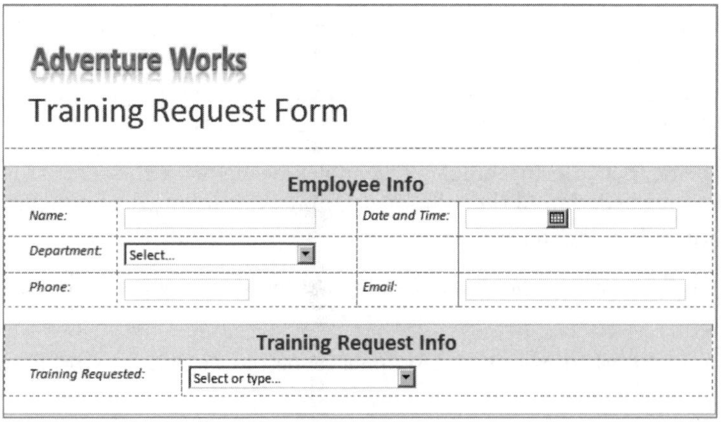

FIGURE 10-15: Form layout

The next step is to create the logic of the form. Appropriate rules are configured for each control. The Name field of the form needs to be a required field. You have a couple of ways to accomplish this. The first is to check the checkbox for Cannot Be Blank in the Control Tools tab. Another way is to create a Quick Rule for it. This example uses the Quick Rule functionality by first clicking the Name textbox to place it in focus and then, from the ribbon, clicking Add Rule ➪ Is Blank ➪ Show Validation Error, as shown in Figure 10-16.

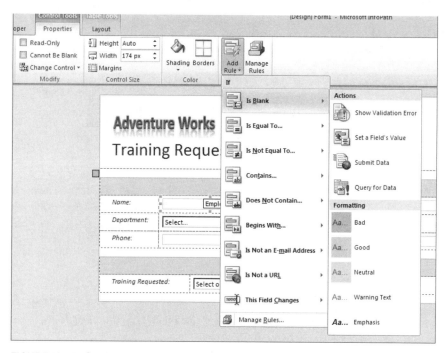

FIGURE 10-16: Configuring a rule

The Quick Rule is created and the task pane is presented showing the rule. The visibility of this Rules task pane can be toggled with the Manage Rules button on the ribbon. The Rules task pane can now be used to change the name of the rule, enhance the rule's condition statement and subsequent action, change the screentip shown, and the error dialog box message. Using this task pane, multiple rules can be created for the control in the current context.

Many different types of conditional operations can be created within a rule. For example, a validation rule can be created on the Phone field to check for a valid phone number using pattern matching. The pattern for phone number is already built into InfoPath. Figure 10-17 shows the available data entry patterns you can use. Additionally, you can create your own custom pattern using regular expressions.

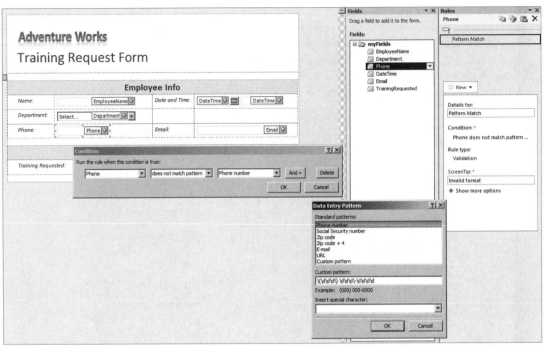

FIGURE 10-17: Data entry patterns

 For more information on regular expressions, check out the Wikipedia page at
http://en.wikipedia.org/wiki/Regular_expression.

In a complex form, you will undoubtedly run into the need for creating similar rules for many different controls on the form. For that need, there is a copy rules feature available within InfoPath that makes the process of rule creation a lot faster. You can copy a single rule or all of the rules on a control, and then simply paste those rules on another control. The copy and paste icons exist at the top right of the Rules task pane. Figure 10-18 shows the phone validation rule being pasted into the Email field.

Of course, the phone validation rule is looking for a valid phone number pattern, so that needs to be changed to look for a valid e-mail address instead — a very easy change to configure in the Rules task pane by reconfiguring the condition of the rule and picking the available E-mail data entry pattern.

The next thing this form needs is for the DateTime field to automatically be populated with the current date and time as the default value. InfoPath ships with a large library of built-in functions that can be used for this functionality. The Default Value button is accessible through the ribbon to bring up the property page for the control. Once at the property page, the *fx* button takes you to the dialog box where you can build the formula for the default value of the control. Figure 10-19 shows the now() function being selected, which returns the current system date and time to be populated within the DateTime control.

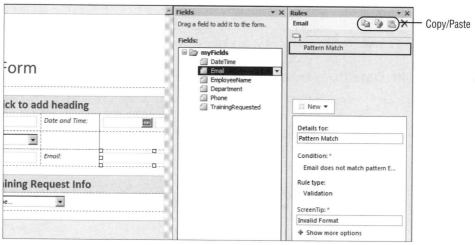

FIGURE 10-18: Icons for copy and paste

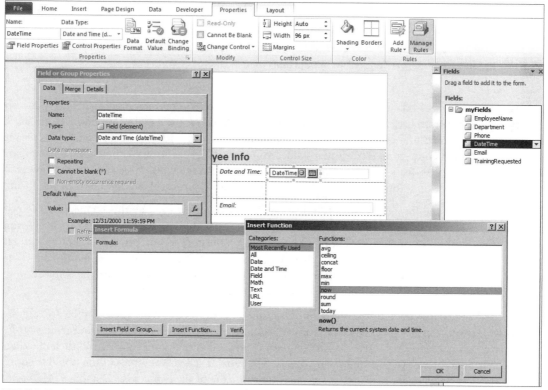

FIGURE 10-19: Populating current system date and time

The InfoPath Designer environment provides a facility to preview your form at any time during the design process. The preview functionality is accessible through the Home tab, and can be used to verify that all of the logic implemented earlier is in working order.

Populating Forms with Data from External Sources

By default, an InfoPath form lets you work with the underlying XML schema that represents the form and is referred to as the Main data connection for the form. Secondary data connections to various data repositories can also be created. Then the data retrieved from these sources can be interspersed with the data on the form. As shown in Figure 10-20, you can find on the ribbon all of the options to get external data from the Data tab.

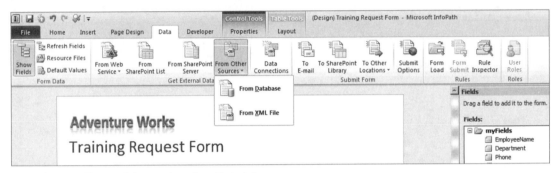

FIGURE 10-20: External data options from Data tab

For this scenario, the Training Request Form must get the `Training Requested` field options populated from a custom list called Trainings Offered in a SharePoint site called Human Resources. The connection to the site is created using the From SharePoint List button on the ribbon. This presents you with a data connection wizard that guides you through connecting to appropriate SharePoint site, and then to the list you want to get the data from. Once the wizard is completed, a new secondary data connection to the list (named Trainings Offered, in this case) becomes part of the form.

Any control on the form can now take advantage of the data retrieved by this connection. To populate the `Training Requested` combo box with the training choices, you can configure it by using the Edit Choices button on the ribbon, which brings up the combo box properties dialog box. Here, you can point to an already configured external data source (`Trainings Offered`, in this case). Then the `Entries` field on the dialog is configured to point to the proper element within the connection that contains the names of the training classes. Figure 10-21 shows the configuration.

Much like the connection to the SharePoint list, a connection to SQL database can be created just as easily. Instead of starting at the Data tab, you can also start the connection creation from within the control's properties page by selecting to get data from an external data source, and then clicking the Add button to bring up the connection wizard. The wizard screen shows all of the possible sources of data — same as the ones available on the Data tab. One of the choices is "Database (Microsoft SQL Server only)." This option is the one you use to connect directly to SQL.

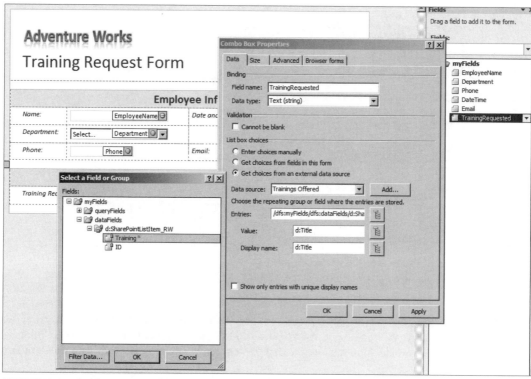

FIGURE 10-21: Configuring the combob box connection

 Keep in mind that just because there is no explicit option for getting data from non-Microsoft databases (such as Sybase or Oracle), that doesn't mean that you can't get to it. In such a case, you would use the web service option to connect to web services provided by those databases to get to their data.

Once you select the SQL database option, the Data Connection Wizard guides you through creating a new connection, or using an existing one you created earlier, to point to a database server and then the appropriate database. In this scenario, the sample AdventureWorks database is used, which contains the Department table that has the department values needed for this form's Department field (Figure 10-22). The Name field in the table contains the names of each department at AdventureWorks.

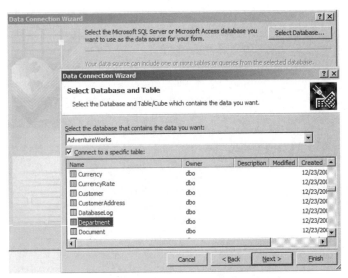

FIGURE 10-22: Selecting a database through the wizard

At this point, if you preview the form, you should see both of the connections in action. As shown in Figure 10-23, the `Training Requested` field should be retrieving data from the SharePoint list, while the `Department` field should show the department names being retrieved from the database.

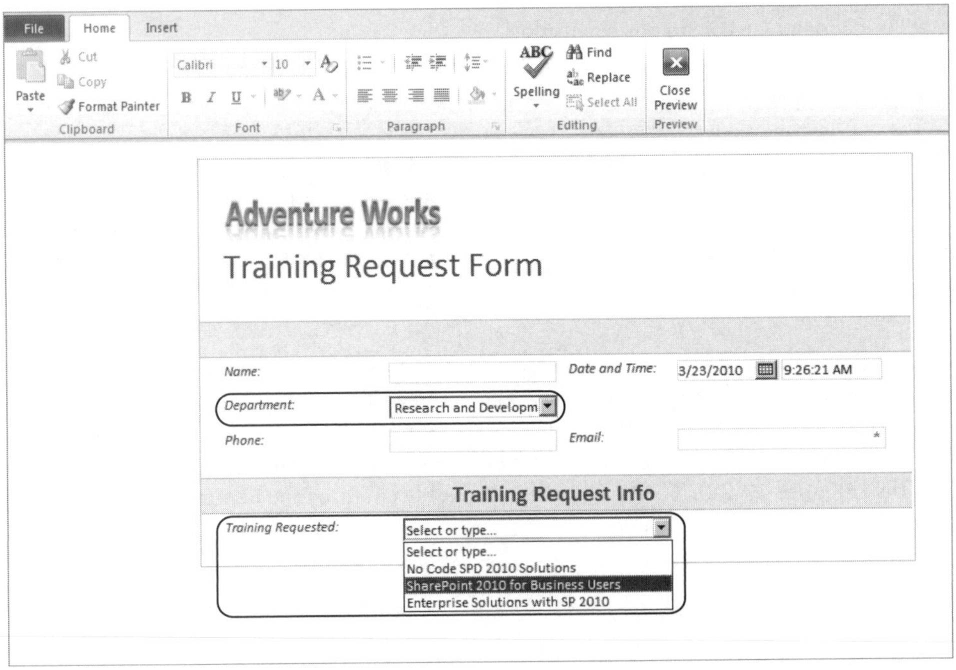

FIGURE 10-23: Both connections working

This scenario doesn't call for creating any more data connections. However, this form can be further enhanced as needed by the form designer. For example, one of the web services available within SharePoint called User Profile (`userprofileservice.asmx`) can be used to retrieve the current logged-in user's profile information. This information can then be used to fill in the user's name in the `Name` textbox field. Many additional steps are required to configure this functionality, but it can all be done without a single line of code!

Publishing Forms to SharePoint Server

InfoPath forms should ultimately be published to a location where the intended users can easily get to them. Earlier in this chapter, you learned about the various publishing locations. In this section, the form is going to be published to SharePoint Server, which is the recommended location.

You execute the publishing process to SharePoint by clicking the SharePoint Server button under the Publish section of the File menu. Much like most of the other processes within InfoPath, the publishing process is also wizard-driven and guides you along the way.

The first step in the wizard is to provide the URL where the form is intended to be published. The second step presents you with the choices on how to publish the form. Figure 10-24 shows all of the options.

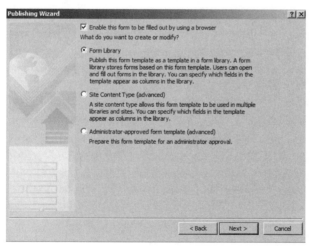

FIGURE 10-24: Publishing options

The wizard provides a brief explanation of each of these options right below its name. Following is the reasoning behind when each of these options should be used:

➤ *Form Library* — Use this option when publishing a form that is going to be unique to a library. You can still publish the form to a different library later, but then, when you need to make a change, you must change each form separately.

➤ *Site Content Type (advanced)* — InfoPath forms can be packaged up in a content type using this option. Subsequently, this content type can then be used in multiple libraries. When the form needs updating, only the content type must be updated and the change is propagated to all libraries using the content type.

➤ *Administrator-approved form template (advanced)* — Forms that are either mobile-enabled and/or have code behind them are required to be approved by the SharePoint administrator through Central Administration. Of course, you can also use this option when that's not the case, and you still want the server administrator to approve all templates that are being produced by form designers.

The scenario for this chapter just calls for publishing to a single library, so the Form Library option is used. After picking this option, the next couple of screens in the wizard provide you the option of either creating a new form library with this form template, or updating an existing library. In this instance, a new form library called Training Requests is created.

The last step before completing the Publishing Wizard is referred to as *property promotion*. It allows the form fields to be made available as columns in SharePoint sites and Outlook folders, or even as passable parameters within the InfoPath form Web part (which is a new Web part introduced with SharePoint Server 2010 that can display InfoPath forms). Figure 10-25 shows this step with some of the properties already filled in.

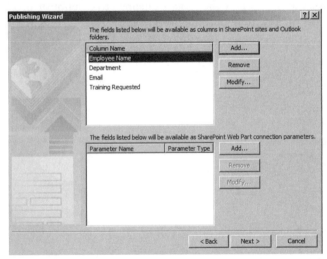

FIGURE 10-25: Property promotion

The benefits of promoting fields as columns include being able to then use the contents of those columns to sort, filter, or create views in the library based on the surfaced information. In addition, the information in these columns is then available to any workflows attached to the library. This, in fact, is exactly what is demonstrated in the later sections of this chapter when the workflow is created and attached to this library.

The next step in the wizard is to just click the Publish button to complete the publishing process. The new form library called Training Requests is created, and the InfoPath form template becomes the default template for that library.

InfoPath forms can be filled in by the end users through the browser or the InfoPath Filler application. As mentioned earlier in this chapter, the enterprise license of SharePoint Server is required for filling out forms in the browser. If the enterprise license is configured, a component called Forms Server is automatically the default mechanism used by SharePoint to serve up the forms in the browser. This is the preferred behavior. However, this default mechanism can be altered through the *advanced settings* of the form library if needed.

Because the form is making a call to a database server, if you want to use the browser functionality and have Forms Server present the forms to the user, a few additional steps are required for this functionality to work. Currently, the data connection file that is being used to create the connection is stored locally at the workstation where the form is designed. This connection file (Department, in this case) must first be exported to be shared through a data connection library in SharePoint.

So, the first step is to create that data connection library anywhere within the same site collection where the form is published. Then, back in the InfoPath Designer environment, bring up the Data Connections dialog box (Data tab ➭ Data Connections).

The process to export the connection is a very simple one. All you have to do is to click the data connection that needs to be exported, click the "Convert to Connection File..." button, and then provide the location of the data connection file in the data connection library. Figure 10-26 shows this process.

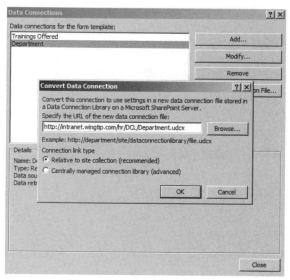

FIGURE 10-26: Exporting the data connection

The connection file should now be available in the data connection library. The initial status of the file is set to Pending. You can click the file and then use the Approve/Reject option available on the ribbon to approve the file. To allow Forms Server to use this connection in the data connection library, the Forms Server settings must be configured by the server administrator through Central Administration. The InfoPath Forms Server configuration is accessible through the General Application Settings section in Central Administration. Once at the configuration page, enable the cross-domain access for user form templates, as shown in Figure 10-27.

Cross-Domain Access for User Form Templates

Form templates can contain data connections that access data from other domains. Select this check box to allow user form templates to access data from another domain.

☑ Allow cross-domain data access for user form templates that use connection settings in a data connection file

FIGURE 10-27: Enabling cross-domain access

The training request form is finally ready now to be accessed through the browser. When you click the New Document button in the ribbon, the form opens up in the same browser window, as shown in Figure 10-28. All of the controls on the form, the logic configured in the form, and the data connections are all displayed in good working order. An end user can now easily fill out the form and save it back in the library.

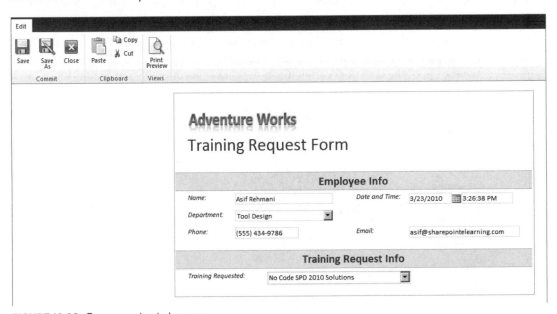

FIGURE 10-28: Form opening in browser

The next section shows how a workflow can be used to automate the approval of this form.

Automating Processes Using SharePoint Designer Workflows

The SPD application (which has a multitude of usage scenarios as covered earlier in this chapter) can also be used to create powerful workflows on top of SharePoint sites. SPD provides a native workflow design environment to create workflows without the need for any programming skills. As shown in Figure 10-29, the following three types of workflows can be created using SPD:

➤ *List* — List workflows are the simplest of the three. They are created scoped to a specific list or library, and are not meant to be ported anywhere else.

➤ *Reusable* — As the name suggests, reusable workflows are very portable. A reusable workflow is created and can be attached directly to a content type, which can then be utilized in a number of lists/libraries. If a change is later made to the workflow, it propagates automatically to all places where the content type is already in use. In addition to this functionality, reusable workflows can be packaged and deployed to other site collections.

➤ *Site workflows* — Site workflows do not need a list or library to be attached to. They are deployed directly to a site, and can work on all site components when executed.

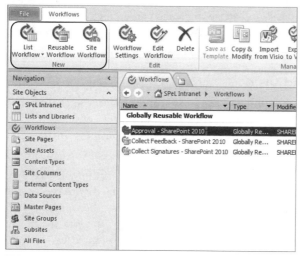

FIGURE 10-29: Available workflows

The main focus for the remainder of this chapter is on creating a workflow that would work on the information provided in the training request form, and routing that form accordingly. Even though many of the aspects of SPD workflows are discussed, this chapter is not meant to provide an exhaustive list of them. You should reference a book such as *Beginning SharePoint Designer 2010* by Woodrow Windischman, Bryan Phillips, Asif Rehmani, and Marcy Kellar (Indianapolis: Wiley, 2010) to get a better grasp on this subject.

Exploring Other Ways to Create SharePoint Workflows

Before discussing the workflows created in SPD, let's take a look at three other ways to implement workflows in SharePoint.

SharePoint Foundation ships with one workflow called Three State. SharePoint Server (standard or enterprise) ships with a few additional workflow templates, including Approval, Collect Feedback, Collect Signatures, and Disposition Approval. These templates can be used in the browser directly by an administrator to start creating workflows. No other software is required. All of these workflows provide a good start, and can be implemented immediately as a complete process to meet the immediate concerns of many organizations.

Another way to create workflows on top of SharePoint is to use Visual Studio (VS). VS is an extremely versatile platform with which programmers can create enterprise-level workflows. The workflow designer environment in VS lets developers visualize the flow of their processes, and then place code behind those processes. So, of course, a prerequisite of creating workflows in this manner is the knowledge of the VS environment and programming skills. Once the workflow is deployed, you or someone else must maintain that code throughout its lifetime.

Aside from creating the workflows using any of the mentioned Microsoft-provided tools, you also have the option to buy a workflow solution from a third-party vendor. Many vendors have now entered the SharePoint workflow market, and strive to provide an even easier and better solution to creating workflows. Vendors with well-known SharePoint workflow solutions include AgilePoint (`http://www.agilepoint.com`), Nintex (`http://www.nintex.com`), and K2 (`http://www.k2.com`).

Workflow Process Design Using Visio

The opportunity to create no-code workflows on top of SharePoint is very appealing, because it opens the door for people without a programming background to create business process solutions. A business analyst or a power user who possesses the knowledge of business processes can start by jumping directly into the SPD environment to create the workflows.

However, one thing that SPD lacks is the capability to visualize the workflow with a diagram. The SharePoint 2010 platform addresses this limitation by providing the facility to create a workflow diagram in Microsoft Visio 2010 instead. So, an alternative to starting the workflow in SPD is to start designing it in Visio, and then transport it to SPD. This process can work the other way as well — starting the workflow in SPD, and then taking it to Visio to visualize it.

Microsoft Visio 2010 ships with the template needed to create a SharePoint workflow. When Visio 2010 starts up, it presents you with many categories of templates. The Microsoft SharePoint Workflow template is located under the Flowchart category. This template contains the workflow shapes for actions, conditions, and terminators. The terminators are first used to define the start and end point of the workflow. Actions and conditions are then sprinkled throughout (using simple drag-and-drop operation) to create the workflow, as shown in Figure 10-30.

Once the shapes are placed as needed on the design surface, they are connected to each other using the Connector tool in the ribbon. If a condition is used in the workflow, it has two or more branches coming off of it, because the outcome of this condition is going to be either Yes or No — the condition is true or not true. This eventually gets translated as an `If...else` statement in the workflow. So, the branches from a condition must be designated as Yes or No by right-clicking each, and selecting the proper choice, as shown in Figure 10-31.

After you are finished designing the workflow, it can be exported to a format that SPD understands. That format is a Visio Workflow Interchange (VWI) file. This file is actually a ZIPped file containing all of the required workflow files. If the file extension is temporarily changed to `.zip`, you can open it up and see the files that are contained within, as shown in Figure 10-32. The XOML files define the workflow, and the VDX file contains the actual Visio drawing.

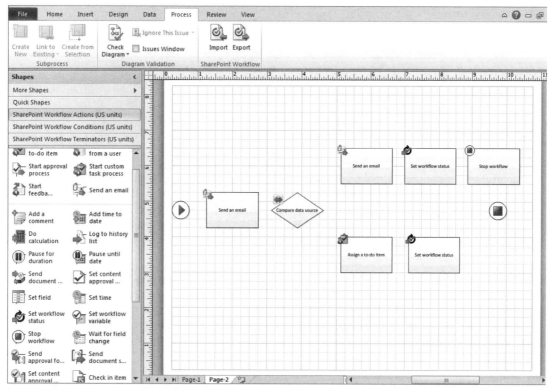

FIGURE 10-30: Using Visio to create workflows

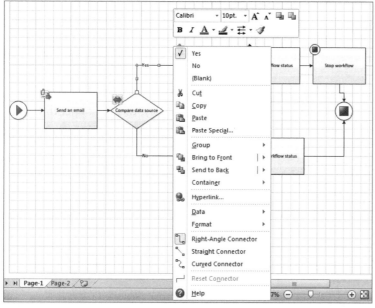

FIGURE 10-31: Designating outcomes of conditions

FIGURE 10-32: Seeing the contents of the ZIP file

The process for exporting to VWI begins at the Process tab on the ribbon. Using the options provided here, you can check the diagram for any errors. If there are errors in the workflow, this view shows you these errors within a task pane at the bottom of the workflow. You can export and also import a workflow by clicking the appropriate button and pointing to the location of the VWI file. Figure 10-33 shows the Process tab and all of the available options.

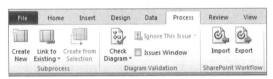

FIGURE 10-33: Options under the Process tab

Once the VWI file has been placed at a location where SPD can access it, it is ready to be consumed and configured within SPD.

Implementing the Workflow in SharePoint Designer

The story now continues within SPD. As you have probably noticed, none of the details around the activities have been set when the workflow is being designed in Visio. The facility to configure the rules and logic in the workflow, and then to eventually publish the workflow, exists in SPD. Visio is primarily used for workflow modeling and visualization.

As mentioned earlier, SPD provides a robust workflow designer interface. The question then becomes, "Who should be the one creating the workflows?" Usually, the personnel that would get the most benefit out of using this environment are site administrators, power users, and developers. The workflow designer environment lets you design the workflow logic within steps. The logical building blocks of workflows are placed within each step as conditional statements and subsequent actions. Figure 10-34 shows the workflow designer interface and the available actions in the drop-down.

Of course, workflows can be designed from scratch within this environment. However, in this scenario, the workflow designed in Visio is imported to create the shell of the workflow.

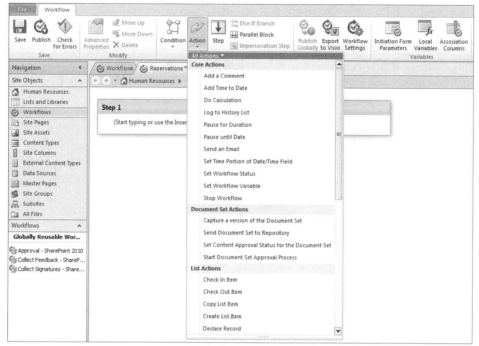

FIGURE 10-34: Actions available in the workflow designer

Transporting Your Workflow to the SPD Environment

In the Workflow section of SharePoint Designer, you can find a button on the ribbon labeled "Import from Visio." This is the starting point for importing a workflow previously designed in Visio.

Upon clicking this button, you are presented with a wizard screen and asked to point to the location of the .vwi file. Once you do that, as shown in Figure 10-35, the next step asks you to choose the type of workflow to import. You can decide to import the workflow directly attached to a list or library, or you can make this a reusable workflow and pick what content type (and its child content types) this workflow should be able to attach to later.

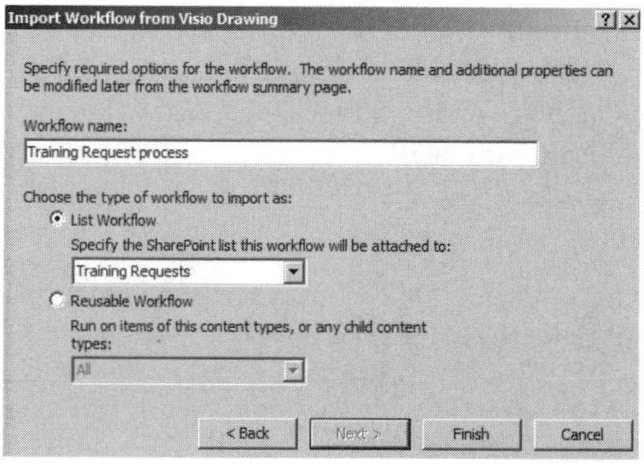

FIGURE 10-35: Choosing the type of workflow to import

This is an important step, because you cannot go back later and change your decision. In other words, you cannot change a list workflow to a reusable workflow, and vice versa. The only way to change a workflow is to start the import process all over again.

Following this chapter's scenario, the workflow is attached to the Training Requests library that contains the InfoPath form designed earlier. Figure 10-36 shows how the workflow looks once it is imported into the workflow designer environment.

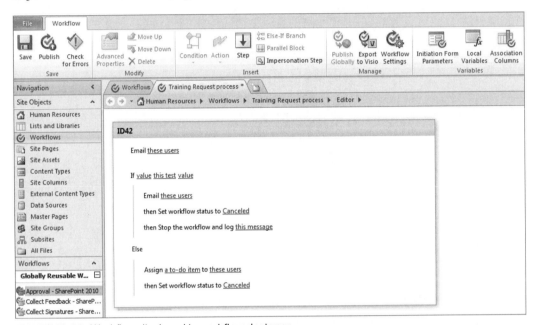

FIGURE 10-36: Workflow displayed in workflow designer

All of the conditions and actions transfer exactly as placed in the Visio diagram. However, as explained earlier, none of the logic is actually configured yet. The underlined parts of the conditions and actions must be configured within SPD, which is examined in the next section. SPD and Visio provide bi-directional support for workflows. In other words, this workflow configured in SPD can later be taken back to Visio for visualization of the process and further manipulation of the workflow diagram.

You still cannot configure the details around the activities in Visio. However, the good news is that your logic designed in SPD is not stripped off either. When you make a roundtrip back to SPD, your logic configuration will still be intact. Any additional action/condition blocks inserted while in Visio will just appear to not be configured and ready to be dealt with in SPD.

Enhancing Your Workflow

Now you reach the task of configuring the logic of this workflow. Many tools are provided in the workflow designer to enhance the workflow. Some of these tools are presented in this scenario to give you a good feel for the power of this design environment. However, you are encouraged to dive further into SharePoint Designer's workflow capabilities by experimenting with it and reading up on it further in *Beginning SharePoint Designer 2010* (Indianapolis: Wiley, 2010).

The workflow conditions and actions are all currently placed in one step, and the step is arbitrarily labeled automatically by the workflow import process. The step name can be changed by simply clicking it and typing in a new name. You should make the step names very self-explanatory. These names are not visible to the end user executing the workflow, and having a detailed name for the step helps in future maintenance of it. A new step can be created by placing the cursor either above or below the step and clicking the Step button on the ribbon. Each step is executed sequentially in the order that it appears on the workflow designer surface. Steps can also be nested within each other if needed, so that one step is carried out within another.

Actions and conditions can be moved up and down either within a step, or across step boundaries by clicking the Move Up and Move Down buttons on the ribbon. Figure 10-37 shows the workflow after a new step has been created and the e-mail action has been moved to it.

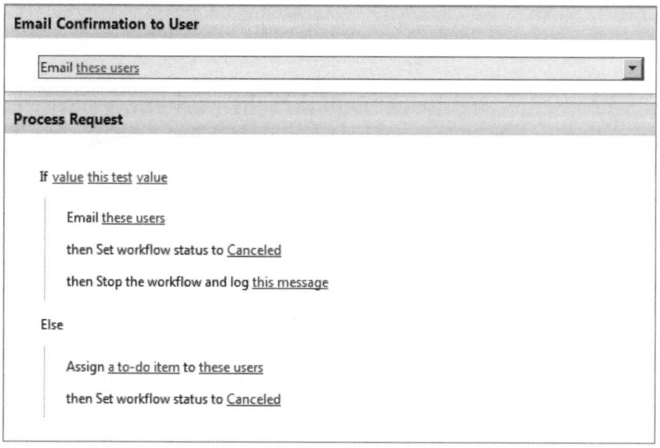

Email Confirmation to User

Email these users

Process Request

If value this test value

    Email these users

    then Set workflow status to Canceled

    then Stop the workflow and log this message

Else

    Assign a to-do item to these users

    then Set workflow status to Canceled

FIGURE 10-37: Moving steps

By default, all actions and conditions run sequentially in the order of their placement within the step. However, you can combine multiple items together to execute all in parallel. This functionality really comes in handy when you want to execute an action without waiting for the previous one to complete. The parallel execution feature requires the placement of a Parallel Block onto the design surface. Once the block is placed within a step, you can move the appropriate actions and conditions within the block. Figure 10-38 shows this functionality.

The workflow is configured from top to bottom. It starts with the first action, "Email these users," which is used to notify the users that their request has been received and is now being processed. Once "these users" is clicked, the e-mail message window lets you compose the message. The address book icon beside the addressee fields lets you pick persons or groups to send the message to. The lookup can be done directly from Active Directory, but a host of other options are also available.

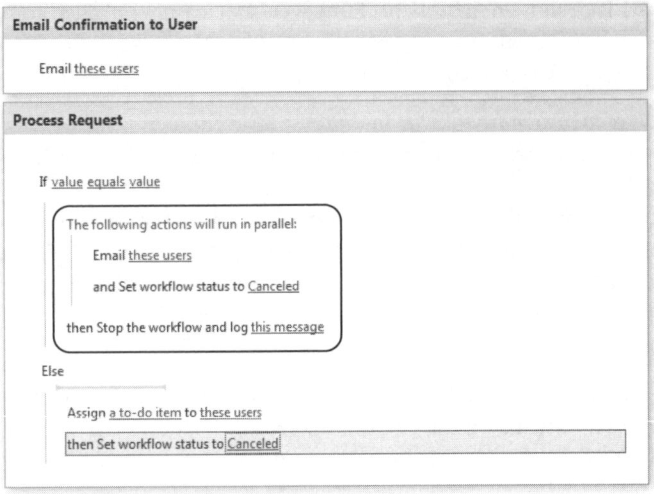

Email Confirmation to User

Email these users

Process Request

If value equals value

The following actions will run in parallel:

Email these users

and Set workflow status to Canceled

then Stop the workflow and log this message

Else

Assign a to-do item to these users

then Set workflow status to Canceled

FIGURE 10-38: Combining steps to run in parallel

One of the options is to select the user who created the current item that the workflow will eventually run upon. That's the option selected for this scenario. The subject line can be a simple static value, or you can click the *fx* button to do a lookup for the value. Better yet, you can click the ellipsis (...) button to bring up a text area called String Builder to let you compose a message with a combination of static and dynamic values.

In this example, the subject line has been formed with the title of the form, along with some text. The body of the e-mail can also hold static and dynamic values mixed together. In addition, the static text can be enhanced with formatting options available in the toolbar above the body field. The e-mail that eventually gets sent is rendered completely in HTML. Figure 10-39 shows the completed e-mail message composition window.

Define E-mail Message

To: Current Item:Created By

CC:

Subject: [%Current Item:Title%] form has been received

Tahoma 10 **B** *I* U Automatic

[%Current Item:Employee Name%],

Your **Training request** has been received and is now being processed.

Add or Change Lookup   OK   Cancel

FIGURE 10-39: Completed e-mail message composition window

Next, the Process Request step starts with finding out if the employee is eligible to take training. An Employee Credits list exists in the Human Resources site, which contains the number of training credit hours already taken by the employee, as shown in Figure 10-40. If the employee has already taken 100 credit hours of training or more, the employee is not eligible to take any further training.

FIGURE 10-40: Employee Credits list

The workflow condition does a lookup to this list to find the number of credits for the person who is filling out the form, and compares to see if the value is greater than 100. The lookup uses the following logic:

1. Select Credits from Employee Credits list

2. Where the Employee Name in Employee Credits list is equal to the Employee Name of the current form

Figure 10-41 shows this logic configured in the workflow lookup dialog.

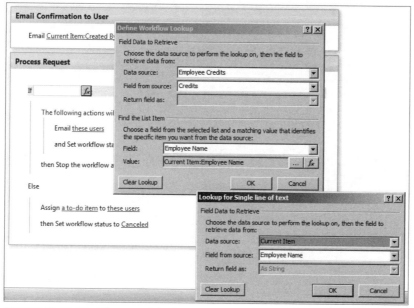

FIGURE 10-41: Workflow condition logic

If the condition returns true, the next action is to e-mail the requestor to reject the training request. This action is much like the e-mail action described earlier, only with differing content. The subsequent action sets the workflow status. Three status options are available as choices: Canceled, Approved, and Rejected.

In this sample scenario, the Rejected option is chosen. However, keep in mind that you are not limited to picking only one of these choices. You can also type an arbitrary status directly into the field if needed. That new status then gets added on to the existing choices and becomes available throughout the workflow.

The next action is to stop the workflow and log a message. The message would describe why the workflow was stopped at this point. This message text can also be a combination of static and dynamic values.

If the condition returns false, and the employee is eligible to take the training, the first action assigns a task to the employee's manager to sign off on the training. In a company, the organization hierarchy is usually contained in Active Directory. SharePoint's User Profile service is used to pull that information and keep it within a user profile database. This information is then available to be fetched through a workflow lookup. The process in this scenario for looking up and assigning the task to the manager is as follows:

1. Select Manager's login name from User Profiles

2. Where the Account Name is equal to the login name of the workflow's initiator

Figure 10-42 shows this logic configured in the workflow lookup dialog.

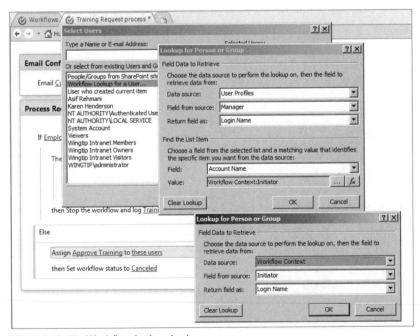

FIGURE 10-42: Workflow lookup logic

Finally, the last action of the workflow sets the workflow status to Approved. Figure 10-43 shows the completed workflow. You can check the workflow for errors by clicking the "Check for Errors" button on the ribbon.

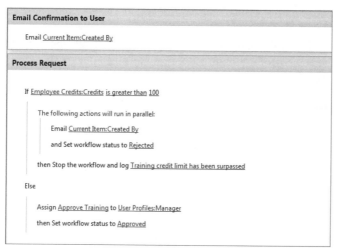

Email Confirmation to User

Email Current Item:Created By

Process Request

If Employee Credits:Credits is greater than 100

    The following actions will run in parallel:

        Email Current Item:Created By

        and Set workflow status to Rejected

    then Stop the workflow and log Training credit limit has been surpassed

Else

    Assign Approve Training to User Profiles:Manager

    then Set workflow status to Approved

FIGURE 10-43: Completed workflow

After the workflow is completed, the settings of the workflow can be changed by clicking the Workflow Settings button on the ribbon to get to the settings screen. Among other things, this screen shows the task and history list that will be utilized for this workflow — both of which can be changed — and also shows the start options for the workflow. For this scenario, the start option is changed to start the workflow when a new item is created.

The only thing left to do now is to publish the workflow. When you click the Publish button on the ribbon, the workflow generates the required files and forms, and then attaches itself to the Training Request library.

The Final Product

The solution is all set up at this point. A user starts by filling out the InfoPath form that's served by the Training Request library. Once the form is saved to the library, the SPD workflow picks it up automatically and checks the user's eligibility for attending training, and then routes the form accordingly. Following are a couple of scenarios used to test out this functionality.

Scenario 1

The form is filled out by a user who already has taken more than 100 hours of training.

Once the form is saved to the library, a couple of e-mails are received by the user. The first one notifies the user that the training request has been received. The second e-mail states that the user is not eligible for further training. At the same time, the form status displays a rejected message in the workflow column of the library, as shown in Figure 10-44.

Department	Employee Name	Email	Training Requested	Training Request Process
Research and Development	Asif Rehmani	asif@sharepointelearning.com	No Code SPD 2010 Solutions	Rejected

FIGURE 10-44: Message that request is rejected

You can click the Rejected status to see more information. The workflow status page opens up. In the Workflow History section shown at the bottom of Figure 10-45, a message appears that says, "Training credit limit has been surpassed."

FIGURE 10-45: Workflow History section

Scenario 2

The form is filled out by a user who has taken less than 100 hours of training.

Once the form is saved to the library, an e-mail is received by the user to notify that the training request has been received. Subsequently, the user's manager is retrieved by the system from the profile database, and a task is assigned to that manager to approve the training. Figure 10-46 shows the task that automatically appears in the task list.

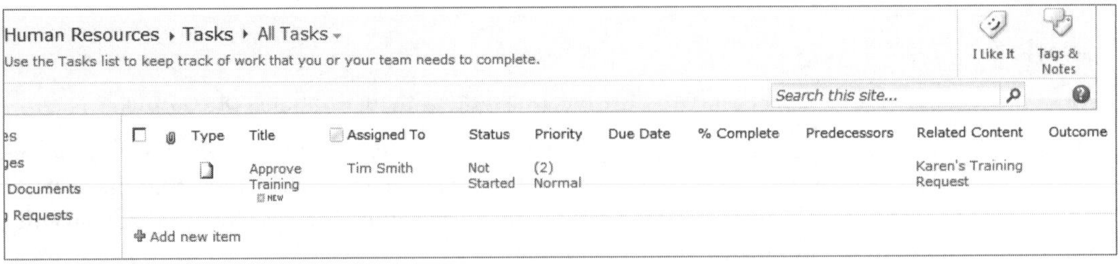

Human Resources ▸ Tasks ▸ All Tasks ▾

Use the Tasks list to keep track of work that you or your team needs to complete.

	Type	Title	Assigned To	Status	Priority	Due Date	% Complete	Predecessors	Related Content	Outcome
	📄	Approve Training 🆕 NEW	Tim Smith	Not Started	(2) Normal				Karen's Training Request	

➕ Add new item

FIGURE 10-46: Approve Training task

When the manager approves the training request by completing the task, the form's status in the Training Request library is automatically set to Approved, as shown in Figure 10-47.

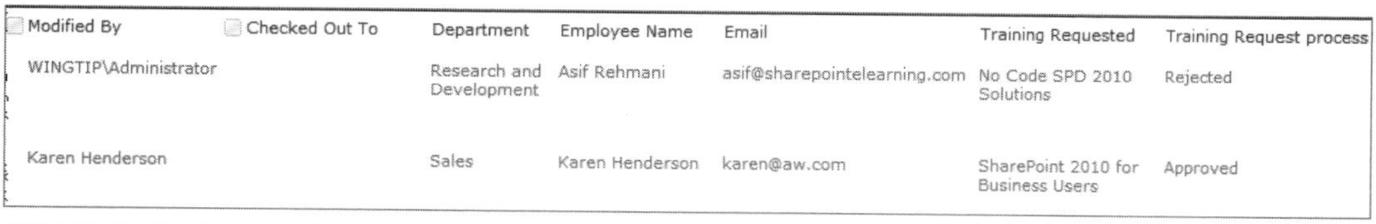

Modified By	Checked Out To	Department	Employee Name	Email	Training Requested	Training Request process
WINGTIP\Administrator		Research and Development	Asif Rehmani	asif@sharepointlearning.com	No Code SPD 2010 Solutions	Rejected
Karen Henderson		Sales	Karen Henderson	karen@aw.com	SharePoint 2010 for Business Users	Approved

FIGURE 10-47: Approved status

Lots of pieces make up this whole puzzle, and sometimes it's best to visualize those pieces in action. The entire scenario presented in this chapter is available to be viewed as a free video at `http://www.sharepoint-videos.com`.

SUMMARY

Microsoft InfoPath 2010 and Microsoft SharePoint Designer 2010 are great products on their own. Put them together, and you get an even more powerful way to create no-code, end-to-end solutions.

This chapter demonstrated the implementation of a simple business process with the help of these tools. Only a fraction of the functionality for each product was covered to keep the chapter at a reasonable length. Much more sophisticated processes can be handled using these tools, and you should definitely continue to explore each tool to enhance your knowledge of the complete set of possibilities they bring to the table.

ABOUT THE AUTHOR

Asif Rehmani has been training and consulting primarily on SharePoint technologies since 2004. He is a SharePoint Server MVP and MCT. Rehmani runs a SharePoint Videos website (`http://www.sharepoint-videos.com`) that provides SharePoint, SharePoint Designer, and InfoPath Video Tutorials. He also provides public in-person and online SharePoint training, as well as private workshops, through Critical Path Training (`http://www.criticalpathtraining.com`). He is also the co-author of the books *Professional Microsoft Office SharePoint Designer 2007* (Indianapolis: Wiley, 2009) and *Beginning SharePoint Designer 2010* (Indianapolis: Wiley, 2010).

11

Building Custom Service Applications for the Right Situations

By Andrew Connell

SharePoint 2010 introduces an improved (yet, somewhat new) concept to the SharePoint platform called the *service application framework*. Service applications are designed to replace SharePoint 2007 Shared Service Providers, and provide much more flexibility in terms of deployment, management, topology, and capabilities to the platform. One of the biggest changes is the capability for developers to build custom service applications. This chapter first looks at the history of service offerings for the SharePoint platform, and then introduces the new service application framework. It then addresses the subject of creating custom service applications, and walks through the process of creating one.

Readers who are familiar with previous versions of SharePoint (SharePoint Portal Server 2003 and Office SharePoint Server 2007) may elect to jump straight to the section, "SharePoint 2010 Service Architecture Framework." Readers who are familiar with the new service application framework and who want to dive into creating custom service applications can jump to the section, "SharePoint 2010 Service Application Extensibility."

The sample service application referenced in this chapter is much too big to include all the accompanying code samples and files in the chapter itself. Instead, the most important parts have been included, with a considerable amount of code and things like error checking and validation having been omitted. Readers will likely get the most out of this chapter by downloading the code associated with this book from the companion website (www.wrox.com) and following along while progressing through the chapter.

UNDERSTANDING SERVICES IN SHAREPOINT

SharePoint has historically been a collaboration product to its core. All SharePoint users are familiar with the concepts of sites, lists, and libraries, as well as the various ways they can collaborate with each other though SharePoint. However, the story does not end there. Many versions ago, Microsoft saw the potential for SharePoint to be the hub of many corporate intranets. To facilitate this, some service offerings needed to be shared among many users.

The first services introduced in SharePoint (search, user profiles, audiences, and My Sites) were needed to extend across the boundaries of SharePoint sites. These service offerings added value to the platform as a whole, rather than just to specific sites. With every release, SharePoint has become more popular and, thus, customers have demanded more and more evolution from Microsoft on the platform.

Those who are familiar with previous versions of SharePoint may want to skip the next section on the history of services in SharePoint and instead jump straight to the section, "SharePoint 2010 Service Architecture Framework."

HISTORY OF SERVICES IN SHAREPOINT

As with most products, having an understanding of the intent and reasons behind a capability or feature helps in gaining some perspective into how it works, as well as how it should be used. The following sections take a brief look back at the history of service offerings in the major SharePoint releases prior to SharePoint 2010, as well as the limitations of the approaches. Ultimately, the SharePoint 2010 service application framework was based off of the previous designs, including their advantages and disadvantages, as well as customer demand.

Service offerings (specifically, shared services) were first introduced in SharePoint v2.0, more commonly known as SharePoint Portal Server (SPS) 2003. Office SharePoint Server 2007 improved the architecture by adding a level of abstraction. The next two sections provide a brief look at services within these two products.

SharePoint Portal Server 2003

SPS 2003 was the first major release of SharePoint. Aside from the sites and site collections provided by Windows SharePoint Services (WSS) 2.0, SPS 2003 contained something called a *portal*. Portals could be seen as special super-site collections that took over an entire SharePoint web application. They offered federated search, a single user profile store to cache details on the user, audiences to target content to specific groups of users, and My Sites, which is a special site collection to which every user has access.

An SPS 2003 farm could contain a maximum of 20 portals. One challenge was that, because each portal had its own group of service offerings, multiple portals in one organization could cause confusion, because multiple search/user profile/audience stores would have to be maintained. In addition, users were quickly confused because it was not clear which My Site they were going to from each portal.

To address this, an SPS 2003 farm could be configured so that one portal in the farm could be flagged as the Shared Service Portal for the rest of the farm. Once this was done, all portals in the farm used the service offerings of the Shared Service Portal. This option was not ideal, because an SPS 2003 farm with 20 portals presented two choices: one set of services, or 20 configurations.

Office SharePoint Server 2007

Microsoft Office SharePoint Server (MOSS) 2007 included many changes to the service offering model in SharePoint that improved and expanded on the limitations of service offerings in SPS 2003. One big change was the removal of the portal construct from SharePoint; there were only site collections and sites. Another difference was that Microsoft removed the association of the services from specific web applications. Instead, all the service offerings were grouped together in something called a *Shared Service Provider* (SSP).

Administrators could then create a new SSP, hosted in its own web application, and configure the services within it individually. MOSS 2007 also introduced two new services: the Business Data Catalog (BDC) and Excel Services. When administrators created new SharePoint web applications, they configured them to use an existing SSP. Then, all site collections hosted by a given web application would leverage the service offerings in the SSP with which the web application was associated.

This model was a welcomed change to the service offering story in SharePoint, but it did have some limitations. First, it was an all-or-nothing proposition. If one web application simply wanted to use the same user profile store as another web application, but have a unique search configuration, administrators would have to create two separate SSPs, and simply duplicate the user profile configuration in the second.

Another limitation was that the service offerings were not extensible. There was no option for developers to create custom service offerings and deploy them in SharePoint. This was a common challenge for many organizations that wanted to share data or functionality across web applications. Many vendors simply created external stores and applications, and created custom controls or web parts that hooked into their systems.

SHAREPOINT 2010 SERVICE ARCHITECTURE FRAMEWORK

SharePoint 2010's approach to service offerings is an even bigger change from MOSS 2007, as well as the change from SPS 2003 to MOSS 2007. First, Microsoft discarded the SSP construct and instead set up each service, now called a *service application*, independently. Web applications could now be associated with individual service applications, rather than a collection, thus removing the limitation in MOSS 2007 that forced administrators to create an entirely new SSP when only one service offering had a different configuration. This made SharePoint a much more multi-tenant-friendly solution, allowing multiple customers to run in the same SharePoint installation, rather than having a separate SSP setup for each customer.

Another big improvement is a significant level of abstraction and control over which servers host specific service applications. Service applications are installed on all servers in the farm, but administrators are free to configure each server independently (that is, they can specify which services will run on each farm). This is done through the Central Administration ⇨ System Settings ⇨ "Manage Services on Server" page. When a service's status is set to Started, it can now serve up requests or be executed on that application server.

Once a service has been installed and configured to run on one or more application servers, an administrator then creates a new configuration of the service application. This configuration, a logical construct, is unique, and can run on any of the servers that have a Started instance running. Administrators are free to create multiple configurations of the same service application, such as in the case of search. One search configuration may be for confidential resources that should be available only to company employees. Another configuration may be available to vendors and customers. The web application that hosts the corporate intranet could then be associated with both search configurations, whereas a web application that is accessible by customers is only associated with the public search configuration.

One of the major abstraction points is that services are always consumed from the SharePoint Web Front End (WFE) servers, or those that run the web services and host the web-based experience for users. This is implemented through the use of *service application proxies*. A service application has an associated service application proxy that knows how to talk to the service application. All communication is done over Windows Communication Foundation (WCF) services via HTTP or HTTPS, which is very secure and does not require any special ports to be opened within or across farms.

This abstraction also enables service applications to be federated across SharePoint farms. As long as it has the proper service application proxies installed, and the necessary cross-farm trusts have been configured, one farm can connect to another farm's service applications. This enables administrators to create dedicated SharePoint farms built simply to host services for the rest of the organization.

Another interesting aspect of the service application framework in SharePoint 2010 is that it is built-in and part of SharePoint Foundation (SPF) 2010. Previous versions of SharePoint included service offerings only within the licensed versions of the product. Although SharePoint Server (SPS) 2010 does include quite a few service applications not found in SPF 2010, a few are included in SPF 2010. However, the important point here is that developers can build services that run on all SharePoint 2010 installations, not just the licensed versions customers have paid for.

 For more information about the SharePoint 2010 service application framework, refer to the documentation on TechNet at `http://technet.microsoft.com/en-us/library/ee704554.aspx`.

SHAREPOINT 2010 SERVICE APPLICATION EXTENSIBILITY

Aside from all the other previously mentioned improvements to the service offerings in SharePoint 2010, another big change is that developers are now free to build their own custom service applications. As this chapter will demonstrate, it enables many vendors to create robust solutions that can snap right into SharePoint. One common example would be creating an anti-virus solution for SharePoint. This is a classic case of a service offering that all SharePoint sites would want to leverage, and administrators could easily configure it to run on individual application servers because it is a very processor-intensive task.

Building a custom service application is not an easy or trivial task. It takes quite a bit of time because there is a lot of plumbing involved, and many components must be built to satisfy the level of abstraction provided by the framework. The sample service application built in this chapter clearly demonstrates this.

The sample, the Wingtip Calculator Service, simply provides two operations: adding or subtracting two numbers. As shown in the chapter, quite a bit of work is done to implement this simple task. In addition, developers must have a solid understanding of not only the SharePoint API, but also the administration API, SharePoint administration web controls, advanced WCF programming, and consuming of services, as well as working with and creating custom Windows PowerShell cmdlets.

What the Service Application Framework Offers

Although there are quite a few things to build when creating a custom service application, the SharePoint 2010 service application framework has quite a bit to offer to developers who choose to build one. Following are many of the things the service application framework has to offer to developers:

➤ *Application pool provisioning* — Service applications are hosted within application pools in Internet Information Services (IIS). SharePoint can handle creating a new application pool and associating it with a custom service application, saving the developer quite a bit of work.

➤ *Database provisioning* — Some service applications may need their own database or multiple databases. The framework includes an SPDatabase object that the provisioning process can pass back to SharePoint. The framework will create the SQL Server database, and run the specified T-SQL script to generate the schema.

➤ *Claims-based security support* — SharePoint 2010 can support claims-based security, and the service application framework can also leverage it.

➤ *Backup/restore/upgrade support* — Custom service applications can opt into the SharePoint farm backup/restore/upgrade process. Developers must only decorate specific service application objects with the correct attribute, and optionally implement a few methods, to partake in this process.

 For more information on backup/restore/upgrade support, refer to the SharePoint 2010 SDK on MSDN at http://msdn.microsoft.com/en-us/library/ee536630.aspx.

➤ *Out-of-the-box load balancer* — The service application framework offers up a round-robin load balancer that spreads out the workload of each service application across all the application servers configured with a running instance.

➤ *Custom permission rights* — Developers can even create custom permission rights, and grant those to specific users (or groups of users) to fine tune what things people can and cannot do with the service application.

Determining Whether or not to Build a Custom Service Application

Before embarking on building a custom service application, developers should take a step back and be sure that they have a solid understanding of when it does and does not make sense to build one.

Building a custom service application involves creating multiple objects that inherit and extend provided objects in the SharePoint API. This is in addition to the work that must be done to implement the business logic of the service application itself.

Because of the amount of work involved, developers should evaluate the business requirements to decide if the benefits that the service application framework has to offer are worth the effort. Any business requirement that is unique to a specific site collection, site, or site template, it likely does not make sense to build a custom service application, nor one that does not share data across site collections or web applications.

Following are some business requirements that would make more sense as a custom service application:

➤ Those that share data across site collections or web applications (such as the Web Analytics or Managed Metadata service applications in SPS 2010)

➤ Those that provide specialized calculations or analytics services (such as Web Analytics, Excel Services, or PerformancePoint Services)

➤ Those that aggregate data (such as Search)

➤ Those that are long-running or very intensive processes (such as Web Analytics, Search, or Word services)

➤ Those that are used for middle-tier applications

CREATING THE WINGTIP CALCULATOR SERVICE APPLICATION

At a high level, creating a custom service application can be broken down into a few different tasks. The first task is to create all the components and installers required to deploy those components to the SharePoint application servers. Next, the components and installers required to deploy these components to the SharePoint WFE servers must be created. Once these two core portions of the service application are deployed to the server, the next step is to create a consumer that will expose the service offering to users or other services. Finally, as with any custom development project, the last step is to test everything to ensure that it is working as desired.

The following sections detail how to create all the necessary service application components, as well as deploy and install them to the various SharePoint servers. Creating a custom service application involves creating quite a few classes and files. The service application created in this chapter is a very simple calculator, the Wingtip Calculator Service, providing addition and subtraction operations. This is a very simple example (and not much of a real-world example), but this approach will make it easier to follow the service application plumbing.

 Although some code snippets are included in this chapter, a considerable amount of code has been omitted for readability. The complete Wingtip Calculator Service application is included in the code download associated with this book (which you can find at www.wrox.com). Refer to the complete sample for all code required to implement the Wingtip Calculator Service application.

Configuring the Visual Studio 2010 Project

The new SharePoint Developer Tools in Microsoft Visual Studio 2010 do not include a project template or items that can serve as a starting point for creating a custom service application. Before beginning the process of creating a custom service application, take a few minutes to set up your project.

Start by creating a new project using the Empty SharePoint Project template. When prompted by the SharePoint Customization Wizard, specify the local startup site to be the URL of the Central Administration site, and set it as a farm solution because service applications cannot be deployed to the sandbox.

The Empty SharePoint Project template adds only the most basic assembly references to the project. Building a custom service application requires adding some additional references. Add references to the following assemblies found on the .NET tab of the Add Reference dialog:

- ➤ System.Configuration
- ➤ System.Management
- ➤ System.Web

Two additional references are necessary, but they are not nearly as easy to add. Both will support creating custom Windows PowerShell cmdlets that will be used in creating the command-line installer part of the custom service application.

The first one, System.Management.Automation.dll, is part of the Microsoft Windows Software Development Kit (SDK) and can be found in c:\Program Files\Reference Assemblies\ Microsoft\WindowsPowerShell\v1.0. Developers can download and install the Windows SDK to get this file. However, this is a rather large install. Another option is to get this assembly from the server's global assembly cache (GAC). Unfortunately, it does not appear in the Add Reference dialog. Because the Add Reference dialog simply makes changes to the project file, developers can manually add this reference.

The other required assembly is the Microsoft.SharePoint.PowerShell.dll, which is also in the server's GAC, placed by there by the SharePoint installer.

To manually add these references to the project, follow these steps:

1. Right-click the project in the Solution Explorer tool window and select Unload Project. If prompted, save your project first.

2. Right-click the project in the Solution Explorer tool window and select "Edit […].csproj."

3. Scroll down to the <ItemGroup /> section that contains a handful of <Reference /> elements. Add the following entries:

   ```
   <Reference Include="System.Management.Automation" />
   <Reference Include="Microsoft.SharePoint.PowerShell" />
   ```

4. Right-click the project in the Solution Explorer tool window and select Reload Project. If prompted, save your project first.

With the references added, add a new farm-scoped Feature to the project. This will serve as the installer for the service application and service application proxy. Follow these steps:

1. Right-click the Feature node in the project within the Solution Explorer tool window and select Add Feature.

2. Right-click the Feature1 node and rename it **WingtipCalculatorServiceInstaller**.

3. Right-click the WingtipCalculatorServiceInstaller Feature and select View Designer. Set the following values:

   ➤ *Name* — Wingtip Calculator Service Installer

   ➤ *Scope* — Farm

Now, because the SharePoint Development Tools do not include SharePoint Project Item (SPI) templates for items required by a service application, items will need to be created and placed in special folders. Thankfully, the SharePoint Developer Tools do provide a way to do this for just this reason.

Add the following mapped folders by right-clicking the project in the Solution Explorer and selecting Add ⇨ SharePoint Mapped Folder. (This process must be repeated for each folder.)

➤ `\{SharePointRoot}\TEMPLATE\Admin` — This will contain the pages used to create and configure the service application within the Central Administration site.

➤ `\{SharePointRoot}\CONFIG\POWERSHELL\Registration` — This will contain the Windows PowerShell custom cmdlet registration XML files.

➤ `\{SharePointRoot}\WebClient` — This will contain the configuration file required to make a connection from the WFE server to the service application's WCF service endpoint.

➤ `\{SharePointRoot}\WebServices` — This will contain the WCF service endpoint for the service application.

Following generally accepted practices, add a subfolder under the `Admin`, `WebClient`, and `WebServices` folders named `WingtipCalculatorService`. Custom files should not be deployed alongside the SharePoint installation files. Therefore, keeping things separate with subfolders is a recommended practice. To make things easier to keep track of, rename the mapped folder `Registration` to `PowerShellRegistration`. This only changes the name of the folder in the Visual Studio project, not the target of where the files will be deployed.

There is one last step to perform to prepare the project. The SharePoint Development Tools build process performs a token replacement on various file types in the project for commonly used items. One of the tokens available to developers is `$SharePoint.Project.AssemblyFullName$`. At compile time, this token will be replaced with the fully qualified four-part name of the generated assembly. By default only `*.ASPX`, `*.ASCX`, `*.XML`, `*.WEBPART`, and `*.DWP` files are searched for tokens to be replaced. This limited list is there only for performance reasons. Developers are free to modify their project files to instruct Visual Studio to include additional files.

Using the technique previously demonstrated to unload and reload a project file, add the following within a `<PropertyGroup />` collection without a condition (such as immediately after the `<SignAssembly />` element):

```
<TokenReplacementFileExtensions>svc</TokenReplacementFileExtensions>
```

At this point, the project is ready to host a new service application. The project should now look like Figure 11-1.

After creating the service application, the chapter will walk through the process of creating two consumers. These should be located in different SharePoint packages (*.WSP), and, therefore, another project is required. Add a new project to the solution named `WingtipCalculatorServiceConsumer` using the Empty SharePoint Project template, and repeat the following steps that were implemented on the service application project:

1. When prompted by the SharePoint Customization Wizard, specify the URL of a SharePoint site collection to test a web part against, and set it as a farm solution.

2. Add all the same references to the `WingtipCalculatorServiceConsumer` project that were added to the `WingtipCalculatorService` project.

3. In the `WingtipCalculatorServiceConsumer` project, add an additional project reference to the `WingtipCalculatorService` project.

4. Add a mapped folder named `PowerShellRegistration` to `\{SharePointRoot}\CONFIG\ POWERSHELL\Registration`.

At this point, the project `WingtipCalculatorServiceConsumer` is ready to host the consumer components. The project should now look like Figure 11-2.

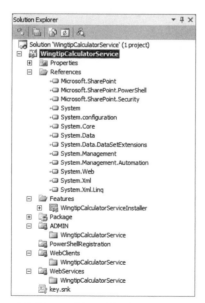

FIGURE 11-1: Visual Studio 2010 WingtipCalculatorService project

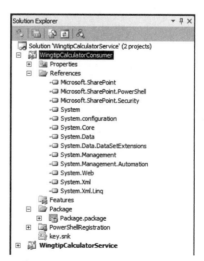

FIGURE 11-2: Visual Studio 2010 WingtipCalculatorServiceConsumers project

Now that the two Visual Studio projects have been created and configured, it is time to create the custom service application.

Creating the Application Server Components

The first portion of the service application to create are the parts that will reside on the SharePoint application servers. The bulk of the work the service application does will be done on application server(s). These back-end components include the service program itself (the thing that does all the work), any associated timer jobs or databases, a WCF service endpoint that will expose the service operations to the SharePoint WFE servers, the administration interfaces (including a web-based user interface and command-line interface), and the installers.

Service

All service applications must have an implementation of the SPService object. This object is the center of gravity for the entire service application. This object should implement the SPIisWebService class (which inherits from SPService) and implement the IServiceAdministration interface. IServiceAdministration specifies all the members that are needed tell SharePoint some basic information about the service, such as its name (GetApplicationTypeDescription()), how to create a new instance (CreateApplication()), and how to create a proxy on the WFE servers to the service application (CreateProxy()), as well as the URL of the page (GetCreateApplicationLink()) administrators should be sent to when creating a new instance from the page Central Administration ⇨ Application Management ⇨ Manage Service Applications.

Create a new class named CalcService.cs in the WingtipCalculatorService project. Add the code shown in Listing 11-1 to it.

LISTING 11-1: Creating the Service Object

```
public class CalcService : SPIisWebService, IServiceAdministration {
  public CalcService() { }
  public CalcService(SPFarm farm) : base(farm) { }

  public SPServiceApplication CreateApplication(string name,
      Type serviceApplicationType,
      SPServiceProvisioningContext provisioningContext) {
    // ... validation code omitted ...

    // if the service doesn't already exist, create it
    CalcServiceApplication serviceApp = this.Farm.GetObject(name, this.Id,
        serviceApplicationType) as CalcServiceApplication;
    if (serviceApp == null)
      serviceApp = CalcServiceApplication.Create(name, this,
          provisioningContext.IisWebServiceApplicationPool);

    return serviceApp;
  }

  public SPServiceApplicationProxy CreateProxy(string name,
      SPServiceApplication serviceApplication,
      SPServiceProvisioningContext provisioningContext) {
```

```
    // ... validation code omitted ...

    // verify the service proxy exists
    CalcServiceProxy serviceProxy = (CalcServiceProxy)this.Farm.GetObject
        (name, this.Farm.Id, typeof(CalcServiceProxy));
    if (serviceProxy == null)
      throw new InvalidOperationException("CalcServiceProxy does not
          exist in the farm.");

    // if the app proxy doesn't exist, create it
    CalcServiceApplicationProxy applicationProxy =
        serviceProxy.ApplicationProxies.
        GetValue<CalcServiceApplicationProxy>(name);
    if (applicationProxy == null) {
      Uri serviceAppAddress = ((CalcServiceApplication)serviceApplication).Uri;
      applicationProxy = new CalcServiceApplicationProxy(name,
          serviceProxy, serviceAppAddress);
    }

    return applicationProxy;
  }

  public SPPersistedTypeDescription GetApplicationTypeDescription(Type
        serviceApplicationType) {
    if (serviceApplicationType != typeof(CalcServiceApplication))
      throw new NotSupportedException();

    return new SPPersistedTypeDescription("Wingtip Calculator Service",
        "Custom service application providing simple calculation
        capabilities.");
  }

  public Type[] GetApplicationTypes() {
    return new Type[] { typeof(CalcServiceApplication) };
  }

  public override SPAdministrationLink GetCreateApplicationLink(Type
        serviceApplicationType) {
    return new SPAdministrationLink
        ("/_admin/WingtipCalculatorService/Create.aspx");
  }
}
}
```

Service Interface/Operation Contracts

Before going much further the service contract that defines what operations the service application can implement needs to be created. This will define the public interface of the WCF service endpoint that the application proxies on the SharePoint WFE servers will use to communicate with the service instances running on the back-end servers. In the case of the simple Wingtip Calculator Service, this interface is quite simple. Add a new class named IWingtipCalcContract.cs to the WingtipCalculatorService project, and add the code shown in Listing 11-2 to it.

LISTING 11-2: Wingtip Calculation Service Contract

```
[ServiceContract]
public interface IWingtipCalcContract {
  [OperationContract]
  int Add(int x, int y);

  [OperationContract]
  int Subtract(int x, int y);
}
```

Service Application

With the service contract defined the service application can be created. This is the part that will do all the work when prompted by the application proxies residing on the various WFE servers in the farm.

This critical component tells SharePoint quite a bit about the service application. The service application can run on multiple application servers in the farm. It must run on at least one server in order to process requests, but it could run on multiple ones. One way to think of this is to compare it to web applications. A SharePoint web application runs on every single WFE server in the farm. Similarly, a service application can run on multiple application servers. Setting this up is covered later in this chapter.

A custom service application must implement two things: SPIisWebServiceApplication and IWingtipCalcContract (the service contract). This class is responsible for creating a new configuration of the service application (the Create() method) and telling SharePoint where to find different pieces associated with this service application.

Following are the properties that should be overridden from the SPIisWebServiceApplication class for the specific Wingtip Calculator Service implementation:

➤ TypeName — This is the name of the service application as it should appear in the list of available services to create when clicking the New button in the ribbon on the Central Administration ➪ Application Management ➪ Manage Service Applications page.

➤ InstallPath — This is the relative path where the service endpoint can be found on the application servers.

➤ VirtualPath — This is the name of the WCF service endpoint file.

➤ ManageLink — This is the Central Administration relative URL of the page administrators should be taken to when they select the service, or when they click the Manage button in the ribbon on the Central Administration ➪ Application Management ➪ Manage Service Applications page.

➤ PropertiesLink — This is the Central Administration relative URL of the page administrators should be taken to when they click the Properties button with a service selected in the ribbon on the Central Administration ➪ Application Management ➪ Manage Service Applications page.

In addition, the service must implement the IWingtipCalcService interface, which, in this case, is quite simple. Listing 11-3 shows a sample of what should be in a new class file added to the WingtipCalculatorService project named CalcServiceApplication.cs.

LISTING 11-3: Excerpt of Contents of CalcServiceApplication.cs

```
public class CalcServiceApplication : SPIisWebServiceApplication,
    IWingtipCalcContract {
  public CalcServiceApplication()
    : base() { }
  private CalcServiceApplication(string name, CalcService service,
      SPIisWebServiceApplicationPool appPool)
    : base(name, service, appPool) { }

  public static CalcServiceApplication Create(string name, CalcService service,
      SPIisWebServiceApplicationPool appPool) {
    // ... validation code omitted ...

    // create the service application
    CalcServiceApplication serviceApplication = new
        CalcServiceApplication(name, service, appPool);
    serviceApplication.Update();

    // register the supported endpoints
    serviceApplication.AddServiceEndpoint("http", SPIisWebServiceBindingType.Http);
    serviceApplication.AddServiceEndpoint("https",
        SPIisWebServiceBindingType.Https, "secure");

    return serviceApplication;
  }

  public override string TypeName {
    get { return "Wingtip Calculator Service Application"; }
  }

  protected override string InstallPath {
    get { return SPUtility.GetGenericSetupPath(@"WebServices\Wingtip"); }
  }

  protected override string VirtualPath {
    get { return "CalcService.svc"; }
  }

  public override SPAdministrationLink ManageLink {
    get { return new SPAdministrationLink("/_admin/WingtipCalculatorService/
        Manage.aspx"); }
  }
  public override SPAdministrationLink PropertiesLink {
    get { return new SPAdministrationLink("/_admin/WingtipCalculatorService/
        Manage.aspx"); }
  }

  #region IWingtipCalcContract implementation
```

continues

LISTING 11-3 *(continued)*

```
public int Add(int x, int y) {
  return x + y;
}

public int Subtract(int x, int y) {
  return x - y;
}
#endregion
}
```

Service Endpoint

As previously explained, all inter-server communication in the service application framework occurs using WCF services over HTTP or HTTPS. In order to expose the service application on the application servers to the service's application proxies installed on the SharePoint WFE servers, a WCF endpoint must be created. Because the `CalcServiceApplication` class already implements the `IWingtipCalcService` contract, all that is required is a simple WCF service that references this class.

Create a new text file named `CalcService.svc` in the `WebServices\WingtipCalculatorService` folder in the `WingtipCalculatorService` project with the following contents:

```
<%@ServiceHost Language="C#"
    Service="CriticalPath.SharePoint.Samples.WingtipCalculator.
        CalcServiceApplication, $SharePoint.Project.AssemblyFullName$"
    Factory="CriticalPath.SharePoint.Samples.WingtipCalculator.
        CalcServiceHostFactory, $SharePoint.Project.AssemblyFullName$" %>
```

To expose this service, create another text file in the same location named `web.config` that will expose the service, and define the service endpoints, bindings, and authentication mechanisms supported. Add the code in Listing 11-4 to the `web.config` file.

LISTING 11-4: CalcService.svc web.config Contents

```
<?xml version="1.0" encoding="utf-8" ?>
<configuration>
  <system.serviceModel>
    <services>
      <service name="CriticalPath.SharePoint.Samples.WingtipCalculator.
          CalcServiceApplication">
        <endpoint binding="customBinding"
            bindingConfiguration="CalcServiceHttpBinding" contract=
    "CriticalPath.SharePoint.Samples.WingtipCalculator.
    IWingtipCalcContract" address="" />
        <endpoint binding="customBinding"
            bindingConfiguration="CalcServiceHttpsBinding" contract=
    "CriticalPath.SharePoint.Samples.WingtipCalculator.
    IWingtipCalcContract" address="secure" />
      </service>
    </services>
```

```
<bindings>
  <customBinding>
    <binding name="CalcServiceHttpBinding">
      <security authenticationMode="IssuedTokenOverTransport"
          allowInsecureTransport="true" />
      <binaryMessageEncoding>
        <readerQuotas maxStringContentLength="1048576"
            maxArrayLength="2097152" />
      </binaryMessageEncoding>
      <httpTransport maxReceivedMessageSize="2162688"
          authenticationScheme="Anonymous" useDefaultWebProxy="false" />
    </binding>
    <binding name="CalcServiceHttpsBinding">
      <security authenticationMode="IssuedTokenOverTransport" />
      <binaryMessageEncoding>
        <readerQuotas maxStringContentLength="1048576"
            maxArrayLength="2097152" />
      </binaryMessageEncoding>
      <httpsTransport maxReceivedMessageSize="2162688"
          authenticationScheme="Anonymous" useDefaultWebProxy="false" />
    </binding>
  </customBinding>
</bindings>
</system.serviceModel>
<system.webServer>
  <security>
    <authentication>
      <anonymousAuthentication enabled="true" />
      <windowsAuthentication enabled="false" />
    </authentication>
  </security>
</system.webServer>
</configuration>
```

Service Instance

Following Microsoft's practice of installing everything related to SharePoint on every server, and then configuring each server to serve a different role, custom service applications will be deployed to all servers in the farm using the SharePoint solution packaging infrastructure (*.WSP). Although the service applications are installed on every server in the farm, they do not necessarily run on all servers.

The service application framework enables administrators to designate the service applications to run on specific servers in the farm. This is done through the Central Administration ⇨ System Settings ⇨ "Manage Services on Server" page by starting or stopping instances. To get a custom service application to be listed on this page it must expose a service instance.

The service instance (a class that is derived from SPServiceInstance) associates an instance entry on the page in Central Administration with a specific service application. When a service application proxy requests the WCF endpoint of a service application as the location where it should send its instructions, SharePoint looks at all servers in the farm, and generates a list of those that have been flagged as having an online or started instance. It then picks one using a round-robin load balancer, and returns the address of the WCF endpoint on that server to the service application proxy.

Creating a new instance is very easy. First, create a new class named `CalcServiceInstance` that inherits `SPIisWebServiceInstance` and overrides a few properties, as shown in Listing 11-5.

LISTING 11-5: CalcServiceInstance.cs

```
public class CalcServiceInstance : SPIisWebServiceInstance {
  public CalcServiceInstance() { }
  public CalcServiceInstance(SPServer server, CalcService service)
    : base(server, service) { }

  public override string DisplayName {
    get { return "Wingtip Calculator Service"; }
  }
  public override string Description {
    get { return "Wingtip Calculator providing simple arithmatic services."; }
  }
  public override string TypeName {
    get { return "Wingtip Calculator Service"; }
  }
}
```

At this point, all the necessary components required by the service application on the application servers in the farm have been created. The next step is to create a way for administrators to create and interact with the service application, as well as install and configure it in the farm.

Service Application Administration Pages

The SharePoint 2010 Central Administration interface provides a few ways for administrators to interact with the custom service application through a web browser interface. This is broken down into three main pages:

➤ *Create page* — This page is used to create new configurations of the service application. This page is shown when the user selects the service application by clicking the New button in the ribbon on the Central Administration ➪ Application Management ➪ Manage Service Applications page.

➤ *Manage page* — This page is used as the primary gateway to administer the service application. The recommendation is to treat this page like a dashboard page that provides details about the currently selected service application, and provides links to other pages that can be used to administer different pieces of the service application. This page is shown when the user selects the service application from the list of created service applications on the Central Administration ➪ Application Management ➪ Manage Service Applications page, and clicks the Manage button in the ribbon.

➤ *Properties page* — This page is used to manage the general configuration of the created service application (such as changing its name, connecting to different databases, associating it with different application pools, changing the identity of an application pool, or something else specific to the service application). This page is shown when the user selects the service application from the list of created service applications on the Central Administration ➪ Application Management ➪ Manage Service Applications page and clicks the Properties button in the ribbon.

All of these pages (and associated pages they link to, in the case of the Manage page) should be deployed to the {SharePointRoot}\TEMPLATE\ADMIN folder on the server. The Manage and Properties pages are unique to the individual service application, and could contain anything. They are not used in the Wingtip Calculator Service because there is not a lot to configure.

However, the Create page is a bit more important because it contains some controls that Microsoft has created for creating an application pool for the administrator. The following code snippet demonstrates using the IisWebServiceApplicationPoolSection web control to create or select an existing application pool and associate it with IIS:

```
<wssuc:InputFormSection Title="Name" Description="Specify a name for the
        service application." runat="server">
  <template_inputformcontrols>
        <wssuc:InputFormControl LabelAssocatiedControlID="ServiceAppName"
            runat="server">
        <template_control>
            <SharePoint:InputFormTextBox ID="ServiceAppName" class="ms-
                input" Columns="35" runat="server" />
        </template_control>
        </wssuc:InputFormControl>
    </template_inputformcontrols>
</wssuc:InputFormSection>
<wssuc:IisWebServiceApplicationPoolSection ID="ApplicationPoolSelection"
        runat="server" />
```

The code-behind for this page does three things:

➤ It first creates a new instance of the service application and sets its status to SPObjectStatus.Online. This is the same thing as "Started" that is shown on the Manage Service Applications page in Central Administration.

➤ It then creates a new instance of the service application on the current application server, and starts the instance by setting its status to Online as well. This is required because, for a service application to run, there must be at least one Online/Started instance on one application server in the farm.

➤ The last step is to create a new instance of the service application proxy because that is how consumers will connect to the service application, including the administration part of the service application.

Refer to the project in the associated chapter code download for the complete code on how this is done.

Service Application Installer

Now that the service application has been created and administrators can interact with it, the last step is to install it in the farm. Because every service application is different, SharePoint does not have any included mechanisms to do this — this is something a developer must do for each custom service application. Installing the service application is a straightforward task that must be done through the SharePoint API.

Installation is broken down into two parts:

➤ First, a new instance of the service application (`CalcService`) must be created and added to the collection of services in the farm. This simply registers the service with SharePoint, in much the same way as installing a Feature does not do anything, except to register the Feature for possible activation at the specified scope.

➤ Second, a new instance of the service application proxy (`CalcServiceProxy`) must be created and added to the collection of proxies in the farm. Again, this makes SharePoint aware of a new application proxy.

Because this task must be done through code, many different options exist for performing this task, such as using a console application, Windows PowerShell, or an `*.MSI` installer. The easiest approach is to use a farm-scoped Feature and implement the installation and uninstallation logic in the `FeatureInstalled()` and `FeatureUninstalling()` methods. Because the Feature is farm-scoped, it will be activated automatically when the Feature is deployed, making the entire deployment of the service application included in a single `*.WSP` file.

Listing 11-6 shows the code that should be added to the `WingtipCalculatorServiceInstaller` Feature previously created in the `WingtipCalculatorService` project.

LISTING 11-6: WingtipCalculatorServiceInstaller Feature Event Handlers Installing the Service Application

```
public override void FeatureActivated(SPFeatureReceiverProperties properties) {
  // install the service
  CalcService service = SPFarm.Local.Services.GetValue<CalcService>();
  if (service == null) {
    service = new CalcService(SPFarm.Local);
    service.Update();
  }

  // with service added to the farm, install instance
  CalcServiceInstance serviceInstance =
      new CalcServiceInstance(SPServer.Local, service);
  serviceInstance.Update(true);
}

public override void FeatureDeactivating(SPFeatureReceiverProperties properties) {
  // uninstall the instance
  CalcServiceInstance serviceInstance =
      SPFarm.Local.Services.GetValue<CalcServiceInstance>();
  if (serviceInstance != null)
    SPServer.Local.ServiceInstances.Remove(serviceInstance.Id);

  // uninstall the service
  CalcService service = SPFarm.Local.Services.GetValue<CalcService>();
  if (service != null)
    SPFarm.Local.Services.Remove(service.Id);
}
```

Once the solution package containing the service application and this Feature are deployed, the Feature will be activated, and the administrators should now see an entry in the New button on the Manage Service Application page, as shown in Figure 11-3.

Creating an Instance of the Service Application

With everything created and deployed, the next step is to create a new configuration of the custom service application. This can be done quite easily through Central Administration. But, by following Microsoft's SharePoint 2010 guidelines, administrators should also have the capability to perform this task using the command line.

FIGURE 11-3: Wingtip service application in Central Administration

The first step is to create a new service application configuration. This is done by first creating a new instance of the service application, granting a user rights to manage it, and then starting an instance of it. As previously mentioned, each service application is different, and, therefore, SharePoint does not include anything out-of-the-box. Instead, developers must implement this.

To do this, create a new Windows PowerShell cmdlet and register it with the SharePoint Windows PowerShell snap-in. Create a new class `NewCalcServiceApplication.cs` in the `WingtipCalculatorService\Admin\WingtipCalculatorService` folder, and have the class it creates inherit from `SPCmdlet`. When this cmdlet is called, it will call the `InternalProcessRecord()` method to execute, which will create the new service application shown in Listing 11-7.

LISTING 11-7: NewCalcServiceApplication Windows PowerShell Cmdlet

```
[Cmdlet(VerbsCommon.New, "CalcServiceApplication", SupportsShouldProcess = true)]
public class NewCalcServiceApplication : SPCmdlet {
  #region cmdlet parameters
  [Parameter(Mandatory = true)]
  [ValidateNotNullOrEmpty]
  public string Name;

  [Parameter(Mandatory = true)]
  [ValidateNotNullOrEmpty]
  public SPIisWebServiceApplicationPoolPipeBind ApplicationPool;
  #endregion

  protected override bool RequireUserFarmAdmin() {
    return true;
  }

  protected override void InternalProcessRecord() {
    // ... validation code omitted ...

    // verify a service app doesn't already exist
```

continues

LISTING 11-7 *(continued)*

```
    CalcServiceApplication existingServiceApp =
        service.Applications.GetValue<CalcServiceApplication>();
    if (existingServiceApp != null) {
      WriteError(new InvalidOperationException("Wingtip Calc Service
          Application already exists."),
        ErrorCategory.ResourceExists,
        existingServiceApp);
      SkipProcessCurrentRecord();
    }

    // create & provision the service app
    if (ShouldProcess(this.Name)) {
      CalcServiceApplication serviceApp = CalcServiceApplication.Create(
        this.Name,
        service,
        appPool);

      // provision the service app
      serviceApp.Provision();

      // pass service app back to the PowerShell
      WriteObject(serviceApp);
    }
  }
}
```

To register this cmdlet with the SharePoint Windows PowerShell snap-in, create a new XML file named `WingtipCalServiceApplication.xml` in the same folder as the cmdlet with the following contents. When the SharePoint Windows PowerShell snap-in loads, it will look at all XML files in the `{SharePointRoot}\CONFIG\POWERSHELL\Registration` and load the cmdlets listed in them.

```xml
<ps:Config xmlns:ps="urn:Microsoft.SharePoint.PowerShell"
        xmlns:xsi="http://www.w3.org/2001/XMLSchema-instance"
        xmlns:schemaLocation="urn:Microsoft.SharePoint.PowerShell
          SPCmdletSchema.xml">
  <ps:Assembly Name="$SharePoint.Project.AssemblyFullName$">
    <ps:Cmdlet>
      <ps:VerbName>New-CalcServiceApplication</ps:VerbName>
      <ps:ClassName>CriticalPath.SharePoint.Samples.WingtipCalculator.
        NewCalcServiceApplication</ps:ClassName>
      <ps:HelpFile />
    </ps:Cmdlet>
  </ps:Assembly>
</ps:Config>
```

Now, to create the service application from PowerShell, open the SharePoint 2010 Management Shell (Start ➪ All Programs ➪ Microsoft SharePoint 2010 Products) and run the script shown in Listing 11-8. A more verbose sample can be found in the project in the code download associated with this chapter.

LISTING 11-8: Windows PowerShell Script to Create a New Configuration of the Wingtip Calculator Service

```
write-host "Ensure service application not already created..."
    -foregroundcolor Gray
$serviceApp = Get-SPServiceApplication | where { $_.GetType().FullName
    -eq "CriticalPath.SharePoint.Samples.WingtipCalculator.
    CalcServiceApplication" -and $_.Name -eq "Wingtip Calculation
    Service Application" }
if ($serviceApp -eq $null){
    write-host "Creating service application..." -foregroundcolor Gray
    $guid = [Guid]::NewGuid()
    $serviceApp = New-CalcServiceApplication -Name "Wingtip Calculation
        Service Application" -ApplicationPool
        "SharePoint Web Services System"
    if ($serviceApp -ne $null){
        write-host "Wingtip Calculation Service Application created."
            -foregroundcolor Green
    }
}

write-host "Configure permissions on the service app..." -foregroundcolor Gray
$user = $env:userdomain + '\' + $env:username

write-host "  Creating new claim for $user..." -foregroundcolor Gray
$userClaim = New-SPClaimsPrincipal -Identity $user
    -IdentityType WindowsSamAccountName
$security = Get-SPServiceApplicationSecurity $serviceApp

write-host "  Granting $user 'FULL CONTROL' to service application..."
    -foregroundcolor Gray
Grant-SPObjectSecurity $security $userClaim -Rights "Full Control"
Set-SPServiceApplicationSecurity $serviceApp $security

write-host "Ensure service instance is running on server $env:computername..."
    -foregroundcolor Gray
$localServiceInstance = Get-SPServiceInstance -Server $env:computername |
    where { $_.GetType().FullName -eq "CriticalPath.SharePoint.Samples.
    WingtipCalculator.CalcServiceInstance" -and $_.Name -eq "" }
if ($localServiceInstance.Status -ne 'Online'){
    write-host "Starting service instance on server $env:computername..."
        -foregroundcolor Gray
    Start-SPServiceInstance $localServiceInstance
    write-host "Wingtip Calculation Service Application instance started."
        -foregroundcolor Green
}
```

The Wingtip Calculator Service application has now been created and configured on the application servers in the SharePoint farm. The next step is to create the WFE components.

Creating the Web Front End Server Components

The second part of building a custom service application is to create the components that will run on the SharePoint WFE servers. The two components that live on a SharePoint WFE related to service applications are the service proxy and application proxy. Once these two components are created, they must be installed and then provisioned.

Service Proxy

The service proxy acts as the hub for the service application on the SharePoint WFE server. The job of the service proxy is to tell SharePoint about the application proxy — that is, what type of service application(s) it can connect to, how to create a new instance of one, and what the user-friendly name of the application proxy is.

To create a new service proxy, add a new class `CalcServiceProxy.cs` to the proxy that inherits from `SPIisWebServiceProxy` and implements `IServiceProxyAdministration`. As previously mentioned, the `IServiceProxyAdministration` interface dictates that the proxy must provide specific details to SharePoint itself. The code in the service proxy is shown in Listing 11-9.

LISTING 11-9: Creating the Service Proxy Object

```
public class CalcServiceProxy : SPIisWebServiceProxy, IServiceProxyAdministration {
  public CalcServiceProxy() : base() { }
  public CalcServiceProxy(SPFarm farm) : base(farm) { }

  public SPServiceApplicationProxy CreateProxy(Type
      serviceApplicationProxyType, string name, Uri serviceApplicationUri,
      SPServiceProvisioningContext provisioningContext) {
    if (serviceApplicationProxyType != typeof(CalcServiceApplicationProxy))
      throw new NotSupportedException();

    return new CalcServiceApplicationProxy(name, this, serviceApplicationUri);
  }

  public SPPersistedTypeDescription GetProxyTypeDescription(Type
      serviceApplicationProxyType) {
    return new SPPersistedTypeDescription("Wingtip Calculator Service Proxy",
        "Custom service application proxy providing simple
        calculation capabilities.");
  }

  public Type[] GetProxyTypes() {
    return new Type[] { typeof(CalcServiceApplicationProxy) };
  }
}
```

Service Application Proxy

The job of the service application proxy is to handle all the communication between the SharePoint WFE and the service application running on one of the back-end application servers. One way to think about this is to envision how a typical application is built to communicate with a web service.

When connecting to a remote web or WCF service, a developer creates a service reference to the remote service in Visual Studio, which creates a proxy within the project to develop against. The service application proxy is similar to this auto-generated web service proxy. However, the service application proxy is much more complicated in that it must interrogate the SharePoint farm for the location of the service application's WCF endpoint.

The service application proxy object can get complicated quite fast because it must create a WCF channel to connect to the service application. First, a WCF host factory must be created, followed by the code to dynamically create a WCF channel and invoke the calls to the service application's WCF endpoint.

Listing 11-10 shows only a fraction of the code in the `CalServiceApplicationProxy.cs` required because the real proxy is nearly 200 lines long. What has been omitted is the WCF plumbing required to obtain the URI of the WCF endpoint, building the WCF channel and invoking it. What is included are the basic declaration, core properties, and the methods that the service application consumers can call.

LISTING 11-10: **Excerpt of the Contents of CalcServiceApplicationProxy.cs**

```
public class CalcServiceApplicationProxy : SPIisWebServiceApplicationProxy {
  private ChannelFactory<IWingtipCalcContract> _channelFactory;
  private object _channelFactoryLock = new object();
  private string _endpointConfigName;

  [Persisted]
  private SPServiceLoadBalancer _loadBalancer;

  public CalcServiceApplicationProxy() { }
  public CalcServiceApplicationProxy(string name, CalcServiceProxy proxy,
      Uri serviceAddress)
    : base(name, proxy, serviceAddress) {
    // create instance of a new load balancer
    _loadBalancer = new SPRoundRobinServiceLoadBalancer(serviceAddress);
  }

  public override string TypeName {
    get { return "Wingtip Calculator Service Application"; }
  }

  #region service application methods
  public int Add(int x, int y) {
    int result = 0;
    // execute the call against the service app
    ExecuteOnChannel("Add", channel => result = channel.Add(x, y));
    return result;
  }
  public int Subtract(int x, int y) {
    int result = 0;
    // execute the call against the service app
    ExecuteOnChannel("Subtract", channel => result = channel.Subtract(x, y));
    return result;
  }
  #endregion
}
```

Service Application Proxy Installer

With the service application proxy created, the next step is to install it on the SharePoint WFE servers. Like the service application, this must be done using the SharePoint API because SharePoint 2010 includes no out-of-the-box mechanism for doing this. The best approach is to use the farm-scoped Feature to create the proxy, so add the code shown in Listing 11-11 to the farm-scoped Feature:

LISTING 11-11: Creating the Proxy

```
public override void FeatureActivated(SPFeatureReceiverProperties properties) {
  // install the service
  CalcService service = SPFarm.Local.Services.GetValue<CalcService>();
  if (service == null) {
    service = new CalcService(SPFarm.Local);
    service.Update();
  }
  // install the service proxy
  CalcServiceProxy serviceProxy =
      SPFarm.Local.ServiceProxies.GetValue<CalcServiceProxy>();
  if (serviceProxy == null) {
    serviceProxy = new CalcServiceProxy(SPFarm.Local);
    serviceProxy.Update(true);
  }
  // with service added to the farm, install instance
  CalcServiceInstance serviceInstance = new CalcServiceInstance(SPServer.Local,
      service);
  serviceInstance.Update(true);
}

public override void FeatureDeactivating(SPFeatureReceiverProperties properties) {
  // uninstall the instance
  CalcServiceInstance serviceInstance =
      SPFarm.Local.Services.GetValue<CalcServiceInstance>();
  if (serviceInstance != null)
    SPServer.Local.ServiceInstances.Remove(serviceInstance.Id);
  // uninstall the service proxy
  CalcServiceProxy serviceProxy =
      SPFarm.Local.ServiceProxies.GetValue<CalcServiceProxy>();
  if (serviceProxy != null) {
    SPFarm.Local.ServiceProxies.Remove(serviceProxy.Id);
  }
  // uninstall the service
  CalcService service = SPFarm.Local.Services.GetValue<CalcService>();
  if (service != null)
    SPFarm.Local.Services.Remove(service.Id);
}
```

Once the solution package containing the service application and this Feature is deployed, the Feature will be activated, and administrators should now see an entry in the Connect button on the Manage Service Application page, as shown in Figure 11-4.

Creating an Instance of the Service Application Proxy

It is now time to create a new instance of the service application proxy. Although this can be done using the Central Administration Web browser interface, that is rather intuitive. This chapter will demonstrate the command-line approach.

First, create the custom Windows PowerShell cmdlet named `NewCalcServiceApplicationProxy`. The contents of its `InternalProcessRecord()` is shown in Listing 11-12. (The rest of the code is omitted for brevity.)

FIGURE 11-4: Wingtip service application proxy in Central Administration

---

LISTING 11-12: Excerpt of NewCalcServiceApplicationProxy Windows PowerShell Cmdlet

```
protected override void InternalProcessRecord() {
  // ... validation code omitted ...

  Uri serviceApplicationAddress = null;
  if (ParameterSetName == "Uri")
    serviceApplicationAddress = _uri;
  else if (ParameterSetName == "ServiceApplication") {
    // make sure can get a reference to service app
    SPServiceApplication serviceApp = ServiceApplication.Read();
    if (serviceApp == null) {
      WriteError(new InvalidOperationException("Service application not
          found."), ErrorCategory.ResourceExists, serviceApp);
      SkipProcessCurrentRecord();
    }

    // make sure can connect to service app
    ISharedServiceApplication sharedServiceApp = serviceApp as
        ISharedServiceApplication;
    if (sharedServiceApp == null) {
      WriteError(new InvalidOperationException("Service application not
          found."), ErrorCategory.ResourceExists, serviceApp);
      SkipProcessCurrentRecord();
    }

    serviceApplicationAddress = sharedServiceApp.Uri;
  } else
    ThrowTerminatingError(new InvalidOperationException("Invalid parameter
        set."), ErrorCategory.InvalidArgument, this);

  // create the service app proxy
  if ((serviceApplicationAddress != null) && ShouldProcess(this.Name)) {
    CalcServiceApplicationProxy serviceAppProxy = new CalcServiceApplicationProxy(
```

continues

LISTING 11-12 *(continued)*

```
            this.Name,
            serviceProxy,
            serviceApplicationAddress);

    // provision the service app proxy
    serviceAppProxy.Provision();

    // pass service app proxy back to the PowerShell
    WriteObject(serviceAppProxy);
    }
}
```

Register this new cmdlet the same way the previous one was registered, and then run the following script shown in Listing 11-13 in the SharePoint 2010 Management Shell to create the proxy.

LISTING 11-13: Windows PowerShell Script to Create a New Configuration of the Wingtip Calculator Service Proxy

```
write-host "Get reference to Wingtip Calculation Service Application"
    -foregroundcolor Gray
$serviceApp = Get-SPServiceApplication | where { $_.GetType().FullName
    -eq "CriticalPath.SharePoint.Samples.WingtipCalculator.
    CalcServiceApplication" -and $_.Name
    -eq "Wingtip Calculation Service Application" }
if ($serviceApp -eq $null){
    Write-Error "CRITICAL ERROR: Failed to acquire reference to Wingtip
        Calculation Service Application!!!!"
}

write-host "Ensure service application proxy not already created..." -
    foregroundcolor Gray
$serviceAppProxy = Get-SPServiceApplicationProxy | where
    { $_.GetType().FullName
    -eq "CriticalPath.SharePoint.Samples.WingtipCalculator.
    CalcServiceApplication" -and $_.Name -eq "Wingtip Calculation
    Service Application Proxy" }
if ($serviceAppProxy -eq $null)
{
    write-host "Creating service application proxy..." -foregroundcolor Gray
    $serviceAppProxy = New-CalcServiceApplicationProxy -Name "Wingtip
        Calculation Service Application Proxy"
        -ServiceApplication $serviceApp
    write-host "Wingtip Calculation Service Application proxy created."
        -foregroundcolor Green

    write-host

    write-host "Adding service application proxy to default group..."
        -foregroundcolor Gray
```

```
Get-SPServiceApplicationProxyGroup -Default |
    Add-SPServiceApplicationProxyGroupMember
    -Member $serviceAppProxy
write-host "Wingtip Calculation Service Application added to default
    group." -foregroundcolor Green
}
```

After running both of these scripts, the Wingtip Calculation Service Application should now appear in the list of configured service applications in Central Administration, as shown in Figure 11-5.

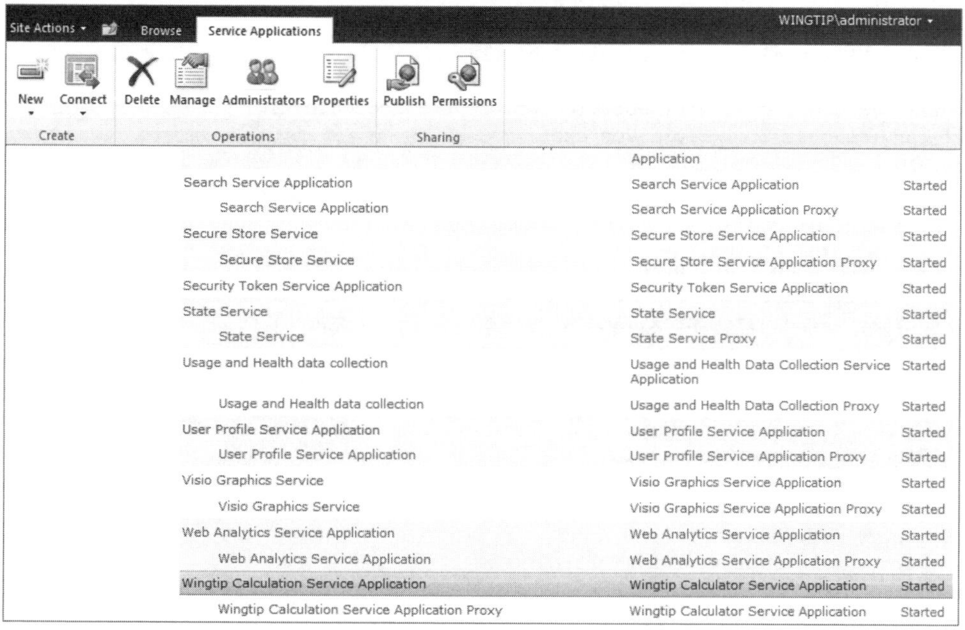

FIGURE 11-5: Wingtip Calculation Service Application in Central Administration

At this point, the service application has been created and deployed, and everything is set up for consumers to be deployed to the SharePoint WFE servers. The next step is to create a consumer.

Creating the Service Consumers

A service application is not terribly useful unless it can be consumed in some shape or form. Consumers can come in various types — such as web parts, web part pages, or even as custom WCF services to expose the service to applications running outside of SharePoint. The consumers could even facilitate a custom administration interface for remote administration of the service.

In the case of the Wingtip Calculator Service, this section demonstrates how to create two different consumers — an Ajax-enabled Web part that can add or subtract two numbers, and a Windows PowerShell cmdlet that can add two numbers together.

Service Consumer Client

Before creating the consumers, one thing developers can do to make the invocation of the service application proxy easier for other developers creating consumers is to provide a service consumer client. This dramatically simplifies the plumbing required for consumer developers. Create a new class `CalcServiceClient.cs` and add the code shown in Listing 11-14.

LISTING 11-14: Service Application Consumer Client

```
public sealed class CalcServiceClient {
  private SPServiceContext _serviceContext;

  public CalcServiceClient(SPServiceContext serviceContext) {
    _serviceContext = serviceContext;
  }

  public int Add(int x, int y) {
    int result = 0;
    CalcServiceApplicationProxy.Invoke(
      _serviceContext,
      proxy => result = proxy.Add(x, y)
    );
    return result;
  }

  public int Subtract(int x, int y) {
    int result = 0;
    CalcServiceApplicationProxy.Invoke(
      _serviceContext,
      proxy => result = proxy.Subtract(x, y)
    );
    return result;
  }
}
```

This will make it much easier to call the service application proxy, because the developers creating service consumers must have to write only a few lines of code:

```
CalcServiceClient client = new CalcServiceClient(SPServiceContext.Current);
result = client.Add(Int32.Parse(FirstIntTextBox.Text),
    Int32.Parse(SecondIntTextBox.Text));
```

Service Consumer Web Part

The first consumer will be based off the SharePoint Developer Tools template Visual Web Part. It will contain two `TextBoxes` (for the two integers to add or subtract), a `DropDownBox` (for the add or subtract operand), a `Button` to execute the operation, and a `Label` to display the results. All of this is wrapped in an Ajax `UpdatePanel` to preserve the page postback.

The code-behind for the Visual Web Part's *.ASCX handles the button click event, as shown in Listing 11-15. Notice how it leverages the client previously created, dramatically simplifying the code required.

LISTING 11-15: Service Application Consumer Visual Web Part Code

```
public partial class WingtipCalcWebPartUserControl : UserControl {
  protected void ExecuteButton_Click(object sender, EventArgs e) {
    CalcServiceClient client = new CalcServiceClient(SPServiceContext.Current);

    int result = 0;

    switch (OperandDropDownList.SelectedItem.ToString()) {
      case "Add":
        result = client.Add(
            Int32.Parse(FirstIntTextBox.Text),
            Int32.Parse(SecondIntTextBox.Text)
        );
        break;
      case "Subtract":
        result = client.Subtract(
            Int32.Parse(FirstIntTextBox.Text),
            Int32.Parse(SecondIntTextBox.Text)
        );
        break;
    }

    AnswerLabel.Text = result.ToString();
  }
}
```

Once deployed and added to a page, the resulting Web part would look like Figure 11-6.

Service Consumer PowerShell Cmdlet

Now, create another Wingtip Calculator Service consumer as a Windows PowerShell cmdlet. Add a new class InvokeCalcService.cs in the WingtipCalculatorConsumer project in the PowerShellRegistration folder. This cmdlet will use the client utility class previously created. Add the code shown in Listing 11-16 to the InvokeCalcService.cs class.

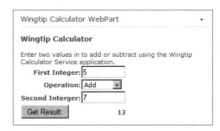

FIGURE 11-6: Wingtip service application consumer Web Part

LISTING 11-16: Wingtip Service Application Windows PowerShell Consumer Cmdlet

```
[Cmdlet("Invoke", "CalcService", SupportsShouldProcess = true)]
public class InvokeCalcService : SPCmdlet {
  private int[] _values;

  [Parameter(Mandatory = true, ValueFromPipeline = true)]
  public SPServiceContextPipeBind ServiceContext;

  [Parameter(ParameterSetName = "Add", Mandatory = true)]
  public int[] Add {
    get { return _values; }
    set { _values = value; }
  }

  protected override void InternalProcessRecord() {
    // get the specified service context
    SPServiceContext serviceContext = ServiceContext.Read();
    if (serviceContext == null)
      WriteError(new InvalidOperationException("Invalid service context."),
          ErrorCategory.ResourceExists, serviceContext);
    else {
      CalcServiceClient client = new CalcServiceClient(serviceContext);

      // validate only two values were passed in
      if (_values.Length != 2)
        WriteError(new InvalidOperationException("Only two values can be
            added/subtracted"), ErrorCategory.InvalidArgument, _values);
      else {
        WriteProgress("Executing Calculation", "Sending calculation commands to
            calculation service application...");
        int result = client.Add(_values[0], _values[1]);
        WriteObject(result);
      }
    }
  }
}
```

Like the previous Windows PowerShell cmdlets, an *.XML file is required to register the Invoke-CalcService cmdlet with the SharePoint 2010 Windows PowerShell snap-in:

```
<ps:Config xmlns:ps="urn:Microsoft.SharePoint.PowerShell"
        xmlns:xsi="http://www.w3.org/2001/XMLSchema-instance"
        xmlns:schemaLocation="urn:Microsoft.SharePoint.PowerShell
            SPCmdletSchema.xml">
  <ps:Assembly Name="$SharePoint.Project.AssemblyFullName$">
    <ps:Cmdlet>
      <ps:VerbName>Invoke-CalcService</ps:VerbName>
      <ps:ClassName>CriticalPath.SharePoint.Samples.WingtipCalculator.
          InvokeCalcService</ps:ClassName>
      <ps:HelpFile />
    </ps:Cmdlet>
  </ps:Assembly>
</ps:Config>
```

To test the custom Windows PowerShell cmdlet service application consumer, open a new SharePoint 2010 Management Shell and run the script shown in Listing 11-17.

LISTING 11-17: Testing the Wingtip Service Application Windows PowerShell Consumer Cmdlet

```
$siteUri = 'http://intranet.wingtip.com'
write-host "  Using service context of site $siteUri..." -foregroundcolor Gray

write-host "Adding 1+1..." -foregroundcolor Gray
$result = Invoke-CalcService -ServiceContext $siteUri -Add 1,1
write-host "Result of 1+1 = $result" -foregroundcolor Gray
write-host "Add method on Wingtip Calculation Service Application working."
     -foregroundcolor Green
```

It may take a moment for the service application to return the result, but eventually it will return the result of adding the two integers together.

SUMMARY

This chapter covered service offerings in the SharePoint platform. After a brief look at the history of service offerings in previous versions of SharePoint, the new SharePoint 2010 service application framework was introduced.

One of the improvements to SharePoint 2010 and the service application framework is the capability for developers to create custom service applications. The majority of this chapter then focused on explaining what is involved in creating a custom service application, and then walked through the process of creating the simple Wingtip Calculator Service application sample.

ABOUT THE AUTHOR

Andrew Connell is an author, instructor, and co-founder of Critical Path Training (www. CriticalPathTraining.com), a SharePoint education-focused company. Connell is a six-time recipient of Microsoft's Most Valuable Professional (MVP) award (2005–2010) for Microsoft Content Management Server (MCMS) and Microsoft SharePoint Server. He has authored and contributed to numerous MCMS and SharePoint books over the years, including his book *Professional SharePoint 2007 Web Content Management Development: Building Publishing Sites with Office SharePoint Server 2007* (Indianapolis: Wiley, 2008). Connell has spoken on the subject of SharePoint development and WCM at conferences such as TechEd, SharePoint Connections, Microsoft Tech Ready, VSLive, SharePoint Best Practice Conference, SharePoint Evolutions Conference, Microsoft TechReady, Office Developer Conference, and Microsoft SharePoint Conference in North America, Europe, and Asia. You can find him on his blog at http://www.andrewconnell.com/blog, as well as on Twitter (@andrewconnell).

12

Managing the SharePoint Application Lifecycle

By Chris O'Brien

Application Lifecycle Management (ALM) is a huge topic, and, not surprisingly, there are various definitions and perspectives. Most definitions emphasize the relationship between software engineering and other aspects of software projects, such as requirements gathering and change management. On MSDN, Microsoft defines ALM as follows:

> *Application Lifecycle Management is the coordination of all aspects of software engineering — including the formulation and communication of business and technical requirements, code design and architecture, project tracking, change management, coding, testing, debugging, and release management — by using tools that facilitate and track collaboration among and within work teams.*

One useful simplification is that ALM is the *consideration of all aspects of an application throughout its lifecycle*. This emphasizes the fact that ALM concerns more than just the Software Development Lifecycle phase (that is, the initial build), and incorporates considerations right from the conception phase at the beginning, to maintenance aspects more relevant after the application has gone live. Frequently, when people refer to ALM, they are focusing on the maintenance aspects. In particular, issues surrounding updating the application, change control processes, and maintaining application integrity are common discussion points.

Undoubtedly, SharePoint has special considerations regarding ALM when compared to regular .NET applications. SharePoint has many additional moving parts, and technical professionals learn that the product's architecture means that existing techniques for aspects such as developing in a team, deploying solutions between environments, and updating applications in use, all often need specific tailoring.

Indeed, an analysis of matters related to SharePoint 2010 and ALM could focus specifically on any one of these aspects, and likely several others, too. In this chapter, the emphasis is on capabilities and approaches that are new to SharePoint 2010, and how development teams can leverage these in the real world.

Much like the common use of the term "ALM," many of the application lifecycle improvements in SharePoint 2010 are oriented toward the upgrade of existing applications. Historically, this has been a complex topic for SharePoint developers, because previous versions had little "framework" support for upgrades, and the SharePoint SDK documentation had minimal coverage. SharePoint 2010 improves this picture considerably. This chapter looks at how the improvements can be used for development teams responsible for maintaining an application throughout its life.

PROVISIONING WITH SOLUTION/FEATURE XML VERSUS .NET CODE

It is commonplace (and generally best practice) for organizations using SharePoint to have one or more test environments in addition to the production environment. As with all application development platforms, a key ALM challenge for developers using SharePoint has always been related to deploying an application through multiple environments.

Though the steps required to build a SharePoint application can be replicated manually in different environments, most teams dismiss this approach as non-scalable and error-prone. Instead, SharePoint applications are typically built using the Features framework, and deployed using Solution packages. This allows modules of functionality to be made available to different scopes within SharePoint (known as *provisioning*), and also facilitates repeatable, consistent deployments.

Broadly speaking, artifacts in SharePoint can be divided into two categories:

- ➤ *Declarative artifacts* — Declarative artifacts are elements that are defined in a physical file somewhere in the SharePoint root. Frequently, these artifacts are used as definitions or templates that are used when new instances of the artifact are provisioned. Examples of declarative artifacts include site definitions, list definitions, and custom actions.

- ➤ *Provisioned artifacts* — Provisioned artifacts are elements that exist inside a Content Database. Typically, they can be created through Feature XML, code, or other means such as the SharePoint UI itself. Examples of provisioned artifacts include content types, list instances, and fields.

Features commonly contain XML to define artifacts such as content types that support functionality and content in the application. However, most SharePoint developers appreciate early on that many of these artifacts can also be created imperatively using the SharePoint API. Consequently the SharePoint developer has options in this area.

Although most articles and code samples use the "traditional" XML route, provisioning via code offers useful benefits. During the 2007 time frame, an increasing number of experienced developers adopted this approach. When the imperative approach is used, this is typically still within the Feature framework. Features are created in generally the same factoring as the declarative approach, but artifacts are provisioned by code in feature receivers, rather than XML. Note also that it isn't possible to avoid XML entirely. Some artifacts can *only* be provisioned with XML.

Let's consider the declarative approach for a moment. Table 12-1 summarizes the pros and cons of declarative provisioning. Each entry in the table could be reversed for imperative provisioning. For example, a disadvantage shown in the table for declarative provisioning is an advantage for the imperative approach, and vice-versa.

TABLE 12-1: Pros and Cons of Declarative Provisioning with XML

ADVANTAGES	DISADVANTAGES
Required for some artifacts (for example, site definition, list template, delegate control, custom action, custom field control)	Not possible to debug the provisioning process
	Little support for upgrade scenarios (for example, some changes to a content type that is in use cannot be done with XML)
Provisioning instructions are not in compiled code, so potentially easier to update	Difficult to control provisioning sequence in some areas
	Arguably steeper learning curve than API

One aspect that SharePoint developers must reconcile is that there is (unfortunately) no way to have a purely declarative *or* imperative approach. There will always be elements of each. Some "template" elements (such as site definitions) require an XML definition, but XML often cannot be used later in the lifecycle for provisioning *changes* to existing artifacts (though SharePoint 2010 does extend the possibilities here as compared to previous versions). Therefore, the decision is essentially about the mix of code versus XML used, and the characteristics of each pattern are important factors.

Ultimately this decision is at least partly a matter of preference. Some developers prefer to work with code to benefit from debugging support. Others may prefer the more widely trodden path of XML-based features. Whichever approach is selected, you should understand *how* artifacts in your solution will be upgraded when the time comes, and where these additions will slot into your Visual Studio solution.

GENERATING FEATURE XML USING SITE TEMPLATES

If you decide that your features will predominantly use XML for provisioning, you must decide how to construct the XML for all of the artifacts you require. When developing for SharePoint 2007, a common approach was to copy and adapt some existing Feature XML (usually from previous work or sample code) to fit the current requirements — a task that became easier with experience, but one that novice developers sometimes found difficult.

A new option in SharePoint 2010 development is to create artifacts the easy way through the browser or SharePoint Designer (SPD) 2010, and then combine SharePoint and Visual Studio 2010 functionality to "reverse-engineer" Feature XML from these customizations in a supported way. Following are the two major advances in the 2010 technologies that enable this:

➤ SharePoint site templates are now `.wsp` files (rather than `.stp` files).

➤ The Import SharePoint Solution Package project type in Visual Studio now enables the easy creation of a new Visual Studio project using the contents of a `.wsp` file.

For many, using this approach could be a big time-saver when developing SharePoint Features, and even seasoned SharePoint developers are likely to find the technique useful. If nothing else, the process provides a great reference for many aspects of Feature schema!

Unfortunately, it remains the case in SharePoint 2010, that saving publishing sites as a template is not supported. For these sites, this approach *can* still be leveraged to obtain portions of Feature XML during development. However, it is unwise to use the overall site template to create further publishing sites.

The process to generate Feature XML from a site template is as follows:

1. Create a SharePoint site in the browser. Make any customizations (for example, create content types) in the browser or SPD.

2. In the Site Settings area for the site, click the "Save site as template" link within the Site Actions category. Name the file and site template (and optionally add a description). Specify if the site content should be included in the template. Once you click the OK button on this page, a .wsp file containing the site template will be stored in the Solutions Gallery for the current site. Figure 12-1 shows the .wsp for a site saved as a template in the Solutions Gallery.

FIGURE 12-1: Site saved as a template

3. Click the link to the .wsp file to download it to your local hard disk.

4. Create a new Visual Studio 2010 project using the Import SharePoint Solution Package project type, as shown in Figure 12-2. Import the generated .wsp.

5. Specify the site and security level of the project. Then browse to the .wsp downloaded to the filesystem (in Step 3) to import the contents of this package. Figure 12-3 shows selection of the .wsp file to import to Visual Studio.

FIGURE 12-2: Import SharePoint Solution Package template option

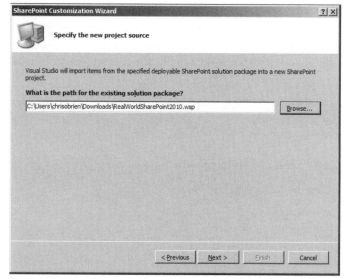

FIGURE 12-3: Selecting the .wsp file to import

6. Optionally, filter the contents to be imported into Visual Studio by deselecting Feature elements in the "Select items to import" dialog. Figure 12-4 shows how to filter the Feature elements during the import process.

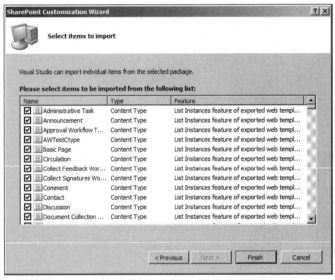

FIGURE 12-4: Filtering Feature elements to import

7. Click Finish in the "Select items to import" dialog. You can then use the Feature XML that was added to the project.

Of course, it's important to remember that saving a SharePoint site as a template only includes artifacts stored in the content database. Any filesystem customizations such as assemblies (for example, for web part code) or files in the SharePoint root (for example, for custom site definitions) are not included.

Keeping this point in mind, consider the following examples of items that can be packaged into Features easily with this method:

➤ Fields (site columns)

➤ Content types

➤ Web properties, including the following:

  ➤ Title, icon, and description

  ➤ Regional settings

  ➤ Theme

  ➤ Quick launch navigation customizations (for example, authored links)

> ➤ Site workflows
> ➤ Available page layouts/site templates

➤ List forms

➤ Event receivers

If the Include Content checkbox is checked on the "Save as Template" page, the following are also added to the `.wsp`:

➤ *Files* — These could include the following:

> ➤ "Content" files such as Office documents
> ➤ "Site infrastructure" files such as master pages, CSS, XSL, images, and so on (assuming that these files were stored in libraries within the site)
> ➤ Web part definition files (`.webpart`)

➤ *List instances* — These would include list items.

➤ *Property bag values* — These enable list items to be updated declaratively

Feature schema has been expanded in SharePoint 2010 to support site templates. Key additions include adding list event receivers to a specific list by URL (previously it was only possible to use a list template ID or content type ID), creating workflow associations, and also allowing property bag values on webs and list items to be set declaratively.

Although, perhaps, not *every* possible customization will be handled correctly by the "save as template/import WSP" method (particularly in the case of SPD); for the most part, this approach delivers an efficient way to "Featurize" many site changes. In particular, it's often possible to "round-trip" using this process during development — a site can be saved as a template, imported into Visual Studio for further customization, and then these further changes deployed to the original site.

In most cases, this process can be repeated as often as required while building the site, although a couple of things can get in the way. Custom field controls and workflow forms are examples. However, when using site templates and WSP import in this particular way, one behavior to look out for in particular with the process is that of customized files.

In SPD, when you are editing a file for the first time that was initially provisioned to the filesystem, from that point on, it becomes a "customized" file stored in the content database. When changes made in Visual Studio are redeployed to the original site, customized files will not reflect any changes. SharePoint will always retrieve the database version, rather than the filesystem version deployed by the WSP.

The only way to incorporate these changes is to create a new site from the template. Resetting the file or site to the site definition (known as "uncustomizing") is not an option, because this will revert files back to the site definition from which the original site was created, which will not contain any changes. If files in the new site subsequently become customized, the recommended approach is to manually synchronize the filesystem versions, and then reset to the site definition.

When importing a site template WSP, the process generates a Visual Studio project with many files — practically every piece of the original site will be in there somewhere. Frequently, this may not be ideal. If you already have one or more Visual Studio projects, it may be more appropriate to extract the Feature files for the artifacts you are specifically interested in, and incorporate these manually into an existing project. This can result in less "Feature bloat," because only required files are used. Additionally, if content was included in the site template, something to remember is that this content will overwrite the current site content whenever the WSP is deployed, which may be undesirable.

Following are two methods for extracting only the required Feature elements:

➤ *Use the dialog displayed by Visual Studio 2010 in the "import WSP process"* — This provides checkboxes to filter Feature elements. (Note that multiple items can be selected by pressing and holding the Ctrl key, and then clicking.)

➤ *Treat the generated Visual Studio project as a temporary working area* — You allow Visual Studio to import all Feature elements, and then you manually copy/paste the relevant Feature XML to the desired Visual Studio project.

 Note that, if artifacts are excluded using the first method, and if the site definition is retained, it will still contain references to all of the Feature elements in the WSP. A warning dialog is shown to inform you that some dependencies are not being imported. These references must be removed for the site definition to be valid.

In addition to "non-custom" artifacts being imported and issues when "round-tripping," SharePoint developers should take note of the following critical caveats with regard to the WSP import process:

➤ It is not supported to import SharePoint 2007 WSP files.

➤ The import process is not full-fidelity. Business Connectivity Services (BCS) entities, code workflows, list definitions, and site definitions are all examples of artifacts that may require modification to work correctly. (See the MSDN topic, "Importing Items from an Existing SharePoint Site," for a full list.)

➤ When web parts are included in an imported WSP, web part properties are stored in binary format. Although they can be subsequently deployed without errors, it does mean that they cannot be edited between the import and deployment.

Despite these caveats, use of site templates and Visual Studio's capability to import .wsp files can reduce initial development effort for some elements of a SharePoint site, and are worthy of consideration.

The next sections focus on later phases in the SharePoint application lifecycle and related considerations — how to upgrade and version an application.

UPGRADING A SHAREPOINT APPLICATION

This section examines two primary types of upgrading in SharePoint:

➤ Feature upgrades

➤ Artifact upgrades

Feature Upgrade in SharePoint 2010

Regardless of whether XML or code-centric Features were used in the initial build, adding new functionality to an existing SharePoint application is typically accomplished with further Feature development.

In SharePoint 2007, this was a somewhat complex landscape for developers. Although new Features could always be created and added to existing WSPs, developers were typically forbidden from updating existing Feature files that had been previously deployed. As a result, the API was the only supported means of enhancing an existing Feature with new functionality. In the absence of a formal location for such "upgrade code," Feature receivers were typically chosen as the most appropriate vehicle for changes. Overall, however, support for upgrading existing applications left much to be desired in SharePoint 2007.

To address these shortcomings, SharePoint 2010 introduces "versioned" Features. The option of creating brand new Features to deploy new functionality still exists, but when this isn't the most appropriate design choice, developers now have a clear path for upgrading existing Features by editing existing files in specific ways, and redeploying to create a new version.

Using this approach, Features can undergo multiple upgrade cycles throughout their lives. With each iteration, the version number of the Feature should be incremented. Table 12-2 shows the new Feature schema elements that support the artifact upgrade process.

TABLE 12-2: Feature XML Changes in SharePoint 2010

XML ELEMENT	DESCRIPTION
UpgradeActions	Parent element for defining provisioning upgrade steps. All subsequent XML elements in this table are children of UpgradeActions.
VersionRange	Defines the range of existing Feature versions to upgrade with the steps defined within this element. This has BeginVersion and EndVersion attributes. Enables a Feature to be repeatedly upgraded through its lifecycle.

continues

TABLE 12-2 *(continued)*

XML ELEMENT	DESCRIPTION
ApplyElementManifests	Allows new Feature elements to be added to an existing Feature. Items declared in the referenced element manifest files will be provisioned on upgrade.
AddContentTypeField	Provides a declarative shortcut for the common task of adding a field to an existing content type.
MapFile	Allows an uncustomized file (that is, one that is served from the web server filesystem, rather than from the content database) to be pointed to a new location.
CustomUpgradeAction	Provides a means of allowing custom code to execute during Feature upgrade. This allows the developer to handle advanced scenarios that cannot be dealt with by declarative XML alone.

In addition to the new XML elements, developers starting out with versioned Features should note the following:

➤ If the `Feature` node does not have a `Version` attribute, the Feature will default to version 0.0.0.0.

➤ The Visual Studio 2010 Feature designer support does not extend to upgrade elements. You must work with the XML by hand, but generally the "merge" capability in the Visual Studio SharePoint tools is sufficient to incorporate changes. (It is not necessary to take full control of the file and lose designer support.)

➤ There is no automatic triggering of Feature upgrade (for example, when a Feature is reactivated after redeploying a WSP). Instead, the developer is responsible for calling the `SPFeature.Upgrade()` method to ensure the Feature is upgraded.

➤ The `SPWebService`, `SPWebApplication`, `SPContentDatabase`, and `SPSite` objects have a `QueryFeatures()` method that is used to identify Features requiring upgrade. These methods return a collection of Features, and are typically used in conjunction with `SPFeature.Upgrade()`.

➤ Feature dependencies can be specified with a `MinimumVersion` attribute. This can be used to ensure depended-on artifacts are present.

An Example of Feature Upgrade

To understand a Feature upgrade, let's take a look at a fictional example. Let's say that the Adventure Works website specializes in providing travel information to young people. Several of the page components rely on SharePoint lists to store their data, and custom controls are generally used for presentation in the public view. One such list is the "tourist activities" list that is present in all "destination guide" webs within the site. Several SharePoint artifacts were provisioned to support the list with the following two Features:

➤ `TouristActivities_Site` — This includes a series of site columns to hold information about the activity and a "tourist activity" content type that uses the columns.

➤ `TouristActivities_Web` — This includes a list definition and a list instance.

Two Features must be used to deploy these artifacts, because some artifacts are Site-scoped and some are Web-scoped. After the initial development of these Features, in Visual Studio, the Feature Designer for the Site Feature looks like Figure 12-5.

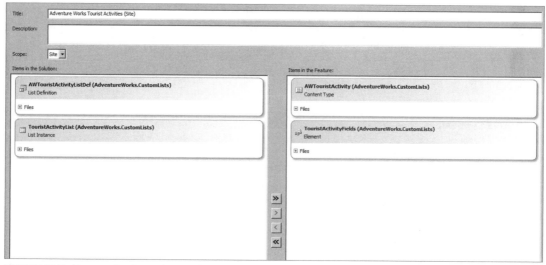

FIGURE 12-5: Feature Designer for the Site Feature

At this point, the manifest for the Site Feature looks like this:

```xml
<?xml version="1.0" encoding="utf-8"?>
<Feature xmlns="http://schemas.microsoft.com/sharepoint/"
    Title="Adventure Works Tourist Activities (Site)" Id=
    "cae1f65d-0365-42e9-9907-356c7983e902" Scope="Site">
  <ElementManifests>
    <ElementManifest Location="AWTouristActivity\Elements.xml" />
    <ElementManifest Location="TouristActivityFields\Elements.xml" />
  </ElementManifests>
```

Code file [597132_ch12_AccompanyingCode.zip] available for download at Wrox.com

At the same point, the Feature Designer for the Web Feature shown in Figure 12-6 displays the initial Web-scoped artifacts.

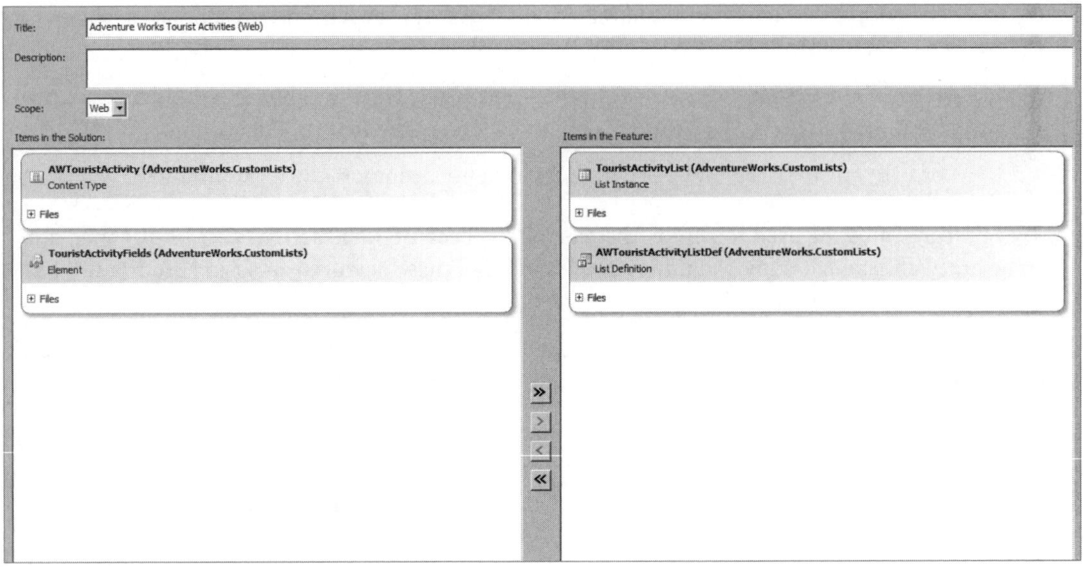

FIGURE 12-6: Web-scoped artifacts

The corresponding XML for the Web Feature is as follows:

```
<Feature xmlns="http://schemas.microsoft.com/sharepoint/
    " Title="Adventure Works Tourist Activities (Web)"
    Id="2c4eff13-48af-4dec-ada8-80688e172560" Scope="Web">
  <ActivationDependencies>
    <ActivationDependency FeatureId=
        "cae1f65d-0365-42e9-9907-356c7983e902"
        FeatureTitle="Adventure Works Tourist Activities (Site)" />
  </ActivationDependencies>
  <ElementManifests>
    <ElementManifest Location="TouristActivityList\Elements.xml" />
    <ElementManifest Location="AWTouristActivityListDef\Elements.xml" />
    <ElementFile Location="AWTouristActivityListDef\Schema.xml" />
  </ElementManifests>
</Feature>
```

The XML for the various artifacts is contained in the referenced element files, but the contents of these are not significant in terms of the upgrade process. In the site itself, an example of the resulting list instance (in the "United Kingdom" destination guide of the site) looks like Figure 12-7 (United Kingdom) and Figure 12-8 (London).

The artifacts supporting this functionality will now be upgraded over two upgrade iteration cycles, using declarative and imperative approaches.

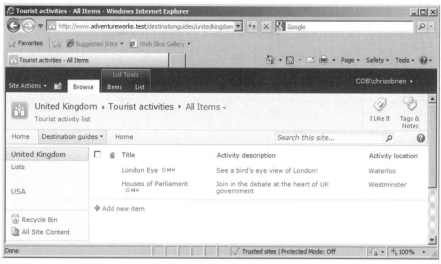

FIGURE 12-7: United Kingdom tourist activities

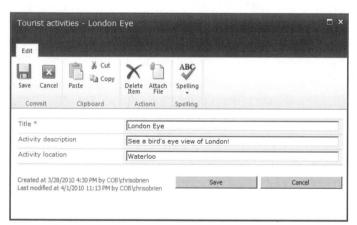

FIGURE 12-8: London tourist activities

Upgrading Features Using Declarative XML Elements

Several common upgrade scenarios can be achieved without code, using declarative XML added to the Feature. The following walkthrough of an upgrade iteration uses this approach. To facilitate new functionality being added to the "tourist activities" list, the following changes must be made to the provisioned artifacts:

➤ Provision two new site columns — a choice field named "Activity type" and a Yes/No (Boolean) field named "Free."

➤ Add the two columns to the "tourist activity" content type, ensuring that all existing list instances reflect this change.

The `ApplyElementManifest` and `AddContentTypeField` elements will be used in this upgrade cycle.

To implement these changes, the following steps are taken in Visual Studio.

To begin, you must add a new element manifest to the existing `TouristActivities_Site` Feature, and add appropriate XML to provision the new fields.

1. Right-click the project and select Add ⇨ New Item. Select the Empty Element project item and name it `TouristActivityFields_Iteration2`. (Note the 2 to distinguish from the other file defining the original fields.)

2. In the `elements.xml` file that is created, add XML for the new fields similar to the following:

```xml
<?xml version="1.0" encoding="utf-8"?>
<Elements>
  <Field Type="Choice" DisplayName="Activity type" Required="FALSE"
      EnforceUniqueValues="FALSE" Indexed="FALSE"
      Format="Dropdown" FillInChoice="FALSE"
      Group="Adventure Works Site Columns"
      ID="{B0DA8DBC-EFDC-46B0-A3EC-2EA80C483B8E}"
                  StaticName="ActivityType" Name="ActivityType"
          Overwrite="TRUE" xmlns="http://schemas.microsoft.com
          /sharepoint/">
    <Default>Unspecified</Default>
    <CHOICES>
      <CHOICE>Art</CHOICE>
      <CHOICE>Family</CHOICE>
      <CHOICE>Evening</CHOICE>
      <CHOICE>Unspecified</CHOICE>
    </CHOICES>
  </Field>
  <Field Type="Boolean" DisplayName="Free" EnforceUniqueValues="FALSE"
      Indexed="FALSE" Group="Adventure Works Site Columns"
      ID="{E167E082-F7F0-442A-A762-12F5680A3922}"
                  " StaticName="Free" Name="Free" Overwrite="TRUE"
              <Default>0</Default>
  </Field>
</Elements>
```

3. Ensure that the new element manifest was added to the correct Feature (the Site-scoped Feature) in the project. If not, use either the Feature Designer or Package Explorer view in Visual Studio to move the element to correct the Feature, and ensure it is not referenced by other Features.

Now, you must edit the Feature manifest to define the steps required to upgrade the Feature for this iteration. Follow these steps:

1. Open the Feature in the Visual Studio project and select the Manifest tab to open the XML view. Click the plus sign (+) next to Edit Options to expand the editable region, and then click the "Open in XML Editor" link to open the XML template file, which will be merged into the designer-managed XML.

2. Add a `Version` attribute to the `Feature` node with a value of `1.0.0.0`.

3. Add the following XML under the `Feature` node:

```
<UpgradeActions>
    <VersionRange BeginVersion="0.0.0.0" EndVersion="0.9.9.9">
        <ApplyElementManifests>
            <ElementManifest Location=
                "TouristActivitiesFields_Iteration2\Elements.xml" />
        </ApplyElementManifests>
        <AddContentTypeField ContentTypeId=
            "0x0100151d9a3e61f54b4b8629d1e0200a70ad"
            FieldId="{B0DA8DBC-EFDC-46B0-A3EC-2EA80C483B8E}" PushDown="TRUE" />
        <AddContentTypeField
            ContentTypeId="0x0100151d9a3e61f54b4b8629d1e0200a70ad"
            FieldId="{E167E082-F7F0-442A-A762-12F5680A3922}" PushDown="TRUE" />
    </VersionRange>
</UpgradeActions>
```

4. Ensure that the following is true about the `UpgradeActions` XML:

➤ The `Location` attribute of the `ElementManifest` element matches the location of the newly added `elements.xml` file. Because this file should now be referenced in the `ElementManifests` section in the merged XML in the Feature Designer, this line can be copied from there into the `UpgradeActions` XML to be certain.

➤ The `ContentTypeId` attributes match the ID of the content type to which the fields should be added.

➤ The `PushDown` attribute of the `AddContentTypeField` elements is set to `TRUE`. This ensures that when the new fields are added to the site content type, they are also added to the list content types found in any existing "tourist activity" list instances.

5. Right-click the project in Visual Studio and select Build to build the updated project, and then upgrade the package in SharePoint using `STSADM` or PowerShell.

 If you use a Visual Studio-based approach to upgrade the package (for example, the CKS:DEV toolkit provides this capability), by default, the conflict resolution process within Visual Studio 2010 deployment will delete existing list instances to reflect schema changes made in this iteration. This will cause data within lists deployed by the project to be lost. In this scenario, if no changes are being made to a list instance, this behavior can be avoided by finding the respective definition in the Visual Studio project, and setting the Deployment Conflict Resolution property to None in the Properties window.

At this point, the changes have been deployed to the local SharePoint instance, but in itself, this will not upgrade the Site Feature. To cause the upgrade to occur, the you must call `SPFeature.Upgrade()` on the Feature instance. For more detail on this, see the sidebar, "Triggering Feature Upgrades."

TRIGGERING FEATURE UPGRADES

Feature upgrade does not happen automatically when a new version of a Feature is deployed. This ensures a greater degree of control is afforded and different targets (for example, Sites/Webs) can be upgraded at different times, or some may be upgraded but not all. Perhaps surprisingly, there is no out-of-the-box user interface, STSADM command, or PowerShell cmdlet to upgrade Features. The only way is to use the API and call SPFeature.Upgrade() for each Feature instance to be upgraded.

Before running SPFeature.Upgrade(), you must identify Feature instances that require an upgrade. For example, in the case of a Web-scoped Feature, it could be that some webs require upgrade, but others have either already been processed, or should not have the new functionality.

You use the QueryFeatures() method to identify Features requiring an upgrade. It does this by comparing the current version number in the Feature definition file with that of each Feature instance currently deployed.

QueryFeatures() exists on different objects to locate Features requiring upgrade at different logical partitions within the farm. For example, SPWebService.QueryFeatures() can locate Features of all scopes across the farm, and SPContentDatabase .QueryFeatures() can locate all scopes within a specific database. The method also exists on SPWebApplication and SPSite. These methods can locate Features with a scope of Site or Web in the respective location. In all cases, a collection of Features is returned, with each SPFeature instance being in a suitable state to call SPFeature.Upgrade().

One option to help manage the Feature upgrade process is an Open Source solution written by the author of this chapter. This consists of custom application pages to provide a UI onto Feature upgrade, and also a PowerShell cmdlet. This tool is available at http://spfeatureupgrade.codeplex.com.

Once the Feature upgrade has run, each "tourist activities" list (and the associated content type) will contain the new fields, as shown in Figure 12-9.

When SPFeature.Upgrade() executes for a Feature, the provisioning instructions within the UpgradeActions are processed *in the order they are defined in the file*. This includes custom code referenced by the CustomUpgradeAction node, thus providing full control over the sequence of upgrade steps. The next part of this walkthrough examines the use of custom code in the upgrade process.

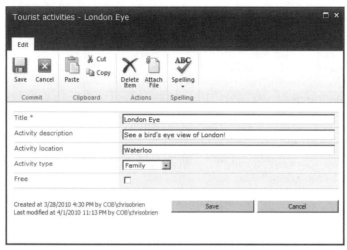

FIGURE 12-9: "Tourist activities" list with new fields

Upgrading Features Using the FeatureUpgrading Event

Aside from using declarative XML (such as with additional element manifests), the alternative technique for upgrading Features involves a Feature receiver to run code during the upgrade process. This approach is used wherever the desired changes cannot be accomplished by Feature XML alone. In practice, this will be the case for many permutations of an upgrade. To accomplish this, the developer must do the following:

➤ Add a `CustomUpgradeAction` element to the Feature definition.

➤ Implement code in the `FeatureUpgrading` event within the Feature receiver to process the upgrade.

The following walkthrough of an upgrade iteration uses this approach.

The content authors on the Adventure Works website are complaining that the description field for a "tourist activity" is too small, and that they cannot enter all the text they need to. Analysis reveals this is caused by the field being of type `Text` (that is, a single line of text) rather than `Note` (that is, multiple lines of text). The goal of this upgrade is to provide the content authors with a larger "Activity description" of type `Note`.

Such an upgrade scenario presents an interesting real-world challenge. It is typically unwise to attempt to change the type of a field that already exists and contains data. Consequently, the development team must be creative.

The solution is to provision a new field of the larger type, and then, for each list item in a "tourist activity" list, copy the data from the old field into the new. Clearly this requires more than just XML. The following steps will be used:

1. Provision a new site column of type `Note` named "Activity description" (with an internal name of `ActivityDescriptionLarge`). The `ApplyElementManifest` element will be used to do this on the Site-scoped Feature.

2. Use the `AddContentTypeField` element to add the column to the "Tourist activity" content type, ensuring that all existing list instances reflect this change.

3. Implement the `CustomUpgradeAction` element in the Web-scoped Feature manifest, specifying the name of the action to run in code.

4. Add code to the `FeatureUpgrading` event within the Feature receiver for the Web-scoped Feature to do the following:

    ➤ Copy list item values from the old activity description field to the new one.

    ➤ Mark the old field as hidden.

Note that changes are being made to both the Site- and Web-scoped Features in this iteration. New artifacts (fields) are being provisioned at the site level, but because the "tourist activity" list instances are present within multiple webs, the Web-scoped Feature will be upgraded to make the changes to each list.

To implement these changes, the following steps are taken in Visual Studio.

To begin, you must add a new element manifest to the existing `TouristActivities_Site` Feature, and add appropriate XML to provision the new field. Follow these steps:

1. Right-click the project and select Add ➪ New Item. Select the Empty Element project item and name it `TouristActivityFields_Iteration3`. (Note the 3 to distinguish from the files defining fields provisioned already.)

2. In the `elements.xml` file that is created, add XML for the new field similar to the following:

```xml
<?xml version="1.0" encoding="utf-8"?>
<Elements xmlns="http://schemas.microsoft.com/sharepoint/">
  <Field Type="Note" DisplayName="Activity description (large)"
      Required="FALSE" EnforceUniqueValues="FALSE"
      Indexed="FALSE" MaxLength="255"
        Group="Adventure Works Site Columns"
            ID="{BC994ADC-C7F2-404E-89C3-9B65275F3B42}"
            SourceID="http://schemas.microsoft.com/sharepoint/"
        StaticName="ActivityDescriptionLarge"
            Name="ActivityDescriptionLarge" Overwrite="TRUE"
            ShowAlways="True" xmlns="http://schemas.microsoft.com/
            sharepoint/" />
</Elements>
```

3. Again, ensure that the new element manifest was added to the Site-scoped Feature in the project. If not, use either the Feature Designer or Package Explorer view in Visual Studio to move the element to correct the Feature, and ensure that it is not referenced by other Features.

4. Edit the Site-scoped Feature manifest as before to define the steps specific to this iteration. Increment the `Version` attribute on the Feature to `2.0.0.0`. Add a new `VersionRange` element as a sibling of the one previously added. Ensure that it looks like the following:

```
<VersionRange BeginVersion="1.0.0.0" EndVersion="1.9.9.9">
    <ApplyElementManifests>
      <ElementManifest Location="TouristActivityFields_Iteration3\
          Elements.xml" />
    </ApplyElementManifests>
    <AddContentTypeField
        ContentTypeId="0x010073f25e2ac37846bb8e884770fb7307c7"
        FieldId="{BC994ADC-C7F2-404E-89C3-9B65275F3B42}" PushDown="TRUE" />
</VersionRange>
```

Now, you must edit the Web-scoped Feature manifest to define the steps required to upgrade the Feature for this iteration. Follow these steps:

1. Open the `TouristActivities_Web` Feature in the Visual Studio project and select the Manifest tab to open the XML view. Click the plus sign (+) next to Edit Options to expand the editable region, and then click the "Open in XML Editor" link to open the XML template file that will be merged into the designer-managed XML.

2. Because this Feature version has not yet been incremented, add a `Version` attribute on the Feature node with a value of `1.0.0.0`.

3. Add the following XML under the `Feature` node:

```
<VersionRange BeginVersion="0.0.0.0" EndVersion="0.9.9.9">
    <CustomUpgradeAction Name="MigrateToLargeDescriptionField">
      <Parameters>
        <Parameter Name="ContentTypeName">Tourist activity</Parameter>
        <Parameter Name="OldField">ActivityDescription</Parameter>
        <Parameter Name="NewField">ActivityDescriptionLarge</Parameter>
      </Parameters>
    </CustomUpgradeAction>
</VersionRange>
```

4. Ensure the following is true about the new `VersionRange` node:

➤ The `Location` attribute of the `ElementManifest` element matches the location of the newly added `elements.xml` file.

➤ The `ContentTypeId` attribute matches the ID of the content type to which the fields should be added, and the `PushDown` attribute is set to `TRUE`.

➤ The child elements of the `VersionRange` element are sequenced as `ApplyElementManifest`, `AddContentTypeField`, and `CustomUpgradeAction`.

Now, you must add code to the Web Feature receiver for the `CustomUpgradeAction`. Follow these steps:

1. If the `TouristActivities_Web` Feature does not yet have a Feature receiver, add one by right-clicking the Feature in Solution Explorer and selecting Add Event Receiver.

2. In the `receiver` class, add the following code to the `FeatureUpgrading` method:

```
public override void FeatureUpgrading
    (SPFeatureReceiverProperties properties,
    string upgradeActionName,
    System.Collections.Generic.IDictionary<string,
    string> parameters)
{
    SPWeb parentWeb = (SPWeb)properties.Feature.Parent;

    switch (upgradeActionName)
    {
        case "MigrateToLargeDescriptionField":
            string contentTypeName = parameters["ContentTypeName"];
            string oldFieldName = parameters["OldField"];
            string newFieldName = parameters["NewField"];

            List<SPField> fieldsToUpdate = new List<SPField>();

            // find all the lists in this web using the
            // 'Tourist Activity' content type..
            SPListCollection genericLists =
                parentWeb.GetListsOfType(SPBaseType.GenericList);
            foreach(SPList list in genericLists)
            {
                if (list.ContentTypes[contentTypeName] != null)
                {
                    // copy list data to new field..
                    foreach(SPListItem item in list.Items)
                    {
                        item[newFieldName] = item[oldFieldName];
                        item.SystemUpdate();
                    }

                    // mark old field as hidden..
                    SPField oldField = list.Fields.GetField(oldFieldName);
                    fieldsToUpdate.Add(oldField);
                }
            }

            foreach(SPField oldField in fieldsToUpdate)
            {
                oldField.Hidden = true;
                oldField.Update();
            }
            break;
        default:
            break;
    }
}
```

Code file [597132_ch12_AccompanyingCode.zip] available for download at Wrox.com

3. Right-click the project in Visual Studio and select Build to build the updated project, and then upgrade the package in SharePoint using STSADM or PowerShell.

Now, execute code to upgrade *both* the Site- and Web-scoped Features, in that order. Use the QueryFeatures() and SPFeature.Upgrade() methods to do this (See the "Triggering Feature Upgrades" sidebar for more information.)

Once the Feature upgrade has run for both Features, if it is successful, each "tourist activities" list will contain the new field, and any list items that had a value in the old "Activity description" field will have this value in the new larger replacement field. Figure 12-10 shows the result of a successful upgrade.

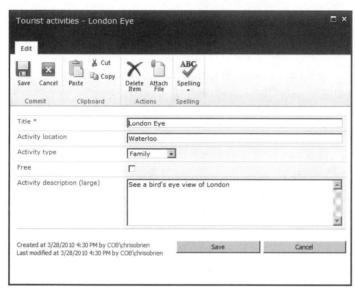

FIGURE 12-10: Successful upgrade

As this example shows, on each upgrade iteration, parameters can be passed from the CustomUpgradeAction XML element to the code, potentially giving a greater degree of flexibility than a hard-coded approach. In terms of structuring code within the FeatureUpgrading method, a Feature that undergoes many upgrade cycles will inevitably generate more and more code over time, and so it may be wise to factor code out into separate methods/classes. Fundamentally, however, it's likely that a switch statement will be employed somewhere to provide branching on the ActionName for each particular upgrade operation.

Considerations When Using Feature Upgrade

The following are points to consider when upgrading Features:

➤ *Logging is off by default* — The Feature upgrade framework performs some Unified Logging Service (ULS) logging, which may be useful when diagnosing issues, but it is not enabled by default. To see these messages, go to Diagnostic Logging in Central Administration, and, under the SharePoint Foundation category, set the following subcategories to Verbose:

  ➤ Feature Infrastructure

  ➤ Fields

  ➤ General

➤ *On the* `VersionRange` *element,* `BeginVersion` *is inclusive but* `EndVersion` *is not* — If there are Feature instances "in the wild" with a version of 1.0.0.0, these would not be captured by using, for example, `BeginVersion="0.0.0.0" EndVersion="1.0.0.0"`, but would be by using `BeginVersion="1.0.0.0" EndVersion="1.9.9.9"`.

➤ *All matching* `VersionRange` *elements are processed* — If multiple `VersionRange` elements are defined that match the version number of a Feature instance, each will be processed during upgrade. For example, if two `VersionRange` elements exist for `BeginVersion="1.0.0.0" EndVersion="1.9.9.9"` and `BeginVersion="1.0.0.0" EndVersion="3.0.0.0"`, the contents of both elements will be processed when that Feature instance is upgraded, in the order they are defined in the file.

➤ *Obey "Feature elements by scope" rules* — It appears that the logic SharePoint uses to upgrade Features is less tolerant than the logic for initial provisioning. As an example, it may be possible to define a Web-scoped Feature containing a content type (whereas the SharePoint SDK states that a content type is a Site-scoped element). Such a Feature may be successfully provisioned initially, but will not upgrade correctly. Developers must pay attention that Feature elements are added to Features of the correct scope to avoid such issues.

➤ *Design upgrade steps carefully* — One scenario to consider is where a Feature definition is upgraded several times (to version 3.0.0.0, for example), and is then activated for the first time on a particular target (for example, the web) at this version. Are all the upgrade steps executed during the activation phase?

For declarative steps such as newly added Feature element manifests, these are indeed processed, courtesy of the fact that when new manifests are added with `ApplyElementManifests` element, Visual Studio also adds them to the `ElementManifests` element. This is effectively what would happen if the manifest were being added during the initial design of the Feature.

Imperative steps in the `FeatureUpgrading` event work differently, however. These are not executed in a chain when a Feature is activated for the first time with an upgraded Feature definition. Consequently, if it is critical that this code executes, it may be necessary for the logic to be called from both the `FeatureActivated` and `FeatureUpgrading` methods.

This illustrates that testing must be performed against all the version scenarios that could be encountered before upgraded Feature definitions are deployed — a perfect example of one of the many complexities of upgrading live applications.

Upgrading Different Artifacts

Imagine a scenario where your SharePoint application has been live for a while now, and the client is asking for some changes. The site definition used as the template for new sites isn't quite right — new columns are needed on some key lists, and various list templates are in need of update. How would these upgrades be implemented?

Although SharePoint 2010's support for versioning Features and assemblies may provide the vehicle for deploying such changes (as discussed later in this chapter), the specifics of the upgrade steps for such a scenario often require a great deal of thought. Managing changes to SharePoint applications that are in use is complex. The key to identifying the steps required is to understand the nature of the artifacts that must be changed.

Declarative artifacts have different characteristics than provisioned artifacts, and typically the means of updating them involves updating one or more files in the SharePoint root. When the files are deployed using WSP packages, it is common practice to overwrite the file(s) on all servers in the farm by upgrading the WSP with a newer package.

Once a provisioned artifact has been provisioned into the Content Database, in most cases, the only way it can be updated (in a supported manner) is to use code to perform the update.

> *Declarative artifacts are typically updated by updating one or more files in the SharePoint root, such as a Feature elements file. Provisioned artifacts are typically updated by using code to modify the artifact instance within the content database.*

Table 12-3 considers a variety of declarative artifacts, and the exceptions to the defined rules. Table 12-4 provides information about provisioned artifacts.

TABLE 12-3: Declarative Artifacts in SharePoint 2010

ARTIFACT	NOTES
Site definition	Site definitions should not be modified once in use. Instead, use Features and/or Feature upgrade.
List definition	Changes to `schema.xml` for a list definition in use may work, but are not recommended. It may be more appropriate to deploy a new list definition and mark the old one as hidden.
Control (delegate control)	Simple file update.
Custom Action	Simple file update.
Feature staple	Simple file update.
Layout page	Simple file update.
Workflow template	Simple file update.

TABLE 12-4: Provisioned Artifacts in SharePoint 2010

ARTIFACT	NOTES
Content type	Use the API or `AddContentTypeField` (for new fields).
Module	Use the API to update a list item, but a simple file update can be used to update a file if the file was deployed with `GhostableInLibrary="True"`. Also, the `MapFile` element can be used within a Feature to re-point the file reference.
Web part	Use API.
Field	Use API.
List instance	Use API.
List view	Use API.
Event receiver registration	Use API.
Timer job registration	Use API.
Content type binding	Use API.
Document converter	Use API.

With this information in mind, it is clear that the upgrade of many declarative artifacts can be accomplished by simply overwriting the appropriate file(s). Because this must be done on all web servers in the farm, the upgrade or deployment of a WSP containing an updated version of the file(s) is the way to do this. So long as the application pool is recycled, the changes will be reflected immediately in such cases.

However, other artifacts are more complex to upgrade, particularly provisioned artifacts. In these cases, code must be written to modify the artifact in the content database. In SharePoint 2010 development, implementing this code in the `FeatureUpgrading` event of the appropriate Feature (as shown in the earlier example) is a good choice.

The list of permutations of possible upgrades to a SharePoint application is a very long list indeed. After all, many different artifacts can all be modified in different ways. Once the artifacts to update have been identified, the next step is to understand the "upgrade characteristics" of each artifact and whether or not they are provisioned into the Content Database. This is the information needed to establish how to leverage Solution and Feature upgrade to implement the required changes.

ASSEMBLY VERSIONING IN A SHAREPOINT APPLICATION

This section examines versioning in a SharePoint application, with particular attention paid to the following:

➤   Versioning of .NET assemblies

➤   Using the `BindingRedirect` element in a WSP manifest

➤   Versioning strategies

Versioning of .NET Assemblies

In comparison to many .NET or Java projects, a common characteristic of SharePoint projects is a lower level of maturity in terms of ALM processes. A classic example of this is assembly versioning practices. Many development teams on other platforms have established tried-and-tested guidelines for developers to use when deciding whether to increment the version number of an assembly.

Yet, this is rarely the case in SharePoint. Instead, it is common for assemblies to remain at version 1.0.0.0 after many iterations of development, which means that the assembly version effectively bears no relation to the assembly contents. This presents several potential issues:

➤   It is difficult or impossible to identify the version of code in a particular assembly. Techniques such as reflection must be used to reverse-engineer code.

➤   There is a greater likelihood of breaking changes. If a member is removed from a class in a shared assembly, any clients that are not recompiled to deal with this change will fail (for example, with a `MissingMethodException`). Effectively, all clients are directed to use the same version of the assembly, which is unlikely to permanently be compatible with all clients in an enterprise application.

➤   There is a greater likelihood of a shared assembly being unwittingly removed when a client application is being removed. Although SharePoint 2010 still does not provide a framework for dealing with this scenario, the risk is worsened when administrators have no indication of the version of a shared assembly to help them understand which clients might rely on it.

In summary, these represent a return to the symptoms of "DLL hell" that .NET's introduction of the Global Assembly Cache (GAC) and side-by-side execution was designed to solve.

Perhaps the most likely reason for the historic lack of versioning in SharePoint applications is that full assembly names (for example, `MyCompany.MyAssembly, Version=1.0.0.0, Culture=neutral, PublicKeyToken=xxxxxxxxxxxx`) tend to be used in many places in SharePoint, and, therefore, are stored in many configuration and Content Databases with no easy way to update these references. The following are examples of where four-part assembly names might appear in SharePoint:

➤   Assembly references in `.master`/`.aspx`/`.ascx` files

➤   Workflow definitions

➤   Event receiver definitions

➤   SafeControl entries in web.config

➤   Web part definitions (.webpart files)

For many of these definitions, the full assembly name is stored in the database for each instance of a definition in each site (for example, one for every event receiver defined). Quite clearly, it would not be an easy task to manage the process of updating these references if assembly versions were incremented regularly. A more realistic alternative would be to use the .NET capability of being able to redirect the assembly loading process to a different version than that initially requested by the application.

This allows an administrator, for example, to specify that the most recent version of an assembly be used, regardless of the version the application was actually compiled against. This is accomplished by use of the BindingRedirect element in the application configuration file, and, in fact, it was entirely possible to use this technique in earlier versions of SharePoint. This was not widely known, possibly because there was little support for implementing it.

In effect, the issue preventing its use in SharePoint 2007 was that the WSP framework did not support it, and, therefore, web.config files on each Web Front-End (WFE) had to be edited by hand to add the BindingRedirect entries. Needless to say, this manual approach did not constitute a mature ALM process.

The only alternative was to use the SPWebConfigModification class to try to automate the web.config changes, though this was more complex than it should have been. Happily, the SharePoint team has now added support for binding redirects in the WSP framework, meaning that robust assembly versioning practices can now be enjoyed by SharePoint projects with little effort. Let's take a look at how this works in practice.

 Unfortunately, you may encounter issues in versioning assemblies in sand-boxed solutions using the technique described here. See the section, "ALM and Sandboxed Solutions," later in this chapter for more information and alternative approaches.

Using the BindingRedirect Element in a WSP Manifest

To ensure the .NET run time loads the desired version of a particular assembly, an entry such as the following is required in the web.config file (with the sample values replaced as appropriate):

```
<dependentAssembly>
        <assemblyIdentity name="MyCompany.MyAssembly"
            publicKeyToken="xxxxxxxxxxx" culture="neutral" />
        <bindingRedirect oldVersion="1.0.0.0" newVersion="2.0.0.0" />
</dependentAssembly>
```

In the XML structure, the dependentAssembly element is a child of runtime/assemblyBinding. When this instruction is specified for an assembly, all references to the old version(s) are redirected to the new version. Notably, it is possible to specify a range in the oldVersion attribute (for example, oldVersion="0.0.0.1-1.0.0.0").

The SharePoint 2010 WSP framework facilitates easily adding binding redirect entries like these into the web.config file for your web application. In much the same way as with SafeControl entries, if the entry is added to the manifest.xml file for the WSP, at deployment time it is automatically pushed out to the relevant web.config file on each server in the farm. When the WSP is retracted, the entry is removed.

> *Binding redirects are added to WSP packages by manually editing the manifest XML. Designer support in Visual Studio 2010 Tools for SharePoint does not extend to this scenario.*

The following steps (in Visual Studio) describe the process for versioning an assembly in SharePoint and ensuring that the appropriate binding redirect is deployed:

1. Increment the assembly version number by editing the project properties, or by editing the AssemblyInfo.cs file directly.

2. Open the package for the project that deploys the assembly being versioned (typically the same project) by expanding the Package node and double-clicking the Package.package child node.

3. Click the Manifest tab to view the XML that is being generated by Visual Studio. In the top pane (which shows the preview XML), copy the Assembly element node for the assembly to the clipboard. This should look something like the following:

```
<Assembly Location="AdventureWorks.Data.dll"
        DeploymentTarget="GlobalAssemblyCache" />
```

4. Click the "Open in XML Editor" link between the two panes.

5. Edit the Package.Template.xml file to add an Assemblies element as a child of Solution. Within the start/end tags of the Assemblies element, paste the Assembly node copied earlier.

6. Open up the Assembly tag by removing the self-closing end tag. The binding redirect details are added below the Assembly element, so that the Assembly element looks like the following (where 1.0.0.0 is the old version number):

```
<Assembly Location="AdventureWorks.Data.dll"
        DeploymentTarget="GlobalAssemblyCache">
    <BindingRedirects>
      <BindingRedirect OldVersion="1.0.0.0" />
    </BindingRedirects>
  </Assembly>
```

7. Build the package by right-clicking the project in Solution Explorer and selecting Package. When the resulting WSP is deployed to SharePoint, a dependentAssembly element containing the binding redirect will be added to the application's web.config file (including extended web applications). All requests for the old version of the assembly (or for every version in the range, if a range is specified) will be redirected to the current version, as deployed by the WSP.

Although this is hugely significant for ALM and SharePoint, developers should be aware that, in some scenarios, extra configuration work must be done when versioning assemblies.

Although binding redirects can now easily be added to `web.config` files, not all SharePoint code runs within the web application. For example, if a versioned assembly is called from a timer job, binding redirects in a `web.config` file will not have any effect, and code is likely to fail. This is because `web.config` is only pertinent to the `w3wp.exe` process (more specifically, to an IIS web application or directory hosted by `w3wp.exe`), whereas timer jobs run in the `owstimer.exe` process.

Table 12-5 shows some examples of SharePoint code hosted by other processes.

TABLE 12-5: Code Outside Scope of Binding Redirects Deployed by WSP Framework

CODE	HOST PROCESS	NOTES
Timer jobs	`14\BIN\OWSTIMER.EXE`	—
Workflows	`14\BIN\OWSTIMER.EXE` (typically)	Workflows can be hosted by different processes. `w3wp.exe` and `owstimer.exe` are commonly used, but custom processes (for example, a console application) are other possibilities.
Sandbox solutions	`14\UserCode\ SPUCHostService.exe`	Binding redirects *do* work in the sandbox, but not via binding redirects in `web.config`.
STSADM commands	`14\BIN\STSADM.exe`	—
PowerShell	`PowerShell.exe`	PowerShell has the capability of loading specific versions of assemblies, meaning that binding redirects are not necessarily required.

If you are writing code that will be hosted in one or more of these host processes, any binding redirects must be manually added to the appropriate file(s) on each SharePoint web server. Following are the available options:

➤ Add the entries to the configuration file for each process where the code may execute (for example, `owstimer.exe.config` for timer jobs).

➤ Add the entries to `machine.config`, giving them scope over all processes running on the machine. Although this may be useful, note that server administrators may have policies that forbid using this option because of its global nature.

In summary, although the SharePoint 2010 WSP framework is not capable of placing binding redirects in all the locations they may be required, the capability to easily deal with the most common case (`web.config` files) is a big win for SharePoint developers. The door is now open to using real versioning practices in SharePoint, and this is a big step forward for non-trivial SharePoint applications.

Versioning Strategies in SharePoint Applications

Managing the lifecycle of a live SharePoint application that is incrementally updated with new functionality is complex. With the advent of versioned Features and increased support for versioned assemblies, SharePoint 2010 provides more options in this space than before, but clearly there are new decisions to be made. This is especially the case for teams that haven't used .NET assembly versioning in the past.

Following are some key questions to keep in mind in this area:

➤ What do the four parts of the version number mean?

➤ How do I decide which part(s) to increment?

➤ What is the difference between `AssemblyVersion` and `AssemblyFileVersion`?

➤ Do the same guidelines apply for incrementing assembly version numbers and Feature version numbers?

➤ Should Feature versions and assembly versions be kept in sync?

➤ If you are only adding new XML to a Feature, but no code, should you still increment the version number?

Ultimately, it's probably fair to say that the only critical thing is that version numbers be incremented in *some* way. However, when version numbers are being incremented consistently to the same plan by all team members, the benefits are greater, and overall complexity to the team is lower. A good way to establish a versioning strategy for SharePoint applications is to first derive guidelines for versioning assemblies, and then consider the strategy for Feature versions.

Assembly Versioning

As a fundamental, it's important to remember that .NET uses the assembly version when deciding which assembly to bind to. Specifically, this is the `AssemblyVersion` attribute. (Notably, the "sister" attribute of `AssemblyFileVersion` is not used whatsoever in the assembly loading process, but does provide an alternate place to "document" the assembly version.)

Following are some key reasons to version assemblies in .NET:

➤ To enable multiple versions of the same code to co-exist (side-by-side execution)

➤ To make it possible to easily identify which version of code is contained within

When proper versioning is not in place, and the version number provides no clue as to the assembly contents, the most common developer recourse is to disassemble the code and visually check using a tool such as Reflector. Of course, this is an extremely poor form of tracking!

It would be much better to combine an agreed versioning plan with some form of documentation (Excel, Team Foundation Server, and so on) capturing key changes between versions. With this in place, teams are able to quickly understand which code is in which file without having to disassemble.

With these fundamental drivers in mind, each team (or individual) must establish an assembly versioning strategy that makes the most sense for them. The four parts of a version number based on the `System.Version` class (such as Feature and assembly version numbers) are *Major.Minor.Build. Revision.*

Arguably, the most common strategy is to use the "change severity" as a guide to deciding which part(s) to increment. Here, the bigger the change, the further to the left is the number that is incremented. Whenever a number part is incremented, all digits to the right are reset to zero. Table 12-6 covers some examples, assuming a starting version of 1.0.0.0.

TABLE 12-6: Deciding Which Part of an Assembly Version Number to Increment

EXAMPLE OF CHANGE	NEW ASSEMBLY VERSION NUMBER
Adding some internal code (for example, logging) to a class, with no change to signature	1.0.0.1
Adding a new member to an existing class	1.0.1.0
Adding a new class to a namespace	1.1.0.0
Removing a class or public/protected class member	2.0.0.0

This approach is solid, and is the strategy of choice for many teams. However, other approaches may provide greater benefit. In particular, when automated builds are used, it is common to "need more" from the assembly version.

Other strategies may use one or more parts to convey things such as the following:

➤ Whether this version is part of shipping/internal release (for example, for a product)

➤ The sprint or iteration

➤ Changeset number from source control (though beware — each part is a 16-bit number with a maximum value of 65535, and a mature source control environment may have higher changeset numbers)

➤ The date/time the assembly was built (for example, when assemblies are being built several times per day/week)

Needless to say, many other possibilities exist, and each development team must decide what is right for it. For SharePoint development, it may be useful to also consider the strategy for Feature versioning in parallel, particularly in environments where there isn't an established regime for versioning assemblies (for example, because of the difficulties of versioning in SharePoint 2007).

Feature Versioning

The drivers for versioning Features are similar, but not quite the same. Remember that the Feature version number *must* be incremented in order for Feature upgrade to do anything when

`SPFeature.Upgrade()` is called. There is no "do nothing" approach if the upgrade framework is to be leveraged. This means that teams may be forced to version Features where they chose not to version assemblies.

Interestingly, the "side-by-side" aspect applies to Features as it does assemblies, but in a different way. Consider the scenario of a new version of a Site- or Web-scoped Feature being deployed throughout a large farm. It may be desirable to stagger this upgrade so that the rollout is controlled. Perhaps some sites should not receive the upgraded Feature at all. In cases such as this, the Feature version number is the key to tracking which version of a particular Feature is being used where in a SharePoint farm.

In terms of strategies for Feature version numbers, the following should be considered:

➤ Feature upgrade is always triggered when `SPFeature.Upgrade()` runs if *any* part of the version number has been incremented.

➤ Feature version numbers should not be tied to assembly version numbers. (Assembly version numbers may be incremented when code changes, but there may be no Feature changes in that iteration.)

➤ If change severity is being used as the basis for assembly versioning, consider adopting a similar approach for Feature versioning.

➤ If other assembly versioning plans are used (such as incorporating the sprint/iteration number), this may similarly provide the best basis for Feature versions.

If you plan to increment Feature version numbers depending on change severity, Table 12-7 provides some example scenarios.

TABLE 12-7: Deciding Which Part of a Feature Version Number to Increment

EXAMPLE OF CHANGE	NEW FEATURE VERSION NUMBER
Changing a display name of the Feature or an artifact	1.0.0.1
Adding a new artifact to an existing Feature	1.0.1.0
Modifying a template artifact (for example, a list definition)	1.1.0.0
Removing an artifact from a Feature, or any other major change (for example, one that would cause a dependent Feature to break)	2.0.0.0

ALM AND SANDBOXED SOLUTIONS

There are some important differences when dealing with lifecycle management issues with sandboxed solutions (as opposed to farm solutions, which are the main focus of this chapter). These can be broken down into the following areas.

Solution Upgrade Model

Perhaps the most immediate difference is that the semantics for upgrading solution packages are different in the sandbox. When an upgrade is performed on a sandboxed solution (for example, with `Update-SPUserSolution` or `STSADM -o upgradesolution`), SharePoint mandates that the filename of the WSP is changed, and uses the solution ID internally to tie together different versions of the same package. This is likely to be related to the fact that the Solution Gallery is, of course, a SharePoint list (which does not allow multiple items with the same name), and the designers may have wished to avoid using list item versioning for solutions.

Therefore, you should use a suitable naming convention when renaming sandboxed solutions — simply appending a version number and/or release date would be an appropriate starting point.

Feature Upgrade

When using the Feature upgrade framework in the sandbox, things work differently here, too. Earlier in this chapter, you learned how `SPFeature.Upgrade()` can be used in conjunction with the `QueryFeatures()` methods to selectively upgrade certain Feature instances. This isn't the case in sandboxed solutions. When this type of WSP is upgraded, if the version number for a Feature definition has been incremented, all associated Feature instances are upgraded automatically at this time. There is no need to run `SPFeature.Upgrade()` as a separate step, and it is, therefore, not possible to be selective in the upgrade process.

Assembly Versioning

Unfortunately, performing assembly versioning with certain assemblies appears to cause issues in sandboxed solutions (in the initial release of SharePoint 2010 at least — the situation may be subsequently improved by updates released by Microsoft). Specifically, it is not recommended that assemblies containing web parts (or other ASP.Net controls) are versioned in the manner described in this chapter (that is, by incrementing the `FileVersion` attribute). This will cause pages hosting the web part or control to fail, even when required configuration such as appropriate `SafeControl` and `BindingRedirect` entries are in place.

An alternative approach in this scenario would be to increment the `FileAssemblyVersion` attribute of the assembly. Because this value is not used when .NET loads the assembly, it is safe to modify this value to document the assembly version. This approach is also appropriate in sandboxed solutions, because many of the benefits of true assembly versioning (such as side-by-side execution) do not apply here.

SUMMARY

Managing the overall lifecycle of a SharePoint 2010 application is easier than in previous releases. There is better support for upgrade scenarios and more formal patterns for developers to use.

During the initial build of a SharePoint application where Features are used to package functionality, a decision must be made as to whether Features will be predominantly XML or code-based.

Although this is not new to many SharePoint developers, in SharePoint 2010, this may influence patterns used later on when the time comes to upgrade Features. If code is used initially, this is most likely also the best approach for an upgrade. Ultimately, however, most complex upgrade scenarios can only be accomplished with code in any case.

The new capability of being able to build up a site in the browser and/or, to a certain extent, in SPD, and then save the site as a `.wsp` (which can be imported by Visual Studio 2010), is likely to prove useful in the initial build. Although the result is not in the easiest form to work with, this technique *can* be useful to selectively obtain the Feature XML for individual artifacts. The Feature XML schema has been expanded in SharePoint 2010 to facilitate this capability, with new XML elements for event receivers, property bag configuration, web templates, and more. Developers must remember that the WSP import capability cannot be used with SharePoint 2007 WSPs.

Later in the application lifecycle, Feature upgrade provides the framework to make changes to artifacts that already exist in the website. The new `UpgradeActions` element contains the changes to be made, and `ApplyElementManifests` and `AddContentTypeField` can deal with many common upgrade scenarios. When the change being made does not match up with any of the provided XML elements, it's time to shell out to C# code. The `CustomUpgradeActions` element allows details to be passed to the new `FeatureUpgrading` method. In here, any custom upgrade logic to suit the requirements can be added, thus providing a more suitable location for upgrade code than existed in the SharePoint 2007 API.

In addition to Feature versioning, SharePoint 2010 adds better support for versioning of assemblies. The WSP framework now has the capability to add `bindingRedirect` entries to all `web.config` files for a web application within the farm. This opens the door to proper assembly versioning in SharePoint, meaning that teams can benefit from better understanding and control of how changes to their application are managed. Some consideration of strategies for versioning Feature and assembly versions should be given to get the most benefit.

ABOUT THE AUTHOR

Chris O'Brien (MCSD.NET, MCTS, MVP) is an independent SharePoint consultant with more than ten years of experience working with complex projects on Microsoft technologies. O'Brien is still very much a hands-on developer, and has led several large-scale web initiatives, including e-commerce, WCM, intranet, back-end integration, and workflow projects. Past clients include BP, Microsoft, London's Metropolitan Police Service, the Ministry of Defence (UK), Northern Ireland government, and Standard Chartered Bank. With a background in ASP.NET/Content Management Server/Commerce Server, O'Brien's work often involves building public-facing websites on SharePoint.

In addition to his day job, O'Brien runs a highly regarded blog focused on the development aspects of SharePoint at www.sharepointnutsandbolts.com, and has created several popular community tools such as the SharePoint Content Deployment Wizard. O'Brien is also a regular speaker at the UK SharePoint user group, and is based in London, England.

13

Using Silverlight 4 with SharePoint 2010

By Karine Bosch

Released in April 2010, Silverlight 4 is an exciting and promising new technology. Silverlight is a browser plug-in that runs on the client and can render animations, audio, and video. To shorten the learning curve for the developer, Silverlight exposes a subset of the .NET Framework, but it is also able to execute JavaScript and interact with other elements on the HTML page.

SharePoint 2010 is tightly integrated with the familiar Microsoft Office applications and provides a consistent user experience that simplifies how people interact with content, processes, and business data. It offers a robust, out-of-the-box functionality to create large intranets, extranets, and public-facing sites.

Silverlight is heavily integrated in SharePoint 2010, and the client object model makes it easy to manage SharePoint data from within Silverlight.

In this chapter, you learn how to build a Silverlight application that displays items from a SharePoint list in a scrolling marquee, as shown in Figure 13-1. The first sample Silverlight application is hosted from within a web part. Later, you learn how to add the Silverlight application to the master page.

FIGURE 13-1: The Silverlight News Banner

You also learn how to build a custom field type and an application page to make managing SharePoint list items easier. Later in this chapter, you learn how the same Silverlight application can also be used to render the list items from an external list.

The last example shows how you can also host a Silverlight application from within a sandboxed solution.

This chapter walks you through these examples and explains the different possibilities for how Silverlight applications can play a functional role in SharePoint.

THE SILVERLIGHT NEWS BANNER

The first sample application shows a simple Silverlight application that retrieves data from a SharePoint list containing news items, and displays them in an attractive way. The news items will continuously scroll over the page.

> *The file* `Sample 1 - News Banner.zip` *available for download at* www.wrox.com *contains the source code for both the Silverlight application and the SharePoint list definition in this example.*

In this first example, the Silverlight application is hosted in the Silverlight Web Part, an out-of-the-box web part that comes with SharePoint 2010. Figure 13-2 shows this web part hosting the scrolling news banner.

FIGURE 13-2: The Silverlight Web Part hosting the scrolling news banner

You can create simple Silverlight applications using Visual Studio 2010. For more advanced Silverlight applications, I recommend that you use Expression Blend. Expression Blend has the advantage of providing the capability to design more complex user interfaces, and then export them to Visual Studio 2010 to add the necessary functionality. In Visual Studio 2010, you can then choose the Silverlight Application project template.

The main user control in this Silverlight application is very simple. It contains a canvas with a StackPanel control 600 pixels wide and 150 pixels high. This stack panel will be populated with a number of custom controls, each representing a news item in a SharePoint list.

Neither the Silverlight control nor the canvas have an initial width or height set because you want the Silverlight application to resize based on the width and height attributed to the SharePoint web part. The RenderTransform element will take care of the scaling when resizing takes place.

A Storyboard will make the news item controls scroll over the screen and the clip region will make sure that the moving StackPanel control will not be visible outside the canvas.

```xml
<Canvas x:Name="LayoutRoot" Background="White">
    <Canvas.RenderTransform>
        <TransformGroup>
            <ScaleTransform x:Name="RootScale" CenterX="0" CenterY="0" />
            <TranslateTransform x:Name="RootTranslate" />
        </TransformGroup>
    </Canvas.RenderTransform>

    <Canvas.Resources>
        <Storyboard x:Name="MarqueeAnimation"
                    Storyboard.TargetProperty="(Canvas.Left)"
                    RepeatBehavior="Forever" >
            <DoubleAnimation x:Name="MarqueeDoubleAnimation"
                             Storyboard.TargetName="NewsItemPanel"
                             From="600" To="-70" Duration="0:0:07"  />
        </Storyboard>
    </Canvas.Resources>

    <Canvas.Clip>
        <RectangleGeometry Rect="0,0,600,150" />
    </Canvas.Clip>

    <StackPanel x:Name="NewsItemPanel" Orientation="Horizontal"
        Width="600" Height="150">

    </StackPanel>
</Canvas>
```

The Silverlight application in this example retrieves items from a SharePoint list. The name of the SharePoint list will be passed to the Silverlight application from within the web part, and retrieved from the InitParams dictionary when the Silverlight application loads.

```csharp
private void Application_Startup(object sender, StartupEventArgs e)
{
    if (e.InitParams != null)
    {
        if (e.InitParams.ContainsKey("list"))
        {
            ListName = e.InitParams["list"].Replace("%20", " ");
        }
    }
}
```

The `ListName` variable has been declared as a public static variable to make it accessible from within the Silverlight controls in this application:

```
public static string ListName = null;
```

When the Silverlight application loads, the canvas is resized to meet the size of the web part hosting the Silverlight application, and an event handler is added to the `SizeChanged` event to resize the canvas when the size of the web part changes.

```
public MainPage()
{
    InitializeComponent();

    ResizeCanvas();
    this.SizeChanged += new SizeChangedEventHandler(MainPage_SizeChanged);
}

void MainPage_SizeChanged(object sender, SizeChangedEventArgs e)
{
    ResizeCanvas();
}

private void ResizeCanvas()
{
    if (App.Current.Host.Content.ActualWidth > 0)
    {
        double width = App.Current.Host.Content.ActualWidth;

        LayoutRoot.Width = width;
        NewsItemPanel.Width = width;
        // resize CanvasRectGeometry
        CanvasRectGeometry.Rect = new Rect(0, 0, width, 150);

        // reset the begin of the scrolling animation
        DoubleAnimation doubleAnimation =
            (DoubleAnimation)this.FindName("MarqueeDoubleAnimation");
        if (doubleAnimation != null)
        {
            doubleAnimation.From = App.Current.Host.Content.ActualWidth;
        }
    }
}
```

The list items are retrieved using the Silverlight client object model. Therefore, you must add a reference to the following assemblies:

➤   `Microsoft.SharePoint.Client.Silverlight.dll`

➤   `Microsoft.SharePoint.Client.Silverlight.Runtime.dll`

Both assemblies are located in the `14\TEMPLATE\LAYOUTS\ClientBin` folder of the SharePoint root.

Calls to the SharePoint server using the Silverlight client object model execute asynchronously, and on a different thread. Therefore, you must first capture the current SynchronizationContext to ensure that you can come back on the UI thread.

```
public MainPage()
{
    InitializeComponent();

    ResizeCanvas();
    this.SizeChanged += new SizeChangedEventHandler(MainPage_SizeChanged);
    uiThread = System.Threading.SynchronizationContext.Current;
    if (uiThread == null)
        uiThread = new System.Threading.SynchronizationContext();
    PopulateNewsBanner();
}
```

The uiThread variable is declared as a class-level variable of type SynchronizationContext residing in the System.Threading namespace:

```
private System.Threading.SynchronizationContext uiThread;
```

The code also contains a property for the client context. The client context is the starting point for the communication between Silverlight and SharePoint, and is located in the Microsoft.SharePoint.Client namespace. On certain occasions, you can use ClientContext.Current, instead of passing in the URL to the SharePoint site. This is explained later when you learn about hosting the Silverlight application within the out-of-the-box Silverlight Web Part.

```
private ClientContext clientContext;
private ClientContext ClientCtxt
{
    get
    {
        if (clientContext == null)
            clientContext = ClientContext.Current;

        if (clientContext == null)
            throw new Exception("Connection failed!");

        return clientContext;
    }
}
```

The PopulateNewsBanner method retrieves the list items from the SharePoint list. First, the list is retrieved using the GetByTitle method of the client object model. The list name is passed in when the Silverlight application loads. This method is available on the Lists collection of the Web object of the current client context.

The news items themselves are retrieved by means of a CamlQuery object. The ViewXml property can be used to specify a sort order and/or filter criteria. In the first instance in this example, only a sort order is set, and all items will be retrieved. The GetItems method is then executed using the CamlQuery object. The Load method of the client context is used to specify which columns of the list items will be returned. This allows you to limit the data returned over the wire. In this example, columns like the title, the body, the publish date, and the picture URL are retrieved.

The `ExecuteQueryAsync` method of client context is responsible for starting the call to the server. Because this method runs asynchronously, you must specify two methods on which the call can come back when it returns from the server — one method for when the call returns successfully, and one method for when the call to the server failed.

```
private void PopulateNewsBanner()
{
    newsList = ClientCtxt.Web.Lists.GetByTitle(App.ListName);
    CamlQuery camlQuery = new CamlQuery();

    camlQuery.ViewXml = "<View><Query><OrderBy>"
        + "<FieldRef Name='PublishDate' Ascending='False' />"
        + "<FieldRef Name='Title' />"
        + "</OrderBy></Query></View>";
    listItems = newsList.GetItems(camlQuery);
    ClientCtxt.Load(listItems,
        items => items.Include(
            item => item["Title"],
            item => item["Body"],
            item => item["PublishDate"],
            item => item["PictureURL"]
            ));

    ClientCtxt.ExecuteQueryAsync(
        HandleClientRequestSucceeded, HandleClientRequestFailed);
}
```

If you want to retrieve all list items that have been published before today and that are not expired, you can add a `<Where>` clause within the `<Query>` node of the `ViewXml` property.

```
private void PopulateNewsBanner()
{
    web = ClientCtxt.Web;
    ClientCtxt.Load(web);

    newsList = ClientCtxt.Web.Lists.GetByTitle(App.ListName);
    CamlQuery camlQuery = new CamlQuery();

    camlQuery.ViewXml = "<View><Query>"
        + "<OrderBy>"
        + "    <FieldRef Name='PublishDate' Ascending='False' />"
        + "    <FieldRef Name='Title' />"
        + "</OrderBy>"
        + "<Where>"
        + "    <And>"
        + "        <Leq><FieldRef Name='PublishDate'/>"
        + "            <Value Type='DateTime' IncludeTimeValue=
                        'FALSE'><Today /></Value>"
        + "        </Leq>"
        + "        <Or>"
        + "            <Geq><FieldRef Name='ExpirationDate' />"
```

```
      + "               <Value Type='DateTime' IncludeTimeValue=
                              'FALSE'><Today /></Value>
      + "               </Geq>"
      + "               <IsNull><FieldRef Name='ExpirationDate' /></IsNull>"
      + "           </Or>"
      + "       </And>"
      + "</Where>"
      + "</Query></View>";
listItems = newsList.GetItems(camlQuery);
ClientCtxt.Load(listItems,
      items => items.Include(
          item => item["Title"],
          item => item["Body"],
          item => item["PublishDate"],
          item => item["PictureURL"]
          ));

ClientCtxt.ExecuteQueryAsync(HandleClientRequestSucceeded,
      HandleClientRequestFailed);
}
```

The `HandleClientRequestFailed` method will be executed when the call to the server fails. The `EventArgs` argument contains an error message that is temporarily stored in a private string message. Then the `Post` method on the main UI thread is used to redirect the request back to the `OperationFailed` method on the main UI thread. There a message box is displayed to render the error message.

```
private string errorMessage;

private void HandleClientRequestFailed(object sender,
      ClientRequestFailedEventArgs e)
{
    errorMessage = e.Message;
    uiThread.Post(new System.Threading.SendOrPostCallback
        (delegate(object state)
    {
        EventHandler h = OperationFailed;
        if (h != null)
            h(this, EventArgs.Empty);
    }), null);
}

public void OperationFailed(object sender, EventArgs e)
{
    MessageBox.Show(string.Format("Failure! /n{0}", errorMessage));
}
```

The `HandleClientRequestSucceeded` method will be executed when the call to the server returns successfully. Also, here the `Post` method on the main UI thread is used to redirect the request back to the `OperationSucceeded` method:

```
private void HandleClientRequestSucceeded(object sender,
      ClientRequestSucceededEventArgs e)
{
```

```
        uiThread.Post(new System.Threading.SendOrPostCallback
            (delegate(object state)
        {
            EventHandler h = OperationSucceeded;
            if (h != null)
                h(this, EventArgs.Empty);
        }), null);
    }
```

The `OperationSucceeded` method loops through the `listItems` collection that was populated by executing the `ExecuteQueryAsync` method of the client context. For each list item in this collection, a Silverlight control is created, setting its `DataContext` property to the list item, and adding it to the `StackPanel` control of the Silverlight application.

Before the news items start scrolling over the page, a number of parameters of the storyboard are changed. The width of the `StackPanel` control is modified to fit the number of news item controls. To make the complete `StackPanel` scroll through the canvas, the `To` property of the `DoubleAnimation` is recalculated based on the number of news items, and the duration of the `DoubleAnimation` is recalculated. Then the storyboard is started.

```
        public void OperationSucceeded(object sender, EventArgs e)
        {
            foreach (ListItem item in listItems)
            {
                NewsItemControl newsItem = new NewsItemControl();
                newsItem.DataContext = item;
                NewsItemPanel.Children.Add(newsItem);
            }

            if (listItems.Count > 0)
            {
                int count = listItems.Count;
                // set the width of the NewsItemPanel
                NewsItemPanel.Width = count * 360;
                // set the endpoint of the animation in the storyboard
                DoubleAnimation doubleAnimation =
                    (DoubleAnimation)this.FindName("MarqueeDoubleAnimation");
                if (doubleAnimation != null)
                {
                    doubleAnimation.To = count * -360;
                    doubleAnimation.Duration = new Duration(new TimeSpan(0,
                        0, 7 * count));
                    if (App.Current.Host.Content.ActualWidth > 0)
                        doubleAnimation.From =
                            App.Current.Host.Content.ActualWidth;
                }
            }

            // start the storyboard
            Storyboard sb = (Storyboard)this.FindName("MarqueeAnimation");
            if (sb != null)
                sb.Begin();
        }
```

The XAML used to define the NewsItemControl contains a grid with two rows. The first row will display a vertically oriented StackPanel to display the title and the publish date of the news item. The second row will display a horizontally oriented StackPanel to display the body and the image.

```
<Grid x:Name="LayoutRoot" Background="White">
    <Grid.RowDefinitions>
        <RowDefinition Height="50" />
        <RowDefinition Height="Auto" />
    </Grid.RowDefinitions>
    <StackPanel Grid.Column="0" Grid.Row="0" Orientation="Vertical"
        Background="#FFCD2300" >
        <!-- The controls displaying Title and PublishDate -->
    </StackPanel>
    <StackPanel Grid.Column="0" Grid.Row="1" Orientation="Horizontal"
        Background="Black" Width="360">
        <!-- The controls displaying Body and Picture -->
    </StackPanel>
</Grid>
```

Figure 13-3 shows the result of the XAML.

The DataContext property is used for data binding purposes. Besides that, data binding expressions can be used on the XAML elements. In the following code snippet, the TitleTextBlock control is bound to the Title property of the list item by using a listItemConverter:

FIGURE 13-3: The NewsItemControl

```
<TextBlock x:Name="TitleTextBlock" Margin="5" Width="120"
           Text="{Binding Converter={StaticResource listItemConverter},
           ConverterParameter='Title'}"
           Foreground="White" FontWeight="Bold" />
```

If you didn't use a list item converter, the class name of the list item would be rendered as the title of the list item. The ListItemConverter class inherits from IValueConverter and is responsible for the rendering of the individual columns in the list item. The Convert method accepts the value, the data type, and the name of the column.

If the column is of type Text or Number, the value will be returned without conversion. If the data type of the incoming column is Lookup, the incoming value is first cast to the type FieldLookupValue, and the LookupValue property is returned for display. If the incoming column is of type URL, the incoming value is cast to the type FieldUrlValue, and the Url property is returned for display.

The ListItemConverter class in this example does not convert all types of columns, and contains only the conversions necessary in this example. It looks like this:

```
public class ListItemConverter : IValueConverter
{
    public object Convert(object value, Type targetType, object parameter,
        System.Globalization.CultureInfo culture)
    {
        // get the list item's field to be displayed
        string fieldToDisplay = parameter as string;
```

```
            if (string.IsNullOrEmpty(fieldToDisplay))
                fieldToDisplay = "Title";

        ListItem sourceListItem = value as ListItem;
        if (sourceListItem == null)
            throw new ArgumentException("value");

        if (fieldToDisplay.StartsWith("Lookup."))
        {
            string lookupFieldName = fieldToDisplay.Replace("Lookup.",
                string.Empty);
            FieldLookupValue lookupValue =
                sourceListItem[lookupFieldName] as FieldLookupValue;
            if (lookupValue != null)
                return lookupValue.LookupValue;
            else
                throw new ArgumentException("Invalid lookup field.");
        }
        else if (sourceListItem[fieldToDisplay] is FieldUrlValue)
        {
            FieldUrlValue urlValue = sourceListItem[fieldToDisplay] as
                FieldUrlValue;
            if (urlValue != null)
                return urlValue.Url;
            else
                throw new ArgumentNullException("Invalid URL field.");
        }
        else
        {
            // return what's being asked for
            return sourceListItem[fieldToDisplay];
        }
    }

    public object ConvertBack(object value, Type targetType, object parameter,
        System.Globalization.CultureInfo culture)
    { throw new NotImplementedException(); }
}
```

Before the `ListItemConverter` can be used in XAML, it should be referenced in the `Resources` element of the `UserControl` element:

```
<UserControl.Resources>
    <local:ListItemConverter x:Key="listItemConverter" />
</UserControl.Resources>
```

Notice the XAML that displays the publish date. It uses the new Silverlight 4 feature `StringFormat` that allows developers to specify a custom format when displaying a date.

```
<TextBlock x:Name="PublishDateTextBlock" Margin="5,0" Width="120"
        Text="{Binding Converter={StaticResource listItemConverter},
        ConverterParameter='PublishDate', StringFormat='MM-dd-yyyy'}"
        TextAllignment="Left" FontSize="8" Foreground="White"
            FontStyle="Italic" />
```

Notice the XAML that displays the body of the news item. It uses the new Silverlight 4 feature `TextTrimming`. This property accepts enumerator values of `None` or `WordEllipsis`. When this property is set to `WordEllipsis`, and the text in the `TextBlock` exceeds the visible limit, the text appears truncated with a trailing ellipsis.

```
<TextBlock x:Name="DescriptionTextBlock" Width="170" Height="90"
    Margin="5"
        Text="{Binding Converter={StaticResource
            listItemConverter},
        ConverterParameter='Body'}" Foreground="White"
        VerticalAlignment="Center" FontFamily="Comic Sans MS"
        TextWrapping="Wrap" TextTrimming="WordEllipsis" />
```

The complete XAML for the `NewsItemControl` looks like this:

```
<UserControl x:Class="NewsBanner.NewsItemControl"
    xmlns="http://schemas.microsoft.com/winfx/2006/xaml/presentation"
    xmlns:x="http://schemas.microsoft.com/winfx/2006/xaml"
    xmlns:d="http://schemas.microsoft.com/expression/blend/2008"
    xmlns:mc="http://schemas.openxmlformats.org/markup-compatibility/2006"
    xmlns:local="clr-namespace:NewsBanner"
    Width="360" Height="150">
    <UserControl.Resources>
        <local:ListItemConverter x:Key="listItemConverter" />
    </UserControl.Resources>
    <Grid x:Name="LayoutRoot" Background="White">
        <Grid.RowDefinitions>
            <RowDefinition Height="Auto" />
            <RowDefinition Height="50" />
        </Grid.RowDefinitions>
        <StackPanel Orientation="Vertical" Grid.Column="0" Grid.Row="0"
                Background="#FFCD2300" >
            <TextBlock x:Name="TitleTextBlock" Margin="5" Width="360"
                Text="{Binding Converter={StaticResource listItemConverter},
                ConverterParameter='Title'}"
                Foreground="White" FontWeight="Bold" />
            <TextBlock x:Name="PublishDateTextBlock" Margin="5,0" Width="120"
                Text="{Binding Converter={StaticResource listItemConverter},
                ConverterParameter='PublishDate', StringFormat='MM-dd-YYYY'}"
                TextAlignment="Left" FontSize="8" Foreground="White"
                    FontStyle="Italic" />
        </StackPanel>
        <StackPanel Grid.Column="0" Grid.Row="1" Orientation="Horizontal"
            Background="Black"
                Width="360">
            <TextBlock x:Name="DescriptionTextBlock" Width="170" Height="90"
                Margin="5"
                    Text="{Binding Converter={StaticResource
                        listItemConverter},
                    ConverterParameter='Body'}" Foreground="White"
                    VerticalAlignment="Center" FontFamily="Comic Sans MS"
                    TextWrapping="Wrap" TextTrimming="WordEllipsis" />
            <Image x:Name="NewsPicture"  Width="180" Height="100"
                Source="{Binding Converter={StaticResource listItemConverter},
```

```
                    ConverterParameter='PictureURL'}"
                    Stretch="Fill" />
            </StackPanel>
        </Grid>
    </UserControl>
```

The sample application is ready to be deployed. Build the Silverlight application and return to your SharePoint site. You have different ways to deploy a Silverlight application, and one way is to upload it to a document library. This is the easiest and most recommended way if you are going to host your Silverlight application in the out-of-the-box Silverlight Web Part. For this example, create a document library with the name XAPS that is dedicated for Silverlight applications that have a .xap extension.

The sample code also comes with a custom list definition that you can use to upload pictures and add a title, the body, publish date, and expiration date, as shown in Figure 13-4.

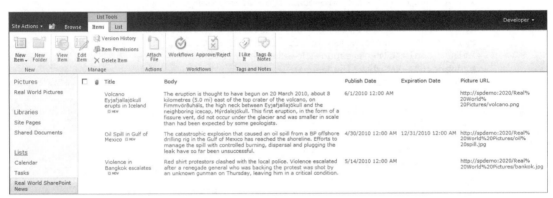

FIGURE 13-4: The Real World SharePoint News list instance

Once the Silverlight application is uploaded into your SharePoint environment, navigate to the page where you want to render your Silverlight application. Edit the page and choose to insert a web part. On the left of the screen that appears (Figure 13-5), select the "Media and Content" category, and from the list on the right, select the Silverlight Web Part, and add it to the page.

A dialog appears where you can enter the URL to the Silverlight application.

Before the Silverlight application can render, you must also specify the name of the list containing the news items. Therefore, you must edit the web part and navigate to the Silverlight section in the web part tool pane, as shown in Figure 13-6. There you can enter the name of the list.

FIGURE 13-5: Choose the Silverlight Web Part from the "Media and Content" category

FIGURE 13-6: Fill out the parameters needed by the Silverlight application

When you click OK, the `initParameters` are passed to the Silverlight application. Figure 13-7 shows the finished web part.

FIGURE 13-7: Finished Silverlight web part

This is the first and very simple example. Further examples in this chapter build on this one.

DEVELOPING A SHAREPOINT WEB PART HOSTING A SILVERLIGHT APPLICATION

The following example shows how you can build your own custom web part to host a Silverlight application, as shown in Figure 13-8.

FIGURE 13-8: The custom web part hosting the Silverlight News Banner

The file `Sample 2 - Silverlight enabled web part.zip` *available for download at* www.wrox.com *contains the source code for this example.*

The hosting web part can be a classic web part, but this example uses the new Visual Studio 2010 project template for a visual web part. Visual web parts come with an `.ascx` user control that is loaded in the `CreateChildControls` method of the web part. It is far easier to build a user interface with an `.ascx` user control than it was before, when all controls needed to be instantiated and added to the `Controls` collection programmatically.

The `NewsBannerWebPartUserControl.ascx` contains the necessary code to host the Silverlight application. Don't forget to set the width and height of the `<div>` element that hosts the Silverlight control; otherwise, you will not see the Silverlight application on the page. These width and height attributes can be positive or relative. A *positive size* is indicated in pixels, and a *relative size* is indicated in percentage. Here, a mix of both is used. The width has a relative size indicated by the value of `100%`, and the height has an absolute value of `150`.

The `<object>` tag represents the Silverlight application. Here you can specify a `width` and `height` attribute, and set them to a percentage to have a relative width and height. This will make the Silverlight application take over the width and height of the container control.

Within the `<object>` tag, a number of `<param>` elements must be specified to render the Silverlight application correctly.

The `source` parameter is a required `<param>` element. The value must be set to an absolute or relative path to where the Silverlight application is located. The `source` parameter is a relative URL to the location in the XAPS document library.

You can specify a `width` and a `height` parameter as `<param>` elements, but this will make your Silverlight application fixed.

Also, the `initParams` parameter must be set in this example. If you recall from the previous example, the only parameter that must be passed to the Silverlight application is the name of the list containing the news items. This list name will be filled out by the user in the tool part of the web part.

```
<asp:Panel ID="SilverlightPanel" runat="server">
    <div id="silverlightControlHost" style="width:100%;height:150">
        <object id="SLNewsBanner"
            data="data:application/x-silverlight-2,"
                type="application/x-silverlight-2"
            width="100%" height="100%">
            <param name="source"
                value="/XAPS/Chapter13.Sample2.NewsBanner.xap" />
            <param name="initParams" value="<%= InitParameters %>" />
            <param name="onError" value="onSilverlightError" />
            <param name="background" value="white" />
            <param name="minRuntimeVersion" value=" 4.0.50401.0" />
            <param name="autoUpgrade" value="true" />
            <a href="http://go.microsoft.com/fwlink/?LinkID=149156&v=
                4.0.50401.0"
```

```
                             style="text-decoration: none">
                              <img src="http://go.microsoft.com/fwlink/?LinkId=108181"
                                    alt="Get Microsoft Silverlight"
                                    style="border-style: none" />
                     </a>
                  </object>
              </div>
          </asp:Panel>
```

The onError attribute refers to a JavaScript function onSilverlightError, which also must be included in the .ascx control within script tags.

```
        <script type="text/javascript">
// <![CDATA[
        _spBodyOnLoadFunctionNames.push("onSilverlightError");
        function onSilverlightError(sender, args) {
            var appSource = "";
            if (sender != null && sender != 0) {
                appSource = sender.getHost().Source;
            }

            var errorType = args.ErrorType;
            var iErrorCode = args.ErrorCode;

            if (errorType == "ImageError" || errorType == "MediaError") {
                return;
            }

            var errMsg = "Unhandled Error in Silverlight Application " +
                appSource + "\n";

            errMsg += "Code: " + iErrorCode + "     \n";
            errMsg += "Category: " + errorType + "        \n";
            errMsg += "Message: " + args.ErrorMessage + "     \n";

            if (errorType == "ParserError") {
                errMsg += "File: " + args.xamlFile + "     \n";
                errMsg += "Line: " + args.lineNumber + "     \n";
                errMsg += "Position: " + args.charPosition + "     \n";
            }
            else if (errorType == "RuntimeError") {
                if (args.lineNumber != 0) {
                    errMsg += "Line: " + args.lineNumber + "     \n";
                    errMsg += "Position: " + args.charPosition + "     \n";
                }
                errMsg += "MethodName: " + args.methodName + "     \n";
            }

            throw new Error(errMsg);
        }
// ]]>
        </script>
```

The code behind of the user control contains an InitParameters property:

```
public partial class NewsBannerWebPartUserControl : UserControl
{
    private string initParameters = string.Empty;

    public string InitParameters
    {
        get { return initParameters; }
        set { initParameters = value; }
    }

    protected void Page_Load(object sender, EventArgs e)
    {
    }
}
```

It also contains a second property in which the web part stores its ID:

```
private string webPartID = null;

public string WebPartID
{
    get { return webPartID; }
    set { webPartID = value; }
}
```

When the user control loads, it will check if the list argument is already specified in the InitParameters string, because it is needed by the Silverlight application to download the SharePoint list items. If not, the panel containing the Silverlight application is made invisible, and a hyperlink will be shown inviting the user to open the web part tool pane to set the Silverlight parameters.

```
if (string.IsNullOrEmpty(initParameters) ||
    !initParameters.Contains("list="))
{
    SilverlightPanel.Visible = false;
    openEditorPartControl =
        new LiteralControl(string.Format(
        "To show a Silverlight control <a
            href=\"javascript:MSOTlPn_ShowToolPane2
            ('Edit','{0}');\">open the tool pane</a>
            and set the Silverlight properties.",
            webPartID));

    this.Controls.Add(openEditorPartControl);
}
else
{
    SilverlightPanel.Visible = true;
}
```

The two properties of the user control will be set by the web part in its `CreateChildControls()` method:

```
protected override void CreateChildControls()
{
    //Control control = this.Page.LoadControl(_ascxPath);
    NewsBannerWebPartUserControl control =
    this.Page.LoadControl(_ascxPath) as NewsBannerWebPartUserControl;
    if (control != null)
    {
        control.WebPartID = this.ID;
        CompleteInitParameters();
        control.InitParameters = this.InitParameters;
        Controls.Add(control);
    }
}
```

The web part itself contains a property that will appear in the tool pane of the web part in the Silverlight category. This property will then be filled out by the user with the name of the list containing the news items.

```
private string initParameters;

[Personalizable(PersonalizationScope.Shared),
 Category("Silverlight"),
 WebBrowsable(true)]
public string InitParameters
{
    get { return initParameters; }
    set { initParameters = value; }
}
```

But that is not all. As you can see, there is a call to a private method with the name `CompleteInitParameters()`. If you want the Silverlight application to work within the current SharePoint context, you must pass a parameter with the name `MS.SP.url`. If you don't pass a parameter with this name, the Silverlight application will not be able to set the current SharePoint context using the following code:

```
ClientContext clientContext = ClientContext.Current;
```

In that case you, must pass the URL to your SharePoint site so that the Silverlight application can set the SharePoint context as follows:

```
ClientContext clientContext =
        new ClientContext("http://MyServer/sites/MySiteCollection");
```

The `CompleteInitParameters()` method takes care of completing the `initParameters` variable with an extra `MS.SP.url` parameter with the current SharePoint URL as a value:

```
private void CompleteInitParameters()
{
    if (string.IsNullOrEmpty(initParameters))
    {
```

```
                        // add the MS.SP.url parameter
                        initParameters = "MS.SP.url=" +
                            HttpUtility.UrlEncode(SPContext.Current.Web.Url);
                    }
                    else if (initParameters.Contains("MS.SP.url"))
                    {
                        // if the initParams argument contains the MS.SP.url, it should be
                        // checked whether the URL is encoded or not.
                        int startpos = initParameters.IndexOf("MS.SP.url") + 10;
                        int endpos = initParameters.IndexOf(",", startpos);
                        if (endpos == -1)
                        {
                            // this means that the MS.SP.url is specified as
                            // last parameter
                            endpos = initParameters.Length;
                        }
                        string url = initParameters.Substring(startpos, endpos - startpos);
                        if (url.Contains("http://"))
                        {
                            // the url is not encoded
                            initParameters = initParameters.Replace(
                                url, HttpUtility.UrlEncode(url));
                        }
                    }
                    else
                    {
                        // the MS.SP.url parameter must be added to list of parameters
                        initParameters += ",MS.SP.url="
                            + HttpUtility.UrlEncode(SPContext.Current.Web.Url);
                    }
                }
            }
```

You can deploy the visual web part using the Visual Studio 2010 Tools for SharePoint 2010.

Open your SharePoint site and navigate to the page where you want to add your web part. If you haven't changed the feature properties in the Visual Studio project, you will find your web part in the Custom category.

Click the hyperlink that invites you to open the web part tool pane and set the `InitParameters` property. You will see that the `MS.SP.url` parameter is already set, as shown in Figure 13-9.

FIGURE 13-9: The Silverlight Web Part tool pane

If you created a list with, for example, the name "Real World SharePoint News" based on the custom list definition from sample one, your `InitParameters` property would look like the following:

```
list=Real SharePoint News,MS.SP.url=http%3a%2f%2fspdemo%3a2020
```

When the `InitParameters` property is set correctly, you can click the OK button to dismiss the tool pane, and the News Banner will become visible, as shown in Figure 13-10.

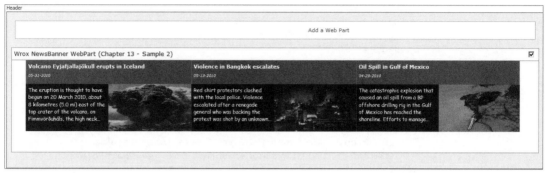

FIGURE 13-10: The Silverlight Web Part

You can click the Stop Editing button on the ribbon to save the changes to the page.

Adding a Custom Ribbon to the Web Part

The next step is to add a custom ribbon tab to the Web Part Tools group where users can select a list from a drop-down menu, as shown in Figure 13-11. This ribbon tab becomes available only when a web part is in Edit mode.

FIGURE 13-11: The News Banner Web Part ribbon

When one of the buttons is clicked to select a list, a message will be sent to the Silverlight application that will then load the list items from the selected list, and display them in the banner.

A custom ribbon group consists of a number of controls. The location in the `CommandUIDefinition` element defines where the ribbon group will be added. In this case, the custom group will be added to the Web Part Tools ribbon. The custom ribbon must be defined in Collaborative Application Markup Language (CAML). Each group and each control also specifies a `Command` attribute. This `Command` attribute will be used later on in JavaScript to decide which action to take.

For this example, a custom ribbon tab is created by adding an empty element item to the project with the name `NewsBannerRibbon`.

```
<Elements xmlns="http://schemas.microsoft.com/sharepoint/">
  <CustomAction
      Id="Ribbon.NewsBannerWebPart"
```

```
      Location="CommandUI.Ribbon"
    Title="Silverlight NewsBanner Ribbon">
  <CommandUIExtension>
    <CommandUIDefinitions>
      <CommandUIDefinition Location="Ribbon.WebPartOption.Groups._children">
        <Group
          Id="Ribbon.NewsBannerWebPart"
          Sequence="70"
          Command="Ribbon.NewsBannerWebPart"
          Description="Sample 6 News Banner"
          Title="Sample 2 News Banner"
          Template="Ribbon.Templates.ManageViewsGroup">
          <Controls Id="Ribbon.NewsBannerWebPart.Controls">
            <Button
              Id="Ribbon.NewsBannerWebPart.ViewRealSharePoint"
              Command="Ribbon.NewsBannerWebPart.ViewRealSharePoint"
          Image16by16="/_layouts/images/
              Chapter13.Sample2.NewsBannerWebPart/SLSP16.png"
          Image32by32="/_layouts/images/
              Chapter13.Sample2.NewsBannerWebPart/SLSP32.png"
              LabelText="Real World SharePoint News"
              Sequence="1"
              TemplateAlias="o1"/>
            <Button
              Id="Ribbon.NewsBannerWebPart.ViewRealNature"
              Command="Ribbon.NewsBannerWebPart.ViewRealNature"
              Image16by16="/_layouts/images/
                  Chapter13.Sample2.NewsBannerWebPart/nature16.png"
              Image32by32="/_layouts/images/
                  Chapter13.Sample2.NewsBannerWebPart/nature32.png"
              LabelText="Real World Nature"
              Sequence="2"
              TemplateAlias="o1"/>
          </Controls>
        </Group>
      </CommandUIDefinition>
      <CommandUIDefinition Location="Ribbon.WebPartOption.Scaling._children">
        <MaxSize Id="Ribbon.NewsBannerWebPart.MaxSize"
                GroupId="Ribbon.NewsBannerWebPart"
                Sequence="20"
                Size="LargeLarge" />
      </CommandUIDefinition>
      <CommandUIDefinition Location="Ribbon.WebPartOption.Scaling._children">
        <Scale Id="Ribbon.NewsBannerWebPart.MediumMedium"
                GroupId="Ribbon.NewsBannerWebPart"
                Sequence="30"
                Size="MediumMedium" />
      </CommandUIDefinition>
      <CommandUIDefinition Location="Ribbon.WebPartOption.Scaling._children">
        <Scale Id="Ribbon.NewsBannerWebPart.Popup"
                GroupId="Ribbon.NewsBannerWebPart"
                Sequence="50"
                Size="Popup" />
```

```
        </CommandUIDefinition>
      </CommandUIDefinitions>
    </CommandUIExtension>
  </CustomAction>
</Elements>
```

The ribbons and the ribbon controls are driven by JavaScript. This is called a *page component*. A page component is a JavaScript object that handles the events of a ribbon and its buttons. These JavaScript files can best be deployed to a subfolder of the LAYOUTS folder in the SharePoint root. Table 13-1 describes the functions of a page component.

When you use the Visual Studio 2010 Tools for SharePoint 2010, you can add a new item and choose the SharePoint Layouts mapped folder. This creates a subfolder to the Layouts folder. Add a JavaScript file with the name NewsBannerPageComponent.js to the subfolder, as shown in Figure 13-12.

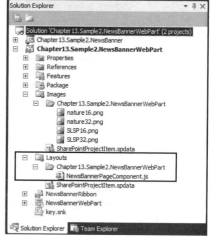

FIGURE 13-12: Map a folder to the SharePoint Layouts folder and add a JavaScript file to it

TABLE 13-1: Page Component Functions

FUNCTION	PURPOSE
Init	Initializes the page component.
getFocusedCommands	Returns a list of the focused commands. Your page component is called for the commands only if it has the focus.
getGlobalCommands	Returns a list of the global commands. Your page component is called for commands, regardless of focus.
isFocusable	Specifies whether the page component can receive focus.
canHandleCommand	Defines whether the page component can handle a command sent to it.
handleCommand	Handles the commands sent to the page component.
getId	Returns the ID of the page component. This is used to associate a control with a page component.

The following code will go into the JavaScript file implementing all functions described in Table 13-1:

```
Type.registerNamespace('NewsBannerWebPart.CustomPageComponent');

var _webPartPageComponentId;

NewsBannerWebPart.CustomPageComponent = function () {
    NewsBannerWebPart.CustomPageComponent.initializeBase(this);
}

NewsBannerWebPart.CustomPageComponent.initialize = function () {
    var ribbonPageManager = SP.Ribbon.PageManager.get_instance();
    if (null !== ribbonPageManager) {
        ribbonPageManager.addPageComponent(
                NewsBannerWebPart.CustomPageComponent.instance);
        ribbonPageManager.get_focusManager().requestFocusForComponent(
                NewsBannerWebPart.CustomPageComponent.instance);
    }
}

NewsBannerWebPart.CustomPageComponent.refreshRibbonStatus = function () {
    SP.Ribbon.PageManager.get_instance().get_commandDispatcher().executeCommand(
    Commands.CommandIds.ApplicationStateChanged, null);
}

NewsBannerWebPart.CustomPageComponent.prototype = {

    canHandleCommand: function (commandId) {

        if ((commandId === 'Ribbon.NewsBannerWebPart')
            || (commandId === 'Ribbon.NewsBannerWebPart.ViewRealSharePoint')
            || (commandId === 'Ribbon.NewsBannerWebPart.ViewRealNature')
            ) {
            return true;
        }
        return NewsBannerWebPart.CustomPageComponent.callBaseMethod(
            this, 'canHandleCommand', [commandId]);

    },

    handleCommand: function (commandId, properties, sequence) {
        if (commandId == 'Ribbon.NewsBannerWebPart.ViewRealSharePoint') {
            // this command gets called when the tab is activated, so populate the
            // dropdown here.
            refreshNewsBanner('Real World SharePoint News');
        }
        if (commandId == 'Ribbon.NewsBannerWebPart.ViewRealNature') {
            refreshNewsBanner('Real World Nature');
        }
    },

    getGlobalCommands: function () {
        var baseCommands = new Array();
        Array.add(baseCommands, 'Ribbon.NewsBannerWebPart');
        Array.add(baseCommands, 'Ribbon.NewsBannerWebPart.ViewRealSharePoint');
```

```
            Array.add(baseCommands, 'Ribbon.NewsBannerWebPart.ViewRealNature');
            return baseCommands;
        },

        getFocusedCommands: function () {
            return [];
        }
    }

    function refreshNewsBanner(listName) {
        if (!listName || listName.length == 0)
            alert('Please, select a news library.');

        var sl = document.getElementById('SLNewsBanner');
        if (sl) {
            sl.Content.NewsBanner.RefreshNewsBanner(listName);
        }
    }


    // Register classes
    NewsBannerWebPart.CustomPageComponent.registerClass(
        'NewsBannerWebPart.CustomPageComponent', CUI.Page.PageComponent);

    NewsBannerWebPart.CustomPageComponent.instance =
        new NewsBannerWebPart.CustomPageComponent();

    if (typeof (Sys) != "undefined" && Sys && Sys.Application) {
        Sys.Application.notifyScriptLoaded();
    }

    // Notify waiting jobs
    NotifyScriptLoadedAndExecuteWaitingJobs("NewsBannerPageComponent.js");
```

A number of JavaScript functions are specific to the working of the web part ribbon, but the most important function to note is the refreshNewsBanner function. The ribbon button passes the name of the desired list to this function. Upon its return, this function retrieves the Silverlight application from the .ascx user control and calls the RefreshNewsBanner method, passing in the selected list name to have it repopulated with the news items of the selected list.

RefreshNewsBanner is a method in the Silverlight application that has been exposed to the outside members on the page using a special technique explained later in this example.

This custom page component must be loaded and registered before it is rendered to the page. The OnPreRender method of the web part is the ideal place for this.

```
        protected override void OnPreRender(EventArgs e)
        {
            string script =
                @"function initRibbonWebPart{0}(){{
                    CUI.Page.PageManager.get_instance().addPageComponent(
                        new NewsBannerWebPart.CustomPageComponent('WebPart{0}'));
                    SP.Ribbon.PageManager.get_instance().addPageComponent(
                        new NewsBannerWebPart.CustomPageComponent('WebPart{0}'));
                }}
```

```
        ExecuteOrDelayUntilScriptLoaded(
            initRibbonWebPart{0},
            'NewsBannerPageComponent.js');";

    script = String.Format(script, ClientID);

    // Register scripts
    ScriptLink.RegisterScriptAfterUI(this.Page, "CUI.js",
        false, true);
    ScriptLink.RegisterScriptAfterUI(this.Page, "SP.Ribbon.js",
        false, true);
    ScriptLink.RegisterScriptAfterUI(this.Page,
        "Chapter13.Sample2.NewsBannerWebPart/NewsBannerPageComponent.js",
        false, true);

    Page.ClientScript.RegisterStartupScript(
        typeof(NewsBannerWebPart), "initializeScript", script, true);
}
```

Changes Made to the Silverlight News Banner

To make this work, a number of changes must be made to the Silverlight NewsBanner application. For starters, the MainPage control class must be marked with the ScriptableType attribute to make it scriptable by JavaScript.

```
[ScriptableType]
public partial class MainPage : UserControl
{
    // rest of the code omitted for brevity
}
```

Then, you must register the Silverlight object with the HTML page by calling the RegisterScriptableObject method on the HtmlPage object. This class resides in the System .Windows.Browser namespace. You can place the code right after the InitializeComponent() call in the MainPage constructor, and register it with a name like NewsBanner.

```
public MainPage()
{
    InitializeComponent();
    // register the Silverlight control
    HtmlPage.RegisterScriptableObject("NewsBanner", this);
    ResizeCanvas();
    this.SizeChanged += new SizeChangedEventHandler(MainPage_SizeChanged);
    uiThread = System.Threading.SynchronizationContext.Current;
    if (uiThread == null)
        uiThread = new System.Threading.SynchronizationContext();

    // populate the banner
    PopulateNewsBanner();
}
```

You also need an extra method that must be called by the contextual ribbon. To make a method callable from within JavaScript, you must decorate it with the `ScriptableMember` attribute. This method must also be public to make it accessible from outside the Silverlight application. The method itself calls the `PopulateNewsBanner` method to retrieve the news items from the SharePoint list.

```
[ScriptableMember]
public void RefreshNewsBanner(string listName)
{
    App.ListName = listName;
    PopulateNewsBanner();
}
```

After deployment of both the web part to SharePoint, and the new version of the `NewsBanner.xap` to the XAPS library, you can try out the web part. Navigate to the page where you added the web part. The contextual ribbon is not visible. Bring the web part in Edit mode to make the contextual ribbon available, as shown in Figure 13-13.

You can click the News Banner tab to make the controls on it visible. Selecting another list from the drop-down will make the Silverlight application load the news items from another list, as shown in Figure 13-14.

FIGURE 13-13: Bring the web part in Edit mode to make the custom ribbon group available

FIGURE 13-14: Select the Real World Nature list from the drop-down list on the ribbon

You can click the Stop Editing button on the ribbon. This will cause the page to initialize the Silverlight application again. If you want to make the choices permanent, you must implement a caching mechanism using, for example, Isolated Storage.

DEPLOYMENT POSSIBILITIES AND ACCESSIBILITY SCOPE IMPACT

In the first example, you deployed the Silverlight application to a document library on the root site. The way you deploy your Silverlight application has an effect on its accessibility for other users.

You have a number of different ways to deploy Silverlight applications, each with its own advantages and disadvantages. Most of the possibilities are covered in the different examples presented in this chapter. Table 13-2 shows the page component functions listed from a less-restricted access scope to most-restricted access scope:

TABLE 13-2: Page Component Functions

DEPLOYMENT	SAMPLES
`14\TEMPLATE\LAYOUTS` folder	The Silverlight application is accessible to the whole SharePoint server.
`BIN` folder of the SharePoint web application	Silverlight applications deployed to the `BIN` folder of the SharePoint web application are accessible to the whole SharePoint web application.
Document library in root web	Silverlight applications deployed to a document library are accessible to the complete web. If deployed in a document library in the root web, web parts and application pages in a sub-web can also make use of these Silverlight applications.
Master Page Gallery	When developing custom master pages, you deploy your master pages to the Master Page Gallery. You can deploy your Silverlight applications to this gallery, or, even better, to its subfolder named `Preview Images`.
Embedded resource	You can also deploy a Silverlight application as an embedded resource of a web part or application page. In that case, the Silverlight application can only be used by that web part or application page.

Make your choice carefully based on the required access scope. The examples in this chapter illustrate the different deployment possibilities.

DEVELOPING A SHAREPOINT CUSTOM FIELD TYPE HOSTING A SILVERLIGHT APPLICATION

This example shows how you can build a custom field type that hosts a Silverlight application. The Silverlight application in this example will retrieve all pictures from all picture libraries and display them in a Silverlight wrap panel, as shown in Figure 13-15.

FIGURE 13-15: The Silverlight-enabled custom field type

 The file `Sample 3 - Silverlight enabled custom field type.zip` *available for download at* www.wrox.com *contains the source code for this example.*

When a user wants to create a new news item, he or she will be able to choose a picture from the custom field. When a news item is edited, the previously selected picture will be shown a bit larger than the other pictures in the wrap panel.

The custom field type will be added to the custom list definition prepared for this chapter.

The Silverlight application will call a custom Windows Communication Foundation (WCF) service hosted in the context of SharePoint, to be able to display all pictures in all picture libraries.

The Picture Service

For the Silverlight application to be able to display all pictures in all picture libraries, a custom WCF service has been developed executing an SPSiteDataQuery.

FIGURE 13-16: The WCF service project

To develop a custom WCF service that runs in the context of SharePoint, you can best create a project based on the Empty SharePoint Project template using the Visual Studio 2010 Tools for SharePoint 2010.

Custom WCF services that need to be used from within SharePoint must be deployed to the ISAPI folder. Right-click the project in the Solution Explorer, choose Add ⇨ Add Mapped Folder, and choose the ISAPI folder from the dialog. Figure 13-16 shows the structure of the complete project.

The WCF service project contains an interface where the Picture object is defined. The class itself is decorated with the DataContract attribute. This attribute resides in the System.Runtime.Serialization namespace, which controls the general WCF serialization. The DataContract attribute is applied at the class level and it controls the serialized name of the object, as well as the namespace. Each property is decorated with the DataMember attribute. It allows you to specify the serialized name of the property, the order in which it appears within the object, as well as whether or not it is a required attribute.

```
[DataContract]
public class Picture
{
    private string title;
    private string url;

    [DataMember]
    public string Title
    {
        get { return title; }
        set { title = value; }
    }

    [DataMember]
    public string ImageUrl
    {
        get { return url; }
        set { url = value; }
    }
}
```

After that, you must define the service contract for the WCF service. This is an interface annotated with the `ServiceContract` attribute. This contract must specify all methods that will be exposed by the WCF service. This WCF service contains only one method, `GetAllPictures`.

```
[ServiceContract]
public interface IPictureService
{
    [OperationContract]
    List<Picture> GetAllPictures();
}
```

The `PictureService` class implements the interface. The only method to implement is the `GetAllPictures` method. It retrieves all pictures from all picture libraries using `SPSiteDataQuery`. To ensure that an `SPSiteDataQuery` retrieves data from all picture libraries, you can set its `Lists` property to `"<Lists ServerTemplate=\"109\" />"`, where `109` is the server template ID for picture libraries.

The method also loops through the retrieved pictures to build readable strings for the picture title and picture URL. The picture URL is constructed using the `EncodedAbsUrl` property (containing the URL of the SharePoint site) and the `FileRef` property (which contains the relative URL of the picture, including the name of the picture library where the pictures are uploaded). The picture title is filtered from the `FileLeafRef` property, which is a concatenation of the picture ID and the picture name, as shown in Figure 13-17.

FIGURE 13-17: The values of the FileRef and FileLeafRef properties

The collection of `Picture` objects is returned to the calling application.

```
[ServiceBehavior]
[AspNetCompatibilityRequirements(RequirementsMode =
        AspNetCompatibilityRequirementsMode.Allowed)]
public class PictureService: IPictureService
{
    public List<Wrox.Picture> GetAllPictures()
    {
        // get all pictures from all Picture libraries
        SPSiteDataQuery query = new SPSiteDataQuery();
        query.Lists = "<Lists ServerTemplate=\"109\" />";
        query.ViewFields =
          "<FieldRef Name=\"EncodedAbsUrl\" /><FieldRef Name=\"FileRef\" />" +
          "<FieldRef Name=\"FileLeafRef\" />";
        DataTable resultTable = SPContext.Current.Web.GetSiteData(query);

        List<Wrox.Picture> pictures = null;
        if (resultTable != null && resultTable.Rows.Count > 0)
        {
```

```
                    pictures = new List<Wrox.Picture>();
                    foreach (DataRow row in resultTable.Rows)
                    {
                        string fileref = row["EncodedAbsUrl"] +
                            row["FileRef"].ToString().Substring(row
                                ["FileRef"].ToString().IndexOf(";#") + 2,
                            row["FileRef"].ToString().Length - row
                                ["FileRef"].ToString().IndexOf(";#") - 2);

                        string fileleafref = row["FileLeafRef"].ToString().Substring(row
                                ["FileLeafRef"].ToString().IndexOf(";#") + 2,
                            row["FileLeafRef"].ToString().Length - row
                                ["FileLeafRef"].ToString().IndexOf(";#") - 2);

                        Wrox.Picture picture = new Wrox.Picture();
                        picture.Title = fileleafref;
                        picture.ImageUrl = fileref;

                        pictures.Add(picture);
                    }
                }

                return pictures;
            }
        }
```

A WCF service needs a .svc file. Add a subfolder with the name of your project or service to the ISAPI folder in your project, and add a text file with the name PictureService.svc. Add a ServiceHost directive to the .svc file. This directive can have a number of attributes that instruct the factory how the code must be compiled. The ServiceHost directive in this example specifies that the used .NET language is C#, and that the code can be found in the PictureService.cs file. The assembly is deployed in the Global Assembly Cache (GAC), so the Service attribute references the full name of service in the assembly.

```
<%@ServiceHost Debug="true" Language="C#" CodeBehind="PictureService.cs"
    Service="Wrox.PictureService, PictureService, Version=1.0.0.0,
        Culture=neutral, PublicKeyToken=e606a7960a492082" %>
```

A WCF service also needs a web.config file. You can add an .XML file to the subfolder of the ISAPI folder.

Silverlight applications only support basicHttpBinding for WCF. The binding element is responsible for how the messages are sent over the wire.

```
<configuration>
    <system.serviceModel>
        <behaviors>
            <serviceBehaviors>
                <behavior name="PictureService.PictureServiceBehavior">
                    <serviceMetadata httpGetEnabled="True"/>
                    <serviceDebug includeExceptionDetailInFaults="False" />
                </behavior>
            </serviceBehaviors>
        </behaviors>
```

```
    <services>
        <service behaviorConfiguration="PictureService.PictureServiceBehavior"
                name="Wrox.PictureService">
            <endpoint address=""
                    binding="basicHttpBinding" contract="Wrox.IPictureService">
                <identity>
                    <dns value="http://wingtipserver" />
                </identity>
            </endpoint>
            <endpoint address="mex" binding="mexHttpBinding"
                contract="IMetadataExchange" />
            <host>
                <baseAddresses>
                    <add baseAddress=
                        "http://wingtipserver/_vti_bin/
                            PictureService/PictureService/" />
                </baseAddresses>
            </host>
        </service>
    </services>
</system.serviceModel>
</configuration>
```

The WCF service is ready to be deployed to the ISAPI folder. You can deploy the WCF service using the Visual Studio 2010 Tools for SharePoint 2010. Before you do so, verify the Site URL in the project properties and set it to the URL of your SharePoint site, as shown in Figure 13-18.

Before the WCF service can be used by the Silverlight application, you must enable Anonymous access from within Internet Information Services (IIS) Manager, as shown in Figure 13-19.

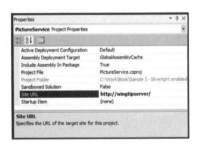

FIGURE 13-18: Change the Site URL property before deploying the custom field using the Visual Studio 2010 Tools for SharePoint 2010

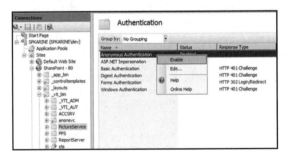

FIGURE 13-19: Enable anonymous access for the Picture Service

You will have to stop and restart IIS before you can test your WCF service.

The Silverlight Picture Picker

The Silverlight application in this example has the name SL Picture Picker and will consume the WCF service to retrieve all pictures available in all picture libraries on the current SharePoint site.

It has the following two different controls:

➤ `WrapPanelControl` — This control is rendered when the custom field is in Edit or New mode, as shown in Figure 13-20.

➤ `ViewPictureControl` — This control is rendered when the custom field is in Display mode, as shown in Figure 13-21.

FIGURE 13-20: The WrapPanelControl in action

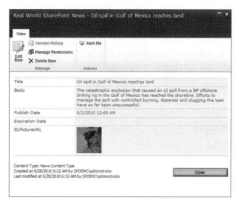

FIGURE 13-21: The ViewPictureControl in Display mode

The custom field will pass the following parameters to the Silverlight application:

➤ `url` — This parameter will contain the URL to the SharePoint site. This time, you cannot use the `MS.SP.url` parameter for the `ClientContext` because the Silverlight application will retrieve the available pictures using the custom WCF service developed previously. The value of this parameter will be stored in a static variable with the name `SiteUrl`.

➤ `ctlid` — This parameter will contain the ID of a hidden field on the page. The Silverlight application can retrieve the hidden field based on this ID, and place the URL of the selected picture in this hidden field. The SharePoint custom field can then, in turn, retrieve the URL from the hidden field and store it in the list item. The value of this parameter will be stored in a static variable with the name `ControlId`.

➤ `purl` — This parameter will only be available when the custom field renders in Display mode, and will contain the URL of the selected picture. The value of this parameter will be stored in a static variable with the name `PictureUrl`.

To decide which Silverlight control to render, the content of the `PictureUrl` variable can be verified. If it contains a URL, it means that only one picture must be displayed, and that the `ViewPictureControl` must be rendered. Otherwise, the `WrapPanelControl` will be rendered.

```
private void Application_Startup(object sender, StartupEventArgs e)
{
    if (e.InitParams != null)
    {
        if (e.InitParams.ContainsKey("url"))
            SiteUrl = e.InitParams["url"];
        if (e.InitParams.ContainsKey("ctlid"))
```

```
                    ControlId = e.InitParams["ctlid"];
                if (e.InitParams.ContainsKey("purl"))
                    PictureUrl = e.InitParams["purl"];
            }
            if (PictureUrl == null)
                this.RootVisual = new WrapPanelControl();
            else
                this.RootVisual = new ViewPictureControl();
        }
```

The `ViewPictureControl` control is a very simple control and contains only an `Image` control.

```
<Grid x:Name="LayoutRoot" Background="White">
    <Image x:Name="ViewPicture" Width="70" Height="70" Stretch="Fill" />
</Grid>
```

When the control loads, the URL from the `PictureUrl` variable is used to set the `Source` property of the `Image` control.

```
public partial class ViewPictureControl : UserControl
{
    public ViewPictureControl()
    {
        InitializeComponent();
        ViewPicture.Source = new BitmapImage(new Uri(App.PictureUrl,
            UriKind.Absolute));
    }
}
```

The `WrapPanelControl` control is a bit more complex. The `Canvas` contains a `WrapPanel` control and a `MessageTextBlock`. The `MessageTextBlock` will be used to display error messages. The `WrapPanel` control is not part of the out-of-the-box Silverlight controls, but is available from the Silverlight 4 Toolkit (which you can download from `http://silverlight.codeplex.com/`).

 The Silverlight 4 Toolkit is a product of the Microsoft Silverlight product team and contains a collection of Silverlight controls, components, and utilities made available outside the normal Silverlight release cycle. It includes full Open Source code, unit tests, samples, and documentation for more than 26 new controls covering charting, styling, layout, and user input.

To make use of the controls in this toolkit, you must add a reference to the `System.Windows.Controls .Toolkit.dll` assembly. The namespace must be added to the definition of the `<UserControl>` element.

```
<UserControl x:Class="SLPicturePicker.MainPage"
    xmlns="http://schemas.microsoft.com/winfx/2006/xaml/presentation"
    xmlns:x="http://schemas.microsoft.com/winfx/2006/xaml"
    xmlns:d="http://schemas.microsoft.com/expression/blend/2008"
    xmlns:mc="http://schemas.openxmlformats.org/markup-compatibility/2006"
```

```
        xmlns:vsm="clr-namespace:System.Windows;assembly=System.Windows"
        xmlns:toolkit="clr-namespace:System.Windows.Controls;assembly=
            System.Windows.Controls.Toolkit"
    Width="400" Height="120">
        <Canvas x:Name="LayoutRoot" Background="Transparent" Width="400" Height="120">
            <toolkit:WrapPanel x:Name="PicturePickerPanel" Width="400" Height="120"
                    Background="Transparent"
                    VerticalAlignment="Stretch"
                    HorizontalAlignment="Stretch"
                    Orientation="Horizontal">
            </toolkit:WrapPanel>
            <TextBlock x:Name="MessageTextBlock" Text="No images found."
                Foreground="Red"
                    Visibility="Collapsed"
                    Width="400" Height="120" VerticalAlignment="Center" />
        </Canvas>
    </UserControl>
```

The Silverlight application also contains a reference to the WCF Picture service. When the reference is added to the Silverlight project, it automatically generates a proxy that can be used from within the Silverlight application.

When the `WrapPanelControl` initializes, the `WrapPanel` is populated and the hidden field is retrieved. If the hidden field contains a value, it is stored in a class-level variable with the name `selectedUrl`. This URL will be used to emphasize the selected picture.

```
        public WrapPanelControl()
        {
            InitializeComponent();

            if (!string.IsNullOrEmpty(App.SiteUrl))
                PopulateWrapPanel();

            if (!string.IsNullOrEmpty(App.ControlId))
                fieldElement =
                    System.Windows.Browser.HtmlPage.
                        Document.GetElementById(App.ControlId);

            if (fieldElement != null)
                selectedUrl = fieldElement.GetProperty("Value").ToString();
        }
```

The `PopulateWrapPanel` is called from within the constructor of the Silverlight control. This method is responsible for the following:

➤   Instantiating the WCF service

➤   Setting the `EndPoint.Address` property to the URL of the current SharePoint site

➤   Defining a handler for the `GetAllPicturesCompleted` event

➤   Calling the `GetAllPictureAsync` method.

```
        private void PopulateWrapPanel()
        {
```

```
            MessageTextBlock.Text = "Loading...";
            MessageTextBlock.Visibility = Visibility.Visible;
            PicturePickerPanel.Visibility = Visibility.Collapsed;
            PicturePickerPanel.Children.Clear();

            PictureService.PictureServiceClient picturews =
                new PictureService.PictureServiceClient();
            picturews.Endpoint.Address = new System.ServiceModel.EndpointAddress(
                App.SiteUrl + "/_vti_bin/PictureService/PictureService.svc");
            picturews.GetAllPicturesCompleted += new
                EventHandler<PictureService.GetAllPicturesCompletedEventArgs>(
                picturews_GetAllPicturesCompleted);
            picturews.GetAllPicturesAsync();
        }
```

The GetAllPictureAsync method runs asynchronously on the server, and will come back with a result in the GetAllPicturesCompleted event handler. If the GetAllPictureAsync method returns a result, the list of Picture objects is retrieved from the result.

In this example, the WrapPanel control is not populated using data binding, but by programmatically creating an Image control for each picture in the list, and adding it to the Children collection of the WrapPanel. The Picture object is assigned to the DataContext property of the Image control, to be able to retrieve certain Picture properties afterward. If the list item is in Edit mode, the custom column can contain a value. That value is then passed in the hidden field on the page. In that case, the Image control is rendered a bit larger to emphasize the selected picture.

If the GetAllPictureAsync method returns an error, the MessageTextBlock will be made visible and will display the error message.

```
        void picturews_GetAllPicturesCompleted(object sender,
            PictureService.GetAllPicturesCompletedEventArgs e)
        {
            if (e.Error == null && e.Result != null)
            {
                pictures = e.Result.ToList<PictureService.Picture>();

                MessageTextBlock.Visibility = Visibility.Collapsed;
                PicturePickerPanel.Visibility = Visibility.Visible;
                PicturePickerPanel.Children.Clear();

                foreach (PictureService.Picture picture in pictures)
                {
                    Image img = new Image()
                    {
                        Source = new System.Windows.Media.Imaging.BitmapImage(
                            new System.Uri(picture.ImageUrl)),
                        Stretch = System.Windows.Media.Stretch.Fill,
                        Margin = new Thickness(5),
                        VerticalAlignment = VerticalAlignment.Center,
                        HorizontalAlignment = HorizontalAlignment.Center,
                    };

                    if (selectedUrl == picture.ImageUrl)
                    {
```

```
                    img.Opacity = 1.0;
                    img.Width = 50.0;
                    img.Height = 50.0;
                }
                else
                {
                    img.Opacity = 0.8;
                    img.Width = 40.0;
                    img.Height = 40.0;
                }

                img.DataContext = picture;
                img.MouseLeftButtonDown +=
                    new MouseButtonEventHandler(img_MouseLeftButtonDown);
                img.MouseEnter += new MouseEventHandler(img_MouseEnter);
                img.MouseLeave += new MouseEventHandler(img_MouseLeave);

                PicturePickerPanel.Children.Add(img);
            }
        }
        else
        {
            PicturePickerPanel.Visibility = Visibility.Collapsed;
            MessageTextBlock.Visibility = Visibility.Visible;
            if (e.Error != null)
                MessageTextBlock.Text = e.Error.Message;
            else
                MessageTextBlock.Text = "No pictures found";
        }
    }
```

A number of mouse event handlers are added to the `Image` control for events such as the
`MouseLeftButtonDown`, the `MouseEnter`, and the `MouseLeave` events. When the user clicks the
image, the `MouseLeftButtonDown` event will be fired. The previously selected image will be resized
to become like the unselected pictures, and the newly selected image will be resized a bit larger.
The URL of the selected image will be stored in the hidden field on the page.

```
void img_MouseLeftButtonDown(object sender, MouseButtonEventArgs e)
{
    if (selectedImage != null)
    {
        selectedImage.Width = 40;
        selectedImage.Height = 40;
        selectedImage.Opacity = 0.8;
    }

    Image image = sender as Image;
    if (image != null)
    {
        image.Width = 60;
        image.Height = 60;
        image.Opacity = 1.0;

        if (fieldElement != null && image.DataContext != null)
        {
```

```
                    PictureService.Picture picture =
                        (PictureService.Picture)image.DataContext;
                    fieldElement.SetProperty("Value", picture.ImageUrl);
                }

                selectedImage = image;
            }
        }
    }
```

The `MouseEnter` event is fired when the user moves the cursor above the image, causing the picture to enlarge a bit.

```
        void img_MouseEnter(object sender, MouseEventArgs e)
        {
            Image image = sender as Image;
            if (image != null)
            {
                image.Opacity = 1.0;
                image.Width = 60;
                image.Height = 60;
            }
        }
```

When the cursor is moved away from the picture, the `MouseLeave` event fires and causes the picture to resize to its normal size.

```
        void img_MouseLeave(object sender, MouseEventArgs e)
        {
            Image image = sender as Image;

            if (image != null && image != selectedImage)
            {
                image.Opacity = 0.8;
                image.Width = 40;
                image.Height = 40;
            }
        }
```

The Silverlight application is ready to build.

The PicturePicker Field

The custom field is derived from the standard `Text` field because it will only be used to store the URL of the selected picture. A custom field type is defined in an XML file that must be deployed to the `14\TEMPLATES\XML` folder. It is the entry point of a custom field type.

An XML file that contains the definition of a field type must be prefixed with `fldtypes_`. In this case, the XML file has the name `fldtypes_picturepicker.xml`.

```
    <?xml version="1.0" encoding="utf-8" ?>
    <FieldTypes>
        <FieldType>
            <Field Name="TypeName">SilverlightPicturePickerField</Field>
            <Field Name="TypeDisplayName">Silverlight Picture Picker</Field>
            <Field Name="TypeShortDescription">Picture picker</Field>
```

```
        <Field Name="ParentType">Text</Field>
        <Field Name="UserCreatable">TRUE</Field>
        <Field Name="FieldTypeClass">Wrox.SharePoint.Fields.
            SilverlightPicturePickerField, SilverlightPicturePickerField,
            Version=1.0.0.0, Culture=neutral,
            PublicKeyToken=b677969f2536ed3b</Field>
    </FieldType>
</FieldTypes>
```

The assembly of the custom field type will be deployed in the GAC. The FieldTypeClass element holds a reference to the PicturePickerFieldType class. This class inherits from SPFieldText and defines all different parts that make up the custom field type.

```
public class SilverlightPicturePickerField : SPFieldText
{
    public SilverlightPicturePickerField(SPFieldCollection fields,
        string fieldName)
        : base(fields, fieldName)
    {
    }

    public SilverlightPicturePickerField(SPFieldCollection fields,
        string typeName,
        string displayName)
        : base(fields, typeName, displayName)
    {
    }

    public override BaseFieldControl FieldRenderingControl
    {
        get
        {
            BaseFieldControl fieldControl = new
                SilverlightPicturePickerFieldControl();
            fieldControl.FieldName = this.InternalName;

            return fieldControl;
        }
    }
}
```

The PicturePickerFieldControl class will take care of the user interface. It will host the Silverlight applications, which will be deployed as embedded resources of the custom field type.

```
[assembly: WebResource("Wrox.SharePoint.Fields.Resources.SL Picture Picker.xap",
        "application/x-silverlight-app")]
namespace Wrox.SharePoint.Fields
{
    public class SilverlightPicturePickerFieldControl : TextField
    {
        private LiteralControl silverlightHost;
        private HtmlInputHidden valueField = null;

        public override object Value
        {
```

```
        get
        {
            EnsureChildControls();
            return valueField.Value;
        }
        set
        {
            EnsureChildControls();
            valueField.Value = value.ToString();
        }
    }

    public override void UpdateFieldValueInItem()
    {
        this.EnsureChildControls();

        try
        {
            this.Value = this.valueField.Value;
            this.ItemFieldValue = this.Value;
        }
        catch { }
    }
```

The `CreateChildControls` method adds two controls to the `Controls` collection: a hidden field and a Silverlight control.

The hidden field will be used by the Silverlight application to store the URL of the selected picture. This allows the custom field to read the URL when the new list item is created, or an existing list item is updated. When the custom field is in Edit mode, this hidden field will also be used by the custom field to store the URL of the selected picture. In that case, it will be read by the Silverlight application to render the image a bit larger than the other available pictures.

The second control to be created is the Silverlight control. Because the Silverlight application is compiled as an embedded resource within the custom field type, the location of the Silverlight application is retrieved from the page using the `GetWebResourceUrl` method of the `ClientScriptManager`. Another important parameter to be set is the `InitParams` parameter. Information like the client ID of the hidden field, and the URL of the current SharePoint site, are concatenated into a comma-separated string.

```
        protected override void CreateChildControls()
        {

            valueField = new HtmlInputHidden();
            valueField.ID = "PictureValueField";
            this.Controls.Add(valueField);

            string xapLocation = this.Page.ClientScript.
                    GetWebResourceUrl(this.GetType(),
                "Wrox.SharePoint.Fields.Resources.SLPicturePicker.xap");

            string initparams = string.Format("ctlid={0},url={1}",
```

```
                    valueField.ClientID, SPContext.Current.Web.Url);

            CreateSilverlightHost(xapLocation, initparams, 600, 130);

            if (this.ItemFieldValue != null)
                valueField.Value = (string)this.ItemFieldValue;
        }
```

The creation of the Silverlight control itself is separated in a private method called CreateSilverlightHost.

```
        private void CreateSilverlightHost(string xapLocation, string initparams,
          int width, int height)
        {
            string slstring = string.Format("<object id=\"SilverlightHost\""
                + " width=\"{0}\""
                + " height=\"{1}\""
                + " data=\"data:application/x-silverlight-2,\""
                + " type=\"application/x-silverlight-2\" >"
                + " <param name=\"source\" value=\"{2}\"/>", width.ToString(),
                    height.ToString(), xapLocation);

            if (!string.IsNullOrEmpty(initparams))
            {
                slstring += " <param name=\"initParams\" value=\"" +
                    initparams + "\"/>";
            }
            slstring += " <a href=\"http://go.microsoft.com/
                fwlink/?LinkID=149156\" "
                + " style=\"text-decoration: none;\">"
                + " <img src=\"http://go.microsoft.com/fwlink/?LinkId=108181\" "
                + " alt=\"Get Microsoft Silverlight\" "
                + " style=\"border-style: none\"/>"
                + " </a>"
                + "</object>";

            silverlightHost = new LiteralControl(string.Format
                ("<div id=\"silverlightHost\"
                style=\"width:100%,height:100%\
                "></div>{0}", slstring));
            this.Controls.Add(silverlightHost);
        }
    }
}
```

The Render method is responsible for rendering the custom field.

```
        protected override void Render(HtmlTextWriter output)
        {

            if (this.ControlMode == SPControlMode.Display)
            {
                base.Render(output);
            }
```

```
        else
        {
            silverlightHost.RenderControl(output);
            valueField.RenderControl(output);
        }
    }
}
```

The custom field type is ready to be built and deployed. To test the custom field type, you can deploy it using the Visual Studio 2010 Tools for SharePoint 2010. Verify the Site URL in the project properties and set it to the URL of your SharePoint site.

Now, let's modify the list definition for the Real World SharePoint News list.

The News List Definition

As shown in Figure 13-22, the `NewsListDefinition` contains site column definitions, a content type definition, and a list definition that makes use of this content type.

In the current list definition, the URL to the picture in a picture library is represented by a simple `Text` field, and can now be replaced by the Silverlight `Picture Picker` field.

FIGURE 13-22: The News List Definition project

With the Visual Studio 2010 tools for SharePoint 2010 you can add a new Empty Element to the project to add a new XML file. Give it a name like SL Site Columns. You can add a `Field` definition for the custom field, as shown here:

```xml
<?xml version="1.0" encoding="utf-8"?>
<Elements xmlns="http://schemas.microsoft.com/sharepoint/">
   <Field ID="{9495ECA0-F7E4-44c9-8136-DDB12BE3344B}"
          Name="SLPictureURL" DisplayName="Picture URL"
          Group="SL News Columns"
          Type="SilverlightPicturePickerField" DisplaceOnUpgrade="TRUE" />
</Elements>
```

The feature definition must be changed in order to update the content type and list definition. First of all, the version must be incremented from 1.0.0.0 to 2.0.0.0. You can do this in the Properties box of the Feature Designer, as shown in Figure 13-23.

Because the existing content type needs to be upgraded, you must add an `<UpgradeActions>` element to the Feature definition. This element must contain child elements for the following:

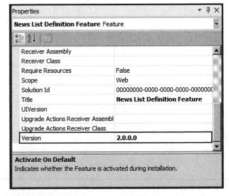

FIGURE 13-23: Increment the version of the feature

➤ `VersionRange` — To specify which versions need to be upgraded

➤ `ElementManifest` — To specify the `elements.xml` that contains the new site column definition

Use the `AddContentTypeField` element to indicate that you want to add a new field to the existing content type. You must specify the content type ID and the Field ID. You can find both IDs in the `elements.xml` files.

```
<UpgradeActions
    ReceiverAssembly="NewsListDefinition, Version=1.0.0.0, Culture=neutral,
        PublicKeyToken=c65ccd0c7ba5ad51"
    ReceiverClass="NewsListDefinition.Features.Feature1.Feature1EventReceiver">
    <VersionRange BeginVersion="1.0.0.0" EndVersion="1.9.9.9" >
        <ApplyElementManifests>
            <ElementManifest Location="SL Site Columns\Elements.xml" />
        </ApplyElementManifests>
        <AddContentTypeField
            ContentTypeId="0x01008d7ca420d2d041b4b48306ed02784d97"
            FieldId="{9495ECA0-F7E4-44c9-8136-DDB12BE3344B}"
            PushDown="TRUE" />
        <CustomUpgradeAction Name="RemoveField">
            <Parameters>
                <Parameter Name="FieldName">SL Picture URL</Parameter>
            </Parameters>
        </CustomUpgradeAction>
    </VersionRange>
</UpgradeActions>
```

You can only achieve this by editing the Feature manifest in XML, as shown in Figure 13-24.

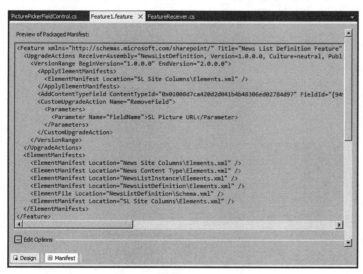

FIGURE 13-24: Edit the feature XML

You must also remove the existing Picture URL field from the content type. Because there is no upgrade element for this, you will have to do this in a Feature receiver. The Feature receiver class now has an extra event: `FeatureUpgrading`. In this event handler, you can add the necessary code to copy the values of the existing list items from the existing field to the new field. When all data is copied, the old site column can be removed from the content type.

If you use the Visual Studio 2010 tools for SharePoint 2010, you can add a Feature receiver by right-clicking the Feature in the Solution Explorer and choosing Add Feature Receiver. You can uncomment the FeatureUgrading event handler and add the following code:

```
public override void FeatureUpgrading(SPFeatureReceiverProperties
        properties,
    string upgradeActionName,
    System.Collections.Generic.IDictionary<string, string> parameters)
{
    if (properties.Feature.Parent is SPSite
        && upgradeActionName == "RemoveField")
    {
        using (SPSite site = properties.Feature.Parent as SPSite)
        {
            using (SPWeb web = site.OpenWeb())
            {
                web.AllowUnsafeUpdates = true;
                SPList list = web.Lists["Real World SharePoint News"];
                if (list != null)
                {
                    // as both fields have the same display name,
                    // update the new field with the old value using
                    // the field IDs
                    SPField oldfield = list.Fields.GetFieldByInternalName(
                        "PictureURL");
                    SPField newfield = list.Fields.GetFieldByInternalName(
                        "SLPictureURL");

                    // copy the picture URL from the old field to
                    // the new field
                    foreach (SPListItem item in list.Items)
                    {
                        item[newfield.Id] = item[oldfield.Id].ToString();
                        item.Update();
                    }

                    // remove the old column from the list
                    list.Fields.Delete("PictureURL");

                    // add the new column to the default view
                    SPView view = list.DefaultView;
                    view.ViewFields.Add(newfield);
                    view.Update();

                    list.Update();
                }

                web.AllowUnsafeUpdates = false;
            }
        }
    }
}
```

When you are ready to deploy the upgrade, it is better to not use the Visual Studio 2010 Tools for SharePoint 2010 because this would retract the solution and then add it again. It is better to package the solution in Visual Studio, and then use PowerShell to upgrade the solution. Right-click the `NewsListDefinition` project and choose Package to generate the `NewsListDefinition.wsp` solution file.

Open the SharePoint 2010 Management Shell from the Start menu to execute following PowerShell statements:

```
$path = "[Your complete path to the WSP file]"
$solution = "NewsListDefinition.wsp"
Update-SPSolution -LiteralPath ($path + $solution) -Identity $solution -
    GACDeployment
```

The `Update-SPSolution` cmdlet will update the solution in the farm solution store. But this has not yet upgraded the Feature. This can be done by using the `PSCONFIG` executable.

Open a Command Prompt and navigate to `C:\Program Files\Common Files\Microsoft Shared\ Web Server Extensions\14\BIN`. Then, execute the following to start the upgrade process:

```
psconfig.exe -cmd upgrade -force -wait -inplace b2b
```

If you receive an error mentioning that the Admin SVC must be running in order to create a deployment timer job, you must start the Windows services and start the SharePoint 2010 Administration service. Then, cancel the deployment job in Farm Solution Management of the SharePoint Central Administration.

Another possibility for upgrading Features is to use the SharePoint 2010 Feature Upgrade Kit from my fellow MVP, Chris O'Brien. This offers an integrated user interface to manage the upgrade of solutions from within the Central Administration or on site-collection level. You can download this very interesting tool from `http://spfeatureupgrade.codeplex.com`.

In that case, use the `Update-SPSolution` PowerShell cmdlet to update the solution in the farm solution store. To speed the execution of the deployment timer job, you can temporarily stop the SharePoint Administration service, execute the `Start-SPAdmin` PowerShell cmdlet, and then use O'Brien's Feature. Don't forget to start the Administration service again.

Navigate to the Real World SharePoint News list and edit one of the news items. As you can see in Figure 13-25, the Silverlight control renders when the custom field type is in New mode or in Edit mode. As shown in Figure 13-26, when in Display mode, only a URL is rendered.

FIGURE 13-25: The Silverlight Picture Picker renders when creating a new list item or editing an existing list item

FIGURE 13-26: In Display mode only a URL is rendered

This can be changed by adding a `RenderPattern` element in the `fldtypes_picturepicker.xml`. With SharePoint 2010, you must also add an extra `<Field>` element to the field definition to inform SharePoint that the rendering of the field is defined in CAML.

```xml
<?xml version="1.0" encoding="utf-8" ?>
<FieldTypes>
   <FieldType>
      <Field Name="TypeName">SilverlightPicturePickerField</Field>
      <Field Name="TypeDisplayName">Silverlight Picture Picker</Field>
      <Field Name="TypeShortDescription">Picture picker</Field>
      <Field Name="ParentType">Text</Field>
      <Field Name="UserCreatable">TRUE</Field>
      <Field Name="FieldTypeClass">Wrox.SharePoint.Fields.
         SilverlightPicturePickerField, SilverlightPicturePickerField,
         Version=1.0.0.0, Culture=neutral, PublicKeyToken=
         b677969f2536ed3b</Field>
      <Field Name="CAMLRendering">TRUE</Field>
      <RenderPattern Name="DisplayPattern">
         <HTML>
          <![CDATA[
            <object id="SilverlightHost" width="70" height="70"
              data="data:application/x-silverlight-2,"
                 type="application/x-silverlight-2">
              <param name="source" value="/_layouts/SL
                 Picture/SLPicturePicker.xap"/>
              <param name="initParams" value="purl=]]>
         </HTML>
         <Column HTMLEncode="TRUE" />
         <HTML>
          <![CDATA[" />
            <a href="http://go.microsoft.com/fwlink/?LinkID=149156"
              style="text-decoration: none;">
              <img src="http://go.microsoft.com/fwlink/?LinkId=108181"
                 alt="Get Microsoft Silverlight" style="border-style: none"/>
            </a>
            </object>
          ]]>
         </HTML>
      </RenderPattern>
   </FieldType>
</FieldTypes>
```

The only problem here is that you cannot retrieve the Silverlight application as an embedded resource, so you must deploy the Silverlight application to a document library on your SharePoint site, or to a subfolder of the SharePoint LAYOUTS folder.

As shown in Figure 13-27, when the change in the CAML is deployed, the custom field will render differently in the list view. As shown in Figure 13-28, when you choose to view one of the list items, the Silverlight application will also render in Display mode.

FIGURE 13-27: The list view rendering a Silverlight application

FIGURE 13-28: The list item rendering a Silverlight application in Display mode

DEVELOPING A SHAREPOINT APPLICATION PAGE THAT HOSTS SEVERAL COMMUNICATING SILVERLIGHT APPLICATIONS

This example shows how you can build a custom application page hosting several Silverlight applications that communicate with each other. One Silverlight application will list all news items entered in the Real World SharePoint News list. When the user selects one of the news items, the details of the selected news item are displayed in a second Silverlight application on the same page, as shown in Figure 13-29. The user will be able to update the selected news item.

As shown in Figure 13-30, this example consists of three Visual Studio projects — two Silverlight applications and a SharePoint project for an application page.

The file `Sample 4 - Silverlight enabled custom application page.zip` *available for download at* www.wrox.com *contains the source code for this example.*

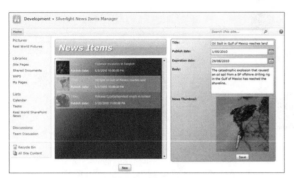

FIGURE 13-29: Details of the selected news item displayed in a second Silverlight application

FIGURE 13-30: The Visual Studio solution for the News Manager

The SLNewsItemsListBox Silverlight Application

The first Silverlight application contains a list box that will render all news list items of the Real World News Items list. When a user clicks a news item, a context menu will appear, as shown in Figure 13-31. From this context menu, the user may update or delete the selected news item, or create a new one.

The list box is formed by a `StackPanel` control with a `ScrollViewer` control. Within that `ScrollViewer`, another `StackPanel` is used to display the different news items.

```
<StackPanel Canvas.Top="80" Canvas.Left="10" Height="370" Width="Auto"
            Orientation="Horizontal"
            HorizontalAlignment="Stretch" VerticalAlignment="Top">
    <ScrollViewer Height="370" Width="380" HorizontalAlignment="Left"
                VerticalAlignment="Top">
        <StackPanel x:Name="ItemsPanel" Height="Auto" Width="430"
            Orientation="Vertical">
        </StackPanel>
    </ScrollViewer>
</StackPanel>
<TextBlock x:Name="MessageTextBlock" Canvas.Top="470" Canvas.Left="10"
    Width="230" Height="25"
    Text="Loading..." Visibility="Collapsed" />
<Button x:Name="NewButton" Canvas.Top="470" Canvas.Left="250"
        Width="50" Height="25"
    Content="New" Click="NewButton_Click" />
```

This results in the design shown in Figure 13-32.

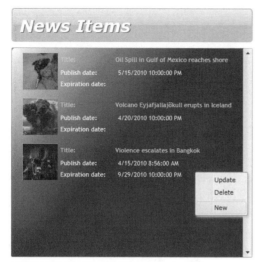

FIGURE 13-31: The SLNewsItemsListBox application in action

FIGURE 13-32: The list box in Design mode

When the Silverlight application loads, there is only one incoming parameter that must be retrieved from the InitParameters dictionary and stored in a static class-level variable — the name of the SharePoint list containing the news list items.

```
public static string ListName;

private void Application_Startup(object sender, StartupEventArgs e)
{
    if (e.InitParams.Count > 0)
    {
        if (e.InitParams.ContainsKey("list")
            && !string.IsNullOrEmpty(e.InitParams["list"]))
            ListName = e.InitParams["list"];
    }
    this.RootVisual = new NewsItemsListBox();
}
```

To retrieve the news list items from the SharePoint list, the Silverlight Client object will be used. This needs references to the following assemblies:

➤ Microsoft.SharePoint.Client.Silverlight.dll

➤ Microsoft.SharePoint.Client.Silverlight.Runtime.dll

The ClientContext will be grabbed using ClientContext.Current. This means that an initParameter with the name MS.SP.url must be passed in from within the SharePoint application page.

```
private ClientContext clientContext;
private ClientContext ClientCtxt
{
```

```
                    get
                    {
                        if (clientContext == null)
                            clientContext = ClientContext.Current;

                        if (clientContext == null)
                            throw new Exception("Connection failed!");

                        return clientContext;
                    }
                }
```

As in previous example Silverlight applications in this chapter, calls to the Silverlight client object model run asynchronously and on a different thread. Therefore, a pointer to the UI main thread must be stored when the Silverlight application loads.

Silverlight applications can also communicate with each other when they are placed on the same page. The `LocalConnection` API enables Silverlight applications to communicate with each other through an asynchronous messaging system. The `LocalConnection` APIs have a `LocalMessageSender` and `LocalMessageReceiver` that operate as sort of a publisher-subscriber model. A Silverlight application can send messages, and other Silverlight applications can listen for these messages. When a message is received, the applications can respond to it and act accordingly.

This example applies this technique to send a message to the second Silverlight application when a user selects a news list item from the list box. The message will contain the ID of the selected list item. The second Silverlight application on the application page will listen for this message, and then display the details of the selected list item.

Before the Silverlight application can send messages, a `LocalMessageSender` must be initialized with a name, which is `NewsItemMessaging` in this example.

In addition, this Silverlight application will also listen for messages sent by the second Silverlight application, indicating that a news item has been changed, or a new one has been created. Therefore, a `LocalMessageReceiver` is also initialized.

This receiver will listen for messages that are passed on the channel with the name `NewsItemUpdateMessaging`. When a message arrives over this channel, the `PopulateListBox` method will be executed to repopulate the list box. The `LocalMessageReceiver` starts listening for messages after the `Listen` method is executed.

```
                public NewsItemsListBox()
                {
                    InitializeComponent();

                    // Get synchronization thread
                    uiThread = System.Threading.SynchronizationContext.Current;
                    if (uiThread == null)
                        uiThread = new System.Threading.SynchronizationContext();

                    // Register control as sender
                    messageSender = new LocalMessageSender("NewsItemMessaging");

                    // define the message receiver for receiver messages that a user
                    // selected a
```

```
// news item from the list box
messageReceiver = new LocalMessageReceiver("NewsItemUpdateMessaging");

messageReceiver.MessageReceived +=
    new EventHandler<MessageReceivedEventArgs>((o, ev) =>
{
    ev.Response = string.Empty;

    Dispatcher.BeginInvoke(new Action(() =>
    {
        this.PopulateListBox();
    }));
});
messageReceiver.Listen();

PopulateListBox();
}
```

The code for retrieving the list items from the SharePoint list is implemented in the `PopulateListBox` method. All list items are retrieved and sorted by publish date.

```
private void PopulateListBox()
{
    serverAction = ServerActions.RetrieveListItems
    web = ClientCtxt.Web;
    ClientCtxt.Load(web);

    newsList = ClientCtxt.Web.Lists.GetByTitle(App.ListName);
    CamlQuery camlQuery = new CamlQuery();
    camlQuery.ViewXml = "<View><Query><OrderBy>"
      + "<FieldRef Name='PublishDate' Ascending='False' />"
      + "<FieldRef Name='Title' /></OrderBy></Query></View>";
    listItems = newsList.GetItems(camlQuery);
    ClientCtxt.Load(listItems,
        items => items.Include(
            item => item["ID"],
            item => item["Title"],
            item => item["PublishDate"],
            item => item["ExpirationDate"],
            item => item["SLPictureURL"]
            ));

    ClientCtxt.ExecuteQueryAsync(HandleClientRequestSucceeded,
        HandleClientRequestFailed);
}
```

As in the `NewsBanner` Silverlight application from the first example in this chapter, the necessary event handlers are implemented.

If the request doesn't return successfully from the server, an error message is displayed in a message `TextBlock`.

When the request returns successfully from the server, it is redirected to the `OperationSucceeded` method on the UI thread. The Silverlight application uses an enumeration to indicate which type of server call is made.

```
public enum ServerActions
{
    RetrieveListItems,
    DeleteItem
}
```

The `OperationSucceeded` method can then act differently upon the value in the `serverAction` variable.

When the server returns from retrieving the news list items, a `NewsItemControl` is created for each list item, and the list item is stored in the `DataContext` property of the `NewsItemControl`. An event handler is added to the `ItemClicked` event to react upon the user selection. There is also a `DeleteItemClicked` event that will be executed when the user clicks the Delete button on the `NewsItemControl`.

When the server returns from deleting a news item, the `PopulateListBox` method is called to refresh the list box with the remaining news list items.

```
public void OperationSucceeded(object sender, EventArgs e)
{
    switch (serverActions)
    {
        case ServerActions.RetrieveListItems:
            // Load the news banner
            foreach (ListItem item in listItems)
            {
                NewsItemControl newsItemControl = new
                    NewsItemControl();
                newsItemControl.DataContext = item;
                newsItemControl.ItemClicked +=
                    new ValueEventHandler
                    (newsItemControl_ItemClicked);
                newsItemControl.DeleteItemClicked +=
                    new ValueEventHandler
                    (newsItemControl_DeleteItemClicked);
                ItemsPanel.Children.Add(newsItemControl);
            }
            break;
        case ServerActions.DeleteItem:
            PopulateListBox();
            break;
    }
}
```

The `ItemClicked` event and the `DeleteItemClicked` event are custom events defined on the `NewsItemControl`. This control displays information (such as title and picture) for the news item. The data is data bound the same way as in the earlier `NewsBanner` example using the

ListItemConverter. For each list item in the list, a NewsItemControl instance is created and added to the list box. The control also defines a number of Storyboards to emphasize the control when the user hovers over an item.

```xml
<UserControl x:Class="SLNewsItemsListBox.NewsItemControl"
    xmlns="http://schemas.microsoft.com/winfx/2006/xaml/presentation"
    xmlns:x="http://schemas.microsoft.com/winfx/2006/xaml"
    xmlns:d="http://schemas.microsoft.com/expression/blend/2008"
    xmlns:mc="http://schemas.openxmlformats.org/markup-compatibility/2006"
        xmlns:local="clr-namespace:SLNewsItemsListBox"
    Width="400" Height="60">
    <UserControl.Resources>
        <local:ListItemConverter x:Key="listItemConverter" />
        <Style x:Key="TitleBlock" TargetType="TextBlock">
            <Setter Property="FontFamily" Value="Trebuchet MS"/>
            <Setter Property="TextAlignment" Value="Left"/>
            <Setter Property="VerticalAlignment" Value="Center"/>
            <Setter Property="Foreground" Value="#FFFFCD00" />
        </Style>
        <Style x:Key="BodyBlock" TargetType="TextBlock">
            <Setter Property="FontFamily" Value="Trebuchet MS"/>
            <Setter Property="TextAlignment" Value="Left"/>
            <Setter Property="VerticalAlignment" Value="Center"/>
            <Setter Property="Foreground" Value="White" />
        </Style>
    </UserControl.Resources>
    <Canvas x:Name="LayoutRoot" Background="Transparent"
            MouseEnter="LayoutRoot_MouseEnter"
            MouseLeave="LayoutRoot_MouseLeave" >
        <Canvas.Resources>
            <Storyboard x:Name="MouseFocus">
                <DoubleAnimation
                    Storyboard.TargetName="ShadeRectangle"
                    Storyboard.TargetProperty="Opacity"
                    From="0" To="0.4" Duration="0:0:0.30"/>
            </Storyboard>
            <Storyboard x:Name="MouseLeaveFocus">
                <DoubleAnimation
                    Storyboard.TargetName="ShadeRectangle"
                    Storyboard.TargetProperty="Opacity"
                    From="0.4" To="0" Duration="0:0:0.30"/>
            </Storyboard>
        </Canvas.Resources>
        <StackPanel x:Name="NewsItemPanel" Orientation="Horizontal" Canvas.Top="4">
            <!-- Thumbnail -->
            <Border Width="65" Height="65" BorderBrush="#D3DBEF"
                    BorderThickness="0.5" >
                <Image Width="64" Height="64" Stretch="Fill" Source="{Binding
                        Converter={StaticResource listItemConverter},
                        ConverterParameter='SLPictureURL'}" />
            </Border>
```

```xml
                    <!-- Other data -->
                    <Grid Width="350">
                        <Grid.ColumnDefinitions>
                            <ColumnDefinition Width="90" />
                            <ColumnDefinition Width="*" />
                        </Grid.ColumnDefinitions>
                        <Grid.RowDefinitions>
                            <RowDefinition Height="25" />
                            <RowDefinition Height="25" />
                            <RowDefinition Height="25" />
                        </Grid.RowDefinitions>
                        <TextBlock Grid.Row="0" Grid.Column="0" Text="Title:"
                                Width="90" Margin="5"
                            Style="{StaticResource TitleBlock}" FontWeight="Bold" />
                        <TextBlock Grid.Row="0" Grid.Column="1" Width="250" Margin="5"
                            Text="{Binding Converter={StaticResource listItemConverter},
                            ConverterParameter='Title'}"
                            Style="{StaticResource TitleBlock}" FontWeight="Bold" />
                        <TextBlock Grid.Row="1" Grid.Column="0" Text="Publish date:"
                                Width="90"
                            Margin="5" Style="{StaticResource BodyBlock}"
                                FontWeight="Bold" />
                        <TextBlock Grid.Row="1" Grid.Column="1" Width="230" Margin="5"
                            Text="{Binding Converter={StaticResource listItemConverter},
                            ConverterParameter='PublishDate'}"
                            Style="{StaticResource BodyBlock}" />
                        <TextBlock Grid.Row="2" Grid.Column="0" Text="Expiration
                                date:" Width="90"
                            Margin="5" Style="{StaticResource BodyBlock}"
                                FontWeight="Bold" />
                        <TextBlock Grid.Row="2" Grid.Column="1" Width="230" Margin="5"
                            Text="{Binding Converter={StaticResource listItemConverter},
                            ConverterParameter='ExpirationDate'}"
                            Style="{StaticResource BodyBlock}" />
                    </Grid>
                </StackPanel>
                <Rectangle x:Name="ShadeRectangle" Canvas.Top="0.5"
                        Canvas.Left="0.5" Width="430"
                    Height="60" Opacity="0" Fill="White" />
                <Rectangle x:Name="SelectedRectangle" Canvas.Top="0.5"
                        Canvas.Left="0.5" Width="430"
                    Height="60" Opacity="0.5" Fill="White" Visibility="Collapsed" />
                <!— The context menu —>
                <toolkit:ContextMenuService.ContextMenu>
                    <toolkit:ContextMenu Name="cm">
                        <toolkit:MenuItem Header="Update" Click="MenuItem_Click"/>
                        <toolkit:MenuItem Header="Delete" Click="MenuItem_Click"/>
                        <toolkit:Separator/>
                        <toolkit:MenuItem Header="New" Click="MenuItem_Click" />
                    </toolkit:ContextMenu>
                </toolkit:ContextMenuService.ContextMenu>
        </Canvas>
    </UserControl>
```

The last boldfaced portion of XAML is the context menu that is displayed when the user right-clicks one of the news items. To be able to work with context menus (which is a new feature of Silverlight 4), you must add additional references to the following assemblies:

➤ `System.Windows.Controls.dll` — This is part of the Silverlight 4 installation. You can find it on the .NET tab when adding a reference in Visual Studio.

➤ `System.Windows.Controls.Toolkit.dll` — This is part of the Silverlight 4 Toolkit. To add a reference to this assembly, you must browse to the `C:\Program Files (x86)\Microsoft SDKs\Silverlight\v4.0\Toolkit\Apr10\Bin` directory.

➤ `System.Windows.Controls.Input.Toolkit` — This is also part of the Silverlight 4 Toolkit and can be found at the same location.

The `NewsItemControl` defines an `ItemClicked` event and a `DeleteItemClicked` event.

```
public delegate void ValueEventHandler(object sender, ValueEventArgs e);

public partial class NewsItemControl : UserControl
{
    public event ValueEventHandler ItemClicked;
    public event ValueEventHandler DeleteItemClicked;

    public NewsItemControl()
    {
        InitializeComponent();
    }
}
```

The `ValueEventHandler` will contain the ID of the selected news item:

```
public class ValueEventArgs
{
    public int Value { get; set; }

    public ValueEventArgs(int value)
    {
        this.Value = value;
    }
}
```

The `MenuItem_Click` event handler is executed when the user chooses one of the menu items in the context menu. When the user chooses to update the selected news item, the `ItemClicked` event is raised. The ID of the selected news item can be retrieved from the `DataContext` property of the control. When the user chooses to delete the selected news item, the `DeleteItemClicked` event is raised. The user can also choose to create a new list item by choosing the New menu item. In that case, the `ItemClicked` event is raised, passing the number zero as the ID.

```
private void MenuItem_Click(object sender, RoutedEventArgs e)
{
    MenuItem menuItem = (MenuItem)sender;
    switch (menuItem.Header.ToString())
```

```
        {
            case "Update":
                if (ItemClicked != null && this.DataContext != null
                    && this.DataContext is ListItem)
                {
                    ItemClicked(this,
                        new ValueEventArgs((int)((ListItem)this.DataContext)["ID"]));
                }
                break;

            case "Delete":
                if (DeleteItemClicked != null && this.DataContext != null
                   && this.DataContext is ListItem)
                {
                    DeleteItemClicked(this,
                        new ValueEventArgs((int)((ListItem)this.DataContext)["ID"]));
                }
                break;

            case "New":
                if (ItemClicked != null)
                    ItemClicked(this, new ValueEventArgs(0));
                break;
            default:
                break;
        }
        cm.IsOpen = false;
    }
```

The `ItemClicked` event is captured in the code behind of the list box through the `newsItemControl _ItemClicked` event handler. For the highlighting of the selected item to work properly, the previously selected item is deselected, and the currently selected one is stored in a class-level variable. The ID of the selected news item can be retrieved from the incoming `EventArgs`. Then, a message is sent containing the ID of the selected news item. Listening Silverlight applications can intercept the message and react to it. In this example, the details of the selected news item will be displayed.

```
        void newsItemControl_ItemClicked(object sender, ValueEventArgs e)
        {
            if (selectedItem != null)
                selectedItem.Deselect();

            selectedItem = (NewsItemControl)sender;

            // Send a message to the listener
            messageSender.SendAsync(e.Value.ToString());
        }
```

The `DeleteItemClicked` event is also captured in the code behind of the list box through the `newsItemControl_DeleteItemClicked` event handler. The list item is retrieved from the `DataContext` property, and the `DeleteObject` method is called to remove the list item from the SharePoint list. The `serverActions` variable is set to `DeleteItem` to inform the `OperationSucceeded` method that the list box must be repopulated. Finally, the `ExecuteQueryAsync` method is called to send the delete operation to the server.

```
void newsItemControl_DeleteItemClicked(object sender, ValueEventArgs e)
{
    selectedItem = (NewsItemControl)sender;
    if (selectedItem.DataContext != null)
    {
        ListItem item = selectedItem.DataContext as ListItem;
        item.DeleteObject();
        newsList.Update();
        serverActions = ServerActions.DeleteItem;
        clientContext.ExecuteQueryAsync(HandleClientRequestSucceeded,
            HandleClientRequestFailed);
    }
}
```

The SLNewsItemDetails Silverlight Application

This Silverlight application will be placed on the same SharePoint application page as the list box. This application will be listening for messages sent by the list box. These messages will contain the ID of the selected news item so that this Silverlight application can retrieve and display the detailed information of the news item, as shown in Figure 13-33.

The XAML consists of a grid with a number of controls like `TextBlock`, `TextBox`, `Image`, and `Button`.

The user can also create a new item by clicking the New button on the `SLNewsItemsListBox` application. In that case, the data entry controls are cleared, and an `Image` control with a question mark is displayed, as shown in Figure 13-34. The user can click this question mark to upload a new picture.

FIGURE 13-33: The SLNewsItemDetails application in action

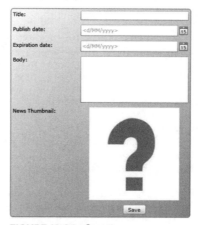

FIGURE 13-34: Creating a new news item

As with the other Silverlight applications, this one also needs to know with which SharePoint list it must communicate. Additionally, the name of a picture library must be passed in case new pictures need to be uploaded. Because you will also need the URL of the SharePoint site to build the complete URL to a picture, the value of the `MS.SP.url` parameter is also stored in a variable.

```
public static string SiteUrl;
public static string ListName;
public static string PictureLibraryName;

private void Application_Startup(object sender, StartupEventArgs e)
{
    if (e.InitParams.Count > 0)
    {
        if (e.InitParams.ContainsKey("MS.SP.url")
            && !string.IsNullOrEmpty(e.InitParams["MS.SP.url"]))
            SiteUrl = e.InitParams["MS.SP.url"];

        if (e.InitParams.ContainsKey("list")
            && !string.IsNullOrEmpty(e.InitParams["list"])
            ListName = e.InitParams["list"].Replace("%20", " ");

        if (e.InitParams.ContainsKey("piclib")
            && !string.IsNullOrEmpty(e.InitParams["piclib"]))
            PictureLibraryName = e.InitParams
                ["piclib"].Replace("%20", " ");                  }
    this.RootVisual = new MainPage();
}
```

When the Silverlight application initializes, an event handler is added for the Load event. The Load event will take care of subscribing to the messaging channel. The `LocalMessageReceiver` object represents the receiving end of a local messaging channel between two Silverlight applications.

After subscription, the Silverlight application will start listening for messages on a different thread. When a message comes in, the routed news item ID is retrieved from the message. The `PopulateNewsItemDetails` method is invoked on the main UI thread using the `Dispatcher` and the item ID is passed to it.

A `LocalMessageReceiver` is defined to listen for messages sent by the `SLNewsItemsListBox` application. A `LocalMessageSender` is defined to send messages when changes are saved to the server.

```
public MainPage()
{
    InitializeComponent();

    // Get synchronization thread
    uiThread = System.Threading.SynchronizationContext.Current;
    if (uiThread == null)
        uiThread = new System.Threading.SynchronizationContext();

    // define the message sender for updated items
    messageSender = new LocalMessageSender("NewsItemUpdateMessaging");


    // define the message receiver for receiver messages
    // that a user selected
    // a news item from the list box
    messageReceiver = new LocalMessageReceiver("NewsItemMessaging");
```

```
messageReceiver.MessageReceived +=
    new EventHandler<MessageReceivedEventArgs>((o, ev) =>
{
    string selectedId = ev.Message;
    int id = 0;

    if (!string.IsNullOrEmpty(selectedId))
    {
        int.TryParse(selectedId, out id);
    }
    ev.Response = string.Empty;

    Dispatcher.BeginInvoke(new Action(() =>
    {
        this.PopulateNewsItemDetails(id);
    }));
});
messageReceiver.Listen();
}
```

This Silverlight application also uses an enumeration to indicate which type of call is made to the server. When the call returns to the `OperationSucceeded` method, the enumeration value will be used to decide what needs to be done next.

```
public enum ServerAction
{
    RetrieveItem,
    CreateItem,
    UpdateItem,
    UploadPicture
}
```

The `PopulateNewsItemDetails` method first clears the controls, and then inspects the incoming ID. If the ID equals zero, it means a new list item must be created, and no data must be retrieved from the SharePoint server. If the incoming ID is a positive integer, the method retrieves the selected news item from the SharePoint server using the `GetItemById` method of the Silverlight client object model.

```
private void PopulateNewsItemDetails(int id)
{
    TitleTextBox.Text = string.Empty;
    BodyTextBox.Text = string.Empty;
    PublishDatePicker.SelectedDate = null;
    ExpirationDatePicker.SelectedDate = null;

    selectedId = id;

    if (id > 0)
    {
        serverAction = ServerAction.RetrieveItem;
```

```
            web = ClientCtxt.Web;
            ClientCtxt.Load(web);

            newsList = ClientCtxt.Web.Lists.GetByTitle(App.ListName);
            listItem = newsList.GetItemById(id);
            ClientCtxt.Load(listItem);

            ClientCtxt.ExecuteQueryAsync(HandleClientRequestSucceeded,
                HandleClientRequestFailed);
        }
        else
        {
            LayoutRoot.Visibility = Visibility.Visible;
            NoThumbnailImage.Visibility = Visibility.Visible;
            ThumbnailImage.Visibility = Visibility.Collapsed;
        }
    }
}
```

As was the case with the SLNewsItemListBox Silverlight application in this chapter, the necessary event handlers are implemented. If the request doesn't return successfully from the server, an error message is displayed in a message TextBlock.

When the request returns successfully from the server, it is redirected to the OperationSucceeded method on the UI thread. In the case that the selected list item is retrieved from the server, the list item is stored in the DataContext property of the grid, which will take care of the data binding of the list item properties to the appropriate controls. In the case that the list item was updated, a message is sent indicating the update. When a new list item has been created, a create message is sent.

```
public void OperationSucceeded(object sender, EventArgs e)
{
    switch (serverAction)
    {
        case ServerAction.RetrieveItem:
            // Load the news banner
            if (listItem != null)
                NewsItemGrid.DataContext = listItem;
            LayoutRoot.Visibility = Visibility.Visible;
            NoThumbnailImage.Visibility = Visibility.Collapsed;
            ThumbnailImage.Visibility = Visibility.Visible;
            break;
        case ServerAction.UpdateItem:
            MessageBox.Show("Update successful!");
            messageSender.SendAsync("update");
            break;
        case ServerAction.UploadPicture:
            break;
        case ServerAction.CreateItem:
            selectedPicture = null;
            MessageBox.Show("Creation successful!");
            messageSender.SendAsync("create");
            break;
    }
}
```

When the user selects an existing news item from the list box, the user will be able to modify the data on the screen. If the user wants to display another picture for the news item, he or she can click the image to open the file dialog. Clicking the Save button saves the changes to the server.

The user can also create a new news item. The user can upload a new picture by clicking the question mark image, which triggers the MouseLeftButtonUp event of the image. The file dialog is opened to allow the user to browse for a picture.

The new picture cannot be saved immediately to the SharePoint picture library because this action must wait until the user chooses to save the changes to SharePoint. Therefore, the new picture is temporarily stored in Isolated Storage. Isolated Storage is ideal for storing data on the local client where the Silverlight application can read and write to it. In Silverlight 4, performance improvements have been made to make accessing data in Isolated Storage faster.

```
private void Image_MouseLeftButtonUp(object sender, MouseButtonEventArgs e)
{
    OpenFileDialog ofd = new OpenFileDialog();
    ofd.Multiselect = false;
    ofd.Filter = "jpeg|*.jpg|All files|*.*";

    bool? retval = ofd.ShowDialog();
    if (retval != null && retval == true)
        selectedPicture = ofd.File;

    else
        selectedPicture = null;

    using (IsolatedStorageFile iso =
        IsolatedStorageFile.GetUserStoreForApplication())
    {
        Stream filestream = selectedPicture.OpenRead();
        int filelength = (int)filestream.Length;
        byte[] data = new byte[filelength];
        filestream.Read(data, 0, filelength);
        filestream.Close();

        IsolatedStorageFileStream isoStream =
            iso.CreateFile(selectedPicture.Name);
        isoStream.Write(data, 0, filelength);
        isoStream.Close();
    }

    using (IsolatedStorageFile iso =
        IsolatedStorageFile.GetUserStoreForApplication())
    {
        if(iso.FileExists(selectedPicture.Name))
        {
            using(IsolatedStorageFileStream isostream =
                iso.OpenFile(selectedPicture.Name, FileMode.Open))
            {
                BitmapImage bmpImg = new BitmapImage();
                bmpImg.SetSource(isostream);
                NoThumbnailImage.Source = bmpImg;
            }
        }
```

```
            }
        }

    }
```

When the user clicks the Save button, the news item must be saved to the SharePoint server.

```
        private void SaveButton_Click(object sender, RoutedEventArgs e)
        {
            if (TitleTextBox.Text.Length == 0)
                MessageBox.Show("Please, fill out a Title before
                    saving the item.");
            else
            {
                if (newsList == null)
                    newsList = ClientCtxt.Web.Lists.GetByTitle(App.ListName);

                if (selectedId == 0)
                {
                    CreateNewsListItem();
                }
                else if (listItem != null)
                {
                    UpdateNewsListItem();
                }
            }
        }
```

If an existing list item is updated, all properties are filled with the changed data. The UploadPicture method will check if a new picture has been selected, and upload it if necessary. Then, the Update method on the list item is called.

Calling the ExecuteQueryAsync method will effectively save the changes to the SharePoint list. When the item is saved successfully, and the call returns to the Silverlight application, a message is sent over the local message channel to inform the list box application that an item has been updated, and the items in the list box must be refreshed.

```
        private void UpdateNewsListItem()
        {
            // upload the picture if the picture has changed
            UploadPicture();

            // update item
            listItem["Title"] = TitleTextBox.Text;
            listItem["Body"] = BodyTextBox.Text;
            //listItem["SLPictureURL"] = GetUrlFromImageSource();
            if (PublishDatePicker.SelectedDate != null)
                listItem["PublishDate"] = PublishDatePicker.SelectedDate;
            else
                listItem["PublishDate"] = DateTime.Now;
            if (ExpirationDatePicker.SelectedDate != null)
                listItem["ExpirationDate"] = ExpirationDatePicker.SelectedDate;

            if (selectedPicture != null)
                listItem["SLPictureURL"] = App.SiteUrl + "/" +
```

```
                    App.PictureLibraryName
        + "/" + selectedPicture.Name;

    listItem.Update();

    serverAction = ServerAction.UpdateItem;
    clientContext.ExecuteQueryAsync(HandleClientRequestSucceeded,
        HandleClientRequestFailed);
}
```

If a new item is created, the selected image is first saved to the picture library by calling the private `UploadPicture` method. Then, an object of type `ListItemCreationInformation` is populated with the filled-out data, and the `Update` method on the item is called.

Calling the `ExecuteQueryAsync` method effectively saves the new item to the SharePoint list. When the item is saved successfully, and the call returns to the Silverlight application, a message is sent over the local message channel to inform that an item has been created, causing the list box to refresh.

```
private void CreateNewsListItem()
{
    // upload the new picture to the picture library
    UploadPicture();

    // create a new list item
    ListItemCreationInformation itemCreateInfo = new
            ListItemCreationInformation();
    ListItem newItem = newsList.AddItem(itemCreateInfo);
    newItem["Title"] = TitleTextBox.Text;
    newItem["Body"] = BodyTextBox.Text;
    if (selectedPicture != null)
        newItem["SLPictureURL"] = App.SiteUrl + "/" +
                App.PictureLibraryName
                + "/" + selectedPicture.Name;

    if (PublishDatePicker.SelectedDate != null)
        newItem["PublishDate"] = PublishDatePicker.SelectedDate;
    else
        newItem["PublishDate"] = DateTime.Now;
    if (ExpirationDatePicker.SelectedDate != null)
        newItem["ExpirationDate"] = ExpirationDatePicker.SelectedDate;

    newItem.Update();

    serverAction = ServerAction.CreateItem;
    clientContext.ExecuteQueryAsync(
        HandleClientRequestSucceeded, HandleClientRequestFailed);
}
```

The `UploadPicture` method retrieves the picture from Isolated Storage, where it was temporarily stored when the picture was selected. The picture is transformed into a byte array and saved to a SharePoint picture library using a `FileCreationInformation` object. The URL of the picture is defined by the following:

➤ The URL of the SharePoint site passed in via the `initParameters` dictionary

➤ The name of the picture library also passed in via the `initParameters` dictionary

➤   The name of the selected picture

```
private void UploadPicture()
{
    if (selectedPicture != null)
    {
        if (pictureLibrary == null)
            pictureLibrary = ClientCtxt.Web.Lists.
                GetByTitle(App.PictureLibraryName);

        FileCollection Files = pictureLibrary.RootFolder.Files;

        using (FileStream fs = selectedPicture.OpenRead())
        {
            byte[] FileContent = new byte[fs.Length];
            FileCreationInformation File = new FileCreationInformation();
            int dummy = fs.Read(FileContent, 0, (int)fs.Length);
            File.Content = FileContent;
            File.Url = App.SiteUrl + "/" + App.PictureLibraryName
                + "/" + selectedPicture.Name;
            File.Overwrite = true;
            Files.Add(File);

            serverAction = ServerAction.UploadPicture;
            clientContext.ExecuteQueryAsync(HandleClientRequestSucceeded,
                HandleClientRequestFailed);
        }
    }
}
```

The two Silverlight applications are ready. They now must be placed on a custom application page.

The News Manager Application Page

The custom application page will render the two Silverlight applications described in the previous sections. They will allow you to manage the existing news items and create new ones, as shown in Figure 13-35.

The application page shown in Figure 13-36 will be accessible from a custom action in the Site Actions menu.

FIGURE 13-35: Custom application page allowing you to manage the existing news items and create new ones

FIGURE 13-36: The News Item Manager page is accessible from a menu item in the Site Actions menu

If you choose to create the Visual Studio project for this example using the Visual Studio 2010 Tools for SharePoint 2010, you can start with an empty project. Choose the Application Page project item template to build the application page.

The following HTML markup for the application page adds an HTML table with two columns to the Main content place holder. Each column hosts a different Silverlight application.

```
<asp:Content ID="Main" ContentPlaceHolderID="PlaceHolderMain" runat="server">
    <table width="100%" height="600">
        <colgroup>
            <col width="50%" />
            <col width="50%" />
        </colgroup>
        <tr>
            <td  height="600" valign="top">
                <!-- News Items ListBox -->
                <div id="slListBoxHost" style="width: 400; height: 600">
                    <object data="data:application/x-silverlight-2,"
                        type="application/x-silverlight-2"
                        width="100%" height="100%">
                        <param name="source"
                            value="/_layouts/News Manager/SLNewsItemsListBox.xap" />
                        <param name="width" value="400" />
                        <param name="height" value="600" />
                        <param name="initParams" value="<%= InitParameters %>" />
                        <param name="autoUpgrade" value="true" />
                        <a href="http://go.microsoft.com/fwlink/?LinkID=149156"
                            style="text-decoration: none">
                             <img src="http://go.microsoft.com/
                                 fwlink/?LinkId=108181"
                                 alt="Get Microsoft Silverlight"
                                 style="border-style: none" />
                        </a>
                    </object>
                </div>
            </td>
            <td height="600" valign="top">
                <!-- News Item Details -->
                <div id="slNewsItemHost" style="width: 420; height: 600">
                    <object data="data:application/x-silverlight-2,"
                        type="application/x-silverlight-2"
                        width="100%" height="100%">
                        <param name="source"
                            value="/_layouts/News Manager/SLNewsItemDetails.xap" />
                        <param name="width" value="420" />
                        <param name="height" value="550" />
                        <param name="initParams" value="<%=
                            DetailsInitParameters %>" />
                        <param name="autoUpgrade" value="true" />
                        <a href="http://go.microsoft.com/fwlink/?LinkID=149156"
                            style="text-decoration: none">
                             <img src="http://go.microsoft.com/
                                 fwlink/?LinkId=108181"
                                 alt="Get Microsoft Silverlight"
                                 style="border-style: none" />
                        </a>
```

```
                    </object>
                </div>
            </td>
        </tr>
    </table>
</asp:Content>
```

The value for both `source` parameters is hard-coded and points to a subfolder of the `_layouts` folder in the SharePoint root. This means that the Silverlight applications will be deployed in the same subfolder as the application page.

But the values for the `initParams` parameters are retrieved from a property defined in the code behind. The `initParams` parameter of the `SLNewsItemsListBox` application needs the URL of the SharePoint site in the `MS.SP.url` parameter to be able to build the current SharePoint context. Additionally, the Silverlight application also needs the name of the SharePoint list that contains the news items.

```
public string InitParameters
{
    get
    {
        return string.Format("MS.SP.url={0},list={1}",
            SPContext.Current.Web.Url, "Real World SharePoint News");
    }
}
```

The `initParameters` parameter of the `SLNewsItemDetails` application needs the same initial parameters, but also an additional one containing the name of the Picture Library that stores the news items pictures:

```
public string DetailsInitParameters
{
    get
    {
        return string.Format("MS.SP.url={0},list={1},piclib={2}",
            SPContext.Current.Web.Url, "Real World SharePoint News",
            "Real World Pictures");
    }
}
```

An `Empty element` project item is added to the project to define the custom action.

```
<Elements xmlns="http://schemas.microsoft.com/sharepoint/">
    <!-- Add Command to Site Actions Dropdown -->
    <CustomAction Id="WroxNewsManager"
        GroupId="SiteActions"
        Location="Microsoft.SharePoint.StandardMenu"
        Sequence="1000"
        Title="Wrox News Item Manager"
        ImageUrl="~site/_layouts/Images/News Manager/Wrox.jpg"
        Description="This Silverlight-enabled application page shows
            news item details.">
        <UrlAction Url="~site/_layouts/News Manager/NewsItemsManager.aspx"/>
    </CustomAction>
</Elements>
```

This completes the example of the Silverlight-enabled application page.

When the application page is deployed, you can access it using the Site Actions menu, as shown in Figure 13-37. All the news items are listed in the Silverlight list box. Clicking the news items will make the second Silverlight application appear, and show the details of the selected news item. You can modify the selected news item or create a new list item using the New button.

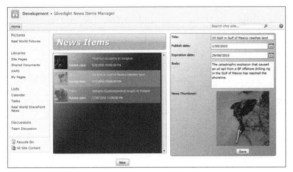

FIGURE 13-37: New button used to modify the selected news item or create a new list item

HOSTING A SILVERLIGHT APPLICATION IN THE MASTER PAGE

You can also host a Silverlight application from within a master page. Wouldn't it be nice to have a scrolling marquee with news items on every page in the SharePoint site, as shown in Figure 13-38?

FIGURE 13-38: The Silverlight News Items Marquee

 The file `Sample 5 - Silverlight enabled master page.zip` *available for download at* www.wrox.com *contains the source code for this example.*

The Marquee Server Control

You could place the Silverlight control directly on the master page. However, because you need the `InitParams` argument to be set in code behind, it is not a bad idea to wrap the Silverlight control into a server control, and place that server control on the master page.

The server control is created using the Visual Studio 2010 Tools for SharePoint 2010. It inherits from the `SPControl` base class. The `CreateChildControls` method is responsible for building the `initParams` string, which contains the URL of the current SharePoint site and the name of the list containing the news items. The private method `BuildSilverlightControl` builds the Silverlight control.

Note that the Silverlight control is added programmatically using a `StringBuilder`. When the string is complete, it is added to the `div` control, which, in turn, is added to the `Controls` collection of the server control.

```csharp
public class MarqueeControl: SPControl
{
    protected override void CreateChildControls()
    {
        // get the location from the embedded resource
        string xapUrl = SPContext.Current.Site.Url
            + "/_catalogs/masterpage/Preview Images/NewsBanner.xap";

        string initparams = string.Format("MS.SP.url={0},list=Real World
            SharePoint News",
                SPContext.Current.Web.Url);

        HtmlGenericControl div = new HtmlGenericControl("div");
        div.ID = "SilverlightControlHost";
        div.Attributes.Add("style", "width: 100%, height: 150");
        div.InnerHtml = BuildSilverlightControl(xapUrl, initparams,"150");

        this.Controls.Add(div);
    }

    private string BuildSilverlightControl(string source, string initParams,
            string height)
    {
        StringBuilder slctl = new StringBuilder();
        slctl.Append("<object id=\"SilverlightHost\"");
        slctl.Append(" width=\"100%\"");
        slctl.Append(" height=\"" + height + "\"");
        slctl.Append(" data=\"data:application/x-silverlight-2,\"");
        slctl.Append(" type=\"application/x-silverlight-2\" >");
        slctl.Append(" <param name=\"source\" value=\"" + source + "\"/>");
        if (!string.IsNullOrEmpty(initParams))
        {
            slctl.Append(" <param name=\"initParams\" value=\"" +
                initParams + "\"/>");
        }
        slctl.Append(" <a href=\"http://
            go.microsoft.com/fwlink/?LinkID=149156\" ");
        slctl.Append(" style=\"text-decoration: none;\">");
        slctl.Append(" <img src=\"http://
            go.microsoft.com/fwlink/?LinkId=108181\" ");
        slctl.Append(" alt=\"Get Microsoft Silverlight\" ");
        slctl.Append(" style=\"border-style: none\"/>");
```

```
            slctl.Append(" </a>");
            slctl.Append("</object>");

            return slctl.ToString();
        }
    }
```

The Custom Master Page

You have different ways to build a custom master page. The best way is to start from an existing master page. SharePoint 2010 comes with a minimal master page that you can use as a starting point if you need to build a completely different master page. Because this example only adds a scrolling marquee to the master page, a copy of the v4.master has been used.

The Silverlight control is wrapped within a server control, and you will place that server control on the master page. Therefore, you must first add a reference to the assembly containing the server control.

```
<%@ Register TagPrefix="WROX" Namespace="Wrox.Chapter13.PictureMarquee"
      Assembly="Wrox.Chapter13.PictureMarquee, Version=1.0.0.0,
          Culture=neutral, PublicKeyToken=970adb296b83a8b6" %>
```

Because you want the marquee to appear at the top of the main content placeholder, you add the server control right within the MSO_ContentDiv.

```
<div class='s4-ba'>
   <div class='ms-bodyareacell'>
      <div id="MSO_ContentDiv" runat="server">
         <WROX:MarqueeControl ID="SLMarquee" runat="server" />
         <a name="mainContent"></a>
         <asp:ContentPlaceHolder id="PlaceHolderMain" runat="server">
         </asp:ContentPlaceHolder>
      </div>
   </div>
</div>
```

Deploying the Custom Master Page

You use the same News Banner Silverlight application as in the first example in this chapter, but this time, it will be deployed to a different location. A master page must be deployed to the Master Page Gallery, and images and other resources (such as a Silverlight .xap file) can be deployed to the Preview Images subfolder of the Master Page Gallery.

When using the Visual Studio 2010 Tools for SharePoint 2010, you can add a Module item to the project, and add your master page and .xap file to it, as shown in Figure 13-39.

FIGURE 13-39: The project structure for deployment of a custom master page

The `elements.xml` file of the module contains the necessary XML to provision the master page to the Master Page Gallery, and to deploy the `.xap` file to the `Preview Images` subfolder. Note that the Master Page Gallery is a list instance based on the list definition with base type `116`.

```xml
<?xml version="1.0" encoding="utf-8"?>
<Elements xmlns="http://schemas.microsoft.com/sharepoint/">
  <Module Name="MasterPages" List="116" Url="_catalogs/masterpage" >
    <File Path="Silverlight Master Page Module\SLMarquee.master"
        Url="SLMarquee.master"  Type="GhostableInLibrary" />
  </Module>

  <Module Name="Xaps" Url="_catalogs/masterpage/Preview Images">
    <File Path="Silverlight Master Page Module\NewsBanner.xap"
        Url="NewsBanner.xap" Type="GhostableInLibrary" />
  </Module>
</Elements>
```

The Build Action of both files must be set to `Content` (as shown in Figure 13-40) to make Visual Studio include them in the SharePoint solution.

Additionally, a `SafeControl` element should be added to the `web.config` file when the solution is deployed to SharePoint to register the `Picture Marquee` server control as a safe control. You must force the package's `manifest.xml` file to include this `SafeControl` element. You can edit the `manifest.xml` by following these steps:

1. Double-click the Package node in Solution Explorer to open the Package Designer.

2. The Package Designer has three buttons at the bottom: Design, Advanced, and Manifest. Click the Manifest button to open the `manifest.xml`.

3. Click the Edit Options button to expand the region where you can make changes to the manifest, as shown in Figure 13-41.

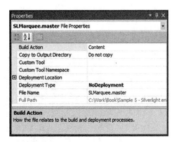

FIGURE 13-40: Set the Build Action to Content

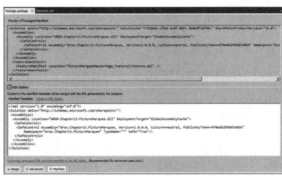

FIGURE 13-41: Edit the manifest.xml file to add a SafeControl element

4. Enter the `SafeControl` element that you expect to be added to the `web.config` of your SharePoint web application.

```xml
<Assemblies>
    <Assembly Location="WROX.Chapter13.PictureMarquee.dll"
            DeploymentTarget="GlobalAssemblyCache">
```

```
<SafeControls>
  <SafeControl Assembly="Wrox.Chapter13.PictureMarquee, Version=1.0.0.0,
      Culture=neutral, PublicKeyToken=970adb296b83a8b6"
    Namespace="Wrox.Chapter13.PictureMarquee" TypeName="*" Safe="True"/>
</SafeControls>
</Assembly>
</Assemblies>
```

Select the Feature to ensure that the Feature is scoped at site collection level. You can apply the master page when the Feature is activated. Therefore, you must add an event receiver class to the Feature. You can achieve this by right-clicking the Feature in the Solution Explorer and choosing "Add event receiver."

Uncomment the `FeatureActivated` method and add the following code to change the master page to `SLMarquee.master`:

```
public override void FeatureActivated(SPFeatureReceiverProperties
    properties)
{
    using (SPSite site = properties.Feature.Parent as SPSite)
    {
        using (SPWeb web = site.RootWeb)
        {
            Uri masterUri = new Uri(web.Url
                + "/_catalogs/masterpage/SLMarquee.master");
            web.MasterUrl = masterUri.AbsolutePath;
            web.Update();
        }
    }
}
```

You can best restore the master page when the Feature is deactivated. Uncomment the `FeatureDeactivating` method and add the following code:

```
public override void FeatureDeactivating(SPFeatureReceiverProperties
    properties)
{
    using (SPSite site = properties.Feature.Parent as SPSite)
    {
        using (SPWeb web = site.RootWeb)
        {
            Uri masterUri = new Uri(web.Url +
                "/_catalogs/masterpage/v4.master");
            web.MasterUrl = masterUri.AbsolutePath;
            web.Update();
        }
    }
}
```

Now, the master page is ready to deploy. Once deployed, you can open your SharePoint site and navigate to different pages to see how the news banner now runs on every page.

USING BUSINESS CONNECTIVITY SERVICES

Business Connectivity Services (BCS) is a new feature in SharePoint 2010 that makes it possible to view and manage data from an external data source like a SQL Server database.

This example returns to the News Banner web part created earlier in this chapter. Here, you will modify the web part and the Silverlight application to make them capable of rendering items from the AdventureWorks SQL Server database, as shown in Figure 13-42.

FIGURE 13-42: Set the new master page as Default Master Page

 The file Sample 6 - Silverlight and BCS.zip *available for download at* www .wrox.com *contains the source code for this example.*

Defining the External Content Type

A *content type* is a definition of a business entity. It groups different metadata columns into a business entity that can be applied to lists and document libraries. An *external content type (ECT)* is a definition of a business entity for which the data is stored in an external data source (for example, a SQL Server database).

This example uses the News Banner Silverlight application from earlier in the chapter to display product information from the AdventureWorks sample database. Ensure that the Secure Store service application and the BCS application are configured correctly.

SharePoint Designer 2010 is an easy tool to use to define ECTs. When opening your SharePoint site in SharePoint Designer 2010, you will see a quick launch with different categories listed. In the External Content Types category, you can define your ECT.

The AdventureWorks Product Information content type is created in a view that gathers product information from different tables: Product, ProductModel, ProductModelProductDescription, ProductDescription, ProductPhoto, and ProductProductPhoto. As shown in Figure 13-43, some of these tables are relation tables.

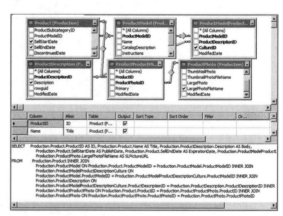

FIGURE 13-43: The vProductInformation view

The columns selected from the different tables are renamed in the view to get column names that correspond to the names that are expected by the Silverlight application. The SQL code for the new view vProductInformation looks like this:

```
SELECT      Production.Product.ProductID AS ID, Production.Product.Name AS Title,
            Production.ProductDescription.Description AS Body,
            Production.Product.SellStartDate AS PublishDate,
            Production.Product.SellEndDate AS ExpirationDate,
            Production.ProductPhoto.LargePhotoFileName AS SLPictureURL
FROM        Production.Product INNER JOIN
            Production.ProductProductPhoto ON Production.Product.ProductID =
            Production.ProductProductPhoto.ProductID INNER JOIN
            Production.ProductPhoto ON
                Production.ProductProductPhoto.ProductPhotoID =
            Production.ProductPhoto.ProductPhotoID INNER JOIN
            Production.ProductModel ON Production.Product.ProductModelID =
            Production.ProductModel.ProductModelID INNER JOIN
            Production.ProductModelProductDescriptionCulture ON
            Production.ProductModel.ProductModelID =
            Production.ProductModelProductDescriptionCulture.ProductModelID
                INNER JOIN
            Production.ProductDescription ON
            Production.ProductModelProductDescriptionCulture.ProductDescriptionID =
            Production.ProductDescription.ProductDescriptionID
WHERE       (Production.ProductModelProductDescriptionCulture.CultureID = 'en') AND
            (Production.ProductPhoto.LargePhotoFileName <>
                'no_image_available_large.gif')
```

When creating the ECT, you must add a connection to the AdventureWorks database, as shown in Figure 13-44.

When the connection to the AdventureWorks database is configured correctly, a list of available tables and views becomes available. Select the vProductInformation view from the list of views, as shown in Figure 13-45. Right-click it to configure the necessary operations. Because you only want to read product information, you only configure the Read List operation and the Read Item operation.

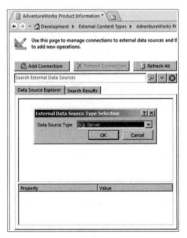

FIGURE 13-44: Create a connection to the AdventureWorks database

FIGURE 13-45: Select the vProductInformation view and create the Read List and Read Item methods

The ECT has two methods: the `Read List` method and the `Read Item` method, as shown in Figure 13-46. No CRUD methods have been defined for this example.

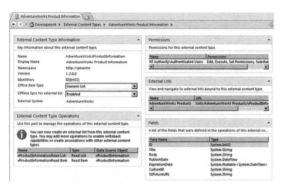

FIGURE 13-46: The external content type definition in SharePoint Designer

You want the News Banner to also display a photo of each product. These photos are also contained in the `AdventureWorks` database and have data type `varbinary`. The view (and so the ECT) does not contain this column, but only the name of the photo. Later in this example, you will use this name to retrieve the photo information using a WCF service, and convert it so that it can be rendered by the `Image` control of Silverlight.

When you save the ECT, it is saved to the BCS application, so you must ensure that this service application is configured before you can start creating ECTs. You can access the BCS from within SharePoint Central Administration.

Defining the External List

Based on this ECT, you can define an external list in SharePoint 2010. When creating the new list, use the External List template and choose the ECT from the External Content Type picker, as shown in Figure 13-47.

This list will now retrieve product information from the different tables in the `AdventureWorks` database, as shown in Figure 13-48.

FIGURE 13-47: Creating the AdventureWorks Products external list

Developing the WCF Service

The `SLPictureURL` column will contain the name of the product photo that is stored in the `AdventureWorks` database. It is not the URL that is expected by the Silverlight application. The photo itself is stored in the SQL Server database as binary data.

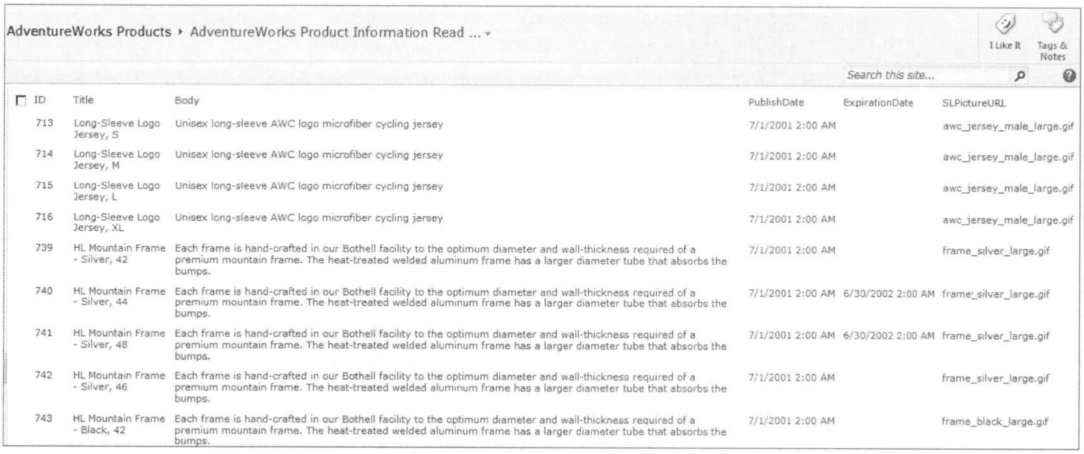

FIGURE 13-48: The AdventureWorks Products list

A custom WCF service is used to retrieve the binary data and convert it to a format that can be understood by the Silverlight application.

The `AdventureWorks` Picture Service exposes the `IAdventureWorksPictureService` interface. It consists of one method, the `GetPicture` method. This method returns an object of type `ImageClass`. This `ImageClass` object exposes two properties: one for the name of the picture, and one for the binary array.

```
[ServiceContract]
interface IAdventureWorksPictureService
{
    [OperationContract]
    ImageClass GetPicture(int productID);

}


[DataContract]
public class ImageClass
{
    [DataMember]
    public string FileName { get; set; }
    [DataMember]
    public byte[] ImageFile { get; set; }
}
```

The `GetPicture` method accepts the product ID as an incoming parameter. This product ID is used to retrieve the corresponding picture in the `AdventureWorks` database.

As mentioned, the `LargePhoto` column contains the picture as a byte array, but it is the byte array of a `.GIF` file format. This is a picture format that cannot be rendered by the Silverlight application. Therefore, this method also takes care of the conversion to a `.JPEG` image. The filename of the picture and the new binary array are stored in an `ImageClass` object, and returned to the Silverlight application.

```
[ServiceBehavior]
[AspNetCompatibilityRequirements(RequirementsMode =
```

```
        AspNetCompatibilityRequirementsMode.Allowed)]
public class AdventureWorksPictureService: IAdventureWorksPictureService
{
    string connectionstring =
        "Data Source=SPKARINE;Initial Catalog=AdventureWorks;Integrated
            Security=True";

    public ImageClass GetPicture(int productID)
    {
        AdventureWorksDataContext datacontext =
            new AdventureWorksDataContext(connectionstring);

        var query = from p in datacontext.Products
                    join ppp in datacontext.ProductProductPhotos
                        on p.ProductID
                      equals ppp.ProductID
                    join pp in datacontext.ProductPhotos on ppp.ProductPhotoID
                      equals pp.ProductPhotoID
                    where p.ProductID == productID
                        && pp.LargePhotoFileName
                    select pp;

        byte[] bytearray = query.FirstOrDefault().LargePhoto.ToArray();

        // this is a byte array for a .gif. Convert it to
        // a .jpg before sending it to
        // the Silverlight application
        MemoryStream ms = new MemoryStream(bytearray);
        Image localImage = Image.FromStream(ms);
        MemoryStream jpgms = new MemoryStream();
        localImage.Save(jpgms, System.Drawing.Imaging.ImageFormat.Jpeg);

        // convert the .jpg into a byte array
        byte[] newbytearray = jpgms.ToArray();

        ImageClass imgClass = new ImageClass();
        imgClass.FileName = query.FirstOrDefault().LargePhotoFileName;
        imgClass.ImageFile = newbytearray;

        // you must keep the stream open
        ms.Close();

        // return the image object
        return imgClass;
    }
}
```

As in the previous example, the WCF service is deployed to the ISAPI folder of the SharePoint root to make it run in the context of SharePoint. However, the main reason this is done is to avoid a cross-domain call from within the Silverlight application.

Modifying the News Banner Web Part

The ribbon of the News Banner web part has been modified to display an extra button. Clicking this button causes the Silverlight application to show the AdventureWorks products from the external list and the corresponding picture, as shown in Figure 13-49.

FIGURE 13-49: The AdventureWorks Products ribbon button in action

The new button is defined in its own custom group.

```xml
<?xml version="1.0" encoding="utf-8"?>
<Elements xmlns="http://schemas.microsoft.com/sharepoint/">
  <CustomAction
        Id="Ribbon.NewsBannerWebPart"
        Location="CommandUI.Ribbon"
        Title="Silverlight NewsBanner Ribbon">
    <CommandUIExtension>
      <CommandUIDefinitions>
        <CommandUIDefinition Location="Ribbon.WebPartOption.Groups._children">
          <Group
          Id="Ribbon.NewsBannerWebPart"
          Sequence="70"
          Command="Ribbon.NewsBannerWebPart"
          Description="News Banner"
          Title="Sample 6 News Banner"
          Template="Ribbon.Templates.ManageViewsGroup">
            <Controls Id="Ribbon.NewsBannerWebPart.Controls">
              <Button
          Id="Ribbon.NewsBannerWebPart.ViewAdventureWorks"
          Command="Ribbon.NewsBannerWebPart.ViewAdventureWorks"
                      Image16by16="/_layouts/images/Chapter13.Sample6.
                      NewsBannerWebPart/AW16.png"
              Image32by32="/_layouts/images/Chapter13.Sample6.
                  NewsBannerWebPart/AW32.png"
          LabelText="AdventureWorks"
              Sequence="3"
          TemplateAlias="o1"/>
            </Controls>
          </Group>
        </CommandUIDefinition>
        <CommandUIDefinition Location="Ribbon.WebPartOption.Scaling._children">
          <MaxSize Id="Ribbon.NewsBannerWebPart.MaxSize"
          GroupId="Ribbon.NewsBannerWebPart"
          Sequence="20"
          Size="LargeLarge" />
        </CommandUIDefinition>
```

```
                <CommandUIDefinition Location="Ribbon.WebPartOption.Scaling._children">
                  <Scale Id="Ribbon.NewsBannerWebPart.MediumMedium"
                  GroupId="Ribbon.NewsBannerWebPart"
                  Sequence="30"
                  Size="MediumMedium" />
                </CommandUIDefinition>
                <CommandUIDefinition Location="Ribbon.WebPartOption.Scaling._children">
                  <Scale Id="Ribbon.NewsBannerWebPart.Popup"
                  GroupId="Ribbon.NewsBannerWebPart"
                  Sequence="50"
                  Size="Popup" />
                </CommandUIDefinition>
              </CommandUIDefinitions>
            </CommandUIExtension>
          </CustomAction>
        </Elements>
```

There is also a change in the `NewsBannerPageComponent.js` JavaScript file. Not only must the new commandId `Ribbon.NewsBannerWebPart.ViewAdventureWorks` be added to the `canHandleCommand` function and the `getGlobalCommands` function, it must also be handled in the `handleCommand` function. In the second example presented in this chapter, the Real World SharePoint News list and the Real World Nature list are based on the same list definition. In this example, however, the AdventureWorks Products list is an external list. As you will see in the next example, both types of lists will be handled differently. Therefore, the `handleCommand` function now also passes the list template ID.

```
        handleCommand: function (commandId, properties, sequence) {
            if (commandId == 'Ribbon.NewsBannerWebPart.ViewRealSharePoint') {
                refreshNewsBanner('Real World SharePoint News', 10000);
            }
            if (commandId == 'Ribbon.NewsBannerWebPart.ViewRealNature') {
                refreshNewsBanner('Real World Nature', 10000);
            }

            if (commandId == 'Ribbon.NewsBannerWebPart.ViewAdventureWorks') {
                refreshNewsBanner('AdventureWorks Products', 600);
            }
        },
```

Also, the `refreshNewsBanner` function has been modified to pass the list template to the Silverlight application.

```
        function refreshNewsBanner(listName, templateId) {
            if (!listName || listName.length == 0)
                alert('Please, select a news library.');

            var sl = document.getElementById('SLNewsBanner');
            if (sl) {
                sl.Content.NewsBanner.RefreshNewsBanner(listName, templateId);
            }
        }
```

Modifying the News Banner Silverlight Application

Nothing has been changed to the XAML definition of the Silverlight application. The first change occurs in the RefreshNewsBanner method that is called by the ribbon buttons. For this example to work, the ribbon buttons pass an extra value, which is the list type. Then, the PopulateNewsBanner is called as usual.

```
[ScriptableMember]
public void RefreshNewsBanner(string listName, string listType)
{
    App.ListName = listName;
    App.ListType = listType);

    PopulateNewsBanner();
}
```

The PopulateNewsBanner method contains an important change. It is not possible to retrieve the list items from an external list, as was done for a normal SharePoint list. The ViewXml property needs some extra information, including the following:

➤ The name of the method that must be used to retrieve the list items. For the AdventureWorks Products external list, it is the vProductInformationRead List method.

➤ All the fields that need to be returned must be listed within the <ViewFields> node.

```
private void PopulateNewsBanner()
{
    web = ClientCtxt.Web;
    ClientCtxt.Load(web);

    newsList = ClientCtxt.Web.Lists.GetByTitle(App.ListName);
    CamlQuery camlQuery = new CamlQuery();
    string viewXml = null;
    if (App.ListType == "10000")
    {
        viewXml = "<View><Query><OrderBy>"
          + "<FieldRef Name='PublishDate' Ascending='False' />"
          + "<FieldRef Name='Title' /></OrderBy></Query></View>";
    }
    else if (App.ListType == "600")
    {
        viewXml = "<View>"
            + "<Method Name='vProductInformationRead List' />"
            + "<ViewFields><FieldRef Name='ID' /><FieldRef Name='Title' />"
            + "<FieldRef Name='Body' /><FieldRef Name='PublishDate' />"
            + "<FieldRef Name='SLPictureURL' /></ViewFields>"
            + "<Query><OrderBy>"
            + "<FieldRef Name='PublishDate' Ascending='False' />"
            + "<FieldRef Name='Title' /></OrderBy></Query>"
            + "</View>";
    }
    camlQuery.ViewXml = viewXml;
```

```
        listItems = newsList.GetItems(camlQuery);
        ClientCtxt.Load(listItems,
            items => items.Include(
                item => item["ID"],
                item => item["Title"],
                item => item["Body"],
                item => item["PublishDate"],
                item => item["SLPictureURL"]
                ).Take(50));

        ClientCtxt.ExecuteQueryAsync(HandleClientRequestSucceeded,
            HandleClientRequestFailed);


    }
```

The SLPictureURL value cannot be rendered as in the previous example using the DataContext property of each NewsItemControl instance. The picture itself must be retrieved using the custom WCF service AdventureWorks Picture Service. Therefore, the setting of the DataContext property has been moved to the constructor of the NewsItemControl instance. The creation of each news item control has been changed in the OperationSucceeded method as follows:

```
        public void OperationSucceeded(object sender, EventArgs e)
        {
            NewsItemPanel.Children.Clear();

            // Load the news banner
            foreach (ListItem item in listItems)
            {
                NewsItemControl newsItemControl = new NewsItemControl(item);
                NewsItemPanel.Children.Add(newsItemControl);
            }

            if (listItems.Count > 0)
            {
                // the rest of the code remains the same and
                // is omitted for brevity.
            }
        }
```

Within the NewsItemControl class, the constructor has been changed to call the AdventureWorks Picture Service by passing the product ID to the GetPicture method.

When a service reference is added to the WCF service from within the Silverlight application, the proxy is automatically created and asynchronous methods are generated. The GetPicture method executes asynchronously and, therefore, an event handler is attached to the GetPictureCompleted event. Then, the GetPictureAsync method is called by passing the ID of the list item.

```
        public NewsItemControl(ListItem item)
        {
            InitializeComponent();
            this.DataContext = item;

            // retrieve the picture if an external list is displayed
```

```
if (App.ListType == "600")
{
    picturews =
        new AdventureWorksPictureService.
            AdventureWorksPictureServiceClient();
    picturews.Endpoint.Address = new EndpointAddress(
        App.SiteUrl +
        "/_vti_bin/AdventureWorksPictureService/
            AdventureWorksPictureService.svc");

    picturews.GetPictureCompleted += new
        EventHandler<AdventureWorksPictureService.
            GetPictureCompletedEventArgs>(
        picturews_GetPictureCompleted);
    picturews.GetPictureAsync(System.Convert.ToInt32(item["ID"]));
}
}
```

The server will come back with the result in the `picturews_GetPictureCompleted` event handler. The result is an object of the custom `ImageClass` type that was defined on the WCF interface. The `ImageFile` property contains the byte array of a `.JPG` image. This byte array can be stored in a memory stream. This memory stream can be attributed to the `SetSource` property of a `BitmapImage` object, which can then be used to set the `Source` property of the `NewsPicture` image control.

```
void picturews_GetPictureCompleted(object sender,
    AdventureWorksPictureService.GetPictureCompletedEventArgs e)
{
    if (e.Error == null && e.Result != null)
    {
        // you should have a byte array for a .gif file
        AdventureWorksPictureService.ImageClass imageClass = e.Result;
        MemoryStream stream = new MemoryStream(imageClass.ImageFile);
        BitmapImage b = new BitmapImage();
        b.SetSource(stream);
        NewsPicture.Source = b;
    }
}
```

When everything is deployed to the SharePoint site, and the modified `NewsBanner.xap` is uploaded to the XAPS library, you can test the web part. Set your web part page in Edit mode to display the web part ribbon, as shown in Figure 13-50.

Clicking the AdventureWorks ribbon button warns the Silverlight application that the items of the AdventureWorks Products external list must be retrieved and displayed in the Silverlight News Banner, as shown in Figure 13-51.

FIGURE 13-50: Select the AdventureWorks ribbon button

FIGURE 13-51: The items from the external list AdventureWorks Products are displayed

USING SILVERLIGHT FROM WITHIN A SANDBOXED SOLUTION

Silverlight applications can also be hosted in a sandboxed solution. In this example, you will turn the News Banner web part into a web part that can be deployed by a sandboxed solution.

> The file `Sample 7 - Silverlight in a sandbox.zip` *available for download at* `www.wrox.com` *contains the source code for this example.*

The News Banner web part in the previous examples is a visual web part. This type of web part cannot be deployed by a sandboxed solution because it needs to deploy the `.ascx` user control file to the SharePoint root, and that's not allowed by a sandboxed solution. A visual web part can easily be replaced by a classic web part, creating and adding the necessary controls programmatically to the user interface of the web part.

When the solution is created using Visual Studio 2010 Tools for SharePoint 2010, you can choose an empty SharePoint project. To that project, you can add a Web Part item, as shown in Figure 13-52.

This adds the necessary web part files to the project. As you can see in Figure 13-53, there is no folder containing an `.ascx` file.

FIGURE 13-52: Add a Web Part item to the empty SharePoint project

FIGURE 13-53: The NewsBannerSandboxedWebPart project structure

In the `NewsBannerSandboxedWebPart.cs` file, you can add the necessary properties that must be filled out by the users before the Silverlight control can be rendered. These properties (such as `source`, `initparameters`, `width`, and `height`) will be rendered in the web part tool pane under the Silverlight category.

```
private string source;

[Personalizable(PersonalizationScope.Shared),
 Category("Silverlight"),
WebDisplayName("XAP Location"),
WebBrowsable(true)]
public string Source
{
```

```
        get { return source; }
        set { source = value; }
    }

    private string initParameters;

    [Personalizable(PersonalizationScope.Shared),
     Category("Silverlight"),
    WebDisplayName("Init parameters (comma separated)"),
    WebBrowsable(true)]
    public string InitParameters
    {
        get { return initParameters; }
        set { initParameters = value; }
    }

    private string width;

    [Personalizable(PersonalizationScope.Shared),
     Category("Silverlight"),
    WebDisplayName("Width Silverlight application"),
    DefaultValue("650"),
    WebBrowsable(true)]
    public string SilverlightWidth
    {
        get { return width; }
        set { width = value; }
    }

    private string height;

    [Personalizable(PersonalizationScope.Shared),
     Category("Silverlight"),
    WebDisplayName("Height Silverlight application"),
    DefaultValue("200"),
    WebBrowsable(true)]
    public string SilverlightHeight
    {
        get { return height; }
        set { height = value; }
    }
```

The Silverlight application must be rendered from within the CreateChildControls method of the web part. If the Source property is not filled out, a hyperlink inviting the user to open the web part tool pane will be displayed. If the Source property is filled out, the Silverlight application is rendered within a DIV element. If no width is specified, a width of 100 percent will be used to render the Silverlight application. The same condition is applied to the height argument.

```
        protected override void CreateChildControls()
        {
            if (string.IsNullOrEmpty(source))
            {
                LiteralControl openEditorPartControl =
                    new LiteralControl(string.Format(
```

```
                    "To show a Silverlight control "
                    + "<a href=\"javascript:MSOTlPn_ShowToolPane2("
                    + "'Edit','{0}');\">open the tool pane</a> "
                    + " and set the Silverlight properties.",
                    this.ID));

            this.Controls.Add(openEditorPartControl);
        }
        else
        {
            CompleteInitParameters();

            HtmlGenericControl div = new HtmlGenericControl("div");
            div.ID = "SilverlightHost";

            // generate the Silverlight control
            StringBuilder sb = new StringBuilder("<object
                id=\"SilverlightHost\"");
            if (!string.IsNullOrEmpty(width))
                sb.Append(" width=\"" + width + "\"");
            else
                sb.Append(" width=\"100%\"");
            if (!string.IsNullOrEmpty(height))
                sb.Append(" height=\"" + height + "\"");
            else
                sb.Append(" height=\"100%\"");
            sb.Append(" data=\"data:application/x-silverlight-2,\"");
            sb.Append(" type=\"application/x-silverlight-2\" >");
            sb.Append(" <param name=\"source\" value=\"" + source + "\"/>");
            if (!string.IsNullOrEmpty(initParameters))
                sb.Append(" <param name=\"initParams\" value=\""
                + initParameters + "\"/>");
            sb.Append(" <a href=\"http://go.microsoft.com/
                fwlink/?LinkID=149156\" ");
            sb.Append(" style=\"text-decoration: none;\">");
            sb.Append(" <img src=\"http://go.microsoft.com/
                fwlink/?LinkId=108181\" ");
            sb.Append(" alt=\"Get Microsoft Silverlight\" ");
            sb.Append(" style=\"border-style: none\"/>");
            sb.Append(" </a>");
            sb.Append("</object>");

            div.InnerHtml = sb.ToString();

            this.Controls.Add(div);
        }
    }
```

Before deploying the web part, check in the Central Administration that the Sandboxed Code Service is started, as shown in Figure 13-54. If this service is not started when trying to deploy the sandboxed solution, you will get an error message telling you that the service SPUserCodeV4 cannot be started.

Service	Status	Action
Access Database Service	Stopped	Start
Application Registry Service	Stopped	Start
Business Data Connectivity Service	Started	Stop
Central Administration	Started	Stop
Claims to Windows Token Service	Stopped	Start
Document Conversions Launcher Service	Stopped	Start
Document Conversions Load Balancer Service	Stopped	Start
Excel Calculation Services	Stopped	Start
Lotus Notes Connector	Stopped	Start
Managed Metadata Web Service	Started	Stop
Microsoft SharePoint Foundation Incoming E-Mail	Started	Stop
Microsoft SharePoint Foundation Sandboxed Code Service	Started	Stop
Microsoft SharePoint Foundation Subscription Settings Service	Stopped	Start
Microsoft SharePoint Foundation Web Application	Started	Stop
Microsoft SharePoint Foundation Workflow Timer Service	Started	Stop
PerformancePoint Service	Stopped	Start
Search Query and Site Settings Service	Started	Stop
Secure Store Service	Started	Stop
SharePoint Foundation Search	Stopped	Start
SharePoint Server Search	Started	Stop

FIGURE 13-54: Checking that the Sandboxed Code Service is started

Sandboxed solutions are not deployed to the Central Administration, but rather in the Solution Gallery scoped to the site collection to which you deployed the sandboxed solution, as shown in Figure 13-55.

When adding the web part to a web part page, you can find the web part in the Wrox Chapter 13 category. Open the tool pane shown in Figure 13-56 to specify the necessary properties.

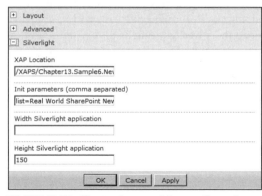

FIGURE 13-55: The site collection Solution Gallery can be accessed from the Site Settings page

FIGURE 13-56: The tool pane of the sandboxed web part

This example runs the news banner from previous example, as shown in Figure 13-57, but you can run any Silverlight application from within the web part.

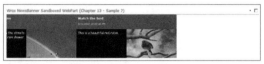

FIGURE 13-57: The sandboxed web part hosting the Silverlight News Banner

SUMMARY

It is not because you are a SharePoint developer that you have to sit back and stay with what the platform offers. I am a SharePoint developer myself, and I encourage you to start using technologies like Silverlight, LINQ, and WCF in combination with SharePoint. You have to use the best of both worlds.

With all the examples presented in this chapter, I wanted to demonstrate that Silverlight is not only a technique to make your sites look prettier, but also that there is really a place for Silverlight to offer extra functionality in SharePoint. Throughout this chapter, you have learned about many of the possible techniques you can use to host and deploy Silverlight applications.

ABOUT THE AUTHOR

Karine Bosch is a SharePoint developer who was recognized as a SharePoint MOSS MVP in April 2009. For several years, she worked as a technical assistant for Patrick Tisseghem, who died in September 2008. One of her best-known achievements is the CAML Query Builder. Together with Tisseghem, she developed the Silverlight BluePrint for SharePoint, which contains several samples on how to integrate Silverlight with SharePoint.

14

Business Connectivity Services

By Nick Swan

As organizations grow and new needs arise for the storage of electronic data, systems are often implemented to store this information in an "as-needed" manner. When investigating how an organization's IT is structured, you will often find a different system for each business department. This makes it very difficult to manage data across applications, reuse the data in business activities, or present the data in a dashboard manner for easy decision making.

Microsoft Office SharePoint Server 2007 (MOSS) Enterprise Edition came with a component called the *Business Data Catalog (BDC)*. This allowed you to define business data that was available from databases and web services, and then reuse it or display it in SharePoint. This feature was a big hit, because, while the integration required a definition file, no custom development or coding was required. Once users experienced how SharePoint could become the central portal for collaboration and integration with other systems, these users requested many features that were not available in the Business Data Catalog.

In SharePoint 2010, the *Business Connectivity Services* (BCS) has replaced the Business Data Catalog found in MOSS 2007. Not only has the technology undergone a name change, but the features have also been improved. The availability of the BCS within SharePoint has been increased so that the integration functionality is now available to more people through SharePoint Foundation, as well as SharePoint Server 2010.

This chapter provides a quick review of some of the limitations the Business Data Catalog suffered. You learn about some terminology and acronym changes that are important to understand when moving from the Business Data Catalog to the BCS. This chapter also examines how things have improved in SharePoint 2010 for those who are interested in data integration. Toward the end of this chapter, you'll experience a real-world look at how you can use new Visual Studio 2010 SharePoint tooling to integrate a database and web service with SharePoint 2010.

A BRIEF LOOK BACK

Back in SharePoint 2007, you could use the Business Data Catalog to integrate line of business (LOB) data with SharePoint. This enabled the re-use of business data within SharePoint, and allowed users to build up dashboards. SharePoint became the central place to go for collaboration and data usage. You no longer needed to go to many disparate systems to get an overview of how your business was running.

The Business Data Catalog was a great solution. However, there were a number of issues to resolve:

➤ The Business Data Catalog was part of MOSS 2007 Enterprise Edition only. If you had a lower license agreement in place, all this cool integration wasn't available to you.

➤ Business Data Catalog was read-only. Although you could write back to your data source through a custom web part or InfoPath solution, this wasn't marketed as out-of-the-box functionality.

➤ Authentication was sometimes difficult to get right. Installing everything on one server was fine, but as soon as you went to a more complex farm environment, many people came across the double-hop issue. The double-hop issue occurred when SharePoint and the data source you were integrating with (typically, SQL Server) were on different servers, and the user's identity could not be passed to authenticate against the back-end system.

➤ There was no setup tooling from Microsoft. Initially, Microsoft suggested using Notepad to create the XML application definition files that the Business Data Catalog needed to know about your data source. Microsoft later released an application in the SDK although many people still complained that this was inadequate. Some third-party tools were available (one of which I helped develop called *BDC Meta Man*). These tools offered a drag-and-drop user interface to generate the XML application definition files in a few minutes.

➤ The Business Data Catalog infrastructure was only capable of reading data from a single source at a time within an application, and had support only for basic Windows Communications Foundation (WCF) services.

Now that you know more about what was available to you in SharePoint 2007 and some of the issues, let's look into some of the naming conventions that were used in the previous version, and how they have changed for SharePoint 2010.

TERMINOLOGY CHANGES

For those who have previously worked with the Business Data Catalog, a few terminology changes with BCS are worth noting:

➤ *Business Connectivity Services (BCS)* — BCS includes everything shown in Figure 14-1. This includes the SharePoint user interface (UI) features, the Microsoft Office client components, the data access components, and any service the BCS may integrate.

➤ *Business Data Connectivity (BDC)* — As mentioned previously, back in the world of SharePoint 2007, BDC stood for "Business Data Catalog." In SharePoint 2010, BDC is an acronym for *Business Data Connectivity*. This component of the BCS is the middle tier that is used to access your LOB system. The BDC tier exists on both the client and server side, so both SharePoint and the Microsoft Office client applications talk through their own BDC layer.

➤ *Models* — Instead of building XML application definition files to define data sources as was done for SharePoint 2007, you now create and configure models.

➤ *External content type* — Instead of an entity, you now have external content types (ECTs). An ECT is a description of the data and BCS methods that make up a real-world object, such as a `Customer`, `Order`, or `Product`. The BCS methods that make up an ECT are the `Finder`, `SpecificFinder`, and so on.

➤ *Single Sign-On (SSO)* — SharePoint Server 2010 still has a Single Sign-On (SSO) service, but it is now called the Secure Store Service (SSS).

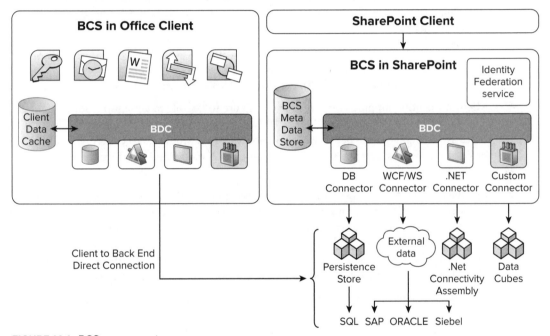

FIGURE 14-1: BCS components

WELCOME TO SHAREPOINT 2010

If there is one thing that Microsoft is good at, it is listening to the feedback of its users. Following are some of the main improvements and new features available in SharePoint 2010 for data integration:

➤ BCS integration is now available in SharePoint Foundation, as well as SharePoint Server. This provides people who are using the free version of SharePoint the capability to integrate with external data. Not all the BCS functionality is in SharePoint Foundation. Later in this chapter, you learn exactly what functionality is included.

➤ Out-of-the-box, BSC is now write-back. The XML model you build up to define the data source with which you wish to integrate now has native method instances available for you to use to execute `Insert`, `Update`, and `Delete` methods. The SharePoint UI also enables you to use these methods.

➤ External lists are a huge new component of SharePoint 2010. To an end user, an external list looks just like any normal list within SharePoint. However, behind the scenes, the information is actually coming through the BCS from an external data source that you have defined. This allows you to use your external data within SharePoint in many of the same ways that you can use normal SharePoint list data.

➤ As mentioned previously, Business Data Catalog was part of the Shared Service Provider model in SharePoint 2007. This had many topology limitations with respect to how you could manage your farm around logical boundaries. With the new service application architecture of SharePoint 2010, SharePoint now has a true multi-tenant model. BCS is now deployed as a service application.

➤ You can now utilize a .NET assembly as a data source. This enables you to write C# or VB.NET code that brings data together from multiple data sources, mixes and merges it, and then presents it through the BCS to SharePoint. This enhances the power of the BCS.

➤ Microsoft is now shipping two tools for you to use to be able to configure your BCS models. You have SharePoint Designer (SPD) 2010 (which can configure SQL Server, WCF, or SOAP-based services), and a pre-deployed .NET model. Visual Studio 2010 comes with a BCS Model project item type, which helps you build up your BCS model and .NET assembly to get at your data.

➤ The Business Data Catalog was really only a component of SharePoint itself. It was pretty tricky to reuse BDC data within Microsoft Office client applications such as Outlook. BCS now has both a client and server component that allows you to take your BCS data down to the client applications, and use this within Office. This not only allows data to be heavily reused within Outlook and SharePoint Workspaces with the use of Office business types, but also allows you to take this BCS data offline and use it when the user is not connected.

➤ You can now have multiple method instances of the same type for each ECT.

Authentication is still going to be an issue for many people. The double-hop issue will still be around, so it is worth taking a little extra time to understand what the issue is.

The double-hop issue only becomes a problem when using pass-through authentication and NT LAN Manager (NTLM) integrated Windows authentication in IIS. Pass-through authentication means that the identity of the user trying to view data in SharePoint will be passed through SharePoint to the back-end system. Unfortunately, NTLM does not allow for delegation of the identity, and so SharePoint cannot execute the request as the user who made it.

If you must use pass-through authentication, you can either enable Kerberos authentication within IIS, or make use of the Secure Store Service, which, as mentioned previously, is an SSO service for SharePoint 2010.

EXISTING BDC APPLICATIONS DURING AN UPGRADE

If you are using SharePoint 2007 and want to upgrade to SharePoint 2010, you may be wondering what happens to all the existing Business Data Catalog applications you have defined and configured. The great news is that any out-of-the box BDC functionality you have configured in SharePoint 2007 will work just fine in SharePoint 2010. The entities you have set up in SharePoint 2007 will be upgraded to ECTs. Any custom code you have written that uses the Business Data Catalog object model should still work.

SharePoint 2010 creates a service application called `SharedServiceName_ApplicationRegistry`, where `SharedServiceName` is the name of your Shared Service Provider (SSP) in SharePoint 2007 before the upgrade. The Business Data Catalog code you wrote for SharePoint 2007 will use this `ApplicationRegistry` service as a proxy to call the upgraded ECTs and get the data it needs to work.

 The only time you may have an issue is if you hard-coded the name of the SSP in your code, because this will change when it is upgraded to have `_ApplicationRegistry` *postfixed to it.*

BCS FEATURES AVAILABLE IN SHAREPOINT FOUNDATION

Let's take a closer look at some of the BCS features available in SharePoint Foundation, as shown in Figure 14-2. These include the following:

➤   External lists

➤   `External Data` column

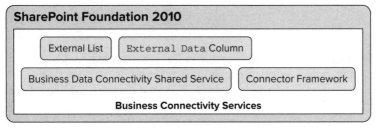

FIGURE 14-2: BCS features available in SharePoint Foundation

External Lists

External lists are an important feature introduced in SharePoint 2010. An *external list* is a SharePoint list, but rather than storing the list items within SharePoint itself, it is hooked up to an ECT so that the data is coming from and being written back to an external data source. End users are able to work with familiar SharePoint lists, and developers are able to access this data through the standard SharePoint List object model. This makes it possible to write web parts and solutions that can ubiquitously pull data from normal SharePoint lists and external lists.

To be able to use an external content type as a data source for an external list, your ECT must have `Finder` (`ReadList`) and `SpecificFinder` (`ReadItem`) methods. Once your ECT is defined and deployed to SharePoint, it is simply a matter of creating a new external list and selecting the ECT you would like it to utilize. You can create the external list through the SharePoint UI and SPD 2010.

If you want to be able to insert or update external data via an external list, your ECT must have `Creator` and `Updater` methods defined. When your ECT has the capability to insert or update new buttons, you will see options available on the ribbon, as shown in Figure 14-3.

Within your insert and update methods, you can define fields to be required. When these fields have the proper attribute set, they will appear in the UI with a red star next to them to indicate that the control must contain a value.

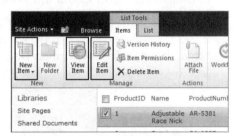

FIGURE 14-3: List tool ribbon options

You can add external list information to any web part page using the Extensible Stylesheet Language Translation (XSLT) viewer web part. This provides the capability to create good-looking dashboards with a little bit of configuration, and perhaps some work using SPD.

Although external lists may look and work exactly the same way as standard SharePoint lists, a few key areas do not match out-of-the-box, including the following:

➤ Workflows

➤ Alerts

➤ RSS feeds

➤ Folders

➤ Attachments

It makes sense that this functionality is missing because you are linking to an external system. Applications other than SharePoint could be writing back to this data source, so it would be impossible for SharePoint workflows and alerts to act on data changes it doesn't even know have happened.

External lists are available in SharePoint Foundation as well as SharePoint Server 2010.

External Data Column

The capability of users to tag documents with metadata is one of the great strengths offered by SharePoint. You may have rows of data that you want to use as a source of metadata in an external system. The `External Data` column allows you to create a column for your list or library that will look up the information defined in an ECT, and reuse this as metadata against documents and list items saved in SharePoint. To be able to use the `External Data` column in your ECT, you must have a `Finder` and `SpecificFinder` method created for it.

The `Business Data` column was available in SharePoint 2007 and came with one annoying issue. If you did not make use of the `ShowInPicker` property within your `Finder` method, you would get only the primary key column returned in the data picker. This made it almost impossible for users to be able to pick the correct metadata they wanted to use.

In SharePoint 2010, however, if you do not use the `ShowInPicker` property, all the columns are returned. This is great because, by default, it makes the data picker more useful. It is also not so great if your ECT has a lot of columns!

To get around this issue, if your ECT does have a lot of columns, you can still use the `ShowInPicker` property to display only a subset of columns. You can do this from within SPD when you are configuring your ECT, as shown in Figure 14-4.

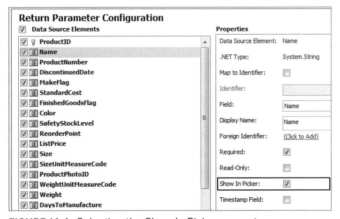

FIGURE 14-4: Selecting the Show In Picker property

Later in this chapter, you learn a lot more about using SPD to configure your ECTs.

The Entity Data Picker still has the limitation of returning only 200 rows of data, so you must configure some filters for your ECT if you want users to be able to choose from a larger data set. You learn more about this configuration later in this chapter.

BCS FEATURES AVAILABLE IN SHAREPOINT SERVER 2010

If you are using SharePoint Server 2010, you get all the functionality from SharePoint Foundation, plus lots more. As shown in Figure 14-5, this increased functionality includes the following:

➤ Business data web parts

➤ Search

➤ User profiles

➤ Office client integration

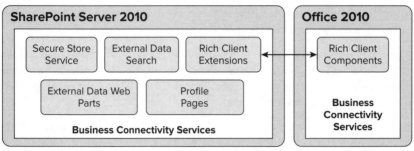

FIGURE 14-5: SharePoint Server 2010 functionality

Business Data Web Parts

The business data web parts that were available for the Business Data Catalog in MOSS 2007 are still there as part of SharePoint Server 2010. Although these web parts are not part of SharePoint Foundation, you can gain a lot of similar functionality with clever configuration of the XSLT web part and external lists. The web parts are almost identical in name and functionality to their predecessors, so this discussion does not delve into each one individually.

The web parts now have the capability to cache the data they retrieve. This will help increase performance a lot if you know that the data you are pulling through won't change too often.

The styling of these web parts is driven by XSLT. This means you can open up a page with the web parts in SPD 2010 and configure the web parts how you want by setting properties with the visual designer, or by applying an XSLT style sheet directly for the web part in the web part's toolbar properties.

Search

The BCS model has undergone a number of changes related to allowing SharePoint to crawl your external data source and return the results when executing a search query.

In the Business Data Catalog, entities needed to have SpecificFinder and IDEnumerator methods defined. The crawler would first execute the IDEnumerator method to get back all the rows of data it needed to crawl. It would use the identifier columns returned by this method and execute the SpecificFinder method to get the entities columns that it needed to crawl. If you didn't have the SpecificFinder and IDEnumerator methods defined, your Business Data Catalog application would not appear when you wanted to create a new search content source.

For SharePoint 2010 and the BCS, an extra property must be added to the LOBSystem model:

```
<Property Type="System.String" Name="ShowInSearchUI"/>
```

Without this property, you won't be able to pick your BCS application to be indexed.

Profile Pages

When you search for something and you are returned a link to a BCS item, you click the link and you are taken to what is called a *profile page*. In MOSS 2007, the default location of this was within the same site as the SSP admin site. This quite often meant that users were directed to a different URL completely than the one they were originally on (sometimes with no nice link to get back). This quite often also included a port number, because administrators who set this up didn't expect users to be browsing to it. You could create your own profile page, but this involved a few manual steps.

Things have improved for SharePoint Server 2010. Now, with profile pages, you must set the URL of the site at which you would like to hold the profile pages. This has to be done within the BCS service application by completing the following steps:

1. Open Central Administration and click the "Manage service applications" link.

2. Click Business Data Connectivity Service from the Service Applications page.

3. When the page opens, you'll see a Configure button in the ribbon menu. Click it and a dialog box will open where you can set the URL location where you'd like ECT profile pages to be created.

Once the profile page location has been set, you can set a new crawl of the BCS content and the search results will link through to this new page.

RootFinder Property

To get your BCS data indexed by SharePoint, you create `SpecificFinder` and `IDEnumerator` methods in the same way as you did in MOSS 2007. However, with SharePoint 2010, you can make your content indexable without having to create an `IDEnumerator`. You do this by making use of the `RootFinder MethodInstance` property, which SPD will use to configure your ECTs to be searchable.

SharePoint Designer 2010 will only create `Finder` and `SpecificFinder` methods. In the `Finder MethodInstance` element, a new property called `RootFinder` will be added, as shown here:

```
<MethodInstances>
    <MethodInstance Type="Finder" ReturnParameterName="Read List" Default="true"
            Name="Read List" DefaultDisplayName="Products Read List">
        <Properties>
            <Property Name="UseClientCachingForSearch"
                Type="System.String"></Property>
            <Property Name="RootFinder" Type="System.String"></Property>
        </Properties>
        <AccessControlList>
        ............
        </AccessControlList>
    </MethodInstance>
</MethodInstances>
```

By setting this property, the `Finder` method will now act in the same way the `IDEnumerator` did before. The `Finder` will execute and return the identifier values for the rows that need to be indexed by executing the `SpecificFinder` method.

Using the `Finder` method and `RootFinder` property does have a downside, however. The `Finder` method often executes and returns lots of columns. This is inefficient for indexing purposes because the SpecificFinder method only needs to know about identifiers for each row it needs to crawl — this is exactly all that the IDEnumerator will provide.

So, SPD and the RootFinder property are good for the purposes of creating a model quickly, and testing out the indexing and searching functionality of the BCS. But, for production purposes, you should always use SpecificFinder and IDEnumerator methods because the IDEnumerator method is pulling back much less data than your Finder method and, therefore, will perform much better when indexing and crawling.

User Profiles

As with SharePoint 2007, if you have an external system that contains information about your users such as phone numbers and birthdays, it is possible to bring this data into SharePoint and merge it with information held within Active Directory (AD). This allows your user profiles to be populated with more information that can be used for display and personalization purposes.

Office Client Integration

The integration with Microsoft Office client applications (such as Outlook, Word, and SharePoint Workspaces) is now very exciting. You now have the capability to take the data offline for use in all Office applications, and also the capability to use external data as though it were native Outlook objects (such as appointments, Calendar items, and Contacts).

Outlook 2010

Many Knowledge Workers spend a huge amount of time using Microsoft Outlook to communicate with internal and external contacts. The data integrated through the Business Data Catalog was quite often types that were similar to objects used in Outlook, but all you could do out-of-the-box was view them in web parts as lists of data.

With Office 2010 and the BCS, it is now possible to map your ECTs as an Office Business Type such as an Appointment, Contact, Task, or Post. You can then map fields within your ECT to the fields of the Office Business Type.

Once the ECT has been published to SharePoint and you have created an external list, the ribbon will display a button for you to click to take the list offline, as shown in Figure 14-6.

This will package the ECT into a Click Once installation package that can be installed on your client PC. Once you do this, the list will appear within Outlook, but, more importantly, when you are viewing it, it will appear in the context of the Office Business Type (that is, events are shown on a calendar, contacts are shown as contact cards, and so on).

FIGURE 14-6: "Connect to Outlook" button on the ribbon

Once the ECT is installed to Outlook, it is then possible to take the data offline and, if the correct methods have been created within the ECT, you can add to or edit the data. If you are online, the changes are reflected back into the external data source straight away. If you are offline, the changes are held in the local BCS cache until you are back online and can sync back up again.

Word 2010

Word 2010 allows you to insert SharePoint list properties straight into the document as Quick Parts. This includes metadata added against a document using the `External Data` column. Not only does Word display the information right in the document, but, by using the Quick Parts, you can actually pick the row of data being returned by the ECT. You use the Entity Data Picker directly in Word itself, and once you select the field you want to bring back, the Entity Data Picker will also retrieve and display all the related fields you set up for the `External Data` column.

To use BCS data in your Word documents, follow these steps:

1. Set up an `External Data` column for a Documents Library in SharePoint.

2. Create a new document from the SharePoint ribbon.

3. From the ribbon choose the Insert section.

4. Within the Text section, click the drop-down arrow for Quick Parts and move the mouse over Document Property, as shown in Figure 14-7.

5. Select the main BCS column you created, and also insert the other related fields you want displayed in the document.

Now, when you hover over the Quick Part of the main BCS field, you will see the BCS icons to validate information entered, or use the Entity Data Picker to select the values to bring back from your external system.

FIGURE 14-7: Drop-down selections for Quick Parts

SharePoint Workspace 2010

SharePoint Workspace 2010 is what was formerly known as Microsoft Groove in Office 2007. The name change reflects Microsoft's desire for this to be considered the tool that you use to take your SharePoint content offline, including external list data. If you have the necessary components installed, you'll notice the "Sync to SharePoint Workspace" button is available on the ribbon, as shown in Figure 14-8.

FIGURE 14-8: "Sync to SharePoint Workspace" button

When you click this button, the site will be available to you. The ECT information will be downloaded to the client. The external list data will be available to view from within SharePoint Workspace 2010, and forms to insert and edit data will be generated for you.

USING TOOLS TO CREATE ECTS

SharePoint 2010 provides a few tools you can use to create ECTs, including the following:

➤ SPD 2010

➤ Visual Studio 2010

You can also use a third-party tool such as BCS Meta Man.

Let's take a look at how to use SPD 2010 and Visual Studio 2010 in a bit more detail.

SharePoint Designer 2010

SPD continues to be free for the 2010 version of SharePoint, which is great news for everybody. In addition to this becoming a more powerful tool for building and customizing your SharePoint sites, you can now also use it to create BCS models and ECTs for SQL Server, WCF services, and pre-deployed .NET assemblies.

Let's walk through the configuration of a new ECT in SPD by using the `Employees` table in `AdventureWorks2000` (which you can download from `http://www.microsoft.com/downloads/details.aspx?FamilyID=487C9C23-2356-436E-94A8-2BFB66F0ABDC&displaylang=en`).

Follow these steps:

1. In SPD, connect to the site where you want to make use of your external data.

2. In the left-hand Navigation pane, click the External Content Types button.

3. When you come to the ECT main page, you'll notice that the ribbon has changed to reflect the operations you can do. Click the External Content Type button, as shown in Figure 14-9.

FIGURE 14-9: External Content Type button on the ribbon

4. You are then presented with the view to configure the ECT. Click the text that looks like a hyperlink, "New external content type," so that it changes to be a textbox. Name your new ECT `Contacts`.

5. As you are configuring some contacts, you want these to appear in Outlook as contact objects. This involves setting the Office Item Type. From the Office Item Type drop-down list, select Contact, as shown in Figure 14-10.

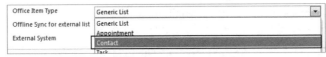

FIGURE 14-10: Office Item Type drop-down list

6. Now, you must connect to an external data source so that you can create the methods for the ECT. Click the link that says, "Click here to discover external data sources and define operations." When you click this link, you'll see the Operation Designer open up. This is where you must configure what you are going to connect to, and configure the operations your ECT will be able to perform.

7. Click the Add Connection button. You'll then be presented with the types of data sources you can connect to with SPD. Select SQL Server from the drop-down and click OK.

8. Enter the database server and database name you want to connect to, as shown in Figure 14-11. Leave the authentication mechanism as "Connect with User's Identity," which, for Business Data Catalog users, will mean that you are connecting with pass-through authentication.

FIGURE 14-11: SQL Server Connection dialog

9. Upon connecting, you'll notice that the Data Source Explorer fills with your database. Expand this to see Tables, Views, and Routines. Then expand the `Tables` folder. Find the `Contact` table and right-click it to expose a context menu, as shown in Figure 14-12.

10. Click the Create All Operations option.

11. A configuration wizard will now pop up that will guide you through the creation of your method. The first step of the wizard is an introduction, so you can just click the Next button.

12. When you get to the Parameters screen, notice the warnings and errors that are reported to you at the bottom of the wizard. The aim of these is to help you configure your ECT to get the functionality and performance you want.

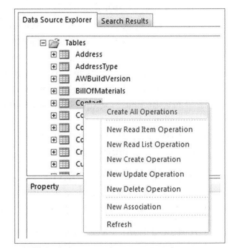

FIGURE 14-12: Context menu for the Contact table

In the left column you'll see the columns available from the table, and in the right column you'll see the properties available for you to configure for each column. A number of these columns are more important than others, so let's take a closer look:

➤ *Required* — If you want to ensure that a field has a value before users can write back, check this property.

➤ *Read Only* — If you do not want users to be able to edit a particular field when writing back, set this property.

➤ *Office Property* — If you are mapping your ECT to an Office Item Type, this is where you will match fields. For example, in the sample Contact ECT, you want to match the `EmailAddress` column with the Office Item Type field `Email 1 Address`, as shown in Figure 14-13. If a field you want to make available does not match an Office Item Type field, you can just leave it as a custom property.

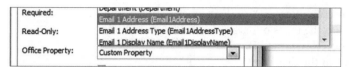

FIGURE 14-13: Matching a column with an Office Item Type

If a field you want to make available within Outlook does not match an Office Item Type field, then you can just leave it as a custom property.

➤ *ShowInPicker* — If your ECT will be used with the `Business Data` column, and it has a lot of fields, you may want to select a subset of these to appear in the Business Data Entity Picker. You can do this by setting this property for the columns you want to be displayed.

➤ *Timestamp field* — If you want your users to be able to search for the data defined by your ECT, you may want to set up incremental crawls. This will ensure that only rows of data that have changed are crawled and indexed, rather than the whole lot again. To be able to do incremental crawls, each row of data does need a column that contains date/time information of when it was last modified so that SharePoint can use this to figure out if it needs to be re-indexed since the last crawl. If you have a column such as this (the sample `Contact` table has the field `ModifiedDate`), you can check this property for it.

Once you have set the various properties for the columns you want to make use of in your ECT, click the Next button.

The final configuration step for your ECT is for filters. You'll notice that SPD recommends that you create at least a Limit filter for your ECT. This is to help with performance, because it will limit the number of rows being retrieved from the database.

Creating a Limit filter on its own, however, is somewhat pointless. If you did this for a table that had 2,000 rows of data, but your Limit filter restricted the number of rows coming back to 100, you'd only get the first 100 rows of data coming back! Therefore, you should always create a Limit filter in conjunction with another type of filter, such as a Comparison or Wildcard. This allows your users to filter the data coming back. With the Limit filter in place, it helps to restrict queries that may return excessive numbers of rows.

Once you have set up your filters, click the Finish button in the wizard to complete configuring your method. You will now be able to see the methods that have been created for you, as shown in Figure 14-14.

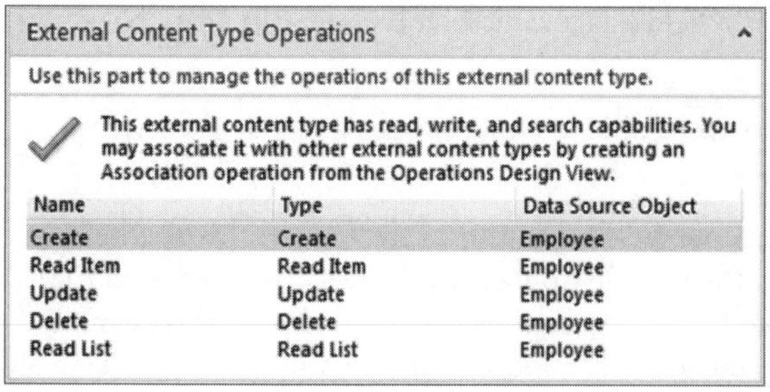

External Content Type Operations

Use this part to manage the operations of this external content type.

✓ This external content type has read, write, and search capabilities. You may associate it with other external content types by creating an Association operation from the Operations Design View.

Name	Type	Data Source Object
Create	Create	Employee
Read Item	Read Item	Employee
Update	Update	Employee
Delete	Delete	Employee
Read List	Read List	Employee

FIGURE 14-14: External Content Type Operations summary

If you need to edit any of these, simply double-click the method name.

Although you have configured the ECT in SPD, nothing has actually been saved or deployed yet. To do that, simply click the Save button in the top-left portion of the SPD application.

Once saved, you'll then need to give your users permissions to execute methods for the ECT

Setting BCS Permissions

By default, you will not have permissions to execute methods and view data from the ECT you have just created. The BCS includes a security layer that requires you to set who can access what.

To set permissions to allow users to execute methods, follow these steps:

1. Open Central Administration and click the "Manage service applications" link.

2. Click Business Data Connectivity Service from the Service Applications page.

3. When the BCS Service page loads, the Contacts ECT will be listed. Click the checkbox to the left of its name to select it.

4. You can now click the Set Object Permissions button that is displayed on the ribbon.

5. A dialog form will open that will allow you to enter the username you want to give permissions to, and also set the permissions you want to apply.

Once you have set the necessary BCS permissions for your users, you will then be able to view your external data in SharePoint.

Other Data Sources

SharePoint Designer 2010 is limited in that it can connect only to SQL Server, WCF services, and pre-deployed .NET types. If you want to use Oracle or an Open Database Connectivity (ODBC) data source, and you want to configure these using SPD 2010, the recommended approach is to create a WCF service or .NET assembly to present the data to the BCS. SPD can connect and configure from both of these types.

Adding a Little Extra

Within the SharePoint 2010 Central Administration screens it is possible to export individual ECT and main model LOBSystem settings, but as individual elements. This isn't much good if you want to export all of the model, which includes model information about associations.

With SPD 2010, however, you can select multiple ECTs, right-click, and choose the Export option from the context menu. This will export the connection settings, ECTs, and any association information about ECTs that are related together.

Visual Studio 2010

Visual Studio 2010 now comes with some great tools for building solutions for SharePoint 2010. From Visual Studio 2010, you can now build BCS models and .NET assemblies that will get the data and present it to the BCS.

Following are some advantages of using the .NET assembly route:

➤ Your ECT can be built from a mashup of different data sources.

➤ Because you can use .NET code, you can transform and manipulate your data in code any way you need to.

➤ You can debug your code.

➤ With regard to application life cycle management, it is easy to move a model built in a development environment through to a live environment.

Building a .NET assembly and the relevant BCS model is certainly more difficult and more involved than using SPD 2010. You must have quite a good understanding of the BCS model, as well as your data systems, and be able to write C# code. This is definitely a job for a developer!

When you open Visual Studio 2010, you can choose to create a new BCS Model Project Type from the SharePoint 2010 section. After you give your project a name, you'll be presented with the screen shown in Figure 14-15.

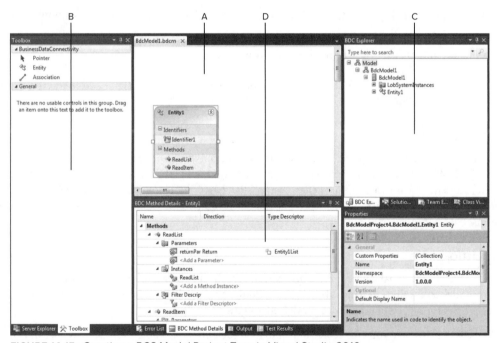

FIGURE 14-15: Creating a BCS Model Project Type in Visual Studio 2010.

Following are descriptions of the parts of this screen:

➤ *Design surface (A)* — The design surface is where you'll create your new ECTs. As you can see, when you first create the project, an ECT called `Entity1` is created for you with the necessary code files.

➤ *Toolbox (B)* — The toolbox doesn't contain many items when you are working with a BCS model. The only things you can drag and drop onto your design surface are new ECT shapes and components to configure associations.

➤ *Solution Explorer and BDC Explorer (C)* — The Solution Explorer is something you may be used to using in Visual Studio for accessing the files in your projects. It is worth just pointing out a couple of files that are of interest. For each ECT created on the design surface, a service class will also be generated. For example, for the ECT called `Entity1`, you see a service class called `Entity1Service.cs`. You must write the `Finder` and `SpecificFinder` BCS methods in this service class. Next to the Solution Explorer, you'll find the BDC Explorer. You use this to configure the fields that are returned by each of your BCS methods.

➤ *BDC Method Details (D)* — The BDC Method Details window is used to create parameter and `MethodInstance` elements of your ECTs.

When you create a new entity on your design surface, Visual Studio automatically creates the service class for you. If you rename the existing entity (for example, from `Entity1` to `Departments`), you'll notice that the name of the service class changes as well.

You'll also notice another class called `Entity1.cs`. This is simply a class that contains lots of properties that define the structure of the data you want to return to the BCS.

As an example, let's say that you have some companies stored in a SQL Server database table that contains information about your customers. You would like to be able to display this list of customers with some extra information that includes their current stock price, which can be obtained through a web service call. This will provide your salespeople with something to talk to the customer about.

Because you want to create one ECT called `Customers` and yet pull the information from two data sources, let's create a .NET assembly so that the ECT fields are populated through C# code.

The `Customer` database table should include the following column formatting:

➤ `CustomerId` — int32 (primary key, auto-increment)

➤ `Name` — varchar(64)

➤ `Address` — varchar(64)

➤ `Phone` — varchar(16)

➤ `StockSymbol` — varchar(4)

Figure 14-16 shows a small subset of data to use for this walkthrough.

4	Microsoft	Redmond	12345	msft
5	Google	San Francisco	666	goog
6	Apple	California	99999	aapl
NULL	NULL	NULL	NULL	NULL

FIGURE 14-16: Subset of data

Now, follow these steps:

1. Open up Visual Studio 2010 and create a New Project. Select the SharePoint 2010 project items and pick Business Data Connectivity Model, as shown in Figure 14-17. Give the project a useful name, such as `MVPBook.Customers`.

FIGURE 14-17: Creating a project based on Business Data Connectivity Model

2. When the SharePoint Customization form appears, click Finish.

3. From the toolbox, drag and drop a new entity onto the `BdcModel1.bdcm` design surface. Double-click the shape and change the name of the entity to `Customers`.

4. Right-click the Method section of the entity shape and choose "Add new Method" from the context menu that appears, as shown in Figure 14-18. Give the method a name of `GetCustomers`.

5. Right-click the Identifiers section of the entity shape and choose Add New Identifier from the context menu that appears. Give the Identifier a name of `CustomerId`.

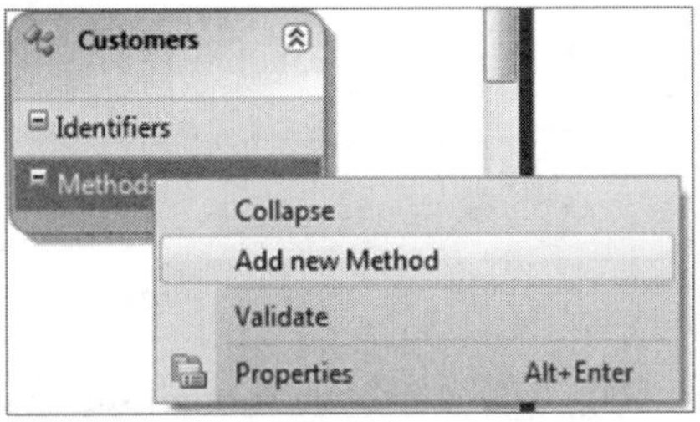

FIGURE 14-18: Selecting "Add new Method" from the context menu

6. In the Properties pane, change the Type Name to be `System.Int32`.

7. Ensure that you have the `Customers` entity selected, and then move to the BDC Methods Details window. In the Parameters section, click "Add a Parameter." Select Create Parameter. A new parameter will be added for you.

8. With this new parameter row selected, change the Name of it in the Properties toolpane from `parameter` to `returnParameter`.

9. Change the Parameter Direction to Return to indicate that this parameter will be returning data to you.

10. Move to the BDC Explorer Window. Expand the model so that you can see the `return-Parameter` you have just created. You'll see the `returnParameter` has a `TypeDescriptor` automatically added that has a name of `returnParameterTypeDescriptor`. Select this and set its values to the following:

➤ Name — `CustomerList`

➤ Type Name — `System.Collections.Generic.IEnumerable`1 [[MVPBook. Customers.BdcModel1.Customer, BdcModel1]]`

➤ IsCollection — true

11. Because `CustomerList` will contain a `Customer` object, you must define this as a `TypeDescriptor`. Right-click the `CustomerList` `TypeDescriptor` and pick Add Type Descriptor from the menu. Set the following properties for this `TypeDescriptor`:

➤ Name — `Customer`

➤ Type Name — `MVPBook.Customers.BdcModel1.Customer,BdcModel1`

12. Now, you must add in each property that the `Customer` object will return. Right-click the `Customer` `TypeDescriptor` and choose Add Type Descriptor. Add the following `TypeDescriptors` and set the following values:

➤ Name — `CustomerId`

➤ Type Name — `System.Int32`

➤ Identifier — `CustomerId`

➤ Name — `Name`

➤ Type Name — `System.String`

➤ Name — `Address`

➤ Type Name — `System.String`

➤ Name — `Phone`

➤ Type Name — `System.String`

➤ Name — `StockSymbol`

➤ Type Name — `System.String`

➤ Name — `StockPrice`

➤ Type Name — `System.Decimal`

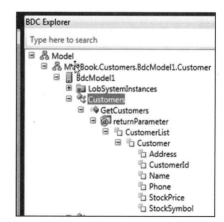

FIGURE 14-19: BDC Explorer after configuration

The BDC Explorer should now resemble Figure 14-19.

13. Finally, you must add a `MethodInstance` element to the new method. This lets the BCS know which functionality your method implements (for example, whether it is a `Finder`, `SpecificFinder`, and so on). In the BDC Method Details window, click "Add a Method Instance" and click the Create Finder Instance link that shows in the corresponding drop-down.

14. Visual Studio gives the method instance a nice name of `GetCustomerInstance`, but you must set the following other properties:

- ➤ Default — True
- ➤ Return Parameter Name — `returnParameter`
- ➤ Return Type Descriptor — `CustomerList`

The model is now finished. Are you wondering what happened to all that XML you used to have to write for the Business Data Catalog? If you save the `BdcModel1.bdcm` file, close it, then right-click the filename in Solution Explorer, pick 'Open With...', and then XML Editor, the file will open up in XML view inside Visual Studio. You can then see all this XML that you have generated by building up your BCS model!

The BCS model configuration is now complete. You can now write some code!

Follow these steps:

1. In Solution Explorer, right-click the `BdcModel1` folder and choose to add a new class file. Call this file `Customer.cs`.

2. In `Customer.cs` file, ensure that the following code exists:

```
using System;
using System.Collections.Generic;
using System.Linq;
using System.Text;

namespace MVPBook.Customers.BdcModel1
{
    public class Customer
    {
        public int CustomerId { get; set; }

        public string Name { get; set; }

        public string Address { get; set; }

        public string Phone { get; set; }

        public string StockSymbol { get; set; }

        public decimal StockPrice { get; set; }
    }
}
```

3. Now, you must use some LINQ to SQL code to retrieve the list of companies from the database table. Right-click the main root solution node in Solution Explorer and choose to add a new item. In the Data project items, find the LINQ to SQL Classes project item. Select this and give it a name of `Database.dbml`.

4. When the new LINQ to SQL designer opens up, bring the Server Explorer into view. Connect to the database that contains your `Customers` table. When this appears in the Server Explorer, drag and drop the `Customers` database table onto the design surface, as shown in Figure 14-20. This will generate all of the LINQ to SQL data access code you require.

5. Save the changes to the `.dbml` file.

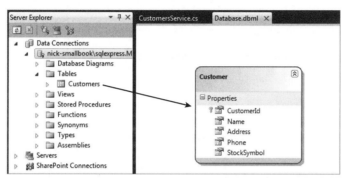

FIGURE 14-20: Dragging and dropping the Customers database table onto the design surface

 It is interesting to note that the LINQ to SQL designer has been built with the same Domain Specific Language Toolkit that the BCS designer has been created with.

Now, you must add a reference to the web service you want to call to get the stock price quotes. Follow these steps:

1. Right-click the reference folder and choose Add Service Reference.

2. Click the Advanced Button, and, in the new form that opens up, click Add Web Reference at the bottom left of the form. This will open up the familiar form window for adding older web services.

3. In the URL textbox, add `http://www.webservicex.net/stockquote.asmx` and click the Go button.

4. Once the URL has resolved, click the Add Reference button. Upon returning to the main Visual Studio window, the web service proxy will be generated for you to work with.

> *It is nice and easy to use an older SOAP ASP.NET 2.0 web service in this case,*
> *because the proxy code that is generated for you by Visual Studio is compiled*
> *and deployed within the assembly. If you were to use WCF, you would have*
> *to worry about the deployment of* app.config *settings or setting up WCF*
> *endpoints in code. In a real-world scenario, however, it is more likely that you*
> *would use a WCF service.*

Open the CustomerService.cs file. Notice that the BCS designer has created the GetCustomers method for you.

```
public static IEnumerable<Customer> GetCustomers()
{
    throw new System.NotImplementedException();
}
```

Let's add a method to the CustomerService.cs class to use the web service to get a stock quote. Add the following new method:

```
public static decimal GetQuote(string symbol)
{
    net.webservicex.www.StockQuote stockQuote =
        new net.webservicex.www.StockQuote();

    string stockData = stockQuote.GetQuote(symbol);

    XElement element = XElement.Parse(stockData);
    return Decimal.Parse(element.Descendants("Last").First().Value);
}
```

This method will simply call the web service you added earlier and use LINQ to XML to get the "Last" price value from the XML response.

You'll need to add the following using statement to the top of the class so that you can use the LINQ to XML XElement object:

```
using System.Xml.Linq;
```

Now, you can add code to the GetCustomers method, as shown here:

```
public static IEnumerable<Customer> GetCustomers()
{
    DatabaseDataContext db = new DatabaseDataContext(@"your connection string");
    var customers = from c in db.Customers
                    select new Customer
                    {
                        Address = c.Address,
                        CustomerId = c.CustomerId,
                        Name = c.Name,
                        Phone = c.Phone,
                        StockSymbol = c.StockSymbol,
```

```
                            StockPrice = GetQuote(c.StockSymbol)
                    };

        return customers;
    }
```

The code is quite concise. It utilizes some LINQ to SQL, as well as Object and Collection initialization. The first line simply creates `DatabaseDataContext` for you to execute your queries against. The next ten lines are, in effect, one line, but split up to make things more readable.

First, you are performing a LINQ to SQL query to get all the customers in the `Customers` database table. You are then using the results to initialize a collection of your own custom `Customer` class that you coded up — setting the values at run-time and also being able to call your `GetQuote` method by passing in the `StockSymbol` value for each `Customer`. This collection is then returned.

And that is all the work you must do. You can now press F5 to compile, package, and deploy the BCS model and code to SharePoint. When the page opens up, put it into edit mode and choose to add a new Business Data List web part. When you choose to configure the web part, you'll be able to open the External Content Type Picker and select the `MVPBook.Customers.BdcModel1.Customer` ECT. Also, notice that `Entity1` is listed. This is the entity that was created by default by the Business Data Model project in Visual Studio.

One of the great things about being able to press F5 to deploy in Visual Studio is that you can set breakpoints and they will be hit without having to attach to any processes. If you are having any problems with getting this example to work, you can do a number of things:

➤ Put a breakpoint in your code and see if it is being hit. If so, step through the code using F10/F11 to see if any errors occur, as shown in Figure 14-21.

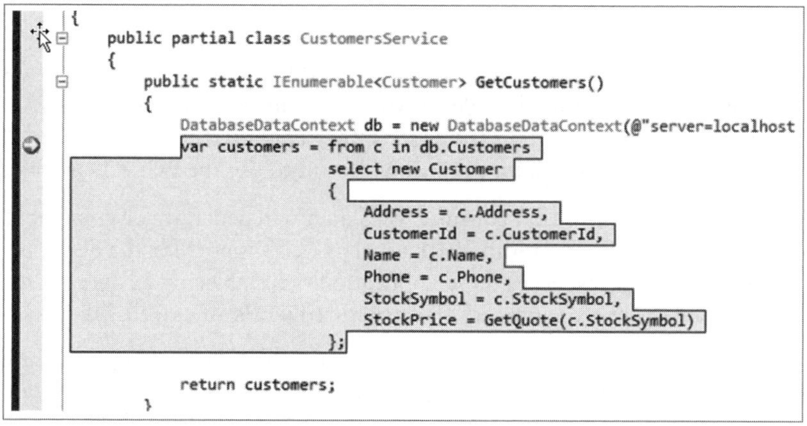

```
{
    public partial class CustomersService
    {
        public static IEnumerable<Customer> GetCustomers()
        {
            DatabaseDataContext db = new DatabaseDataContext(@"server=localhost
            var customers = from c in db.Customers
                            select new Customer
                            {
                                Address = c.Address,
                                CustomerId = c.CustomerId,
                                Name = c.Name,
                                Phone = c.Phone,
                                StockSymbol = c.StockSymbol,
                                StockPrice = GetQuote(c.StockSymbol)
                            };

            return customers;
        }
```

FIGURE 14-21: Stepping through the code with breakpoints

➤ Check to see whether you need to set any BCS permissions. Within Central Administration and the BCS application service, check that your users have the necessary permissions on the Model and External Content Type to be able to use it.

➤ As always in SharePoint, log files are your friends. Any BCS issues are likely to be reported in here, often with exactly the information you'll need to fix things.

In this Visual Studio example, you have seen how a .NET assembly is really useful to join content from multiple data sources to produce a single ECT. The example ECT is relatively simple in that it only has a basic `Finder` method. To take your ECTs to the next level with Search and the capability of writing back, look through the examples in the SDK, or check out the support articles on the Lightning Tools site at `www.lightningtools.com/bcs-meta-man/support.aspx`.

BCS Meta Man

As mentioned earlier, I learned all about the Business Data Catalog through building the BDC Meta Man tool, which some of you may have had the chance to use. With Microsoft offering tooling for building your models, the creators of Meta Man had to significantly improve tooling as well. The new tool is called BCS Meta Man, and extends tooling from Microsoft to generate all the BCS model and C# code for you automatically. You can download the free Developer Version from `http://www.lightningtools.com/bcs/bcs-meta-man.aspx`

DEVELOPING AGAINST THE BCS OBJECT MODELS

One of the great powers of the BCS is that once you define your ECTs, they can be reused many times within SharePoint. They can also be reused by developers through the BCS object models.

Usually, if developers want to write some code to interact with data in an external system, they must learn the API and security specifically for that data source. In a typical corporate environment, this could mean developers would have to remember up to four or five ways to interface with data. If you define your data as ECTs, developers can use the methods within these models to retrieve and possibly write back the data they need. As they are working through the BCS, they only need to learn the BCS programming API, instead of a specific one for each system.

Because data can be accessed through both the server (SharePoint) and client applications (Office), two object models are now available for you to use when developing your solutions. If you are building a web part that will be deployed to SharePoint, you will want to make use of the BCS Server object model. When you are building applications for Office applications such as Word, you may be accessing data in the client cache, which means you will want to use the BCS Client object model.

Developing Office client applications that consume BCS data will generally be completed as Office Business Applications (OBAs). Visual Studio 2010 now has rich support for the development and deployment of OBAs. Microsoft promotes these application types as being a route for merging the unstructured world of document creation with the structured world of external data systems.

Finally, a powerful administration API allows you to programmatically build up your models and ECTs, as well as change them. When pairing this administration API with PowerShell, you can script changes that you may need to make when moving a BCS model from a development to production environment.

SUMMARY

The Business Data Catalog was good. Business Connectivity Services is even better. Improvements have been made by Microsoft across the board for connectivity, user interface, tooling, and availability. Integration is not only easier, but also the number (and type) of things you can do with your data within SharePoint (and now the Office client applications) has increased immensely.

ABOUT THE AUTHOR

Nick Swan is a SharePoint Server MVP who has been developing with Microsoft-based technologies for ten years since completing work on a software engineering degree. Nick co-founded Lightning Tools with Brett Lonsdale in 2007 and they have been building great tools and web parts since then. You can find out more at www.lightningtools.com. Lonsdale and Swan also host a SharePoint Pod Show with Rob Foster, which you listen to at www.sharepointpodshow.com. Swan lives in Reading, United Kingdom, with his fiancée, Sophie, and their cats, Fluffy and Carragher.

15

Using PerformancePoint Services 2010

By Darrin Bishop

One of the key workloads for Microsoft SharePoint Server 2010 is Insights. The Insights workload is all about unlocking and using your business information. The Insights workload includes key technologies and services such as PerformancePoint Services (PPS), Excel Services, Visio Services, and Business Connectivity Services (BCS). PerformancePoint Services 2010 is a key business intelligence (BI) product for Microsoft.

PerformancePoint Services 2010 provides the capability to create rich, interactive dashboards that allow Information Workers to view and work with structured and unstructured data in a secure and easy-to-consume format. Power users, BI workers, administrators, and developers can create, manage, and deploy dashboards and dashboard components (such as charts, graphs, reports, and scorecards) to SharePoint libraries. The capability to slice and dice the business data allows data to become actionable information.

Microsoft made some significant changes to PerformancePoint Services 2010 when compared to PerformancePoint Server 2007. Although users of the previous version of PPS will certainly recognize the similarity of the designer and the available dashboard components, there have been vast improvements to this latest version as a result of building the product on SharePoint Server 2010, rather than simply integrating the user interface.

This chapter provides an overview of PerformancePoint Services 2010 and gets you started with the creation of dashboards and components to provide detailed insight into your business.

THE CASE FOR BUSINESS INTELLIGENCE

BI has been an elusive concept for many companies. High cost, propriety systems, unfamiliar programming models, and separate security models are but a few reasons why BI has been so elusive. Ultimately, many companies point to simple report generation as their BI solution.

Why Does a Company Need BI?

Companies spend an inordinate amount of time and resources capturing data as part of their business processes. Unfortunately, data is not information. To be used as information, that data must be presented in an easy-to-consume format. Better still is to visualize the data to gain a better understanding of the information.

BI allows a company to drill into their data and produce actionable information. A scorecard with indicators can quickly tell an executive when he or she should be worried that expenses are off track. Reports can tell a mid-level manager that a production line is experiencing more quality issues when compared to other similar production lines. In each case, a decision can be made based on easily understood information.

BI supports the company by visualizing data as information that can be acted upon. Without BI, decision making is based on assumptions and guesses. At times, there is no decision making because the company is simply unaware of the issue.

Asking the Right Questions

Effective BI is all about asking the right questions at the right time. Graphs, charts, and indicators are only pretty pictures and do nothing to solve business problems when the wrong questions are asked. As SharePoint developers, designers, and administrators, we are generally called on to create a BI solution with little or no insight into the business. It is important to recognize that Information Technology staff are generally not knowledgeable enough about the overall business issues to develop a BI solution without generous help from the business unit.

Before any report, scorecard, or dashboard is ever created, the business should have its key strategic and tactical objectives defined. From these objectives, the author should have a clear understanding of the intent of the BI solution. Successful BI solutions happen when they are directly related to a company's strategic and tactical objectives. It is from these objectives that the questions can be asked, and, even more important, we can determine what the correct answer is. If the company has an objective to increase production by 10 percent of the top 10 products by gross profit margin, we can easily help develop a visualization of the metric. More importantly, we can easily agree on the metrics used to indicate success or failure. This simple (but detailed) goal is measurable and actionable. Compare the previous objective to a more undefined objective of "let's increate our profit." How do we determine success? How do we measure success or failure? Ambiguous objectives generally lead to a failed BI solution.

How Can PerformancePoint Services Help?

Where does PPS fit in? PPS is now a service application in the Enterprise edition of SharePoint 2010. Many of the constraints of a typical BI suite are no longer constraints.

➤ *PPS runs on the same hardware as SharePoint (the Enterprise version of SharePoint 2010)* — PPS can be turned on without the need to purchase another product unless the design requires another SharePoint 2010 server.

➤ *PPS is administered as a SharePoint service* — Administrators do not need to learn a new interface. PPS has the common SharePoint service administration interface.

➤ *PPS is secured using SharePoint security* — There is no separate security model, SharePoint list and library security is used to secure the reports, filters, dashboards, and scorecards.

➤ *PPS has a common .NET development model* — PPS allows for custom development using common .NET development techniques. There is no need to learn a new language or script.

PPS provides authoring tools to create dashboards, which contain related PPS content such as reports, filters, and scorecards. Reports, filters, and scorecards (and other types of content) are used to connect to a data source and visualize the data. This allows authors to rapidly create new dashboards and dashboard content to change data into information.

PERFORMANCEPOINT SERVICES 2010 OVERVIEW

PerformancePoint Services 2010 is a key service in Microsoft SharePoint Server 2010 that helps to provide insights into the vast amount of business data through the use of dashboards and dashboard components. Creating dashboards and dashboard components provides a means to visualize raw data in an easy-to-understand format.

PerformancePoint Services 2010 is a service available with the Enterprise version of Microsoft SharePoint Server. Microsoft SharePoint Server 2010 provides the foundation to run PerformancePoint Services 2010, SharePoint Server 2010 also provides the mechanism to create, store, secure, and view dashboards and dashboard components.

PerformancePoint Services Architecture

PerformancePoint Services 2010 includes both client-side and server-side technologies. Clients can be browsers used to display dashboards, Dashboard Designer (a rich Windows application used to create and edit dashboards), and custom applications used to integrated or extend PPS.

The server-side technology includes components that run on the Web Front End (WFE), application, and data tiers. As a SharePoint service, the bulk of PerformancePoint processing happens on the application server. Like other SharePoint services, PPS can be deployed in a single-server scenario or scaled out to multiple servers in multiple topologies. Figure 15-1 shows an overview of the PerformancePoint Services 2010 architecture.

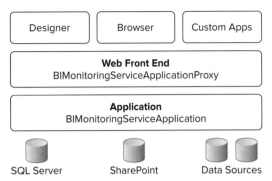

FIGURE 15-1: PeformancePoint Services architecture

Web Front End Tier

The WFE is the main connection between the client and the core service running on the application server. It's responsibly include serving up the user interface of a dashboard. The user interface of a dashboard is composed of web part pages and web parts. The PerformancePoint web parts are containers that can communicate asynchronously using web services via the WFE servers.

The WFE also hosts the Dashboard Designer's ClickOnce application, which is a Windows application that deploys to a client machine, and is used to author dashboards and dashboard components.

The last major function of the WFE server is to connect to the actual PPS running in the application tier. The connection happens though a Windows Communication Foundation (WCF) proxy like all other SharePoint services. The use of proxies and services provides the capability to scale out services to multiple application servers.

Application Tier

SharePoint application servers host the PPS service. PPS can be balanced across one or more application servers. The service interface of PPS allows access to the actual BIMonitoringServiceApplication.

The BIMonitoringServiceApplication connects to both the SharePoint repository (where PerformancePoint Services 2010 content, including dashboards, reports, scorecards, and filters, are stored) and to a database (where a small amount of data such as persisted filter settings is stored). Most PPS data is stored and secured in the SharePoint repository as list and library items using PerformancePoint lists, libraries, and content types.

Data Tier

The actual PerformancePoint Services 2010 service uses SharePoint lists and libraries, along with specific content types for data sources, filters, and content, to store most of the PerformancePoint Services 2010 content. Administrators have the capability to limit which sites, webs, or libraries can contain PPS content. Each PPS application has access to a SQL Server database to store items, including temporary objects, parameters settings, and annotations. Each application has a configured Unattended Service Account stored in the Secure Store service that will be used to access the application-specific database.

The data tier also consists of data sources used in the dashboard itself. These data sources include SQL Server data, SharePoint list data, and Analysis Services data, to name just a few.

CONFIGURING AND ENABLING PERFORMANCEPOINT SERVICES

PerformancePoint Services 2010 is deployed as a service, and is available only in the Enterprise version of SharePoint Server 2010. Because PerformancePoint Services 2010 is an integral part of SharePoint 2010, the process of starting and enabling the service is similar to any other SharePoint 2010 service. The SharePoint service framework supports multiple configurations, as well as supporting multiple services on various applications

This chapter provides an overview of PPS and assumes the service is already started and configured. The Farm Configuration Wizard will create the service and the service proxy, leaving only a few items to be configured before dashboards can be created. The example dashboard built in this chapter will use the preconfigured SharePoint 2010 virtual machine freely available for download (see section, "Setting Up the Example," later in this chapter).

Configuring the Unattended Service Account

The Unattended Service Account is required to have read access to all data stores that will be used with content such as reports, scorecards, and filters. The PerformancePoint Dashboard Designer uses this account to access the data during the authoring of a dashboard. Also, PerformancePoint connections can be authored to use the Unattended Execution Account as a trusted account to access data during run time. This account is not configured by the Farm Configuration Wizard, and must be configured before the service will function.

The Secure Store Service is a service and must be started before it can be used to store the Unattended Service account. Administrators can choose in which Secure Store application to store the PPS Unattended Service Account credentials. Unattended Service Account credentials are configured on a PPS application basis. Each application requires configured credentials.

 The use of the Unattended Service Account does not remove the need to use Kerberos when accessing data remotely from the SharePoint server

To set the Unattended Service Account credentials in the Secure Store for the PerformancePoint Service Application example, follow these steps:

1. From the Home page of the Central Administration site, select "Manage service applications" located in the Application Management section.

2. Select "PerformancePoint Service Application" from the list of service applications. Then, select PerformancePoint Service Application Settings. This will display the settings page for the PerformancePoint Service Application instance, as shown in Figure 15-2.

3. Enter the Secure Store application name and credentials.

4. Click OK to store the credentials.

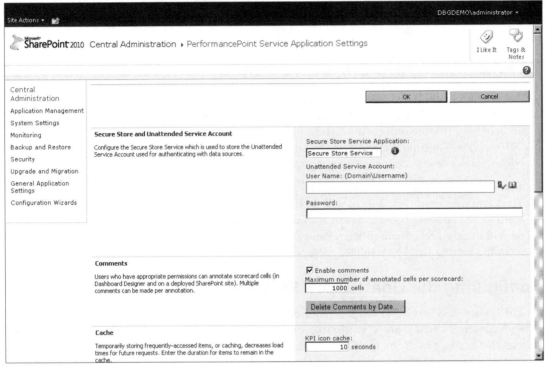

FIGURE 15-2: Setting the Unattended Service Account

Configuring Trusted Locations

PPS stores content that includes reports, scorecards, filters, key performance indicators (KPIs), indicators, data connections, and dashboards inside of lists and libraries configured specifically for PPS data sources and content. PerformancePoint data sources are stored in instances of the Data Connections Library for PerformancePoint. PPS content is stored in instances of PerformancePoint Content lists. Administrators have control over which lists or libraries are trusted for use with PPS.

PPS will only recognize trusted libraries and lists. This is a security feature that allows the administrator to control where PPS is allowed to retrieve or store dashboards and dashboard content. Trusted Data Connection libraries and PerformancePoint Content lists are controlled separately from each other. Administrators have the capability to select all PPS data source locations, or to make a more granular selection down to the library level. Administrators have the same capability for Content lists as well. Trusted locations are managed on a per-application service setting using the Application Management pages. This allows different trusted locations for different PerformancePoint application services.

To set the PerformancePoint Application's trusted Data Source Locations, follow these steps:

1. From the Home page of the Central Administration site, select "Manage service applications" located in the Application Management section.

2. Select "PerformancePoint Service Application" from the list of service applications. Then, select "PerformancePoint Service Application Settings." You will then see the settings page for the PerformancePoint Service Application.

3. Next, select Trusted Data Source Locations. As shown in Figure 15-3, you can select to trust "All SharePoint locations," or "Only specific locations." If you select "Only specific locations," the next page will allow the addition of trusted locations.

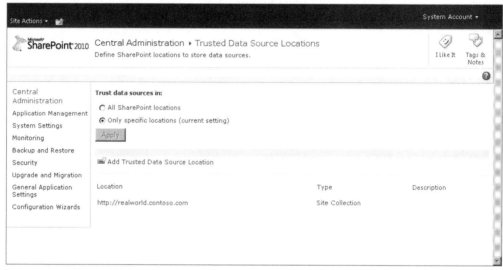

FIGURE 15-3: Trusted Data Source Locations dialog

You would follow the same steps to set the trusted content locations after you click the Trusted Content Locations link in Step 3.

Enabling PerformancePoint Services on a Site

The PPS Service should now be running, but a few steps are required to actually consume the service in a SharePoint Server 2010 site. Out-of-the-box, SharePoint Server 2010 provides a Business Intelligence Center site template that provides common and necessary Features to work with the various BI pieces. This includes all the necessary Features for PPS.

Figure 15-4 shows the home page of a site based on the Business Intelligence Center site template. If the Business Intelligence Center fits your design needs, simply create a new site collection using the Business Intelligence Center template, and then the site will be ready for new PerformancePoint content. The Business Intelligence Center template is located under the Enterprise tab of the template listings.

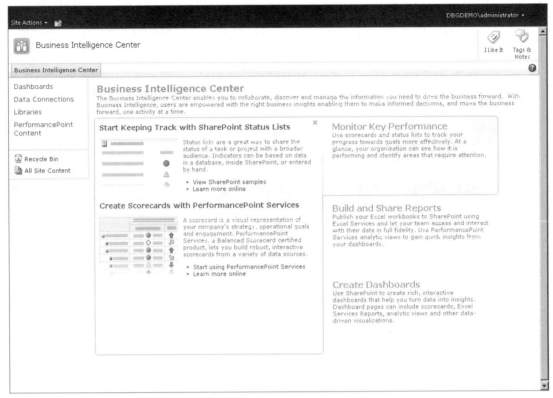

FIGURE 15-4: The Business Intelligence Center site

You do not have to use the Business Intelligence Center template to work with PPS. The same Features that are applied to the Business Intelligence Center site template can be activated on any other site when you need to work with PPS content.

To prepare a site to use the functionality of PPS, you must activate the PerformancePoint Services Site Collection Feature at the site-collection level, and the PerformancePoint Services Site Feature at the specific site level. This will install and enable the needed resources to access and use PPS.

Configuring the Client

PPS is primarily a web-based application that can be accessed using any web browser that is supported by SharePoint Server 2010. In general, there is no client setup or configuration required, with three optional exceptions:

➤ *.NET Framework 3.5 Service Pack 1 (SP1)* — Most clients will have .NET 3.5 SP1 already installed. To work with the PerformancePoint Dashboard Designer, you must have .NET 3.5 SP1 on the client machine to support the Dashboard Designer application.

➤ *Silverlight* — Silverlight is not required by SharePoint Server 2010, but if the client does have Silverlight enabled, the user interface will "light up" and provide a Silverlight interface in areas. PPS requires the use of Silverlight for the Decomposition chart. This chart provides a type of drill-through functionality that allows a user to examine the composition of the information.

➤ *Visio* — Microsoft Visio is required to view strategy maps. Strategy maps are another form of visualizing scorecards and KPIs.

There is no hard-and-fast requirement to install Silverlight or Visio on every potential client. However, the designer of the dashboard should be aware that certain PPS content (such as Decomposition Charts and Strategy Maps) may not be available to all readers.

CREATING A PPS DASHBOARD

Creating dashboards that visualize information and allows Information Workers to effectively make business decisions requires an understanding of the business and the need. Simply knowing how to create a dashboard to display data is not enough to be successful.

A team approach is commonly used to develop successful dashboards. The team would include business analysts, a data specialist, SharePoint architects, designers, and possibly developers.

From a purely SharePoint perspective, the following are the general steps required to create a dashboard:

1. *Create the data source* — Before you can start working with PPS, you need one or more data sources that contain the information to display in your elements. These data sources may or may not already exist. The types of data sources that PPS can consume include SQL Server Analysis Services, Excel Services, Excel, SharePoint list data, and SQL table data.

2. *Create a workspace* — A workspace contains a collection of associated components that are stored in SharePoint lists specific to PerformancePoint Services 2010. The workspace is the organizational structure that keeps track of the settings of the workspace, along with the content and libraries the author can use. Think of a workspace as a logical gathering of pieces you might need for a particular project.

3. *Create PPS data source element* — Data source elements contain the connection information between the dashboard components and the data source. Authors create and configure data source connections that are stored in a Data Source Library associated with the workspace.

4. *Create PPS content* — PPS dashboards are composed of content such as reports, graphs, charts, and scorecards. Once the data sources are created, the author can create new PPS content that is associated with an existing data source. Once the content is created, the author may configure the content to display or work with the data as needed. The PPS content is saved to one or more PPS-specific SharePoint lists. Throughout the lifecycle of the dashboard, authors may create, modify, and remove PPS content from the workspace.

5. *Create a dashboard* — The author creates a dashboard that will contain the PPS content. Dashboards contain one or more pages, each with one or more PPS elements, as well as navigation and other text. The dashboard is a container for a logical grouping of associated dashboard elements, some of which may be connected to each other.

6.   *Place elements onto dashboard pages* — Once the components and dashboards pages are created, the author can place the components onto the pages, and optionally connect or filter the components.

7.   *Deploy dashboards* — As dashboards are completed, they can be deployed to allow everyone (with the correct permissions) to view and interact with the data. Dashboards are stored in PPS-specific document libraries, and can be secured like any other content in SharePoint.

Setting Up the Example

The example for this chapter will create a simple PerformancePoint Dashboard with a scorecard, two reports, and a filter. Figure 15-5 shows the deployed dashboard. Readers can follow along with the example. This example demonstrates a fictional scenario where the primary view would be interested in profit and revenue for the company's bike sales.

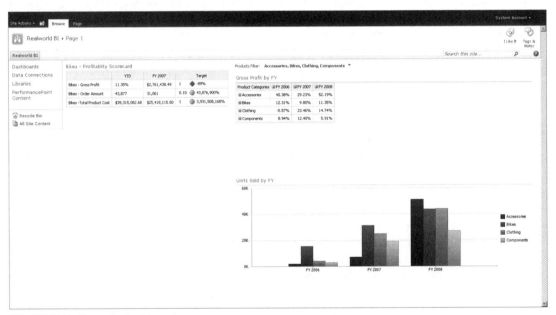

FIGURE 15-5: Example Dashboard

The example is demonstrated using the freely available 2010 Information Worker Demonstration and Evaluation Virtual Machine (RTM) located at http://www.microsoft.com/downloads/details.aspx?FamilyID=751fa0d1-356c-4002-9c60-d539896c66ce&displaylang=en. This virtual machine is already configured with all the necessary server requirements, including SharePoint, PPS, and SQL Analysis Services. The example is running on a new web application with a host header of realworld.contoso.com and a site template of Business Intelligence Center.

The example data source used in this chapter is the freely available `AdventureWorks` database located at `http://msftdbprodsamples.codeplex.com/releases/view/37109`. To follow along with the example, download the `AdventureWorks` database and follow the instructions to install the database and analytic cubes to your SQL Analysis Services server.

Creating PPS Content

PPS content includes the items you generally think of when you build a dashboard. Content can include various reports, scorecards, filters, and data connections. The content is created in Dashboard Designer and stored in one or more PPS-specific lists or libraries. Finally, the content is added to a dashboard and deployed to SharePoint.

Creating the Workspace

A workspace is needed to create dashboards, PPS content, and data sources. Opening the Dashboard Designer automatically creates a new empty workspace if no saved workspace is available. The Business Intelligence Center site template includes a link to the Dashboard Designer. The link is located on the `ppssample.aspx` page located in the site's `Pages` directory. For the "RealWorld" example, this would be located at `http://<Server>realworld.contoso.com/Pages/ppssample.aspx`.

The ClickOnce application will download and install on the client machine. If this is the first time the Dashboard Designer has been run on the client, the ClickOnce application downloads the client and creates a shortcut in the Start ⇨ All Programs ⇨ SharePoint menu. The Business Intelligence site template includes the Data Connection library and PerformancePoint Content list. These are included in the designer's workspace.

 If the workspace is not displaying the correct list and libraries, check the workspace's associated site.

To view or change the workplace's associated site, follow these steps:

1. Select the File button in the top-left corner of the Dashboard Designer. Select the Designer Options button located at the bottom of the File menu.

2. Select the Server tab and view or modify the workspace's associated site.

At this time, you should save the workspace so that you can reopen it at a later time. Saving the workspace will create a DDWX file on the file system.

 Be sure that you save the workspace occasionally. You will not lose the content you have created (because it is stored in lists and libraries), but you will lose the organization you have created.

Creating Data Sources

Data sources are fairly simple. Data sources connect PPS content to the data. Data sources are created and edited in the Dashboard Designer, and are stored in a list associated with the workspace. The list must be based on the Data Connections Library for PerformancePoint library definition.

 Don't get this confused with other connection libraries. The library definition that is installed when you activate the PPS Features is named Data Connections Library for PerformancePoint.

 The "RealWorld" example utilizes only one data connection to the AdventureWorks *analytic database. It is common to see many different data connections and many different data source types in a dashboard.*

To create the AdventureWorks data connection, follow these steps:

1. Right-click the Data Connection folder in the left-hand workspace browser pane and select New Data Source

2. Select the Analysis Services template type from the data source template dialog shown in Figure 15-6. This creates the new data source and opens the configuration form shown in Figure 15-7. Each data source has a slightly different configuration.

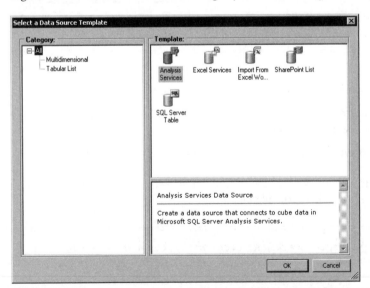

FIGURE 15-6: Available Data Source types in PerformancePoint Services 2010

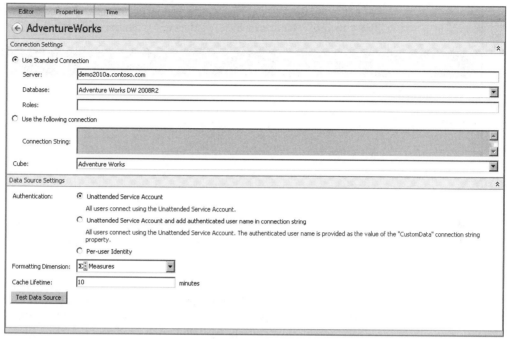

FIGURE 15-7: Data source configuration form

3. Add the SQL Server Analysis server containing the data (for example, `demo2010a.contoso.com`).

4. Select the Database drop-down list and select "Adventure Works DW 2008." The designer will not connect to the data source if the Unattended Execution Account does not have read permissions. Other common issues with connections include an incorrect configuration of Kerberos.

5. Select the Cube drop-down list and select Adventure Works.

6. Test the connection by clicking the Test Data Source button. A successful connection message should appear.

7. Select the Properties tab and edit the properties to provide a meaningful Name and Description of the data source. There might be more than one data source in the library, so a meaningful name will make selecting the correct data source easier. This example uses the name `AdventureWorks`.

8. Click the Save button to save the changes to the `Data Connections` library.

Notice that the authentication has been set for Unattended Service Account. This connection will connect to the data source as the Unattended Service Account for each end user who will view a report or scorecard using this connection. The Per-User Identity will connect to the data source as the user. The middle option is only available for an Analysis Services connection. This option will connect as the Unattended Service Account, but pass back the username in the connection string for filtering purposes.

Data sources are stored in the library. To confirm that the connection is indeed saved to the library, you can navigate to the library to verify. Figure 15-8 shows the view from the Data Connections library.

FIGURE 15-8: The RW PPS Data Connection Library with the AdventureWorks data source

Notice that, because the store for the connection information is a SharePoint library, the connections can be versioned like any other document. Any properties that are set on the Properties tab are promoted to the library as column information. Also, note that the Property tab in the connection configuration form allows the author to select a folder to contain the connection. Folders provide some level of organization. As the workspace grows, there may be many data connections that are saved in the same library, and folders will help the author select the correct data connection.

Creating Reports

Once the workspace has a data source available, the next step is to create PPS content. Content is stored in a PerformancePoint Content list. Authors can easily create content by clicking the Create tab, or right-clicking a content list in the workspace browser pane.

Reports are a category of content that is used to display data in a variety of ways. The most common reports are Analytic Charts and Analytic Grids, which provide the basis for a chart view and a tabular grid view. Authors can select one of the report types by selecting one of the report types from the ribbon, as shown in Figure 15-9.

FIGURE 15-9: Report section of the ribbon

Each report employs a wizard that allows the author to select the appropriate information to start the report. The "Other Reports" option provides a Select Template dialog to select the appropriate report.

For this example, let's create a single Analytic Chart to display AdventureWorks data from the previously created data connection. This chart will be a bar chart that displays the number of units sold per fiscal year. To create a new Analytic Chart, follow these steps:

1. Select the Create tab in the PerformancePoint Dashboard Designer to display the items that can be created.

2. Select the Analytic Chart button. The Create Analytic Chart Report wizard will start.

3. Select the data source to use. For this example, select the `AdventureWorks` data source that was created in the previous steps.

4. Click Finish. The new Analytic Chart item will display in the design pane. The chart will not have any meaningful displayed data.

 If the data connection is not available in the wizard, check to see if the data source has been saved at least once.

5. Select the Property tab to provide a meaningful name and description. For this example, name the chart "Units Sold by FY."

6. Provide a folder name to organize your reports. For this example, use the folder `Reports`.

7. Select the Design tab to design the report.

The right-hand pane in the designer provides the details of the data source selected for the report. A single chapter is not enough time to explain the intricacies of data warehouses, measures, and dimensions. This area is generally the play area for the BI professional or the report designer.

SharePoint professionals are often given the criteria to create the necessary report for the dashboard. Don't be concerned if the next steps presented here make little sense. The point is that the tool allows you to create the content based on design decisions created by others.

Let's now configure the chart to display some information.

 The functionality of these components is immense. This discussion simply looks at a simple scenario so that you can see how much functionality is available.

To create a report that displays the number of units sold by fiscal year, follow these steps:

1. From the right-hand Details pane, expand the Product dimension and drag the Category dimension to the `Series` column below the chart. Right-click the category dimension listed in the Series column and choose Select Members. Uncheck the Default Member checkbox and select Accessories, Bikes, Clothing, and Components located under All Products. Click OK to exit the dialog box,

2. From the right-hand Details pane, drag the Date Fiscal dimension (located under Date ⇨ Fiscal ⇨ Fiscal) to the bottom `Axis` column below the chart. Right-click the category dimension listed in the Series column and choose Select Members. Uncheck the Default Member checkbox and select FY 2006, FY 2007, and FY 2008, located under All Periods.

3. From the right-hand Details pane, drag the `Order Quantity` measure to the `Background` column below the chart.

4. Save the finished report. The final chart should look similar to Figure 15-10.

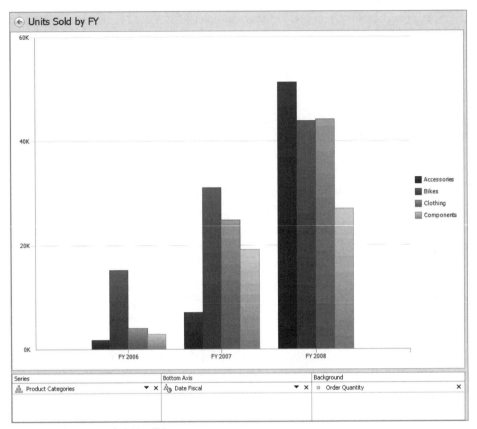

FIGURE 15-10: Units Sold by FY report

Analytic Grids are another similar type of content for PerformancePoint Services. They are created in a manner very similar to a chart, but grids appear in a row and column format. Authors can use the same steps described for the chart report example to create a grid report, with the only exception being the type of report (which would be Analytic Grid).

Figure 15-11 shows an Analytic grid named Gross Profit by FY. This grid uses has the following properties:

➤ Series — Product Categories

➤ Bottom Axis — Date Fiscal Year

➤ Background — Gross Profit Margin

Product Categories and Date Fiscal Year have been filtered similar to the Units Sold by FY report.

Product Categories	⊞ FY 2006	⊞ FY 2007	⊞ FY 2008
⊞ Accessories	40.38%	29.23%	52.19%
⊟ Bikes	12.31%	9.80%	11.35%
⊞ Mountain Bikes	4.84%	16.51%	23.59%
⊞ Road Bikes	18.38%	5.24%	8.36%
⊞ Touring Bikes			1.52%
⊟ Clothing	-5.57%	23.46%	14.74%
⊞ Bib-Shorts		30.74%	
⊞ Caps	-10.60%	-3.00%	-1.52%
⊞ Gloves		27.15%	46.85%
⊞ Jerseys	-10.36%	-2.22%	-15.47%
⊞ Shorts		30.93%	39.08%
⊞ Socks	38.15%		41.46%
⊞ Tights		30.08%	
⊞ Vests			38.12%
⊞ Components	8.94%	12.40%	5.91%

FIGURE 15-11: Gross Profit by FY report

Both charts and reports provide many configuration options, including changing the display type and design. The data area of the report also allows for clickable actions. Data points can be determined by clicking the appropriate area to see the associated tooltip. Feel free to click around the report to view the various actions and data.

Creating Scorecards

Scorecards provide a simple visual method to view goals and metrics to gain an understanding of where your actual performance is, compared to where you would expect or like it to be. PPS provides all the key functionality to create and display a scorecard on a dashboard.

PPS scorecards deserve more attention than can be delivered in this chapter. This discussion briefly covers scorecards to provide an understanding of how to create one.

Following are the major pieces of a scorecard:

➤ *Data sources* — Generally, the data that is displayed in a scorecard comes from one or more data sources created in the PerformancePoint Dashboard Designer. Data for a scorecard can be *dynamic* (meaning that it is pulled from a data source such as an analytic cube) or *static* (meaning that the data is manually assigned).

➤ *Indicators* — Indicators provide the visual aspect of a scorecard. Indicators determine how you display the current status of a KPI. These determine how you show if you are on or off target. Indicators are generally a set of images that will be mapped to a specific performance category. Typically, indicators are green, yellow, or red to denote if you are on target, in danger of going off target, or off target. Center-weighted indicators show if you are off or on target as compared to the center point. Authors can create indicators from a list of Indicator templates, as shown in Figure 15-12.

➤ *KPIs* — KPIs are metrics. KPIs use indicators to visually display performance of the actuals against the target. Whereas indicators are used to visually indicate on or off target, KPIs define the actual value and the target value. KPIs are the metrics that help determine your overall scorecard. Scorecards are made up of one or more KPIs.

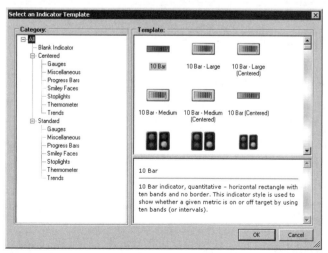

FIGURE 15-12: Preconfigured Indicators in PerformancePoint Services 2010

KPIs in a scorecard can be one of three types:

➤ *Leaf KPIs* — These are the actual metrics. They generally compare an actual value to a set of target values. For example, a leaf metric might show the actual number of bikes sold for the month of February, and the targeted number of bikes to be sold in February.

➤ *Non-leaf KPIs* — These are an aggregation of leaf KPIs to display a single number to indicate success or failure using numbers and indicators. For example, a non-leaf KPI could be a "Total Dollars of Revenue in Europe," which might be an aggregation of the products sold in Europe.

➤ *Objective KPIs* — These roll up varied weighted KPIs to provide an overall view of the collection of KPIs. The rollups bring together non-similar KPIs into a category with an overall indication of success or failure using indicators. An example of an objective KPI might be "Increase in Customer Satisfaction," which could roll up various other KPIs that drive customer satisfaction.

Scorecards consist of one or more KPIs to provide insight into the business data, and allow Information Workers to drill down into the data that is used to define the KPIs. Scorecard support in PerformancePoint Services 2010 allows authors to create custom indicators, KPIs with multiple actuals, and targets, as well as the actual scorecards. Custom indicators are needed only when one of the supplied indicators does not fit the requirement. KPIs must be created or imported into the workspace if they are to be used on a scorecard in the workspace.

An in-depth look at building scorecards in PerformancePoint Services 2010 would entail more discussion than can be offered in this chapter. However, the following example demonstrates how to create three KPIs and one scorecard to measure a very simple objective to increase profitability. Each KPI will look at the sub set of Bikes and display a Year To Date value based on FY 2008, a FY 2006 value, and a Target value as compared against the Year To Date value.

 The AdventureWorks *data does not contain sales data for FY 2009 or FY 2010. This example pretends the current year is 2008.*

To create the first KPI, follow these steps:

1. In the Dashboard Designer, right-click the PerformancePoint Content folder in the workspace browser pane, and select New ➪ KPI.

2. From the KPI Template dialog, select Blank KPI. This creates a new KPI in the workspace with one Actual and one Target value.

3. Select the Property tab and then name the KPI "Bikes: Gross Profit Margin." Set the folder to "KPIs."

4. Select the Editor tab to edit the new KPI.

5. Rename the Actual to "YTD" by clicking in the Name column for the Actual and changing the name.

6. Click the data mapping link for the new YTD row. This will show the current data mapping.

7. Click the Change Source button and select the AdventureWorks data source.

8. Select "Gross Profit Margin" from the Measure drop-down list and click OK.

9. Click the New Dimension Filter button on the form and select Product.Product Categories. Then, click the associated Default column value to set the default Category value. Uncheck the "Default Member (All Product)" value and select Bikes.

10. Click the New Dimension Filter button on the form and select Date.Date.Fiscal Year. Then, click the associated Default column value to set the default Fiscal Year value. Uncheck the "Default Member (All Periods)" value and select "FY 2008". The YTD Actual value will now be retrieved from the AdventureWorks data source and only contain data from the Bikes category for FY 2008.

11. Set the format to Percentage by clicking the YTD's Number Format link.

12. Create a new Actual named FY 2007 by clicking on New Actual menu button. Set the data source, dimension, format, and Product.Products Categories filter to the same values as YTD. Set the default Fiscal Year value to FY 2007. The FY 2007 Actual value will now be retrieved from the AdventureWorks data source, and only contain data from the Bikes category for FY 2007.

13. Select the data mapping link for the Target row.

14. Set the value to .15 and click OK. This targets a value of 15 percent.

The AdventureWorks database does not contain any values that are appropriate for Target values. This chapter's examples will set the Target values manually.

15. Set the format to percentage by clicking the Target's Number Format link.

16. Save the KPI.

Figure 15-13 shows the KPI in the designer.

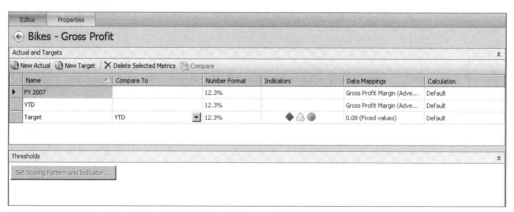

FIGURE 15-13: Gross Profit Margin KPI in the PerformancePoint Dashboard Designer

Now, create a new KPI following the previous steps and name the new KPI "Bikes: Order Amount". This time, use the Order Quantity dimension and set the Target value to 33,547, which is an 8 percent increase over FY 2007. Set the format for this KPI to Number format.

The last KPI should be called "Bikes: Total Product Cost" using the same steps as the previous KPIs. For this KPI, select the Total Product Cost dimension and a Target value of 24,401,390.88, which is a 4 percent decrease in value. The format for this KPI should be Currency. For this KPI a lower number is better, and the indicator must be modified.

1. Click the Target Row to display the indicator below the KPI.

2. Click Set Scoring Pattern Indicator.

3. Select "Decreasing is Better" in the Scoring Pattern Indicator drop-down box and click Next.

4. Accept the default indicator and click Next.

5. Set the Worst value to 39315000 and click Finish.

Let's now create a new scorecard and add the KPIs to the scorecard. To create the scorecard, follow these steps:

1. In the Dashboard Designer, right-click the PerformancePoint Content folder in the workspace browser pane and select New ⇨ Scorecard.

2. Select Bank Scorecard from the templates and click OK. This creates a new blank scorecard in the workspace.

3. Click the Property tab and name the scorecard "Bikes: Profitability Scorecard."

4. Set the folder to Scorecards.

5. Select the Editor tab to add the KPIs. The leaf KPIs just created are located in the right-side Details pane. Select each KPI and drag them to the scorecard.

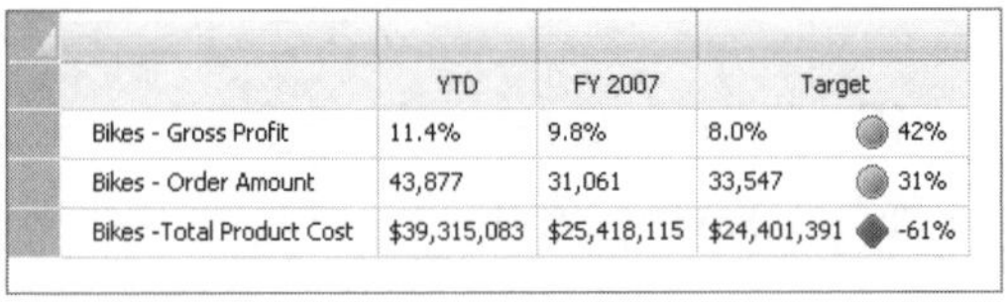

	YTD	FY 2007	Target	
Bikes - Gross Profit	11.4%	9.8%	8.0%	● 42%
Bikes - Order Amount	43,877	31,061	33,547	● 31%
Bikes -Total Product Cost	$39,315,083	$25,418,115	$24,401,391	◆ -61%

6. Save the scorecard.

FIGURE 15-14: Profitability Scorecard in the PerformancePoint Dashboard Designer

Figure 15-14 shows the scorecard in the Dashboard Designer.

Creating Filters

Filters in PerformancePoint Services 2010 are now first-class citizens. Filters are dashboard content that can connect to reports and scorecards to limit or filter the data, thus allowing readers to modify the view. As shown in Figure 15-15, six different filter templates are available.

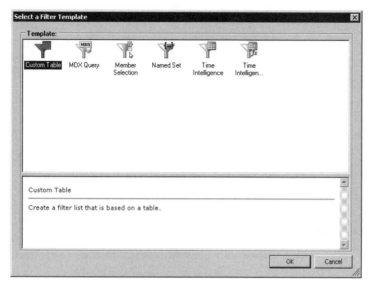

FIGURE 15-15: Available filter templates

Filters can have one of three different display types:

➤ *List* — This displays as a drop-down list for selecting a single item.

➤ *Tree* — This displays as a tree control to select a single item.

➤ *Multi-Select Tree* — This displays as a tree control to select multiple items.

Each template type requires different information to be provided. For example, let's create a filter that will connect to an original chart to allow an Information Worker to view data for one or more product categories.

To create the filter, follow these steps:

1. In the Dashboard Designer, right-click the `PeformancePoint Content` folder in the workspace browser pane and select New ➪ Filter.

2. Select a template from the Filter Template panel. For this example, select the Member Selection template and click OK. The Member Selection template will filter based on a selection from the `AdventureWorks` data.

3. Select the `AdventureWorks` data source and click Next.

4. Click the Select Dimension button and choose the `Product.Category` dimension. Click OK.

5. To select the Members that will be displayed by the filter, click Select Members and check Accessories, Bikes, Clothing, and Components. Click OK and then Next.

6. Select the Multi-Select Tree display type to allow users to select a multiple members at a time. Click Finish.

7. Set the filter as "Product Category" in the Filters folder and save.

Creating Dashboards

In PerformancePoint Services 2010, dashboards are really a collection of one or more web part pages with web part zones. Once a dashboard has been deployed to SharePoint, the dashboard pages will contain PerformancePoint web parts, which will display the data based on the design you have created.

The Dashboard Designer provides the design surface to add, remove, and configure dashboard pages. The Dashboard Designer also enables the author to add the dashboard content previously created, including reports, scorecards, and filters.

To create a dashboard, follow these steps:

1. Right-click the `PerformancePoint Content` folder in the workspace browser, and select New ⇨ Dashboard.

2. Select the Dashboard Page Template from the wizard. Dashboard pages are deployed as web part pages. The various page templates utilize different web part pages with different web part zones. For this example, select the Column, Split Column template and click Next to create the dashboard in the workspace. Figure 15-16 shows the Dashboard Designer with the newly created dashboard.

3. Select the Property tab and name the dashboard "RealWorld Dashboard" and set the folder to "Dashboards."

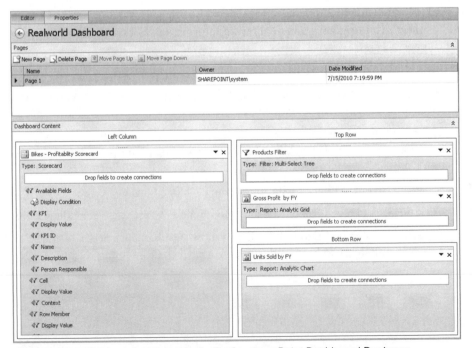

FIGURE 15-16: The new dashboard in the PerformancePoint Dashboard Designer

Dashboard pages contain dashboard content that is known to the workspace. The right-hand Details pane shows the available components that can be added to the dashboard pages. To add a dashboard component to a page, drag the component from the Details pane to the zone on the page.

For the "RealWorld Dashboard" example, drag the "Bikes -Profitability Scorecard" scorecard to the Left Column. Drag the Product Category filter to the right Top Row zone. Place the Gross Profit by Fiscal FY under the filter in the same zone. The Units Sold FY can be place in the right Bottom Row zone.

To connect the Product Category filter to the two reports simply drag and drop the filter in the editor pane to each report and drop it on the area representing the report that displays the "Drop fields to create connections." Dropping the filter onto this area will display the Connection dialog box where the author can configure the connection. In this example connect to Product Categories using the Display Value and click OK. Figure 15-17 displays the Connection dialog box. This should be done for both reports.

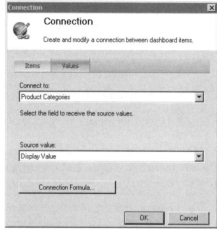

Once the configuration of the connection is done the RealWorld Dashboard is complete. Make sure you save the dashboard.

FIGURE 15-17: The Connection dialog

Deploying Dashboards and Dashboard Components

Creating a dashboard and its components does not actually create a dashboard that can be viewed by Information Workers. It creates the instructions on how to create the dashboard. Dashboards are actually a collection of folders and pages that are created during deployment to a Dashboard library.

Deploying a Dashboard

The deployment process creates the dashboard. What you may think of as a dashboard in the Dashboard Designer translates to SharePoint as a folder in a Dashboard library, with one web part page for each page of the dashboard. Content that is added to the zones in the dashboard are actually web parts configured to display the content based on the "instructions" you create in the Dashboard Designer.

To deploy a dashboard, simply right-click the dashboard item in the workspace browser pane, and then click "Deploy to SharePoint." Figure 15-18 shows the dialog used to deploy the dashboard.

The dialog box displays all Dashboard libraries in the site. Select a Dashboard library to deploy to and click OK. The dashboard will deploy and display in the browser.

FIGURE 15-18: Dashboard deployment dialog box

Deploying Specific Dashboard Content to a Content Page

Generally, dashboard content is placed on dashboard pages. The content that created for this chapter's example exists on the dashboard page as a PerformancePoint web part configured to display a specific set of information as defined in the designer. Because the content is displayed using web parts, the content can exist on a content page outside of the containing dashboard. This allows a designer to reuse a chart, graph, or scorecard and display it practically anywhere it is required.

The following four PerformancePoint web parts are installed in the Web Part Gallery for deploying dashboard content to content pages:

➤ PerformancePoint Filter web part

➤ PerformancePoint Report web part

➤ PerformancePoint ScoreCard web part

➤ PerformancePoint Stack Selector web part

The first three web parts are used to display filters, reports, and scorecards on a web part page. The fourth web part is used to organize multiple PPS web parts in the same web part zone.

To add content to an existing non-dashboard page, you simply add the appropriate web part to the page. If, for example, the content to be added is a report such as a chart or graph, add a PerformancePoint Report web part to the content page.

Each of the web parts has a property to allow you to select the appropriate content from a PerformancePoint Content library. Once the content is selected from the library, click Apply or OK to refresh the page, and the web part will display the selected piece of content. Figure 15-19 shows the PerformancePoint Report web part, and the associated property to select reports.

Figure 15-20 shows the Home page with the PerformancePoint Services Report web part.

Securing Dashboards

Security starts with the actual connection to the data source. As described previously in this chapter, you can configure a data connection to use the Unattended Service Account to connect to the data source. In this scenario, the Unattended Service Account must have read permissions on the data source, and anyone connecting to the data source using this connection will have access to the data. Moreover, from the data source perspective, all connections will appear to be from the same account (the Unattended Service Account), and, therefore, no server-side security or filtering by user account can be applied.

Connections can be created using the Per-Identity configuration. The Per-Identity will connect to the data source as the current user. The current user must have read privileges on the data source to connect. The data source can limit the results based on the user ID.

Analysis Services has one unique connection configuration that connects as the Unattended Service Account. In this scenario, the user ID is provided as part of the connection, so the Analysis Services can limit the results based on the user, while still connecting as a trusted account.

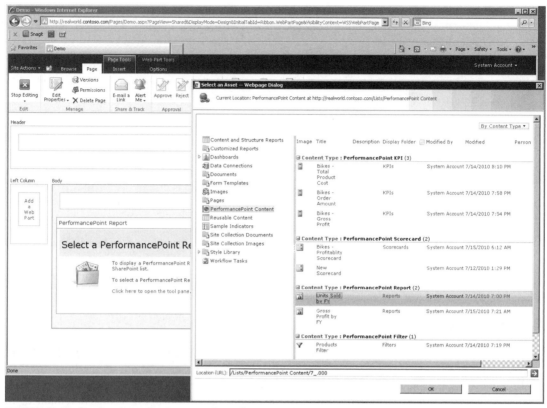

FIGURE 15-19: Configuring a PerformancePoint Services 2010 Report web part

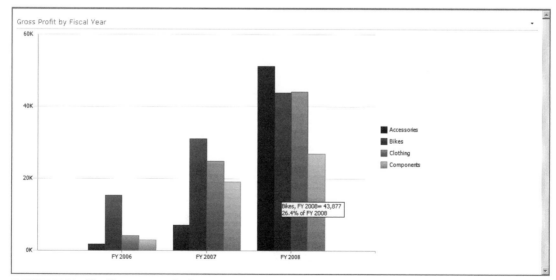

FIGURE 15-20: The Home page displaying a report

Regardless of the chosen connection configuration, data source administrators and those who create and maintain PPS connections must work together to ensure that the data is secured, but accessible to the correct individuals.

Permission to create, edit, and view PPS content is managed by SharePoint 2010 security. PerformancePoint Services 2010 stores data connections and dashboard content inside of SharePoint lists and libraries. Security is maintained by SharePoint for the lists and libraries that contain the content.

Lists and libraries associated with PPS workspaces include a link to set security. This link simply points to the permission page of the list or library. To access the permission page of a list or library from the Dashboard Designer, right-click the folder in the designer's workspace browser pane and select Manage Permissions. You must have contribute permissions on any list or library that you work with. End users must have read permissions on any list or library from which they will view items.

One of the benefits of moving the storage of the PPS content to SharePoint lists and libraries is that you can now have multiple lists and libraries, each with their own levels of permissions. This provides a way for you to limit who can work with what data source or dashboard component.

ABOUT THE AUTHOR

Darrin Bishop is an author, speaker, and developer who has focused on Microsoft SharePoint Technologies since SharePoint Portal Server 2001. He is the president and lead developer for Darrin Bishop Group, Inc., a Midwest-based Microsoft Partner focusing on SharePoint technologies, portals, and collaboration. He speaks frequently at conferences large and small on various development and administration topics. Bishop maintains a blog at www.darrinbishop.com/blog where you can send him feedback or questions. You can follow him on Twitter by subscribing to @bishopd.

16

Managing Metadata with SharePoint Server 2010

By Joris Poelmans

From a document-management perspective, SharePoint Server 2007 already provided a number of exceptional improvements — such as the introduction of both content types and site columns. From a metadata-management perspective, SharePoint Server 2010 again adds extra capabilities that effectively bridge the gap with other high-end document-management systems.

This chapter looks at how you can use the built-in metadata support from SharePoint Server 2010 to effectively organize all your content. SharePoint Server 2010 provides support for building a detailed taxonomy structure, as well as supporting folksonomies. Both of these approaches have their advantages and disadvantages, which are touched upon in this chapter.

Because the Enterprise Managed Metadata (EMM) service plays a central role within setting up both folksonomies and taxonomies, you learn how you need to configure EMM in an efficient way. You also learn how EMM mitigates issues with large-scale, content-type deployment. Finally, this chapter explores how you can extend the out-of-the box functionality with regard to metadata management.

INFORMATION ARCHITECTURE

The term "information architecture" was probably first used in the 1970s by Richard Saul Wurman when he described the role of an information architect as an emergent twenty-first century professional occupation focused on the science of information. But, it was not until 1996 that the term became mainstream, when it was used by Louis Rosenfield and Peter Morville in their book *Information Architecture for the World Wide Web* (Sebastopol, CA: O'Reilly Media,

2006) to define the process of organizing and labeling information on websites to increase "find-ability" and usability.

When looking at SharePoint, it becomes apparent that its strength as a broad platform also poses a significant challenge when designing the information architecture. The diversity of available compo-nents from collaboration, to portal and website building blocks over workflow capability, to business data integration and business intelligence capability, support a very diverse set of usage scenarios. This also means that there is no one size that fits all from an information architecture perspective, because a website built with SharePoint Server 2010 is probably not the same as a project portal with focus on collaboration.

SharePoint also has some specific technical characteristics that impact the design of the informa-tion architecture. The first-level information architecture building blocks in SharePoint consist of SharePoint web applications, site collections, and subsites. These components provide a macro view of the SharePoint information architecture. On a lower level, you see objects such as content types, site columns (or fields), lists, and list items to store and classify information at the site level. Each of these information architecture components has its own specifics with regard to design decisions.

One of the key limitations in SharePoint Server 2007 was the fact that the definition of lower-level objects such as content types and site columns was tied to the site collection level. Because site collec-tions also provided the mechanism to scale, this provided information architects with the dilemma to choose between easy management of metadata structures and the capability to scale.

The new EMM service in SharePoint 2010 enables easy management of organization-wide metadata across web applications and site collections. This means that one of the major drawbacks of using multiple site collections or web applications within your information architecture has been resolved.

TAXONOMY AND METADATA

Metadata is data about data, plain and simple — or is it? Typically, metadata is a set of standards that people agree upon for describing certain types of information. So, metadata is what you need other than the data itself to understand the use of that data (or content).

Look at an example to make this a little bit easier to understand. Let's say that, to add metadata to describe Shakespeare's famous play, *Romeo and Juliet*, you would probably add the following information:

➤ Author: William Shakespeare

➤ Title: Romeo and Juliet

➤ Publication Date: 1591-1594

➤ Category: Drama

You probably notice that filling in the "Category" might pose a challenge when you are offered a free text field. This is one of the design challenges with regard to metadata. After determining the different types of metadata for content, you must determine whether you want to control the possible metadata values, or whether you want to leave the values completely free. In most cases, you want to guide the user to fill in the correct metadata values by offering a limited list of values, because the person publishing the information might not have sufficient domain knowledge about the content itself.

A list of possible metadata values is the simplest form of a *controlled vocabulary*. The purpose of a controlled vocabulary is to prevent authors from defining meaningless metadata values, from offering too specific or too general metadata values, and to prevent different authors from misspelling and choosing slightly different forms of the same metadata value.

The *Guidelines for the Construction, Format and Management of Monolingual Controlled Vocabularies (NISO Z39.19-2005)* (Baltimore, MD: National Information Standards Organization, 2005) describes the different formats of such controlled vocabularies, each with increasing complexity and features from lists over synonym rings, to taxonomy and thesaurus structures.

FIGURE 16-1: Literature taxonomy

"Taxonomy is a collection of controlled vocabulary terms organized into a hierarchical structure. Each term in taxonomy is in one or more parent/child (broader/narrower) relationships to other terms in the taxonomy." (Source: NISO Z39.19)

If you apply this to the earlier example of *Romeo and Juliet*, the taxonomy for the "Category" field when classifying *Romeo and Juliet* would probably look like Figure 16-1.

SharePoint Server 2010 supports the following types of controlled vocabularies:

➤ *Simple list* — This is something that was also available in SharePoint 2007, using a simple lookup list.

➤ *Synonyms* — It is possible to define synonyms, abbreviations, and preferred terms using the new managed metadata infrastructure in SharePoint 2010.

➤ *Taxonomy* — Support is provided through the managed metadata infrastructure in SharePoint 2010. In SharePoint Server 2007, taxonomy was implemented through building a hierarchy of sites and subsites that introduced a number of drawbacks. SharePoint 2010 has a built-in hierarchical field control.

➤ *Thesaurus and ontology* — A thesaurus is an extension of a taxonomy because it adds a specific set of properties to the terms within the hierarchy to describe them (such as broader term, narrower term, and so on). Ontologies take this a step further by adding an extra notion of different relationship types between elements within the hierarchy. Out-of-the-box, SharePoint Server 2010 does not support the notion of associative relationships (it supports only hierarchical relationships), nor does it completely support the notion of thesauri.

Creating and maintaining a taxonomy can be a very labor-intensive task, and is probably best done by experts in this field. This is probably one of the reasons for the rise in interest in the phenomenon of folksonomy.

TAXONOMY VERSUS FOLKSONOMY

Folksonomy is a term used to describe the result of adding metadata in the form of open-ended labels called *tags* by a large group of people. Folksonomy is a form of taxonomy that is built by the end users themselves. It is a typical Internet-based phenomenon (rooted within the Web 2.0 phenomenon) where users of websites such as Flickr, del.icio.us, and Technorati use tags to describe web content and, thereby, they make it easier to search, discover, and navigate this web content over time.

Typically, these tags are displayed in the form of *tag clouds*. The idea behind folksonomy is that large groups of people are smarter than an elite few in classifying and categorizing information, a phenomenon that is commonly referred to as "the wisdom of the crowds." As you will see later, SharePoint 2010 allows for a hybrid approach where you can use both a taxonomy and a folksonomy, and where the folksonomy can be used as source to organically build a formal taxonomy.

Table 16-1 provides a comparison between a taxonomy and a folksonomy.

TABLE 16-1: Taxonomy Versus Folksonomy

CHARACTERISTIC	TAXONOMY	FOLKSONOMY
Flexibility	Less flexible; continuous investment needed for updates	Very flexible; very easy to add information
Accuracy	Built by a small group of subject matter experts	No control over the accuracy; possibility of skewed perspective
Control perspective	Centrally controlled	Lack of control
Possible errors	Usability validation needed	Misspellings; different punctuations; different capitalization; variations in spelling

METADATA AND TAXONOMY PLATFORM ENHANCEMENTS

A number of new features in SharePoint Server 2010 are built around the new *Enterprise Managed Metadata (EMM) service*, which enables a more consistent metadata experience with support for shared taxonomies. Following are the most important improvements within SharePoint 2010 with regard to metadata and managing content:

➤ *Managed metadata* — This includes built-in support for taxonomy structures with the *managed metadata* field.

➤ *Term store* — This is a central database that contains one or more taxonomies, which is referred to as *term set* in SharePoint 2010.

➤ *EMM service* — This allows multiple SharePoint web applications to consume the information stored in the term store.

➤ *Location-based metadata* — This makes the tagging process more productive by adding metadata automatically.

➤ *Metadata navigation settings* — This allows you to make use of metadata values within the SharePoint navigation menus.

➤ *Document sets* — This includes support for working with multiple documents as a single work unit with support for shared metadata at the work unit level.

➤ *Content organizer* — This automatically routes documents or web pages to a specific location within SharePoint based on the metadata that is filled in by the user.

➤ *Content type syndication* — This allows for central management of content types together with capability to use these content types across site collections, web applications, and even farms.

➤ *Social tagging* — This includes the integration of the social aspect within the metadata story, because social tagging is backed by the term store as well.

➤ *Support for different business choices* — These go from tightly managed metadata systems (closed term sets) to very open systems where users can add any keyword they want.

➤ *Support for working with multiple documents as a single work unit* — This is accomplished with *document sets*, with support for shared metadata at the work unit level.

➤ *Location based metadata* — This makes the tagging process more productive by adding metadata automatically.

The following sections look at each of these enhancements in a bit more detail.

Applying Centrally Stored Metadata

The SharePoint *term store* contains a collection of *terms*, which are words or phrases that can be tagged onto an item in SharePoint 2010. These terms exist in two flavors: managed terms and managed keywords.

Managed Terms

Managed terms are predefined by a small group of people, and are organized into a hierarchy. They can be selected by users via the new *managed metadata column type*. The managed metadata column is a single-column or multi-value column that binds to a term set in the term store, which works like a "super choice" field. Users can either fill in a value using the textbox (which provides term suggestions), or they can use the taxonomy picker control shown in Figure 16-2 (which shows a dialog with a tree picker control for the complete hierarchy of terms within the term set linked to the managed metadata column). SharePoint Server uses an identifier for each term, instead of just storing the label. This allows for the use of synonyms for each label, as well as support for multilingual scenarios.

FIGURE 16-2: Taxonomy picker control

Managed terms support synonyms and abbreviations, as well as the new *Multilingual User Interface* (*MUI*). It is possible to add multiple managed metadata columns to a SharePoint list, library, or content type — but it is also possible to use a term set as a data source for a user profile property in the SharePoint user profile store.

You can provide translations for each term within the term store. Based on the language selected by a user within the MUI, the user will see the translation within the user interface and be able to work with the metadata in his or her own language. This might be one of the reasons why you should use managed terms instead of a simple choice field to display a controlled list of selectable options to the end user.

Enterprise Keywords

Enterprise keywords are like a "super text" field — they allow you to enter any value, but there is still a link with the term store. Because of this link with the term store, you will get auto-completion and preferred keyword suggestions as you start typing, as shown in Figure 16-3. Possible suggestions are keywords that have already been added to the term store. If the keyword already exists, it will store the ID from the keyword, together with the value in the Enterprise Keywords field. If it is a new keyword, it will be added to the non-hierarchical keyword term set.

Enterprise keywords are defined as a site column. It is possible to add it to specific lists or libraries, or to other content types. However, it is only possible to add one managed keywords column to a specific SharePoint object.

Enterprise keywords are appropriate for more ad-hoc folksonomy scenarios where the users are allowed to tag an item with whatever keywords they believe are appropriate. However, you can promote a specific keyword to a managed term within the term hierarchy. This allows for building a taxonomy in an organic fashion.

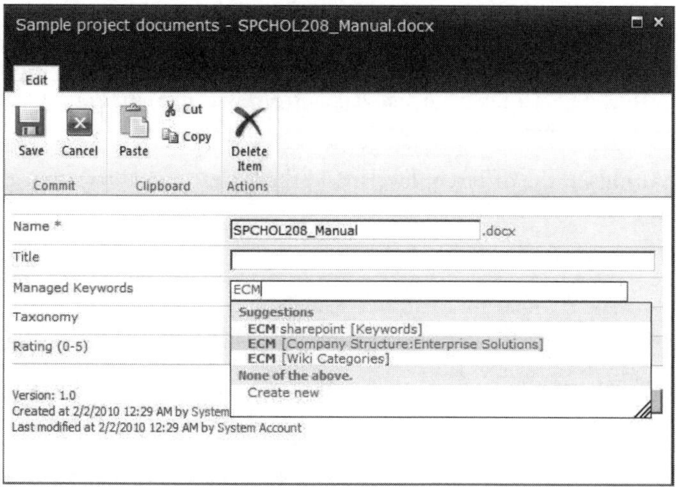

FIGURE 16-3: Enterprise keywords field control

Working with the Term Store Management Tool

As explained earlier, the SharePoint term store contains a collection of terms that are centrally managed. There is only one term store per managed metadata service.

As shown in Figure 16-4, a term store can contain one or more *term groups*. Term groups act as security boundary. It's at the level of a term group that you can define *term group managers* and *term group contributors*. The term group managers have contributor rights and can add additional contributors. A contributor is responsible for managing all of the terms and term sets within the term group. A term group can again contain one or more term sets. The term set is the hierarchy of different terms that are being used.

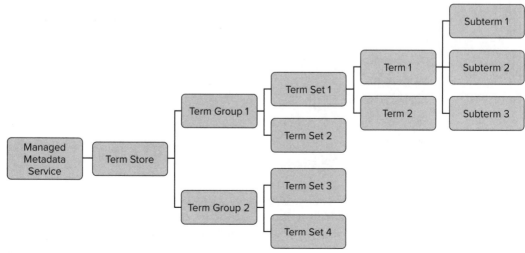

FIGURE 16-4: Term store hierarchy

Term Set and Term Management

The term store management tool is the Central Administration page for controlling all of the different term stores. It is accessible from the Site Settings page, as well as from within SharePoint Central Administration.

Table 16-2 lists all the possible operations at the different levels, and the lowest necessary security rights.

TABLE 16-2: Available Term Operations and Required Permissions

LEVEL	AVAILABLE OPERATIONS	REQUIRED PERMISSIONS
Term store	Define term store administrator Create new term store	Farm administrator
	Create new term group Define working languages	Term store administrator
	Create new term set Import term set Define group contributors	Term group manager
Term set	Define term set owner, contact, stakeholders, submission policy, and availability for tagging Create term Copy term set Reuse terms Move term set Delete term set	Term set contributor
Term	Create term Copy term Reuse terms Merge terms Deprecate term Move term Delete term Define custom sort order	Term set contributor

The *submission policy* — with two options, *open* or *closed* — determines who can add terms to the term set. When a term set is closed, only term set contributors can add terms to this term set. When it is open, users can add terms from within the taxonomy picker dialog screen.

The term set owner, term set contacts, and term set stakeholders are not security roles. The users defined in these term set properties cannot perform any activities on the term set or the terms within.

Table 16-3 explains specific term operations in more detail. It is important to note that changes you make to terms in the term store are pushed down in the metadata of all of the content that is using this term.

TABLE 16-3: Specific Term Operations Explained

TERM OPERATIONS	EXPLANATION
Reuse term	You can reuse a term in another place in the term store hierarchy. Once a term is being reused, you will need to edit the term information only once — either in the source or the different reused terms — and all source terms and reused terms will be updated.
Merge terms	Merging a term into another term adds the term (and all synonyms and translations of this term) as a synonym to the target term.
Deprecate term	This makes the term unavailable for metadata tagging. You can reverse this operation by enabling the term again. Contents that have been tagged with a deprecated term will keep the existing metadata. There are no specific warnings in the SharePoint user interface from an end user's perspective.
Delete term	This operation is irreversible. Once you delete a term, all contents tagged with this term give a warning, "This term is not a valid term." If the deleted term had children, or it was the source term for a reuse scenario, its children are moved into the orphaned terms category.
Move terms	This option is not only used to re-arrange the hierarchy of terms, but also to promote managed keywords to a managed term. However, It is not possible to move a managed term into the managed keywords store.
Define custom sort order	You can specify a custom sort order for terms, so it isn't necessary to show them in alphabetical order. A typical example would be days of the week.

Multilingual Scenarios

After you have installed the necessary SharePoint language packs, you are able to define alternate languages for the terms within the term store. Once you have translated a specific term into an alternate language, the new MUI uses the available translation. If there is no translation available for a specific term, the user interface always falls back to the default language.

Following are the different steps to take:

1. Install the SharePoint Server language pack for each language that you want to support.

2. From the Term Store Management Tool, add each language to the list of working languages for the term store, and define which language is the default language for the term store, as shown in Figure 16-5.

3. Translate the labels for each term and language combination that you want to support.

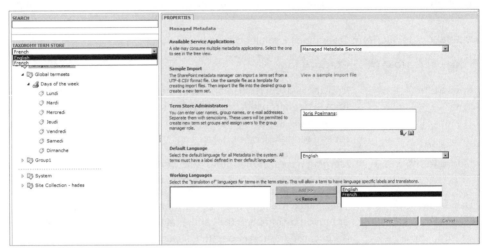

FIGURE 16-5: Default languages and alternate working languages in the term store

 Although you can import a term set using a specific comma-delimited file format, it is not possible to import translations for specific terms. This is something that needs to be done using the SharePoint object model or using Powershell.

Boundaries

The term store has been built with large-scale deployments in mind. However, some design boundaries must be taken into consideration when setting up the managed metadata service infrastructure. Table 16-4 describes these boundaries.

TABLE 16-4: Term Store Boundaries

OBJECT	BOUNDARY
Term	You can nest terms a maximum seven levels deep. You can have a maximum of 1 million terms in the term store.
Term set	A maximum of 30,000 terms are allowed per term set, and maximum of 1,000 term sets are allowed per term group.

Using the Service Application

It is important to understand the new SharePoint 2010 services infrastructure before you get started with the EMM service. SharePoint Server 2010 uses a new services model that allows you to deploy only the services that are needed to a farm. This is different from the 2007 model, where the deployment of services through the Shared Service Provider (SSP) was an all-or-nothing decision.

These services can be shared across web applications, and even across farms (not all service applications can be shared across farms, but the managed metadata service does support cross-farm consumption). SharePoint web applications typically consume these services through a *service connection*. It is possible to have multiple instances of the same service in a farm.

The managed metadata service actually controls two distinct features: the term store and *content type syndication*. Content type syndication solves a typical problem in SharePoint Server 2007 where there was no out-of-the box solution for creating an enterprise library of content types that could be synchronized across different site collections. It is possible to create packaged content types using the SharePoint Features framework and WSPs, and to activate them on every site collection in 2007. However, this is a very time-consuming and error-prone process that becomes especially challenging once you need to update the content types you already deployed.

SharePoint 2010 solves this problem by introducing a new feature called the *content type hub*. The content type hub is a site collection that is designated as the "source" from where you can share content types throughout different web applications. The content type hub is exposed to every web application using the managed metadata service infrastructure. You learn more about content type syndication later in this chapter.

The logical architecture of service applications facilitates very flexible scenarios, as shown in Figure 16-6. In this example scenario, both the intranet portal and Internet website can make use of the content types defined in the intranet content type hub, but the keywords and terms are separated. However, it is also possible to create extra managed metadata service applications to accommodate for multiple term stores specific for some parts of your organization.

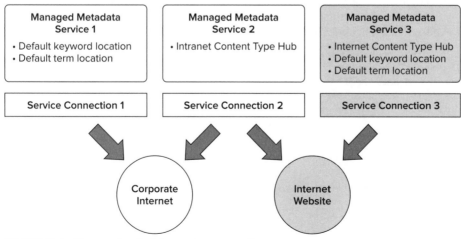

FIGURE 16-6: Managed metadata service connections

Managed metadata service applications are administered from within SharePoint Central Administration, where you get an overview of all available service applications. When you initially create a new managed metadata service, you must specify the name, database, application pool, and the URL for the content type hub from which the service application will consume content types. Because a web application can have connections to multiple managed metadata services, you must configure a number of options (such as the default keyword location, the term set location, and how content type syndication will function). These settings are controlled in the Managed Metadata Service Connection properties screen shown in Figure 16-7.

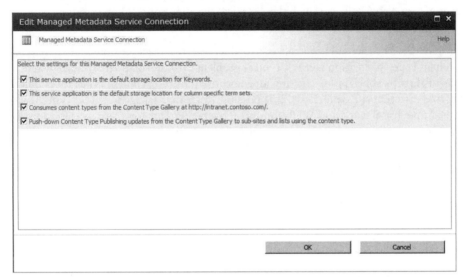

FIGURE 16-7: Service connection properties

Installation and configuration of all these different options can be a tedious and error-prone task. This is why SharePoint Server 2010 provides more than 500 different *cmdlets* to fully automate the administration of SharePoint. All the different operations from within Central Administration with regard to the managed metadata service are also available as PowerShell cmdlets.

```
$snapin = Get-PSSnapin | Where-Object {$_.Name -eq
    'Microsoft.SharePoint.Powershell'}
if ($snapin -eq $null){
    Write-Host "Loading Microsoft SharePoint Powershell Snapin"
    Add-PSSnapin "Microsoft.SharePoint.Powershell"
}

$ManagedAccount = Get-SPManagedAccount | select -First 1
if ($ManagedAccount -eq $NULL) { throw "No Managed Accounts" }

$ApplicationPool = Get-SPServiceApplicationPool "SharePoint Hosted Services" `
 -ea SilentlyContinue
if($ApplicationPool -eq $null){
    $ApplicationPool = New-SPServiceApplicationPool `
        "SharePoint Hosted Services" -account $ManagedAccount
    if (-not $?) { throw "Failed to create an application pool" }
```

```
}

Write-Progress "Creating Taxonomy Service Application" -Status "Please Wait..."

$MetadataServiceInstance = (Get-SPServiceInstance |?{$_.TypeName -eq
    "Managed Metadata Web Service"})
if (-not $?) { throw "Failed to find Metadata service instance" }

if($MetadataserviceInstance.Status -eq "Disabled"){
   $MetadataserviceInstance | Start-SPServiceInstance
   if (-not $?) { throw "Failed to start Metadata service instance" }
}

while(-not ($MetadataServiceInstance.Status -eq "Online")){
      write-host "Waiting for provisioning …"; sleep 5;
}

$MetaDataServiceApp  = New-SPMetadataServiceApplication -Name `
    "Wrox Metadata Service Application" -ApplicationPool $ApplicationPool
if (-not $?) { throw "Failed to create Metadata Service Application" }

$MetaDataServiceAppProxy  = New-SPMetadataServiceApplicationProxy -Name `
    "Wrox Metadata Service Application Proxy" -ServiceApplication
        $MetaDataServiceApp -DefaultProxyGroup
```

Table 16-5 provides a breakdown of cmdlets used to administer the managed metadata service.

TABLE 16-5: Relevant Cmdlets for Administering the Managed Metadata Service

POWERSHELL CMDLET	EXPLANATION
Get-SPMetadataServiceApplication	Get a reference to a `MetadataWebServiceApplication` instance.
New-SPMetadataServiceApplication	Create a new managed metadata service application and a corresponding term store.
Set-SPMetadataServiceApplication	Set properties for a managed metadata service application.
Get-SPMetadataServiceApplicationProxy	Get a `MetadataWebServiceApplicationProxy` instance — a reference to a managed metadata service connection.
New-SPMetadataServiceApplicationProxy	Create a new managed metadata service connection for a local or remote managed metadata service application.
Set-SPMetadataServiceApplicationProxy	Update properties of the managed metadata service connection.

continues

TABLE 16-5 *(continued)*

POWERSHELL CMDLET	EXPLANATION
Clear-SPMetadataWebServicePartitionData, Export-SPMetadataWebServicePartitionData, Import-SPMetadataWebServicePartionData	SharePoint Server 2010 supports multi-tenancy. In a multi-tenant scenario, segmentation is accomplished through the use of site groups (or site subscriptions). Because the managed metadata services are shared at the web application level, you must assign data to its own partition so that other site groups are not able to see this data, even though all site groups are using the same managed metadata service application. To set this up, you will need these PowerShell commands.

Understanding Location-Based Metadata

Adding the correct metadata is not a favorite task for end users when they need to add multiple documents to SharePoint. To make this less of a chore, and to avoid errors when applying metadata, SharePoint 2010 introduces *location-based metadata*. It is possible in SharePoint 2010 to configure location-based metadata defaults for a hierarchy of folders.

To change the metadata defaults, go to Library Settings ➪ Column Default Value Settings. In the example shown in Figure 16-8, a number of folders are added to a document library, and the Beta folder has a default value configured for the TestColumn field equal to z. This is also depicted in the folder hierarchy on the left side by adding a little green wheel icon on the folders that have metadata defaults. You also notice that the Alpha folder has no metadata defaults added to it.

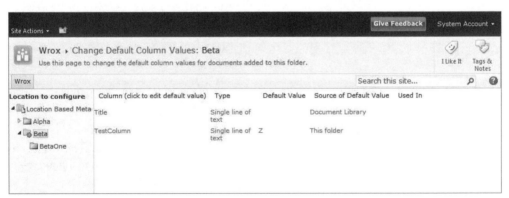

FIGURE 16-8: Location-based metadata

For parent folders with metadata default values, the subfolders also inherit these metadata defaults, unless a different metadata value is explicitly defined. This means that documents added to the

`BetaOne` folder shown in Figure 16-8 will also get this metadata default. The metadata defaults are applied whenever a document is added, either as a single file upload or as a multiple upload, as part of a workflow, or as the result of a document conversion.

To do the same using the SharePoint object model, you need a reference to the `Microsoft.Office` `.DocumentManagement.MetadataDefaults` class. As shown in the following code snippet, you first add a reference to `Microsoft.Office.DocumentManagement.dll` (found in the `14\ISAPI` folder) if you need to use this class:

```
using (SPSite sitecollection = new SPSite("http://intranet.contoso.com/
    sites/wrox"))
{
    using (SPWeb site = sitecollection.OpenWeb(""))
    {
        SPList list = site.Lists["MetadataDefaults"];
        SPDocumentLibrary doclib = (SPDocumentLibrary)site.Lists["MetadataDefaults"];
        SPFolderCollection doclibfolders = site.Folders;
        string sfolderurl = site.Url + "/" + doclib.RootFolder + "/" + "MyFolder";
        SPFolder newfolder = doclibfolders.Add(sfolderurl);
        doclib.Update();

        MetadataDefaults columndefaults = new MetadataDefaults(list);
        columndefaults.SetFieldDefault(newfolder, "Company", "RealDolmen");
        columndefaults.Update();
    }
}
```

Understanding Metadata Navigation Settings

SharePoint 2010 provides two new navigation concepts — navigation hierarchies and key filters — both of which appear in the left-hand pane of the new user interface (Figure 16-9):

➤ *Navigation hierarchies* — These provide a hierarchical tree view that allows users to filter items in a document library or list by selecting nodes in the tree view.

➤ *Key filters* — These offer filtering capabilities for a specific field with built-in type ahead.

After activating the "Metadata Navigation and Filtering" site feature, the different lists in a site will have a new Metadata Navigation settings page (Figure 16-10) for configuring that list to use metadata tree view hierarchies and filter controls to improve navigation and filtering of the contained items.

Go to the `Features` folder in the SharePoint root folder, which is the common name for the folder location `C:\Program Files\Common Files\Microsoft Shared\Web Server Extensions\14\`. If you take a look at the `MetaDataNav` Feature folder, you will notice that both controls are implemented using the notion of delegate controls. The out-of-the-box `v4.master` defines two delegate controls with the IDs `TreeViewAndDataSource` and `ColumnFilterCAMLGenerator` — which the `MetaDataNav` Feature swaps out at run time for the `MetadataNavTree.ascx` and `ColumnFiltering` `.ascx`. This means that, if you built your own custom master pages and you wanted to take advantage of these controls, you must add in these delegate controls.

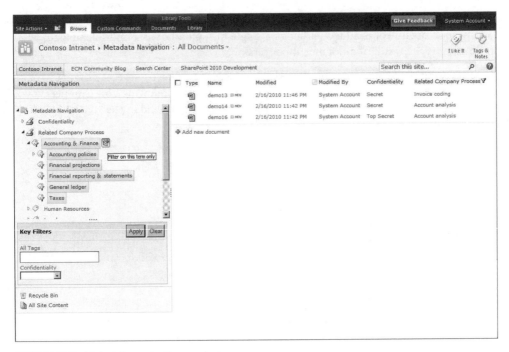

FIGURE 16-9: Metadata navigation controls

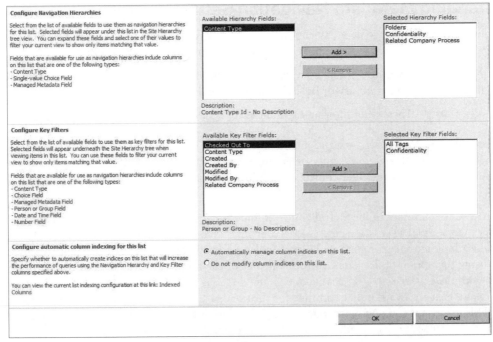

FIGURE 16-10: Revised metadata navigation settings

Document Sets and Metadata Behavior

Document sets are a new type of object in SharePoint where multiple work products (Excel files, Word documents, scans, and so on) are managed as a whole. A typical example of a document set is a proposal dossier that contains the main proposal document, the contract agreement, and possibly all of the input documents from the customer.

Document sets provide the following functionality:

➤ Provide you with the capability to group documents together and define common metadata fields for the document set as a whole. For these document set metadata fields, you can define that they are shared among all the individual documents within the document sets.

➤ Provide you with a specific welcome page for a document set, which can be customized by adding web parts.

➤ Enable you to link a number of allowed content types to the document set.

➤ Enable you to add a number of default documents to a document set. These documents will be available upon creation of the document set.

➤ Provide the capability to create a version snapshot of the document set as a whole. This requires that versioning is activated at the document library to where the document set is linked.

➤ Enable you to define workflows at the document set level, instead of the individual documents.

Document sets are implemented as a content type in SharePoint 2010, which derives from the Document Collection Folder content type. The following code samples show the content type schema for a document set content type with one shared column. This first snippet shows how to define a new site column (which is no different than in SharePoint 2007):

Available for
download on
Wrox.com

```xml
<?xml version="1.0" encoding="utf-8"?>
<Elements xmlns="http://schemas.microsoft.com/sharepoint/">
  <Field ID="{EA3B6D7D-70DE-49c6-BC18-B6EDAEF09AAC}"
         Name="CustomerName"
         DisplayName="Customer Name"
         Description=""
         Group="SampleDocumentSet"
         Type="Text"
         DisplaceOnUpgrade="TRUE" />
</Elements>
```

Code file [SampleDocumentSet.zip] available for download at Wrox.com

The next code snippet shows how a new document content type (which is added to the allowed list of content types for the document set) also uses this same column:

```xml
<?xml version="1.0" encoding="utf-8"?>
<Elements xmlns="http://schemas.microsoft.com/sharepoint/">
  <!-- Parent ContentType: Document (0x0101) -->
  <ContentType ID="0x0101000e08cb4f603c47a99141fdcc1bde6831"
               Name="ProposalDoc"
               Group="Custom Content Types"
```

```
                    Description="My Content Type"
                    Version="0">
        <FieldRefs>
          <FieldRef ID="{EA3B6D7D-70DE-49c6-BC18-B6EDAEF09AAC}"/><!-- Customer name -->
        </FieldRefs>
      </ContentType>
    </Elements>
```

This last snippet shows the content type schema definition for the custom document set content type. Notice that the newly created site column is added at the document set level, and that it is defined as a *shared field*. This means that the values for this field are automatically pushed down by the document set into the individual documents, which use this same field.

```
<?xml version="1.0" encoding="utf-8"?>
<Elements xmlns="http://schemas.microsoft.com/sharepoint/">
  <!-- Parent ContentType: Document Set (0x0120D520) -->
  <ContentType ID="0x0120D520008c79bffa49114dad9576da98ce634c75"
               Name="ProposalDocumentSet"
               Group="Custom Content Types"
               Description="My Proposal Document Set"
               Version="3"
               ProgId="SharePoint.DocumentSet"
               >
    <Folder TargetName="_cts/ProposalDocumentSet" />
    <FieldRefs>
      <FieldRef ID="{8553196d-ec8d-4564-9861-3dbe931050c8}"
                DisplayName="Proposal Name"
                Description="Enter in the format of [CUSTOMER]-
                    [PROPOSAL TITLE]." />
      <FieldRef ID="{EA3B6D7D-70DE-49c6-BC18-B6EDAEF09AAC}"/><!--
          Customer name field - docset reference -->
    </FieldRefs>
    <XmlDocuments>
      <XmlDocument NamespaceURI="http://schemas.microsoft.com/office/
          documentsets/sharedfields">
        <sf:SharedFields xmlns:sf="http://schemas.microsoft.com/office/
            documentsets/sharedfields" LastModified="1/1/2010 08:00:00 AM">
          <SharedField id="EA3B6D7D-70DE-49c6-BC18-B6EDAEF09AAC" /><!--
              Customer name shared field -->
        </sf:SharedFields>
      </XmlDocument>
      <XmlDocument NamespaceURI="http://schemas.microsoft.com/office/
          documentsets/allowedcontenttypes">
        <act:AllowedContentTypes xmlns:act="http://schemas.microsoft.com/office/
            documentsets/allowedcontenttypes" LastModified=
            "1/1/2010 08:00:00 AM">
          <AllowedContentType id="0x0101" /><!-- Document -->
          <AllowedContentType id="0x0101000e08cb4f603c47a99141fdcc1bde6831" /><!
              -- ProposalDoc-->
        </act:AllowedContentTypes>
      </XmlDocument>
    </XmlDocuments>
  </ContentType>
</Elements>
```

Do not forget to activate the document set feature at the site collection level before deploying custom document set content types. Always use feature activation dependencies to avoid unexpected behavior. Visual Studio 2010 includes designer support for adding feature activation dependencies for custom features that you build.

Using Content Organizers

The *content organizer* is an extension of the old routing functionality linked to the Records Center in SharePoint 2007. If you are sending an item to the SharePoint 2007 Records Center, it would be moved to the correct library based on the records routing list, which contains a list of content types and a link to a destination library. Content organizers decouple this functionality from the Records Center and make it available throughout your entire SharePoint environment.

One of the challenges for end users is to find the correct location where they need to store their document or create web pages. Content organizers solve this problem by moving documents and web pages automatically to the correct location based on the metadata associated with it.

So SharePoint 2010 provides a number of big improvements with regard to the routing functionality, including the following:

➤ The content organizer not only routes documents based on content types, but also based on other metadata attributes — it will even be able to build a folder structure based on these metadata attribute values. The content organizer uses content organizer rules to define the routing logic.

➤ The content organizer is available in all sites, not just the Records Center.

To get started, you must activate the content organizer feature at the site level. (Look at the `DocumentRouting` and `DocumentRoutingResources` folders within the Features folder underneath the SharePoint root for more details.) This will enable two extra links on the site administration section of the site settings (*content organizer settings* and *content organizer rules*), as well as create an extra document library called the Drop Off Library.

The content organizer settings page contains general configuration settings, such as the following:

➤ Automatically redirect to the Drop Off Library

➤ Allow sending to other site

➤ Partition folders

The content organizer also includes a feature for folder partitioning that automatically creates folders after the target location has reached a specified number of items. This can also be used for web content management scenarios, because the SharePoint 2010 pages library now also supports folders.

➤ Determine what to do with duplicate submissions — that is, append unique characters, or simply use the built-in SharePoint versioning

➤ Preserve context to include audit logs and properties with the submission

➤ Define rule managers that must sort out content that did not get routed correctly

➤ Determine submission points — the URL of the web service that allows third-party applications to interact with the content organizer

The content organizer rules are stored a within a normal SharePoint list, which has the Organizer Rule content type linked to it. Here you define the routing logic to route documents based on metadata and content type. When you activate the content organizer feature, all uploads to the site are automatically sent to the Drop Off Library. (However, you can change this setting.) Afterward, uploads are routed to the correct location. The user will also get notifications of this within the SharePoint user interface (Figure 16-11) when uploading a document and modifying the required metadata for routing.

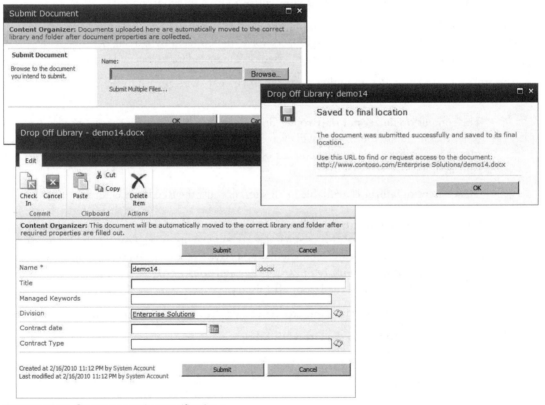

FIGURE 16-11: Content organizer notifications

Understanding Content Type Syndication

The EMM service application facilitates a new feature called *content type syndication*. This allows for central management of content types, while providing the capability to publish (syndicate) these content types to multiple site collections (even on other web applications or farms). This means that SharePoint Server 2010 enables up-to-date and consistent content type schemas, even in large deployments, without the need to revert to custom-built solutions or third-party add-ons.

A content type that is being syndicated from the content type hub is commonly referred to as an *enterprise content type*. Follow these steps to enable content type syndication:

1. Define a content type hub by going to the properties of the managed metadata service entry in the Manage Service Applications page. Here you can enter the URL of the hub site collection. Don't forget to check the box directly below to report syndication import errors.

2. Enable consumption of content types from the content type hub through the managed metadata service connection. Select properties for the managed metadata service connection entry in the Manage Services Applications page. Check the box "Consumes content types from the content type gallery at http://intranet.contoso.com" and click OK.

Publishing Content Types

After setting up content type syndication, you will see a new option in the settings page for a content type: Manage Publishing for This Content Type. After you publish the content type, it will become available for consumption.

The content types and their settings are pushed across using two different timer jobs:

➤ The *content type hub timer job* retrieves all the content types that are marked for publishing or re-publishing.

➤ The *content type subscriber timer job* actually grabs these content types and pulls them into the different site collections.

There will be an instance of the content type subscriber job for each web application that is associated with the managed metadata service connection linked to the content type hub. The content hub timer jobs run every 15 minutes by default. If you need to speed up things, you can go to Central Administration and use the new Run Now functionality on the timer job definition page. You can also start these timer jobs using PowerShell, as shown here:

```
start-sptimerjob -identity metadatahubtimerjob
start-sptimerjob -identity metadatasubscribertimerjob
```

A number of different elements at the content type level are pushed over using content type syndication:

➤ The content type itself with all the different site columns.

 Lookup columns will not be syndicated.

➤ Workflow associations for the content type, but not the workflow definitions (you must manually ensure that these are deployed)

➤ Information management policies linked to the content type

After setting up a content type for syndication, you will see it listed on the Content Type Publishing Hubs page (Figure 16-12), which is available through a link on site collection administration called "content type publishing."

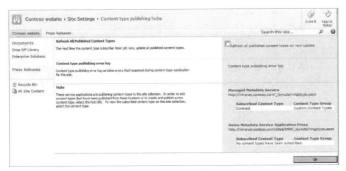

FIGURE 16-12: Content type publishing hubs

Consuming Content Types

Content types that are consumed from the content type hub will be read-only on the consumer side. However, it is possible to create a new content type that derives from the *enterprise content type*.

Understanding Social Tagging and Metadata

Thus far, you have learned about applying metadata to an item for which you typically have the necessary rights to add the metadata. This is commonly referred to as *authorative tagging*. This section now takes a look at social tagging.

Social tagging allows users to add keywords to content. These keywords are an addition to the metadata provided by the content contributors. These tags will help users categorize, promote, and retrieve relevant links, because the SharePoint search will take into account whether content has been tagged to decide about its relevancy with regard to a specific query.

But tagging is about more than just enhancing the "findability" of items and the overall navigation experience. It is also about group-based social networking, such as finding people with common interests and specific expertise.

Tagging and the Term Store

In SharePoint 2010, both authorative tagging (which uses managed metadata) and social tagging use the same backend — namely the term store. This means that the tag itself will be stored within the term store with a specific GUID. Within the tagging control (Figure 16-13), you will see term suggestions, as well as disambiguation of terms, because of this link with the term store.

The social tag is not stored with the item itself, but rather is stored in the social data database. The tag will be added to the keyword term set, and the social data database will store the GUID for the taxonomy term, the URI, link to the user profile, timestamp, and so on.

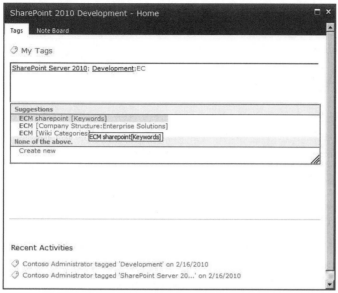

FIGURE 16-13: Social tagging control

 The social tagging feature itself is linked to the user profile service application. Therefore the social data database will typically have a name such as [User profile service application]_[SocialDB]_[GUID], *where the first part is the name of the user profile service application. From within Central Administration, administrators will be able to disable social tags and note boards for specific users or groups of users, delete specific tags (such as all tags for an employee who leaves the company), or remove tags that are not wanted.*

Extending Social Networking

The social networking functionality in SharePoint Server 2010 can be extended using classes within the Microsoft.Office.Server.SocialData namespace. SharePoint Server 2010 provides new functionality for programmatically creating and aggregating social tags (by using the SocialTagManager class), ratings (SocialRatingManager class), and comments (SocialCommentManager class).

The following code sample shows how you can use the SocialTagManager class to display information about the use of social tags. It also shows the link between the SocialTerm class and the Microsoft.SharePoint.Taxonomy.Term class.

```
using System;
using Microsoft.SharePoint;
using Microsoft.Office.Server;
using Microsoft.Office.Server.UserProfiles;
```

```
using Microsoft.Office.Server.SocialData;
using Microsoft.SharePoint.Taxonomy;

namespace SocialDataConsoleApp
{
    class Program
    {

        static void Main(string[] args)
        {
            using (SPSite sitecollection = new SPSite("http://
                intranet.contoso.com"))
            {
                SPServiceContext servicecontext =
                    SPServiceContext.GetContext(sitecollection);
                SocialTagManager mySocialTagManager = new
                    SocialTagManager(servicecontext);

                foreach (SocialTerm socialterm in mySocialTagManager.GetAllTerms())
                {
                    Term keywordterm = socialterm.Term;
                    Console.WriteLine(keywordterm.GetDefaultLabel(1033) + " " +
                        socialterm.Count.ToString());
                }
            }
            Console.ReadLine();
        }
    }
}
```

Code file [SocialDataConsoleApp.zip] available for download at Wrox.com

PROGRAMMATIC ACCESS TO THE EMM SERVICE

The `Microsoft.SharePoint.Taxonomy` namespace contains most of the APIs required to write extensions on the EMM service. A number of methods are also available within the API to manage taxonomies in rich client applications or rich Internet applications.

This section first looks at the `Microsoft.SharePoint.Taxonomy` namespace.

Using the Taxonomy API

The first thing you will need to do when you want to use the taxonomy API is to instantiate a `TaxonomySession` object. The `TaxonomySession` class creates a new session in which to instantiate objects and commit changes transactionally to the `TermStore` object. The constructor for the `TaxonomySession` class is overloaded with an extra `UpdateCache` parameter. The `UpdateCache` parameter forces the `TaxonomySession` to check for cache changes synchronously. The normal update check happens in the background every 10 seconds.

```
public TaxonomySession( SPSite site, bool updateCache)
```

You should set the UpdateCache parameter to true only when you are doing edits to the term store, and you want to be sure that you have the latest data. For example, the Term Store Manager application page sets this to true when it renders, because this is a place where editing happens quite frequently.

The following code sample shows how you can instantiate a TaxonomySession object. It shows how to traverse the hierarchy of main objects linked to the term store. The top-level object is the TermStore, which can contain one or more Groups. Within these Groups, there will be one or more TermSet objects available with a hierarchy of Terms linked to it.

```
private static void WalkTermStoreHierarchy()
{
 using (SPSite sitecollection = new SPSite("http://intranet.contoso.com")){
    string sGroupManagers;
    TaxonomySession taxonomysession = new TaxonomySession(sitecollection);

    foreach (TermStore termstore in taxonomysession.TermStores){
     Console.WriteLine("Termstore: {0}, DefLanguage:{1}, Languages:{2}",
         termstore.Name, termstore.WorkingLanguage,
         ArrayToStringGeneric(termstore.Languages,";"));
       foreach (Group termgroup in termstore.Groups){
          sGroupManagers = "";
          foreach (SPAce<TaxonomyRights> ace in termgroup.GroupManagers){
            sGroupManagers += ",";
            sGroupManagers += ace.DisplayName;
          }
          Console.WriteLine("Termgroup:{0},groupmgrs:{1}",termgroup.Name,
              sGroupManagers);
          foreach (TermSet termset in termgroup.TermSets){
             Console.WriteLine("Termset: {0},Is open:{1}", termset.Name,
                 termset.IsOpenForTermCreation.ToString());
             WalkTermSetTree(termset.Terms);
          }
       }
    }
 }
 Console.ReadLine();
}

private static void WalkTermSetTree(TermCollection tc)
{
   foreach (Term t in tc)
   {
     Console.WriteLine("Parent:{0} - {1}", (t.IsRoot ? "Root" : t.Parent.Name),
         t.Name);
     if (t.Terms != null)
        WalkTermSetTree(t.Terms);
   }
}
```

Code file [TermStoreConsoleApp.zip] available for download at Wrox.com

The next sample shows how to create and update items in the term store. As you see in the following code sample, it is also possible to add your own `CustomProperties` to a `Term`, which enables you to completely extend the available EMM functionality.

```
private static void UpdateTermStoreItems()
{
  using (SPSite sitecollection = new SPSite("http://intranet.contoso.com"))
  {
    try
    {
      TaxonomySession taxonomysession = new TaxonomySession(sitecollection);
      TermStore termstore = taxonomysession.TermStores["Managed Metadata Service"];
      // Creates and commits a Group object named Group1, a TermSet object
      // named termSet1, and several Term objects. Term1, Term2, and Term3 are
      // members of termSet1. Term1a and Term1b are children of Term1.
      Group group1 = termstore.CreateGroup("Group1");
      TermSet termset1 = group1.CreateTermSet("TermSet1");
      group1.AddGroupManager(@"contoso\brianc");
      Term term1 = termset1.CreateTerm("Term1", 1033);
      Term term2 = termset1.CreateTerm("Term2", 1033);
      Term term1a = term1.CreateTerm("Term1a", 1033);
      Term term3 = termset1.CreateTerm("Term3", 1033);
      term1.SetCustomProperty("RelatedTerms", term2.Id.ToString());
      termstore.CommitAll();
      Console.WriteLine("Terms created ...");
      Console.ReadLine();

      // Sets a description and some alternate labels for term1 and commits
      // the changes to termStore.Add a French translation for the term2 label
      term1.SetDescription("This is term1", 1033);
      term1.CreateLabel("TermOne", 1033, false);
      term2.CreateLabel("Term Deux", 1036, true);
      termstore.CommitAll();
      Console.WriteLine("Terms updated ...");
      Console.ReadLine();

      // Deletes term3, from termStore and commits changes
      term3.Delete();
      termstore.CommitAll();
      Console.WriteLine("Term deleted ...");
      Console.ReadLine();
    }
    catch (TermStoreOperationException ex)
      {
        Console.WriteLine("{0}",ex.ToString());
      }
  }
}
```

In this code, you can see the `CreateLabel` method is used to create synonyms or abbreviations for the `Term` object. Most of the operations require LCID parameters to support multilingual scenarios. It is important to note that the taxonomy API is built with transactional support, so, after you have made some changes or created objects within the term store, you must explicitly call the `TermStore` `.CommitAll` method. All changes will be committed in the current transaction, and either all changes are committed successfully, or none are committed.

 Export does not seem to be implemented within the `Microsoft.SharePoint` *`.Taxonomy` namespace. However, there is an* `ImportManager` *class that provides the functionality to import a comma-separated value (CSV) file with terms into the term store, which is accessible from* `TermStore.GetImportManager` *Export functionality is something that you must build yourself using the SharePoint object model.*

The taxonomy API also contains some classes for tracking changes in the term store. You will typically need to call the `GetChanges` method, which has been implemented on the `TermSet`, `TermStore`, and `Group` class, which will return a `ChangedItemCollection`.

The following sample code shows how to retrieve all additions of terms in the last five days:

```
private static void GetTermStoreChanges()
{
  using (SPSite sitecollection = new SPSite("http://intranet.contoso.com"))
  {
    TaxonomySession taxonomysession = new TaxonomySession(sitecollection);
    TermStore termstore = taxonomysession.TermStores["Managed Metadata Service"];
    ChangedItemCollection changeditems = termstore.GetChanges
        (DateTime.Today.AddDays(-5), ChangedItemType.Term,
        ChangedOperationType.Add);
    foreach (ChangedItem ci in changeditems)
    {
      Console.WriteLine("Id {0},ChangedTime{1}", ci.Id.ToString(), ci.ChangedTime);
    }
    Console.ReadLine();
  }
}
```

 Take a look at the `TermStoreManagerPlus` *solution on* http:// sharepointextensions.codeplex.com *for a complete working example of how you can extend the taxonomy API.*

Remote Access to the Term Store

SharePoint 2010 extends the services layer, which allows developers to call into SharePoint from remote applications. The SharePoint 2010 remote services layer is composed of web services, Windows Communication Foundation (WCF) services, and the new client object model. Unfortunately, the taxonomy API is not exposed in the client object model.

At first sight, there seem to be two alternative ways of accessing SharePoint remotely: by using the `TaxonomyClientService.asmx` web service, or by using the `MetadataWebService.svc` WCF service. For your own application, you must use the `TaxonomyClientService.asmx` web service. The `MetadataWebService.svc` is meant to only be used by the Web Front End server to communicate with the Application server.

Following are properties of the `TaxonomyClientService` web service:

➤ *Description* — Web service designed for Office client applications and custom built applications to use

➤ *Location* — `http://<site>/_vti_bin/TaxonomyClientService.asmx`

➤ *Methods* — `AddTerms, GetChildTermsInTerm, GetChildTermsInTermSet, GetKeywordTermsByGuids, GetTermSets, GetTermsByLabel`

If the `TaxonomyClientService` web service does not provide enough functionality, you will probably need to write your own WCF service.

SUMMARY

In this chapter, you have learned about the different improvements in SharePoint Server 2010 with regard to the way that it handles metadata. One of the major enhancements is the addition of Managed Metadata column, which provides support for establishing taxonomies and folksonomies. The addition of Enterprise Content Types has made defining and controlling content types in large environments a lot easier. Since these features are linked to the new Service Application infrastructure, the administration experience will require less effort.

But there are also a lot of functional additions which will lower the barrier for end users to add metadata, and show them the value of adding metadata. Metadata navigation has made it easier for users to discover content within large document libraries, while location-based metadata has made the process of adding metadata easier. With document sets, it becomes easier to manage a group of documents as one logical work unit, which again improves the end user experience (since end users can define metadata at the document set level, instead of for every separate document).

ABOUT THE AUTHOR

Joris Poelmans has more than ten years of experience with Microsoft development. He works at RealDolmen (`www.realdolmen.com`), a Belgian IT services company and Microsoft Gold Partner. His main competence area is Information Worker solutions, where he currently focuses on the SharePoint Products and Technologies platform. In October 2005, he was awarded the Microsoft MVP award for Windows SharePoint Services, and has again received the award every year through 2010. He is also one of the founding members of Belux Information Worker User Group (BIWUG at `http://www.biwug.be`). He regularly posts some SharePoint stuff on his blog at `http://jopx.blogspot.com`.

17

Understanding SharePoint 2010 Search

By Ágnes Molnár

Nowadays, we store more and more content in our computer systems. The stored bits themselves are data pieces, but they store information and very important knowledge for us, and for our companies:

➤ *Data* is a set of properties that represent objects, items, events, elements, and so on.

➤ *Information* is data that can be used.

➤ *Knowledge* is information put to action, mostly integrated with other information. It provides a basis for decisions and planning actions.

As you can see, it's not enough to store the data. You must process it, and make it usable and useful for the end users. The goal is to store as much information as possible, and build a strong and powerful Knowledge Base around the data.

But efficient storing is not enough; information that cannot be found is worthless. Either the users know where to find what they are looking for, or not. SharePoint 2010 provides a lot of capabilities to help end users find required information.

SharePoint 2010 has a much-improved search engine and infrastructure built on a much-improved information architecture. Extreme scalability, document sets, metadata management, and so on, all help end users to achieve a much more robust and powerful experience.

This chapter takes a detailed look at the improvements made to search capabilities in SharePoint 2010. In this chapter, you learn about the following:

➤ Improvements in SharePoint 2010

➤ Search architecture

➤ Administering SharePoint 2010 Search

➤ Administering FAST Search

➤ Building an information architecture for Search

➤ User interfaces (UIs) for Search

➤ Improving the "searchability" and "findability" with Search

To begin this discussion, let's take a look at what's new in SharePoint 2010 Search.

NEW AND IMPROVED SHAREPOINT 2010 SEARCH

Similar to previous versions, SharePoint 2010 has various licensing options with various search capabilities. FAST Search Server 2010 for SharePoint has also been added.

Table 17-1 outlines some of the improved features found in SharePoint 2010 Search.

TABLE 17-1: SharePoint 2010 Search Features

FEATURE	FUNCTIONALITY	ENHANCEMENTS
Microsoft SharePoint Foundation 2010 Search	Basic search capabilities	A maximum of 10 million items per search server can be indexed.
Microsoft Search Server 2010 Express	Basic search capabilities	Scopes, custom properties, federated search locations, query suggestions, shallow refinement, Windows 7 federation search. With SQL Express, a maximum of 300,000 items can be indexed. With SQL Server, a maximum of 10 million items can be indexed.
Microsoft Search Server 2010	Basic search capabilities	Scopes, custom properties, federation search, query suggestions, shallow refinement, Windows 7 federation search. A maximum of 10 million items can be indexed.
Microsoft SharePoint Server 2010	Search Server 2010 capabilities	Improved people search, social search, taxonomy integration. A maximum of 10 million items can be indexed.

FEATURE	FUNCTIONALITY	ENHANCEMENTS
FAST Search Server 2010 for SharePoint	SharePoint Server capabilities	Visual Best Bets, User Context–based search enhancements, property extraction, similar results, improved sorting capabilities, relevance tuning, deep results refinement, previewers, Rich Web Indexing support. More than 500 million items can be indexed.

SharePoint Server 2010 has also retained a lot of capabilities found in the previous version, Microsoft Office SharePoint Server 2007 (MOSS 2007). Table 17-2 shows a few of the basic capabilities inherited from the past.

TABLE 17-2: SharePoint 2007 Search Features

FEATURE	FUNCTIONALITY
Windows SharePoint Services 3.0 Search	Indexing of local SharePoint content Rich result set Alerts and RSS feeds of results Removing duplicated results Security trimming of search results
Microsoft Office SharePoint Server 2007 for Search	WSS 3.0 Search capabilities, plus: Indexing of Microsoft Exchange public folders, file shares, and custom content Keywords and Best Bets Query reports Search Center without tabs People Search Search Federation
Microsoft Office SharePoint Server 2007 Enterprise Search	MOSS 2007 for Search capabilities, plus: Indexing of Line-of-Business (LOB) system content Search Center with tabs Business Data Search Custom security trimming

SHAREPOINT 2010 SEARCH ENGINES

Although SharePoint 2007 was a great product for search, as mentioned previously, SharePoint 2010 offers a lot of improvements and new capabilities. Basically, two major engines can be used for SharePoint 2010 Search:

➤   SharePoint 2010 Search Engine

➤   FAST Search Server 2010 for SharePoint

SharePoint 2010 Search Engine

The SharePoint 2010 Search Engine has a lot of new capabilities and improvements for the user experience, and for administration.

For end users, it gives great out-of-the-box search experience with the following:

➤   *User interface* — SharePoint 2010 Search Engine provides a new, rich UI.

➤   *Refinement Panel* — This new part of a Search result page is a detailed, metadata-based panel that helps to filter the results by various metadata fields.

➤   *Boolean query syntax* — In SharePoint 2010, Boolean expressions are valid and can be processed in the query. For example, users can execute queries such as this:

```
("SharePoint Search" OR "Live Search") AND (title:"Keyword Syntax"
    OR title:"Query Syntax")
```

➤   *Suggestion while typing your query* — Based on previous user search expressions, users get suggestions while typing the query expression.

➤   *"Did you mean" suggestions* — Users are now offered improved "Did you mean" suggestions after running the query in case keywords in a search query appear differently from what the user intended.

➤   *Enhanced out-of-the-box relevance* — Improved algorithms for better matching and ranking capabilities.

➤   *Federated results* — If you want to conserve bandwidth, or you want to access external content with different credentials, SharePoint cannot crawl the remote source. MOSS 2007 Service Pack 2 contained a new feature that is improved in SharePoint 2010. You can federate the search results from a remote search service and display them in separate web parts as part of the search result page, and on a separate result page.

➤   *Related searches* — With the results for your query, SharePoint 2010 also provides related searches for additional results from previous searches.

➤   *"View in Browser" for documents* — Because the Office Web Application service can be deployed and integrated with SharePoint 2010, all kinds of Office documents can be opened in the browser, without any installed Office client.

➤ *Improved People Search* — Not only does this feature have a renewed UI, it also includes a lot of new capabilities, including phonetic search, presence, organization and recent content information, Refinement Panel with filtering status skill, and so on, as shown in Figure 17-1.

FIGURE 17-1: Improved People Search

➤ *Phonetic and nickname matching* — In English and many other languages, names can be spelled in various ways (for example, Christine and Kristine), and people may have various nicknames (for example, William and Bill). This new feature helps to simplify those complications.

➤ *Social behavior improves relevance* — The more active a user is in a special topic area, the more relevance he or she will get in the search results.

➤ *Windows 7 integration* — Windows 7 users can create a federated search connector for SharePoint 2010's search scopes so that they will be able to search that scope any time from their client machines. The search results and all associated data will be displayed in Windows Explorer, where the users can take advantage of the operating system (for example, preview and drag-and-drop). Figure 7-2 shows an example.

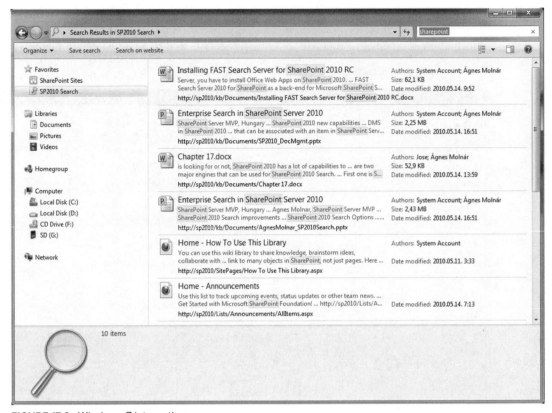

FIGURE 17-2: Windows 7 integration

Following are some features that are particularly notable for administrators:

➤ *Search as shared service application* — Instead of the Shared Service Providers (SSPs) in MOSS 2007, SharePoint 2010's shared service applications provide much more flexible and extensible capabilities, so that Search also can be stronger as a service.

➤ *Enterprise scale-out to hundreds of millions of docs* — With the optimization of the SharePoint 2010 Search engine and SQL 2008, the search has been scaled out to hundreds of millions of documents, especially if you use FAST Search Server 2010 for SharePoint.

➤ *Full fault tolerance* — In SharePoint 2010, it's possible to provision multiple Query components for a single search service application. It is highly recommended that you mirror your Query component in order to provide fault tolerance.

➤ *Wizard-driven installation* — Deploying SharePoint 2010 doesn't require scripting or coding. It can be fully done on the Central Administration UI.

➤ *PowerShell support* — As with SharePoint 2010 in general, Search also has PowerShell support, so that you can also write scripts to create or manage search service applications.

➤ *Consolidated Search Dashboard* — The search service application's dashboard page contains a lot of useful information about the status of the system, crawling, queries, and so on.

➤ *Topology editor* — This is used for adding and managing search components in a deployment.

➤ *Systems Center Operation Manager (SCOM) support* — SharePoint 2010 Search can be monitored through SCOM.

➤ *Full Search reporting* — Search administration reports help to monitor the performance of crawl and query components.

➤ *Easy to add new external sources as Business Data* — External data sources can be connected to SharePoint 2010 via the Business Connectivity Services (BCS). The connected data source can be easily added as a content source to the search service application.

FAST Search Server 2010 Engine

In April 2008, Microsoft completed the acquisition of an enterprise search company, FAST Search & Transfer. For those who used MOSS 2007, FAST Enterprise Search Platform (ESP) could be integrated as a separate server product, via various web parts. But as an important result of this acquisition, Microsoft has developed FAST Search Server 2010 for SharePoint that is a fully integrated search server engine, one that deeply supports SharePoint search functions.

For end users, FAST Search Server 2010 provides a very visual and dynamic user experience, with the following capabilities added to SharePoint 2010 Search:

➤ *Thumbnails and previews for documents* — Word and PowerPoint files in the search result will be displayed with a thumbnail of the cover page. Moreover, PowerPoint files can be previewed in the results list without opening the file, either with a PowerPoint client or with Office Web Applications. These capabilities can help end users visually find the expected content. Figure 17-3 shows an example.

FIGURE 17-3: Thumbnails and previews in search results

➤ *View in browser* — By using Office Web Applications, Office files can be opened in the browser, without installing the thick client on the computer.

➤ *Visual Best Bets* — Best Bets are well-known from MOSS 2007, and can also be found in SharePoint 2010. But with FAST Search, you also can define Visual Best Bets, which are pictures or videos that are Best Bets for several keywords.

➤ *Deep refiners with counts* — The Shallow Refinement Panel is also available in SharePoint 2010 Search with the capability of refining results by the most important metadata. However, only FAST Search provides the capability of result refining on metadata associated with all results. Moreover, FAST Search provides more customization capabilities, and shows counts for each of the refiners.

➤ *User Context from User Profiles* — User Profiles might store a lot of information about each user, and SharePoint 2010 provides some very powerful social capabilities based on these profiles. From a Search perspective, results can be targeted by contextual user information (for example, department, skills, competencies, city, and so on). User Contexts can be built by using User Profile properties, so that they make sub-groups of users, and can be associated with the following:

  ➤ Keywords

  ➤ Best Bets

  ➤ Visual Best Bets

  ➤ Document promotion/demotion

➤ *Sorting on any property* — Each property can be the base of sorting, configured in the "Sort by" field.

➤ *Similar Search* — With this link for each result, users can get a new result set based on the search of the selected search result item.

➤ *Broader, better language support* — FAST Search supports language-specific word breaking and stemming (via FAST lemmatization by reduction), spellcheck, and antiphrasing.

➤ *Richer query language* — In FAST Search, custom queries can be set up using the native query language for FAST. This provides a complete toolbox, even in the case of advanced queries.

For administrators, FAST Search Server 2010 is a highly capable and easy-to-manage search engine that offers the following:

➤ Extreme scale-out up to more than 500 million items

➤ A content processing pipeline

➤ Entity extraction

➤ Tunable relevance ranking

➤ Easy setup of User Context, Visual Best Bets, promotion/demotion

➤ Easy-to-configure sorting and refinement

Now that you are familiar with the improvements in SharePoint 2010 Search, let's take a look at how to deploy SharePoint 2010 Search.

DEPLOYING SHAREPOINT 2010 SEARCH

MOSS 2007, the previous version of SharePoint 2010, included Shared Service Providers (SSPs). SharePoint 2010 has improved on that technology, and SharePoint 2010 Search is now one of the service applications offered in SharePoint 2010.

In SharePoint 2010, services can be managed one by one, instead of organizing them into SSPs, and each can have its own database. Moreover, it's also possible to create more than one instance of the same service application type, and web applications can be associated to these services one by one.

Deploying a New Search Service Application

Once you've installed your SharePoint 2010 farm, you can deploy and configure service applications, including search services. In SharePoint 2010, you can integrate either the SharePoint 2010 Search Engine or the FAST Search Server Engine with your farm.

To provide a better understanding of the importance of service applications, this section describes how to deploy and configure a SharePoint Search service application. Later in this chapter, you learn about deployment and configuration of FAST Search Server.

The search service application can be created on the Manage Service Applications page of the Central Administration site. During the creation process, you must fill in the following settings:

➤   Name of the search application

➤   FAST type of application:

>   ➤   *None* — This option means that you don't want to use FAST Search Server's capabilities in your search service application. This option should be used if you have not installed FAST Search Server in your farm, or if you have it, but want to deploy a search application without using it.

>   ➤   *FAST Search Connector* — This is examined later in this chapter.

>   ➤   *FAST Search Query* — This is examined later in this chapter.

➤   Application pools for Search Admin Web Service and for Search Query and Site Settings Web Service with security accounts.

After the search service application is successfully created, you must configure some other settings (discussed shortly), and in order to use the newly created search service application in your web applications, you must be sure it's associated with your web application.

Go to Central Administration, and choose Application Management ➪ "Configure service application associations." On the Configure Service Application Associations page shown in Figure 17-4, you can change the associations between your web applications and service applications. This is where you can set which search service application will be used by your web applications.

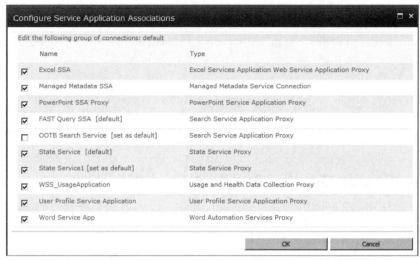

FIGURE 17-4: Configure Service Application Associations page

As with all other service applications in SharePoint 2010, the search service application can be managed by the people who are granted permission to be the administrators of the service independently from other service applications. This can be done from the Service Applications list.

As shown in Figure 17-5, the ribbon contains the management operations for the service applications. Here is where you can define administrators, edit properties and permissions of search service applications, or publish a service application to be available from other SharePoint 2010 farms.

FIGURE 17-5: Service Applications group on the ribbon

If you open the search service application for managing it, the Welcome Page comes up. This page contains a lot of useful information about the status of the service, last crawls, search topology, and some useful shortcuts for your quick reference:

➤ Crawl status and Background activity

➤ Recent crawl rate (items per second)

➤ Number of Searchable items

➤ Recent query rate (queries per minute)

➤ Propagation status

➤ Default content access account

➤ Contact e-mail address

➤ Proxy server

➤ Scopes update status

➤ Scopes update schedule

➤ Scopes needing update

➤ Search alerts status

➤ Query logging

Also, this is the page where the Quick Launch contains all of the search operations that you'll need.

Crawling and Indexing

A search engine is designed to search for information in electronic content sources. It stores some information about the crawled contents, and queries are passed over this stored index database. SharePoint 2010 also contains a complex search engine, so, in order to understand all the settings, following are some descriptions of general search engine components:

➤ *Crawler* — This is the component that browses the contents automatically on a regular basis. The goal of the crawling process is to provide up-to-date data from the data source to the indexer(s).

➤ *Indexer* — This component is responsible for collecting and storing relevant data of crawled contents, in order to make available fast and precise information retrieval during the queries.

➤ *Query* — The Query component provides the UI for entering the user queries, and presents the result set to the end users. It communicates with the Indexer component directly to get the results for the user query, and to put the proper result set together.

In the Crawling Quick Launch group of search service application settings, you are able to define the settings for crawling and indexing. Configuring crawling and building index files is the first step to building a SharePoint 2010 search architecture.

Following is a description of configuration settings:

➤ *Content sources* — Content source definitions contain three important types of information: the type of the content source, the location, and the crawling schedule. Also, you can start full or incremental crawling from here.

➤ *Crawl rules* — With crawl rules, you can exclude or include paths from being crawled, and set different authentication accounts as defaults. The rules will run in the order they appear in this list. The Test field enables you to specify whether you have any rule matching to a specific URL.

➤ *Crawl log* — In this detailed log, you can check each content source, what should be crawled, what warnings and errors should be noted, and so on. The log contains information on all crawled items.

➤ *Server name mappings* — Server name mappings are useful when you must override how URLs are shown in search results. They are typically used when the URLs used by the crawler to access content are different from the URLs used by users to navigate to the same files.

➤ *Host distribution rules* — In SharePoint 2010, crawl databases contain data related to the content sources, crawl schedules, and other information specific to crawl operations for each search service application. Host distribution rules can be applied to farms with more than one crawl database. They can be used to associate a host with a specific crawl database.

➤ *File types* — The SharePoint 2010 content index can contain a lot of file types. You can modify the included file types in this list.

➤ *Index reset* — Use this operation if you want to reset the index, clear all its content, and rebuild it from scratch.

➤ *Crawler impact rules* — These can be used to adjust the load that the crawler applies to content sources, including the number of simultaneous requests, or time to wait between each request.

Queries and Results

The role of the index server is complex, and includes the following responsibilities:

➤ Processing the crawls

➤ Making the indices available to the query servers

➤ Managing content source properties such as location and scheduling

➤ Creating and maintaining an index database

After your crawl settings are customized, and the content sources are indexed, you'll be able to use the indexed content in your queries initiated by users or other services. The query server returns the result set to the query originator (both end users and services can send queries to SharePoint 2010).

The "Queries and Results" group of search service application settings also can be found on the Quick Launch bar, and this is where you can configure the use of the following query operations:

➤ *Authoritative pages* — Search uses the lists of authoritative pages to enhance the overall ranking of results. You can define three levels of authoritative pages, and a list of sites to denote.

➤ *Federated Locations* — These are usually remote search engines that provide results to the queries initiated in SharePoint 2010, but also can be local if you want to run simultaneous searches on the same content.

➤ *Metadata properties* — These are the properties of crawled content that users can use in search queries.

➤ *Scopes* — Search scopes must be created in order to organize indexed content, refine the queries, and allow accessing them from the SharePoint 2010 Search UI.

➤ *Search result removal* — If your index contains some URLs you don't want to be in the queries anymore, you can enter them here. Crawl rules will be also created to exclude these URLs from future crawling processes.

Reports

To get statistics about your search services and queries, SharePoint 2010 provides some improved reporting capabilities for Search as well. They can be found in the Reports group of the Quick Launch and include the following:

➤ *Administration reports* — This report library contains basic and advanced reports (for example, Crawl Rate per Content Source, Query Latency, or Crawl Processing per Component).

➤ *Web Analytics reports* — These reports provide insights into the behavior of users of your SharePoint sites. To get a Web Analytics report, the Web Analytics service application also must be deployed to the farm. On the Central Administration site, go to the Application Management ➪ Service Applications, click on New ➪ Web Analytics Service Application, and fill in the required fields.

DEPLOYING FAST SEARCH SERVER

FAST Search Server 2010 for SharePoint is a new additional search component that can be installed separately, and provides richer user experience and more scalable architecture.

This section examines what additional administration tasks you must do when you have FAST Search Server 2010 for SharePoint installed on your farm. As you will see, to use the extra capabilities, you will need to perform some extra work, but all the basics are the same as when you use the SharePoint 2010 out-of-the-box search.

Installing FAST Search Server 2010 for SharePoint

FAST Search Server 2010 for SharePoint can be installed as a collection of additional servers in your SharePoint 2010 farm. In an extremely small environment, FAST Server Search engine can be installed in a standalone way, even to the standalone SharePoint Server 2010. In most cases, however, it must be deployed to one or more different servers.

When you install FAST Search Server 2010 on two or more servers, one of them must be deployed as a FAST Admin Server, where administrative services are installed and run. The other servers are non-Admin FAST Servers, with the responsibility of connecting to an Admin Server in a multiple-server deployment, and running services such as query matching, indexing, and document/item processing. In each deployment, one Admin Server must be added, and one or more non-Admin Servers can be added.

If you want to have a multi-server FAST topology, you must install the FAST Admin Server before the non-Admin Servers, and then connect them to each other and to your SharePoint Server 2010 farm. The most important benefit of this architecture is that a SharePoint 2010 farm with FAST Search Server 2010 can include more than one index server, so that the amount of crawled and indexed content can be practically infinite.

The good news is that FAST Search Server 2010 for SharePoint has an Install Wizard, so the installation can proceed pretty smoothly. However, you should consider some things before you start the installation. Even if you choose to install it by using the wizard, it is very useful to know and understand what happens behind the wizard, and what the configuration steps are.

First, you will need a FAST Search Admin domain user, who will be able to perform the administration tasks on the FAST Servers (for example, `demo2010\fastuser`). This user must be a member of the `FASTSearchAdministrators` group on the servers, as well as `DBcreator` on the SQL Database.

After these preparation steps, you must start the FAST Search Server 2010 for SharePoint Installation Wizard, and choose Install Prerequisites. This step will install the following components on your server:

➤ Application Server Role, Web Server (IIS) Role

➤ mimefilt.dll

➤ Distributed Transaction Support

➤ Windows Communication Foundation Activation Components

➤ XPS Viewer

➤ Hotfix for Microsoft Windows (KB976462)

➤ Windows Identity Foundation (KB974405)

➤ Microsoft Primary Interoperability Assemblies 2005

➤ Microsoft Visual C++ 2008 SP1 Redistributable Package (x64)

➤ Microsoft Filter Pack 2.0

After completing these steps, you can install FAST Search for your SharePoint 2010 farm, and then run the FAST Search Server 2010 for SharePoint Config Wizard. Following are the steps for the installation and the configuration settings:

1. Install FAST Search Server 2010.

2. Add FAST Search Server 2010 as a backend for SharePoint Server 2010. This includes the following:

➤ Create a FAST Search content service application.

➤ Set up at least one content source.

➤ Create a FAST query service application.

3. Connect the FAST query service application to the SharePoint web application.

4. Configure the following FAST Search Server 2010 settings:

➤ Enable click-through relevancy.

➤ Enable queries from SharePoint 2010 Server via HTTP or HTTPS.

➤ Configure FAST Search Authorization.

If you perform all of these steps successfully, you can begin to deploy your FAST Search Services for SharePoint 2010. The following sections provide a detailed examination of this deployment.

Deploying FAST Search Service Applications

As mentioned previously, SharePoint 2010 search services can be deployed as service applications. FAST Search Server 2010 for SharePoint behaves the same, so you must deploy service applications for FAST Search Server 2010 to work properly.

Following are the two kinds of FAST Search service applications in SharePoint 2010:

➤ *FAST Search content service application* — This service crawls content and feeds it into the FAST Search Server 2010 for SharePoint backend.

➤ *FAST Query service application* — This service provides query results from the content that is crawled by the content service application.

The following sections describe the settings of both kinds of service applications. It's really important to note that these settings might look like useless steps during configuration. However, they are very important in a multi-server environment, or in the case of the publishing of FAST Search Server's services.

FAST Search Content Service Application

The FAST Search content service application crawls content and feeds into the FAST Search Server 2010 for SharePoint backend. So, this should be the first step in configuring SharePoint 2010 services.

Before deploying the FAST Search content service application, locate the `install_info.txt` file in the `FASTSearch` installation folder on the administration server. When deploying a FAST Search content service application, you must define the following settings. This assumes that you set the base port 13300 during the installation of the FAST Search Server.

➤ *Name* — This is the name of your search service application (for example, "FAST Content SSA").

➤ *Type* — This is the type of the search service application. In this case, it must be "*FAST Search Connector.*"

➤ Application Pool — This is the application pool for the search service application. It can be chosen from the existing application pools, or created as a new one.

➤ *Content Distributors* — The location of the Content Distributor(s) can be found in the `install_info.txt` file in the `FASTSearch` folder on your server (for example, `sp2010 .demo2010.local:13391`). However, be careful, because `install_info.txt` contains the port number (`13391`) for the HTTPS communication. If you would like to communicate over HTTP, the correct port number is `13390` (that is, the port number provided in the `install_info.txt` minus 1).

➤ *Content collection name* — This is the name of the content collection that will hold the content of this connector (by default, it's value is "sp").

FAST Query Service Application

The FAST Query service application receives queries and provides query results from the content that is crawled by the FAST Search content service application. It must be defined and associated with your web application in order to use FAST Search Server results in your SharePoint 2010 search.

When deploying a FAST Query service application, you must define the following settings. This assumes that you set the base port 13300 during the installation of FAST Search Server.

➤ *Name* — This is the name of the search service application (for example, "FAST Query SSA").

➤ *Type* — This is the type of the search service application. In this case, it must be "FAST Search Query."

➤ *Application Pool for Search Admin Web Service* — This can be chosen from the existing application pools, or created as a new one.

➤ *Application Pool for the Search Query and Site Settings Web Service* — This can be chosen from the existing application pools, or created as a new one.

➤ *Query Service Location* — The requested value can be found in the install_info.txt file (for example, http://sp2010.demo2010.local:13287).

➤ *Administration Service Location* — The requested value can be found in the install_info.txt file (for example, http://sp2010.demo2010.local:13257).

➤ *Resource store location* — The requested value also can be found in the install_info.txt file (for example, http://sp2010.demo2010.local:13255).

➤ *Account for Administration Service* — This is the FAST admin account (for example, demo2010\fastuser).

Again, be careful before setting the port numbers while configuring. Check the install_info.txt file before creating the FAST Query service application.

USING POWERSHELL COMMANDS

As is common in SharePoint 2010, PowerShell commands also can be used to deploy, configure, and maintain the search infrastructure. Table 17-3 shows the most important PowerShell commands for search management.

TABLE 17-3: PowerShell Commands

FUNCTION	COMMAND AND PARAMETERS
Retrieving the search service application object	`$searchApp = Get-SPEnterpriseSearchServiceApplication <Search Application Name>`
Checking the search service instance	`$searchInstance = Get-SPEnterpriseSearchServiceInstance <SearchServerName>`
Starting a search service instance	`Start-SPEnterpriseSearchServiceInstance <SearchServerName>`

For more commands and information, download a whitepaper from Microsoft Download Center at `http://www.microsoft.com/downloads/details.aspx ?displaylang=en&FamilyID=94e6a73b-dabd-48c5-9ea4-8b7c3294fc97.`

BUILDING THE SEARCH ARCHITECTURE

After installing and deploying SharePoint 2010 Search, you must deploy an information architecture that is important for the end user experience. To give the best search experience to the end users, developers must build the architecture very carefully. All the following pieces must fit:

➤ *Physical architecture* — Index, query, FAST Search, service applications, and so on

➤ *Logical architecture* — Content sources, scopes, federation, keywords, and so on

➤ *Information architecture* — Lists and libraries, metadata, organizing rules, tagging, navigation, Search pages, and so on

To achieve an effective search experience, first of all, you need the proper search architecture as a backend. Let's take a look at the main components of the SharePoint Search infrastructure.

Defining Content Sources

SharePoint 2007 provided the capability to index various content sources, including the following:

➤ Local and remote SharePoint sites

➤ Websites

➤ File shares (to include in the search results your documents stored in shared folders)

➤ Exchange Public Folders

➤ Business data (which was very useful for integrated solutions to achieve external data search requirements)

SharePoint 2010 can crawl a wide variety of content sources. These can be defined on the level of search service application by following these steps:

1. Go to your search service application admin site, and choose Content Sources from the Crawling group on the left navigation bar.

2. Select New Content Source.

3. Type a name for the content source, and choose one of the types. The crawling of content is available via various indexing connectors for SharePoint 2010. Table 17-4 shows some different connectors for FAST Search Servers.

TABLE 17-4: Indexing Connectors for SharePoint 2010

TYPE OF CONTENT	INDEXING CONNECTOR	RECOMMENDED
SharePoint content	SharePoint indexing connector	
File shares	File share indexing connector	
Exchange Public Folders	Exchange indexing connector	
People profiles	People profiles indexing connector	
Websites	Website indexing connector	If you have a limited number of websites to crawl, without dynamic content that often changes.
	FAST Search Web Crawler	If you have a large number of websites to crawl. If your website content contains dynamic data (for example, JavaScript). If you need advanced web crawling, configuration, and scheduling options. If you want to crawl RSS content. If the website content uses advanced login options.
Database	BDC-based indexing connectors	If you prefer to use SharePoint Designer 2010 for configuration. If you want to use timestamp-based change detection for incremental database crawls. If you prefer using SharePoint Server 2010 Central Administration for operations. If you want to enable change log–based crawling by modifying the connector file and creating a stored procedure in the database.
	FAST Search database connector	If you prefer using SQL queries for configuration. If you want to use advanced data joining operation options. If you want to use advanced incremental update features.

TYPE OF CONTENT	INDEXING CONNECTOR	RECOMMENDED
Lotus Notes content	Lotus Notes indexing connector	If you prefer to use SharePoint Server 2010 Central Administration for operations.
	FAST Search Lotus Notes connector	If Lotus Notes security support is required (including Lotus Notes roles). If you want to crawl Lotus Notes databases as attachments.
Custom content	BDC-based indexing connectors	If the data in your content source contains data in a line-of-business (LOB) application, like SAP. If you want to enable change log–based crawling by directly modifying the connector model file.

Source: http://technet.microsoft.com/en-us/library/ff383278.aspx

As you've seen, you can also develop your custom indexing connector for your content sources. Some additional indexing connectors are also available, with Business Intelligence Indexing Connector (BI IC) being a good example.

BI IC is used to make business intelligence (BI) assets more discoverable through FAST Search Server 2010 for SharePoint. BI IC can be deployed to enhance enterprise search capabilities for Excel, PowerPivot, and Reporting Services reports, as well as their underlying data sources. When it is installed, an additional Reports search tab is added to SharePoint search sites. Using BI IC provides users with improved results, descriptions, thumbnails, and previews, and they will be able to refine the search results to quickly and easily find the information they need.

Following are the steps for configuring a content source in SharePoint 2010:

1. After selecting the type of the content to be crawled, you must enter the start addresses of the chosen source types.

2. Define the crawling behavior of the entered start addresses — either crawl the folder with its subfolders, or only the entered folder itself.

3. After that, you can schedule the full and incremental crawling for this content source, and can start a full crawl immediately.

4. Finally, you can change the priority of this content source. The SharePoint 2010 Crawling component will prioritize the processing of the content sources with High priority over the Normal ones.

 Remember that your content sources will only be available to search after a crawling process.

In SharePoint 2010, one more option has been added — the Custom Repository. That means that developers can develop any additional custom connectors in .NET to crawl and index any repositories not supported by Business Connectivity Services (BCS). The connector framework supports crawling of structured and unstructured content as well.

If you'd like to edit your content sources later, just go to the Content Sources page and select which one to edit. You will be able to change all of the settings just described.

Using Scopes

Content from all sources must be organized into search scopes to refine the queries and allow access to the content from the Search UI. In SharePoint 2010, the scope definitions can be very similar to the previous versions.

To define some scopes, go to the search service application admin site, and select Scopes from the "Queries and Results" group in the left Navigation pane. This is where you can create new search scopes and edit the existing ones.

When you choose New Scope, you can set the basic properties of the scope, including name, description, and a target results page (for example, `http://sp2010/search/results.aspx`).

After you have set the basic properties, the next step is to assign various rules to your scope. Following are some of your options:

➤ *Web address* — This works independently of the defined content sources. Even uncrawled content can be added, although it's not recommended.

➤ *Property query* — Some properties can be defined to use in search scopes. If you define a property query rule, you can choose from these properties and define a filter (for example, `contentclass=urn:content-class:SPSPeople`).

➤ *Content source* — You can select from the content sources defined before, and all content of this source will be included in your scope (for example, Local SharePoint Sites).

➤ *All content* — This includes all crawled content in your search service.

Each of these rules can behave in three different ways:

➤ *Included* — Any item that matches the rule will be included, unless the item is excluded by another rule.

➤ *Required* — Every item in the scope must match this rule.

➤ *Excluded* — Items matching this rule will be excluded from the scope.

Let's take a look at an example to make the scope rules more understandable. Let's say that you'd like to define a scope that is for the people results all over your farm. To do this, you should create a scope "People" with the following rules with an Included behavior:

```
contentclass = urn:content-class:SPSPeople
```

Scheduling Crawls

In SharePoint 2010, content sources can be scheduled in two ways:

➤ *Full crawl* — During the full crawl, the whole content source will be crawled, independently from the previous crawls.

➤ *Incremental crawl* — During the incremental crawl, the crawler only sends to the index database the new content created since the last crawl.

When you define the schedule settings for your content sources, one of the most important things to keep in mind is maintaining the optimal balance between utilizing the resources you have, and providing the best results to the end users. For example, if you have limited resources, you shouldn't schedule crawling for every 5 minutes. This is because you might suffer huge performance degradation, or you could even bring down the full farm.

To avoid these kinds of problems, you must consider the following:

➤ How much content do you have to crawl in each source?

➤ How strong is your index server in the farm (as far as the power and speed of the processor, as well as available RAM)?

➤ What network connection do you have between the servers of the farm, and between the index server and your content?

Finding the optimal scheduling setup sometimes takes days, or even longer (depending on your requirements). However, if you experience an extremely slow crawling environment, the first thing to consider is a migration of the crawling server to a much more powerful machine.

Crawler impact rules also can help to optimize the scheduling. Crawler impact rules can be used to adjust the load that the crawler applies to content sources. With the request frequency of a crawler impact rule, you can define how the crawler will request documents from this site — simultaneously up to the specified number, or request only one document at a time and wait a specified time between requests.

Using Search Federation

Sometimes, SharePoint Search Engine cannot be used (or you don't want to use it). For example, you may have to conserve the resources used by crawling and indexing, or content you want to use cannot be crawled by SharePoint. In these cases, you can use federated resources from remote search engines, and include their result sets into your search result page.

Following are the advantages of search federation:

➤ Remote sites that block SharePoint crawler in their `robots.txt` files can also be crawled by a federated search engine.

➤ You can include specific keywords and keyword patterns in the query.

➤ The content that changes very often can immediately be crawled.

➤ You can query content under a different security context.

➤ You don't have to crawl infrequently queried content.

Of course, in some circumstances federation cannot be used, including the following:

➤ You don't have enough bandwidth, or your SharePoint farm cannot access the Internet.

➤ Content cannot be crawled by the remote server.

➤ The remote server does not return search results with Atom or RSS.

Figure 17-6 shows a result set from a federated search.

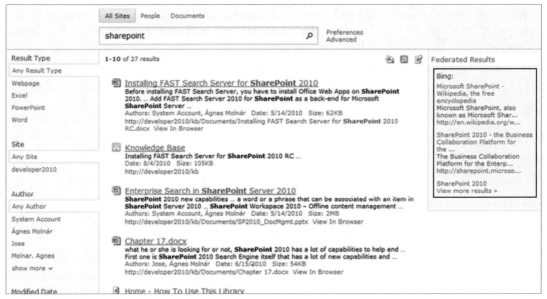

FIGURE 17-6: Result set from a federated search

Federated Locations also can be configured in the search service application. Although out-of-the-box locations are defined when the search service application is created, you can also create your own locations, or import location settings. Let's take a look at how.

Federated Location connections can be saved in .FLD (Federated Location File) format, and you can import these files into your search service application. If you don't have any .FLD files, you can download some from the Online Gallery (follow the link on the Manage Federated Location page of the search service application).

To define your own Federated Location, you must first know which search engines can be used and which ones cannot. All search engines that are compatible with OpenSearch 1.0/1.1 can be used as Federated Locations. Essentially, if a search engine can return a result set as an RSS or Atom feed, it can be a Federated Location.

Let's assume that you'd like to search Flickr for picture results. In this case, the URL for the result set will be something like the following (where {searchTerms} shows where your query string will be placed):

```
http://api.flickr.com/services/feeds/photos_public.gne?tags=
    {searchTerms}&lang=en-us&format=rss_200
```

This is because Flickr provides search result sets that are compatible with OpenSearch 1.0/1.1, so you can use them as a Federated Location.

After configuring Federated Locations in your search service application, you can immediately use them on your search pages. Simply insert a Federated Results web part, choose the location you want to use, and set the web part properties.

Keep the following in mind:

➤ If you configure a Federated Location but it doesn't appear in the web part's drop-down menu, check whether the Federated Location is defined in the same search service application that is used by your web application.

➤ If you configured a Federated Location, and you assigned it to a web part as well, but there are no results at all, check whether your location is compatible with OpenSearch 1.0/1.1.

If you want to use a location that is not compatible with OpenSearch 1.0/1.1, you still have an alternative. Get a remote search engine that is able to crawl the content you want to include. Then, extract the URL of the result list, and change your query terms to {searchTerms}.

For example, to get Wikipedia results, you can use Bing as a search engine. In your Federated Location definition, use the following URL for the result set:

```
http://www.bing.com/search?q=site%3aen.wikipedia.org+{searchTerms}&format=rss
```

The results will be similar to that shown in Figure 17-7.

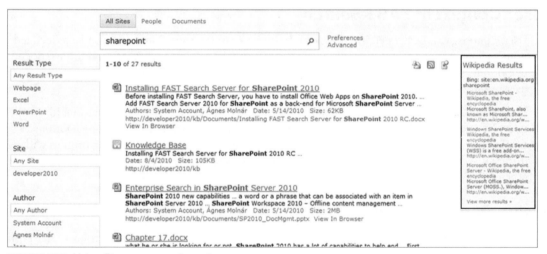

FIGURE 17-7: Using Bing as a search engine

Understanding Keywords and Best Bets

With the help of keywords, you can mark specific items as more relevant in your SharePoint environment. That means that they show up more prominently in the search results. For example, if you run a financial company, the keywords can be "money," "stock," or "finance." Moreover, you can define synonyms for these keywords, so that your keyword dictionary can be expanded.

For the subjects defined by your keywords, you can also define some relevant items, known as *Best Bets*. In SharePoint 2007, Best Bets were URLs linking to some useful places, but in SharePoint 2010, you can also define images or videos as a visual Best Bet.

Keywords can be defined at the site collection level. Go to the Site Collection Settings and choose Search Keywords. Choose Add Keyword, and you will then be able to specify the following for a keyword:

➤ *Keyword phrase* — This defines what the queries have to match to return the keyword results.

➤ *Synonyms* — These are words that can be typed by users when searching for the keyword (for example, "MOSS, WSS, SPS, SPF" can be synonyms for the keyword "SharePoint").

➤ *Best Bets* — These are recommended results for this keyword.

➤ *Keyword definition* — This is an optional description of the keyword that will appear in the keyword result.

➤ *Contact* — This is the person who must be informed when a review date is passed.

➤ *Publishing Start, End, and Review Date* — If these are defined, the keyword will appear in the result set only between the Start and End Date. The Review Date is the date when the keyword must be reviewed by the contact.

User Context in FAST Search

User Contexts can be defined in FAST Search Server 2010 for SharePoint, and can be associated with various search settings, including Best Bets, Visual Best Bets, document promotions, document demotions, site promotions, and site demotions. User Contexts match the properties defined on the user's SharePoint User Profile page.

For example, you can define a User Context for Marketing managers, and another one for the IT guys. You can define the keyword "SharePoint" with different Best Bets and site promotions to display for each of these User Contexts, so users with different properties in their profiles will see different search results. In this way, users can be addressed with the relevant information in a very efficient way.

Using People Search

Social networking capabilities are really improved in SharePoint 2010 — with a robust User Profile page, status updates, tagging, organization, and so on.

In addition to these new capabilities, social search has been improved as well. Following are some of the most important benefits of the new People Search in SharePoint 2010:

➤ The Refinement Panel can also be used in People Search, with some custom views (for example, Name Matches and Profile Matches), Ask Me About filters, and so on.

➤ The display of people in the result set has also been improved. They show up with a picture, some basic data, Ask Me About field values, and some really useful links, as shown in Figure 17-8.

➤ By clicking the name of the user, you will be redirected to his or her profile page.

➤ You can add each result to your colleagues directly from the result set.

➤ You can browse the user in the organizational chart directly from the result set.

➤ If you hover the mouse over the "By [Name]" link, you'll immediately see the content created by the user, without being redirected to anywhere, as shown in Figure 17-9.

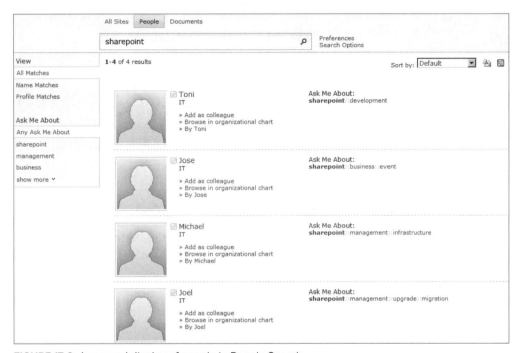

FIGURE 17-8: Improved display of people in People Search

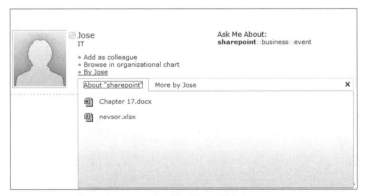

FIGURE 17-9: Hovering over the "By [Name]" link

For an effective use of People Search, you must first properly manage User Profiles. If the User Profile Service is ready, and profiles are imported, they can be crawled and indexed by the SharePoint Search Engine.

To enable People Search, you must first crawl for people by modifying your "Local SharePoint sites" content source, or by creating a new one. Following is the URL that is crawled:

```
sps3://sp2010
```

After you have set up crawling, you must define a scope — for example, with the name "People." Unless you have special requirements, you need only one rule in this scope:

```
contentclass = urn:content-class:SPSPeople - Included
```

> *It's important to mention that FAST Search Server 2010 for SharePoint doesn't have its own People crawling method. It also uses the out-of-the-box SharePoint crawling for that.*

CUSTOMIZING USER INTERFACES

From the user's perspective, the UI is the most important part of the architecture. This section examines various kinds of UIs that can be deployed in SharePoint 2010, and how you can ensure that end users are satisfied with their search experiences.

Understanding Centralized and Decentralized UIs

Following are the two primary kinds of search UIs:

➤ *Centralized* — A centralized UI is a site where the only function available is Search. Typically, this is a Search Center based on one of the SharePoint 2010's Search site templates. Of course, some customizations can be made, but the main function of the site is Search itself.

➤ *Decentralized* — When you build a decentralized UI for Search in SharePoint 2010, you create some functional sites that include search elements as well. For example, as shown in Figure 17-10, you can create a Document Center and insert a Search Box and a Search Core Results web part, addressing the Documents scope.

FIGURE 17-10: Decentralized UI

Using Search Centers

In SharePoint 2010, the following three kinds of Search Centers are all available as a site template:

➤ *Basic Search Center* — This site provides basic search experience. It contains pages for search results and advanced search.

➤ *Enterprise Search Center* — This site is for enterprise search experience. It contains a welcome page with two tabs for general and people searches, and pages for search results and advanced search. You can also add new pages and tabs on the welcome page.

➤ *FAST Search Center* — This site is for delivering a FAST Search experience. It is very similar to the Enterprise Search Center, but utilizes full FAST Search capabilities. Of course, it can use FAST capabilities only when FAST Search Server 2010 for SharePoint is installed on your farm.

Using Search Web Parts

You can use SharePoint 2010 Search web parts to extend your Search Center capabilities. Also, you can insert these web parts in any SharePoint pages even if they are not in a Search Center. Just choose Edit ➪ "Add a web part to any zone" and then select the Search category. Here is the list of all Search web parts in SharePoint 2010:

➤ Advanced Search Box

➤ Dual Chinese Search

➤ Featured Content

➤ Federated Results

➤ People Refinement Panel

➤ People Search Box

➤ People Search Core Results

➤ Refinement Panel

➤ Related Queries

➤ Search Action Links

➤ Search Best Bets

➤ Search Box

➤ Search Core Results

➤ Search Paging

➤ Search Statistics

➤ Search Summary

➤ Top Federated Results Using Scopes

With these capabilities, you can build a fully customized search experience for your users. For example, you can insert Search Box and Search Core Results web parts for the scope Documents into your Document Center, or for the scope People into your HR site.

Customizing the Refinement Panel

Both SharePoint 2010 Search result pages and FAST Search result pages have Refinement Panels. This panel also can be inserted into any result page — and it can be customized.

The most important customization setting of the Refinement Panel is the Filter Category Definition, in the Refinement settings group. After expanding this field, you can see and edit an XML description of the Refinement Panel's filters. In this XML code, you can find `CustomFilter` tags, which can be edited or removed. You can even put your own filter settings here. The only thing you have to be careful about is that the fields in a Refinement Panel customization that are set as `CustomFilter` must be Managed Properties.

For example, one CustomFilter field is for images, defining the file extensions of images. By default, the only file types it contains are TIF and TIFF, so you may want to expand it with GIF and JPEG. To achieve this, insert the following boldfaced rows into the XML:

```
<CustomFilter CustomValue="Image">
        <OriginalValue>tif</OriginalValue>
        <OriginalValue>tiff</OriginalValue>
        <OriginalValue>gif</OriginalValue>
        <OriginalValue>jpg</OriginalValue>
</CustomFilter>
```

After saving the settings, you must uncheck the Use Default Configuration checkbox in the Refinement group (Figure 17-11) of web part properties before using the new values.

Integrating the Client

If you use SharePoint Workspace 2010 as a client for your SharePoint 2010 server, you can use client-side search functions in this application as well. This means that, even if you're not connected to the SharePoint server, the content is available on your desktop and can be searched.

If your client operating system is Windows 7, you can also search the SharePoint content from Windows Explorer, without opening a browser.

To achieve this functionality on the client side, you must define the SharePoint site as a federated search connector for Windows 7, then create a search connector to it. You can add federated search connector definitions in Windows 7 by creating a search connector description file (`.osdx`).

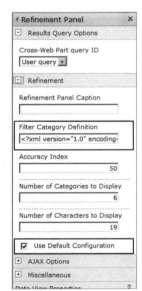

FIGURE 17-11: The Use Default Configuration checkbox

This `.osdx` file is a special XML file that describes the connection. For example, in the case of SharePoint 2010, the description file must be similar to this:

```
<?xml version="1.0" encoding="UTF-8"?>
<OpenSearchDescription xmlns="http://a9.com/-/spec/opensearch/1.1/" xmlns:ms-
    ose="http://schemas.microsoft.com/opensearchext/2009/">
<ShortName>SP2010 Search</ShortName>
<Description>SP2010 Search</Description>
<Url type="application/rss+xml"
    template="http://sp2010/search/_layouts/
    srchrss.aspx?k={searchTerms}&amp;web.count=50"/>
<Url type="text/html"
    template="http://sp2010/search/Pages/results.aspx?k={searchTerms}"/>
</OpenSearchDescription>
```

Here, the URL of the SharePoint Search site is `http://sp2010/search`. It can be both SharePoint 2010 Search Center and FAST Search Center as well.

After creating and editing the description file, save it to anywhere on your computer. Then right-click this file and choose Create Search Connector. After that, the Search connector will appear in your Favorites in Windows Explorer, and you can use it any time you want.

IMPROVING "FINDABILITY" AND "SEARCHABILITY"

Enterprise search is no longer simply about search pages. The capability of users to search and find required information has a huge business value, so you should plan and maintain the information architecture very carefully.

This section examines how metadata and keywords can help the "findability" of information stored in SharePoint 2010. After that, you will see why Search Engine Optimization (SEO) is important for Internet sites based on SharePoint 2010, and how you can improve it.

Using Managed Metadata

One of the most relevant improvements of SharePoint 2010 is metadata management. According to MSDN, "Enterprise metadata management (EMM) is a set of features introduced in Microsoft SharePoint Server 2010 that enable taxonomists, librarians, and administrators to create and manage terms and sets of terms across the enterprise."

Following are some of the most important key features regarding the improved metadata management:

➤ The Managed Metadata Service is deployed as a service application, which means that you can define it in the same farm, and you can share it between SharePoint farms.

➤ Metadata services are term stores, or special databases that contain one or more taxonomies.

➤ A *taxonomy* is a hierarchical group of metadata that provides meaning and gives structure to the information.

➤ Metadata management now includes a term management tool with service management, security settings, term sets, and so on.

From the search perspective, metadata management is very important. This is primarily because crawling, indexing, and querying managed metadata is very efficient, and search results are better and more consistent. Also, various navigation tools (for example, metadata-based navigation of document libraries, Refinement Panel, and so on) are available to use and empower the user experience.

Building efficient, powerful, and useful taxonomies is always really difficult to do. The two most important categories of taxonomies are functional and organizational:

➤ Tags for *functional taxonomies* are categorized based on the functions and activities that produce them. The business processes of the organization are used to create and manage the taxonomy.

➤ *Organizational taxonomies* are used to represent the organization structures like divisions, departments, and so on.

Both of them can be used in the same organization at the same time, but you must identify them and plan for them carefully.

Here are some best practices for building taxonomies:

➤ Always plan before you create anything. Involve the business stakeholders and power users to check their everyday work, extract their knowledge and opinions, and also ask them about what they would need, but don't have right now.

➤ Plan from a business perspective, not from a technology perspective.

➤ Establish a governance team with members from the whole organization to manage taxonomies.

➤ Regularly check the status of all taxonomies. Sometimes some refreshing and reorganizing is needed, but only in cases of business changes.

➤ Train the taxonomy owners.

➤ Train the end users and keep them motivated.

Using Metadata Properties

Managed properties are the properties of crawled content that users can use in search queries. They can be defined in each search service application.

Let's take a look at an example of using managed metadata properties. Assume that you'd like to crawl a set of documents, without any other content (for example, list items). In this case, you use the IsDocument metadata property, but this one cannot be used in search scopes by default. To make it available, you must first allow it to be used in scopes.

By using the IsDocument metadata property, the Documents scope will be something like this:

```
ContentSource = Local SharePoint sites (Included)
IsDocument = 1 (Required)
```

Of course, it's also possible to include more content sources. In this case, the only thing you have to do is add as many ContentSource rules to your scope as you want, and select Included as a behavior to all.

Improving Keywords and Best Bets

As mentioned, keywords help to mark specific items as more relevant in your SharePoint environment. This means that they show up more prominently in the search results. Best Bets are some tips to follow when users search for some specific keyword.

When you use this capability, you can improve the user experience in a very easy way. But be careful. If keywords and Best Bets are irrelevant to the users, the users won't like them and won't use them. Moreover, the kinds of tips provided in Best Bets may annoy the users, rather than help them.

Before defining keywords and Best Bets, ask the key users and stakeholders. It should be a business decision, not a technical one. Finally, use audiences if applicable, to avoid the irrelevant and annoying information in the result set. If you have FAST Search Server 2010 for SharePoint installed, you should also define User Context to be able to address each user with relevant and useful information.

Improving People Search

Maybe it's too obvious, but just think about how People Search can improve the user's capability to reach information. Sometimes the best way to learn more about a topic is to find an expert. If User Profiles are well-organized and managed, the experts in your organization will be available to help each other, so that the overall organizational efficiency will be much higher,

To take full advantage of People Search, train and force the end users to maintain their profiles, and motivate them to help each other. The People Search result page also can be customized, so, if you have special requirements, don't hesitate to build up your custom result set UI.

Improving the User Context in FAST Search

If you have FAST Search Server 2010 for SharePoint installed, you should also define the User Context to be able to address each user with relevant and useful information. This is a very powerful capability of FAST Search, and can be defined at the site collection level. Each site collection can then have its own User Context definitions, with different settings.

Understanding SEO and SharePoint 2010

Search Engine Optimization (SEO) is the process of optimizing sites and pages for search engines to result in better relevance and ranking for the site. Because SEO is mostly a strong planning process, you should consider some best practices before trying to implement SEO for your sites:

➤ SEO is mostly for Internet-facing sites, but it is sometimes also needed in intranet environments. You must carefully consider whether you need it. Don't waste resources if it's not necessary, but identify the requirements and plan deep in case of need.

➤ Use relevant keywords.

➤ Never use irrelevant or "popular" keywords to improve the number of visitors on your site.

➤ Use proper semantic codes for formatting.

➤ Use descriptive URLs and page titles.

➤ Place your content high up on the page. Some engines crawl only the first lines or paragraphs of the pages.

➤ Use a clear site hierarchy, and make every page reachable.

➤ Remove broken links.

➤ Text browsers (such as LYNX) are the best tool you can use to examine your site. Crawlers see the content the same way text browsers do.

➤ Use valid HTML and XML.

SEO is a really complex topic, but remember that your content is primarily for users, not for search engines.

SUMMARY

As you have seen in this chapter, SharePoint 2010 is really powerful and has a lot of improved and new functions. This chapter introduced you to these capabilities and improvements, including SharePoint 2010 Search, as well as FAST Search Server 2010 for SharePoint.

ABOUT THE AUTHOR

Ágnes Molnár has been working with Microsoft technologies and SharePoint since 2001. After a few years of experience as a developer and SharePoint expert, she founded a SharePoint consulting company in Hungary, Central Europe. She's been working as senior consultant and has led the implementation of SharePoint for numerous Central European companies. Her main focus is on Architecture, Governance, Information and Knowledge Management, and Enterprise Search. She's a frequent speaker at conferences around the globe, and also the author of SharePoint articles and co-author of various books.

18

Understanding Branding in SharePoint 2010

By Randy Drisgill

Thus far, this book has focused primarily on developers and IT professionals. This chapter is geared toward the user interface designers and those who need to know how to make SharePoint 2010 look as great as it performs.

This chapter begins by explaining what branding for SharePoint is, and then describes some of the newer branding features that have been introduced in the 2010 version. Finally, this chapter describes the basic steps necessary for creating a website that doesn't look like the default SharePoint experience.

INTRODUCTION TO SHAREPOINT BRANDING

In general, *branding* is the act of creating a specific image or identity that people will recognize in relation to a company. When referring to websites, branding usually involves the colors, fonts, logos, and supporting graphics that make up the general look and feel of the site. Branding for SharePoint sites is not very different from any other website, except that the branding topic for SharePoint includes the creation of master pages, page layouts, cascading style sheets (CSS), web parts, and eXtensible Stylesheet Language Transformations (XSLT).

Branding certainly sounds a lot like traditional design, so why is branding the popular term when it comes to SharePoint design? The answer is a simple case of alleviating confusion.

Often, when it comes to enterprise software, the word "design" can be confused with a lot of different activities. Depending on the specialty of the technical person that is asked, design could be the act of creating an effective user interface, or it could be the act of planning and architecting a software application, often known as "software design." By using the term "branding," it can be easily understood that the topic relates to creating a visual website design.

Comparing SharePoint Foundation 2010 and SharePoint Server 2010

Just like SharePoint 2007, SharePoint 2010 is available as two distinct products; one of them is free and the other is not. SharePoint Foundation 2010 is the new version of the free Windows SharePoint Services version 3 (WSSv3) and SharePoint Server 2010 is the new version of Microsoft Office SharePoint Server 2007 (MOSS).

Although SharePoint Server 2010 is more costly, it includes the Publishing features, which have several useful additions for branding projects:

➤ Publishing sites enable designers to create a form of a page template known as *page layouts*.

➤ Publishing sites contain navigation providers that are more flexible, and can be managed more easily from the SharePoint web user interface.

➤ Publishing sites enable site administrators to change a master page for their site and all subsites easily from the SharePoint web user interface.

➤ SharePoint Server enables more flexibility with themes, including the capability to change the colors and fonts in the SharePoint web user interface. Also, Publishing sites include the capability to apply themes to all subsites at the same time.

Types of SharePoint Sites

When creating branding for SharePoint it is important to understand what kind of website is being created. SharePoint is typically set up as one of two types of websites, each with a unique purpose: Internet sites and intranet sites. Either of these types of SharePoint site can focus on a range of functions from communication to collaboration.

Internet Sites

Internet sites are public-facing, and typically have anonymous users visiting them using a variety of Internet browsers. These sites are usually driven by marketing, with few content authors and tightly controlled content.

Typically, public Internet-facing sites offer the opportunity to create very stylistic, design-heavy websites. Two great examples of corporate-branded Internet sites that were built with SharePoint are

Chilis.com (Figure 18-1) and Ferarri.com (Figure 18-2). Both of them show heavy branding, so much so that, without some poking around in the HTML source, it is hard to see any evidence that they are even using SharePoint.

Intranet Sites

Intranet sites are typically available only to employees and partners who are internal to corporate firewalls or virtual private networks (VPNs), though sometimes parts of them (known as *extranets*) are available externally as well. The focus of intranet sites is typically to facilitate information delivery or collaboration for specific sets of users. They often have many content authors, as well as many users who will be consuming content and collaborating on new content.

FIGURE 18-1: The www.chilis.com website built with SharePoint

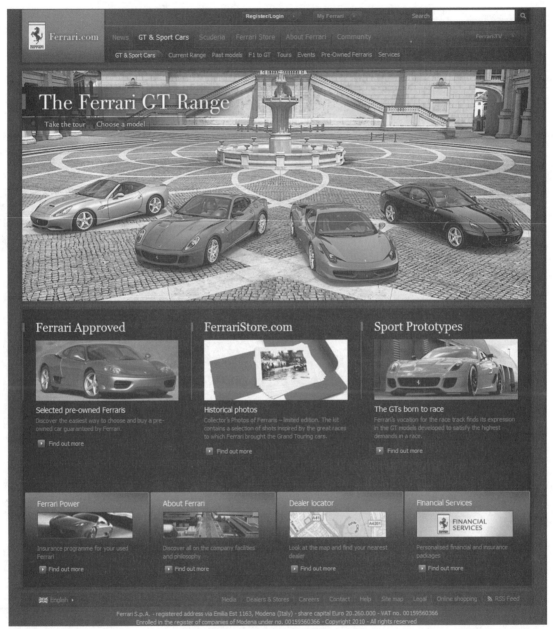

FIGURE 18-2: The www.ferarri.com website built with SharePoint

Unlike with public Internet sites, browsers and system capabilities can be limited to a specific supported set. The out-of-the-box layout of SharePoint 2010 team sites has a collaboration-heavy look and feel that often fits the bill as a good starting point for an internal intranet design. Figure 18-3 shows an out-of the-box SharePoint 2010 team site. However, this doesn't mean that companies want their intranet sites to all look the same. Often, it is important to add a certain amount of corporate branding, even to intranet sites. Figure 18-4 shows a typical custom branded SharePoint intranet site.

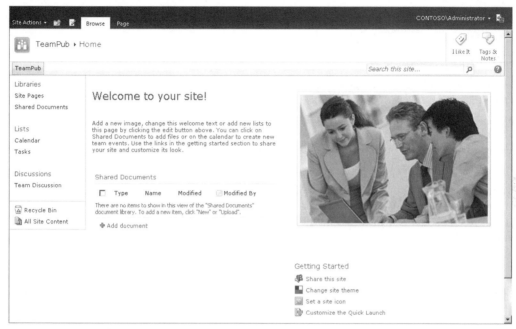

FIGURE 18-3: Out-of-the-box SharePoint 2010 team site

FIGURE 18-4: Custom branded SharePoint 2010 intranet site

How Branding Works in SharePoint

Before diving into the specifics of creating branding in SharePoint 2010, it's important to understand some of the key ways in which branding can be applied in SharePoint. The following sections examine these key concepts in detail.

Understanding Themes

Themes are a great way to introduce small amounts of style into a SharePoint site without investing a lot of time and effort into doing a full-scale branding effort. Technically speaking, themes can be thought of as changes that are applied to the existing look and feel through the use of CSS. In SharePoint 2007, themes played a similar function, but behind the scenes, they worked completely differently than they do in SharePoint 2010.

In SharePoint 2007, themes were created on the server in the `SharePoint 12` folder (the root folder for SharePoint), and consisted of XML, CSS, and images that were applied over the top of the default master page. When a page was loaded, both the SharePoint core CSS file and the theme CSS file would be loaded by the browser, with the theme's CSS showing on the page because it was loaded last.

In SharePoint 2010, themes are created with the Microsoft Office client software (2007 and above), using Word, PowerPoint, or Excel to create `.THMX` files that describe the 12 theme colors and 2 fonts available in the new SharePoint themes. Once created with Office, they can be loaded into SharePoint 2010 and applied to any site by site owners.

Unlike SharePoint 2007, the new theming engine in SharePoint 2010 doesn't apply CSS after the existing CSS. Instead, when a theme is applied to a SharePoint 2010 site, SharePoint looks for specific CSS markup comments, and replaces colors and fonts in the line immediately following each of the comments.

Following are the possible theme comment tokens, along with a sample of how each works in CSS. In each example, the comment changes the color or font of the element below it.

➤ `ReplaceFont` — Replaces fonts with one of the two font choices.

```
/* [ReplaceFont(themeFont: "MajorFont")] */
font-family: arial;
```

➤ `ReplaceColor` — Replaces colors such as backgrounds and fonts with one of the 12 color options.

```
/* [ReplaceColor(themeColor:"Accent1")] */
color: red;
```

➤ `RecolorImage` — Recolors images using one of three methods: Tint, Blend, and Fill.

```
/* [RecolorImage(themeColor:"Accent2",method:"Tinting ")] */
background-image:url("header.png");
```

Another difference in the new theming engine is that SharePoint 2010 themes do not contain custom background images. Instead, SharePoint 2010 will apply color shading to specific images using the CSS comments.

Along with the capability to create themes in the Office client, the Server version of SharePoint 2010 allows site owners to modify the themes directly in the SharePoint web user interface. Figure 18-5 shows this interface. Site owners can change the colors or fonts in the SharePoint web user interface and see their changes immediately.

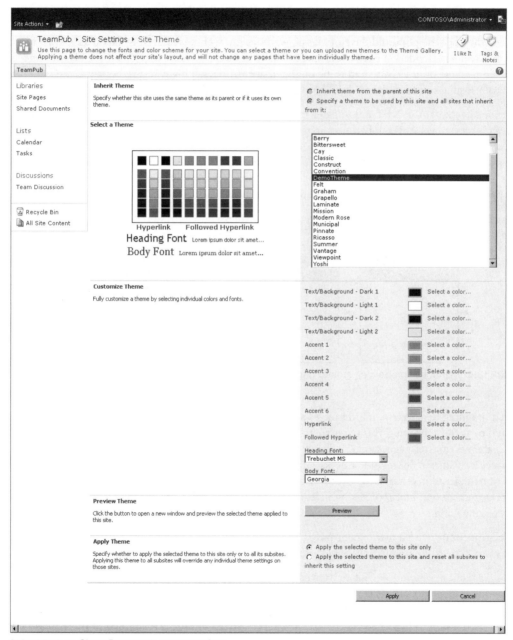

FIGURE 18-5: SharePoint web user interface

The new theming engine effectively drops the entry barrier for creating simple color and font changes in SharePoint. Now, anyone with rudimentary knowledge of how themes work in Office can create a SharePoint theme in minutes, instead of in hours. Some examples of how theming works in SharePoint 2010 are discussed later in this chapter.

Understanding Master Pages

If you remember the good old days of classic web design, web pages used to be created with all the look and feel hard-coded in each every page. This meant that when changes inevitably were needed, every single page on a website had to be changed accordingly. This was a tedious process, and often it led to mistakes, or even situations where some pages would end up not looking the same.

With the advent of ASP.NET 2.0, master pages were introduced to alleviate this problem. Because SharePoint leverages ASP.NET, it uses master pages in much the same way that ASP.NET does. Just like in a typical ASP.NET website, master pages allow designers and developers to create a consistent look and feel for all the pages in a SharePoint website. Every page on a typical SharePoint site references a master page. When that page is loaded in a browser, ASP.NET merges the master page with the page content, and the resultant styled page is returned to the user.

Figure 18-6 shows the relationship between master pages and page content.

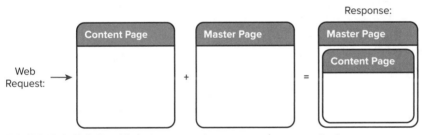

FIGURE 18-6: Relationship between master pages and page content

From a branding perspective, master pages are the outer shell design of a SharePoint website. Sometimes referred to as the "chrome," this outer shell defines the overall look for every page loaded by SharePoint. Unlike themes, master pages can actually change the layout of many of the elements that are loaded on the page. If themes in SharePoint are like painting the walls of a house, *master pages* are like the blueprint or actual architecture of the house. Master pages consist of standard HTML, SharePoint-specific controls, and *content placeholders*, which are containers that will load specific pieces of content from the referring content page.

SharePoint comes with a few master pages out-of-the-box that can be used for website branding right away. The following list describes each of them:

➤   `default.master` — This master page is used only when a SharePoint 2007 site is being upgraded to 2010. It is virtually identical to how the default master page in SharePoint 2007 looked. It is worth noting that this master page can be used only when SharePoint 2010 is in SharePoint 2007 mode via Visual Upgrade. Visual Upgrade is examined in more detail later in this chapter.

➤ `minimal.master` — This master page is used only on pages that have their own navigation, or need extra space (such as dedicated application pages or the search center). Unlike the concept of minimal master pages in SharePoint 2007, this master page is not intended to be the starting point for branding, because it is missing several common SharePoint controls.

➤ `v4.master` — This is the default master page that is used for much of SharePoint 2010, and is the same as what was shown earlier in Figure 18-3. In many ways, it is similar to the default master page in SharePoint 2007, except that the HTML markup has been improved, and the branding has been updated to a more modern look and feel.

➤ `nightandday.master` — This master page is available only in a SharePoint Server 2010 site that has the Publishing features enabled. It is similar to the `Blueband` master page in SharePoint 2007, only with an updated look and feel. Unlike `v4.master` (which is geared toward intranet sites), this master page is simpler and more appropriate for an Internet site. Because the underlying code is less complex, this can be a good place to look when trying to learn about master pages. Figure 18-7 shows the `nightandday` master page.

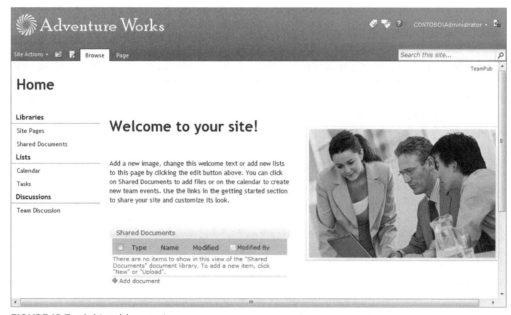

FIGURE 18-7: nightandday master page

Besides the out-of-the-box master pages, one of the key concepts of branding for SharePoint is creating custom master pages. This concept is discussed later in this chapter.

Understanding Page Layouts

If master pages create the outer shell of a SharePoint design, then *page layouts* can be thought of as a design template for the actual content of a page. Page layouts are available only in SharePoint Server sites that have the Publishing features enabled. They allow content authors to create pages based on pre-built and custom layouts.

Several out-of-the-box page layouts can be used right away in a SharePoint Server site, but also remember that designers and developers can always create their own custom page layouts. For example, when creating a new page in SharePoint Server, the same content can be arranged as a news article or as a welcome page, based on the page layout that is selected.

Figure 18-8 shows the relationship between master pages and page layouts.

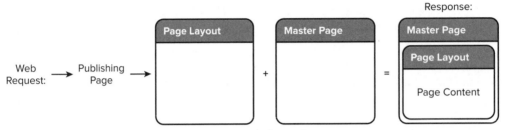

FIGURE 18-8: Relationship between master pages and page layouts

Along with defining how content is arranged in a page, page layouts also define the location of editable fields and web parts. *Web parts*, which can be thought of as self-contained widgets of functionality, can be arranged in pages through the use of *web part zones* that are defined in page layouts. Web part zones allow content authors to add and arrange multiple web parts vertically or horizontally. For those who are used to how this worked in SharePoint 2007, it's also worth noting that, in SharePoint 2010, besides web part zones, web parts can also be placed in HTML content fields in both publishing pages and wiki pages.

Using Cascading Style Sheets

Cascading style sheets (CSS) is pervasive in SharePoint branding. Almost every aspect of SharePoint is styled by CSS. All of the SharePoint controls that are loaded by a master page are styled by CSS, as well as many web parts — even SharePoint themes apply to specially commented CSS files in SharePoint 2010. Because of the importance of CSS in SharePoint, a sound understanding of it is crucial to becoming skilled at branding in SharePoint.

 For more information on learning CSS, check out another Wrox book, Professional CSS: Cascading Style Sheets for Web Design, Second Edition, *by Christopher Schmidt (Indianapolis: Wiley, 2008).*

Unlike SharePoint 2007, which had essentially one large core CSS file that was loaded for each page, SharePoint 2010 splits its default CSS across several smaller CSS files that are loaded depending on what controls are available on a given page. (Though much of the main CSS for SharePoint still resides in one core CSS file named `corev4.css`.)

When creating a heavily branded SharePoint site, it is often critical to create custom CSS to style not only the page design, but also the out-of-the-box SharePoint controls. The primary means for loading custom CSS in SharePoint is by referencing it from a custom master page.

SharePoint Server provides a secondary means to load CSS, known as *Alternate CSS*. Alternate CSS can be applied to any of the out-of-the-box master pages or any custom master page easily through the SharePoint Server web user interface. This can be particularly useful for mimicking the old SharePoint 2007 themes concept by applying CSS and background images to the default v4 master page using Alternate CSS.

Both custom master pages and Alternate CSS are discussed in more detail later in this chapter.

Approaches to Branding SharePoint 2010

One challenge when discussing SharePoint branding is that many people who are approaching the topic come from different skill levels, and often have different goals in mind for how intricate their designs need to be. Fortunately, leveraging all of the preceding concepts, there are several ways to approach branding in SharePoint 2010. They vary from being quite simple, to involving more skill and time.

Following are three different approaches for creating branding in SharePoint:

> *Low effort* — By utilizing the out-of-the-box branding, someone with little knowledge of traditional website development and design can create a multitude of look-and-feels. With a SharePoint Server 2010 website, you have two master pages to choose from: `v4.master` and `nightandday.master`. Both of these master pages can have their colors and fonts changed by applying any of the 20 out-of-the-box SharePoint themes. Custom themes can also be created using the Microsoft Office client software or the SharePoint server web interface. This approach is fairly easy to learn, and is effective at introducing custom colors and fonts to a site.

> *Medium effort* — To take the site branding one step further, CSS can be used to apply more customized styles, and even to add background images to a SharePoint site. SharePoint Server 2010 includes a simple way to apply custom CSS from the web interface, known as *Alternate CSS*. The medium-effort approach obviously involves having some knowledge of CSS and how it applies to SharePoint.

> *Full effort* — This involves utilizing all of the possible SharePoint branding options, including creating custom master pages, custom CSS, and potentially some custom page layouts. The approach is good for people who are experienced with traditional website design and have some knowledge of SharePoint or ASP.NET master pages. It is also well-suited for public Internet sites and internal employee portals.

These approaches are discussed in more detail later in this chapter.

EXPLORING NEW BRANDING FEATURES

When Microsoft created Office 2007, it put a lot of effort into making the user interface feel like an intuitive extension of the activities that users were trying to accomplish. It called this enhancement the *Microsoft Office Fluent User Interface* (or *Fluent UI*). One of the most infamous additions to the Fluent UI in Office 2007 was the ribbon interface, which replaced traditional menus and toolbars with an organization of contextual tabs.

After a short period of adjustment, users got used to the ribbon, and many found that it allowed them to spend more time and energy focused on actually accomplishing tasks in Office, rather than hunting for menu items. With SharePoint 2010, the Fluent UI has been introduced into the SharePoint web user interface, as well as SharePoint Designer. By introducing the Fluent UI and the ribbon to SharePoint, many common tasks have been reduced to one or two clicks in the ribbon. Figure 18-9 shows the ribbon interface in SharePoint 2010.

FIGURE 18-9: Ribbon interface in SharePoint 2010

Besides the addition of the Fluent UI and the ribbon, several other user experience changes will affect branding in SharePoint 2010. The following sections describe some of these new features and how they impact branding.

Adhering to HTML Standards

One of the first SharePoint 2010 enhancements that affects branding is the fact that SharePoint 2010 embraces HTML standards much more than previous versions. The out-of-the-box master pages all have a valid XHTML strict DOCTYPE declared. A DOCTYPE is a piece of code declared at the top of a document that instructs browsers or other software to use a specific language to interpret the rest of the included code. Having a valid DOCTYPE in SharePoint 2010 goes a long way toward being able to make websites that are compliant with modern HTML standards.

Those readers who are well-versed in classic web design may be asking if this means that SharePoint 2010 is fully compliant with the standards of the World Wide Web Consortium (W3C). Unfortunately, the answer is that the rendered SharePoint 2010 page, even for anonymous Internet users, is still not completely compliant out of the box. While the rendered page is much more standards-compliant than previous versions, SharePoint 2010 still utilizes some legacy code that is not 100 percent compliant. However, this doesn't mean that W3C compliance should be ignored, because Microsoft's goal moving forward is to introduce new controls that are XHTML-compliant.

Although SharePoint 2010 is not fully W3C compliant, it is compliant with another very important standard known as the Web Content Accessibility Guidelines (WCAG). WCAG is a series of guidelines published by the W3C's Web Accessibility Initiative aimed at making content on the web more accessible for all users, despite any potential disabilities. More precisely, SharePoint 2010 is compliant to the WCAG 2.0 AA specification (you can find more information at http://www.w3.org/TR/WCAG20/). This feature really goes a long way toward helping designers and developers build SharePoint sites that are accessible for the widest range of users.

Expanded Browser Support

One of the big knocks against SharePoint 2007 was its support for browsers other than Internet Explorer for anything more than just browsing page content. For SharePoint 2010, Microsoft has vastly improved the capability for other browsers to interact with the SharePoint data from a content authoring and administration standpoint.

Microsoft divides browser support for SharePoint 2010 into three main categories:

➤ *Supported* — A supported web browser is a web browser that is known to have been fully tested with all features and functionality to work with SharePoint Server 2010. If you encounter any issues, Support can help you to resolve these issues.

➤ *Supported with known limitations* — A supported web browser with known limitations works with most features and functionality. However, if there is a feature or functionality that does not work or is disabled by design, documentation on how to resolve these issues is readily available.

➤ *Not tested* — A web browser that is not tested means that its compatibility with SharePoint Server 2010 is untested, and there may be issues with using the particular web browser.

SharePoint Server 2010 works best with up-to-date, standards-based web browsers. The following are supported browsers running on the Windows operating system:

➤ Internet Explorer 7 (32-bit)

➤ Internet Explorer 8 (32-bit)

The following are supported browser options with known limitations:

➤ Internet Explorer 7 (64-bit)

➤ Internet Explorer 8 (64-bit)

➤ Firefox 3.6 (32-bit) on Windows operating systems

➤ Firefox 3.6 on non-Windows operating systems

➤ Safari 4.04 on non-Windows operating systems

Any browser that is not listed as supported or supported with known limitations is not supported from a content authoring standpoint, and may not behave as expected, even in simple browsing scenarios with the out-of-the-box SharePoint user interface.

It is important to note that Internet Explorer 6 (IE6) is not one of the supported browsers for SharePoint 2010. Though a master page could be crafted that can support basic browsing of a SharePoint 2010 site with IE6, the ribbon and other functionality relies on web standards that are not supported properly by IE6. While some organizations may find the lack of IE6 support to be limiting, it was a necessary choice for Microsoft to make to ensure SharePoint 2010 could enter the world of standards-based markup, while not having to support outdated fixes and hacks that older browsers would have required.

Master Page Improvements

Because master pages are so critical to the effort of branding SharePoint, any improvements added to them in SharePoint 2010 have a large impact on the branding process. Important changes to how master pages work in SharePoint 2010 are outlined in the following sections.

Applying Branding Throughout a SharePoint Site

One of the most exciting improvements for branding in SharePoint 2010 is the capability for custom master pages to be applied to almost all aspects of a SharePoint site. In SharePoint 2007, applying custom branding to the Application pages (those with _layouts in the URL, including many of the Site Settings menus) was challenging. The only ways to effectively accomplish this was to either edit the application.master that lived in the SharePoint root folder, create a SharePoint 2007 theme, or apply Alternate CSS to the site along with a custom master page. These solutions often left designers and developers with using unsupported methods, or forced them to create many more branding assets to accomplish unified branding across an entire SharePoint site.

SharePoint 2010 alleviates this pain by allowing custom master pages to apply to Application pages as well as the rest of a site. If a custom master page is created to adhere to the requirements of SharePoint 2010, this is as simple as either applying the master page to all Site and System pages from the master page settings menu in SharePoint Server, or by using SharePoint Designer 2010 to apply it to a SharePoint Foundation site. Figure 18-10 shows the master page settings menu in SharePoint Server 2010.

Simpler Rendering for Navigation Menus

SharePoint master pages utilize the `<SharePoint:AspMenu>` control to render navigation for SharePoint sites. This control has a new property named `UseSimpleRendering`. When set to `True`, the SharePoint navigation will render the menu with simple modern HTML code, leveraging unordered lists instead of nesting a ton of tables. This has the benefit of lessening the page weight, as well as making styling with CSS much easier than in previous versions. Following is an example of some of the output when `UseSimpleRendering` is on:

```
<ul class="static">
 <li class="static">
  <a class="static menu-item" href="/entwiki/Pages/Home.aspx">
   <span class="additional-background">
    <span class="menu-item-text">Ent Wiki</span>
   </span>
  </a>
 </li>
</ul>
```

Though this is certainly a great addition to SharePoint, if branding is being upgraded from SharePoint 2007, it may be beneficial to leave the `UseSimpleRendering` set to `False`. This will cause `AspMenu` to render navigation exactly like it did in SharePoint 2007, removing the need to update any complex CSS that was created to brand the navigation for SharePoint 2007.

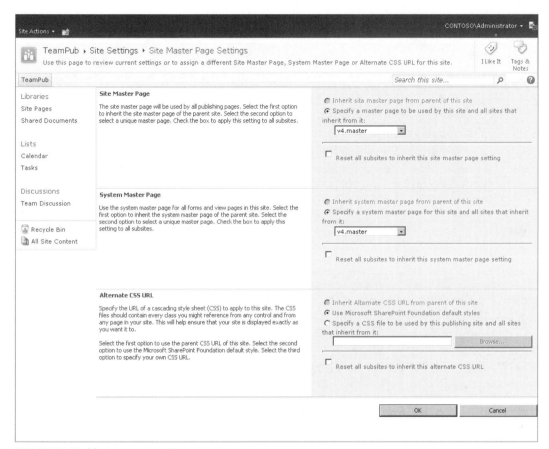

FIGURE 18-10: Master page settings menu

Wiki Pages

The concept of *wikis* in SharePoint is certainly not new. They existed in SharePoint 2007 as an easy way for organizations to create constantly evolving content. Many companies used them to allow efficient collaboration, and even to create corporate knowledge bases.

In SharePoint 2010, the concept of wikis has been expanded greatly to encompass many more aspects of day-to-day SharePoint content management. This expansion begins with the common SharePoint team site template. In SharePoint 2010 team sites, content editing is based on the new wiki functionality. This allows content to be updated quickly, including the addition of images and even web parts directly into the page content without the use of web part zones. Figure 18-11 shows the new wiki page editing experience.

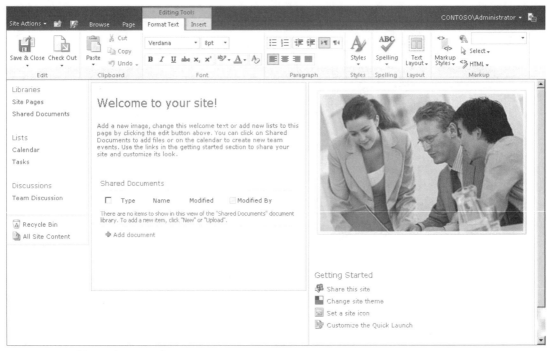

FIGURE 18-11: New wiki page editing experience

Wiki pages in SharePoint 2010 also allow content authors more control over content layout than in previous versions of SharePoint. This functionality is known as *text layout*, and it includes several pre-baked content layouts that can easily be switched from the ribbon interface. Figure 18-12 shows the Text Layout options for a wiki page.

Along with the Team Site template, SharePoint 2010 includes a new site template called the Enterprise Wiki. This replaces the popular Collaboration Portal site template that was included with SharePoint 2007. This template (which is available only with SharePoint Server) is an excellent starting point for corporate intranets. Unlike the wiki pages in team sites, pages in Enterprise Wiki's use page layouts to provide customizable page-level templates, instead of the Text Layout Feature. Watch out for this, because it can easily trip someone up. The Text Layout button grays out in the ribbon without a pointer telling where to find the Page Layout button instead. Figure 18-13 shows the Page Layout button in the ribbon.

Dialog Boxes

Another very cool enhancement in SharePoint 2010 is the focus on reducing the number of page loads that are needed to perform various tasks. One way that this is accomplished is through the use of *dialog boxes*. These allow related menus and content to be loaded into a floating frame that is essentially a *modal window*, or a window that gains focus over the main window that must be interacted with or canceled before continuing.

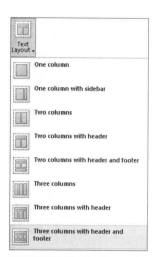

FIGURE 18-12: Text Layout options

FIGURE 18-13: Page Layout button in the ribbon

Dialog boxes in SharePoint 2010 can be dragged around within the browser window, and even maximized to the full browser size. Figure 18-14 shows a dialog box in SharePoint 2010.

Though dialog boxes are certainly helpful, they present a unique challenge in the context of SharePoint branding. This is because, by default, dialog boxes in SharePoint 2010 will show all branding that is applied to a master page, including logos, footers, navigation, and so on. Dialog boxes are intended to have minimal styling, and, as such, Microsoft has provided a simple way of hiding branding from them.

Anything that shouldn't show in a dialog box can have a specific CSS class, s4-notdlg, added to its HTML element, and SharePoint will simply hide that element only when showing dialog boxes. For example, the following <div> probably shouldn't show up in dialog boxes, so the special CSS class was added to it:

```
<div class="footerStyle s4-notdlg" >Copyright 2010 Randy's Waffles</div>
```

Because SharePoint dialog boxes will hide anything with the class of s4-notdlg, this <div> will not show in dialog boxes.

FIGURE 18-14: Dialog box in SharePoint 2010

Multi-Lingual User Interface (MUI)

For those SharePoint projects that involve multiple languages, the new *Multi-Lingual User Interface (MUI)* Feature in SharePoint 2010 will be very helpful. MUI allows for dynamic replacement of various web user interface elements based on the language specified by the user. Following are some of the elements that can be controlled by MUI:

➤ Site title and description

➤ Site column display names

➤ Navigation

➤ Menu items

➤ Managed Metadata Services tagging

This feature is separate from the old Variations Feature that is carried forward from SharePoint 2007, in that separate pages are not created for each language. Instead, the page elements are swapped out as the page is rendered. MUI has the capability to swap out many types of content, including menus, controls, titles, descriptions, navigation, breadcrumbs, metadata, and more.

It's important to remember that MUI is not a replacement for Variations. Rather, it can be used alongside of Variations to provide a more robust multi-lingual environment. MUI provides different labels for the same content, while Variations require completely different pages for different languages.

Visual Upgrade

Another new feature that affects the user experience in SharePoint 2010 is the concept of *Visual Upgrade*. In previous versions, an upgrade meant having to upgrade the user interface of SharePoint before being able to work with the upgraded server. With SharePoint 2010, server administrators and site owners can decide when and if the SharePoint 2010 user interface is applied to a particular SharePoint site.

By utilizing this feature, SharePoint 2010 capabilities can be leveraged while retaining the old SharePoint 2007 look and feel. All of the old SharePoint 2007 user interface options will work, including v3 master pages and themes. Though the user interface will look like SharePoint 2007, under the hood, everything will be using the SharePoint 2010 features. Figure 18-15 shows a SharePoint 2010 site with SharePoint 2007 visuals applied.

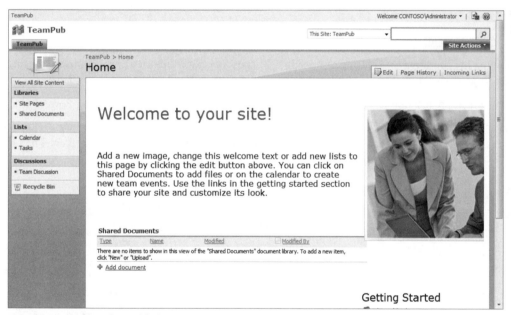

FIGURE 18-15: SharePoint 2010 site with SharePoint 2007 visuals applied

It is important to note that, although Visual Upgrade is certainly useful, SharePoint sites should not remain in the SharePoint 2007 user experience long term. This is meant to be a temporary fix while the new SharePoint 2010 branding is created. Not all SharePoint 2010 functionality will work properly with the SharePoint 2007 visual experience, including the wiki page functionality.

CREATING A BRANDED SHAREPOINT 2010 SITE

Whereas the previous sections of this chapter have discussed some of the new enhancements to branding in SharePoint 2010, the following sections focus on actually creating a branded SharePoint 2010 site. The first focus is on low- and medium-effort branding, including themes and Alternate CSS. Following that, you learn about the full-effort branding and creating custom master pages.

Working with SharePoint 2010 Themes and Alternate CSS

As discussed earlier, themes are a great way to change the colors and fonts that are applied to SharePoint. The following section discusses the use of the Microsoft Office client to create themes. Because themes in SharePoint 2010 cannot have custom background images, a later section discusses using Alternate CSS to take the branding further.

 One thing to watch out for when following along with the theme demos in this chapter is that SharePoint Foundation 2010 does not support showing themes for anonymous users. However, themes will work fine for anonymous users in SharePoint Server 2010.

Using Microsoft Office Themes in SharePoint 2010

Following are the steps for creating and using a Microsoft Office theme in SharePoint 2010 using PowerPoint 2010. The steps are similar for PowerPoint 2007, Word 2010, and Word 2007.

1. Open PowerPoint (2010) and either use a new PowerPoint file, or an existing PowerPoint presentation.

2. On the ribbon, switch to the Design tab and click Colors. Then select Create New Theme Colors, as shown in Figure 18-16.

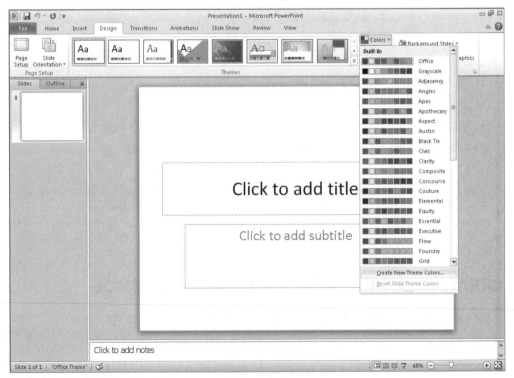

FIGURE 18-16: Selecting Create New Theme Colors

In the dialog for creating new theme colors shown in Figure 18-17, notice that there are two dark and two light Text/Background colors, six Accent colors, and two Hyperlink colors. One thing to consider here is that the Accent 1 through 6 colors correspond well to the bullet indention levels in PowerPoint, but they are more subjective in SharePoint. Some experimentation is typically needed before getting the right combination. One good strategy here is to pick colors that are similar or complementary.

3. After selecting a color scheme, click Save.

4. Back on the ribbon, click Fonts ⇨ Create New Theme Fonts, as shown in Figure 18-18.

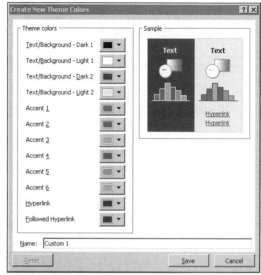

FIGURE 18-17: Dialog for creating new theme colors

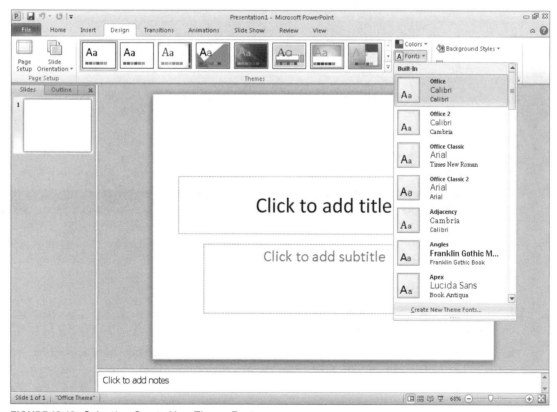

FIGURE 18-18: Selecting Create New Theme Fonts

In the dialog for creating new theme fonts shown in Figure 18-19, notice that there are options to set both the Heading and Body font, and that the selection includes many of the fonts installed on the client computer. Because these fonts will be used in SharePoint and loaded from the user's browser, be sure to pick fonts that are common across multiple operating systems.

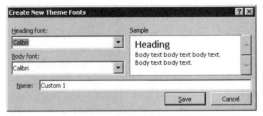

FIGURE 18-19: Dialog for creating new theme fonts

5. After selecting the two fonts, click Save.

6. Up until now, the choices were being saved in the local PowerPoint file. To export the theme for use in SharePoint, click the small More button on the right side of the Themes section of the Design tab in the ribbon, as shown in Figure 18-20.

FIGURE 18-20: More button in the ribbon

7. At the bottom of the All Themes menu, click Save Current Theme. Select a location and name it demo.thmx. Click Save. This saves the .THMX file so that it can be used in SharePoint.

8. Open a SharePoint 2010 site in a browser, log in, and click Site Actions ➪ Site Settings. Under Galleries, click Themes. This will load a document library view of the available themes.

9. To add the new theme, from the ribbon, click the Documents tab and then click Upload Document, as shown in Figure 18-21.

FIGURE 18-21: Upload Document option on ribbon

10. From the Upload Document dialog box, click Browse. Find the saved demo.thmx file and click Open. Then click OK in the main dialog box.

11. The Save dialog box will now open. The filename can be changed here, or the selection can just be saved by clicking Save. Now, the new theme is ready to be selected for use in SharePoint.

12. To select the theme, click Site Actions ➪ Site Settings. Then, under Look and Feel, click Site Theme.

13. From the Select a Theme menu, select demo from the list. The theme can be previewed by clicking Preview, or it can be applied to the site immediately by clicking the Apply button.

If you have followed the steps outlined here, your SharePoint site will show the selected colors throughout the page, including menus and hover states.

The out-of-the-box SharePoint v4.master *look and feel does not actually utilize any fonts that are applied from a custom theme. Although this certainly reduces the usefulness of themes with the default look and feel, theme fonts work with* nightandday.master *and, as you will see later in the chapter, you can use themes with your own custom CSS. In these cases, you can utilize the two theme fonts if you like.*

Adjusting a Theme with SharePoint Server 2010

As noted earlier, SharePoint Server 2010 specifically adds the capability to change theme colors and fonts from inside the SharePoint web user interface. SharePoint Foundation 2010 does not have this feature. Changes to themes for SharePoint Foundation 2010 must occur in the Office client software (that is, Word, PowerPoint, or Excel).

To change the theme attributes in SharePoint Server 2010, simply click Site Actions ➪ Site Settings. Under Look and Feel, click Site Theme. From there, the Customize Theme section displays all of the same options that are available from the Office client software. Figure 18-22 shows the Customize Theme menu. One really cool feature here is the color picker shown in Figure 18-23 that appears when Select a Color is clicked.

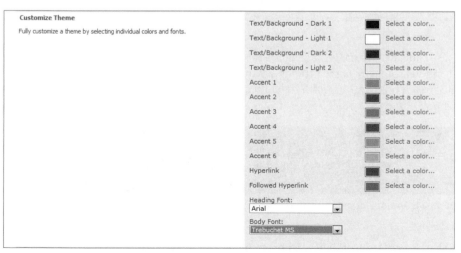

FIGURE 18-22: Customize Theme menu

The two font choices can also be changed from the Customize Theme menu. Note that all of the fonts installed on the server are available for selection. This can be particularly troublesome because site owners can select inappropriate fonts such as Wingdings.

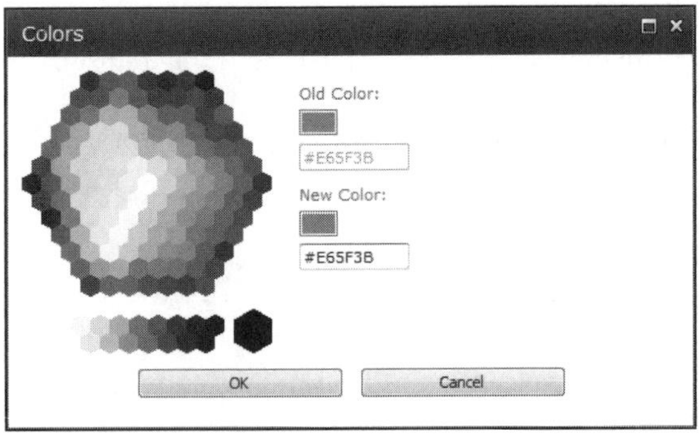

One last option that is available in SharePoint Server 2010 is the capability to apply the theme to the current site, and to reset all of the subsites below it to the same theme. There was no equivalent option for SharePoint 2007 themes, and this can be quite useful for projects with many subsites. Once all of the changes are made, clicking Apply refreshes the site with the new colors and fonts that were selected.

FIGURE 18-23: Color picker

Using Alternate CSS in SharePoint Server 2010

Alternate CSS is a feature of SharePoint Server that allows custom CSS to be easily applied to a site. Alternate CSS is a great way to add background images and other minor stylistic changes to SharePoint that can't be done with just a theme. Also, because the new themes engine in SharePoint 2010 allows the use of comments to change colors on-the-fly, Alternate CSS can be an easy way to leverage that feature. SharePoint Foundation 2010 does not have a menu in the web user interface for switching Alternate CSS, but the same techniques could be used with custom code or a Windows PowerShell command.

The following steps describe how to apply a custom header background graphic to a SharePoint Server 2010 site using Alternate CSS.

 The files for the examples in this chapter are available for download with the rest of the examples in this book at wrox.com.

1. First, a suitable header image named Header.jpg is required. This example will use a header for a fictitious company named Randy's Waffles. The image will need to have a logo on the left and stretch pretty far in width to handle higher-resolution monitors. Figure 18-24 shows the example Randy's Waffles header image.

FIGURE 18-24: Example Randy's Waffles header image

2. Open SharePoint Designer 2010 and open the root of a SharePoint Server 2010 website.

3. From the Site Objects panel on the left, click All Files.

4. In the All Files list, click Style Library ➪ en-us ➪ Themable.

5. From the ribbon, click Folder to add a new folder and name it `Demo`.

6. Click the new `Demo` folder. Then drag the `Header.jpg` image into the SharePoint Designer main section. This will add the image to the `Style Library/en-us/Themable/Demo` folder.

7. Next, add a new CSS file by clicking File from the ribbon and selecting CSS. Name the new file `Demo.css`.

8. Click `Demo.css` to open it, and then click Edit File from the ribbon to begin editing it.

9. Add the following CSS to the file:

```
/* set the header to show the custom background */
.s4-title {
    background:transparent url("Header.jpg") no-repeat scroll top left;
}

/* make the header height larger */
.s4-titletable {
    height: 120px;
}

/* hide the logo and site title */
.s4-titlelogo, .s4-titletext {
    visibility: hidden;
}

/* social link color */
.ms-socialNotif-text {
    color:black;
}
```

This CSS will change the header to show the background image, change the header height to show all of the image, set the site icon and title to hidden, and, finally, change the tagging link text color to make it more readable.

10. Save `Demo.css` by pressing Ctrl+S.

11. Next, right-click both `Header.jpg` and `Demo.css` from SharePoint Designer. Select Check In and then select Publish a Major Version. This will allow other users on the SharePoint site to see the CSS and image.

12. In a web browser, load the SharePoint 2010 site and click Site Actions ➪ Site Settings. Under Look and Feel, click Master Page.

13. Ensure that Site and System master pages are both set to `v4.master`. Under Alternate CSS URL, choose "Specify a CSS file to be used by this publishing site and all sites that inherit from it." Click the Browse button.

14. From the asset picker dialog, navigate to Style Library ➪ en-us ➪ Themable ➪ Demo and select `Demo.css`. Click OK.

15. From the master page menu, click OK. The site will refresh with the CSS styles applied to it. Figure 18-25 shows the newly styled site.

There is a problem in the current implementation of how background images are applied when the Themable *directory is used. You will learn more about theme comments later in this chapter, but it's important to note that, for the previous example, you need to ensure that no theme is applied to the site. If a theme is applied to a site that uses the previous alternate CSS in the* Themable *directory, the custom background header graphic will not show. This problem has to do with how SharePoint looks for theme comments in a themable folder. Since the previous example doesn't have any theme comments, SharePoint gets confused and has problems showing the image.*

FIGURE 18-25: Newly styled site

Working with SharePoint Theme Comments

Because the example in the previous section used the Themable directory in the Style Library, SharePoint 2010 theme colors can be applied to the Alternate CSS through the use of special comments that SharePoint understands. The following example takes the Alternate CSS from the previous example and adds two comments, one that will tint the header background image, and another that changes the color of the tagging links:

1. From SharePoint Designer 2010, right-click Demo.css from the previous example and select Check Out. This will allow the file to be modified.

2. Click `Demo.css`, and then click Edit File from the ribbon.

3. Add the following two bolded CSS comments above the corresponding existing CSS:

```
/* set the header to show the custom background */
.s4-title {
    /* [RecolorImage(themeColor:"Accent1",method:"Tinting")]*/
    background:transparent url("Header.png") no-repeat scroll top left;
}

/* make the header height larger */
.s4-titletable {
    height: 120px;
}

/* hide the logo and site title */
.s4-titlelogo, .s4-titletext {
    visibility: hidden;
}

/* social link color */
.ms-socialNotif-text {
    /* [ReplaceColor(themeColor:"Light1")] */
    color:black;
}
```

The first will tint the `Header.png` image the color of Accent 1, and the second will change the link color on the tagging links to the color that is set for Text/Background - Light 1.

4. Save the file by pressing Ctrl+S. Then right-click it and select Check In. Select Publish a Major Version.

5. The changes typically won't take effect until the theme is reapplied, so click Site Actions ⇨ Site Settings. Under Look and Feel, click Site Theme and either change one of the theme colors, or select a different theme and click Apply. (This is needed to apply the theme code. After it's applied, the previous theme can be selected and re-applied if needed.)

When SharePoint encounters these comments, it knows to make a new version of the header image tinted in the color of Accent 1, and it changes the tagging links at the top of the page to the same color as Text/Background - Light 1. SharePoint does this as the theme is applied. This is why the theme must be re-applied in order to see any changes that were made to the theme.

Creating a Custom Master Page

Themes are great for applying custom colors and fonts to a SharePoint site. However, to really make wide-sweeping changes, custom master pages are required. In many ways this topic is larger than can be addressed in a single chapter. For that reason, this section focuses on simply providing an overview of the topic. Also, note that the examples in this section all use SharePoint Designer to customize master pages. This is fine for local development in a virtual machine or development server. However, for large-scale production servers, these customizations should be packaged into a SharePoint solution package (or WSP) for proper deployment.

For more information on customization and solution packages check out Andrew Connell's MSDN article, "Understanding and Creating Customized and Uncustomized Files in Windows SharePoint Services 3.0," at `http://msdn.microsoft.com/en-us/library/cc406685.aspx`*. Although the article was written for an earlier version of SharePoint, the concepts are still applicable to SharePoint 2010.*

When getting started with master pages in SharePoint, it's easy to think that the best place to start would be a blank master page. But SharePoint master pages are complex animals. One reason they are complicated is because of *content placeholders* which, as mentioned earlier, are containers that will load specific pieces of content from the referring content page. SharePoint master pages have many required content placeholders, and, if any of them are omitted, the site will error. Because of this, it's often better to start from a pre-built master page shell that can have custom branding wrapped around it.

Starting with an Out-of-the-Box Master Page

The out-of-the-box master pages (like `v4.master` and `nightandday.master`) are great starting points for simple custom branding. One benefit to starting with one of these master pages is that if only minor changes are being made, the custom branding should work with little testing.

However, there are some major downsides to starting with out-of-the-box master pages. First, they are commented poorly — as in there are pretty much no comments to help with understanding which parts are being used for what. Second, the out-of-the-box master pages contain a lot of formatting that is specific to their individual looks, and, unless a project requires that same look and feel, there will be a lot of time spent understanding what is there and removing or changing things. That being said, if the only requirement is for something minor to be changed, removed, or added, starting with one of the out-of-the-box master pages can be a great way to go.

The following example uses `v4.master` as a starting point to create a new master page that uses a fixed-width layout centered in the page. These types of layouts are popular for public-facing sites that want to have a cleaner look and feel. SharePoint Server 2010 is used for this example. Follow these steps:

1. Open SharePoint Designer 2010 and load a SharePoint Server 2010 site.

2. From the Site Objects menu on the left, click Master Pages.

3. From the list of master pages, click next to `v4.master`. Then, from the ribbon, click Copy and then click Paste. This will create a duplicate of `v4.master` named `v4_copy(1).master`.

4. Click Rename from the ribbon and then rename `v4_copy(1).master` to `v4_centered.master`.

5. Click `v4_centered.master` and the click Edit File from the ribbon. A prompt will ask if you want to check it out. Click Yes.

6. Change the background color to maroon. Near line 36, add `style="background-color: maroon;"` to the `<body>` tag, as shown here:

```
<body scroll="no" onload="if (typeof(_spBodyOnLoadWrapper) != 'undefined')
    _spBodyOnLoadWrapper();" class="v4master" style="background-color: maroon;">
```

7. Add a surrounding `<div>` that centers the inner page and makes the background white. Near line 37, add the following line between the `<form>` tag and the `<asp:ScriptManager>` tag:

```
<div style="width: 960px; margin: auto; background-color:white;">
```

8. Close out the previous `<div>`. Near line 626, add a closing `</div>`.

9. Lastly, add a class called `s4-nosetwidth` to the main page `<div>`. Otherwise, SharePoint will take over and inject a variable width to the page. Near line 293 change `<div ID="s4-workspace">` to `<div ID="s4-workspace" class="s4-nosetwidth">`.

10. Save the master page by pressing Ctrl+S.

11. Right-click `v4_centered.master` in SharePoint Designer and select Check In. Then select Publish a Major Version. SharePoint will warn that "This document requires content approval. Do you want to view or modify its approval status?" Click Yes, and a browser window is opened to the Approval status page.

12. Click the arrow that appears to the right of `v4_centered` and select Approve/Reject. From the next screen, click Approved and OK. This will allow other users to see the changes.

13. Click Site Actions ➪ Site Settings. Under Look and Feel, click Master Page.

14. Select `v4_centered.master` for both the Site Master Page and System Master Page. Ensure that Alternate CSS URL is set to "Use Microsoft SharePoint Foundation default styles." Click OK.

15. This will apply the new master page through the site, even to the Site Settings pages. Figure 18-26 shows the new fixed-width master page. The screen width in the screenshot is low; you can just barely see that the main page width is smaller than the full screen width. The dark areas on the sides of the screenshot are the background, while the large white area in the middle is the actual page width.

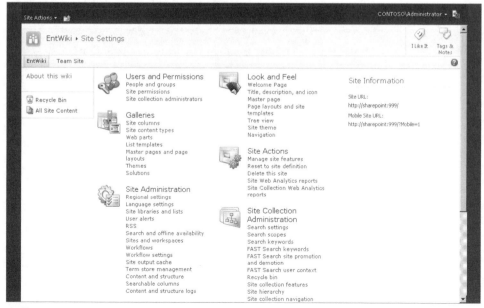

FIGURE 18-26: New fixed-width master page

Using a Starter Master Page

Another way to start a new SharePoint branding project is to use a starter master page. In SharePoint 2007, these were referred to as *minimal master pages*. But, in SharePoint 2010, there is already something named `minimal.master` that is intended for use with applications having their own navigation or needing extra space. It is not intended as a starting point for all SharePoint branding.

Starter master pages are typically better commented than the out-of-the-box master pages, and have minimal styling and layout. However, they contain all of the required content placeholders and have some of the functional SharePoint controls already loaded for easy use.

As of this writing, the following are two popular choices for starter master pages in SharePoint 2010:

➤ *Microsoft's starter master page* (`http://code.msdn.microsoft.com/odcSP14StarterMaster`) — This starter master page was built for SharePoint Foundation 2010, but it will also work in SharePoint Server 2010. It is extremely minimal, having most of the elements hidden, and with virtually no page formatting. For example, by default, this master page does not even include the Site Actions button. Microsoft's starter master page is a good beginning point for learning about SharePoint 2010 master pages.

➤ *My starter master pages* (`http://startermasterpages.codeplex.com`) — I have created a few Starter Master Pages: one for SharePoint Foundation 2010, one for SharePoint Server 2010 publishing sites, and some other minor iterations for specific cases. They are less minimal than Microsoft's starter master page, and have most of the common SharePoint functional controls displayed.

The following steps detail how to create a new custom master page based on a starter master page in a SharePoint Server 2010 site:

1. Open SharePoint Designer 2010 and load a SharePoint Server 2010 site.

2. From the Site Objects menu on the left, click Master Pages.

3. Click Blank Master Page from the ribbon and name it `demo.master`.

4. Click `demo.master` and then click Edit File from the ribbon. A prompt will ask if you want to check it out. Click Yes.

5. Download the starter master page from `http://startermasterpages.codeplex.com` and unzip the files the local computer.

6. Copy the contents of `_starter.master` to the clipboard and switch to SharePoint Designer 2010. Then paste over the contents of `demo.master`, replacing the basic master page content that was included in `demo.master`.

7. Save the master page by pressing Ctrl+S.

8. Right-click `demo.master` in SharePoint Designer and select Check In. Then select Publish a Major Version. SharePoint will warn that "This document requires content approval. Do you want to view or modify its approval status?" Click Yes, and a browser window is opened to the Approval status page.

9. Click the arrow that appears next to demo and select Approve/Reject. From the next screen, click Approved and OK. This will allow other users to see the changes.

10. Click Site Actions ⇨ Site Settings. Under Look and Feel, click Master page.

11. Select demo.master for both the Site Master Page and System Master Page. Ensure that Alternate CSS URL is set to "Use Microsoft SharePoint Foundation default styles." Click OK.

12. This will apply the new master page throughout the site, even to the Site Settings pages. Figure 18-27 shows the SharePoint site with the starter master page applied. Notice that it contains very little styling and formatting.

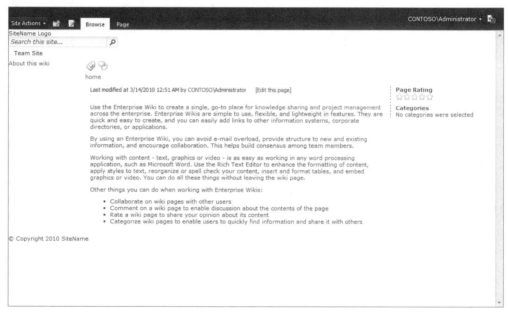

FIGURE 18-27: SharePoint site with the starter master page applied

Next Steps

The starter master page is like a blank canvas. By adding HTML for layout and CSS for styling, almost any look can be created. HTML can pasted into the starter master page surrounding the various pieces of SharePoint functionality to arrange them as desired. Custom CSS can be added to the Style Library and then loaded into SharePoint via the following command (which is already included in the starter master page from the previous example):

```
<SharePoint:CssRegistration name="/Style Library/sitename/
    style.css"  After="corev4.css" runat="server"/>
```

This command ensures that custom CSS is always loaded after the core SharePoint CSS, which is a key concept in overriding the out-of-the-box styles.

One common method for creating complex SharePoint branding is to first create the design using just HTML and CSS, and test it to ensure that everything looks right. By testing a design in HTML before applying it in SharePoint, a lot of design decisions can be made quicker without being slowed by SharePoint check-ins and check-outs. From there, the HTML and CSS can be moved directly into the master page to apply layout and styling. After all of the HTML and CSS is added, finishing the design is just a matter of tweaking the CSS to ensure that all of the SharePoint-specific styling matches the rest of the design.

Though the vast volume of CSS used by SharePoint is out-of-the-box, sometimes it can be daunting to figure out how to override the default SharePoint styles. Luckily, tools can help analyze a SharePoint site and identify the CSS classes to help with overriding them:

➤ *IE8 Developer Tools (formerly a separate download for IE7 called IE Developer Toolkit)* — This is now included with every copy of Internet Explorer 8 (IE8), and can be activated in IE8 by clicking Tools ⇨ Developer Tools.

➤ *Firebug for Firefox* (www.getfirebug.com) — This is a third-party add-on for Firefox that can be downloaded and installed.

Both of these tools allow you to analyze the rendered page, and discover and adjust CSS on-the-fly. Many designers consider Firebug to be a more powerful tool, but because of the differences between IE and Firefox, both are often required to truly understand all of the styles being applied to a SharePoint site. Once styles are identified, they can be moved back into the master page CSS to apply to SharePoint permanently.

Upgrading SharePoint 2007 Master Pages

So far, you have learned about creating a new SharePoint 2010 master page. But what happens if there is already existing SharePoint 2007 branding? Can you use these files with SharePoint 2010? The answer is certainly "yes," but you have a couple options when using a SharePoint 2007 master page with SharePoint 2010.

SharePoint 2007 master pages can be used immediately as-is if a SharePoint 2010 site is using Visual Upgrade to stay in SharePoint 2007 mode. Because Visual Upgrade is meant to only be a temporary solution, SharePoint 2007 master pages should eventually be upgraded to work directly with the SharePoint 2010 visuals.

 For more information on this process, check out the MSDN article, "Upgrading an Existing Master Page to the SharePoint Foundation Master Page," at http://msdn.microsoft.com/en-us/library/ee539981(office.14).aspx.

SUMMARY

This chapter focused on the topic of creating branding for use in SharePoint 2010. It started with an introduction to SharePoint branding, including a definition of what branding means in SharePoint. Next, the focus turned to how branding is accomplished in SharePoint 2010, including the topics of themes, master pages, page layouts, and CSS. This chapter also examined some of the user experience changes in SharePoint 2010 that affect branding. Lastly, several examples were provided that looked at the various approaches to actually applying branding to SharePoint 2010, including themes, Alternate CSS, and both default master pages and starter master pages.

By now, you should have a good understanding of how branding works in SharePoint 2010, and what some of the first steps are for creating custom branded SharePoint 2010 sites.

ABOUT THE AUTHOR

Randy Drisgill has been working with SharePoint911 as their branding and design lead since 2008. He has more than ten years experience developing, designing, and implementing Internet-based software for clients ranging from small businesses to Fortune 500 companies. Randy has been working with SharePoint since the beta of SharePoint 2007, and has worked on many large-scale internal and public-facing SharePoint branding projects. In 2009, he was recognized by Microsoft as an authority on SharePoint branding by being awarded MVP status for SharePoint Server. Randy has also worked on several articles and books on the topic of SharePoint. You can visit his blog at `http://blog.drisgill.com`.

19

Planning, Designing, and Administering a Multimedia Assets Management Solution

By Claudio Brotto and Igor Macori

At the SQL Server and SharePoint level, support for Remote BLOB Storage (RBS) and Filestream (together with the introduction of new content types and libraries designed specifically for multimedia content) will dramatically reduce the effort required to create an advanced multimedia assets management solution.

By combining these features with the improvements in the Internet Information Services (IIS) technology stack related to bit-rate throttling, a SharePoint architect is now able to envision and plan for a system that is scalable and responsive. This system can leverage the out-of-the-box Silverlight components to create a rich and intuitive user experience, taking the ideas introduced by Web 2.0 solutions to the next level.

This chapter provides an introduction to the new multimedia capabilities of SharePoint Server 2010, with a set of suggestions and best practices derived from real-world projects and experiences. This chapter was co-authored by a SharePoint administrator and a SharePoint developer, with the goal of providing a 360-degree overview of Digital Assets Management (DAM) solutions in SharePoint 2010.

LOOKING AT DIGITAL ASSETS MANAGEMENT SCENARIOS

Solutions incorporating multimedia content often have playful purposes, something that makes them fit into the private world of enjoyment and fun. This is the first thing that comes to mind when you think of systems such as YouTube and Flickr.

Several opportunities related to business matters where solutions and systems for multimedia and Digital Assets Management (DAM) also can be realized. It's also possible to extend storing and archiving systems based on SharePoint technology to multimedia content, allowing for interesting scenarios such as the following:

➤ Archiving of multimedia documentation that can be used for product catalogues (including product photos and artwork, photo galleries on realized projects, demonstrative movies, and interviews with designers and users).

➤ Archiving and sharing solutions for movies that can be used as video lessons and web casts for intracompany e-learning or knowledge-sharing systems. This is allowed by new tagging, rating, and social computing features included in SharePoint 2010.

➤ Archiving of audio recordings (lessons, meetings, and audio-guides), and then publishing them on podcasts created with data contained in Asset Libraries. An RSS feed would allow users to subscribe and then download them to their iPods and ZUNE players.

Facing Challenges in Multimedia Solutions Design and Implementation

Multimedia solutions are usually associated with large files. This is a typical characteristic of high-quality videos and images, something that makes their circulation on the Internet quite difficult because of bandwidth or hardware limitations in slower computers. Additionally, multimedia content is often handled as binary data or simple links. There is information encrypted in that data that should be considered as descriptive metadata (for example, video length, format, frame size, frame rate, keywords, and so on), which can be really helpful when you're trying to organize or search for this content.

It was rather complex to conceive of a DAM system on Microsoft Office SharePoint Server 2007. There were three main gaps:

➤ No storage solution specifically optimized for large objects (as multimedia content usually is)

➤ No specific optimization for reducing the bandwidth usage and facilitating remote content delivery

➤ No out-of-the-box multimedia player component for multimedia content within SharePoint sites

These issues have been solved in Microsoft SharePoint 2010, creating new development opportunities on the platform, and solutions oriented toward a DAM. Out-of-the-box integration for multimedia content in the new SharePoint 2010 user interface offers several interesting features, allowing designers and developers to save time and work while implementing their solutions.

You shouldn't be deceived by the higher number of available resources. User interfaces should always be thoroughly designed, without underestimating each step of the design phase. An interface should be fully integrated with product logic, and designers should also consider several elements to plan on a proper size for storing systems — and pay attention to the performance of these systems.

You will learn more about solutions for these issues as this chapter progresses, as well as more about the technologies that allow you to fill these gaps.

Let's first dive into a bit more detail about issues related to storage, the user perception, and content presentation.

Storage

If you want to face every issue that complicates your solution, the first thing you must deal with is storage.

By design, all SharePoint content added by the user is logically stored in site collections. This has physical implications, because a site collection cannot be split over more than one Content Database. Therefore, if a user uploads a huge amount of content inside a specific site collection, this eventually leads to a rapid growth in the size of the Content Database.

From a management perspective, an excessive growth of a Content Database causes several issues:

➤ Manageability costs (longer backup/recovery times)

➤ Hardware costs (with SQL Server storage usually being more expensive)

➤ Performance issues (high load on SQL Server box, as well as not leveraging the value of SQL Server's query engine)

In such scenarios, Remote BLOB Storage (RBS) comes to the rescue! This is a new SQL Server 2008 and SQL Server 2008 Express feature, allowing you to store BLOB content outside of Content Databases, on the Database Server filesystem. SharePoint 2010 fully supports RBS because of a specific RBS Provider released alongside SQL Server 2008 R2 that makes the new data management totally transparent, both to the user interface and the object model. RBS will be discussed later in this chapter.

User Perception

The next issue to tackle is related to multimedia content fruition. Different from the storage issue, this point is directly perceived by the end user. If response times and content availability are not correctly thought out in advance, users may find themselves in front of a slow or hardly usable system, becoming unsatisfied and likely abandoning your application.

As a result of this, you may think about creating smaller-sized content, making publishing and distribution easier, especially in situations where bandwidth is not that large. However, you would also be forcing some restrictions in terms of quality for archived content, as well as in terms of the user experience for those who have high-speed connections.

Things will get more difficult when your solution is used both by users coming from the company network and by remote users connected through Internet. Solution planning and design will be much more complicated.

The primary goal, then, is about storing multimedia content in the system with the best possible quality. It should be the system itself, properly configured, that delivers content to all users in the best possible way, dynamically adapting the quality (that is, frame size, frame rate, and so on) to the available network conditions for that specific user in that specific time.

You could use Microsoft Internet Information Services (IIS) Bit Rate Throttling Module, available alongside Media Services 3.0 for IIS 7.0 (and above). This component adds to classic web server features a handful of elements that are typical in streaming servers. So, there's an optimization for multimedia content streaming based on the actual material quality (bit rate), allowing, at the same time, progressive downloading and viewing.

Overall performance could be optimized using more Web Front-End (WFE) servers in load balancing, and BLOB Cache to reduce traffic from WFE servers to SQL Server. When a Windows Server 2008 (R2) and Windows 7 infrastructure is available, you may implement `BranchCache`. This service enables you to spread `BranchCache` servers in each organization facility, allowing WAN users to access content easily and with great performance.

The Bit Rate Throttling Module, as well as the BLOB Cache and `BranchCache` features, will be detailed later in this chapter.

Content Presentation

A third issue was lack of a native, rich media player, which left room for custom implementations that enriched the SharePoint 2007 out-of-the-box features. These components have evolved over time, starting with an ActiveX-based player, and eventually becoming sophisticated Silverlight players embeddable into SharePoint pages as web parts.

In SharePoint 2010, this issue is solved through the out-of-the-box integration with Silverlight, and the availability of a multimedia player usable not only as a web part, but also as a component of web content management pages.

Later in this chapter, you'll find a thorough discussion of the media components as well as the data structures on which typical DAM solutions are based.

INFRASTRUCTURE DEPLOYMENT

This chapter does not address installation and configuration of a SharePoint 2010 basic infrastructure. Instead, the following discussions assume that installation and configuration have already been performed.

 For more information about SharePoint 2010 implementation, see http:// technet.microsoft.com/en-us/sharepoint/ee263917.aspx.

The discussion in this section examines the following:

➤ Implementation of the Remote BLOB Storage (RBS)

➤ Installation and configuration of the IIS 7 Bit Rate Throttling Module

➤ Use of the Disk-Based BLOB Cache feature

➤ Use of `BranchCache`

Figure 19-1 shows a possible architecture for the solution described here. Components for RBS data caching and storage have been added to the typical SharePoint 2010 farm infrastructure.

Remote BLOB Storage

RBS is one of the most anticipated and appreciated new features included in SharePoint 2010. Because of RBS and SQL Server 2008 availability in the farm, stored BLOB (binary data) contents can be separated from their description information (for example, filename, metadata). This component allows you to create and manage smaller Content Databases, straying really far from limits suggested by best practices in database growth (100 GB for each Content Database).

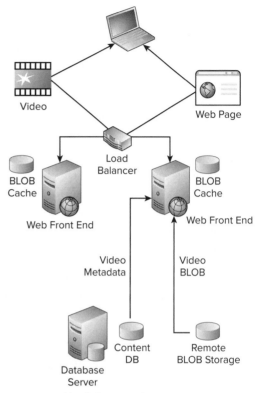

FIGURE 19-1: Solution architecture

 For more information on RBS, see the Technet sites at `http://technet` `.microsoft.com/en-us/library/ee748607(office.14).aspx` and `http://` `technet.microsoft.com/en-us/library/ee748649(office.14).aspx`.

BLOB contents are stored on the Content Database server filesystem in a fully transparent environment, which involves managing settings configured on SQL Server 2008.

 RBS Storage makes use of disk devices that should be accessible to SQL Server. In cluster environments, you should define a shared volume that can be accessed by every node in the cluster. For best performance, RBS and Content Databases should be defined on separate disks.

SharePoint 2010 can handle this feature because of a specific RBS Provider (downloadable from the Microsoft website, and released alongside SQL Server 2008 R2) that should be installed on each WFE server in the farm. The RBS Provider allows SharePoint 2010 to answer specific user requests, retrieving file metadata from the Content Database and binary contents from RBS. (A pointer to the file is added to the Content Database, which creates a link to the object stored on RBS.)

SQL Server 2008 allows administrators to determine which contents of a particular web application will use RBS, defining different levels of granularity for each Content Database, as shown in Figure 19-2.

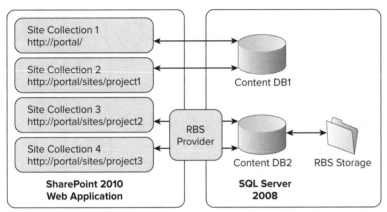

FIGURE 19-2: Partitioning logical diagram for web application contents

SharePoint 2010 allows system administrators to activate RBS features both on newly created Content Databases, and on already existing Databases, whose BLOB content will be moved on to RBS. These activities can be executed only after configuring SQL Server 2008, installing the RBS Provider on the Content Database server and each WFE server, and using specific PowerShell commands on SharePoint 2010 servers to properly enable these new features.

For more information on how to enable RBS Filestream on SQL Server 2008, see `http://go.microsoft.com/fwlink/?LinkID=166110&clcid=0x409.`

To install the RBS Provider, open a command prompt with Administrator privileges and execute the following command for each Content Database that should be extended to use RBS features. (The command should be entered in a single line. Here it is displayed on multiple lines for formatting reasons.)

```
msiexec /qn /lvx* rbs_install_log.txt /i RBS_X64.msi TRUSTSERVERCERTIFICATE=true
     FILEGROUP=PRIMARY DBNAME="WSS_Content"
     DBINSTANCE="DBInstanceName"
     FILESTREAMFILEGROUP=RBSFilestreamProvider
     FILESTREAMSTORENAME=FilestreamProvider_1
```

> *To download the 64-bit RBS Provider for SharePoint 2010, see* http://
> go.microsoft.com/fwlink/?LinkID=165839&clcid=0x409.

The RBS Provider should be implemented by executing another command from the command prompt with Administrator privileges:

```
msiexec /qn /lvx* rbs_install_log.txt /i RBS_X64.msi DBNAME="WSS_Content"
    DBINSTANCE="DBInstanceName" ADDLOCAL="Client,Docs,Maintainer,
    ServerScript,FilestreamClient,FilestreamServer"
```

To enable RBS, open the SharePoint 2010 Management Shell console from Programs group in the Start menu, and execute the following command:

```
$cdb = Get-SPContentDatabase -WebApplication http://sitename
$rbss = $cdb.RemoteBlobStorageSettings
$rbss.Installed()
$rbss.Enable()
$rbss.SetActiveProviderName($rbss.GetProviderNames()[0])
```

When an RBS solution has been employed, you should review the policies for backup/restore and disaster recovery in the SharePoint farm, and implement proper maintenance plans on SQL Server 2008. You should define the correct backup strategy according to the capabilities and features that the RBS Provider makes available, so that you can ensure a safe synchronization between the SQL Server Databases and the RBS Provider data.

> *Several third-party solutions on SharePoint 2007 are available to move BLOB contents on the filesystem, but the majority of them adopt External BLOB Storage (EBS), a legacy technology that Microsoft will discontinue. As of this writing, there are also several vendors that provide proprietary RBS solutions, often adding advanced capabilities (such as granular restore, flexible disaster recovery strategies, custom rules for BLOB externalization, cloud-computing support, and so on). For updated information about RBS solutions, see the author's blog at* http://blogs.devleap.com/igor/archive/2010/07/04/
> available-rbs-provider-for-sharepoint.aspx.

Bit Rate Throttling Module

The Microsoft IIS 7.0 Bit Rate Throttling Module is an IIS extension that can be downloaded and installed as a single component, or as part of the IIS 7 Media Services package (which also includes the Smooth Streaming, Live Smooth Streaming, and Web Playlist modules).

For a high-level overview of the IIS 7 Media Services features, see http://learn.iis.net/media. *If you want to download IIS 7 Media Services 3.0, see* http://go.microsoft.com/?linkid=9689915.

The installation should be performed on each WFE server in the farm, and, of course, administrators should use the proper component for the target infrastructure (which is a 64-bit environment). After a successful setup, you can use the IIS Manager console to define which websites should use Bit Rate Throttling features.

The Bit Rate Throttling module can act at different scopes (server, site, virtual directory, and file), and makes the following features available:

➤ *Fast Start* — This provides the capability to send the first part of the media file without rate limiting, so that the playback buffer in the player is filled, and playback can begin as soon as possible. (Most players try to pre-buffer a certain amount of the video, often 5 seconds, before starting playback.)

➤ *Disconnect detection* — When the client stops watching the video, the Bit Rate Throttling module detects the connection closure and stops sending the file.

➤ *Static throttling rates* — Built-in support is provided for configuring static throttling rates, as well as detecting the playback rate for several media formats. (This can be expanded to add other media formats through a set of configuration settings.)

 If you need a detailed step-by-step guide for configuration, see http://learn.iis.net/page.aspx/148/bit-rate-throttling-configuration-walkthrough/.

A LOOK AT STREAMING COMPONENTS

The IIS 7 Media Services extensions include specific modules dedicated to media content streaming, based on the standard HTTP protocol.

Traditionally, streaming technologies were based on User Datagram Protocol (UDP) as the transport protocol, and made use of application protocols specifically designed to support streaming of content over the network, such as the Real Time Streaming Protocol (RTSP).

During the last few years, UDP-based streaming has been abandoned in favor of an HTTP-based approach, which makes use of *progressive download*. Progressive download is just an HTTP file download, but it relies on the multimedia player being able to start the playback while the download is still in progress.

HTTP progressive download has several advantages when compared to traditional streaming. It is supported by web servers, and, thus, does not require dedicated (and usually expensive) streaming servers. Moreover, because it's based on HTTP, it can leverage HTTP proxy caches, and, obviously, it is much easier to make it work across firewalls.

HTTP progressive download also has some shortcomings, though. The most relevant is that it is a "dumb" protocol. If you want to see proof of this, you can try to view a video file from YouTube or MSN SoapBox, and pause the playback after some time. You will notice that the progress bar advances, and, under the hood, this means that the download is still in progress — even if the client has stopped the video playback! The Bit Rate Throttling Module mitigates this issue by detecting client disconnection and interrupting the download, although it cannot be considered a real streaming implementation.

It's clear that an optimal solution should try to provide the advantages of both the streaming protocols and the HTTP progressive download. This is achieved by HTTP-Based Adaptive Streaming.

HTTP-Based Adaptive Streaming is not a brand new protocol because it relies on HTTP and uses HTTP progressive download. The idea behind it is that multimedia content should be split into small chunks (typically, video chunks are 2 to 4 seconds long), which are then served to the client using HTTP standard download. The "adaptive" part comes into play when each chunk is saved on the server in different versions with different bitrates. During playback, the server is able to detect the client connection quality, and sends the chunk with the highest bitrate that is supported by that client at that particular moment.

IIS Media Services provides adaptive streaming capabilities with the Smooth Streaming and Live Smooth Streaming modules.

You should be aware that the Smooth Streaming and Live Smooth Streaming modules that come with the IIS 7 Media Services package are not natively integrated with content stored inside a SharePoint library. However, it's possible to develop custom solutions that add to SharePoint applications the capability to interact with content directly served by the (Live) Smooth Streaming endpoint.

For more information about the Smooth Streaming and Live Smooth Streaming components, see `http://www.iis.net/expand/SmoothStreaming`.

BLOB Cache

The Disk-Based BLOB Cache feature may greatly improve the performance of your solution, especially in situations with a high number of concurrent users asking for a relatively small number of large files. This is a very common situation in DAM projects.

This feature dramatically decreases the number of data requests from SQL Server, making data immediately available to users because a copy of these files is stored in the WFE server cache. This copy is generated when some content is requested by a user for the first time, and remains stored in the WFE server's disk cache until that content is modified, or when cache configuration settings will consider that expired.

Activating the Disk-Based BLOB Cache feature requires modifying the web application's `web.config` file on each WFE server, adding or modifying the following XML node:

```
<BlobCache location="C:\blobCache" path="\
    .(gif|jpg|png|css|js|wmv|wma|mp3)$"
    maxSize="100" max-age="86400" enabled="true"/>
```

Several settings can be defined through this configuration:

➤ The location where cache content copies will be stored on the filesystem.

➤ The file types that can be cached.

➤ The maximum disk space for cached files, expressed in gigabytes. (When space is full, old contents will be overwritten by new elements added to the cache.)

➤ The maximum duration (expressed in seconds) for objects in the client browser cache. (For example, if you set this parameter to 86,400 seconds, that means 24 hours.)

The last parameter allows administrators to enable or disable the cache. (The default value is disabled.)

Branch Cache

`BranchCache` in the Windows 7 and Windows Server 2008 R2 operating systems can help increase network responsiveness of centralized applications when accessed from remote offices, giving users in those offices the experience of working on your local area network (LAN). `BranchCache` also helps to reduce wide area network (WAN) utilization.

When `BranchCache` is enabled, a copy of data accessed from intranet web and file servers is cached locally within the branch office. When another client on the same network requests the file, the client downloads it from the local cache without downloading the same content across the WAN.

As shown in Figure 19-3, `BranchCache` can operate in one of two modes:

➤ *Distributed Cache* — Using a peer-to-peer architecture, Windows 7 client computers cache copies of files and send them directly to other Windows 7 client computers as they need them. Improving performance is as easy as enabling `BranchCache` on your Windows 7 client and Windows Server 2008 R2 computers. Distributed Cache is especially beneficial for branch offices that do not have a local server.

➤ *Hosted Cache* — Using a client/server architecture, Windows 7 client computers cache content to a computer on the local network running Windows Server 2008 R2, known as the *Hosted Cache*. Other clients that need the same content retrieve it directly from the Hosted Cache. The Hosted Cache computer can run the Server Core installation option of Windows Server 2008 R2, and can also host other applications.

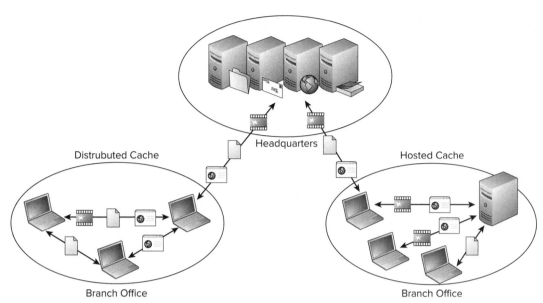

Distrubuted Cache

Headquarters

Hosted Cache

Branch Office

Branch Office

FIGURE 19-3: Logical diagram for BranchCache

BranchCache can improve the performance of applications that use one of the following protocols:

➤ *HTTP and HTTPS* — The protocols used by web browsers and many other applications (such as Internet Explorer, Windows Media, SharePoint, and more).

➤ *Server Message Block (SMB), including signed SMB traffic* — This is the protocol used for shared folders.

BranchCache only retrieves data from a server when the client is requesting it. It is a passive cache, thus it's not going to increase WAN utilization. BranchCache only caches read requests and, thus, will not interfere with a user saving a file.

BranchCache improves the responsiveness of common network applications accessing intranet servers across slow links. It does not require any infrastructure. Thus, you can improve the performance of remote networks simply by deploying Windows 7 to client computers and Windows Server 2008 R2 to server computers, enabling BranchCache at the end.

BranchCache seamlessly works alongside network security technologies, including Secure Socket Layers (SSL), Server Message Block (SMB) Signing, and end-to-end IPsec. You can use BranchCache to reduce network bandwidth utilization and improve application performance, even if the content is encrypted.

 For more information about BranchCache *services, see* http://www.microsoft .com/windowsserver2008/en/us/branch-office.aspx *and* http://technet .microsoft.com/en-us/network/dd425028.aspx.

DESIGNING THE DATA FOUNDATION

Behind every Content Management System (CMS), there should be a proper infrastructure and content hierarchy design. Applications dealing with digital data should follow that requirement.

SharePoint Server 2010 includes several new content types and libraries for multimedia content management. Taking advantage of these innovations allows you to focus design activities on specific project requirements, with a common foundation ensuring main features, both from a structural and a user interface perspective.

Planning Asset Content Types

Data structures provided by SharePoint 2010 for multimedia content management are logically distributed through a Feature that can be enabled from site collection configuration, whose definition can be examined in `[SharePointRoot]\Template\Features\AssetLibrary`. During SharePoint Server 2010 installation, that Feature is associated with the majority of available site templates through a farm-level stapling Feature (`[SharePointRoot]\Template\Features\BaseSiteStapling`).

> *Sites based on the Blank (STS#1) template behave differently in relation to the Asset Library Feature. The stapling Feature doesn't associate the Asset Library Feature to template STS#1, so blank sites created as top-level sites can't take advantage of its multimedia capabilities. On the other hand, blank sites created as subwebs will "inherit" their capabilities from top-level sites containing them.*

Despite implications from its name, the Asset Library Feature does not include just definitions for list templates. Once enabled, several elements are created:

➤ Content types for images, audio, and video

➤ Specific fields for multimedia content

Image, audio, and video content types are linked to document libraries created from the Asset Library template, in agreement with the list definition. Users take advantage of these content types to organize and store their multimedia content. From a hierarchical perspective, image, audio, and video content types share a common parent, represented by the Asset content type, which inherits its properties from the generic Document.

The availability of a basic content type provides a great advantage, because it's possible to perform operations (such as rollup, aggregations, workflow, or policies) on all digital content, regardless of the form.

Table 19-1 lists all available fields in each content type.

Even though it's possible to use the out-of-the-box multimedia content types, you should carefully plan your own content type definitions — best practices used when designing content type hierarchies also apply to DAM systems!

TABLE 19-1: Available Fields for Content Types

FIELD	AUDIO	IMAGE	VIDEO	DESCRIPTION
Author	X	X	X	Indicates the user who uploaded the asset into the SharePoint library.
Copyright	X	X	X	Indicates the copyright that is applied to the asset, if any.
Credit		X		Indicates the person acknowledged for creating the asset (for example, a photographer, a producer, and so on).
Data Rate	X		X	Indicates the data rate (in kilobytes per second, or KB/s).
Description	X	X	X	Indicates a description about the asset.
Frame Height			X	Indicates the frame height (in pixels).
Frame Width			X	Indicates the frame width (in pixels).
Frame Rate			X	Indicates the frame rate (in KB/s).
Frame Size			X	Indicates the frame size in pixels.
Height		X		Indicates the height of the image (in pixels).
Length	X			Indicates the duration of the audio file (in seconds).
Preview Image URL			X	Contains the URL of the preview image for a given video file.
Width		X		Indicates the width of the image in pixels.

You should carefully evaluate the available approaches for the creation and provisioning of custom content types. Although it's possible to use the browser or SharePoint Designer to create custom fields and content types, you should use content types deployed through Features and solutions, because this allows for better packaging and reuse.

Delivering Content through Asset Libraries

After designing a proper structure for content, you should create libraries to contain them. Using a standard document library, and having the Asset content types explicitly associated with it, is a suitable approach, because it ensures consistency in the data structure. But this would lead to a very low level of customization from the user-interface perspective. Most DAM solutions need features such as video preview, inline players, or image thumbnails.

These features are already available, without any development effort, using the Asset Library as base template. The Asset Library is just a simple document library with Image, Audio, and Video content types associated.

The Asset Library also contains a specific View definition used for multimedia content presentation, which features the following:

➤ Thumbnail viewing for images

➤ Preview Images visualization for Audio and Video content types

➤ A "live fly-out" (enabled with a mouse-over on an asset thumbnail) that displays details about the element, and a box allowing its fruition (a player for audio and video, or a larger thumbnail for images)

➤ "Inline" fruition for audio and video, taking advantage of client-side components provided by Silverlight 3.0, with a possible "downgrade" to a preview image when the Silverlight player is not available on the client system

Figure 19-4 shows a fly-out and thumbnails.

FIGURE 19-4: Fly-out and thumbnails

You can further examine the Asset Library by digging into the list schema, available at `[SharePointRoot]\TEMPLATE\FEATURES\AssetLibrary\AssetLibrary\schema.xml`.

An external XSLT file takes advantage of the new XSLT List View web part. The XSLT style sheet, available at `[SharePointRoot]\TEMPLATE\LAYOUTS\XSL\AssetPicker.xsl`, can be used as a good starting point for subsequent interface customizations.

CONFIGURING AND DEVELOPING THE USER EXPERIENCE

DAM solutions often extend far beyond the features provided by the Asset Library. Customizations are not limited to graphical and web design layouts, but may involve tasks such as the aggregation and the integration of multimedia content in specific pages or page templates.

SharePoint Server 2010 provides several tools and techniques that make this customization possible and, sometimes, very easy to accomplish. Following are the most significant components that you can use to perform these customizations:

➤ A Media web part, based on Microsoft Silverlight 3.0

➤ A media field and a media field control

➤ The ubiquitous Content Query web part

➤ A JavaScript API to manipulate the media player

The following sections provide an overview for these components, identifying usage and applicability scenarios for each.

Using the Out-of-the-Box Multimedia Web Part

Multimedia content distribution through web pages should deal with HTML specifications and with the way the current browsers implement them. Though images are supported and viewable through the use of a standard tag (for example, an IMG tag in an HTML code block), audio and video content often need a more sophisticated presentation inside the web page itself, which is not possible using HTML capabilities. By using specific browser extensions and the required markup to load and configure these extensions, though, a web designer can create interactive players to provide a rich user experience.

The use of specific server-side components such as ASP.NET controls (which take care of the client-side markup) is a great accelerator for site-building activities. In SharePoint Server 2010, this is the role of the Media web part.

Availability

The Media web part becomes available after enabling Publishing Features at the site collection level. This dependency results in part from the tight integration among multimedia components used in an Internet-facing portal, as you'll see in the following discussion.

If you consider that the Media web part provisioning in the Site Collection Web Part Gallery depends on the Publishing Resources Feature — which is also distributing other resources (for example, the Content Query web part) — a more specific intervention for enabling the Media web part could be required.

In scenarios where the Publishing Features can't be activated, you could do the following:

➤ Manually add the web part definition (.webpart file) to the Web Part Gallery, possibly using self-discovery Features

➤ Implement a Feature to perform provisioning for a handcrafted .webpart file through a Module element

Configuration

After it is available in a Site Collection Web Part Gallery, the Media web part can be added to pages through the SharePoint 2010 ribbon interface. By default, the Media web part is available from the Media and Content category on the ribbon.

The Media web part features several customizable properties:

➤ `MediaSource` — This contains the URL of the multimedia resource to play. You can use files from a user's computer (the user is prompted to choose a SharePoint library where the file will be uploaded), SharePoint, or an external URL.

➤ `PreviewImageSource` — This contains the URL of an image acting as an audio or video preview when playing has been stopped. A default image, available in `Style Library/Media Player/VideoPreview.png`, is shown when this field is empty.

➤ `AutoStart` — When set to `true`, multimedia content starts playing when the page is displayed. (If the property is not set, users can press Play on the embedded media player.)

➤ `Loop` — When set to `true`, multimedia contents are repeated indefinitely.

➤ `Style` — This allows you to choose the embedded media player style.

➤ `Height/Width` — These are the controls for the visible media player area size.

➤ `Lock Aspect Ratio` — This property locks the player's height/width ratio.

Listed properties are configurable through the SharePoint 2010 ribbon interface, as shown in Figure 19-5, which can be considered as an alternative to the usual toolpane.

FIGURE 19-5: Media web part configuration ribbon

The Media web part streams content through a multimedia player created with Microsoft Silverlight 3.0 technology. This choice assures an optimal content fruition, and opens some customization scenarios.

Media Web Part Internals

The Media web part is a wrapper control that generates the HTML markup required to view and use a Silverlight application in a web page.

During the server-side rendering phase, properties set by users are considered to build an `application/x-silverlight-2` type HTML `object` tag, as shown here:

```
<object id="…"
type="application/x-silverlight-2"
data="data:application/x-silverlight-2,"
```

```
        width="100%" height="100%">
<param name="source" value="/_layouts/clientbin/mediaplayer.xap"/>
<param name="enableHtmlAccess" value="true"/>
<param name="windowless" value="true" />
<param name="background" value="#80808080" />
<param name="initParams"
      value=",previewImageSource=/Style%20Library/
      Media%20Player/VideoPreview.png,autoPlay=true" />
```

The Silverlight plug-in is configured to load a XAP (`MediaPlayer.xap`) file, available at `[SharePointRoot]\Template\Layouts\ClientBin`, which is responsible for the multimedia content rendering. `MediaPlayer.xap` receives some initialization values through the `initParams` parameter. In addition to the multimedia file URL, these include user-inserted properties defining the playing mode (for example, the `AutoPlay` property is set to `true`).

Multimedia Field Type

In some Web Content Management solutions (or, more generally, in SharePoint portals using Publishing Features and page layout mechanisms), multimedia content integration is made easier by the availability of a field type dedicated to audio and video. This field is shown to the final user with the name "Rich media data for publishing," as shown in Figure 19-6.

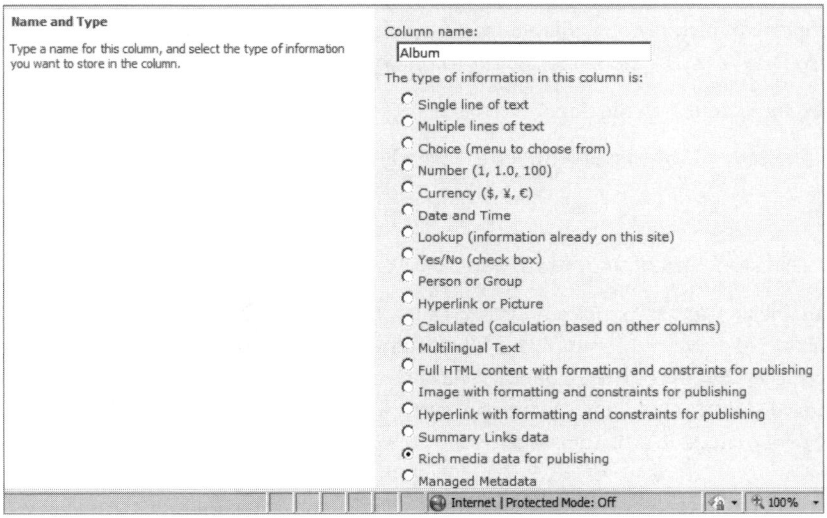

FIGURE 19-6: The Media field

A media field control (`MediaFieldControl`) can be included in a page layout by using SharePoint Designer, or directly adding the proper tag in the page, to obtain something similar to the following:

```
<PublishingWebControls:MediaFieldControl
    id="MediaFieldControl1"
    FieldName="…"
    runat="server"
    AutoPlay="True"
```

```
        Loop="False"
        DisplayMode="Overlay"
        Height="500px"
        Width="400px"
        PresentationLocked="True">
</PublishingWebControls:MediaFieldControl>
```

The inclusion of the field through SharePoint Designer automatically adds an ASP.NET `Register` directive, needed for using the `MediaFieldControl` in the page. If you must manually write the ASP.NET markup, you should explicitly include the following snippet:

```
<%@ Register Tagprefix="PublishingWebControls"
    Namespace="Microsoft.SharePoint.Publishing.WebControls"
    Assembly="Microsoft.SharePoint.Publishing, Version=14.0.0.0,
    Culture=neutral, PublicKeyToken=71e9bce111e9429c" %>
```

Configurable properties for `MediaFieldControl` are similar to the ones already discussed for the Media web part. The majority of them — especially the ones connected to the playing/viewing mode (`Size`, `Loop`, `AutoPlay`) — can be overwritten by the content editors when creating pages.

When editors must follow a standard layout (for example, when a shared and uniform branding should be produced), the `PresentationLocked` property should be set to `True`. This disables the corresponding controls in the Media ribbon tab.

Another important property (which is not available from the Media web part customization interface) is the `DisplayMode` property. `DisplayMode` can be set to one of the following values:

➤   `Inline` (the player is added to the page)

➤   `Overlay` (the player is added to a layer over the page)

➤   `Full Screen`

Take a look at the internal structure of `MediaFieldControl` to fully understand how it works.

Its field definition, available at `[SharePointRoot]\Template\Xml\fldtypes_publishing.xml`, highlights how the `MediaFieldControl` is simply a Note (multiline text) field specialization, represented in the server object model through `Microsoft.SharePoint.Publishing.Fields.MediaField` class. `MediaFieldControl` doesn't show any specific properties, delegating its functions to accessory classes, `Microsoft.SharePoint.Publishing.WebControls.MediaFieldControl` and `Microsoft.SharePoint.Publishing.Fields.MediaFieldValue`, each of which is respectively responsible for field rendering and internal data representation.

Data flow (from user editing to the multimedia player visualization on the pages) is a sequential process that includes the following:

➤   *Inclusion of a media field in a content type or list/document library* — Media fields can be referenced both by lists and document libraries, and are often used on page libraries, properly associated with a Publishing content type.

➤   *Item editing, through edit form or Publishing page customization* — This interaction (as already mentioned for the Media web part) is performed by using the ribbon. When settings are saved, the client side stores those settings using a hidden HTML field. This field includes a serialized version of user-defined parameters (media URL, style, visible area size, and so on).

➤ *Item viewing, through the server-side* `MediaFieldControl` — Immediately before the rendering stage, this control deserializes all the properties stored in the hidden HTML field, instantiating a new `MediaFieldValue` object. This object is passed as a parameter to the `MediaFieldControl` method, which is finally responsible for the generation of the proper HTML markup.

During the editing stage, the tight connection between `MediaFieldControl` and the Media web part becomes quite clear, because both share the same mode and tab within the ribbon. When you analyze how those two components work, their connection becomes even more clear. `MediaFieldControl` doesn't have a specific rendering logic, but acts as container for a child control of Media Web Part type. Data flows from the container control to the child control through the previously loaded `MediaFieldValue` instance.

This extremely tight dependency explains why the Media web part has been included in SharePoint Server 2010 Publishing Features, even if it would also make sense in situations different from the usual Web Content Management application.

Content Query Web Part

The Content Query web part is definitely one of the "premium" tools for creation of Web Content Management applications. Available after the Publishing Features have been activated, the Content Query web part has been greatly improved in SharePoint 2010. Now it's even more flexible and simple to configure than before.

Several improvements have been made, as a proof of the central role played by DAM. Multimedia content rendering can be directly accessed by users from the Web Part configuration toolpane.

Specifically related to DAM applications is the "Play media links in browse" Boolean property. When it's set to `true`, a small client-side script is generated and added to the page. This script attaches all media links on the page to a Silverlight player, whose display mode is, by default, set to Overlay, thus providing a smart "click-and-play" behavior.

So, there is no reason to edit `ItemStyle.xslt` to change the rendering logic. Although it is still possible, it's no longer the only available way to alter rendering logic!

Designing Custom Skins for Multimedia Players

Multimedia components discussed thus far provide a set of branding and customization modes, useful for changing the user interface look according to project guidelines. Most notably, the multimedia player on which the Media web part and the `MediaFieldControl` are based supports skins. Developers and web designers can take advantage of this skinning mode to create various different styles.

The following logic acts as a foundation for retrieving and using skins:

➤ During the editing stage, the ribbon client-side code extracts a list of XAML files contained in a `Style Library` folder (`Style Library/Media Player`), allowing the user to choose a skin from a drop-down control list.

➤ During the rendering stage, through the setting of an HTML object tag parameter, the selected skin is used to customize the player appearance.

The realization of a custom skin corresponds, therefore, to the creation of a XAML file following the `Silverlight MediaPlayer.xap` application interface, which is going to take advantage of it. The best approach in this situation is to modify one of the already available skin files for subsequent approximations, because it includes the structural markup needed by the media player to work.

A XAML file can be edited manually or through an XML editor. You should check out Microsoft Expression Blend, which has advanced tools and an easier-to-use WYSIWYG interface. Follow these steps to customize media player skins using Microsoft Expression Blend:

1. Open Microsoft Expression Blend and create a new Silverlight project. (The project will act as a container for the XAML file, which will be edited.)

2. Add the XAML file used as a foundation for the customization process to the project. The Expression Blend designer will not resolve the `clr-namespace` mapping used to define the `TargetType` property. Fortunately, this property can be temporarily removed, and adding it back before publishing should be enough to make it work again.

3. Now you can customize the skin. The Expression Blend interface simultaneously shows a preview area and a markup area, providing inexperienced users with an intuitive editor that doesn't require them to understand generated code. A major level of detail can be reached, but only with manual and expert editing on the generated XAML file.

Figure 19-7 shows what happens when a logo has been added next to the title of a multimedia resource.

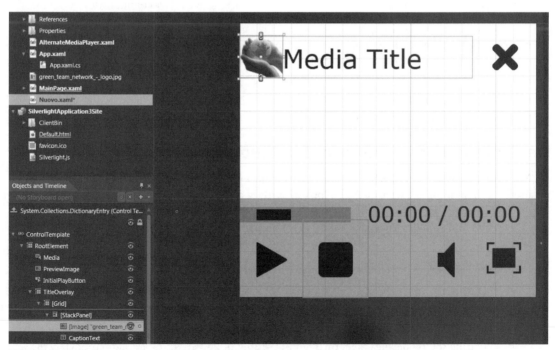

FIGURE 19-7: Custom media player skin

A XAML `Image` tag has been used in this situation. Because the image URL should point to a resource accessible during the web rendering phase, usually the image is loaded inside a SharePoint document library during the Publishing step.

Once the file has been saved and then loaded in `Style Library/Media Player`, the user can select the skin (if the used field control `PresentationLocked` property hasn't been set to `True`).

Media Player Advanced Configuration

As you have seen, when properly connected to multimedia resources, using the Media web part or the `MediaFieldControl` allows for a good interactivity with audio and video, especially because of the embedded features provided by the Silverlight player. Because interaction occurs through controls managed by the player, the work for web designers is very simple, because they can rely upon a solid component, and just worry about page aggregation and presentation logic.

On the other hand, several situations exist in which a higher control on operations is needed.

Just think about when you need to include the player in a page template, but also employ external user interface elements to play content. Or, consider a scenario when, in an analog manner, users may choose from a list of multimedia content, and fruition occurs after selection from that list. In both of these situations, you should be able to interact with the multimedia player "from the outside," possibly taking advantage of APIs featuring an easy-to-use interface.

Fortunately, these APIs exist. A handful of JavaScript functions become available after including a file (`MediaPlayer.js`) found in `[SharePointRoot]`\Template\Layouts\MediaPlayer.js. To enable that, the following script reference should be added to the HTML head tag:

```
<script type="text/javascript" src="/_layouts/MediaPlayer.js" />
```

The choice of a client-side object model makes for several customization possibilities:

➤ *Content mash-up* — Multimedia items are played through the Media Player and retrieved from external sources (RSS, SharePoint Lists, REST sources, and so on).

➤ *Creation of dynamic web user interfaces* — These are based on an asynchronous communication paradigm (Ajax).

➤ *General use of web part tools* — These include the Content Editor web part, XSLT ListView web part, and Content Query web part. These do not require development and distribution of custom server-side components (but a good knowledge of JavaScript is obviously recommended).

To briefly describe functionalities offered by these JavaScript APIs, use the following HTML block as a starting point:

```
<div id="songsList">
<ul>
<li>
    <a href="/AlbumTracks/Track01.mp3">First Track</a>
</li>
<li>
    <a href="/AlbumTracks/Track02.mp3">Second Track</a>
</li>
```

```
</ul>
</div>
<div id="host"></div>
```

This is static HTML code, but, as previously noted, it could be generated dynamically through aggregation and data access web parts such as the XSLT List View web part or the Content Query web part.

Thus, you can create a client-side media player component with a simple call like the following:

```
var host = document.getElementById('host');
mediaPlayer.createMediaPlayer(
        host,
        host.id,
        '400px',
        '300px',
        {
            displayMode: 'Inline',
            mediaSource:'',
            previewImageSource:'',
            autoPlay: false,
            loop: false,
            mediaFileExtensions:'mp3;',
            silverlightMediaExtensions:'mp3;'
        }
    );
```

The createMediaPlayer function receives the following as input:

➤   A reference to a container HTML element (in the example, the host object is a div)

➤   The size of the media player

➤   Needed playing parameters (in this case, they will be passed to the Silverlight player as initialization parameters, through generated <params> attributes)

Also, the MediaPlayer.js library offers easy ways to automatically connect a MediaPlayer creation script to a series of links. This call is extremely simple:

```
var list = document.getElementById('songsList');
mediaPlayer.attachToMediaLinks(songsList, ['mp3']);
```

This function extracts every HTML anchor contained in the input node, adding to each a JavaScript code block associated with the client-side click event. The added code creates and displays a media player instance in Overlay mode. As mentioned previously, the rendering of Content Query web part, when the property "Play media links in browser" has been set to True, makes use of this feature.

The interaction with the player is supported by a set of playing control features. The first thing to do is to get an instance of the MediaPlayer that should be controlled:

```
var panel = document.getElementById("host")
var players = panel.getElementsByTagName("object");
var playerToControl = players[0].Content.MediaPlayer;
```

After getting the `MediaPlayer` instance, developers can set a data source or a viewing template:

```
playerToControl.MediaSource = 'SomeSong.mp3';
playerToControl.TemplateSource = 'SomeTemplate.xaml';
```

It is also possible to manage the typical controls of a multimedia player:

```
playerToControl.Play();
playerToControl.Pause();
playerToControl.Stop();
```

Fast-forward and rewind controls are also available. To display them, set the property `PositionMilliseconds`, as shown in the following example:

```
p.PositionMilliseconds += 10000; //FWD
p.PositionMilliseconds -= 10000; //REW
```

DESIGNING CUSTOM ASSET LIBRARY VIEW STYLES

Even if the Thumbnail view defined by the Asset Library template is practical and complete, some-times it's worth customizing its user interface in a more advanced way to provide, for example, some typical features such as Slide Show or Image Gallery. In these situations, out-of-the-box tools are not enough. You can work on more specific customizations that are created through SharePoint Designer, or other editing and web design tools.

A suitable approach requires using the Content Query web part or other content aggregation tools. But sometimes the only need is to define a View directly usable from the Asset Library interface, choosing from the View selector control. Though it was rather complex in the previous versions of SharePoint, this operation is much easier now, because of the inclusion of the XSLT List View web part.

Although this discussion does not delve into too much detail about this component, it is important to underline that a View rendering can now be defined through an XSLT transformation. When a custom style sheet is implemented and then used through an XSLT List View web part, default XSLT transformations can be useful when combining available templates with their own ones (using the XSLT `call-template` instruction), or completely replacing them (through a template override).

Consider a practical example that shows how a custom Asset Library View style (with the capabil-ity of visualizing available images in Slide Show mode) is created. For this example, the following operations are performed:

➤ Create the static markup needed for the slide show effect to work

➤ Make the markup parametric, taking advantage of the HTML-generation features provided by the XSLT List View web part

➤ Save the style sheet and apply it to the libraries that should be customized

Because this example does not focus on web design elements (this is a task that should be left to web design professionals), consider the creation of the static HTML markup as a prerequisite.

The following code snippet shows the HTML markup for a library called Open Source Lightbox, whose files were previously loaded in the Style Library:

```
<script type="text/javascript" src="/Style Library/js/prototype.js">
</script>
<script type="text/javascript"
    src="/Style Library/js/scriptaculous.js?load=effects,builder">
</script>
<script type="text/javascript" src="/Style Library/js/lightbox.js">
</script>

<link rel="stylesheet" href="css/lightbox.css" type="text/css" media="screen" />

<a href="img1.jpg" rel="lightbox" title="caption 1"><img .. ></a>
<a href="img2.jpg" rel="lightbox" title="caption 2"><img .. ></a>
<a href="img3.jpg" rel="lightbox" title="caption 3"><img .. ></a>
```

 Needed files and support documentation are available on the project website at http://www.lokeshdhakar.com/projects/lightbox2.

This HTML snippet should be dynamically generated by an XSLT transformation, which is able to fetch a data set from any Asset Library it will be applied to, as shown in the following code snippet:

```
<xsl:stylesheet xmlns:x="http://www.w3.org/2001/XMLSchema"
  xmlns:d="http://schemas.microsoft.com/sharepoint/dsp"
  version="1.0" exclude-result-prefixes="xsl msxsl ddwrt x d asp SharePoint ddwrt2"
  xmlns:ddwrt="http://schemas.microsoft.com/WebParts/v2/DataView/runtime"
  xmlns:asp="http://schemas.microsoft.com/ASPNET/20"
  xmlns:xsl="http://www.w3.org/1999/XSL/Transform"
  xmlns:msxsl="urn:schemas-microsoft-com:xslt"
  xmlns:SharePoint="Microsoft.SharePoint.WebControls"
  xmlns:ddwrt2="urn:frontpage:internal">

  <xsl:import href="/_layouts/xsl/main.xsl"/>
  <xsl:output method="html" indent="no"/>

  <xsl:template match="/">
    <div id="images">
      <xsl:for-each select="/dsQueryResponse/Rows/Row">
        <xsl:variable name="FullImage" select="@FileRef"/>
        <xsl:variable name="ImageTitle" select="@Title"/>
        <a rel="lightbox" href="{$FullImage}" title="{$ImageTitle}">
          <xsl:call-template name="RenderThumbnail">
            <xsl:with-param name="thisNode" select="."/>
            <xsl:with-param name="subDir" select="'_t'"/>
            <xsl:with-param name="resizeSquareSideLength" select="100"/>
          </xsl:call-template>
        </a>
      </xsl:for-each>
    </div>
  </xsl:template>
</xsl:stylesheet>
```

Notice that including small size images (in thumbnail version) is performed through an XSLT template call to `RenderThumbnail`, which is defined in system files and is available after the `<xsl:import>` directive has been executed. Newly created styles readily become available to SharePoint Designer users, who could apply them to standard visualizations in a few clicks.

The following operations can be performed:

➤ Associate the `ListViewStyle` content type to the Style Library.

➤ Load the XSLT file in the `XSL Style Sheets` folder, setting the content type attribute to `ListViewStyle`.

➤ Configure document metadata to turn it into a SharePoint Designer `ListView` style, as shown in Figure 19-8.

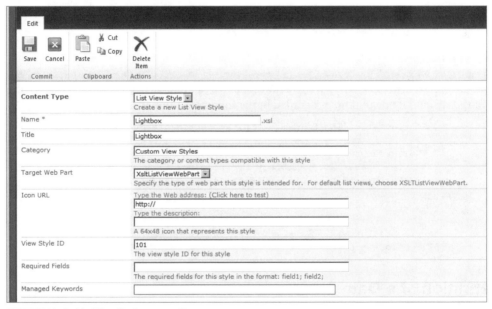

FIGURE 19-8: ListViewStyle properties

Finally, you should create a View for the Asset Library you want to personalize, and finish the customization using SharePoint Designer. You just need to select the View, highlight the `XsltListViewWebPart` tag from the code pane, and the customized style will appear in the View Styles group. Its application will require just a single click!

PACKAGING THE SOLUTION IN A CUSTOM SITE DEFINITION

Throughout this chapter, you have learned about several features connected to the customization of a DAM application. Regardless of the number and type of customization changes, you should always adopt a rational approach in development. This often entails reusable objects that can be distributed through packaging-and-deploy tools provided by SharePoint.

So, take a look at the steps required to enclose some of the proposed customizations into a set of Features, which can be distributed through the Solution (WSP) mechanism, and used during the deployment stage in the target infrastructure. This activity will not be explored in a fully exhaustive way. The goal here is merely to provide a starting point for building site templates based on SharePoint 2010 DAM functionalities, showing how some of the most frequently used features are created.

Asset Library Feature Activation

Site columns, content types, and the Asset Library list definition are enabled by automatically activating the Asset Library Feature. You can use Feature stapling in order to have the Asset Library Feature automatically activated on each site based on a specific site definition, as detailed in the following snippet:

```
<Elements xmlns="http://schemas.microsoft.com/sharepoint/">

<FeatureSiteTemplateAssociation ID="4BCCCD62-DCAF-46dc-A7D4-E38277EF33F4"
    TemplateName="<Template Name>" />

</Elements>
```

Or, if you are writing your own site definition, you can reference the Asset Library Feature directly in the custom site definition, as detailed in the following snippet:

```
    <Configuration ID="0" Name="DigitalAssetsManagementSite">
...
    <SiteFeatures>
      <!-- Enable Asset Library Creation for site collection -->
      <Feature ID="4BCCCD62-DCAF-46dc-A7D4-E38277EF33F4"></Feature>
    </SiteFeatures>
    <WebFeatures>
...
    </WebFeatures>
    </Configuration>
```

Definition of a Data Structure

After designing a proper data structure, you should definitely add custom site columns and custom content type definitions using custom Features referenced by the site definition. The following example shows a custom content type definition for `SampleVideo`. In this particular situation, the reference to a custom site column `Additional Notes` has been added:

```
    <Field
     ID="{FEC8ED03-B9BF-4835-89CB-5943051AD426}"
     Name="AdditionalNotes"
     DisplayName="Additional Notes"
     Type="Note"
     UnlimitedLengthInDocumentLibrary="True"
     Group="Real World SharePoint 2010">
    </Field>

    <ContentType ID="0x0101009148F5A04DDD49CBA7127AADA5
        FB792B00291D173ECE694D56B19D11
```

```
        1489C4369D00d85be58bf384438993f592c9b44828a3"
    Name="SampleVideo"
    Group="Real World SharePoint 2010"
    Description="A custom Video Content Type"
    Version="0">
    <FieldRefs>
      <FieldRef ID="{FEC8ED03-B9BF-4835-89CB-5943051AD426}"/>
    </FieldRefs>
</ContentType>
```

Creation of Asset Library Instances

When creating an Asset Library instance, without further customizations other than the ones available in the initial list definition, two different approaches are available.

First, a list instance can be created through a Feature, subsequently referred in the site definition manifest:

```
<ListInstance
  Title="AssetLibraryInstance"
  OnQuickLaunch="TRUE"
  TemplateType="851"
  FeatureId="4bcccd62-dcaf-46dc-a7d4-e38277ef33f4"
  Url="Lists/AssetLibraryInstance"
  Description="A simple asset library">
</ListInstance>
```

On the other hand, if you are writing a custom site definition, the list instance creation operation can be added to the onet.xml file, as in the following example:

```
<Configuration ID="0" Name="DigitalAssetsManagementSite">
...
  <Lists>
    <List
      Title="AssetLibraryInstance"
      Type="851"
      FeatureId="4bcccd62-dcaf-46dc-a7d4-e38277ef33f4"
      Url="Lists/AssetLibraryInstance"
      Description="A simple asset library">
    </List>
  </Lists>
...
</Configuration>
```

Definition of Custom Asset Libraries

A custom list definition should be implemented in more complex situations where a customized Asset Library template can be defined (for example, when an association with previously defined content types should be added, or when specific views and functionalities should become available). Implementing a custom list definition could require a lot of time, depending on customizations being included.

The first step is to configure some properties for the list, taking a few cues from the out-of-the-box Asset Library list definition:

```
<List
  xmlns:ows="Microsoft SharePoint"
  xmlns="http://schemas.microsoft.com/sharepoint/"
  Title="SampleVideoList"
  Direction="$Resources:Direction;"
  Url="SampleVideoList"
  BaseType="1"
  EnableContentTypes="TRUE"
  EnableThumbnails="TRUE"
  ThumbnailSize="128"
  WebImageWidth="320"
  WebImageHeight="320">
```

Next, the following block can be used to associate the "Sample Video" content type with this custom list definition:

```
<MetaData>
  <ContentTypes>
    <ContentTypeRef
        ID="0x0101009148F5A04DDD49CBA7127AADA5FB
        792B00291D173ECE694D56B19D111489C4369D00d85be
        58bf384438993f592c9b44828a3" />
  </ContentTypes>
...
</MetaData>
```

Finally, for view customization, you can use some of the techniques presented earlier in the chapter in the discussion about customizing Asset Library view styles. One of the already existing View nodes can be used (or a new one can be added), including a reference to the XSLT, which will be responsible for the custom rendering logic, as shown in the following example:

```
<View
  BaseViewID="15"
  Type="HTML"
  Name="LightboxView"
  WebPartZoneID="Main"
  MobileView="FALSE"
  MobileDefaultView="FALSE"
  DisplayName="LightBox"
  SetupPath="pages\viewpage.aspx"
  Url="Lightbox.aspx"
  ImageUrl="/_layouts/images/dlicon.png">

  <XslLink>Lightbox.xsl</XslLink>

  <ParameterBindings>
...
  </ParameterBindings>
  <ViewFields>
    <FieldRef Name="Title"/>
    <FieldRef Name="FileLeafRef"/>
  </ViewFields>
  <Query/>
```

```
<RowLimit Paged="TRUE">30</RowLimit>
<Toolbar Type="Standard"/>
</View>
```

 In this context, the XSLT transformation isn't distributed in the Style Library, but should be copied on each WFE server's filesystem, at [SharePointRoot]\Templates\Layouts\XSL\Lightbox.xsl.

NOTES FROM THE FIELD

To wrap up this chapter, let's take a look at a set of suggestions and good practices that come from the authors' experiences in real-world projects.

Of course, every consideration should be evaluated on the specific application scenario that you are approaching. No general rule exists that applies to all circumstances!

Choosing a Farm Topology

You should collect all the information derived from the capacity planning phase, and try to improve your solutions with the new features offered by the SharePoint 2010 architecture.

For example, you could rely on the Managed Metadata Service application, taking advantage of Service Applications features such as cross-farm sharing and redundancy capabilities, while using these shared taxonomies to tag multimedia content, making it findable either online or offline.

You should also consider Search service requirements for the SharePoint farm. This could encourage designers to create a more complex topology, with WFE servers carrying the higher burden, as shown in Figure 19-9. So, the WFE servers should be the first receiving balance and redundancy.

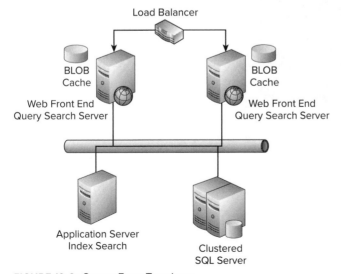

FIGURE 19-9: Server Farm Topology

A high reliability requires that you pay careful attention to data availability, thinking about a SQL Server 2008 infrastructure in a cluster environment with shared storage (for example, Storage Area Network, or SAN).

Also, it's very important to think about the communication between your servers. It's easy to imagine that connections and communications between servers in the farm could become a bottleneck that should be monitored and optimized.

You should implement a network segment dedicated to the solution infrastructure, eliminating possible disturbances and network broadcasts. You should also add at least a Domain Controller Server to this subnetwork to provide complete efficiency to each operation that requires authentication. Communication between servers should be facilitated on a network infrastructure that has a dedicated bandwidth of at least 1 Gbps, through the use of specific switches.

Remember that I/O on disk is the main culprit for slowdown in SharePoint communications. So, pay careful attention to the shared network storage access speed. Fast systems such as SAN with fiber-optic connections should be preferred.

Monitoring the Bandwidth Usage

Bandwidth usage should be deeply analyzed during the planning phase, and should be supported by specific stress tests alongside tuning activities when the system has already gone live.

During those tests, the bandwidth usage of WFE servers could be monitored through several diagnostic tools, ranging from the Windows Task Manager Networking charts (Figure 19-10) and Performance Monitor indicators, going down to the hardware level where switch diagnostics can be put in place.

FIGURE 19-10: Bandwidth usage analysis through Windows Task Manager

Planning Content Storage

The volume of content should be carefully analyzed at the beginning, and a forecast about the growth of that content should be performed for a time range of at least three years (the average duration for a similar solution).

If you follow best-practices advice (which suggests a capacity fewer than 200 GB for each Content Database), the forecast about content volume growth should pay attention to the following design elements:

➤ The distribution of web application content on more site collections associated with distinct Content Databases

➤ The choice between storing BLOB content in Content Databases, or dividing metadata from binary data through an RBS solution

➤ The total size of storage

Facing a High Number of Concurrent Users

If you plan for a high number of concurrent users (or if you notice this growth after the system has gone live), the first thing you should analyze is the availability of bandwidth that allows incoming traffic to your web servers to be managed.

But bandwidth availability is not enough to ensure that your application will be able to serve content in an acceptable time. You should ensure that the server load is under control, and eventually improve the response time by configuring the BLOB cache appropriately.

As a final improvement, you can think about scaling-out your farm topology by adding new WFE servers.

Improving the Responsiveness for Users in Branch Offices

First of all, considering that remote users are typically connected through slow networks (this may be a virtual private network, or VPN, over an Internet connection), you should try to reduce the bandwidth consumption by using a proper configuration of the Bit Rate Throttling Module.

Also, if you are providing a solution "inside" your organization (this could be, for example, an e-learning system to support human resources training), you could try to distribute this system in each of the company facilities. BranchCache could be adopted, and the basic infrastructure (Windows Server 2008 R2 and Windows 7) could be upgraded to meet the new requirements.

Handling Large Files Stored Inside SharePoint

SharePoint is capable of storing files with a maximum size of 2 GB, and this is a hard limit that, of course, you cannot exceed in DAM solutions. But you should take into account that SharePoint 2010 is optimized for the management of multimedia files with a size under 150 MB.

Also, you should consider that the standard settings that are applied to web applications limit the size of the uploaded documents to 50 MB. If you want to increase these settings, you must change it using either the SharePoint Central Administration user interface, or the PowerShell command line. Remember that IIS also has settings that prevent HTTP requests over a configurable size. If you need detailed information about these settings, see `http://technet.microsoft.com/en-us/library/cc754791(WS.10).aspx`.

Once you have correctly set the size limits, you should consider tuning the chunk size settings to improve the connection between SQL Server and SharePoint Server in situations where large files are exchanged. This will reduce the number of times that a WFE server must connect to the SQL Server to read all the large file data.

To do so, you can make use of the `stsadm` command-line utility. The following example shows how to set this limit to 1024 MB:

```
stsadm -o setproperty -pn large-file-chunk-size -pv 1073741824
```

ABOUT THE AUTHORS

Claudio Brotto is a SharePoint developer based in Bologna, Italy. His main areas of expertise range from low-level platform development (C/C++/COM) to application analysis and design, using the Microsoft .NET Framework (since the early days of Beta 1). Over the past few years, his focus has moved from raw application development to higher-level solutions based on Microsoft SharePoint Products and Technologies. Today he's involved in consulting and training services on SharePoint projects that his company, Green Team, is delivering to local and worldwide customers. He's a regular speaker in SharePoint events and conferences. He's founder of the Italian SharePoint Community (`www.sharepointcommunity.it`). For 2009 and 2010, he was awarded the Microsoft Most Valuable Professional (MVP) in SharePoint Services. You can find him at `www.devlizard.com`.

Igor Macori lives in Bologna, Italy, with his three girls (his partner and his two cats). He is co-founder and Training and Consulting Manager for Green Team (`www.greenteam.it`), an Italian Microsoft Gold Certified Partner founded in 1991. He has managed various IW Solutions projects (SharePoint, OCS, Project Server, and others), and completed various solutions implemented for enterprise companies and public-sector organizations. He is a regular trainer and speaker for Italian Microsoft courses and technical events dedicated to partners and customers, and has achieved several technical certifications since 1996 (MCP, MCSA, MCSE, MCITP, MCTS SharePoint, MCAS, and MCT). In 2008, he was recognized as a Microsoft MVP for Microsoft SharePoint Server. He is the owner of one of the most visited Italian SharePoint and collaboration Internet blogs (`www.macori.it`). He is co-organizer of the Italian Microsoft SharePoint Conference (`www.sharepointconference.it`) and he is founder and community leader of `SharePointCommunity.it`, the Italian SharePoint Community. He has written 18 books about Microsoft Office and Microsoft Windows, and has co-authored a book about Business Process Management with SharePoint.

20

Accessing SharePoint Data

By Reza Alirezaei

SharePoint 2010 introduces a great deal of new functionality to meet common challenges in working with SharePoint data, particularly with new client-side and server-side data access methods, and the capability to enforce referential integrity between SharePoint lists. To make optimal decisions, you must have a strong understanding of the new options, as well as the trade-offs.

The techniques described in this chapter should underpin most of the things you do in the particular functional area of accessing SharePoint data. This chapter focuses on accessing and consuming data stored in SharePoint, and provides insights into different data access techniques that can be utilized in your SharePoint applications. It also introduces some guidelines and best practices to mitigate the performance degradation when accessing SharePoint data.

DATA MODELING

Typically, when you consider a data model in SharePoint, the starting point is always where you need to store the data. This decision leads to two options:

➤ Database

➤ SharePoint lists

Databases can handle advanced data models that carry complex relationships with high availability, and SharePoint lists enable a great experience in the browser. So, the question is, which way do you go?

In SharePoint 2007, if you wanted to implement a data model using a database, generally you had to handle security and CRUD (Create/Read/Update/Delete) operations yourself, unless you wanted to use the Business Data Catalog (BDC) for your read-only scenarios. SharePoint lists could store information in pretty much the same structured way a database does — in rows and columns. However, you were on your own to figure out how to use SharePoint's weakly typed object model, and how to work with cumbersome Collaborative Application Markup Language (CAML) to perform simple data operations.

The options for storing and working with data represent a major evolution in SharePoint 2010. However, there is a general misconception that SharePoint is only capable of storing unstructured data (that is, documents, images, and videos), and that structured data must be kept in databases all the time. In reality, these two worlds are changing ever so fast. Nowadays, databases handle more aspects of unstructured data (that is, storing Binary Large Objects, or BLOBs), and SharePoint can contain more and more structured information.

Standard SharePoint lists have a lot more improved behaviors, including capabilities that were traditionally exclusive to a database. Let's not forget that creating and managing those lists is a lot easier now, and it requires no specialized skills in designing, implementing, and maintaining custom databases.

Business Connectivity Services (BCS, which is an improved version of BDC) supports full CRUD operations through both its server-side and client-side object models. You can store data in a highly structured way in Excel files and expose it (in a true service model) to the consumers of the service in the current farm or in another farm. External lists (another new feature in SharePoint 2010) are capable of showing data that is stored in SharePoint Content Databases, as well as an external line of business (LOB) application. Conveniently, you can use the same techniques to query data, regardless of their storage locations. In SharePoint 2010, both the Language Integrated Query (LINQ) and CAML query languages support join operations.

Of course, more choices always come with trade-offs and restrictions that must be understood up front. Understanding these factors can help you build better, more cost-effective, and more maintainable applications faster in the long run.

Figure 20-1 highlights the primary differences between a database and SharePoint lists. In particular, this figure shows the main cases that will drive you one way or another.

DATA ACCESS OPTIONS

Once you decide to store data in SharePoint lists, you have taken an important step in your data modeling process. However, the journey still is not over!

To take it a step further, you must think about which data access options are appropriate, and when to use them. Typically, data access options are not mutually exclusive. That means that it's very common to see your SharePoint application use a mixture of server-side and client-side query options, or even no-code solution altogether.

Figure 20-2 shows some of these options based on different scenarios.

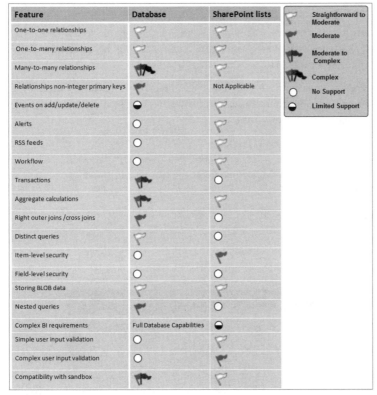

Feature	Database	SharePoint lists
One-to-one relationships	Straightforward to Moderate	Straightforward to Moderate
One-to-many relationships	Straightforward to Moderate	Straightforward to Moderate
Many-to-many relationships	Complex	Straightforward to Moderate
Relationships non-integer primary keys	Moderate to Complex	Not Applicable
Events on add/update/delete	Limited Support	Straightforward to Moderate
Alerts	No Support	Straightforward to Moderate
RSS feeds	No Support	Straightforward to Moderate
Workflow	No Support	Straightforward to Moderate
Transactions	Complex	No Support
Aggregate calculations	Moderate to Complex	Straightforward to Moderate
Right outer joins /cross joins	Moderate	No Support
Distinct queries	Straightforward to Moderate	No Support
Item-level security	No Support	Moderate
Field-level security	No Support	No Support
Storing BLOB data	Straightforward to Moderate	Straightforward to Moderate
Nested queries	Moderate	No Support
Complex BI requirements	Full Database Capabilities	Limited Support
Simple user input validation	No Support	Straightforward to Moderate
Complex user input validation	No Support	Moderate
Compatibility with sandbox	Moderate to Complex	Straightforward to Moderate

Legend:
- Straightforward to Moderate
- Moderate
- Moderate to Complex
- Complex
- No Support
- Limited Support

FIGURE 20-1: Primary differences between a database and SharePoint lists

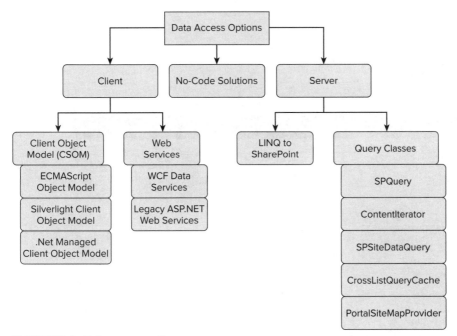

FIGURE 20-2: Data access options

Note a few things about Figure 20-2:

➤ Some of the server-side APIs to data access (such as `SPSiteDataQuery`, `CrossListQueryCache`, and `PortalMapProvider`) are not covered in this chapter. That's mainly because those APIs haven't changed much in SharePoint 2010.

➤ Another topic not covered in this chapter is Business Connectivity Services. Flip back to Chapter 14 to learn more about this technology, and how you can use it to accomplish various common tasks when accessing SharePoint data.

➤ Web services can also be called from server-side code.

In the remainder of this chapter, you learn more detail about some of these options.

CREATING SAMPLE LISTS

Before diving into some examples of data access options in SharePoint, create three lists: `Customers` (Figure 20-3), `Orders` (Figure 20-4), and `Products` (Figure 20-5).

FIGURE 20-3: Customers list

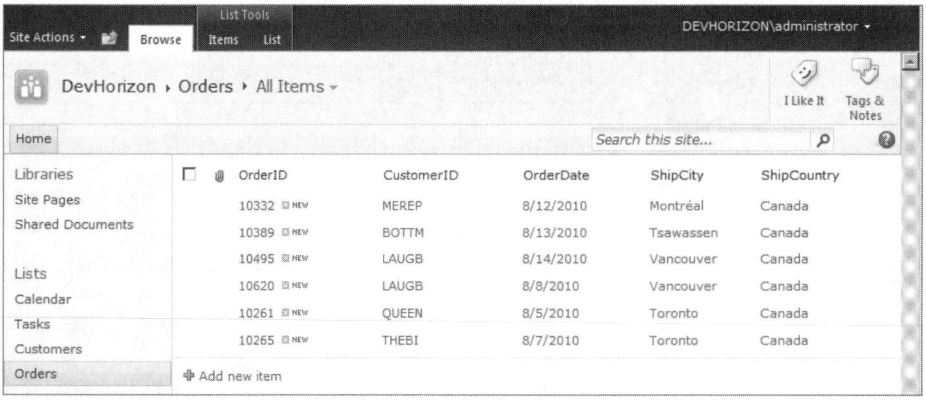

FIGURE 20-4: Orders list

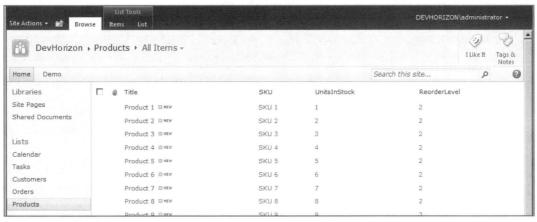

FIGURE 20-5: Products list

There is a join property between `Customers` and `Orders` lists, as shown here:

```
       One                          Many
--------------------------------------------------
CUSTOMERS.[CustomerID]  ®    ORDERS.[CustomerID]
```

In the `Orders` list, the join property is handled using a lookup column named `CustomerID` that retrieves values from the `Customers` list. The `Products` list contains 10,000 items.

 You can find the complete code to populate this list in the code download for this book at `www.wrox.com`.

ACCESSING SHAREPOINT DATA USING THE SERVER-SIDE OBJECT MODEL

Accessing SharePoint data using the server-side object model is a very common technique used by SharePoint developers. SharePoint 2010 provides a powerful array of server-side APIs that enable you to interact with your data programmatically when your code executes on the server.

This section provides an overview of some of these options, and provides some guidance on how to use them.

Query Optimization

Everyone wants the performance of their SharePoint sites to be optimal. Unfortunately, for many production SharePoint implementations, performance becomes an issue sooner rather than later, and off-course, which becomes a major point of frustration.

One of the main factors contributing to slow performance is the way you query SharePoint data. Having long-running queries against a SharePoint Content Database not only consumes system resources, which makes the servers and services in the farm run slowly, but also may lead to table locking and unexpected behaviors in your application. So, query optimization becomes an important task.

A number of tools, Microsoft white papers, and blog posts exist about how to correctly use the SharePoint object model for different data-retrieval use cases. On the top of that, there are lots of best practices on how to distribute your content so that your solutions can scale while the best access performance is achieved. For example, see "Working with Large Lists in Office SharePoint Server 2007" at http://www.devhorizon.com/go/27.

However, there are limited sources that focus on how you can make your queries run faster, as well as ensure that they work as expected for all users of your application.

Working with Collections

In SharePoint, nearly everything is a collection. The SharePoint object model provides a series of specialized collection classes for data storage and retrieval such as SPWebApplicationCollection, SPSiteCollection, SPWebCollection, SPListCollection, SPListItemCollection and so on.

Improper coding with SharePoint collections can impact your application in three ways:

➤ First, it may increase resource utilization on the farm, which affects your application and potentially other applications hosted in the same farm.

➤ Second, it may result in a large amount of data returned to the client, and affect the responsiveness of your application.

➤ Third, it can lead to behaviors that may not be caught during development. For example, if you query for more than 5,000 items, end users may receive an SPQueryThrottleException exception caused by exceeding the list's default throttling limit. The list throttling limit is covered later in this chapter.

Consider the situation in production in which you have thousands of items with dozens of metadata in a collection you are trying to load into memory. This will produce quite a memory footprint on the server, and can affect the performance of your application.

As an example, suppose you want to show the name of each product in the Products list with 10,000 items in it using the following code:

```
SPList list = web.Lists["Products"];
for (int i = 0; i < 10; i++)
{
    Console.WriteLine(list.Items[i].Title);

}
```

How this code affects the performance begins at the database level. Figure 20-6 (captured by SQL Profiler) demonstrates what is executed in the Content Database when this code runs.

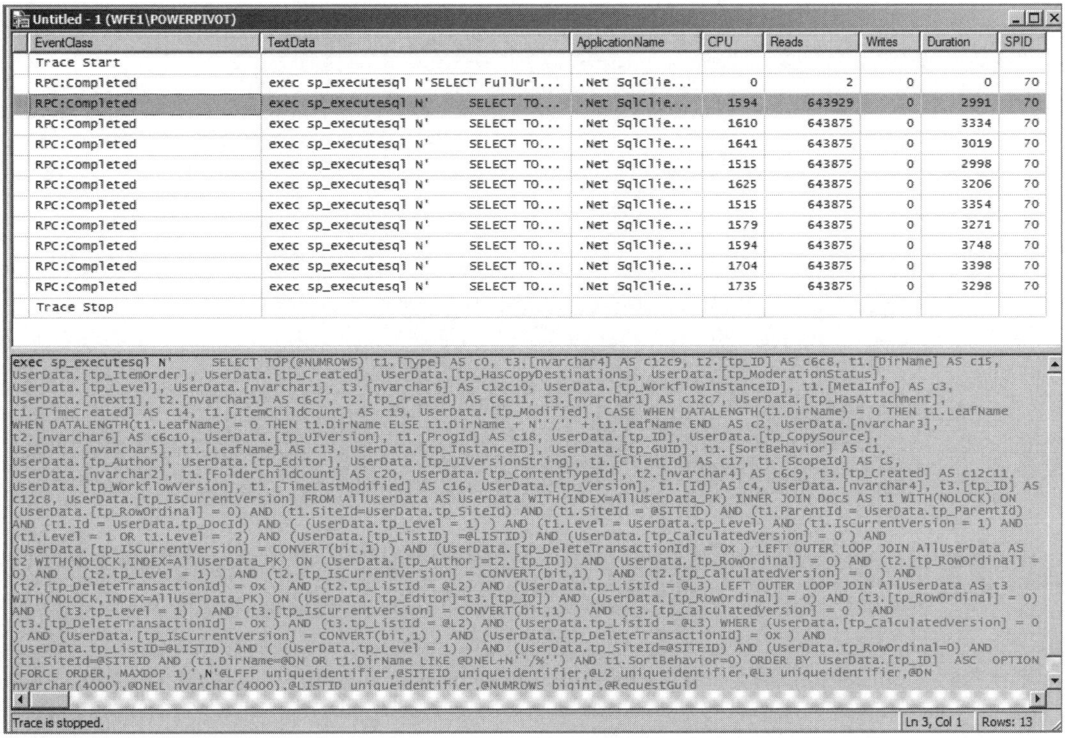

FIGURE 20-6: What is being executed in the Content Database the first time

As you can see, every time `list.Items` is called, a new instance of `SPListItemCollection` is initialized, and a round trip to the Content Database is made to retrieve the entire collection. In this particular example, this results in 10 unnecessary object initializations and 10 database round trips, which will cause the query to run longer. Obviously, if you had looped over all 10,000 items, object initializations and query duration could be even worse, and it could lead to horrible situations with an increase in the amount of CPU and memory consumptions.

Let's replace the previous code with the following code:

```
SPList list = web.Lists["Products"];
SPListItemCollection items = list.Items;
        foreach (SPListItem item in items)
        {
            Console.WriteLine(item.Title);
        }
```

The change was to move the `list.Items` call outside of the loop and to use `foreach` for iteration. Figure 20-7 demonstrates what is executed in the Content Database when the preceding code runs.

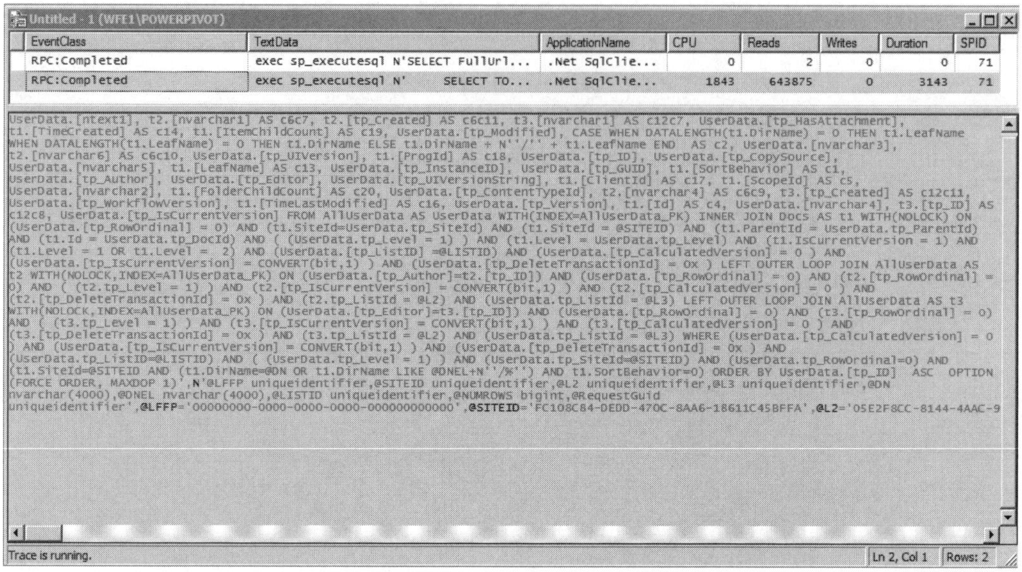

FIGURE 20-7: What is being executed in the Content Database the second time

Note that, in optimized code, you are iterating through all 10,000 items, not just 10 items, but this provides better performance and the code is easier to read, too. There is only one object initialization and only one database round trip is made.

Horizontal and Vertical Filtering

In the preceding discussion, you applied a few query optimization techniques, but the amount of data that is returned by a query is not yet optimized. It would be ideal if, instead of returning many rows and columns, you could filter out all but some of them.

The SPListItemCollection object has an XML property that gets all the data in the collection in XMLDATA format. In the previous example, if you stored the value of this property in a text file using the following code, you would see that you are pulling 15 MB of data to the client as the result of your query:

```
string data = items.Xml;
System.IO.File.WriteAllText(@"C:\SPListItemCollectionXMLDump1.txt", data);
```

> *You can find all auto-generated* SPListItemCollectionXMLDumpX.txt *files in the code download for this book.*

Although some business requirements may dictate working with the entire data set, in most cases, you only need a subset of list data. So, wouldn't it be nice if your query only returned the rows that it required? That's where SPQuery query class and CAML can help!

The following code demonstrates how to create and configure an instance of the SPQuery class that filters the returned data:

```
SPList list = web.Lists["Products"];
StringBuilder sb = new StringBuilder();
sb.Append("<Where>")
.Append("  <BeginsWith>")
.Append("    <FieldRef Name='SKU' />")
.Append("    <Value Type='Text'>SKU 3</Value>")
.Append("  </BeginsWith>")
.Append("</Where>")
.Append("<OrderBy>")
.Append("  <FieldRef Name='Title' Ascending='TRUE' />")
.Append("</OrderBy>");
SPQuery qry = new SPQuery();
qry.Query = sb.ToString();
SPListItemCollection items = list.GetItems(qry);
string data = items.Xml;
System.IO.File.WriteAllText(@"C:\SPListItemCollectionXMLDump2.txt", data);
```

The code creates an instance of the SPQuery class and sets its Query property to a string that represents a simple CAML query. The query simply returns all the products for which the SKU column has a value that starts with the word "SKU 3." Then, a call is made to the GetItems method on the SPList instance, passing in the SPQuery instance as a parameter. Finally, just as with the previous example, the XMLDATA result is written into a text file for further analysis.

If you look at the generated file, you will see that the size is approximately 1.7 MB, which is quite a bit smaller than the full data set file. Obviously, this is because of the filter that exists in the CAML query within the <Where> clause.

Figure 20-8 demonstrates what is executed behind the scenes in the Content Database when this code runs. It's crystal clear that the CAML query has translated into a much faster stored procedure call with considerably less CPU consumption and database I/O.

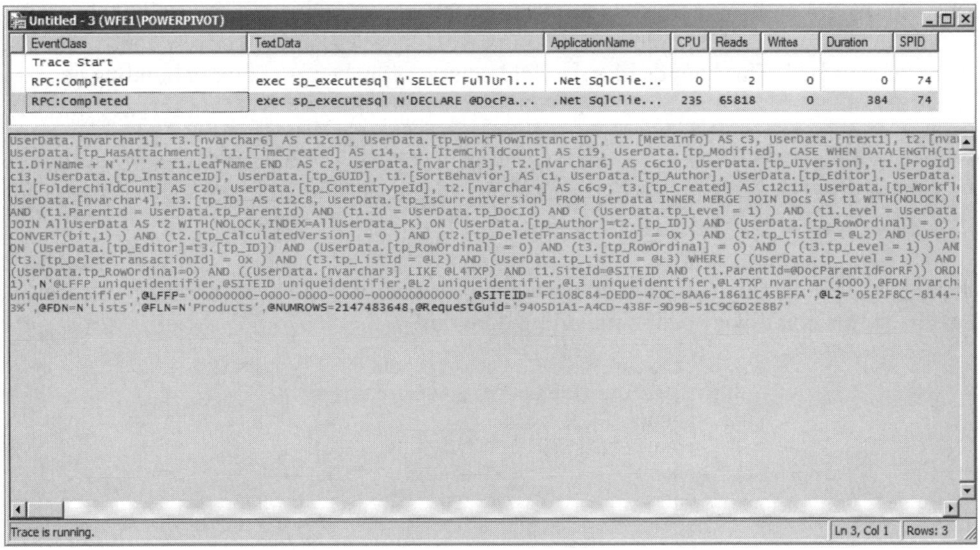

FIGURE 20-8: Result of using Where clause in your CAML query

In the previous code, you applied a horizontal filter by returning a subset of data using a CAML query, instead of pulling the entire collection down. If you look back into the content of one of the generated text files, you will see that, for each row, there is a line that looks like the following XML snippet:

```
<z:row ows_ContentTypeId='0x0100167954BB8AAB144A8E7BEA05DE49F16B'
ows_Title='Product 3999' ows_SKU='SKU 3999' ows_UnitsInStock='3999'
ows_ReorderLevel='2' ows_ID='3999' ows_ContentType='Item'
ows_Modified='2010-08-18 01:10:46' ows_Created='2010-08-18 01:10:46'
ows_Author='1;#DEVHORIZON\administrator'
ows_Editor='1;#DEVHORIZON\administrator' ows_owshiddenversion='1'
ows_WorkflowVersion='1' ows__UIVersion='512' ows__UIVersionString='1.0'
ows_Attachments='0' ows__ModerationStatus='0'
ows_LinkTitleNoMenu='Product 3999' ows_LinkTitle='Product 3999'
ows_LinkTitle2='Product 3999' ows_SelectTitle='3999'
ows_Order='399900.000000000' ows_GUID='{AB3E22EC-388A-48BD-9D53-
    C4975E02E54E}' ows_FileRef='3999;#Lists/Products/3999_.000'
ows_FileDirRef='3999;#Lists/Products'
ows_Last_x0020_Modified='3999;#2010-08-18 01:10:46'
ows_Created_x0020_Date='3999;#2010-08-18 01:10:46'
ows_FSObjType='3999;#0' ows_SortBehavior='3999;#0'
ows_PermMask='0x7ffffffffffffff' ows_FileLeafRef='3999;#3999_.000'
ows_UniqueId='3999;#{C80E3C08-5A60-4338-9F67-CDF86C0D7BDA}'
ows_ProgId='3999;#' ows_ScopeId='3999;#{26B44B03-31C0-4E48-A4D8-
    8ACC762E6EBC}' ows__EditMenuTableStart='3999_.000'
ows__EditMenuTableStart2='3999' ows__EditMenuTableEnd='3999'
ows_LinkFilenameNoMenu='3999_.000' ows_LinkFilename='3999_.000'
ows_LinkFilename2='3999_.000' ows_ServerUrl='/Lists/Products/3999_.000'
ows_EncodedAbsUrl='http://wfe1.devhorizon.local/Lists/Products/3999_.000'
ows_BaseName='3999_' ows_MetaInfo='3999;#' ows__Level='1'
ows__IsCurrentVersion='1' ows_ItemChildCount='3999;#0'
ows_FolderChildCount='3999;#0' />
```

This is just a ton of stuff for one row of data! You certainly don't need every column returned by the CAML query. So, how would you filter it vertically and clean it up before it is sent over the wire?

This brings up the use of the `ViewFields` property of the `SPQuery` object. Essentially, this property allows you to include and exclude columns in your CAML queries, and effectively control the number of columns returned. This sounds like the right solution for the case you are building here, so let's see it in action.

Continuing with the previous example, add the following line right after where you initialized the `SPQuery` object:

```
qry.ViewFields = "<FieldRef Name='Title'/>";
```

Also, change the data dump file, so that you can compare the returned result with and without `ViewFields`. At this point, your code should look like this:

```
SPList list = web.Lists["Products"];
StringBuilder sb = new StringBuilder();
sb.Append("<Where>")
    .Append("  <BeginsWith>")
    .Append("    <FieldRef Name='SKU' />")
    .Append("    <Value Type='Text'>SKU 3</Value>")
    .Append("  </BeginsWith>")
    .Append("</Where>")
```

```
              .Append("<OrderBy>")
              .Append("  <FieldRef Name='Title' Ascending='TRUE' />")
              .Append("</OrderBy>");
           SPQuery qry = new SPQuery();
qry.ViewFields = "<FieldRef Name='Title'/>";
           qry.Query = sb.ToString();
           SPListItemCollection items = list.GetItems(qry);
           string data = items.Xml;
System.IO.File.WriteAllText(@"C:\SPListItemCollectionXMLDump3.txt",
    data);
           foreach (SPListItem item in items)
           {
               Console.WriteLine(item.Title);
           }
```

Now, build and run the code. Figure 20-9 shows a SQL Profiler trace with the new change in place. Compare the CPU, Reads, and Duration columns of the database call with the previous result where the ViewFields property was not used in the CAML query.

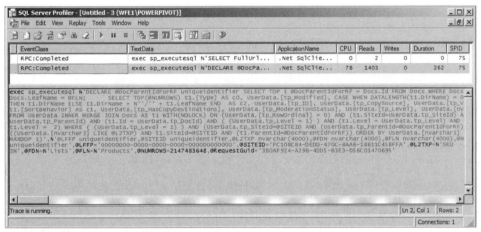

FIGURE 20-9: Result of using ViewFields in your CAML query

Note the size of the new dump file and you see that it is reduced to only 406 KB. If you look at the same row of data you analyzed before, you can see the difference you have made, as shown in the following XML snippet:

```
<z:row ows_Title='Product 3999' ows_MetaInfo='3999;#' ows__ModerationStatus='0'
    ows__Level='1' ows_ID='3999' ows_UniqueId='3999;#{C80E3C08-5A60-4338-9F67-
        CDF86C0D7BDA}' ows_owshiddenversion='1' ows_FSObjType='3999;#0'
    ows_Created='2010-08-18 01:10:46' ows_PermMask='0x7ffffffffffffff'
    ows_Modified='2010-08-18 01:10:46'
    ows_FileRef='3999;#Lists/Products/3999_.000' />
```

SharePoint 2010 introduces a new property for the SPQuery object called ViewFieldOnly, which can be used in conjunction with ViewFields to make your queries run even faster. Again, continuing with the previous example, add the following line right after where you set the ViewFields property:

```
qry.ViewFieldsOnly = true;
```

Also, change the data dump file, so that you can compare the returned result with and without `ViewFieldOnly` property. At this point, your code should look like this:

```
SPList list = web.Lists["Products"];
StringBuilder sb = new StringBuilder();
sb.Append("<Where>")
  .Append("  <BeginsWith>")
  .Append("    <FieldRef Name='SKU' />")
  .Append("    <Value Type='Text'>SKU 3</Value>")
  .Append("  </BeginsWith>")
  .Append("</Where>")
  .Append("<OrderBy>")
  .Append("  <FieldRef Name='Title' Ascending='TRUE' />")
  .Append("</OrderBy>");
SPQuery qry = new SPQuery();
qry.ViewFields = "<FieldRef Name='Title'/>";
qry.ViewFieldsOnly = true;
qry.Query = sb.ToString();
SPListItemCollection items = list.GetItems(qry);
string data = items.Xml;
System.IO.File.WriteAllText(@"C:\SPListItemCollectionXMLDump4.txt",
    data);
foreach (SPListItem item in items)
{
    Console.WriteLine(item.Title);
}
```

Now, build and run this code. If you look at the SQL Profiler trace for this query, you will find that the combination of `ViewFields` and `ViewFieldOnly` slightly outperforms the query with only the `ViewFields` property. However, the dump file proves that by using this combination you have pulled down a much cleaner and smaller data set (290 KB), as shown in Figure 20-10.

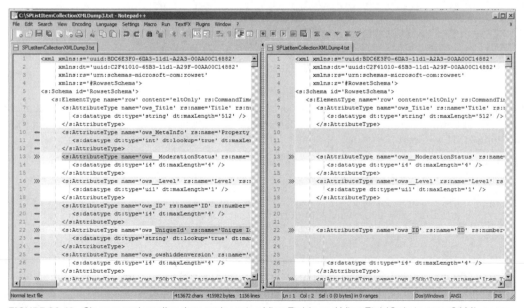

FIGURE 20-10: Cleaner and smaller data set by using ViewFields and ViewFieldOnly in your CAML query

If you look at all the generated files on the filesystem as shown in Figure 20-11, surely the result of your query optimization techniques speaks for itself!

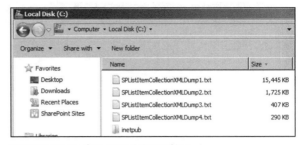

FIGURE 20-11: Generated dump files

Typically, when you query SharePoint data, you would like to present it to the end user in a web part or page that uses `ViewState`. You maintain `ViewState` so that you can interact with the returned data across visible or invisible postbacks. Even though your page may look very simple and lightweight, the result of having a huge data set behind the scenes can inflate the `ViewState` (that is, increase the page size). Also, the amount of data passed back and forth across postbacks can severely affect the performance of your applications and other applications residing in the same Web-Front End (WFE) server.

List-Level Indexing

Conceptually speaking, indexing in a SharePoint list and a database is very similar, and these tasks share some common characteristics, too.

An *index* is a structure that improves the speed of data-retrieval operations at the cost of slower writes. However, an index increases storage space, and can take up processing power when modifying items (that is, adding, deleting, and updating).

By default, SharePoint creates an index on the `ID` column. So, you can always count on it being indexed, and your query to be fast. Other than the `ID` column, SharePoint allows you to create additional indexes (up to 20 per list) on some other column data types.

 For the complete list of supported data types for list-level indexing, see the official documentation on MSDN at `http://www.devhorizon.com/go/28.`

SharePoint supports two types of indexes:

➤   Compound index

➤   Single-column index

Typically, you use a compound index when your query requires a filter on more than one column. Whereas single-column indexes can be applied to any column with a supported data type, compound indexes have two major limitations.

First, only two columns (primary and secondary columns) can participate in a compound index. Second, a `Text` column can't be used in a compound index. If you create an index for a SharePoint list, and then you choose a column with the `Text` data type, the other column becomes unavailable, forcing you to create a single-column index, as shown in Figure 20-12.

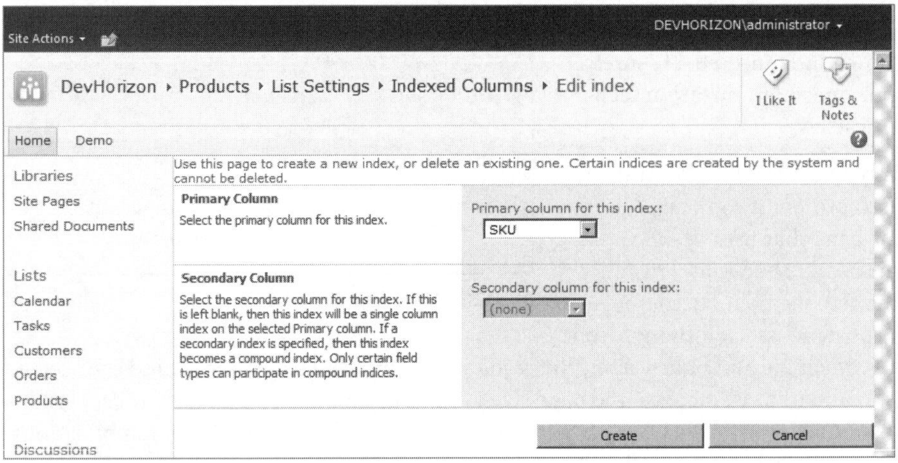

FIGURE 20-12: Being forced to create a single-column index

Although you have up to 20 indexing slots in your lists, it's not recommended to use all of them. That's because some Features in SharePoint generate indexes automatically so that they can function properly. For example, Metadata Navigation works with compound indexes to provide a new way to filter list views by their item metadata and tagging.

List Throttling

As mentioned previously, the behavior of standard SharePoint lists has been improved in SharePoint 2010. One of these improvements is *list throttling*, which allows you to configure large lists to prevent any operation from involving too many rows at any one time.

If you browse to the Central Administration site ⇨ Manage Web Applications ⇨ General Settings ⇨ Resource Throttling ⇨ List View Threshold, you will see that the default list throttling limit is set to 5,000. It's strongly recommended that you do not change this default value. This value relates to when a page lock gets placed on a SQL table when 5,000 rows are affected, rather than row-lock, which will affect other sites in the same site collection and reduce scalability. While you are on the Resource Throttling page, notice that you can also schedule happy hours where throttling is disabled for maintenance activities using the "Daily Time Window for Large Queries" attribute.

When items in a list exceed the list throttling limit, users receive a warning when they browse to the List Settings page, informing them that the list exceeds the list view threshold, as shown in Figure 20-13.

Showing a warning is one thing, but preventing expensive operations from executing is another thing. Let's suppose that you have created a web part that uses the following code to return all products from the `Products` list:

```
try
{
    //The following query returns all 10,000 items from the
    //Products list
    string query = @"<View>
```

```
                <Query>
                    <Where>
                        <And>
                            <BeginsWith>
                                <FieldRef Name='SKU' />
                                <Value Type='Text'>S</Value>
                            </BeginsWith>
                        </And>
                    </Where>
                </Query>
            </View>";
            SPQuery listQuery = new SPQuery();
            listQuery.Query = query;
            SPList list = SPContext.Current.Web.Lists["Products"];
            SPListItemCollection items = list.GetItems(listQuery);
            int count = items.Count;

        }
        catch (Exception ex)
        {
            ErrorMsg.Text = ex.Message + "<br/><br/>" + ex.StackTrace;
        }
```

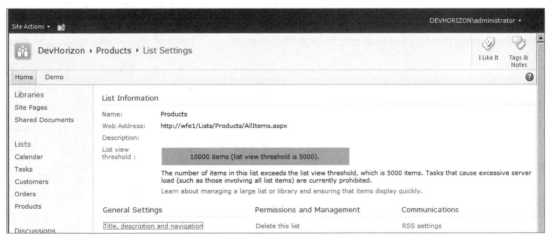

FIGURE 20-13: Exceeding the list view threshold

When an end user (say, Barbara Decker) visits a web part page with this web part, she receives the error shown in Figure 20-14. As you can see, the list throttling limit didn't allow your web part to execute.

Of course, in some circumstances you cannot avoid iterating large lists. Therefore, you need an override of list throttling. Like the old saying goes, there are a number of ways to skin this cat.

As mentioned previously, you can schedule happy hours where throttling is disabled. Alternatively, you can use Microsoft Access 2010 to query SharePoint list data, because Access Services 2010 has its own throttling settings.

FIGURE 20-14: List throttling limit preventing web part execution

If you don't like either of these options, then you must write some code. To do so, consider one of the following three coding options:

➤ Setting the `SPList.EnableThrottling` property to `false` to disable throttling for a particular list.

➤ Setting the `SPQuery.QueryThrottleMode` property to `SPQueryThrottleOption.Override` to disable throttling for a particular query.

➤ Using the new `ContentIterator` API.

The first option is to disable list throttling on a list-by-list basis. Similar to disabling throttling globally, disabling throttling for a list is not recommended. However, it can be a short-term fix while the longer-term issue is remedied.

The following code shows the `FeatureActivated` and `FeatureDeactivating` methods of the web-scoped Feature. This Feature enables and disables list throttling for the `Products` list.

```
public class ProductsListThrottlingEnablerEventReceiver : SPFeatureReceiver
{
    public override void FeatureActivated(SPFeatureReceiverProperties
        properties)
    {
        SPList list = GetProductsList(properties);
        list.EnableThrottling = false;

    }

    public override void FeatureDeactivating(SPFeatureReceiverProperties
        properties)
    {
        SPList list = GetProductsList(properties);
        list.EnableThrottling = true;

    }

    private static SPList GetProductsList(SPFeatureReceiverProperties
```

```
        properties)
    {
        SPWeb curWeb = (SPWeb)properties.Feature.Parent;
        SPList list = curWeb.Lists["Products"];
        return list;
    }
}
```

The second option is to disable list throttling for the SPQuery object on a situational basis. In addition to setting the SPQuery.QueryThrottleMode property to SPQueryThrottleOption.Override, two other conditions must be met; otherwise, your query is still subject to the regular list view threshold. First, the Object Model Override attribute must be set to Yes. Second, your query must execute under the security context of a super user. To make someone a super user, browse to the Central Administration site ⇨ Manage Web Applications ⇨ User Policy and give them either "Full Control" or "Full Read" permission, as shown in Figure 20-15.

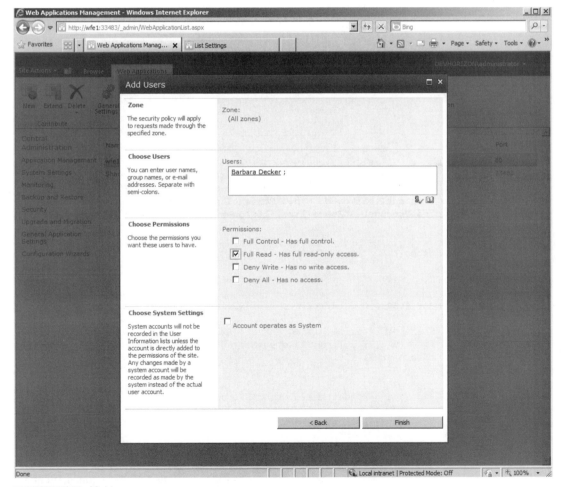

FIGURE 20-15: Making someone a super user

The third option is to use the `ContentIterator` class in the `Microsoft.Office.Server` assembly. You should consider using this class to access the large lists with throttling enabled, or when you suspect that your list is likely to grow large over time.

The following console application demonstrates how to use a CAML query and the `ContentIterator` class to retrieve 10,000 items from the `Products` list without hitting the throttling exception:

```
static void Main(string[] args)
    {
        string siteUrl = "http://wfe1.devhorizon.local";

        using (SPSite site = new SPSite(siteUrl))
        {
            using (SPWeb web = site.OpenWeb())
            {
                //The following query return all 10,000 items in Products list
                string query = @"<View>
                <Query>
                    <Where>
                        <And>
                            <BeginsWith>
                                <FieldRef Name='SKU' />
                                <Value Type='Text'>S</Value>
                            </BeginsWith>
                        </And>
                    </Where>
                </Query></View>";
                SPQuery listQuery = new SPQuery();
                listQuery.Query = query;
                SPList list = web.Lists["Products"];
                string iteratorName = "Chapter 20 Sample iterator";
                ContentIterator ci = new ContentIterator(iteratorName);
                ci.ProcessListItems(list, listQuery, ItemProcessor, ErrorProcessor);
            }
        }
        Console.ReadLine();

    }

    private static bool ErrorProcessor(SPListItem item, Exception e)
    {
        Console.WriteLine(string.Format("Exception thrown when processing
            {0}:{1}", item.Title, e.Message));
        return true;
    }

    private static void ItemProcessor(SPListItem item)
    {
        Console.WriteLine(string.Format("{0} is now processed",
            item.Title));
    }
```

The `ContentIterator` class takes two callback methods for processing the query (one item at a time), and also the errors that may occur during the query process. The `ContentIterator` class is ideal to iterate collections in chunks, to avoid receiving a throttling exception.

Before wrapping up this discussion, it's worth highlighting two important tips here:

➤ There is a general misconception that list throttling applies only to data-retrieval queries. That's why I avoided using the word "query" as much as possible, and instead used "operation."

➤ It's also important to note that throttling is determined by the number of affected rows in the SQL database as the result of an operation, not by the actual number of the items in the result set. For example, you may delete a site containing a list with 10,000 items in it, and the throttle limit is still hit. That's because deleting a site requires deleting the list and all 10,000 items in it. Obviously, there is no item returned by the operation.

LINQ to SharePoint

LINQ is a Microsoft .NET Framework component that adds a native querying language to .NET languages. Unlike other query languages that have a different syntax for each data source, LINQ offers a consistent syntax across different types of data sources.

To make a data source accessible with LINQ, all you need is a LINQ provider. For example, to use LINQ against SQL you can use a LINQ to SQL provider, and to use LINQ against XML you would use LINQ to XML.

Just like SQL and XML, SharePoint lists are considered as yet another data source. SharePoint 2010 ships with a LINQ provider called LINQ to SharePoint, defined in the `Microsoft.SharePoint.Linq` namespace, in a managed code assembly. The primary job of this provider entails two things:

➤ It provides strongly typed entities to perform CRUD operations against SharePoint data, instead of writing CAML queries.

➤ It translates the LINQ queries into the query language of SharePoint (that is, CAML).

Figure 20-16 shows LINQ to SharePoint process flow.

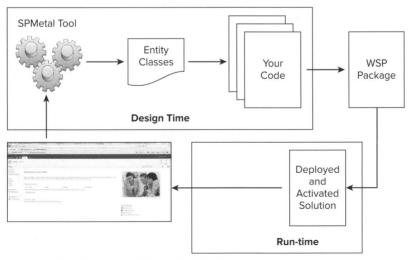

FIGURE 20-16: LINQ to SharePoint process flow

LINQ to SharePoint is considered a server-side data access option, and is not available in the client-side object model.

Generating the Entity Classes

SharePoint 2010 ships with a tool named `SPMetal` that you can use to generate entity classes for the lists and content types in your site. Open a Command Prompt window as an administrator and change the current path to `%ProgramFiles%\Common Files\Microsoft Shared\web server extensions\14\BIN`, if it's not already in the Windows `%PATH%` environment variable. In the command line, type the following command:

```
SPMetal /web:http://SiteUrl  /code:SiteName.cs
```

In this command, note the following:

➤ `http://SiteUrl` is the absolute URL of your site.

➤ `SiteName.cs` is the file generated by the tool, which contains an entity class.

Figure 20-17 shows an example of this command. As you can see, `SiteURL` can be local to the server that `SPMetal` is running on, in which case, the server object model will be used to connect to the server and generate entity classes. If you use the `/useremoteapi` parameter, the tool will generate an entity class against a site that's not local. This makes the tool usable for when you don't have direct access to the server, or for online deployments where you can only deploy a sandboxed solution.

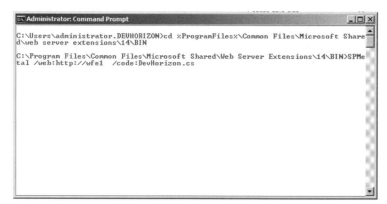

FIGURE 20-17: Using SPMetal from the command line

If you look at the generated code, the top entity class (`DevHorizonDataContext`) is of type `Microsoft.SharePoint.Linq.DataContext`. This class includes strongly typed properties for each list on the site, and acts as a gateway to access other entities such as `CustomersItem`. The

`CustomersItem` class that represents each customer within the `Customers` list includes strongly typed properties for each column value, such as `ContactName` and `CompanyName`.

The following code shows how to use the generated entity classes to perform a simple LINQ query to retrieve all customers located in Toronto:

```
using (DevHorizonDataContext context = new
       DevHorizonDataContext(SPContext.Current.Web.Url))
    {
        string city = "Toronto";
        var results = from customerItem in context.Customers
                      where customerItem.City == city
                      select customerItem;
        foreach (var cust in results)
        {
            writer.WriteLine(string.Format("Customer ID: {0}, Name:
                {1}, Contact: {2} <br/>", cust.Id,cust.CompanyName,
                cust.ContactName));
        }
    }
```

Note two things about this code:

➤ First, like all other LINQ providers, a LINQ to SharePoint query is not executed until it is enumerated in the `foreach` loop.

➤ Second, the `DataContext` base class implements the `IDisposable` interface, so you should always consider disposing of the data context instance you create for your LINQ queries. That's why it's being placed in a `Using` statement. Figure 20-18 shows the result.

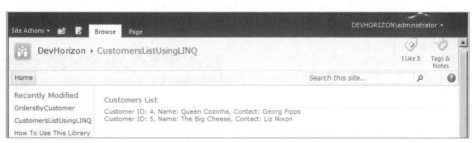

FIGURE 20-18: Result of LINQ query

List Relationships Using Lookup Columns

Typically, SharePoint data exists in multiple lists. To establish a relationship between list items in one list and related items in another list, you must use lookup columns. SharePoint 2010 introduces three improvements for lookup columns.

First, when you link two lists using a lookup column, you can display other columns from the target list, in addition to the lookup column. These columns are commonly referred to as *projected columns*.

Second, lookup columns now support *referential integrity*, which prevents users from deleting an item in the target list if it is referenced in one or more items in the related list — which would otherwise orphan data. You can also configure it to follow a cascade delete behavior in which, if an item is deleted in the target list, all the referenced items in the related list are deleted as well.

Figure 20-19 shows new lookup column improvements for the `CustomerID` column in the `Orders` list. Note that right underneath where you select your lookup column are a bunch of other columns that you can select and add to the list's default view. Also, note that there is a separate checkbox for enforcing relationship behavior with two options available: "Restrict delete" and "Cascade delete."

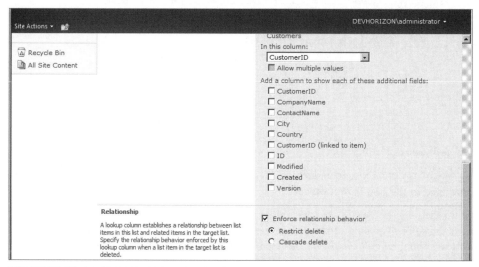

FIGURE 20-19: Lookup column improvements

Third, there is a new configurable limit called List View Lookup Threshold. This setting is located in Central Administration site ⇨ Manage Web Applications ⇨ General Settings ⇨ Resource Throttling, as shown in Figure 20-20. Essentially, this setting specifies the maximum number of lookup columns a query can involve at any one time, before hitting an exception.

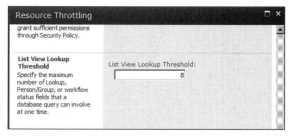

FIGURE 20-20: List View Lookup Threshold configurable limit

Associations between SharePoint lists are analogous to relationships between tables in a database. Thankfully, `SPMetal` understands these relationships very well, and generates entity classes that can aggregate data across such relationships.

The following code shows a property named `CustomerID` in the `OrderItem` entity that allows you to find the associated customer for a particular order:

```
private Microsoft.SharePoint.Linq.EntityRef<CustomersItem> _customerID;
//Code Omitted for brevity
[Microsoft.SharePoint.Linq.AssociationAttribute(Name = "CustomerID", Storage =
    "_customerID", MultivalueType = Microsoft.SharePoint.Linq.AssociationType.
   Single, List = "Customers")]
    public CustomersItem CustomerID
    {
       get
       {
          return this._customerID.GetEntity();
       }
       set
       {
          this._customerID.SetEntity(value);
       }
    }
```

Note how the `EntityRef<TEntity>` class is used to represent the singleton side of the `1:n` relationship between the `Customers` and `Orders` lists.

The following code shows how to retrieve all orders for a particular customer, and how LINQ to SharePoint handles a join:

```
using (DevHorizonDataContext context = new
       DevHorizonDataContext(SPContext.Current.Web.Url))
    {
         string customerID = "LAUGB";
         var results = from orderItem in context.Orders
                       where orderItem.CustomerID.Title = customerID
                       select orderItem;

         foreach (var order in results)
         {
             writer.WriteLine(string.Format("Order ID: {0},
                 Date: {1} <br/>",
                 order.Title, order.OrderDate));
         }
    }
```

As you can see, thanks to `SPMetal`, performing a join across two lists that are connected by a lookup column is very simple using LINQ, which added the required association logic to the entity classes for you.

When you run the preceding code in a SharePoint site with `Customers` and `Orders` lists, you should see something like Figure 20-21.

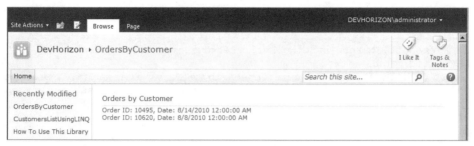

FIGURE 20-21: SharePoint site with Customers and Order lists

On the reverse side of the association, the `CustomerItem` entity has a property named `OrdersItem` that can be used when you need to find all the orders for a particular customer, as shown in the following code. This way, instead of looping through every order from the `Orders` list and checking the value of the `CustomerID` lookup column, you perform your query in one shot using simpler code with less overhead. Note how the `EntitySet<TEntity>` class is used to represent the many side of the `1:n` relationship between the `Customers` and `Orders` lists (known as *reverse lookup association*).

```
private Microsoft.SharePoint.Linq.EntitySet<OrdersItem> _ordersItem;
//Code Omitted for brevity
[Microsoft.SharePoint.Linq.AssociationAttribute(Name = "CustomerID",
Storage = "_ordersItem", ReadOnly = true, MultivalueType =
Microsoft.SharePoint.Linq.AssociationType.Backward, List = "Orders")]
    public Microsoft.SharePoint.Linq.EntitySet<OrdersItem> OrdersItem
    {
      get
      {
        return this._ordersItem;
      }
      set
      {
        this._ordersItem.Assign(value);
      }
    }
```

In the example provided in this chapter, a list-level lookup column (`CustomerID`) and `SPMetal` generated the reverse lookup logic for the relationship. In the real world, where you use site columns and content types (at least you should), and, most likely, they are used in multiple lists, `SPMetal` won't generate the reverse lookup logic. You have an option here. Using a list-level lookup column (as opposed to a site column) is one way to work around this limitation in LINQ to SharePoint.

Finally, if you look at the constructors of both entities (`OrderItem` and `CustomerItem`), you will find `OnSync`, `OnChanged`, and `OnChanging` event handlers to ensure that each entity remains up-to-date, should the associated entity instance ever change. The following code shows the constructor of `OrderItem` entity:

```
public OrdersItem()
    {
        this._customerID = new Microsoft.SharePoint.
            Linq.EntityRef<CustomersItem>();
        this._customerID.OnSync += new System.
            EventHandler<Microsoft.SharePoint.
            Linq.AssociationChangedEventArgs<CustomersItem>>
            (this.OnCustomerIDSync);
        this._customerID.OnChanged += new
            System.EventHandler(this.OnCustomerIDChanged);
        this._customerID.OnChanging += new
            System.EventHandler(this.OnCustomerIDChanging);
        this.OnCreated();
    }
```

The following code shows another join between `Orders` and `Customers` with the capability to restrict the number of columns returned by the query:

```
using (DevHorizonDataContext context = new
    DevHorizonDataContext(SPContext.Current.Web.Url))
    {
        var log = new StringBuilder();
        TextWriter logWriter = new StringWriter(log);
        context.Log = logWriter;

        var results = from orderItem in context.Orders
                    select new { orderItem.Title,
                        Company = orderItem.CustomerID.CompanyName,
                        Contact = orderItem.CustomerID.ContactName
                            };

        foreach (var order in results)
        {
            writer.WriteLine(string.Format("Order ID: {0}, Company :
                {1}, Contact: {2} <br/>", order.Title,
                order.Company, order.Contact));
        }

        ExtractCAML(log.ToString());
                delimiter.RenderControl(writer);
                camlDisplayArea.RenderControl(writer);
    }
```

Note two things about this code:

➤ The `new` keyword is used in the LINQ expression to create an anonymous type that contains a `Title` column (`Order ID`) from the `Orders` list, as well as `CompanyName` and `ContactName` from the `Customers` list.

➤   For debugging purposes, and to review the CAML query that lies behind the LINQ query, the `Log` property of the `DataContext` class is set to `TextWriter`. The result is then sent to a helper method (`ExtractCAML`), which then renders the generated CAML in a `Literal` control, as shown in Figure 20-22. Of course, you could redirect the log to other outputs (such as a physical file on the filesystem). You can take the generated CAML query and execute it using the `SPList.GetItems(SPQuery)` method to get the same result.

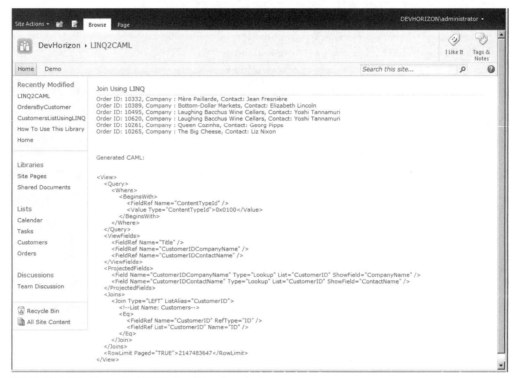

FIGURE 20-22: Generated CAML in a Literal control

As you can see, the LINQ query is turned into a simple CAML query with one join predicate (`<join>` element). Additionally, the columns specified in the anonymous type have been translated into an enumeration of three `<FieldRef>` elements within the `<ViewFields>` element. Also, note that `CustomerID` is the only field present in the `<ProjectedFields>`. That's because you didn't specify other columns from the `Customers` list for display in the `Orders` list.

The capability to join lists using a lookup column and specify the projected columns in CAML is new in SharePoint 2010.

Limitations of LINQ to SharePoint

As you can see, LINQ to SharePoint is a powerful way to execute your SQL-like queries against SharePoint, and work with the result in a strongly typed way. However, LINQ has its own limitations.

First of all, similar to many SharePoint Features, LINQ to SharePoint currently does not support anonymous users, even if it's enabled on the site.

Second, entity classes are heavily dependent on the schema of the site. If the schema of the site changes for whatever reason, you must rebuild the entity classes by running SPMetal again. Essentially, LINQ works pretty much like an O/R mapper when it comes to schema changes in the underlying data source.

Another limitation is that SPMetal cannot generate the entity classes for more than a site (SPWeb). If your lists and content types are spread across multiple sites, you must temporarily move them to a staging site, and run the tool against it. To establish the right context for your queries, you must use the DataContext.RegisterList method to tell the run-time where to find the missing lists and content types when you move them back to their original sites.

A fourth limitation is again with SPMetal. External lists are generally ignored when the tool is building the entity classes, except if they have a column of ID, in which case the tool errors out. You have two options to fix this: rename the column, or use parameters.xml (the SPMetal configuration file) to specifically ask for the lists, thus ignoring the problematic external list.

Another limitation is the number of CAML queries generated for a single LINQ query. A LINQ query with more than one CAML query is considered inefficient and blocked by the run-time. An example of an inefficient query is when you want to aggregate two lists without a relationship defined by a lookup column. In this case, you get an InvalidOperationException exception with the following message:

```
The query uses unsupported elements, such as references to more than one list,
    or the projection of a complete entity by using EntityRef/EntitySet.
```

Your choices to work around this limitation are as follows:

➤ Get the CAML behind the LINQ query and use it in the SPList.GetItems(SPQuery) method.

➤ Use two-stage queries. (For more information, see the official documentation on MSDN at http://www.devhorizon.com/go/29).

A sixth limitation is cross-site queries. Although it is perfectly possible to use LINQ to perform cross-site queries, this is not the most performant way. Use query classes specialized for cross-site queries (within the same site collection) such as SPSiteDataQuery, PortalSiteMapProvider, and CrossListQueryCache.

Another limitation occurs in sandboxed solutions. The sandbox implementation has some limitations when using certain LINQ to SharePoint queries. For example, when you use the StartsWith operator, an exact match is returned instead. This bug will likely be addressed in future updates.

An eighth limitation is the additional overhead that LINQ queries may cause because of the dynamic conversion to CAML at run-time.

Last, but certainly not least, the LINQ to SharePoint provider converts whatever it can to CAML, and for those parts that cannot be converted, LINQ to Objects will be used. As a best practice, you should avoid causing the LINQ to SharePoint provider to use LINQ to Objects if possible. This can create substantial overhead on the client, and severely impact the performance of your LINQ queries.

> *For more information on the efficiency of different LINQ to SharePoint constructs, and how to review the generated CAML, see "Query Efficiency with LINQ to SharePoint" section in Microsoft Patterns and Practices SharePoint Guidance at* http://www.devhorizon.com/go/30.

ACCESSING SHAREPOINT DATA USING THE CLIENT-SIDE OBJECT MODEL

As mentioned, you have a number of new ways to access SharePoint 2010 data, to present it to the end users, and to let them interact with it. The client-side object model (CSOM) is a new option. CSOM provides a consistent programming experience across three distinct sets of APIs:

➤ ECMAScript object model

➤ Silverlight client object model

➤ .NET managed client object model

These APIs interact with SharePoint using a subset of the server-side object model, and using the same familiar object hierarchy starting at the site collection level all the way down to webs, lists, list items, fields, and so on. If you have done coding using the server-side object model, you should be able to pick up the CSOM pretty quickly.

> *Although all client-side data access options discussed in this section can be used in server-side code as well, most of the time, the server-side object model remains the fastest and the most efficient option when your code executes on the server.*

In this section, you'll use the ECMAScript object model to build a client-side application that reads from the Customers list and presents it to the end user. You will also use the new Dialog APIs to add new customers to the list. So, from client-side script, you will perform two operations: querying list data and manipulating it.

Because this isn't a chapter on the new CSOM Feature in SharePoint, this discussion won't go into more detail on the Silverlight and .NET Managed client object model for accessing SharePoint data, because they are all very similar. However, it's important to point out the major differences.

The main difference between these APIs is their coverage of the SharePoint object model. ECMAScript and Silverlight object models are lighter in comparison to the .NET managed client object model, because they are meant to execute in a web page where every bit transferred over the wire matters. When it comes to interoperability, ECMAScript is the only client-side API that can be used in non-.NET applications where calls into the SharePoint object model are required.

From a functionality perspective, ECMAScript and Silverlight, by design, do not support synchronous operations to avoid blocking the UI thread and the user interaction for the duration of the operation. In Silverlight, however, you have the option to manually implement your synchronous operation in a background thread.

ClientContext Object: The Entry Point

Similar to coding against the server-side object model (in which you always need an entry point to the object model), the new CSOM also uses a ClientContext object to represent the context for SharePoint objects and operations covered in the CSOM. For example, consider the following scenarios:

➤ You need to return context information for a specific site collection, so you would use
`var clientContext = new SP.ClientContext("/sites/SiteCollection1");`

➤ You need to return the current context in which the client-side code is running, so you would use `var clientContext = SP.ClientContext.get_current();`

Querying Lists Using JavaScript

Now that you know how to get a handle into the CSOM, let's build a simple visual web part that fetches customers from the Customers list and displays them to the end user.

Open Visual Studio and create a SharePoint 2010 project with one visual web part named CustomersListUsingECMA. In the Solution Explorer, expand the CustomersListUsingECMA module, and open the CustomersListUsingECMA.ascx file by double-clicking it.

Add the following markup code at the bottom of the file, right underneath the directives that are already there:

```
<SharePoint:ScriptLink ID="ScriptLink1" runat="server" Name="sp.js"
    Localizable="false" LoadAfterUI="true" />
<table id="tblCustomersList" style="border: solid 1px
    silver"><tr><td>Loading...</td></tr></table>
<script language="ecmascript" type="text/ecmascript">
</script>
```

The tblCustomersList HTML tag defines an empty table to which your script will dynamically add rows for each customer returned. The ScriptLink control adds the necessary framework files (SP.js) required to use CSOM in your code. The LoadAfterUI="true" attribute ensures that SP.js is processed after the ScriptResource.axd file, which it depends on. You could also use OnDemand="true" to load SP.js on demand and not as part of the initial page load.

Like most of popular script libraries, SharePoint offers two flavors for its CSOM script. `SP.js` *is the "minified" version and* `SP.debug.js` *is the debug version (full version) where much of the CSOM is kept. Minifying scripts and CSS styles reduces the overall size of the page payload, and potentially results in faster page rendering.*

Obviously, you could also programmatically add this control in the `CreateChildControls()` or `OnPreRender()` methods of the web part. Personally, I prefer to stay away from code behind as much as possible when writing ECMA code.

Next, add the following JavaScript code within the `Script` block you added previously (before the closing `</script>` tag):

```
                    var clientContext = null;
    var customers;
    var customersList;
    var copyOfAddCustomerForm;

    function LoadCustomers() {
    clientContext = SP.ClientContext.get_current();
    var web = clientContext.get_web();
    customersList = web.get_lists().getByTitle("Customers");
    var query = new SP.CamlQuery();
    query.set_viewXml("<View><Query><OrderBy><FieldRef Name='Title'
        Ascending='FALSE'></FieldRef></OrderBy></Query></View>");
    customers = customersList.getItems(query);
    clientContext.load(customers);
    clientContext.executeQueryAsync(onCustomersListLoaded, onCustomersListFailed);
    }

function onCustomersListLoaded() {}
function onCustomersListFailed(sender, args) {}
ExecuteOrDelayUntilScriptLoaded(LoadCustomers, "sp.js");
```

The code starts with declaring useful global variables that will be used throughout the code. The `LoadCustomers()` function retrieves the current context and loads up the current web (just like `SPContext.Current.Web`). In the next line, through the `web` object, the `Customers` list is referenced. For now, to get the functionality running and keep the example easy, the name of the list is hard-coded. I'm sure you won't do this when writing production code.

Once you have a handle to the `Customers` list, a new instance of the `SP.CamlQuery` class is initialized, and it is set to return for all the customers in Toronto. Then, the CAML query is passed into the `customersList.getItems()` method for execution. The result is a collection of customers that will be saved in a `customers` global variable.

In the next line, the `clientContext.load` tells the client object model to load the objects scalar, in this case, loading global variable `customers`. Finally, the `executeQueryAsync` method is invoked asynchronously, passing two callback functions: `onCustomersListLoaded` and `onCustomersListFailed`. The callback functions will be called depending on success or failure of the asynchronous call.

At this point, both callback methods are empty. Don't worry, you will complete them in just a moment.

Because you are using the `ECMAScript` client object model, your JavaScript function (`LoadCustomers`) relies on a full load of the `SP.js` file. Remember, you set it to load after UI loads, commonly known as the *lazy loading nature* of `SP.js()`. The function won't work if `SP.js` is not already loaded. In this particular example, you must ensure that the custom code runs after `SP.js` finishes loading. To solve this timing issue, the `ExecuteOrDelayUntilScriptLoaded(LoadCustomers, "sp.js")` method is called, and the name of the function and `SP.js` are passed to it. This will take care of the timing for you.

> *The lazy loading nature of the* `SP.js` *file (enforced by the* `ScriptLink` *control), along with the* `ExecuteOrDelayUntilScriptLoaded` *method, causes a delay in the download of the script files until users can view the page. Using this technique, your pages are rendered more quickly.*

With the base code in place, let's add the callback methods and wrap up the code. First, add the following code to the `onCustomersListLoaded` callback method:

```
function onCustomersListLoaded() {
        var row = new Array();
        var cellcontent;
        var cell;
        var CustomersTable = document.getElementById('tblCustomersList');
        while (CustomersTable.rows.length > 0)
            CustomersTable.deleteRow(CustomersTable.rows.length - 1);
        var tb = document.createElement('tbody');
        var customerEnumerator = customers.getEnumerator();
        var index = 0;
        while (customerEnumerator.moveNext()) {
            row[index] = document.createElement('tr');
        var customer = customerEnumerator.get_current();
        var CompanyName = customer.get_item("CompanyName");
            cell = document.createElement('td');
            cellcontent = document.createTextNode(CompanyName);
            cell.appendChild(cellcontent);
            row[index].appendChild(cell);

            tb.appendChild(row[index]);
            index++;

        }
        CustomersTable.appendChild(tb);
    }
```

The code in `onCustomersListLoaded()` method is pretty self-explanatory because most of it deals with building the table with the content. Note the first highlighted section. An `enumerator` is created from the `customers` global variable. Using this enumerator, you can iterate through all the selected customers and add their company names to the table. For each customer, the `get_item()` method retrieves the values. In this particular example, the `Customers` list doesn't have a lookup field, but if it did, you could use the `get_lookupValue(FieldName)` method to retrieve the value of the lookup column, as shown in the following example:

```
customer.get_item(LookupFieldName).get_lookupValue();
```

Next, let's complete the `onCustomersListFailed` callback method by adding some error-handling code in case the call fails:

```
function onCustomersListFailed(sender, args) {
    alert(args.get_message());
}
```

Now that you have everything coded, let's build and deploy the project. If everything goes smoothly, you should be able to see the list of customers in your web part, as shown in Figure 20-23.

FIGURE 20-23: List of customers in web part

If you browse to the page where you deployed this web part, and if anonymous access is enabled on the site, you will see the error shown in Figure 20-24.

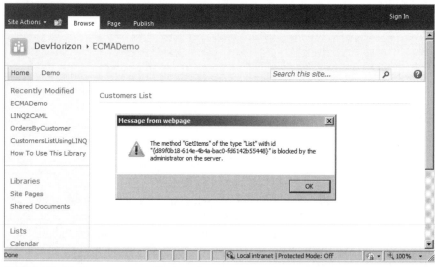

FIGURE 20-24: Error message displayed

Now, to solve this issue, you want to run the following PowerShell script from Run window. The script will remove the anonymous users restriction in calling into the GetItems() method.

```
$wa = Get-SPWebApplication "http://SITE_URL"
$wa.ClientCallableSettings.AnonymousRestrictedTypes.Remove(
    [microsoft.sharepoint.splist], "GetItems")
$wa.Update()
```

Manipulating SharePoint Data Using JavaScript

At this point, everything you wanted to build using the ECMA object model is completed, except for one thing: adding customers to the list. To add a customer, you use the SP.UI.ModalDialog class to create a modal dialog window that dynamically loads the content of a DIV tag, which contains controls that allow users to input data. The data collected by the modal dialog will then be used to add the customer to the list.

First, you must add the content of DIV tag and other required HTML markup to the page to support the functionality. Add the following HTML code snippet after the ending </table> tag:

```
<br />
<a href="javascript:ShowAddCustomer()">Add a customer</a>
<br />
<div id="divAddCustomer" style="display: none; padding: 5px">
    <b>Customer Information</b><br /><br />
    ID <br />
    <input type="text" id="txtCustomerID" /><br />
    Company Name <br />
    <input type="text" id="txtCompanyName" /><br />
    Contact Name<br />
    <input type="text" id="txtContactName" /><br />
    City<br />
    <input type="text" id="txtCity" /><br />
    Country<br />
    <input type="text" id="txtCountry" /><br />
    <span id="spnError" style="color: Red" /><br />
    <input type="button" value="Add New Customer" onclick="AddCustomer()" />
</div>
```

Note that, in the DIV tag, there is a button that calls into a JavaScript function called AddCustomer(), which will be coded later. Next, add the following JavaScript code in the main script block where all the other functions reside:

```
function ShowAddCustomer() {
    var divAddCustomer = document.getElementById("divAddCustomer");
    copyOfAddCustomerForm = divAddCustomer.cloneNode(true);
    divAddCustomer.style.display = "block";
    var options = { html: divAddCustomer, title: 'Add Customer', width:
        200, height: 350, dialogReturnValueCallback: ReAddClonedForm};
    modalDialog = SP.UI.ModalDialog.showModalDialog(options);
}

function ReAddClonedForm() {
    document.body.appendChild(copyOfAddCustomerForm);
}
```

The ShowAddCustomer() function is used to render a modal dialog using the SP.UI.ModalDialog .showModalDialog() method. Because the showModalDialog() method removes the elements passed in from the document object model (DOM), you clone a copy and add it back later in the ReAddClonedForm() function, which is set as modal dialog's callback method (see the options variable).

Now, you must add the main functions that do the actual work of adding the customer to the list. You do this in the AddCustomer() function, as shown in the following code:

```
function AddCustomer() {
        var licInfo = new SP.ListItemCreationInformation();
        customerListItem = customersList.addItem(licInfo);
        customerListItem.set_item('Title',
            document.getElementById("txtCustomerID").value);
        customerListItem.set_item('CompanyName',
            document.getElementById("txtCompanyName").value);
        customerListItem.set_item('ContactName',
            document.getElementById("txtContactName").value);
        customerListItem.set_item('City',
            document.getElementById("txtCity").value);
        customerListItem.set_item('Country',
            document.getElementById("txtCountry").value);
        customerListItem.update();
        clientContext.load(customerListItem);
        clientContext.executeQueryAsync(onCustomerAddedSuccess,
            onCustomerAddedFailed);
    }


    function onCustomerAddedSuccess() {
        modalDialog.close();
        LoadCustomers();

    }

    function onCustomerAddedFailed(sender, args) {
        var spnError = document.getElementById("spnError");
        spnError.innerHTML = args.get_message();
    }
```

In this AddCustomer() function, you continue to use the same client context you built previously, and use it to get a handle to a new list item in the Customers list. Next, you set the column values, and, finally, execute the query using the executeQueryAsync() method.

Figure 20-25 shows the new link on the web part and the modal dialog that opens as the result of clicking it.

Once you fill out the form, click Add New Customer and that's it! You should be able to see the new customer in the Customers list with no postback.

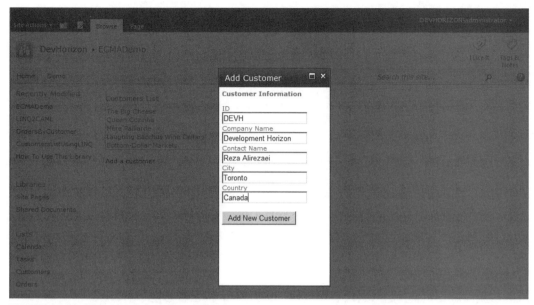

FIGURE 20-25: Web part link and modal dialog

JavaScript IntelliSense

Unfortunately, Visual Studio 2010 doesn't provide JavaScript IntelliSense right out of the box, but it is relatively easy to add. In visual web parts, you must add the following scripts to the user control either before or after your main script block. Once you do that, you'll get IntelliSense within your user control, as shown in Figure 20-26.

```
<script type="text/javascript" src="/_layouts/MicrosoftAjax.js" ></script>
<script type="text/javascript" src="/_layouts/SP.debug.js" />
```

FIGURE 20-26: Adding IntelliSense in Visual Studio

As mentioned previously, `SP.debug.js` is for debugging purposes only. So, when deploying to production, ensure that you remove these lines so that the minified version of `SP.js` (referenced in the `ScriptLink` control) is used.

In standalone scripts, use the following reference tags:

```
<reference path="C:\Program Files\Common Files\Microsoft Shared\Web Server
    Extensions\14\TEMPLATE\LAYOUTS\MicrosoftAjax.js" />
<reference path="C:\Program Files\Common Files\Microsoft Shared\Web Server
    Extensions\14\TEMPLATE\LAYOUTS\SP.debug.js" />
```

In application pages (within the `PageHead` content placeholder), or page layouts or site pages (within the `PlaceHolderAdditionalPageHead` content placeholder), use the following code to tell the conditional formatting to include `SP.debug.js` when debugging and, hence, provide IntelliSense:

```
<% #if DEBUG %>
<script type="text/javascript" src="/_layouts/SP.debug.js" />
<% #endif %>
```

ACCESSING SHAREPOINT DATA USING WEB SERVICES

So far, you have learned a number of ways to interact with SharePoint data. This section focuses on using web services. The section is divided into two topics:

➤ Windows Communication Foundation (WCF) data services

➤ Legacy ASP.NET web services

WCF Data Services

Possibly one of the easiest ways for developers to access SharePoint data in SharePoint is via a new service called `listdata.svc`. This service provides full REST (Representational State Transfer) over HTTP support for manipulating list data (not a document library), as well as browsing list and document library data using regular HTTP verbs such as GET, POST, PUT, DELETE, and MERGE.

WCF data services are based on a platform-neutral protocol called Open Data (OData), which further extends Atom and AtomPub protocols for exchanging XML data over HTTP, and supports advanced features such as batching, concurrency control, and partial updates.

 I personally prefer not to use the terms "OData" or "REST" to refer to the `ListData.svc` service, because the former is the protocol that the service is based on, and the latter is the design pattern that the service follows (which describes how the service can be accessed). I prefer to use SharePoint WCF data service.

To use the new WCF data service, you must first install it. Browse to the download page at `http://www.devhorizon.com/go/31`, and download the `Windows6.1-KB976127-v6-x64.msu` file. Then, double-click the file to run the update.

Once the update is installed, the standard location for the service is _vti_bin (ISAPI folder), so, if you simply type into your browser the URL of your site and append /_vti_bin/listdata.svc, you will get a standard Atom feed format that describes the data available in your site.

To see the returned Atom feed, you may need to turn off the feed reader view in your browser. In Internet Explorer 8, this option can be turned off by unchecking the "Turn on feed reading view" option in Tools ➪ Internet Options ➪ Content Tab ➪ Feed and Web Slices ➪ Settings.

Notice that the lists you created earlier in this chapter are all present. By further appending /Customers to the URL, you can retrieve all the customers in the Customers list, or you can retrieve any specific one by appending a number. For example, the following URL returns the first customer, as shown in Figure 20-27.

```
http://wfe1/_vti_bin/listdata.svc/Customers(1)
```

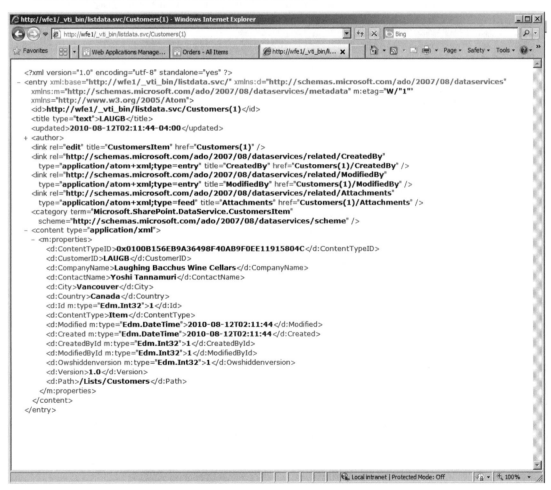

FIGURE 20-27: Returning the first customer in the list

You can perform more advanced queries by appending the `$filter` property, as shown here:

```
?$filter=startswith(propname,'value')
```

For example, the following URL returns the customers for whom their `City` column has a value that starts with "To," such as "Toronto":

```
http://wfe1/_vti_bin/listdata.svc/Customers?$filter=startswith(City,'To')
```

Let's build a console application that uses `listdata.svc` to query the `Customers` list. The first step is to create the WCF data services service proxy.

In the Solution Explorer window, right-click Service References and select the Add Service Reference option. This opens the Add Service Reference Wizard, where you can type in the URL to the `listdata.svc` in the context of your test website, as shown in Figure 20-28.

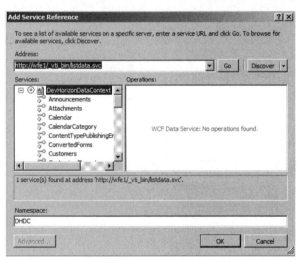

FIGURE 20-28: Add Service Reference Wizard

Like all other data access methods you have seen in this chapter, you must instantiate a data context to perform a data operation. In this particular example, the data context class is named `DevHorizonDataContext`.

```
DevHorizonDataContext clientContext = new
    DevHorizonDataContext("http://wfe1/_vti_bin/listdata.svc");
```

Once the data context is established, you can use LINQ queries to perform data operations. Now, you must add the following code to the `Main()` method of your console application:

```
DevHorizonDataContext clientContext = new DevHorizonDataContext( new
    Uri("http://wfe1/_vti_bin/listdata.svc"));
clientContext.Credentials = CredentialCache.DefaultCredentials;
var customersQuery = (DataServiceQuery<CustomersItem>)
clientContext.Customers.Where(c => c.City.StartsWith("To"));
foreach (var customer in customersQuery)
```

```
    {
            Console.WriteLine(customer.CompanyName + "::" + customer.ContactName);
            }

    Console.ReadLine();
```

The code first establishes the context and specifies the user credentials for authenticating to the service. That's the security context of whoever is running the console application, or, in the case of in-browser applications such as Silverlight, the current logged-on user.

The code uses a LINQ syntax to build a query expression that returns all customers for whom their city starts with "To" (like "Toronto"). The returned query is of type DataServiceQuery<TElement>, which is stored in the customersQuery variable. Finally, the code iterates through the result and outputs it to the console, as shown in Figure 20-29.

FIGURE 20-29: Displaying the result of the query

When you submit a LINQ query to the service proxy, it converts your query into a URL-based REST request (just like the examples shown earlier), and submits the request to the listdata.svc WCF data service on the server. This is counted as one conversion. The service then converts the received URL request into a LINQ to SharePoint expression (the second conversion). Finally, as you saw earlier in this chapter, the LINQ to SharePoint provider converts the LINQ expression into a CAML query, which is considered as the third (the last) conversion.

Obviously, there is a performance hit with your REST queries because they have to hop through three conversions before they find their way to the SharePoint object model. The CSOM is the only data access option that allows you to submit a CAML query directly from your client-side logic, and has less overhead compared to the SharePoint WCF data service.

In addition to an Atom feed, the SharePoint WCF data service can also return the result in JavaScript Object Notation (JSON) format. JSON is a lightweight data-exchange serialization format that is derived from JavaScript, and can be easily used in JavaScript clients.

The following code shows a JSON function that calls into the listdata.svc WCF data service and returns the customers. The return result is then rendered in a DIV tag.

```
<script src="http://ajax.microsoft.com/ajax/jquery/jquery-1.3.2.min.js"
    type="text/javascript"></script>
<script type="text/javascript">
$(document).ready(function () {
  $.getJSON("http://wfe1/_vti_bin/listdata.svc/Customers",function (jsonData)
    {
    $.each(jsonData.d.results, function (i, customer) {
```

```
        var CompanyName = customer.CompanyName;
        var ContactName = customer.ContactName;
        html = "<li><b>" + CompanyName + "::" + ContactName + "</b></li>";
        html += "<hr/>";
        $('#divCustomers').append($(html));
        });
    });
});
</script>
<div id="divCustomers"></div>
```

When you deploy the visual web part and run it in your site, you should get the result shown in Figure 20-30.

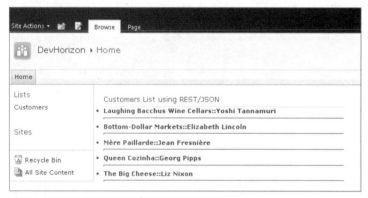

FIGURE 20-30: Using a JSON function to generate a result

As you can see, interacting with the `listdata.svc` WCF data service is not difficult.

Legacy ASP.NET Web Services

Just like in Microsoft Office SharePoint Server (MOSS) 2007, a number of web services are available in SharePoint 2010, all implemented as ASP.NET web services. For backward compatibility, SharePoint 2010 ships with all web services available in MOSS 2007, but some of them are changed (for example, `userprofileservice.asmx`) and a few new ones are added (for example, `TaxonomyClientService.asmx`).

The primary job of these services is to allow accessing SharePoint data remotely. If you have ever coded against SharePoint legacy web services, most likely you have used them either in lieu of the server-side object model or for remote calls.

Following are the top reasons why you should favor the server-side object model instead of web services, if possible:

➤ Web services are more difficult to use, and they may increase development time.

➤ Web services are slower. Referencing DLLs in your server-side code always outperforms referencing and calling into a web service — always!

➤ Web services are not fully featured APIs, so many operations that can be accomplished in the server-side object model simply can't be done via web services. The coverage of the object model by web services is limited.

Because of future compatibility, Microsoft has made it crystal clear (see `http://www.devhorizon` `.com/go/32` for more information) that it's not a best practice to use legacy ASP.NET web services for remote calls when the client object model or REST APIs can do the job. If the client object model or REST cannot meet your needs, you can always build custom WCF services to fill the gap.

 For more information on how to build WCF Services in SharePoint 2010, see the official documentation on MSDN at `http://www.devhorizon.com/go/33.`

So, if legacy ASP.NET web services are that bad, why are they still in SharePoint 2010? Aside from backward compatibility, a number of scenarios still exist in which you may want to use web services, even in your server-side code. As an architect and developer, it's important to know those scenarios.

One of those scenarios is when you need to query for data across the server farm where using search APIs is not an option. Another scenario is to perform administrative operations remotely using web services located in the `%ProgramFiles%\Common Files\Microsoft Shared\web server extensions\` `14\ADMISAPI` folder.

Last, but certainly not least, SharePoint web services offer bulk operations such as updating, deleting, and adding list items. These operations are a lot easier using web services, and they consume fewer resources compared to the object model, because your code invokes a single commit transaction.

 For more information on batch operations, see the official documentation on MSDN at `http://www.devhorizon.com/go/34.`

Plus, if you need to get the list items or the entire list schema, web services spit out a much cleaner result. As you saw earlier in this chapter, `SPListItemCollection.XML` returns the result in `XMLDATA` format with lots of "I do not care" elements and attributes in it.

In the end, like everything else in SharePoint, it's a mixed bag. Use web services where they make sense, and avoid using them where it doesn't.

ACCESSING SHAREPOINT DATA USING NO-CODE SOLUTIONS

Accessing SharePoint data using server or client object models is great, but in a number of scenarios users require virtually no-code solutions to extract data from SharePoint lists and document libraries.

Because this chapter is mainly intended for a technical audience, this discussion won't go into much detail on no-code solutions. But, as a developer and an architect, it is always good to know your choices. Following are a few of them:

➤ You can use out-of-the-box rollup web parts such as the Content Query web part.

➤ You can use Business Intelligence (BI) in SharePoint 2010 with support for accessing SharePoint list data.

➤ Outlook offers synchronization with some SharePoint data.

➤ Microsoft SharePoint Workspace 2010 (formerly Microsoft Office Groove) is a rich client application for SharePoint that allows you to synchronize your SharePoint site (including data) with your desktop computer.

> *If you are interested in learning more about how new BI capabilities of SharePoint 2010 can help you access your SharePoint data, see* Professional SharePoint 2010 Development *(Indianapolis: Wrox, 2010).*

SUMMARY

SharePoint provides a lot of new options in the functional area of accessing its data. One of the toughest tasks for a developer and architect is to first understand the new Features, and then figure out how to apply them. With the pressures of project delivery and cost, it's quite challenging to know everything in sufficient depth in order to make optimal decisions.

This chapter focused on helping you understand some of these new Features and how they differ from each other. As a follow-up to this chapter, you should check out client and list data model reference implementations in Microsoft Patterns and Practices SharePoint Guidance at `http://www .microsoft.com/spg`.

ABOUT THE AUTHOR

Reza Alirezaei (MVP, MCPD, MCPIT, and MCTS for SharePoint 2010) is an architect focused on designing custom applications with SharePoint, Office, and Microsoft Business Intelligence (BI) products and technologies. As a technical leader with more than 12 years of experience in the software industry, he has helped many development teams architect and build large-scale, mission-critical applications. In addition to consulting, Alirezaei is an instructor and speaker. He speaks in many local and international conferences. Alirezaei achieved the status of Microsoft Most Valuable Professional (MVP) for SharePoint in 2006 which he still is today. Other than this book, Alirezaei has co-authored two more SharePoint books: *Professional SharePoint 2010 Development* (Indianapolis: Wiley, 2010) and *Professional Microsoft SharePoint 2007 Reporting with SQL Server 2008 Reporting Services* (Indianapolis: Wiley, 2009). He blogs at `http://blogs.devhorizon.com/reza` and tweets on Twitter @RezaAlirezay.

21

Finding Answers to Your SharePoint 2010 Questions

By Mike Walsh

This is the final chapter in what has hopefully been a very interesting and useful book. My 21 MVP colleagues each have written about a SharePoint 2010 subject close to their hearts. But what if they didn't cover something you need to know more about, or what if you want more than a single chapter can give you?

This chapter will help you to find additional resources to supplement what you have read in this book. It will also help you as you continually track Microsoft developments, and point you to other articles and documents that may help you with your SharePoint experience. This chapter also provides hints on how to search for solutions and post questions to forums.

LOOKING FOR BOOKS

By buying this book, you have already shown yourself to be someone who uses technical books to improve your knowledge. So, the natural first choice when seeking additional information is to look for some more books. Assuming that your local bookstore doesn't have a complete set of SharePoint 2010 books, you'll no doubt be heading off to an Internet bookseller like Amazon or Barnes & Noble.

Amazon probably has the largest selection of books, so a natural choice would be to head for the largest Amazon site, which is the U.S. one, and enter "SharePoint" (or "SharePoint 2010") as the search criteria for the Books section.

That approach has several snags:

➤ *Too many books are listed* — The search will first list books that have "SharePoint" in the title, but will then move on to listing books that mention "SharePoint" in the text. Mostly, these will be uninteresting to SharePoint specialists, and, in some of them, the reference will be simply to "another book in this series" that has "SharePoint" in the title.

➤ *In the first set of books listed, you will only get books with SharePoint in the title* — Toward the top of the search return results, the search will not list books about specialist subjects such as Excel Services or workflow. If you are lucky, the books on specialist subjects might be listed somewhere much later down the list among all the books that mention SharePoint somewhere in the text. To find books on the specialized areas, you'll need to do several specific searches.

➤ *The lists are not sorted according to the kind of book* — If you are interested only in books for developers, you must work your way through a list that contains books that do not interest you.

➤ *The list will contain English-language books, plus very few books in other languages* — Amazon (U.S.) does occasionally have books listed in different languages. But the local Amazon France, Germany, and Japan sites, for example, have many more, including both books written in that language, and books translated from English.

➤ *Some books are never listed in any Amazon site* — Mostly, these are books in languages such as Spanish and Portuguese, for which there is no Amazon site. But there are also privately published books that never achieve an Amazon listing.

➤ *Some books are available only in downloadable versions and are not available at Amazon* — Your Amazon searches will find the Kindle versions of books as well, but a few "books" (such as Wrox Blox offerings) are available only in downloadable PDF versions, and these can often only be found at the publishers' sites.

The net result is that being aware of all the books that are available (or about to become available) requires a major effort. In today's world of technology, that often means searching the Internet for someone who has already made that effort.

I've made that effort for many years. My own WSS FAQ sites have had a book page since Windows SharePoint Services (WSS) 2.0 and SharePoint Server (SPS) 2003, and, as is typical with the Internet, the sites have continually been improved over the years, along with my skills in finding books. The latest v4 (SharePoint 2010 products and technologies) site has a book page consisting of all the books on SharePoint 2010 and related subjects that I have found by searching various Amazon sites, asking other MVPs about which titles they are writing, searching Spanish and Italian publisher sites, reading a selection of RSS feeds, and so on.

That book page (`http://wssv4faq.mindsharp.com/Lists/v4FAQ/V%20Books.aspx`) is grouped according to type of book, so that, for example, all the development books are listed in the same section. There's also an "OUT" column that indicates whether the book is available at any Amazon site (and not just listed there as being in a pre-release state). A late addition, as a result of user feedback, is a Published Date column to indicate at a glance for non-released books when they are likely to be available.

It's a good idea to do some (price) comparison shopping, especially if you live in a European country that does not have its own Amazon site. Sometimes prices in one country site are considerably less than in another.

There are, however, a few caveats to keep in mind when making price comparisons.

The first is that the rules for postage charges vary, depending on which Amazon site you are using. If you live in the same country as the site, you may get free shipping, but otherwise there might be a fixed price per parcel (such as with Amazon Germany), or a basic delivery-charge-plus-item charge that will be different from one Amazon site to another. (For example, France charges more than the United Kingdom.)

Because of different tax rates, the listed price may change because of where you live. For example, the United Kingdom imposes no tax on books, but Finland levies an 8 percent tax on books. So, when you order a book that is listed at a price of 5 English pounds, when you indicate that you want the book delivered to Finland, the price of the book increases to 5.40 pounds (plus additional postage charges). This sort of thing applies to Amazon France and Amazon Germany, too. Amazon U.S., however, doesn't change the price because of where you live (just the postage charge). Kindle prices nowadays do vary with location, with prices for European customers at Amazon US often much more than the "additional tax costs" Amazon US claims. Amazon UK doesn't even (as of August 2010) sell Kindle Books to non-UK addresses.

As far as my site goes, although I try to keep track of new book listings, and whether or not a book has been published, I can't (on a regular weekly basis) update the prices of each book in each Amazon site. So, regard the prices I list for the book as being prices that were correct at the time stated on the web page. If you want to be sure, access the individual URLs to see the latest prices in each store.

Also note that, for Europeans, the Amazon U.S. prices may seem very attractive, but even the lowest postal charges outweigh most of the price differences — and also tend to mean a two- to three-week wait for delivery. If a book is in stock at Amazon U.K., and isn't too expensive there, you may well (even in mainland Europe) get the book cheaper (and certainly much quicker) than if you purchased it from Amazon U.S. Amazon U.S. has also started using less packing material — especially avoiding non-degradable plastic. This might work in the U.S., but, with much longer delivery times to Europe, the fact that the books are just dumped into a box and dispatched can lead to damage (for example, water damage) and the need to ask for replacement copies (as a refund, which the website suggests, is pointless because of the high cost of postage that isn't refunded).

So, what about areas of SharePoint 2010 knowledge that aren't covered by books? Or, what about situations in which you aren't prepared to wait for a book to arrive? The following sections explore some alternatives.

CONTINUALLY EXPANDING YOUR KNOWLEDGE

You probably purchased this book, and you've read it this far, so I presume you are the kind of IT professional who likes to do some research before installing and/or running something. This section is geared for just that kind of mindset, because it covers a lot of resources you could be following to expand your knowledge *before* you have a problem that must be solved.

Following are the resources that are explored here:

➤   Microsoft sites

➤   Webcasts

➤   Knowledge Base articles

➤   Online magazines

➤   Blogs

➤   Newsgroups and forums

➤   RSS feeds

This discussion points you to resources you can use to track what is available, what issues people are commonly experiencing, and how to solve those problems. The purpose of this discussion is not necessarily to force you to remember everything that has caught your attention, but to remember that something about "X" has appeared in one of these resources, and hopefully which resource might have what you're looking for. This will simplify searching for answers (which is discussed later in this chapter) when you do have a specific problem you are researching.

So, let's take a look at these resources in a bit more detail.

Microsoft Sites

Here are three main Microsoft sites that should be of interest to SharePoint users and developers:

➤   Microsoft Developer Network (MSDN)

➤   TechNet

➤   Microsoft Office

You'll notice that I don't mention the Microsoft SharePoint site itself (`http://sharepoint.microsoft.com` *or any of the Resource Centers such as the one for Enterprise Content Management at* `http://msdn.microsoft.com/fi-fi/sharepoint/ff843952(en-us).aspx`*). That's because experience has shown that the Microsoft SharePoint sites tend to be both rather lacking in the information they contain, and also that the people supporting them tend to lose interest quickly (perhaps once they have started working on the next version). All that is left (until they do a re-vamp and start all over again) is an automatically generated site with links. This might not happen for SharePoint 2010, but it has happened for every version so far, so the chances are that it will happen again. By all means, do a search for "SharePoint Resource Centers" to check them out for yourself though.*

MSDN Site

The MSDN site is a good source for two things:

➤ Long, detailed articles (some from Microsoft people, but most from outside experts), often with quality diagrams

➤ Descriptive items (in narrative form with no diagrams) taken from the Software Development Kits (SDKs) for SharePoint 2010 and SharePoint Foundation (SPF) 2010

MSDN is for developers, and so most of the articles (and the SDK) are of interest to developers.

Several good ways to be aware of what new long articles on SharePoint are available from MSDN are:

➤ *Set up an RSS feed* — The URL feed at `http://www.microsoft.com/feeds/msdn/en-us/sharepoint/rss.xml` is described as being for all SharePoint MSDN articles.

➤ *Monitor the downloads coming from Microsoft* — To do this, you can use the RSS feed at `http://www.thundermain.com/rss`. (The download site is located at `http://www.microsoft.com/downloads`.)

> *In whatever your situation may be, it's very worth it to monitor this download site, because this is where you'll find links to service packs and other useful products, such as virtual hard disk (VHD) versions of operating systems, and ready-made SharePoint installations. Last year, there were a couple of such SharePoint (2007) VHD versions, one of which was a complete development environment. This year (2010) there is already a VHD available that contains both Office 2010 and SPS 2010 (`http://www.microsoft.com/downloads/details.aspx?displaylang=en&FamilyID=751fa0d1-356c-4002-9c60-d539896c66ce`). (See `http://msdn.microsoft.com/en-us/sharepoint/bb964529.aspx` for links to several Resource Centers.)*

➤ *Monitor the list of technical articles from MSDN* — Check out `http://msdn.microsoft.com/en-us/library/ff420368.aspx`.

To access details for the online SDK, begin with the following URL:

`http://msdn.microsoft.com/en-us/library/ee557253.aspx`

TechNet Site

The TechNet website does not offer long, detailed articles. Instead, it provides descriptions like those in MSDN, but the difference is that, with TechNet, these descriptions are procedures for administrators, and they are regularly updated whenever necessary. Usually, updates are posted because the original text was not clear, rather than wrong. However, textual errors are also corrected occasionally.

The URL `http://technet.microsoft.com/en-us/library/cc288223.aspx` leads to the "Newly published content for SharePoint Foundation 2010" page. Here you will find updated pages that list and link to every new or modified TechNet article on SPF 2010 during a particular week. The URL `http://technet.microsoft.com/en-us/library/cc262043.aspx` leads to a similar page for SharePoint Server (SPS) 2010.

Again, the best way to be aware of newly posted and amended items is to set up an RSS feed.

Here are the feeds for the previously mentioned two Newly Published Content pages:

➤ `http://services.social.microsoft.com/feeds/feed/`
`SharePointFoundation2010NewContent`

➤ `http://services.social.microsoft.com/feeds/feed/`
`SharePointServer2010NewContent`

Microsoft Office Site

At the Microsoft Office site (`http://office.microsoft.com/en-us/FX100647101033.aspx`), you'll eventually find long and short articles about specific aspects of SharePoint 2010. Many of the longer articles (and some of the shorter ones) from the Office site include links to matching webcasts.

The previous Microsoft Office URL points to the site for all of Office. If you want to just look at the SharePoint information, go to `http://office.microsoft.com/en-us/sharepoint-help/`.

> *As of this writing, neither of these sites offer the clear and direct access to all Office articles for SharePoint that the equivalent 2007 sites used to provide. Until they do, the recommendation is to use the Microsoft Office Developer RSS feed at* `http://www.microsoft.com/feeds/msdn/en-us/office/rss.xml`. *Despite the title, this includes many SharePoint-related links.*

Webcasts

In addition to the webcasts provided in connection with some Office articles, typically longer MSDN, TechNet, and other webcasts are available from Microsoft. The best place to look for most of these is at the following URL:

`http://www.microsoft.com/events/webcasts/ondemand.mspx`

Most of these use the level-of-difficulty scales that might be familiar to many of you through your attendance at the larger Microsoft conferences such as TechEd. So, for example, a 100 webcast is for people new to the product, 200 introduces more difficulties, 300 is starting to be beyond me, and 400 is for geniuses only. Obviously, the level you should watch depends more on your existing knowledge of the product being discussed than anything else. I find SharePoint 100 webcasts to be over-simplistic.

Following are a few more places that provide webcasts:

➤ *Channel 9 webcasts* — The general address for this is `http://channel9.msdn.com/`. If possible, you should use that URL and look around, because the site is rather chaotic and seems to put good things everywhere. For example, `http://channel9.msdn.com/posts/Learn/Using-Access-2010-and-SharePoint-2010-Services/` is a page pointing to a training unit about the Access Services function of SPS 2010. (You can find it via the not-too-obvious "learn" menu item.) Despite its name, this is also a Microsoft site. It provides the chatty, more casual kind of webcasts that some people prefer.

➤ *Get Started Developing on SharePoint 2010* — This site at `http://msdn.microsoft.com/en-us/sharepoint/ee513147.aspx` started out in the early beta phase of the product with a good series of ten webcasts. It is worth tracking to see if it keeps up this early promise. (Even by August 2010 nothing had changed except for a change in the page's title and the SharePoint 2010 Developer Training Course at `http://channel9.msdn.com/learn/courses/SharePoint2010Developer/` was the place where developer web casts were being added.)

➤ *The TechNet "How Do I?" videos* — These are located at `http://technet.microsoft.com/en-us/cc138021.aspx`. You will find a SharePoint section.

➤ *Private webcasts* — Several people (Microsoft MVPs and others) also provide webcasts on SharePoint.

As with books, I try to monitor all these sources and could save you time if you are prepared to accept my selection of webcasts. Look for my recommendations at `http://wssv4faq.mindsharp.com/Lists/v4WebCasts/AllItems.aspx`.

Microsoft Knowledge Base Articles

The typical way to track recent Knowledge Base (KB) articles is via a product-specific RSS feed. However, this can be problematic because having feeds only for, say, SPF 2010, SPS 2010, and SharePoint Designer (SPD) 2010 isn't enough. There might be SharePoint-relevant posts in Office 2010 articles, ForeFront articles, InfoPath articles, or somewhere else.

Again, I have a web page at `http://wssv4faq.mindsharp.com/Lists/v4KBArticles/v4%20Sorted%20by%20Date.aspx` that you might find useful to use instead of trying to track all the different RSS feeds yourself.

Microsoft has provided new RSS feeds for KB articles for both SPS 2010 and SPD 2010. These are `http://support.microsoft.com/common/rss.aspx?rssid=14944&ln=en-us&msid=d080617a8f544ba9b606f1d738d2fbe5` and `http://support.microsoft.com/common/rss.aspx?rssid=14970&ln=en-us&msid=d080617a8f544ba9b606f1d738d2fbe5`, respectively.

Although, as of this writing, there is no separate feed for SPF 2010 KB articles, this isn't a huge problem because SPS 2010 articles that also apply to SPF 2010 will have SharePoint Foundation 2010 (also) listed in the "Applies To" section of the KB article.

Magazines

In today's world of technology, magazines come not only in the traditional printed format, but also are available through the Internet. This section looks at some good sources for magazines.

Microsoft Magazines

A couple of good places to look for information are monthly Microsoft magazines, which used to also be available in paper form (and were rather expensive), but now are only available on the Internet (free). Following are descriptions of these:

➤ *TechNet Magazine* (`http://technet.microsoft.com/en-us/magazine/default.aspx`) — This is considered by some to be the better of the two for SharePoint articles, because there has been at least one SharePoint article almost every month for the past couple of years. Extra articles are occasionally included if justified by the main subject covered by that month's magazine.

➤ *MSDN Magazine* (`http://msdn.microsoft.com/en-us/magazine/default.aspx`) — This has SharePoint articles much less often than *TechNet Magazine,* because the articles only appear if SharePoint (or a product that is closely related to SharePoint) is featured in that month's issue.

Additional Online Magazines

Outside of the realm of Microsoft, several online, advertising-driven SharePoint magazines of varying quality are also available. An example of this breed is *SharePoint Magazine* (`http://sharepointmagazine.net/`) that, despite being a quarterly magazine, looks very much like a fairly normal website. The difference is that most of the text on the site is written by people other than the site's owner.

Blogs

Blogs are another way to find good information about SharePoint 2010. However, the primary problem is the varying degree of information offered. The contents of even a good blog can vary between worthwhile technical content on SharePoint to inside information about newly born children. So, what you must do is find a SharePoint blogger you like, and then perhaps take a look at the other SharePoint bloggers that he or she cross-references or recommends.

Following are some good sources for SharePoint blogs.

MVP Blogs

Most of the authors of this book also write blogs. It would be overkill to have a list of all of them here, so what follows is just a small random selection of some of them.

➤ *Karine Bosch* (`http://karinebosch.wordpress.com/`) — Often posts on Silverlight, but also general information posts.

➤ *Randy Drisgill* (`http://blog.drisgill.com/`) — Mostly discusses branding.

➤ *Gary LaPointe* (`http://stsadm.blogspot.com/`) — Heavily programming-oriented posts.

➤ *Agnes Molnar* (`http://dotneteers.net/blogs/aghy/`) — Offers short pieces on how to do things in SharePoint 2010.

➤ *Chris O'Brien* (`http://www.sharepointnutsandbolts.com/`) — Focuses on programming/ deployment, but sometimes writes about more.

There's also a selection of links to the latest items from several SharePoint blogs at the Alltop (SharePoint) site (`http://sharepoint.alltop.com/`). This includes links to the blogs of several SharePoint MVPs, including some of the other contributors to this book.

Team Blogs

Some SharePoint Blogs are known as *team blogs*. These Microsoft blogs are must-reads, because they sometimes contain scoops (that is, information that you will get first through the blog) and official statements.

I follow quite a few team blogs, including those focused on several Office 2010 client products. Following are my top three SharePoint 2010 team blogs:

➤ *SharePoint Team Blog* (`http://blogs.msdn.com/b/sharepoint/`) — This has far too many marketing posts, but they are easily recognizable, and some of the other posts are essential reading.

➤ *SharePoint Designer Team Blog* (`http://blogs.msdn.com/b/sharepointdesigner/`) — This wasn't very active in the 2007 product times, so I'm hoping for an improvement for the 2010 version of the product.

➤ *SharePoint Developer Documentation Team Blog* (`http://blogs.msdn.com/b/ sharepointdeveloperdocs/`) — This is still in its early days (as of this writing). It started up toward the end of the SharePoint 2007 period.

Perhaps the best team blog is the one for Excel at `http://blogs.msdn.com/b/excel/`. Early indications are that the same team will also be prolific writers on Excel Services.

So, there you have it — some direction on blogs. This should provide you with something to get your teeth into, and help you decide for yourself the kinds of blogs and bloggers you are interested in. Note, too, that all of the previously mentioned team blogs have RSS feeds available.

Newsgroups and Forums

The discussion in this section focuses only on the Microsoft newsgroups and forums. However, a couple of different forum systems are mentioned later.

Newsgroups

Note that some newsgroups such as Google Groups and Egghead Café are actually not different newsgroup systems from the Microsoft examples provided here. In fact, they are front ends to the same newsgroup system. Egghead Café is a front end that produces odd effects when replies are made via the newsgroup (and quotes of earlier posts are lost, even though they appear if you look at the newsgroup via the Egghead Café front-end). Use of these front-end systems for posting to the newsgroups is, therefore, not recommended, although Google Groups *is* recommended for searching the newsgroups.

Following are a couple of the benefits of newsgroups:

➤ They can be accessed very quickly via *newsgroup readers* (such as Outlook Express or Thunderbird).

➤ Messages to them can be read off-line (using some newsgroup readers), and answers also can be written off-line and posted only when connected again.

These days, this second benefit is not much of an advantage, because most people are no longer paying per minute for their Internet access. It's also possible to access newsgroups via browsers, but then they are just as slow (comparatively) as using forums (which are examined shortly).

The disadvantages of newsgroups used to be that they were impossible to moderate. This meant that irresponsible users would post their (identical) questions to many different forums, or to the wrong forum, and there was nothing anyone could do about it. The occasional spam post also lasted longer in the newsgroups than they now do in the forums, and posts with flames remained forever.

However, the primary problem today with newsgroups is that they are in decline. There are now (as of this writing) only three SharePoint newsgroups left, and the number of new posts in those newsgroups is a small fraction of what it used to be. Also, the Microsoft support people who used to frequent them have moved on to the Microsoft forums, as have most of the MVPs and many other experienced people who previously used to provide "peer" support in the newsgroups.

You can access the SharePoint newsgroups through your newsreader by going to `msnews.microsoft.com` and specifying "SharePoint" as a selection criterion. However, for 2010 questions/solutions, the recommendation is that you completely ignore newsgroups. If you also have 2007 questions, then don't access the newsgroups as described here, but instead search using "Google Groups - Advanced Search," which accesses indexed content of all the SharePoint newsgroups, including those that were recently removed.

Forums

Of much more importance these days are forums, which, unlike newsgroups, Microsoft does control.

The main advantages of using forums are the reverse of the situation for newsgroups. There is Microsoft support in most of the forums, and there are moderators with the capability to remove spam, delete duplicate posts, move posts to a different SharePoint forum (where they are more likely to get an answer), and move completely off-topic posts to the (forum-wide) Off-Topic forum. Moderators can also remove personal attacks, remove posts asking for "urgent" or "ASAP" help (something forums are not meant for, as you will see later in this chapter), and so on. There are also a large number of qualified people providing mostly accurate and helpful answers to the questions of other users.

The main problem with the forums is that access to them is via web browsers, and, thus, they are relatively slow compared to using newsgroup readers. This is especially the case when just reading messages to get a feel for a product (which is something I recommend you do before you post to a forum, a topic that is addressed later in this chapter).

The original Microsoft SharePoint forums were established in the early WSS 3.0/MOSS 2007 era, and experience has shown that there were too many of them leading to too many off-topic posts, as well as some forums having virtually no posts at all. There was a lot of discussion before the product names were specified, but, as always when something is actually in use, confusion rose among some forum users. This, too, led to occasional off-topic posts.

Both problems seem to have been at least partially resolved with the new SharePoint 2010 forums. The old SharePoint forums will only be used for all previous SharePoint products and versions that came before SharePoint 2010. The new SharePoint 2010 forums will cover all the products included under the umbrella of SharePoint 2010 (which will mainly mean SPF 2010, as well as the Standard and Enterprise versions of SPS 2010) and even related products such as Search Server 2010 and FAST Search Server 2010 (but not Project Server 2010, which has its own forums).

As of this writing, there are only four SharePoint 2010 forums:

- "SharePoint 2010 — General Questions and Answers"
- "SharePoint 2010 — Setup, Upgrade, Administration and Operation"
- "SharePoint 2010 — Using SharePoint Designer, InfoPath and Other Customization"
- "SharePoint 2010 — Using Visual Studio with SharePoint and Other Programming"

These forums were made available at the time the Public Betas of the SharePoint 2010 were released, but, naturally, they now cover the RTM products.

There were expected to be the following additional forums by RTM, but as of this writing (post RTM), these are still not there. Watch out for them! (There was also pressure for an own forum for InfoPath 2010, which was solved by adding "InfoPath" to the name of the "SharePoint 2010 — Using SharePoint Designer, InfoPath and Other Customization" forum.)

- "SharePoint 2010 Business Intelligence"
- "SharePoint 2010 Enterprise Content Management"
- "SharePoint 2010 Collaboration"
- "SharePoint 2010 Search"

If there is a specialized forum for the functionality you are asking about, use that. If there isn't, use the most accurate of the four more wide-reaching forums. For example, if you are posting a programming question about Excel Services, it will go in the Business Intelligence forum (if a Business Intelligence forum is available), and not in the forum for programming questions.

The reason that SharePoint 2010 is included in the forum name is that experience in the past years of the forum system has shown that people look mainly to the name of the forum when they post. For example, many posts that had nothing to do with the physically challenged went to a forum called "SharePoint Accessibility," even though both the description of the forum and a sticky post located prominently at the top of the forum said that the forum was only for accessibility for the physically challenged.

For those who are wondering what has happened to the Workflow forum that was in the earlier (pre-SharePoint 2010) forum set, its posts are now in the 2010 forums logically divided into built-in workflows ("SharePoint 2010 — Setup, Upgrade, Administration and Operation"), SharePoint Designer 2010 work-flows ("SharePoint 2010 — Using SharePoint Designer, InfoPath and Other Customization"), and Virtual Studio workflows ("SharePoint 2010 — Using Visual Studio with SharePoint and Other Programming").

I also promised you information on non-Microsoft SharePoint forums. One such forum is "Virtual SharePoint User Group Forums" at `http://vspug.com/forums/`. (This was formerly known as the "SharePoint University Forums.")

The final "forum" I'll mention here is the sharepointdiscussions Yahoo Group at `http://tech.groups .yahoo.com/group/sharepointdiscussions/`. Interactions with this "forum" all take place via e-mail. Typically, people set up a rule to deliver messages to a separate folder to have them together for reading. Because it is e-mail–based, when you want to add your comments to the conversation, you just click Reply. Also, because it is e-mail–based, all messages are available offline, and can be searched. It's worth checking out if you don't mind getting lots of e-mails.

If the e-mails go to a Gmail address, you can search them using the (Google) Gmail search function.

RSS Feeds

Although you have read about RSS feeds throughout the discussions thus far in this chapter, this section highlights the benefits of using RSS feeds to keep up to date with new developments in the SharePoint area. Following are a few of those benefits:

➤ *Time savings* — You can use RSS feeds to save you time. For example, you don't need to check to see if the next month's copy of *TechNet Magazine* is available on the Web. Once it is there, you can instead get a set of RSS feeds (one per article, thus saving even more time by allowing you to go directly to the article you want to read) to save you the trouble of, and time spent, looking.

➤ *Not missing anything* — Rather than regularly checking to see if there are any newly released articles on SharePoint Server 2010 (with the risk that, having checked for several weeks with no results, you don't bother looking again), an RSS feed will let you know when something new arrives.

➤ *Fine-tuning* — It's a simple process to add or remove RSS feeds, so you can, over time, create a collection of RSS feeds that exactly suit your needs. (I use Google Reader for my own RSS feeds — it's a link away from Gmail.)

SOLVING SUDDEN PROBLEMS

So far in this chapter, you have learned about how to continually educate yourself so that you know how to do things correctly and, thus, avoid problems. However, problems will always pop up, so you must also know how to quickly get information that will help you to solve those problems.

The simplest method (and one that, in the pre-Internet age of computing, would have meant choosing a suitable IBM manual and reading it) would be just to identify the best single source of information from all those presented earlier, and read through the titles of all the documents there looking for something that matches up with the problem. For example, in many cases, a problem could have been experienced by many users already, and so there is likely to be a Knowledge Base article about it. You could find it, in time, by looking through all the SharePoint 2010 Knowledge Base articles.

That method will work — eventually — but it typically will take far too long for your needs. So, following are some alternatives.

Searching

A better approach to solving a problem not addressed by any of the sources previously identified in this chapter is *searching the Internet*. That may seem easy enough — just load up Google or Bing in your browser, type in something appropriate, and the answer should be there in no time.

Well, this approach might work (and, so, it is well worth trying first), but the chances are that even if your chosen search engine finds something suitable, it will be on page 50 of returned results, and you'll never get to it.

So, maybe you should explore the next level of searching. This level would be to go to a suitable site, and, in the site's search engine (or forum), type in your search string. This cuts down on the number of returned hits, while, at the same time, naturally reducing the scope of your search. But what if that particular forum or site doesn't have the answer at all? Or, what if the search engine of that forum or site isn't any good?

You should then explore the next phase, of which there are two versions — normal and supercharged.

In the normal version, you are saying, "I know that this site is the right place for my search, but I want to use a powerful search engine to search it." In this case, you go to Google (or Bing) and specify the search string followed by (in the URL) `site:http://<sitename>`. (Unlike many parameter additions in a search string, `site:` works for both Google and Bing.) If you think the answer is in a newsgroup, you can go to the Advanced Search function in Google Groups and enter your search string in one line. You restrict the newsgroups it searches by specifying, for example, `microsoft .public.sharepoint.*`.

This method is fine, but you are still only searching a single site (or a single structure of newsgroups) at a time. So, you must repeat the search for each possible site. That leads to the supercharged version of this search phase.

Now, you are SharePoint 2010 users, and even if you are not using SharePoint Server 2010 (as I would expect would be the usual situation for readers of this book), you will certainly be using SharePoint

Foundation 2010 with Search Server 2010 Express installed on top of it. In other words, you have access to Federation Search (as discussed earlier in this book).

When using that, it's a matter of seconds to set up a number of Search web parts on a SharePoint 2010 web page that search suitable sites simultaneously. Use Bing rather than Google for such searches, because it just works, whereas setting up a Google search that uses the normal Google search site is virtually impossible. When it is ready, save the page so that it is accessible via Site Pages, and perhaps have a link to that page under Quick Launch so that it is directly accessible to you.

I've found that having three columns each with a single web part that shows the first ten hits is a sensible way to go about it. That's a nice compromise between having searches of all possible sites on the same page (very messy) and going back to the single site searches.

In version three of my web page for the SharePoint products, I had good search results with two different sets of Bing searches. I'd search MSDN, TechNet, and the Office sites in one page, and the MSDN and TechNet forums in the other page (and, in both cases, ensured that I excluded parts of sites in the URL string). That way, the forum searches only searched forums, and the MSDN and TechNet searches didn't search forums.

But what if you still haven't found anything sensible in your searches, and you still have a problem? Then the next step is probably going to be to ask a question in a forum.

Asking a Question in a Forum

Another alternative to solving sudden problems is to use the *Microsoft SharePoint forums*, rather than relying on newsgroups (and, probably, rather than relying on any other forums). Remember that a very large number of people out there all over the world, in all time zones, answer questions. In most forums, there are even some dedicated Microsoft support people (based in Shanghai, and working Shanghai time and normal working hours and days), and, recently, for questions that even they are having difficulty with, there are also "Microsoft Online Support" people. The quantity of qualified people means that it is often possible to get very quick responses indeed.

However, this is not always the case, and this is a key point with forums. There are no guarantees. There is no guarantee that you will get a reply at all. There is no guarantee that you will get a useful reply. And there is no guarantee that you will find a solution to your problem.

There is a guarantee of responses if you have a TechNet or MSDN subscription. Part of the value of those subscriptions is that Microsoft guarantees a response within 48 hours to a question sent to a forum by a subscription holder. Rather than using separate customer forums for such messages and replies, Microsoft uses the standard forums. The benefit of using the standard forums is that those questions and answers are also available to people without MSDN or TechNet subscriptions. The disadvantage is that people without MSDN and TechNet subscriptions see those replies and follow-ups, and expect the same kind of support for their own questions. (You can't see whether a poster has a subscription.)

It's very important to stress that there are no guarantees, because it is important that you are aware of that when you make your first approach to a forum and write a question.

So, take a look at a progression of steps for using a forum.

Step One: Find the Correct Forum

If you have followed the earlier advice in this chapter, you will have learned how to monitor the SharePoint forums for some time, and have chosen the correct forum for any particular question. Always take the time to look at the names and descriptions of all the SharePoint forums, and then, after you decide on a suitable one, have a quick look at a few threads in the forum to confirm that your thinking was correct, and that you have picked a reasonable forum for your question.

Picking the right forum increases your chances of getting an answer. For example, a question on licensing sent to a programming forum is likely to be ignored completely.

Step Two: Write a Sensible Title

One thing to note here is that the text of your title describes the problem well enough so that people feel inclined to read your question, and possibly answer it. It also should be of reasonable length (several lines of text in a title is excessive) and be meaningful (for example, "SharePoint problem" isn't meaningful).

What you should not do is try to make the title "interesting." All attempts to make a title "interesting" by such methods as adding one or more exclamation marks to the problem description, having more than one question mark, using excessive capitalization, and combinations of all three, are doomed to failure, as are the use of certain words like "weird," "strange," "peculiar," and "is this a bug?" Either the moderator will just delete your post, or the number of people prepared to even look at your post will be reduced substantially. Also, avoid putting text like "Please help" in your titles. Readers know that you want help; otherwise, you wouldn't be posting to the forum. "Please help" is hardly a problem description.

Another thing you should never do is to say that something is "urgent" or, equally bad, that "I want an answer ASAP" (or a text like "waiting for your quick reply"). Very few of the experts in the forums will consider answering a question from a person who demands a reply to their question ASAP, or says that it is urgent. *All* questions in the forums are urgent for the writer of them. Most people, however, have the intelligence not to say so out loud, and certainly have the intelligence not to demand a reply from people, most of whom are helping in their free time.

Finally, if you are asking about a back product, always say so in the title of the post. Many people reading the forum messages will not have used that back product and won't be too happy after opening the thread to find out that it is about a back product. They could instead have spent the time opening a question they could answer. (This doesn't apply to SharePoint 2010 questions, yet, because questions about earlier SharePoint products go to the "pre-SharePoint 2010" forums.)

Step Three: The Text

Once you have selected the correct forum, and you have a sensible title, the final step is to create a message that is likely to be answered. Depending on the question, the amount of text in a quote will vary, but here are some things to avoid:

➤ *Don't demand answers, or say things are urgent* — This issue has been addressed.

➤ *Don't, by virtue of saying who you work for, reduce the number of people who are likely to answer your question* — I've noticed that people from the U.S. who work in some capacity for a branch of the U.S. military quite often say so in their posts. This *might* cause a few U.S. citizens to answer the question who wouldn't otherwise do so, but the flip side will be not getting many answers from the rest of the world.

➤ *Don't use phrases that will seem strange to readers in other parts of the world* — "Hello Dears" seems to be a favorite of posters from the Middle East, but it sounds very odd to the rest of us. Religious statements ("thanks be to god") are extremely weird for many readers from secular countries when placed in a technical question.

➤ *Do write special texts for the forums* — Remember that you are writing to colleagues reading your posts in their free time, or during small breaks from work. They do *not* want to see yet another formal tender because they see enough of those at work. So, if you are given a detailed written tender or similar paper, do not post it as a forum question with a line above the full text of the tender that says, "Can anyone help me with this?" Instead, write out the key questions from the tender in your own words, and decide if those questions are different enough for you to need different posts for them.

➤ *Don't write posts that are too short* — Short posts are sometimes all you need. But don't overdo things. At least ensure that people know which SharePoint product you are asking about — or, indeed, which Office product version you are talking about. I've lost count of the people who write that they have a problem synchronizing "Excel" with "SharePoint."

➤ *Don't write posts that are too long* — Remember that you are not writing an official message to Microsoft. You are writing for colleagues. If we want to know every last detail of your configuration, we'll ask you in a follow-up. The chances are that we don't. Also, don't overdo the length of your text. If I see a post that takes up about a third of a page, I'll ignore it. My (and others) attention span when I'm not being paid isn't that long.

➤ *Don't use formatting shortcuts* — Don't make the mistake of making your post only seemingly shorter by not bothering with paragraphs and (empty) line feeds. Your post needs to be understandable the first time it is read, or people will ignore it. For example, having eight lines crammed full with text is one sure way to make people move on. Don't use SMS "words" either. If I see "u" in a message for "you," I first scream, and then I ignore the question. Use real English words.

 Ensure that the browser you are using doesn't remove the line feeds you put into a text when you post to a forum. At least one version of Firefox did that, and it led to unreadable posts.

Understanding When There Are No Responses

With the aid of the hints provided here (and, of course, a good description of your problem), you should get some useful replies to your questions. But what if you don't get any replies?

Here are some things to consider in that case:

➤ *Remember these are forums* — In other words, wait a few days before you do anything. Some people don't look at the forums every day, and certainly most people don't look at the forums on the weekend (which, oddly enough, seems to mostly start at midday on Friday). So, give them enough time to see your message.

➤ *Don't just bump* — Some people just write a reply to their message that says "bump" (or "anyone?") to remind other forum users that there hasn't been a reply yet. Even assuming this is done after a few days of waiting (which, as you just read, you ought to do — and I've seen bump messages after an hour!), how does it improve your chances of getting a reply? The original post is still exactly the same text that people have already read and didn't answer. In addition, some people who haven't yet read the post (people with long weekends, perhaps) will often be annoyed at seeing a bump (especially after an hour!), and others who just look at the main list of threads will think, "Oh, there's a reply, I won't bother reading that one."

So, instead of just writing a bump, think again about the title and the text you wrote. Maybe the title wasn't too clear, in which case you can edit it. Maybe the text could have been better, in which case you can write a reply to that post adding to the original post and explaining some of the less clear parts of it. Making the effort to do this will encourage people to take another look at your original post who would otherwise just continue to ignore you as though you just "bumped."

Note that if no one has yet replied to your question and you want to improve or add to the original text, it is best done by editing the original text, rather than writing a reply to the original post. This shouldn't be done if there are already replies (which, naturally, were based on the original text), though, and editing a post will not bump it up the list (because the time-stamp isn't then changed).

➤ *Try a paid support service instead* — Maybe your company has access to a premium support contract. If you get no help from the forums, use that. Maybe the problem is so important to you that you are prepared to pay a few hundred dollars to solve it. If so, consider calling Microsoft Customer Support Services.

➤ *Search again* — Perhaps you gave up searching for the solution too easily and, thus, moved to asking in the forums too quickly. If the forums aren't helping you, look at searching for solutions again. Often just trying a different search phrase is all you need.

So, there you have it — a guide to SharePoint knowledge and problem solving using books, online information sources, along with searching or asking questions in forums.

ABOUT THE AUTHOR

Mike Walsh has worked in the computer industry for more years than he cares to remember, with most of his working life spent in Finland, Germany, and Sweden. While contributing to this book, he was working as a technology consultant for Logica in Helsinki.

INDEX

$() for wrapping variables, 136
| (pipe) operator, 136
14 Hive, 70
2010 Information Worker
    Demonstration and Evaluation
    Virtual Machine (RTM), 560
7 *Microsoft Office Business
    Applications for Office
    SharePoint Server 2007*
    (Microsoft Press), 127

A

access
    restricting (SPD), 213–217
    to scope and Silverlight
        applications, 465–466
accessing SharePoint data
    data access options, 704–706
    data modeling, 703–704
    sample lists, creating,
        706–707
    using client-side object model.
        See client-side object
        model, accessing data with
    using no-code solutions,
        743–744
    using server-side object
        model. *See* server-side
        object model, accessing
        data with
    using web services, 738–743
actions
    action rules (InfoPath
        Designer), 339
    for workflow, 232, 233
Active Directory Certificate
    Services (AD CS), 118
Active Directory Domain Services
    (AD DS), 5–7, 107
Active Directory Federation
    Services (AD FS), 113–114,
    115–119

activity feed timer job,
    enabling, 22
adaptive streaming, 679
Add Web Part dialog (ribbon),
    290–291
AddAndCustomizePages
    permission, 80
AddContentTypeField
    element, 481
AddContentTypeField XML
    element, 416
Add-PsSnapin cmdlet, 131
ADFS architecture, EIF with, 126
administration pages (custom
    service applications), 390–391
administrators, SPD and, 207
ADO.NET Data Services,
    265, 266
AdventureWorks databases, 33
AdventureWorks SQL Server
    database
        data connection, creating,
            562–563
        as example data source, 561
        rendering items from. *See*
            SQL Server databases,
            rendering items from
AgilePoint, 362
All Site Content link, 221–224
Alirezaei, Reza, 703, 744
ALM. *See* Application Lifecycle
    Management (ALM)
Alternate CSS in SharePoint
    Server, 647, 660–662
Analytic Charts, creating,
    564–565
Analytic Grids (PPS), 566–567
Anonymous access (IIS), 470
Application Lifecycle Management
    (ALM), 407–439
        applications, upgrading. *See*
            artifacts; Feature upgrades
        basics of, 407–408
        defined, 407

Feature XML, generating,
    409–415
provisioning, 408–409
sandboxed solutions and,
    437–438
versioning in applications. *See*
    versioning in applications
application page hosting Silverlight
    applications (project), 485–505
    application page, 502–505
    SLNewsItemDetails
        application, 495–502
    SLNewsItemsListBox
        application, 485–495
applications
    application definition
        files, 240
    application domain, sandbox
        solutions and, 252
    Application Pages (Web Part
        Framework), 284
    application pool
        provisioning, 379
    Application Registry
        Service, 53
    application tier (PPS), 554
    upgrading. *See* artifacts;
        Feature upgrades
ApplyElementManifests XML
    element, 416
architecture
    information architecture,
        577–578
    PPS, 553–555
    Search, 621
    of service applications, 587
archiving scenarios (DAM), 672
artifacts
    artifact upgrades, 428–430
    creating, 408–409
    declarative artifacts, 408, 409
    provisioned artifacts, 408
    Web-scoped artifacts,
        417–418

.ascx files, 520
ASP.NET
    declarative model, 275
    imperative model, 275
    master pages and, 644
ASPX/HTML Pages, 286
assemblies
    Assembly Deployment Target
        property, 316
    assembly versioning,
        435–436, 438
    deployment of, 294–295
asset content types, planning,
    682–683
Asset Library Feature
    activating, 696
    Asset Library template,
        693–695
    content types and, 682–683
    custom Asset Libraries,
        697–699
    delivering content through,
        683–684
    instances, creating, 697
attributes, SafeControl, 283
authentication. See claims-based
    authentication
authorative tagging, defined
    (metadata management), 598
automating
    business processes, 335
    with SPD work flows, 360–361

B

backup and restore, 165–204
    basics of, 165
    Central Administration,
        171–172, 184–187, 192–194
    change logs, 201–202
    commands, STSADM, 47
    Content Database recovery.
        See Content Database
        recovery
    Content Database sizing
        and, 203
    content recovery, 168–169
    disaster recovery, 169
    farm backups. See farm
        backup and recovery
    farm configuration and,
        170–171
    full farm recovery, 198–201
    further protection, 202
    granular backups. See granular
        backups
    item-level recovery, 194–197

list import and export,
    174–175
new features, 165, 175
operations planning and,
    166–168
PowerShell. See PowerShell
Search recovery, 175
site-collection recovery,
    197–198
solution packages for custom
    code, 202
SQL database snapshots,
    172–173
third-party solutions, 203–204
trial restores, 203
types of backups, 175
upgrade support, 379
bandwidth, monitoring usage of,
    700–701
base classes, inheriting from custom
    cmdlets, 157–159
basicHttpBinding for WCF, 469
Batch Site Manager, 47
BCP (business continuity plans). See
    business continuity plans (BCPs)
BCS (Business Connectivity
    Services). See Business
    Connectivity Services (BCS)
BDC (Business Data Catalog). See
    Business Data Catalog (BDC)
Beginning SharePoint Designer
    2010 (Wiley, 2010), 349, 361
Best Bets (searches), 612, 627,
    628, 635
BI (Business Intelligence)
    Business Intelligence Center
        template, 558–559
    PPS and, 551–553
BIMonitoringServiceAppli-
    cation, 554
BIN/CAS deployments, 248
BindingRedirect element in WSP
    manifests, 432–434
Bing, using as search engine, 627
Bishop, Darrin, 551, 576
Bit Rate Throttling Module, 674,
    677–679
blank sites, 682
Bleeker, Todd, 269, 332–333
BLOB Cache feature, 680–681
blogs as resources, 752–753
Bogue, Robert L., 247, 267
books as SharePoint resources,
    745–747
Boolean query syntax
    (searches), 608
Bosch, Karine, 441, 524
boundaries (term store), 586

BranchCache
    basics of, 680–681
    users in branch offices
        and, 701
branded SharePoint sites, creating,
    655–668
    Alternate CSS, 660–662
    custom master pages, 663–668
    Microsoft Office themes and,
        656–659
    theme comments, 662–663
    themes, adjusting with
        SharePoint Server, 659–660
branding, 637–669
    approaches to, 647
    basics of, 637, 642
    branded SharePoint sites,
        creating. See branded
        SharePoint sites, creating;
        master pages, creating
        custom
    browser support,
        expanded, 649
    CSS, 646–647
    defined, 637
    dialog boxes, 652–654
    HTML standards and, 648
    master pages, 644–645,
        650–651
    MUI, 654
    new features, 647–648
    page layouts, 645–646
    SharePoint Foundation vs.
        SharePoint Server, 638
    themes, 642–644
    types of SharePoint sites,
        638–641
    Visual Upgrade, 655
    wiki pages, 651–652
branding in SPD
    basics, 217–218
    CSS, modifying, 218–219
    example, 224
    master pages, 219–223
    SPD as an option, 244
breadcrumbs, SPD, 212–213
break statements, 141
Brotto, Claudio, 671, 702
browsers
    creating InfoPath forms for,
        350–354
    expanded browser
        support, 649
    used for personalization, 274
Buenz, Adam, 105, 127
Business Connectivity Services
    (BCS). See also SQL Server
    databases, rendering items from
        background, 525

basics, 240
BCS Meta Man, 548
Business Data Catalog (BDC),
   history of, 526
components of, 527
ECTs, tools for creating. *See*
   ECTs, tools for creating
features available in
   SvharePoint Foundation,
   529–531
features available in SharePoint
   Server 2010, 531–535
MS Office client applications
   and, 534–535
object models, developing
   against, 548
permissions, setting, 539
search queries and, 532–534
terminology changes in,
   526–527
business continuity plans
   (BCPs), 167
Business Data Catalog (BDC)
applications, upgrading from
   SharePoint 2007, 529
history of, 526
Business Data Connectivity (BDC),
   53, 526–527
business data web parts (BCS), 532
Business Intelligence (BI), 551–553
business processes, automating, 335

C

CAML (Collaborative Application
   Markup Language)
   `CamlQuery` object, 445
   declarative code and, 253
   declarative elements of, 275v
CardSpace interface, 114
CAS (code access security)
   `IPermission`, 279
   permissions (.NET
      Framework), 317
   policies, sandboxed solutions
      and, 248, 253
cascading style sheets (CSS)
   branding and, 646–647
   master pages, editing (SPD),
      219–223
   modifying (SPD), 218–219
   starter master pages and,
      667–668
Central Administration
   configuring to use SSRS, 30
   exports from, 180–181
   farm backups from, 184–187
   farm restores and, 192–194

new features, 171–172
sandboxed solutions and,
   523–524
SPD access and, 214
updating SPD setting from,
   215–217
upgrade status page
   (SharePoint Server 2010), 45
upgrading Features and, 483
centralized search UIs, 630
change logs, 201–202
`Chilis.com`, 639
claims
   `Claims` property, 108
   claims transformer, 109
   claims-based environment,
      107–108
   claims-based security
      support, 379
   impact on delegation, 112–113
   Internal Enterprise Claims
      (IEC), 120–121
   processing, abridged, 110–111
   SharePoint, architecture of,
      120–126
claims-based authentication
   architecture of, 120
   background, 105–106
   configuring with AD FS 2.0
      STS, 115–119
   environments, components of,
      113–114
`Clear-SPLogLevel` cmdlet, 76
ClickOnce application, 561
clients
   browsing requirements for
      SharePoint Server 2010, 37
   client object model vs. server
      object model, 265
   `Client` object
      (`SLNewsItemsListBox`
      application), 487
   client-side search functions,
      632–633
   configuring (PPS), 558–559
client-side object model, accessing
   data with
      `ClientContext` object, 731
      JavaScript Intellisense,
         737–738
      manipulating data with
         JavaScript, 735–737
      overview, 730–731
      querying lists using JavaScript,
         731–735
Closed Web Part Gallery, 288
cmdlets
   for administering Managed
      Metadata Service, 589–590

custom. *See* custom cmdlets
defined, 130
farm creation, 147–150
finding, 144–146
non-persistent, 158
persistent data, 158
PowerShell, 588
for service applications, 145
site structure creation,
   150–153
code. *See also* CAS (code access
   security)
   code review process, 249
   coding with SharePoint
      collections, 708–710
   compiled, 279
   deploying to servers, 248
   execution of declarative
      code, 253
   no-code solutions, 248–249
   outside scope of binding
      redirects, 434
   solution packages for custom
      code, 202
collections, SharePoint
   coding with, 708–710
   horizontal/vertical filtering,
      710–715
   LINQ to SharePoint. *See*
      LINQ to SharePoint
   list throttling, 716–721
   list-level indexing, 715–716
colors, theme, 656–657, 659–660
columns
   Column Editor (SPD),
      226–227
   managed metadata column
      type, 581
commands
   backup and restore
      (PowerShell), 172, 177, 178
   for search management
      (PowerShell), 620–621
`CommandUIDefinition`
   element, 459
compiled code, 279
`CompleteInitParameters()`
   method, 457
Component Object Model
   (COM), 154
composite applications,
   defined, 240
compound indexes, 715
computer names, setting, 4
Condition Criteria window
   (SPD), 228
conditional formatting, 339–341
conditions, workflow (Workflow
   Designer), 232

configuring
    backup and recovery (farm configuration), 170–171
    Central Administration to use SSRS, 30
    claims-based authentication, 115–119
    clients (PPS), 558–559
    configuration wizard (SharePoint 2010), 17–19
    content sources (searches), 623
    Initial Farm Configuration Wizard, 19–20
    LDAP providers for forms authentication, 122
    log settings with PowerShell, 74–77
    logging database (SharePoint), 88–90
    media players, 691–693
    Media web part, 686
    PPS, 555–557
    profile import architecture, 20–22
    SharePoint claims, 114–119
    SSRS for SharePoint Integration mode, 29
    Visual Studio project (Wingtip app), 381–383
configuring Windows
    Desktop Experience feature, adding, 8
    loopback check, disabling, 7–8
    password expiration, disabling, 8–9
    Remote Desktop, enabling, 10
    User Account Control, disabling, 10
    users, creating, 10–11
    Windows Updates, enabling, 11–12
Connell, Andrew, 206, 375, 405, 664
content
    consuming content types, 598
    content organizers, 581, 595–596
    content planning (DAM), 701
    Content Query web part, 689
    ContentIterator class, 716–721
    FAST Search content service application, 619
    management of (DAM), 682–684
    placeholders, 644, 664
    recovery, 168–169
    sources (Search), 621–624

Content Database recovery
    basics of, 173–174, 198
    recovering documents using, 194–195
    restoring databases, 195
    for site collection recovery, 197–198
    site collection restores and, 179
    sizing and, 203
Content Databases
    mirrored or log-shipped, 62
    RBS and, 673
    running Test-SPContentDatabase against, 44–45
    in SharePoint 2007, 46–47
    upgrading multiple, 66–68
Content Pages (Web Part Framework)
    deploying dashboard content to, 574
    flavors of, 284
    master pages and, 644
content type
    content type hub, 587
    content type hub timer jobs/subscriber jobs, 597
    defining external, 510–512
    syndication, 581, 587, 596–598
continue statements, 141
controlled vocabulary, 579
controls, InfoPath, 338–340
correlation ID GUID, 77–78
crawling (searches), 615–616, 624–625
Create GUID dialog, 307
Create page (Central Admin), 390–391
CreateChildControls method, 274, 454, 457, 478, 521
createMediaPlayer function, 692
CreateSilverlightHost method, 479
CSOM script, 732
CSS. See cascading style sheets (CSS)
ctlid parameter (SL Picture Picker), 471
custom cmdlets
    base classes, inheriting from, 157–159
    creating, 156–157
    custom PipeBind objects, 159–161
    packaging/deploying with Visual Studio 2010, 161–163

custom development of workflows, 244
custom field type hosting Silverlight application (example). See field type hosting Silverlight application (example)
custom permission rights, 379
custom site definitions, 47–50
CustomFilter tags, 632
Customization Wizard dialog, SharePoint, 298
customized pages (SharePoint 2007), 41
customizing page settings (SPD), 217
CustomUpgradeAction XML element, 416, 423

D

dashboards
    basics of, 551
    and components, deploying, 573–574
    creating (PPS), 559–561, 572–573. See also workspaces (PPS dashboards)
    Dashboard Designer, 554, 572
    Developer Dashboard, 79–80
    securing, 574–576
data
    accessing SharePoint. See accessing SharePoint data
    data access options, 704–706
    Data Connection Wizard, 355–356
    Data Connections Library, 562
    data modeling, 703–704
    data pages (database snapshots), 173
    data tier (PPS), 554–555
    DataContext property, 449, 494
    DataContract attribute, 467
    defined, 605
    external data integration (SPD), 240
    manipulating with JavaScript, 735–737
data sources
    customizing structure of (multimedia assets management), 696–697
    dashboards and, 559
    data source elements, 559

Data Sources component (SPD interface), 346–349
PPS workspaces and, 562–564
scorecards and, 567
SPD, 239–243
databases. *See also* Content Databases
database attach upgrade (SharePoint Server 2010), 58–61
Database Connection button (SPD interface), 348
database provisioning, 379
database test cmdlet, 44
debugging (Hello World sandbox project), 257–258
decentralized search UIs, 630
declarative artifacts
basics, 408
rules, 429
updating, 429–430
declarative code, 253, 279
declarative model (ASP.NET), 275
declarative provisioning, 408–409
declarative XML elements, 419–423
Default `PermissionSet` for BIN-Based Assemblies (listing), 318
`default.master` master page, 644
definitions (News List Definition project), 480
delegation, claims impact on, 112–113
`DeleteItemClicked` event, 490, 493–494
`DeleteObject` method, 494
deploying
assets (Visual web part exercise), 309–312
code to servers, 248
custom master pages, 507–509
dashboards/dashboard components, 573–574
FAST Search Server 2010, 617–620
and packaging custom cmdlets with VS 2010, 161–163
Search service applications, 613–615
deployment
access scope (Silverlight applications), 465–466
content-type (EMM), 577
infrastructure deployment, 674–675
sandboxed deployment, 253
Designer, SharePoint. *See* SharePoint Designer (SPD) 2010

Designing Forms for Microsoft Office InfoPath and Forms Services 2007 (Addison-Wesley), 344
Desktop Experience (Windows), 8
detach databases hybrid upgrade (SharePoint Server 2010), 66–68
developers
Developer Dashboard, 79–80
use of SPD and, 207
dialog boxes, branding and, 652–654
Digital Assets Management (DAM) solutions. *See* multimedia assets management solutions
digital identity, defined, 105
disaster recovery (DR)
basics of, 169
importance of planning, 166–168
objectives, defining, 167–168
disconnect detection (Bit Rate Throttling), 678
`Discover(TCmdletObject)` method, 159
Disk-Based BLOB Cache feature, 680–681
Display Password Text (listing), 328–329
disposable objects, handling (PowerShell), 154–156
Distributed Cache mode for `BranchCache`, 680
`<div>` element, 454
DNS Manager, 28
DocAve Recovery Manager, 197
`DOCTYPE`s, defined, 648
document sets, 581, 593–595
domain controller, making VM into, 5–7
double-hop issue (authentication), 528
Drisgill, Randy, 637, 669

E

`ECMAScript` object model, 730–731
ECTs (external content types)
creating with BCS Meta Man, 548
creating with SharePoint Designer (SPD) 2010, 536–539
creating with Visual Studio 2010, 539–548
defining, 510–512, 527
tools for creating, 536–548

Edit mode (web parts), 289–290
editors
editor parts (web parts), 323–330
`EditorPart` Import Directives (listing), 324
opening (SPD), 212
EIF (Enterprise Identity Federation), 124–126
elements
dashboard pages and, 560
`elements.xml` file, 508
EMM (Enterprise Managed Metadata) service
basics of, 580–581
content-type deployment and, 577
efficient configuration and, 577
programmatic access to, 600
employee training forms example (InfoPath/SPD), 349
Empty SharePoint Project template, 380, 383
Enhanced Security Configuration (IE), 4
Enterprise content types, defined (metadata management), 597
Enterprise edition of SharePoint 2010, 553
Enterprise Identity Federation (EIF), 124–126
Enterprise keywords (metadata management), 582–583
Enterprise Managed Metadata (EMM) service. *See* EMM (Enterprise Managed Metadata) service
Enterprise Search Center, 631
entity classes, generating, 722–723
Entity Data Picker, 531
event throttling, 71–72
Excel, Microsoft
Excel Services, 53–54, 72
trace logs and, 81
`ExecuteQueryAsync` method, 446, 448, 494, 500–501
exporting
lists, 174–175
websites and lists, 179–182
workflows to and from Visio 2010, 234
Expression Blend (Microsoft), 442, 690
Expression Web Designer, 206
extended type system (PowerShell), 133–136
Extensible Object Markup Language (XOML), 275

Extensible Stylesheet Language
    Translation (XSLT),
    225–226, 693
external content types (ECT). *See*
    ECTs (external content types)
external data
    `External Data` column
        (BCS), 530–531
    populating InfoPath forms
        with, 354–357
    sources, connecting SPD to,
        347–349
external lists (BCS), 529–530
extranets, defined, 639

farm backup and recovery
    basics, 175, 184
    farm backup sets, 188–190
    farm configuration, 170–171
    farm restore, 192–194
    full farm recovery, 198–201
    performing backups, 184–188
    scripting, 190–192
farms
    farm creation cmdlets
        (PowerShell), 147–150
    Farm Creation Script -
        `BuildFarm.ps1` (listing),
        148–150
    farm solutions vs. sandboxed
        solutions, 250, 252
    farm topologies for
        multimedia assets,
        699–700
    `FarmConfigurations.xml`
        (listing), 133–134, 148
FAST Search Server 2010
    basics, 611–612
    FAST Query service
        application, 620
    FAST Search & Transfer, 611
    FAST Search content service
        application, 619
    FAST Search service
        applications, deploying,
        619–620
    installing for Sharepoint,
        617–619
    user context in, 628
Fast Start feature (Bit Rate
    Throttling), 678
Feature elements
    extracting, 414
    "Feature elements by scope"
        rules, 428

Feature upgrades
    basics, 415–416
    care with upgrade steps, 428
    default logging off and, 427
    example, 416–419
    "Feature elements by scope"
        rules and, 428
    Feature Upgrade Kit, 483
    `FeatureUpgrading` event,
        423–427, 481–482
    `FeatureUpgrading`
        method, 426
    sandboxed solutions and, 438
    triggering, 422
    using declarative XML
        elements, 419–423
    using `FeatureUpgrading`
        event, 423–427
    `VersionRange` element
        and, 428
Feature XML
    editing, 481
    `feature.xml` file, 49
    generating, 409–415
    vs .NET code, provisioning
        and, 408–409
Features, SharePoint
    configuring (Visual web part
        exercise), 301–302
    defined, 277
    Feature versioning, 436–437
    `FeatureActivated`
        method, 509
    `FeatureDeactivating`
        (listing), 308
    `FeatureDeactivating`
        method, 509
    upgrading with declarative
        XML elements, 419–423
Federated Locations
    (searches), 626
`FederatedAuthentication`, 115
federation, search, 625–627
`Ferarri.com`, 640
Fiddler, 33
field type hosting Silverlight
    application (example), 466–485
    News List Definition project,
        480–485
    picker picker, 470–476
    picture service, 467–470
    `PicturePicker` field,
        476–480
fields
    for content types, 682
    field types, multimedia,
        687–689

`FieldTypeClass`
    element, 477
    hidden (`SL Picture`
        `Picker`), 478
files
    File tab, SPD, 213
    `FileRef`/`FileLeafRef`
        properties, 468
    handling large (DAM),
        672–673, 701–702
filtering
    Filter Category Definition
        (Refinement Panel), 632
    `-Filter` parameters, 140
    filters, creating (PPS
        workspaces), 570–572
    horizontal/vertical
        (collections), 710–715
    and iterating objects
        (PowerShell), 139–141
findability, searches and, 633
Firebug for Firefox, 668
Firefox browser, 33, 668
`fldtypes_` prefix, 476
Fluent User Interface (or Fluent
    UI), 345, 647–648
folksonomy vs. taxonomy, 580
fonts, theme, 657–660
footers, adding to sites, 219–221
`ForEach-Object` cmdlet, 140–141
Form Library template
    (SharePoint), 350
`Format-Custom` cmdlet, 138
`Format-List` cmdlet, 138
`Format-Table` cmdlet, 138
formatting
    object data (PowerShell),
        138–139
    rules (InfoPath Designer), 339
forms. *See also* views and forms
    (SPD)
forms, InfoPath
    configuring LDAP providers
        for authentication of, 122
    creating, 336–339
    creating for browser,
        350–354
    enhancing with validation/
        conditional formatting,
        339–341
    final forms (employee training
        application), 371–373
    Forms Server, 359
    populating with external
        data, 354–357

publishing to different
locations, 341–344
publishing to SharePoint
Server, 357–360
templates, 336–338
forms-based authentication
(FBA), 55
forums as resources, 754–756,
758–761
Forward Lookup Zone (DNS), 28
Foster, Rob, 549
FrontPage, SPD and, 205–206
full crawls, searches and, 624
Full Trust Proxy Project, 260–265
functional taxonomies, 634
functions
page component, 461–463
and scripts (PowerShell),
141–144

G

Galleries, Web Part, 287–288
gallery section (SPD), 210–211
GetAllPictureAsync
method, 474
GetAllPictures method, 468
Get-Command cmdlet, 144
Get-Help cmdlet, 145
GetItemById method, 497
Get-Member cmdlet, 131–132,
144, 146
GetPicture method, 513, 518
Get-Set-SPLogLevel cmdlet, 76
Get-SPDiagnosticConfig
cmdlet, 74–75
Get-SPFarm cmdlet, 131–132
Get-SPLogEvent, 82–85
Get-SPLogLevel cmdlet, 75–76
Get-SPServiceApplication-
Proxy cmdlet, 55
Get-SPTrustedIdentity-
TokenIssuer PowerShell
command, 115
Get-SPWeb cmdlet, 132, 137
GetWebResourceUrl
method, 478
ghostable pages, 285
ghostableInLibrary pages, 285
-Global switch, 155–156
globally reusable workflows
(SPD), 231
governance issues (SPD), 213–214

granular backups
basics of, 175, 176
exporting websites/lists,
179–182
importing websites/lists,
183–184
site collection backups,
176–178
site collection restore,
178–179
Green, Hagen, 344
Group Policy Management
Editor, 9
Guidelines for the Construction,
Format and Management
of Monolingual Controlled
Vocabularies, 579
GUIDs, burning, 307

H

HandleClientRequestFailed
method, 447
HandleClientRequestSucceeded
method, 447
handleCommand function, 516
"happy hour", 253
Health Analyzer
overview, 94
reviewing problems, 94–97
rule definitions, 97–98
"Hello World" sandbox project,
255–259
horizontal/vertical filtering
(collections), 710–715
Hosted Cache mode for
BranchCache, 680
hosting Silverlight applications in
master pages, 505–509
HTML (Hypertext Markup
Language)
standards, branding and, 648
starter master pages and,
667–668
HTTP (Hypertext Transfer
Protocol)
BranchCache and, 681
HTTP-Based Adaptive
Streaming, 679
progressive download and,
678–679
HTTPS (Hypertext Transfer
Protocol Secure), 681
hybrid upgrade approach
(SharePoint Server 2010),
61–62

I

IAdventureWorksPicture-
Service interface, 513
IClaimsPrincipal interface, 108
identity metasystem
background, 105–106
identities, defined, 105
identity provider (IdP), 109
Identity Provider Security
Token Service (IdP-
STS), 109
identity selectors, 111
IdentityClaimTypeInfor-
mation value, 115
multiple identities, 110–112
overview, 106–107
security token service (STS),
108–110
security tokens and claims,
107–108
IDEnumerator method, 532
IE8 Developer Tools, 668
IEC (Internal Enterprise Claims),
120–121
IIS. See Internet Information
Services (IIS)
ImageClass object, 513–514
imperative code, 279
imperative model (ASP.NET), 275
impersonation steps (SPD
workflows), 232–233
Imported Web Parts Gallery, 288
importing
lists, 174–175
user profile data to
SharePoint, 534
websites and lists, 183–184
workflows to and from Visio
2010, 234
incremental crawls
(searching), 624
indexing (searches)
basics of, 615–616
connectors, 622–623
index, defined, 715
indicators, scorecards and, 567
InfoPath
combining with SharePoint
Designer, 349
controls, 338–340
final forms (employee training
application), 371–373
forms, creating, 336–339
forms, creating for browser,
350–354

InfoPath (*continued*)
forms, enhancing with
validation/conditional
formatting, 339–341
forms, InfoPath vs SharePoint,
224–225
forms, populating with
external data, 354–357
forms, publishing to different
locations, 341–344
forms, publishing to
SharePoint Server, 357–360
forms, upgrading files and, 59
InfoPath Designer 2010,
336, 354
InfoPath Filler 2010, 336
InfoPath Filler application, 342
*Information Architecture for the
World Wide Web* (O'Reilly), 577
Information Workers (IW), SPD
and, 206–207
Initial Farm Configuration Wizard,
19–20
InitParameters dictionary,
443, 487
InitParameters property,
456–459, 487
InitParams argument, 505–506
initParams parameter, 454, 504
in-place upgrade (SharePoint Server
2010)
fundamentals, 50–52
under the hood, 52–54
post-upgrade process, 54–57
Insights workload, 551
installing
FAST Search Server 2010,
617–619
Install Wizard (FAST Search
Server), 618
install_info.txt file
(searches), 619, 620
installer, service application
(Wingtip app), 391–393
InstallPath property, 386
Office Web Applications, 17
SharePoint Server 2010
Enterprise, 16–17
SQL Server 2008 R2, 12–14
Windows 2008 R2, 3
installing SharePoint 2010
activity feed timer job,
enabling, 22
configuration wizard, 17–19
configuring profile import,
20–22
.exe file, extracting, 16–17

Initial Farm Configuration
Wizard, 19–20
installing Office Web
Applications, 17
managed metadata, 24–25
overview, 16
prerequisites, installing, 17
running search crawl, 22–23
Secure Store, setting up, 23–24
SharePoint Server 2010
Enterprise, installing, 16–17
Windows 2008 R2/Windows 7
patch, 16
instances
creating (Asset Library
Feature), 697
Instance Pages (Web Part
Framework), 285
Integration mode, SharePoint, 29
interfaces. *See* user interfaces
Internal Enterprise Claims (IEC),
120–121
Internet Explorer (IE)
Enhanced Security
Configuration (ESC), 4
testing sites in, 28
Internet Information Services (IIS)
Bit Rate Throttling Module,
674, 677–679
change logs and, 202
Media Services features,
678–679
Internet Protocol (IP), 106
Internet sites, overview of, 638–639
Intranet sites, overview of, 639–641
IsDocument metadata property
(searches), 634
issuer (identity provider), 109
ItemClicked event, 490, 493, 494
item-level recovery, 194–197

JavaScript
functions, web part ribbon
and, 463
Intellisense, 737–738
manipulating data with,
735–737
methods, 465
page component, 461–463
querying lists with, 731–735
JSON (JavaScript Object Notation)
format, 741

K2, 362
Kellar, Marcy, 349, 361
Kerberos authentication, 106–107
Kerberos TGT (Ticket-Granting
Ticket), 109
key filters (metadata
management), 591
keyboard shortcuts for deploying
solution packages, 312
keywords
Enterprise keywords, 582–583
searches and, 627–628, 635
Klindt, Todd, 69, 102–103
Knowledge Base (KB) articles as
resources, 751
KPIs (key performance indicators),
creating, 567–569

languages. *See also* Multilingual
User Interface (MUI)
language support for
searches, 612
multilingual scenarios in
metadata managements,
585–586
SharePoint language
packs, 585
Lapointe, Gary, 129, 164
large site collections, defined, 46
layouts
_layouts virtual
directory, 284
text, 652
lazy loading nature of SP.js()
file, 733
LDAP providers, configuring for
forms authentication, 122
leaf KPIs, 568
legacy ASP.NET web services,
742–743
libraries
Dashboard libraries, 573
Data Connections Library for
PerformancePoint library
definition, 562
RW PPS Data Connection
Library, 564
as SPD data source, 239
Lightning Tools, 549
LINQ to SharePoint
basics of, 721–722
entity classes, generating,
722–723

limitations of, 728–730
list relationships using lookup columns, 723–728
LINQ to SQL designer, 545–547
lists
creating sample, 706–707
custom, for site workflow, 234–239
external, defining, 512
importing/exporting, 174–175, 179–182, 183–184
list relationships using lookup columns, 723–728
list throttling (collections), 716–721
List View Lookup Threshold, 724
list workflows (SPD), 231, 360
ListItemConverter class, 449–450
list-level indexing (collections), 715–716
ListName variable, 444
ListViewStyle content type, 695
querying with JavaScript, 731–735
scrolling lists. See Silverlight News Banner project
as SPD data source, 239
"Working with Large Lists in Office SharePoint Server 2007", 708
Live Smooth Streaming module, 679
load balancers, 379
Load method, 445–446
LoadWithPartialName method, 132
LOB (line of business) systems, 240
LocalConnection API, 488
LocalMessageReceiver, 488, 496
LocalMessageSender, 488, 496
-localonly parameter (STSADM command), 38
location-based metadata, 581, 590–591
logging
crawl log, 615
Log Collection Schedule, 90
log settings, configuring with PowerShell, 74–77
logs, troubleshooting with, 77–80
LOGS directory of SharePoint root, 70

upgrade (SharePoint Server 2010), 40–41
logging database, SharePoint
basics of, 86–88
configuring, 88–90
consuming, 90–94
Lonsdale, Brett, 549
lookup columns, list relationships using, 723–728
lookup from user profiles, 233
loopback check, disabling, 7–8

M

Macori, Igor, 671, 702
magazines as resources, 752
MainPage control class, 464
Major.Minor.Build.Revision parts of version numbers, 436
Manage Data Connection Files library, 59
Manage Form Templates library, 59
Manage page (Central Admin), 390–391
Manage Rules button (ribbon), 351
managed accounts, creating, 25–26
managed metadata column type, 581
Managed Metadata Service application, 699
Managed Metadata Service (MMS), 24, 53, 55
managed terms, 581–582
ManageLink property, 386
Management Shell, SharePoint 2010, 130
manifest.xml file, editing, 508–509
MapFile XML element, 416
Marcy Kellar, 361
markup code, 279
mashups, defined, 240
master pages
basics, 644
branding and, 218–223, 644–645, 650–651
creating custom, 507, 663–664
in Master Page Gallery, 286
Master Page Gallery, 507–508
out-of-the-box master pages, 664–665
page layouts and, 646
server controls on, 505–506
starter master pages, 666–668
upgrading, 668

MasterUrl property (SPWeb object), 285
Medero, Jason, 35, 68
media players
advanced configuration, 691–693
custom skins for, 689–691
Media web part, 685–687
MediaFieldControl, 687–689
MediaPlayer.js file, 691–692
rich media players, 674
Meeting Workspace Tab Pages, 286
menus
MenuItem_Click event handler, 493
navigation menus, master pages and, 650–651
Mergecontentdbs command, 47
Merge-SPLogFile cmdlet, 84–85
Meta Man, BCS, 548
metadata management, 577–604
centrally stored metadata, applying, 581–583
content organizers, 595–596
content type syndication, 596–598
document sets, 593–595
EMM, 577
information architecture, 577–578
infrastructure of services, 587
location-based metadata, 590–591
managed metadata service, 587–590
metadata, defined, 578
metadata basics, 578–579
MetadataWebService.svc WCF service, 604
navigation settings, 591–592
programmatic access to EMM service, 600
remote services layer, 603–604
searches and, 616, 633–634
social networking, extending, 599–600
social tagging, 598–599
taxonomy, defined, 579
taxonomy and folksonomy, 580
taxonomy API, 600–603
taxonomy basics, 578–579
taxonomy platform enhancements, 580–581
term store management tool, 583–586

Microsoft
    Expression Blend, 690
    InfoPath Designer 2010. *See*
        InfoPath
    Internet Information
        Services (IIS). *See* Internet
        Information Services (IIS)
    magazines as resources, 752
    Microsoft Patterns and
        Practices SharePoint
        Guidance, 744
    `Microsoft.SharePoint`
        `.IdentityModel`
        namespace, 115
    `Microsoft.SharePoint.`
        `PowerShell`
        namespace, 157
    `Microsoft.SharePoint.`
        `Security` namespace, 317
    `Microsoft.SharePoint.`
        `Taxonomy` namespace,
        600–603
    `Microsoft.SharePoint.`
        `Taxonomy.Term` class,
        599–600
    SharePoint forums, 758
    SharePoint Workspace
        2010, 744
    sites as resources, 748–750
    starter master page, 664
    Visio 2010. *See* Visio,
        Microsoft
    Windows SharePoint Services
        (WSS), 44
Microsoft Office 2010
    client applications and BCS,
        534–535
    client software, themes
        and, 642
    Fluent User Interface (Fluent
        UI), 647–648
    InfoPath. *See* InfoPath
    `Microsoft.Office/`
        `nl.DocumentManagement.`
        `MetadataDefaults`
        class, 591
    `Microsoft.Office.`
        `Server.SocialData`
        namespace, 599
    Professional Plus, 33
    SharePoint 2010 and, 441
    SharePoint Server (MOSS)
        2007, 377
    themes, creating, 656–659
Microsoft Patterns and Practices
    SharePoint Guidance for
    SharePoint 2010, 252
Microsoft Word 2010. *See* Word
    2010, Microsoft

minimal master pages, 645,
    664, 666
modal windows, defined, 652
modeling, data, 703–704
Modify Style window (SPD),
    228–229
Module Features, 287, 305
Molnár, Ágnes, 605, 636
monitoring SharePoint 2010, 69
Morville, Peter, 577
`Move-SPProfileManagedMeta-`
    `dataProperty` cmdlet, 55
MSDN site as resource, 748,
    749, 758
MSDN ULS Viewer, 81–82
multilingual scenarios in metadata
    managements, 585–586
Multilingual User Interface (MUI)
    managed terms and, 582
    new features, 654
multimedia assets management
    solutions, 671–702
    advanced configuration (media
        players), 691–693
    asset content types, planning,
        682–683
    Asset Libraries, custom,
        697–699
    Asset Library Feature. *See*
        Asset Library Feature
    Asset Library template,
        customizing view styles,
        693–695
    bandwidth usage,
        monitoring, 700
    Bit Rate Throttling Module,
        677–679
    BLOB Cache feature, 679–680
    `BranchCache`, 680–681, 701
    challenges, 672–674
    concurrent users, 701
    content management, 682–684
    Content Query web part, 689
    content storage, planning, 701
    custom skins, 689–691
    customizing for user
        experience, 685
    data structure, customizing,
        696–697
    farm topologies, 699–700
    infrastructure deployment,
        674–675
    large file challenges, 672–673,
        701–702
    Media web part, 685–687
    `MediaFieldControl`,
        687–689
    possible scenarios, 671–672

RBS, 675–677
    remote users, 701
    rich media players and, 674
    storage issues, 673
    user perception challenges,
        673–674
multiple identities (identity
    metasystem), 110–112
MVP blogs as resources, 752–753
My Sites Content Databases, 60
my starter pages, 664

N

names, assembly, 431–432
naming trace log files, 70
Native mode (SSRS), 29–30
navigation
    menus, 650–651
    metadata navigation settings,
        581, 591–592
    Navigation pane (SPD),
        210–211, 221–224,
        346–347
    in SPD 2010, 212–213
.NET
    .NET Framework 3.5 Service
        Pack 1 (SP1), 558
    application domain, 252
    assemblies, BCS and, 540
    assemblies, versioning of,
        431–432
    CAS policies, 248
    code vs. Feature XML,
        408–409
    Framework CAS
        permissions, 317
network-based identity
    (Kerberos), 106
New Style Copy feature, 222, 224
`New-Object` cmdlet, 132–133
News Banner project. *See* Silverlight
    News Banner project
News Banner web part
    custom ribbon, adding to web
        part, 459–464
    modifying, 515–516
    `NewsBannerWebPartUser-`
        `Control.ascx`, 454
    as visual web part, 520
news items
    creating new, 495
    News Item Manager page, 502
    `NewsItemControl` class, 449,
        451, 490, 493, 518
    `NewsItemControl`
        instances, 491

news manager application page, 502–505

newsgroups as resources, 753–754

NewsListDefinition (Silverlight application), 480–485

New-SPLogFile, 84

nightandday.master master page, 645

Nintex, 362

no-code solutions, accessing data with, 743–744

non-leaf KPIs, 568

Notepad, 81

NT LAN Manager (NTLM), 106

numbers, Feature version, 437

O

objective KPIs, 568

objects
handling disposable (PowerShell), 154–156
object data, formatting (PowerShell), 138–139
object models, developing against BCS, 548
object pipeline (PowerShell), 136–138
<object> tag (Silverlight application), 454
PipeBind objects (PowerShell), 146
sandbox restrictions on, 254

O'Brien, Chris, 49, 407, 439, 483

Office, Microsoft. See Microsoft Office 2010

Office Business Applications (OBAs), 548

Office SharePoint Server (MOSS) 2007, 377

Office Web Applications, installing, 17

ONET.xml file, 48

OnPreRender method, 463

onSilverlightError function, 455

ontology, controlled vocabulary and, 579

operations planning, 166–168

OperationSucceeded method, 447–448, 490, 494, 497, 518

organizational taxonomies, 634

orphans, defined, 40

.osdx file, searches and, 632

Outlook 2010, BCS and, 534

out-of-the-box workflow templates, 233, 244

P

Package.package designer, 303

packaging
and deploying custom cmdlets with VS 2010, 161–163
Packaging Explorer, 304
web parts, 276

page component
basics of, 461
functions and access scope, 465–466

page layouts
branding and, 645–646
Web Part Framework, 287

pages
ABCs of, 280–281
customized (SharePoint 2007), 41
page terms (Web Part Framework), 284
types of SharePoint, 284–287

parallel blocks (SPD), 232

parameters
PipeBind, 146
PowerShell for searches, 620
in scripts and functions, 143–144
workflows and, 235

password expiration, disabling, 8–9

PasswordEditorPart Class (listing), 325

PCC (Public Cloud Claims), 122–124

People Search, 609, 628–630, 635

PerformancePoint Services (PPS), 551–576
architecture, 553–555
basics of, 551, 553–555
BI, 551, 552–553
configuring clients, 558–559
configuring trusted locations, 556–557
configuring unattended service accounts, 555–556
dashboards, creating. See dashboards; workspaces (PPS dashboards)
dashboards, securing, 574–576
dashboards/dashboard components, deploying, 573–574
enabling on sites, 557–558

permissions
custom permission rights, 379
manipulating (workflow), 233
setting BCS, 539

Personalizable attribute, 294

Phillips, Bryan, 349, 361

picture picker (Silverlight application)
development of, 470–476
PicturePicker field, 476–480
PicturePickerFieldControl class, 477
PicturePickerFieldType class, 477

picture service (Silverlight application), 467–470

PipeBind objects (PowerShell), 146

players, media. See media players

Poelmans, Joris, 577, 604

policies, CAS, 248

PopulateListBox method, 489, 490

PopulateNewsBanner method, 445, 465, 517

PopulateNewsItemDetails method, 496, 497

PopulateWrapPanel method, 473

Portal Server 2003, SharePoint, 376–377

portals, 376

Power Tools, 259

PowerGUI tool, 144

PowerPivot, 13

PowerShell
background, 129–130
backup and restore, 172
basics of, 130
changing user interface example, 43
cmdlets (metadata management), 589–590
configuring log settings with, 74–77
custom cmdlets. See custom cmdlets
disposable objects, handling, 154–156
exports from, 182
extended type system, 133–136
farm backups with, 187–188
farm creation cmdlets, 147–150
filtering/iterating objects, 139–141
finding cmdlets, 144–146
functions and scripts, 141–144
importing with, 183
object data, formatting, 138–139
object pipeline, 136–138
as object-based scripting language, 131–133

PowerShell *(continued)*
overview, 130
PipeBind objects, 146
PowerShell ISE, 144
scripted farm backups,
190–191
scripting, 115
for search management,
620–621
site structure creation cmdlets,
150–153
PPS. *See* PerformancePoint Services
(PPS)
pre-upgrade checker tool
(SharePoint Server 2010), 38–40
Products Configuration Wizard,
SharePoint (SPCW), 50
*Professional CSS: Cascading Style
Sheets for Web Design, Second
Edition* (Wiley), 646
*Professional Microsoft Office
SharePoint Designer 2007*
(Wiley), 373
*Professional Microsoft SharePoint
2007 Reporting with SQL
Server 2008 Reporting Services*
(Wiley), 744
*Professional SharePoint 2007
Development* (Wiley), 127
*Professional SharePoint 2007
Web Content Management
Development* (Wiley), 405
*Professional SharePoint 2010
Development* (Wiley), 744
profile import architecture,
configuring, 20–22
profile pages (BCS), 532–533
progressive downloads, 678–679
projected columns, 723
properties
managed metadata
(searches), 634
Media web part, 686
MediaFieldControl, 688
Properties box of Feature
Designer, 480
Properties page (Central
Admin), 390–391
PropertiesLink
property, 386
property promotion,
defined, 358
TaxonomyClientService web
service, 604
web part, 293–294
prototyping development tasks
(SPD), 245

provisioned artifacts
basics of, 408
rules, 430
updating, 429–430
provisioning (ALM), 408–409
proxies
basics of, 259–260
proxy example, 260–265
service application, 52, 378
PSBase property (PowerShell),
135–136
PSObject (PowerShell), 135
Public Cloud Claims (PCC),
122–124
publishing
content types, 597–598
forms to SharePoint Server,
357–360
InfoPath forms to different
locations, 341–344
Publishing Pages (Web Part
Framework), 286
purl parameter (SL Picture
Picker), 471

Q

queries
FAST Query service
application, 620
optimization of (server-side
object model), 707–708
"Query Efficiency with LINQ
to SharePoint", 730
query throttling, 252–253
querying lists using JavaScript,
731–735
querying lists with JavaScript,
731–735
and results, 616
Sharepoint 2010 Search, 615
Quick Rules, 340, 351

R

RBS. *See* Remote BLOB Storage
(RBS)
Read List/Read Item methods,
511–512
Read() method, 159, 161
read-only databases hybrid upgrade
(SharePoint Server 2010), 62–66
recovery. *See also* backup and
restore; disaster recovery (DR)
recovery level objectives
(RLOs), 167–168

recovery point objectives
(RPOs), 167–168
recovery time objectives
(RTOs), 167–168
Recycle Bin
backup/restore and, 169
hiding from Navigation pane
(SPD), 221–224
referential integrity, 724
Refinement Panel, customizing
(searches), 632
refiners (searches), 612
refreshNewsBanner function, 517
RefreshNewsBanner method, 463
RegisterScriptableObject
method, 464
regular expressions, 351–352
Rehmani, Asif, 335, 349, 361, 373
Relying Party (RP), 109
Relying Party Security Token
Service (RP-STS), 109
Remote BLOB Storage (RBS)
basics of, 675–676
Content Databases and, 673
RBS Provider, 676–677
Remote Desktop, enabling, 10
RenderPattern element, 484
RenderTransform element, 443
Repair Automatically option, 97
Report Builder 3.0,
downloading, 31
reporting service content types,
30–32
Reporting Services Configuration
Manager, 29
reports, 564–567, 617
RequestSecurityToken (RST)
messages, 115
RequestSecurityTokenResponse
(RSTR) messages, 115
resource-based identities, 106
resources and references, 745–761
blogs, 752–753
books, 745–747
finding quickly, 757
forums, 754–756, 758–761
Knowledge Base (KB)
articles, 751
magazines, 752
Microsoft Office site, 750
Microsoft sites, 748
MSDN site, 748, 749
newsgroups, 753–754
RSS feeds, 756
searching, 757–758
TechNet website, 748,
749–750
webcasts, 750–751

Resources element, 450
REST (Representational State
    Transfer)
        interface, 266–267
        WCF Data Services and, 738
        web services, 349
restore and backup. *See* backup and
    restore
results. *See* queries
reusable workflows (SPD), 231, 361
ReuseThread option, 156
reverse lookup association, 726
ribbons
        AdventureWorks ribbon, 519
        interface in SharePoint
            2010, 648
        News Banner Web Part ribbon.
            See News Banner Web Part
        ribbon section (SPD), 210
        web parts ribbon, 289
rich media players, 674
Roberts, Scott, 344
RootFinder property, 533–534
Rosenfield, Louis, 577
Ross, John, 205, 246
RSS feeds as resources, 756
RTOs/RPOs/RLOs, 167–168
rule definitions (Health Analyzer),
    97–98
rules
        crawl rules, 615
        InfoPath Designer rules,
            339–340
        Rules task pane, 351
        scope rules, 624
RW PPS Data Connection
    Library, 564

S

SafeControl element, 283–284,
    508–509
sandboxed solutions, 247–267
        ALM and, 437–438
        alternatives to, 265–266
        basics of, 249–253
        defined, 202
        execution of declarative
            code, 253
        vs. farm solutions, 250
        limitations of, 250
        local vs. remote execution, 252
        no-code solutions, 248–249
        project, 255–259
        proxies basics, 259–260
        proxy example, 260–265
        query throttling, 252–253
        restrictions, 253–255

sandbox counters, 251
Sandboxed Code Service,
    523–524
sandboxed deployment, 253
Sandboxed Solution
    property, 304
        Silverlight hosted in, 520–524
        termination of sandboxed
            code, 250–251
        when to use, 266
scheduling backups, 190–191
Schmidt, Christopher, 646
scopes (searches), 616, 624
scorecards, creating (PPS
    workspaces), 567–570
scripting
        farm backups, 190–192
        ScriptableType
            attribute, 464
        scripts and functions
            (PowerShell), 141–144
ScrollViewer control, 486
search engines (SharePoint 2010)
        basics of, 608–611
        crawling and indexing,
            615–616
        queries and results, 616
        reports, 617
        Search infrastructure, 621–624
        Search service applications,
            deploying, 613–615
        web parts, 631–632
searching
        Best Bets, 627–628, 635
        centralized/decentralized
            search UIs, 630
        client-side search functions,
            632–633
        content sources (Search),
            621–624
        crawls, scheduling, 624–625
        FAST Search Server 2010. *See*
            FAST Search Server 2010
        findability, 633
        keywords, 627–628, 635
        managed metadata
            properties, 634
        metadata management and,
            633–634
        new features, 606–607
        People Search, 628–630, 635
        PowerShell commands,
            620–621
        Refinement Panel,
            customizing, 632
        scopes, 624
        Search architecture, 621
        Search Centers, 631
        search crawl, 22–23

search federation, 625–627
Search infrastructure, 621–624
search queries, BCS and,
    532–534
Search recovery, 175
Search service applications, 53
Search web parts, 631–632
searching net for resources,
    757–758
SEO, 635–636
Sharepoint 2010 Search. *See*
    Sharepoint 2010
        user context in FAST search,
            628, 635
        user interfaces,
            customizing, 630
Secure Socket Layers (SSL),
    118, 202
Secure Store Service (SSS), 53–54,
    527, 555
Secure Store, setting up, 23–24
security. *See also* claims-based
    authentication
        claims-based security
            support, 379
        PPS and, 553, 556
        Security Assertion Markup
            Language (SAML)
            token, 109
        security token service (STS),
            108–110
        Security Token Service web
            application, 114–115
        security tokens, 107–108
        SecurityTokenService
            application, 115
SEO (Search Engine Optimization),
    635–636
Server Message Block (SMB), 681
server object model vs. client object
    model, 265
serverActions variable, 494
server-side object model, accessing
    data with
        collections. *See* collections,
            SharePoint
        query optimization, 707–708
service applications. *See also*
    Wingtip Calculator service
    application
        administration pages (Wingtip
            app), 390–391
        building custom, 379–380
        creating (Wingtip app),
            386–388
        creating instance of (Wingtip
            app), 393–395
        extensibility, 378–379
        framework, 379–380

service applications (*continued*)
  installer (Wingtip app),
    391–393
  overview, 377
  proxies, defined, 378
  proxy, creating instance of
    (Wingtip app), 399–401
  proxy installer (Wingtip
    app), 398
  server components, creating
    (Wingtip app), 384
  service architecture
    framework, 377–378
  service consumer client
    (Wingtip app), 402
  service consumer PowerShell
    cmdlet (Wingtip app),
    403–405
  service consumer Web Part
    (Wingtip app), 402–403
  service consumers (Wingtip
    app), 401–405
  service instance (Wingtip app),
    389–390
  service interface/operation
    contracts (Wingtip app),
    385–386
  service proxy, creating
    (Wingtip app), 396
  SPService object
    implementation (Wingtip
    app), 384–385
  WCF endpoint, creating
    (Wingtip app), 388–389
  web front end server
    components (Wingtip
    app), 396
service connection (metadata
  management), 587
Service Level Agreement (SLA)
  policies, 47
Service Object, creating (listing),
  384–385
ServiceContract attribute, 468
services infrastructure (metadata
  management), 587–590
SessionAuthentication HTTP
  module, 115
SetSource property, 519
Set-SPDiagnosticConfig settings
  (PowerShell), 86
Set-SPDiagnosticConfig cmdlet,
  70, 74
settings page (SPD), 210
shared fields, defined (metadata
  management), 594
Shared Service Providers (SSPs),
  50, 377

SharePoint 2007
  farm, setting to read-only
    state, 62–64
  read-only production farm, 65
SharePoint 2010
  Administration Toolkit, 47
  Central Administration (SCA)
    Solution Store, 277
  Claim Provider Service
    Web Service Protocol
    Specification
    (MS-CPSWS), 115
  claims, architecture of,
    120–126
  Customization Wizard,
    298, 380
  Developer Tools, 381
  farm, 65
  history of services in
    SharePoint, 376–377
  Management Shell, 130
  monitoring, 69
  new development model, 277
  new features for data
    integration, 527–528
  pages, types of, 284–287
  Portal Server 2003, 376–377
  Products Configuration
    Wizard (SPCW), 50
  Security Token Service
    Web Service Protocol
    Specification
    (MS-SPSTWS), 115
  service application
    extensibility, 378–379
  service architecture
    framework, 377–378
  sites/components, customized
    with SPD, 345–347
  Solution Package (WSP), 157,
    161, 277, 303
  tools to effect change in, 274
  upgrade process. *See*
    upgrading
  upgrading features in, 49
  Workspace, BCS and, 535
SharePoint Designer (SPD) 2010
  basics of new features, 206,
    208, 243
  branding. *See* branding
  combining with InfoPath, 349
  creating ECTs with, 536–539
  current user, checking/
    changing, 213
  data sources, 239–243
  download site, 33
  employee training
    application, 349

external data sources,
    connecting to, 347–349
  File tab, 213
  FrontPage and, 205–206
  interface, 345–346
  managing sites, 243
  navigating, 212–213
  new interface for, 208–212
  overview, 344
  prototyping development
    tasks, 245
  requirements for use of,
    207–208
  restricting access to, 213–217
  rule-based workflows and, 244
  SharePoint sites/components,
    manipulating, 345–347
  types of users, 206–207
  used for customization, 274
  views and forms. *See* views
    and forms (SPD)
  workflows. *See* workflows,
    SharePoint Designer
SharePoint Foundation (SPF)
  BCS features available in,
    529–531
  Content Database and, 44
  service application framework
    and, 378
  vs. SharePoint Server
    (branding), 638
SharePoint Server 2010
  Alternate CSS in, 660–662
  BCS features available in,
    531–535
  Enterprise, installing, 16–17
  publishing forms to, 357–360
  vs. SharePoint Foundation
    (branding), 638
SharePoint Server 2010 test
  environment
  computer name, setting, 4
  configuring Central
    Administration to use
    SSRS, 30
  configuring SSRS for
    SharePoint Integration
    mode, 29
  DNS entry, adding, 28
  hardware used, 2
  making VM a domain
    controller, 5–7
  managed accounts, creating,
    25–26
  overview, 1
  reporting service content
    types, 30–32

SharePoint 2010,
   installing. *See* installing
   SharePoint 2010
site collection, creating, 27–28
software considerations, 33
software used, 2
SQL Server 2008 R2,
   installing, 12–14
testing site in IE, 28
user data, setting up, 25
VM guest operating system,
   creating, 2
web application, creating,
   26–27
Windows, configuring. *See*
   configuring Windows
Windows 2008 R2,
   installing, 3
Windows 7 or Vista, building
   on, 3
<SharePoint:AspMenu>
   control, 650
{SharePointRoot}, 271
ShowInPicker property, 531
Silverlight
   application page hosting
      Silverlight applications
      (project). *See* application
      page hosting Silverlight
      applications (project)
   BCS and. *See* SQL Server
      databases, rendering items
      from
   deployment options and access
      scope, 465–466
   field type project. *See* field
      type hosting Silverlight
      application (example)
   hosted in sandboxed solutions,
      520–524
   hosting applications from
      within master pages,
      505–509
   PPS client configuration and,
      558–559
   rendering items from SQL
      Server databases and. *See*
      SQL Server databases,
      rendering items from
   Sharepoint and, 441, 524
   Silverlight 4 basics, 441–442
   Silverlight 4 Toolkit, 472, 493
   Silverlight MediaPlayer.
      xap application interface,
      690–691
   web parts project. *See* web
      part hosting Silverlight
      application

Silverlight News Banner project
   basic project, 442–453
   changes made to, 464–465
   deploying custom master
      pages, 507–509
   modifying application,
      517–519
Single Sign On (SSO) database,
   23, 54
single-column indexes, 715–716
Site Actions menu, 312
Site Assets library, 347
site collections
   backup and restore (granular
      backups), 176–179
   creating, 27–28
   large , defined, 46
   recovery, 197–198
   Site Collection Solution
      Gallery, 277
   Site Collection Web Analytics
      reports, 93
   site collection Web Part
      Gallery, 287
   SPD access and, 214
site definitions
   custom, 47–50
   defined, 48
sites. *See also* web sites
   Site Pages, 286
   site structure creation cmdlets
      (PowerShell), 150–153
   Site Structure Creation Script —
      BuildWebApps.ps1
      (listing), 151–153
   site templates, 409–415
   Site Web Analytics reports, 93
   site workflows (SPD), 231,
      234–239, 361
   site-collection
      administrators, 43
   testing in IE, 28
   types of SharePoint sites,
      638–641
Skewer Click, 219
skins (custom) for multimedia
   players, 689–691
SLNewsItemDetails application,
   495–502
SLNewsItemsListBox application,
   486–496, 504
Smooth Streaming module, 679
snap-ins, 131
snapshotting, 57
SOAP web services, 349
social networking, extending,
   599–600
social tagging, metadata and, 581,
   598–599
SocialTagManager class, 599–600

solutions. *See also* sandboxed
   solutions
   farm vs. sandboxed solutions,
      250, 252
   no-code, 248–249
   upgrading solution packages in
      sandbox, 438
sparse files (database
   snapshots), 173
SPAssignmentCollection object,
   137, 154–155
spbackup.xml file, 189–190
SPBRTOC.XML file, 188–189
SPCmdletGetSPList.cs (listing),
   158–159
SPD (SharePoint Designer). *See*
   SharePoint Designer (SPD) 2010
SPDiagnosticConfig cmdlt,
   74–75
SpecificFinder method, 532
SPIs (SharePoint Project Items), 277
SPListItemCollection
   object, 710
SPListPipeBind.cs (listing),
   159–160
SPLogEvent cmdlet, 82–85
SPLogLevel cmdlets, 75–77
SPMetal tool, 722, 729
SPQuery class, 711
SPSiteDataQuery, 468, 480–485
SPSitePipeBind object, 137, 159
SPTrustedIdentityTokenIssuer,
   creating, 116–117
SP.UI.ModalDialog class, 735
SPUserHostService.exe
   process, 253
SPWebPartManager control, 288
SPWebService object, 133
SPWindowsClaims-
   Authentication, 115
SQL database snapshots,
   172–173, 177
SQL Server
   2008 R2, installing, 12–14
   clusters, 65
   Management Studio, 93
   virtualization and, 57
SQL Server databases, rendering
   items from
   external content type, defining,
      510–512
   external lists, defining, 512
   News Banner Silverlight
      application, modifying,
      517–519
   News Banner web part,
      modifying, 515–516
   WCF service, developing,
      512–515

SSRS (SQL Server Reporting Service)
  configuring Central Administration to use, 30
  configuring for SharePoint Integration mode, 29
StackPanel control, 443, 448–449, 486
Start-SPAssignment cmdlet, 154–155
StartsWith operator, 729
static analysis, defined, 249
static throttling rates (Bit Rate Throttling), 678
Stop-SPAssignment cmdlet, 154, 156
storage
  as digital assets management challenge, 673, 701
  RBS. See Remote BLOB Storage (RBS)
streaming components, 678–679
StringFormat feature (Silverlight), 450
STSADM
  backup/restore commands, 47
  command for repairing Content Databases, 41
  command-line tool, 129
  exports from, 182
  farm backups with, 187
  operations, PowerShell and, 172
  pre-upgrade command, 38
  site collection backups and, 177
  site collection restores and, 178
submission policy, term sets and, 583
.svc files (WCF services), 469
Swan, Nick, 525, 549
SynchronizationContext (News Banner project), 445
syntax for calling functions (PowerShell), 143
System Pages (Web Part Framework), 285
system requirements, SharePoint Server 2010 upgrade, 36–37
System.Management.Automation namespace, 157
System.Runtime.Serialization namespace, 467
System.Web.UI.WebControls.WebControl, 270, 274

T

tab controls, web part, 291–292
tabs, 212–213
tags, folksonomy and, 580
taxonomy
  API, 600–603
  basics, 578–579
  controlled vocabulary and, 579
  defined, 579, 633
  vs. folksonomy, 580
  picker control, 581, 582
  platform enhancements, 580–581
  searches and, 634
  TaxonomyClientService.asmx web service, 604
team blogs as resources, 753
TechNet Plus subscriptions, 2, 13, 15
TechNet website resource, 748–750, 758
templates
  form (InfoPath), 336–338
  generating Feature XML using site templates, 409–415
  site templates (SPD), 209–210
  web part templates, uploading, 291
  workflow templates, modifying (SPD), 233
term groups, 583
term store
  basics, 580–581
  boundaries, 586
  management tool, 583–586
  remote access to, 603–604
  tagging and, 598–599
  terms, defined, 581
termination of sandboxed code, 250–251
testing
  sites in IE, 28
  solution (Visual web part exercise), 312–316
  Test-SpContentDatabase cmdlet, 64
  Test-SPContentDatabase cmdlet (Powershell), 44
text
  layout, wiki pages and, 652–653
  TextTrimming feature (Silverlight), 450
themes
  adjusting, 659–660
  branding and, 642–644

  for forms, 337
  Microsoft Office, creating, 656–659
  Themable directory, 662
  theme comments, 662–663
thesauruses, controlled vocabulary and, 579
Three State workflow, 361
throttling
  event, 71–72
  list, 720
thumbnails
  searches and, 611
  thumbnail view (Asset Library), 684
timer jobs
  management, 98–100
  Status page, 100–102
Tisseghem, Patrick, 524
titles of forum questions, wording, 759
TitleTextBlock control, 449
Token Policy (TP), 109
Token Practice Statement (TPS), 109
tokens, security, 107–108
ToolZones, 289
trace logs, SharePoint
  basics, 70–74, 80–81
  Excel and, 81
  MSDN ULS Viewer, 81–82
  SPLogEvent cmdlet, 82–85
  SPLogFile cmdlet, 84
trial restores, 203
trial upgrades (SharePoint Server 2010), 57
troubleshooting with logs, 77–80
trusted locations, configuring (PPS), 556–557
TypeName property, 386

U

UIs (user interfaces). See user interfaces
uiThread variable (News Banner project), 445
Unattended Service Account, 555–556, 563
uncustomized pages, 285
"uncustomizing" (site definitions), 414
"Understanding and Creating Customized and Uncustomized Files in Windows SharePoint Services 3.0", 206, 664
Unified Logging Service (ULS)

Feature upgrades and, 427
overview, 69–70
SharePoint logging database.
See logging database,
SharePoint
SharePoint trace logs. *See* trace
logs, SharePoint
Windows Event logs, 85–86
universal identity, 106
`Update-`
`SPInfoPathAdminFileUrl`
`Windows` PowerShell cmdlet, 53
`Update-SPInfoPathUserFileUrl`
cmdlet, 60
`Update-SPProfilePhotoStore`
cmdlet, 55
`Update-SPSolution cmdlet`, 483
`UpdateUserExperience`
parameter, 66
upgrading
applications, 415–430
BDC applications from
SharePoint 2007, 529
content type, 480–483
Feature Upgrade Kit, 483
solution packages, 438
upgrade definition files (UDFs),
48–50
`UpgradeActions` XML
element, 415, 480
"Upgrading an Existing
Master Page to the
SharePoint Foundation
Master Page," 668
upgrading to SharePoint
Server 2010
background information, 36
Central Administration status
page, 45
with custom site definitions,
47–50
database attach post-upgrade
steps, 61
database attach upgrade
approach, 58–61
database test cmdlet, 44
detach databases hybrid
approach, 66–68
expected downtime, 44–45
hybrid upgrade approach
overview, 61–62
in-place post-upgrade process,
54–57
in-place upgrade approach,
50–52
in-place upgrade under hood,
52–54
large Content Databases and,
46–47

pre-upgrade checker tool,
38–40
read-only databases hybrid
approach, 62–66
site access during, 46
system requirements for,
36–37
upgrade improvements, 37–38
upgrade logging, 40–41
Visual Upgrade Feature, 41–43
uploading
Upload Document dialog
box, 658
`UploadPicture` method,
500–501
web part templates, 291
url parameter (SL Picture
Picker), 471
user interfaces
centralized/decentralized
(searches), 630
customizing for searches, 630
new (SPD), 208–212
user profiles
importing data to
SharePoint, 534
User Profile Services, 53–54,
60–61
User Profile Synchronization
Service, 20
User Profile web service, 357
users
checking and changing
(SPD), 213
concurrent users, multimedia
assets and, 701
creating, 10–11
remote users, multimedia
assets and, 701
User Account Control (UAC),
disabling, 10
User Contexts in FAST Search,
628, 635
user profiles, using in
workflows, 233
user solutions, 202
`UserControl` element, 450
`UseSimpleRendering`
property, 650

V

`v4.master` mastert page, 645
validation
enhancing InfoPath forms
with, 339–341
rules (InfoPath Designer), 339
`ValueEventHandler`, 493
variables, workflows and, 235

Variations feature, 654
Verbose trace logging, 97
verbs, web part, 330–332
Verbs Property Override
(listing), 331
versioning in applications
assembly versioning, 435–436
`BindingRedirect` element in
WSP manifests, 432–434
Feature versioning, 415–416,
436–437
.NET assemblies, 431–432
strategies, 435
`VersionRange` element,
415, 428
vertical/horizontal filtering
(collections), 710–715
`ViewPictureControl` (SL
Picture Picker), 471–472
views and forms (SPD)
basics, 224–225
editing, 226–230
views and XSLT, 225–226
`ViewXml` property, 445–446
`VirtualPath` property, 386
Visio, Microsoft
designing workflows with,
362–364
implementing workflow
designs in SPD, 364–365
importing workflow designs to
SPD, 365–366
importing/exporting
workflows to and from
(Visio 2010), 234
PPS client configuration and,
558–559
Visio Premium 2010, 33
Visio Workflow Interchange
(VWI) file, 362
Visual Studio (VS) 2010
assembly versioning and, 433
creating ECTs with, 539–548
creating workflows with, 362
"Hello World" sandbox
project, 255–259
packaging/deploying custom
cmdlets with, 161–163
project, configuring (Wingtip
app), 381–383
SharePoint tools, 259, 275
Silverlight applications
and, 442
solution for News
Manager, 486
trial download, 33
upgrading Features using, 424
used for centralization, 274
web parts, 454

Visual Upgrade Feature (SharePoint Server 2010), 41–43, 655

Visual web parts
- defined, 274
- replacing with classic web parts, 520
- Visual web part template (VS 2010), 270

Visual web parts, creating (exercise)
- Add New Items, 298–300
- coupling with user control, 320–323
- delivering solution, 320
- deploying assets, 309–312
- editor parts, adding, 323–330
- environment, preparing, 295
- Feature, configuring, 301–302
- project, creating, 295–298
- securing code, 316–320
- SharePoint solution, configuring, 302–305
- testing solution, 312–316
- web part verbs, adding, 330–332
- writing code, 305–309

VM (virtual machine)
- making into domain controller, 5–7
- VM guest operating system, creating, 2
- VMWare Workstation 7.1, 2

vocabulary, controlled, 579

vProductInformation code, 511

vProductInformationRead List method, 517

Walsh, Mike, 745, 762

WCAG 2.0 AA specification, 648

WCF (Windows Communication Foundation)
- Data Services, 738–742
- developing in Silverlight project, 512–515
- serialization and, 467
- WCF service project. See field type hosting Silverlight application (example)

Web Analytics reports, 92–93, 617

web applications
- creating, 26–27
- Web Application Summary report, 92
- Web Application Web Part Gallery, 287

Web Content Accessibility Guidelines 2.0, 336

Web Front End
- server components (Wingtip app), 396
- servers, 377
- tier (WFE tier), 554

web page contents, listing (web parts), 292

Web Part Galleries, defined, 284

web part hosting Silverlight application, 453–465
- custom ribbon tab, adding to Web Part Tools group, 459–464
- first steps, 453–459
- Silverlight News Banner application, changes to, 464–465

web parts. See also SQL Server databases, rendering items from
- Add Web Part dialog (ribbon), 290–291
- Application Pages, 284
- benchmarks for, 281
- componentization with, 272
- configurability of, 273–274
- Content Pages, 284
- defined, 280
- development tasks, 276–280
- Edit mode, 289–290
- history of, 270–271
- improvements in current release, 274–275
- Instance Pages (System Pages), 285
- interoperability of, 272–273
- makeup of, 282
- Master pages, 286
- News Banner web part, modifying, 515–516
- out-of-the-box, 276
- overview, 269–270
- packaging, 276
- page layouts and, 287, 646
- page terms, 284
- portability of, 273
- properties, 293–294
- Publishing Pages (Site Pages), 286
- resource files, 294–295
- reusability of, 271–272
- ribbon, 289
- SafeControl element attributes, 283–284
- Search web parts, 631–632
- service consumer web part (Wingtip app), 402–403

Silverlight Web Part (News Banner project), 442, 452, 453

tab controls, 291–292

uploading templates, 291

Visual web part, creating (exercise). See Visual web parts, creating (exercise)

visual web parts, 454, 520

web page contents, listing, 292

Web Part
- CreateChildControls (listing), 317, 325–327

Web Part CreateEditorParts (listing), 328

Web Part Framework, 282

Web Part Galleries, 287–288

Web Part Page Maintenance screen, 293

Web Part Pages, 285

web part tool pane, 453–454, 458

Web Part Tools, 291

web part zones, 646

WebPartManager control, 288

WebPartVerbCollection object, 330

WebPartZone class, 289

WebPartZoneBase, 289

web services
- accessing data with, 738–743
- connecting to, 240–243

web sites
- applying branding throughout, 650
- branding basics and, 637
- enabling PPS on, 557–558
- exporting, 179–182
- importing, 183–184
- managing with SPD, 243

web sites, for downloading
- AdventureWorks database, 33, 561
- ALM projects, 417, 426
- BCS Meta Man, 548
- commands (searches), 621
- DocAve Recovery Manager, 197
- Feature Upgrade Kit, 483
- Fiddler, 33
- Firebug for Firefox, 668
- Firefox, 33
- IE8 Developer Tools, 668
- Media Services features, 678
- Microsoft Office 2010 Professional Plus, 33
- Microsoft SharePoint Designer 2010, 344

W

RBS Provider, 676
SharePoint 2010 Enterprise
    edition, 15
SharePoint Administration
    Toolkit, 47
SharePoint Designer 2010, 33
Silverlight, 33
SPD, 207
SQL Server 2008 R2, 12
ULS Viewer, 81
Visio Premium 2010, 33
Visual Studio 2010, 33
WCF data service, 736
web proxy project code,
    261, 263
Windows 2008 R2 Standard
    edition, 3
Windows 2008 R2/Windows 7
    patch, 16
workflow solutions, 362
web sites, for further information
2010 Information Worker
    Demonstration and
    Evaluation Virtual Machine
    (RTM), 560
Alirezaei, Reza (blog), 744
Asset Library Feature, 684
backup/restore/upgrade
    support, 379
batch operations, 743
BCP, 165
BranchCache services, 681
building on Windows 7/
    Vista, 3
building WCF Services in
    SharePoint 2010, 743
Connell, Andrew (blog), 405
database snapshots, 173
FBA and claims
    authentication, 55
Feature upgrading, 49
Lapointe, Gary (blog), 164
Lightning Tools, 549
list-level indexing, 715
loopback check, disabling, 7
Medero, Jason (blog), 68
Microsoft Patterns and
    Practices Guidance for
    SharePoint 2010, 252, 744
Power Tools, 259
"Query Efficiency with LINQ
    to SharePoint", 730
RBS, 675
regular expressions, 351–352
Rehmani, Asif, 373
SDK, 175

SharePoint 2010 service
    application framework, 378
SharePoint Object Model, 175
SharePoint Server enterprise
    licensing, 336
Smooth Streaming and
    Live Smooth Streaming
    components, 679
solutions, 202
SSO data from Microsoft SSO
    to Secure Store service, 54
TechNet, 13
TermStoreManagerPlus
    solution, 603
third-party recovery solutions,
    203–204
upgrade definition files
    (UDFs), 50
User Profile web service, 357
WCAG 2.0 AA
    specification, 648
"Working with Large Lists
    in Office SharePoint Server
    2007," 708
WebAppConfigurations.xml
    (listing), 150–151
WebBrowsable attribute, 294
webcasts as resources, 750–751
web.config files
    assembly versioning and,
        433–434
    backing up, 310
    WCF services, 469
WebDescription attribute, 294
WebDisplayName attribute, 294
WebProxyCaller, 264
Web-scoped artifacts, 417–418
WFE tier, PPS and, 554
Where-Object cmdlet, 137,
    139–140
WIF (Windows Identity
    Foundation), 114
Wiki Pages, 285, 651–652
Williams, Randy, 165, 204
Windischman, Woodrow, 349, 361
Windows, Microsoft
    2008 R2, installing, 3
    2008 R2/Windows 7 patch, 16
    Access Control Lists
        (ACLs), 106
    Communication Foundation
        (WCF) services, 378
    Event logs, 85–86
    Identity Foundation
        (WIF), 114
    PowerShell ISE, 131

Task Manager, bandwidth
    usage and, 700
Updates, enabling, 11–12
Windows 7/Vista
    building SharePoint Server
        2010 test environment on, 3
    searches and, 609–610
Wingtip Calculator service
    application
    application server components,
        creating, 384
    CalcServiceApplication.cs,
        Contents of (listing),
        387–388
    CalcServiceApplication-
        Proxy.cs, Contents of
        (listing), 397
    CalcServiceInstance.cs
        (listing), 390
    CalcService.svc web.config
        Contents (listing), 388–389
    NewCalcServiceApplication
        Windows PowerShell
        Cmdlet (listing), 393–394
    NewCalcService-
        ApplicationProxy
        Windows PowerShell
        Cmdlet (listing), 399–400
    overview, 380
    service application
        administration pages,
        390–391
    Service Application Consumer
        Client (listing), 402
    Service Application Consumer
        Visual Web Part Code
        (listing), 403
    service application, creating,
        386–388
    service application, creating
        instance of, 393–395
    service application installer,
        391–393
    service application proxy,
        396–397
    service application proxy,
        creating instance of,
        399–401
    service application proxy
        installer, 398
    service consumer client, 402
    service consumer PowerShell
        cmdlet, 403–405
    service consumer Web Part,
        402–403
    service consumers, 401–405
    service instances, 389–390

Wingtip Calculator service
    application (*continued*)
    service interface/operation
        contracts, 385–386
    service proxy, creating, 396
    Service Proxy Object, Creating
        (listing), 396
    SPService object
        implementation, 384–385
    Testing the Wingtip Service
        Application Windows
        PowerShell Consumer
        Cmdlet (listing), 403
    Visual Studio 2010 project,
        configuring, 381–383
    WCF endpoint, creating,
        388–389
    web front end server
        components, creating, 396
    Windows PowerShell Script
        to Create Configuration of
        Wingtip Calculator Service
        (listing), 395
    Windows PowerShell Script
        to Create Configuration of
        Wingtip Calculator Service
        Proxy (listing), 400–401
    Wingtip Calculation Service
        Contract (listing), 386
    Wingtip Service Application
        Windows PowerShell
        Consumer Cmdlet
        (listing), 403
    WingtipCalculatorService-
        Installer Feature
        (listing), 392
Word 2010, Microsoft, 535

workflows, SharePoint Designer
    automating with, 360–361
    best options for, 243–244
    designing with Visio, 362–364
    enhancing, tools for, 366–371
    final forms (employee training
        application), 371–373
    impersonation steps, 232–233
    implementing Visio design in
        SPD, 364–365
    importing Visio design to SPD,
        365–366
    importing/exporting, 234
    new types of, 230–231
    parallel blocks, 232
    site workflow to custom list,
        234–239
    user profiles, using in, 233
    ways to create, 361–362
    Workflow Designer, 231–232
    workflow templates,
        modifying, 233
"Working with Large Lists in Office
    SharePoint Server 2007", 708
workspaces (PPS dashboards),
    561–573
    associated site, viewing or
        changing, 561
    basics of, 561
    dashboards, creating, 559,
        572–573
    data sources, creating,
        562–564
    filters, creating, 570–572
    reports, creating, 564–567
    scorecards, creating, 567–570
World Wide Web Consortium
    (W3C) compliance, 648
WrapPanelControl (SL Picture
    Picker), 471–474

WSPs (SharePoint Solutions)
    code deployment and, 248
    manifests, versioning and,
        432–434
WS-SecurityPolicy, 112
WS-Trust specification, 108
Wurman, Richard Saul, 577

X

XML (Extensible Markup
    Language)
    elements.xml file, 508
    Feature upgrades using
        declarative XML, 419–423
    Feature XML changes, 415
    Feature XML, generating,
        409–415
    Feature XML vs. .NET code,
        408–409
    File Connection button (SPD
        interface), 347
    provisioning and, 408–409
XOML (Extensible Object Markup
    Language), 253
XSL List View (XLV) Web
    Part, 276
XSLT (Extensible Stylesheet
    Language Translation),
    225–226, 693
.xsn files, 341

Y

Young, Shane, 1, 34

Z

Zone, Web Part, 289